THE Myths OF Rome

Look at any dictionary of classical mythology, and what you find will be Greek—all those marvellous stories from Homer and Hesiod about the Olympian gods and the heroes who fought at Troy. Any mention of the Romans will be by contrast, as of a people who had no gods and heroes of their own, and therefore no true mythology. 'This rubbish need not trouble us long,' remarked H.J. Rose in the contemptuous chapter on 'Italian pseudo-myths' at the end of his *Handbook of Greek Mythology*. That was in 1928, but not much has changed since then. In 2003, the *Oxford Dictionary of Classical Myth and Religion* put it like this (pp. 364–5):

> Rome, on the other hand, was situated at the margin of the 'civilized' world and was late to assimilate Greek myth . . . When the Roman elite started to write down its history at the end of the third century BC, it had one fixed mythological complex at its disposal: the foundation of Rome by Romulus and Remus . . . The absence of divine tales has even led some scholars to the suggestion that the Romans lacked a mythology altogether.

It's all the result of a two-hundred-year-old prejudice, born of the Romantic movement and nourished by nineteenth-century classical scholarship, that only the Greeks were authentically creative, and the Romans were merely practical— engineers, jurists, empire-builders.

The purpose of this book is to show that that's all wrong. New discoveries have proved that Rome was *not* 'at the margin of the civilised world', that it was *not* merely the 'elite' that created her world of stories. Nor was the foundation legend unique as a Roman myth, and there was certainly no shortage of 'divine tales'. The proof of that is in the great tradition of European painting, from Tiepolo in the eighteenth century back to Botticelli in the fifteenth, artists with no post-Romantic hang-ups about what might or might not count as 'authentic' mythology.

It is often thought, for no good reason, that myth and history are mutually exclusive. But most mythic stories were believed to be true, and some really were. Was Lucretia a real woman, raped by the king's son? Did Horatius really hold the bridge alone against an army? Nobody knows; but figures like Spartacus, Cleopatra, Caligula and Nero were certainly real flesh and blood before they became figures of myth. The long history of the Roman People and their city—under the kings, the free republic, or the Caesars—generated countless stories, no less mythic than the tale of Troy.

And the Roman stories still *matter*, as they mattered to Dante in 1300 and Shakespeare in 1600 and the founding fathers of the United States in 1776. What does it take to be a free citizen? Can a superpower still be a republic? How does well-meaning authority turn into murderous tyranny? These are themes for our own day as well.

THE Myths OF Rome

T.P. WISEMAN

UNIVERSITY
of
EXETER
PRESS

First published in 2004 by
University of Exeter Press
Reed Hall, Streatham Drive
Exeter, Devon EX4 4QR
UK

www.exeterpress.co.uk

British Library Cataloguing in Publication Data
A catalogue record of this book is available from the British Library

ISBN 0 85989 703 6

Typographic design by Quince Typesetting, Exeter
Typeset in Sabon and Futura by XL Publishing Services, Tiverton

Printed in Great Britain by Butler & Tanner Ltd, Frome

Magistris artium

Herc Ashworth
Craig Axford
Kate Boddy
Larry Bowles
Karen Bradshaw
Hannah Carrington
Andrew Clark
Joanna Clift
Galadriel Conway
Nick Cotton
Steve Davies
Kate Gurney
Ed Hopgood
Davey Kim
Pamela Lemmey
Sarah Mark

Lee McGill
Tanja Morson
Vasiliki Motsiou
Michelle Oskoui
Daragh Pollard
Rob Southgate
Rebecca Symonds
Betony Taylor
Rachel Tynan
Sarah Waltho
Anita Watson
Sian Willbourne
Alex Williams
James Willington
Karl Woodgett
Melanie Young

CONTENTS

ILLUSTRATIONS

"I suppose there's quite a story behind all this."

The New Yorker, 5 September 1953

ACKNOWLEDGMENTS

I am very grateful to the Leverhulme Trust and the University of Exeter, for freeing me from undergraduate teaching in 1999–2001 and thus allowing this book to get started; to Anna Henderson and the University of Exeter Press, for making it such a handsome volume; to the Classical Association and the British Academy, for permission to re-use published material; to my students and colleagues at Exeter, particularly those involved with the MA in Roman Myth and History, for good ideas and helpful criticism; and above all to Anne, for everything.

T.P.W.
February 2004

USER'S GUIDE

When embarking on a complex story, we may need to take our bearings in both time and space. The next three pages provide a time-chart, at a scale of one millennium per page, covering the period from 1000 BC to the present. The central column on each page numbers the centuries; listed on the left are the main sources, literary or visual, on which the story depends (bracketed names are of authors whose work is lost except for quotations); listed on the right are the main events and 'events' (inverted commas denote legendary status) of the story itself. After that there are maps (figures 1–4), of Rome, of Latium and Campania, and of the central and eastern Mediterranean. Both the time-chart and the maps are for reference only, to provide help if anything in the story is unclear. The other resource is the index, which I have done my best to make helpful.

In order not to clutter up the text, I have not used numbered notes. For those who want to chase up particular details, or check the author's reliability, references to sources and modern discussions will be found at the back of the book, keyed by page number and a brief phrase to identify the relevant item. The bibliography which follows the references makes no claim to be a complete guide to the literature of the subject, but it does list all the modern works I have referred to. Many readers, I imagine, will be content to ignore all that. What matters most is the story itself, which starts on p. 1.

TIME-CHART

	BC		
	1000		Late Bronze Age (*Cultura laziale* I)
	900		Early Iron Age (*Cultura laziale* II)
? Gabii graffito, fig. 5	**800**	Euboians on Ischia	
			'Seven Kings of Rome': 'Romulus 753–716'
? Homer ? Hesiod	**700**		'Numa Pompilius 715–673'
		? Demaratos to Etruria	
		? Creation of Rome as city-state	'Tullus Hostilius 673–642' 'Ancus Marcius 642–617'
(Eugammon) (Stesichoros)	**600**		'Tarquinius Priscus 616–579'
		'Macstrna'	'Servius Tullius 578–535'
Hercules statue group, fig. 9 (? Promathion of Samos)	**500**	Pythagoras in Italy End of monarchy at Rome 'Coriolanus 488' 'Cincinnatus 458'	'Tarquinius Superbus 534–510'
('Twelve tables' law code) Herodotos Thucydides	**400**	'Death of Verginia 449' Destruction of Veii Rome sacked by Gauls 387 Walls of Rome built; power-sharing consulship 367	
(Kleidemos) Ficoroni cista, fig. 23 François tomb paintings, fig. 14	**300**	Latins incorporated into Roman citizen body Battle of Sentinuum 295 Sabines incorporated into Roman citizen body	
(Eratosthenes)		Pyrrhos in Italy 280–275 Return of Regulus 249 Battle of Cannae 216	Games of Flora 241/238
(Naevius) (Ennius)	**200**	Great Mother comes to Rome 204 Bacchanalia witch-hunt 186 Conquest of Macedon 168	Hannibal defeated 202
Polybios		Destruction of Carthage 146 Murder of Tiberius Gracchus 133	
	100	Sulla's march on Rome 88	
(Licinius Macer)		Spartacus 73–71	Catiline 63–62
Cicero Varro		Caesar crosses the Rubicon 49	Battle of Philippi 42
Sallust Horace		Death of Kleopatra 30	Young Caesar becomes Augustus 27
Virgil Livy	**1**	Augustus *pater patriae*, Julia banished 2	

AD

1

Ovid　　　Dionysios

Tiberius adopted 4
Murder of Agrippa Postumus 14
Fall of Sejanus 31

Tiberius 14–37
Gaius Caligula 37–41
Claudius 41–54
Nero 54–68

Valerius Maximus
Seneca　　Lucan
Octavia
Martial　　Pliny
Suetonius　Tacitus
Plutarch

Fire of Rome 64
Galba 68–9, Flavian dynasty 69–96, Nerva 96–8

100

200

Acts of Peter

Death of Marcus Aurelius 180

300

? Justin
Arnobius

New walls of Rome 271–5

Constantine emperor 312–37

400

Servius　　Macrobius
Augustine
Orosius

Rome sacked by Goths 410

Rome sacked by Vandals 455

500

600

Pope Gregory 590–604

700

? Franks Casket, fig. 103

800

Charlemagne crowned as emperor 800

Rambona diptych, fig. 104　**900**　Trial of Pope Formosus 896

1000

		AD **1000**	
			Rome sacked by Normans 1085
		1100	
		1200	
		1300	
	Dante		
	Petrarch		
	Chaucer		
		1400	
Botticelli		**1500**	Florentine republic 1494–1512
Bellini			
Beccafumi	Machiavelli		
Titian	North's Plutarch		
	Shakespeare	**1600**	
Rubens	Jonson		
	May's Lucan		English civil wars 1642–51
			English republic (Commonwealth and Protectorate) 1649–60
	Racine		
	Dryden's Virgil	**1700**	
	Addison		
Tiepolo	Massey's Ovid		American republic 1776
	Gibbon		
David		**1800**	French republic 1792
			Napoleon emperor 1804
Haydon	Macauley		People's Charter 1838 Roman republic 1849
	Mommsen		French second empire 1852
	Marx		German second empire 1871
	Kipling	**1900**	
			Mussolini 1922–43
Quo Vadis	Graves		
Spartacus			
I, Claudius			
Gladiator	Hughes	**2000**	

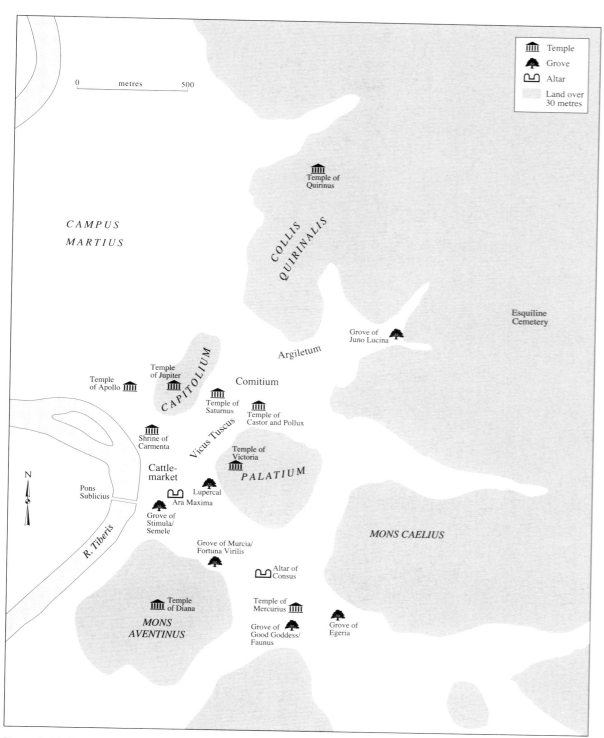

Figure 1. Mythic Rome

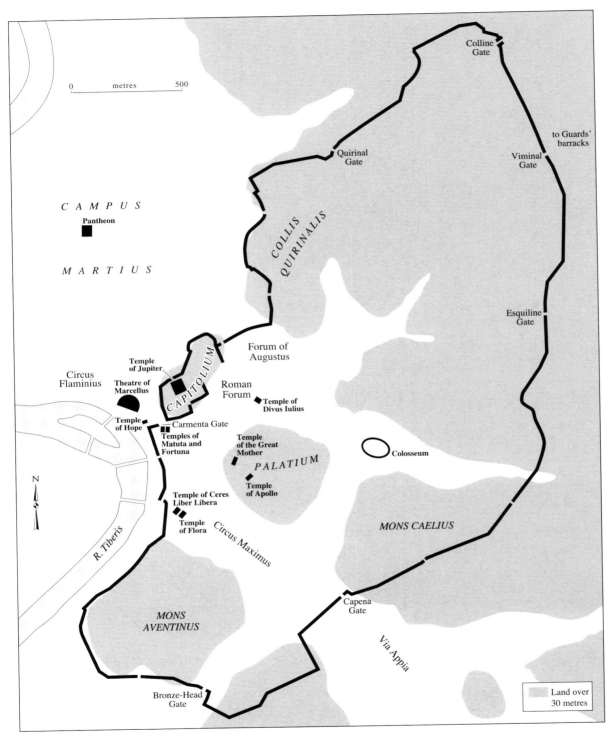

Figure 2. Historical Rome

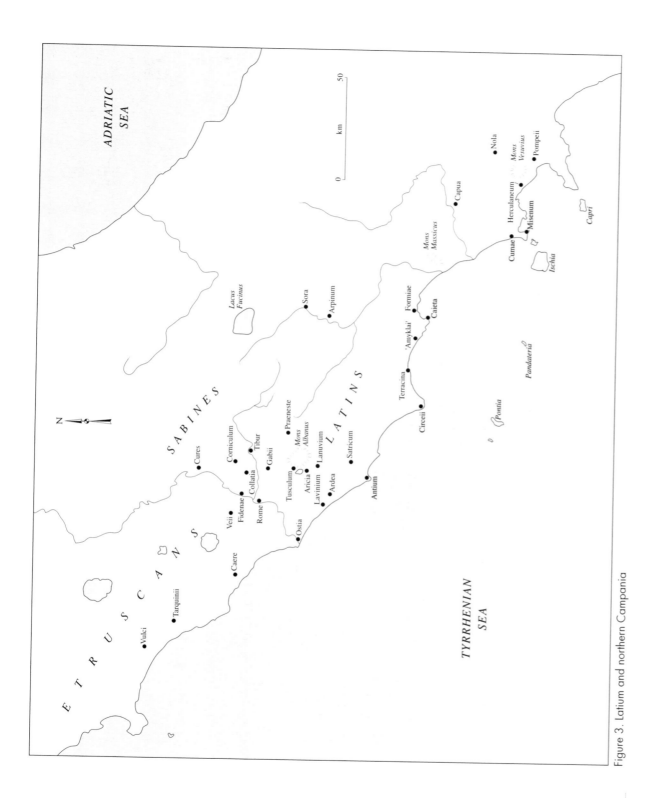

Figure 3. Latium and northern Campania

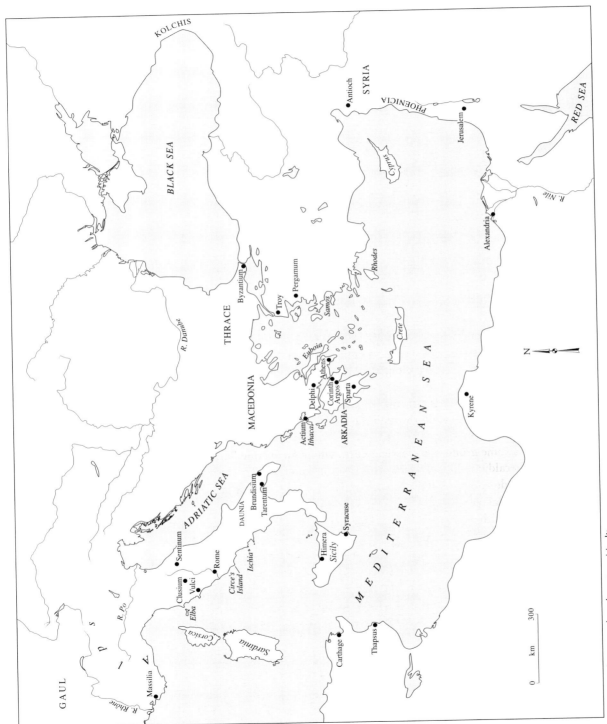

Figure 4. The central and eastern Mediterranean

1

THE TRIUMPH OF FLORA

TIEPOLO IN CALIFORNIA

Let's begin in San Francisco, at the California Palace of the Legion of Honor in Lincoln Park. Through the great colonnaded court, past the Corinthian columns of the porch, we enter the gallery and go straight ahead to the huge Rodin group in the central apse that dominates the visitor's view. Now look left. Along a sight line passing through two minor rooms, a patch of colour glows on the far wall. We walk through the Sichel Glass and the Louis Quinze furniture to investigate.

The scene is some grand neo-classical park, where an avenue flanked at the entrance by heraldic sphinxes leads to a distant fountain. To the right is a marble balustrade adorned by three statues, conspicuous against the cypresses behind: a muscular young faun or satyr, carrying a lamb on his shoulder; a mature goddess with a heavy figure, who looks across at him; and an upright water-nymph in a belted tunic, carrying two urns from which no water flows.

They form the static background to a riotous scene of flesh and drapery, colour and movement. Two *Amorini* wrestle with a dove in mid-air; four others, airborne at a lower level, are pulling a golden chariot or wheeled throne, decorated on the back with a grinning mask of Pan. On it sits a young woman wearing nothing but her sandals; she has flowers in her hair, and a ribboned garland of flowers across her thighs. The golden drapery that might have covered her billows out behind, perhaps blown by the wind or tossed aside by one of the two maids at the back (the other one beats a tambourine). Her route is marked on each side by an urn and a long staff bound with red ribbon. On the right dances a bare-breasted girl (darker-skinned than the beauty enthroned

Colour plate 1

1

behind her), in a flying red petticoat and a golden garter. On the left, two men are kneeling and offering flowers; one has a plumed helmet and a round shield. In the foreground, dark greenery contrasts with the brilliant light in which all this action is bathed.

Whatever is going on? This excellent gallery provides full information, and the panel on the wall reads as follows:

> Giovanni Battista Tiepolo
> Italian, Venetian, 1696–1770
> *The Empire of Flora*, ca. 1743
> Oil on canvas
> Gift of the Samuel H. Kress Foundation to the M.H. de Young Memorial Museum
> 61.44.19
> Forming a pair with *Maecenas Presenting the Arts to Augustus* (Hermitage, Leningrad), *The Empire of Flora* was commissioned from the artist in 1743 by Francesco Algarotti, Venetian author and art connoisseur. The two paintings were ordered by Count Heinrich von Brühl, artistic adviser to Augustus III, Elector of Saxony and King of Poland.
>
> Within the frivolous 18th century interpretation of the mythological subjects of these two paintings are specific references that flatter the Count. For example, the garden fountain in the background of our painting records the Neptune group by sculptor Lorenzo Mattielli that graced the gardens of Brühl's Marcolini Palace in Dresden. More obvious allusions to Brühl's patronage of the arts appear in the Leningrad painting, which depicts Maecenas counseling the ancient Augustus on the arts, in much the same way as Count Brühl advised Augustus III.
>
> Current scholarship suggests the specific subject may be drawn from Torquato Tasso's epic poem *Jerusalem Delivered* and represents Armida's garden.

That's a very helpful account of its origin, but it tells us more about the companion-piece in the Hermitage than about the painting we are looking at. We want to know what the frivolous mythological subject *is*.

'Current scholarship' is a little disingenuous in suggesting Armida's garden from Tasso. When Algarotti wrote to Brühl in July 1743, he promised him that Tiepolo's picture 'will represent the empire of Flora, who changes the wildest places into scenes of delight'; and he should have known. In fact, the chariot suggests that the artist had in mind the *triumph* of Flora—and that is what our painting is called in the standard catalogue of Tiepolo's work.

The central figure must be Flora herself. The gorgeous girl in the chariot flaunts her body and looks out at us as if we were hardly worthy of her notice. *Colour plate 2(a)* Her pose is like that of Venus in Tiepolo's 'Venus and Vulcan' in Philadelphia, where the adulterous goddess seems to taunt her husband with her naked beauty. There is also a hint of it (shoulders back, right arm akimbo) in 'The *Colour plate 2(b)* Meeting of Antony and Cleopatra' in Edinburgh. In the San Francisco picture, the kneeling men to the left are perhaps like Vulcan and Antony, helpless in the presence of such high-voltage erotic power.

But we know about Venus; we know about Cleopatra. The triumph of Flora is not so familiar a story. Algarotti's letter is helpful as far as it goes: the goddess of flowers will preside over the great man's luxurious park. But that doesn't account for her haughty look, the homage of the men or the sheer sensuality of the scene. Nor does it explain why the bold beauty's triumphal chariot is being towed out from somewhere *outside* the park, off to the right, as if it has been garaged in an outhouse. Flora certainly makes her entrance in style—but where has she been?

1.2 OVID, BELLINI AND TITIAN

Tiepolo's source for 'The Triumph of Flora' was a Roman poem much more widely read in the eighteenth century (and indeed the fifteenth, sixteenth and seventeenth) than it is in our time. A wonderful poem, despite its modern neglect, it had long been a source of inspiration for Tiepolo's great predecessors, the 'old masters' of the Venetian school. The author was Publius Ovidius Naso—'Venus clerk Ovyde' in Chaucer's *The House of Fame*, 'the most capricious poet, honest Ovid', for Touchstone in *As You Like It*. The poem is called *Fasti*, 'The Calendar' or 'The Festivals', an artfully kaleidoscopic collection of tales based on the ritual calendar of the Roman religious year. Alas, it never found a Dryden or a Pope, but a London schoolmaster called William Massey— a contemporary of Tiepolo—did his best to render it into English verse in 1757.

Here is a piece of Massey's Ovid, an episode in the first book (9 January, the *Agonalia*), which takes off from Ovid's various explanations of animal sacrifice:

> The sluggish ass to Priapus is killed,
> Of whom a story's told, jocose and odd,
> But vastly suitable to such a god.
> When Greece once celebrated Bacchus' feast
> In honour of his triumphs in the east,
> Thither resorted from the Arcadian plains
> The jovial rural gods, and many swains:
> Pan, sylvan Satyrs, goddesses of woods,
> And nymphs inhabiting the crystal floods;
> Here old Silenus on his ass appears,
> And he who birds from fruitful orchards scares. . .

Ovid *Fasti*
1.391–400

The last reference is to Priapus; Massey has bowdlerised Ovid's line, which actually means 'and the red (god) who scares the timid birds with his penis', or perhaps 'and the (god) with the red penis who scares the timid birds'. Ithyphallic statues of Priapus, with the projecting member painted red, were often set up in gardens as scarecrows.

3

. . . Who gathered all to a delightful place
And feasted jocund, sitting on the grass;
Bacchus afforded wine in plenteous store,
And on their heads they flowery garlands wore.
Some of the Naiads' tresses artless were,
And some were decked with diligence and care;
One, with a sprightly air, tucks up her clothes,
Another does a beauteous breast expose;
By this a naked taper arm is shown,
And that, in a long vestment, sweeps the lawn.
Pan and the Satyrs burned with amorous fire.
Nor would Silenus check his fond desire;
Old as he was, the lecher would renew
Those pleasures which in youthful days he knew.
But of the nymphs in all that lovely train,
Fair Lotis gave the garden-god most pain;
With her inflamed, for her he sighs alone
By nods and signs, and makes his passion known;
But pride and haughtiness attend the fair.
Thus, she despised him with a scornful air.

Ovid Fasti
1.401–420

She could have been a subject for Tiepolo—but it was a Venetian of an earlier age, Giovanni Bellini, who painted 'The Feast of the Gods'.

Colour plate 3

It was done for the 'alabaster chamber' in Alfonso D'Este's ducal palace in Ferrara, along with other Bacchic themes (Titian's 'The Andrians' and 'Bacchus and Ariadne'). In Bellini's scene, Bacchus is the ivy-crowned child on the left, filling a jug from the barrel; behind him, a respectable, grizzled Silenus pets his donkey; two satyrs are fooling about, unused to eating off crockery; Pan quietly plays his pipes in the background; and the waitress-nymphs, their clothes revealingly disordered as the text requires, are behaving with much more decorum than the senior gods satirically portrayed in the front row—Mercurius with his *caduceus*; Jupiter with his eagle; Neptunus with his trident, making free with the unidentified goddess to his right (and perhaps also with the nymph in blue, to judge by her glance); Ceres with her crown of corn-ears; Apollo with his laurel-wreath and 'lyre'.

To understand what is happening at the right of the scene, we must go back to Ovid's narrative:

Toiled with the gamesome pleasures of the feast,
The night came on, and all retired to rest;
All o'er the copse they different places chose,
And laid them down to make their soft repose.
Lotis the last beneath a maple's shade,
Upon the ground, reclined her drowsy head.

> Her lover rose about the dead of night,
> Who holding in his breath, and treading light,
> Came softly to the place where Lotis slept,
> And all the way the utmost stillness kept;
> He lays him gently down by Lotis' side;
> Her eyes the god of sleep had firmly tied.
> Flushed now with joy, to greater he prepares
> And boldly with his hand her covering rears. . .

Ovid *Fasti*
1.421–432

That is Bellini's scene. His Priapus (the gardener) is fully clothed, but the folds of his tunic, picked out in appropriate red, betray his nature. Far above his head is a bird, not at all frightened now the scarecrow god has his mind on other things. Bellini has Priapus holding a tree to balance his weight, just as Ovid says (*corpus librabat*: 'he lays him gently down' is Massey's mistranslation). What happened next? Well, remember that all this is to explain why asses are sacrificed to Priapus:

> . . . When lo! Silenus' ass, with sudden bray,
> Stopped short the lecher in his wanton way.
> The nymph affrighted struggled from his arms,
> And with her cries the sleeping crowd alarms;
> In form obscene Priapus stood confessed,
> By moonlight, to the giggling nymphs a jest.

Ovid *Fasti*
1.433–438

Not all the *Fasti* stories are so farcical. Ovid is always surprising his reader with changes of subject and mood, and he can handle tragedy as well as burlesque. His second book ends with a long episode to explain the day called 'Kingsflight' (*Regifugium*, 24 February). He tells of the rape of Lucretia by Sextus Tarquinius, son of the king of Rome, and the consequent uprising that drove out Tarquin and his family. That is a story we shall look at in Chapter 6. What matters here is Ovid's description of the rape (this time in L.P. Wilkinson's translation), and Titian's interpretation of it:

> He rose, and drew his gilded sword, and hied
> Straight to the chamber of that innocent bride,
> And kneeling on the bed, 'Lucretia,' breathed,
> ''Tis I, Prince Tarquin, with my sword unsheathed!'
> She nothing spake: she had no power to speak,
> Nor any thought in all her heart to seek,
> But trembled, as a lamb from sheepfold strayed,
> Caught by a wolf, lies under him dismayed.
> What could she do? Struggle? She could not win.

Ovid *Fasti*
2.793–801

It was a scene evidently more significant to Titian than the more common subject of Lucretia's suicide. He painted it at least three times, most famously in the version for Philip II of Spain, now in Cambridge. This brutal exercise of power is as far as can be from the comic frustration of Priapus at the bacchanal. Right across the emotional range, the stories in Ovid's *Fasti* provided rich material for the Venetian painters of the golden age, as they did two centuries later for Tiepolo.

1.3 OVID AND BOTTICELLI

Ovid introduces Flora at the end of *Fasti* book 4, on 28 April:

Ovid Fasti
4.945–6

> The goddess Flora decked with flowers appears
> Who a soft scene of jesting freedom bears. . .

'Scene' is meant literally, in the theatrical sense. For this was the start of the games of Flora (28 April to 3 May), at which, as Ovid's text has it, 'the stage's custom is for freer fun'. What exactly that custom was is revealed by an author writing a few years after Ovid, Valerius Maximus in his collection of moral examples. That work too was much better known in the Renaissance than it is today.

Valerius has a section on *maiestas*, the prestige or moral authority of great men, which concludes with an example about Marcus Cato the younger, Stoic philosopher and champion of old-fashioned morality. He was watching the games of Flora in 55 BC, when his friend Marcus Favonius, who was sitting next to him, pointed out that he was causing an embarrassment to the audience. 'The populace was ashamed [in his presence] to call for the showgirls to undress.' When Cato realised, he got up and went out, to the accompaniment of warm applause from the audience. 'They called back on to the stage their traditional custom of fun, confessing that they attributed more prestige to that one man than they claimed for themselves as a body.' Even as he praises Cato, the moralist author reveals that erotic entertainment was itself traditional, an old custom at the games of Flora. The poet Martial makes the same point more cynically:

Martial Epigrams
1.pref

> You know of sprightly Flora's ritual fun,
> The festal jests and licence of the rout.
> Then why, stern Cato, come to watch? Have done.
> Or did you come in simply to walk out?

Ovid puts off his treatment of Flora to the following book, where he gives her her due on the final day of her games (3 May): 'Fair Flora! now attend thy sportful feast. . .' Last month, he says, I postponed your role (*partes tuas*)—as if the goddess herself were one of her showgirls on the stage.

From time to time in the *Fasti*, Ovid gets his information from the gods in

Nymphs and Shepherds

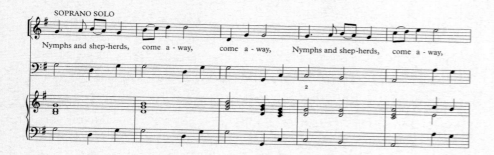

Nymphs and Shepherds, come away;
In the Groves let's sport and play;
For this is *Floras* holyday
Sacred to ease and happy Love,
To Dancing, to Musick and to Poetry.
Your Flocks may now securely rove
Whilst you express your Jollity.

Schoolchildren sing Henry Purcell's pretty song innocently unaware that 'Flora's holiday' was a festival of sexual licence. The song comes originally from Act IV of Thomas Shadwell's play *The Libertine* (1675), but there the third line was 'Where each day is a Holy-day'. Purcell's music was written for the revival of the play in 1692 (and published in the first volume of *Orpheus Britannicus* in 1706); presumably the reference to Flora dates from then.

person. This is just such a passage, and interviewing *this* goddess was a particular pleasure. He begins with the question that puzzles the San Francisco gallery visitor: who *is* Flora? She tells him, and her breath as she speaks is the scent of spring roses.

She used to be Chloris, a nymph of the Elysian Fields. 'It's hard to tell you modestly what my figure was like. . .' One day, the god of the West Wind saw her and pursued her. Rape became marriage, with a garden for a wedding gift. Zephyrus made his bride a goddess, mistress of the flowering spring, and her name was Latinised as Flora.

Colour plate 5

Botticelli's 'Primavera' shows us the scene. Without prejudice to the more arcane, neo-Platonic interpretations of the iconography, we can read the surface meaning clearly enough as an illustration of Ovid's text. From right to left: Zephyrus, Chloris the nymph (her name means 'pale') and Flora the goddess; then Venus, whose month is April, and on the far left Mercurius, whose month is May (he named it after his mother Maia); between them, where the games of Flora belong, dance the three Graces, whose names are Mirth and Splendour and Delight. In the Elysian Fields, there are flowers underfoot and fruit in the trees; and above it all the blind god of desire has his burning arrow on the string. As Flora tells her poet, the flowering of human sexuality is also part of her realm:

> A flower an emblem of young years is seen,
> With all its leaves around it fresh and green;
> So youth appears, when health the body sways,
> And gladness in the mind luxuriant plays.

Ovid Fasti
5.273–274

So ends her first response. The poet has been enjoying looking at her, but when she gently reminds him to get on with the interview, he asks about the origin of the games.

> To this my question Flora quick replies:
> Before that men in luxury were drowned,
> In corn and cattle all their wealth was found;
> Sheep were their money, and their riches land,
> But lawless power had then the sole command.
> The common rights unjustly some invade,
> And on offenders long no mulct was laid;
> The people joining shared one public stock,
> He was a drone, who kept a private flock.
> At length the Aediles by their power restrained
> The usurpation that so long had reigned;
> Upon the guilty members fines were raised,
> And the defenders of the laws were praised.
> Part of the fines the state to me dispensed,
> And by the victors were my games commenced.

Ovid Fasti
5.278–292

Here is a new dimension to the goddess. Her games are the result of an ideological *démarche*: wealthy landowners encroach on public land, the plebeian aediles defend the rights of the people with punitive fines. Ovid (though not his translator) reveals their significant name: they were called *Publicius*. We know from other sources when this happened, in 241 or 238 BC, and that the fines also paid for a splendid new temple to Flora. We know too that the reason for the aediles' drastic act was a crop failure (*sterilitas frugum*): in a famine year, the people's protectors must take appropriate action.

But the Senate refused to recognise the games. Flora was slighted, and she took revenge:

> The task would be too long to mention all
> Who to celestial anger owe their fall.
> The Roman fathers me neglected long;
> What way had I to vindicate my wrong?
> With grief I laid my wonted cares aside,
> For fields and gardens, which had been my pride. . .
> From off the trees the olive-buds were torn
> By raging winds, and hail destroyed the corn;
> And if the vines the hopeful blossoms crowned,
> The rains impetuous dashed them to the ground.
> No cruelty does with my anger dwell,
> Yet these disasters how could I repel?
> The fathers met; and vowed that if the year
> Should plenteous prove, my feasts should be their care,
> And annual made; their pious vows I heard;
> My flowery games the consuls then prepared.

Ovid Fasti
5.311–316,
321–330

Ovid (but not his translator) gives the consuls' names, and thus dates the event to the year of Lucius Postumius Albinus and Marcus Popillius Laenas, 173 BC.

So now at last we know why Flora triumphs. Now we can see why Tiepolo painted her coming, as it were, out of the shadows. And now we can understand her haughty look and her brazen nakedness. The people's goddess is offended, but she has prevailed. Despite the moralists, the games go on—and there they are in the right foreground, as the girl with the golden garter tosses her skirt up for us.

> Let none now from soft merriment refrain;
> Flora's a goddess of the jovial train.
> Nor is it hard to say, why these her games
> Are celebrated by young wanton dames;
> No prudery she feigns, no rigid air,
> And thus she's honoured by the common fair. . .

Ovid Fasti
5.347–352

'By a plebeian chorus' is what Ovid actually says, and he must be referring to the showgirls. Botticelli presents them demurely as the Graces; but perhaps Tiepolo has caught more of Ovid's tone.

| 1.4 | ROMAN MYTHS |

The purpose of this chapter is not just to explain Tiepolo's painting. The point is this, that the triumph of Flora offers an entry into the Romans' story-world which by-passes nineteenth- and twentieth-century preconceptions.

A variety of influences—the New Testament, Edward Gibbon, Hollywood— have conspired to make us see Rome only as an empire, a paradigm of power. The *fasces*, symbols of the Roman magistrate's authority, have given us the icons of fascism; the standards of Roman legions have been parodied and paraded in Nazi rallies; the architecture of triumphal arches and honorific columns speaks its message of victory and conquest as clearly for us as it did for the Romans and their subject peoples.

And during the same two centuries, a Romantic conception of 'Greece' (which means the Athens of Pericles and the Elgin marbles) has frozen our perception of the ancient world into a schematic polarity. The Greeks gave us democracy, philosophy, tragedy, art and myth; the Romans made roads and bridges, aqueducts and sewers, law and order. The clichés of television define it in visual shorthand: white marble against the blue Aegean, or legionaries' boots tramping a paved road in the rain (for the archaeology of Roman Britain is a powerful influence too).

Of course the Romans were proud of their empire, 'the immense majesty of the Roman peace', as Pliny put it in the first century AD, calling it a gift from the gods to the human race. But they also knew the cost of it. 'To robbery, butchery and plunder they give the lying name of empire; they create a desolation and they call it peace.' It was a Roman, the historian Cornelius Tacitus, who wrote that famous indictment, and put it in the mouth of a Celtic chieftain vainly defending the last outpost of liberty.

The Romans had their own story of liberty, how it was gained and how it was lost; and they knew that their power had grown from small beginnings, thanks to the civic virtue of men who put the common good before their own ambition. Behind the emperors' pomp and pageantry lay a long and rich tradition every bit as ideological as that of the Athenian democracy. Kings and consuls, tribunes and tyrannicides, secessions and civil wars produced a world of stories that were both historical and mythic. For myth and history do not exclude each other.

Mythos (Greek) and *fabula* (Latin) mean literally 'that which is said', and thus 'story'. To forestall tedious terminological argument, let us define a myth as a story that matters to a community, one that is told and retold because it

COLOUR PLATES

PLATE 1

Giambattista Tiepolo, 'The Empire [or Triumph] of Flora', in the San Francisco Fine Arts Museum.

Welcome to the forgotten world of Roman myths. Here is a naked goddess with a point to make, a dancing girl defying the puritans, and a delighted 'welcome back' from the citizens of Rome. The story was told by a famous poet in the time of Caesar Augustus; the picture was painted for another Augustus, the Elector of Saxony, in 1743. The title is clearly stated in a letter to the Elector's agent from the Venetian dealer who negotiated the sale—and yet, two and a half centuries later, with the painting on display in a major international art gallery, the experts were baffled. They thought it might be an illustration of a sixteenth-century Italian epic poem: could it be Armida's garden, from Tasso's *Gerusalemme liberata*?

That loss of knowledge—and it is not unique—explains the purpose of this book, to rediscover the mythology of Rome. See pp. 6–10 for the identification of the scene and the Ovidian episode it illustrates.

PLATE 2 Two more Tiepolo paintings, parallels for Flora's haughty shoulder in Plate 1: the goddess of love, married to the blacksmith god but caught in bed with the god of war, and the queen of Egypt, making the acquaintance of the joint ruler of the Roman world. Above (a), **'Venus and Vulcan', in the Philadelphia Museum of Art**: Volcanus' hammer and Mars' sword are at an appropriate angle. Right (b), **'The Meeting of Antony and Cleopatra', in the National Gallery of Scotland**—a sketch for the fresco in Palazzo Labia, Venice, where Cleopatra's pride and Antony's submission are less emphatic.

Giovanni Bellini (reworked by Titian), 'The Feast of the Gods', in the National Gallery of Art, Washington D.C. The original version was painted in 1514, and the gods are in contemporary costume, including Priapus as the gardener at the far right. The girl he hopes to uncover is the nymph Lotis, and their story is another piece of Ovidian eroticism (pp. 3–5).

PLATE 3

Titian, 'Tarquin and Lucretia' (1571), in the Fitzwilliam Gallery in Cambridge. This story of a rape that succeeded, the king's son and the virtuous lady, shows Ovid in a different mode (pp. 5–6, 132–3).

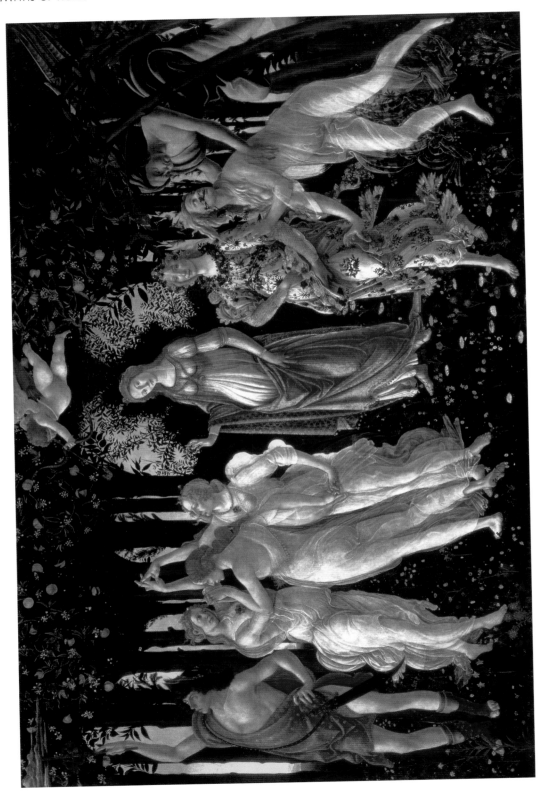

PLATE 5

Sandro Botticelli, 'Primavera' (c. 1481), in the Uffizi in Florence.

Read from right to left, this great icon of the Renaissance illustrates a Roman myth for a Roman festival, the same Ovidian story that Tiepolo would exploit nearly three centuries later (Plate 1, pp. 6–8). In the 'happy field' of Elysium, the god of the west wind lays his hands on the pale nymph, and transforms her into the goddess of spring flowers. 'Before that', says Ovid, 'the world had been monochrome.' The Romans gave her a festival of erotic shows that ran from the end of April to the beginning of May, from Venus' month to Mercurius'.

But this Venus is fully dressed, and matronly; these showgirls are the Graces, their dance duly decorous; this Mercurius is Hermes, the god of 'hermetic' wisdom, looking upwards and outwards. Botticelli's biographer called the painter a '*persona sofistica*', and other sophisticated persons, as Edgar Wind showed in his classic study *Pagan Mysteries in the Renaissance*, might find in his composition allusions to an arcane philosophy far beyond the thoughts of the Roman citizens in the theatre enjoying Flora's games.

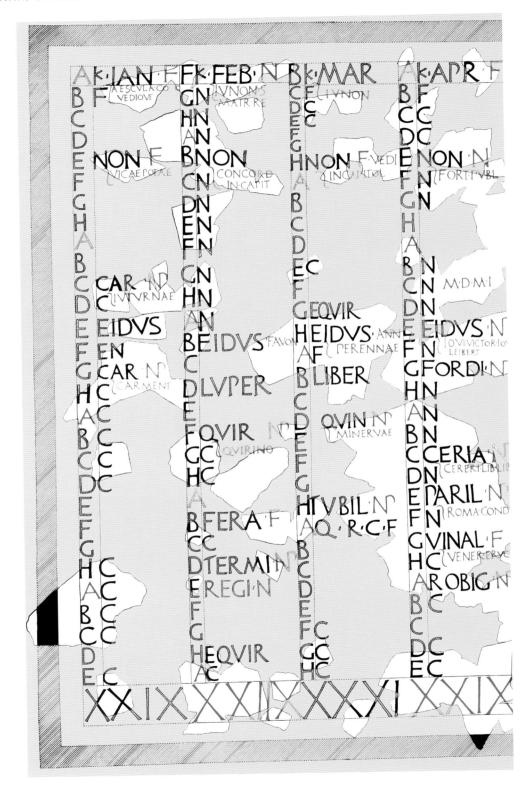

PLATE 6

Fragments of the *Fasti Antiates maiores*, a Roman calendar of the first century BC: reconstruction of January–April (pp.63–5).

The months are set out in columns, with the number of days in each (29, 28, 31, 29) at the bottom. On the left of each column the days are marked by letters, in an eight-day sequence from A to H. The main part of each column marks the Kalends (*K*), Nones (*NON*) and Ides (*EIDVS*) on the first, fifth (or seventh) and thirteenth (or fifteenth) day; these fixed points are the fossilised remains of an even older lunar calendar, originally representing the new moon, first quarter and full moon. Also marked are the characters of each day (*F* for *fastus*, *N* for *nefastus*, *C* for *comitialis*, etc), and the abbreviated names of the festivals, most of which are marked with the unexplained formula *NP* (in ligature).

That these festivals belong to the calendar's archaic nucleus is shown by the annotations in smaller red lettering, which are clearly additions. Look for instance at 11 and 23 April: *M.D.M.I.* (for *Matri deum magnae Idaeae*) and *Vener[i] Eruc[inae]*—sacrifices to the Phrygian goddess, 'the Great Idaean Mother of the Gods' (pp. 174–7 below), and to Venus of Phoenician Eryx in western Sicily. These two cults were brought to Rome during the Hannibalic War, in the late third century BC.

PLATE 7

Tomasso Laureti, 'The Battle of Lake Regillus', a mural in the Sala dei Capitani of the Palazzo dei Conservatori in Rome.

The Palazzo dei Conservatori is on the ancient Capitol, on your right as you come up the steps to the Piazza del Campidoglio. Remodelled in the mid-sixteenth century to a design by Michelangelo, it housed the city government of Rome in a splendid sequence of chambers on the first floor. The first of them is a grand hall decorated with murals of the discovery of Romulus and Remus, the foundation of the city, the seizure of the Sabine women, Romulus' wars and Numa's piety, and the story of the Horatii (pp. 57–8). From there you pass into the council chamber, now known as the Sala dei Capitani, decorated with murals by Tommaso Laureti in 1587–1594. To your right, behind the tribunal, is Lucius Brutus supervising the execution of his own sons (p. 133); to your left, Gaius Mucius

before Porsena, with his hand in the fire (p. 138); on the wall behind you, Horatius Cocles holding the bridge (pp. 58–9); and on the wall facing you, this magnificent evocation of the battle of Lake Regillus (pp. 65–6). Two and a half centuries later, Macaulay would tell that story too, in praise of 'the great Twin Brethren who fought so well for Rome'.

The interior paintings of two Etruscan cups of the 'Clusium Group' (fourth century BC) provide visual evidence for the world of 'show business' in Italy a century or so before the first Latin playwrights wrote their texts. The dancing satyr (opposite, right) implies that the showgirls' performance is in some sense Dionysiac (p. 83); and the eagle in the scene above suggests that their version of Leda and the swan is taken from Euripides *Helen* 17–21.

PLATE 9

Jacques-Antoine Beaufort, 'The Oath of Brutus' (1771), in the Musée municipal at Nevers.

A man's got to do what a man's got to do, and the woman's body lies forgotten in the background. This is the foundation legend of the Roman Republic (pp. 132–3). Lucretia told her husband and her father what Sextus Tarquin had done (Plate 4), and then stabbed herself through the heart. Lucius Brutus—whose story was now merged with hers—drew out the dagger from the wound and swore on it to rid Rome of the tyrant and his brood. A still later development of the story brought in Publius Valerius Publicola ('the People's friend'), though his presence was even  more gratuitous than that of Brutus. Here the four men strike their heroic pose: Brutus holds the knife; the foreground figure on the right should be Collatinus, with Lucretia's father between them; behind is a suitably shadowy Valerius.

PLATE 10

Peter Paul Rubens(?), 'The Flight of Cloelia', in the Dresden Art Gallery.

The Roman hostages are escaping from Lars Porsena (p. 138). The source is Plutarch, in his life of Publius Valerius Publicola, chapter 19 (translation by John and William Langhorne, 1770): 'Upon the faith of this treaty, Porsena had ceased from all acts of hostility, when the Roman virgins went down to bathe . . . As no guard was near, and they saw none passing or repassing, they had a violent inclination to swim over, notwithstanding the depth and strength of the stream. Some say one of them, named Cloelia, passed it [the river] on horseback, and encouraged the other virgins as they swam.' Rubens gives us 23 girls, eight horses, and a very surprised river  god. Cloelia, on the leading horse, gives him an apprehensive glance, no doubt assessing his degree of excitement. In the background is the bridge, broken in the Horatius Cocles story.

PLATE 11

Peter Paul Rubens, 'Mars and Rhea Silvia' (1617), in the Prince's Collection in Liechtenstein.

Romulus and Remus are about to be conceived. Rubens' Mars is not a susceptible young warrior, but a bearded veteran; his Rhea Silvia (early versions of the story call her Ilia) is not a helpless girl, but a mature priestess at the altar of her goddess. The headlong desire that brings them together is the *AMOR* to create *ROMA*, the necessary genesis of Rome. Like Botticelli in Plate 5, Rubens has taken a sexy tale in Ovid and made it respectable (pp. 138–9). Divine rapes as they really happened may not be seen by mortal eyes.

PLATE 12

Pietro da Cortona, 'The Rape of the Sabine Women' (1629), in the Pinacoteca Capitolina in Rome (on the second floor of the Palazzo dei Conservatori; see Plate 7).

Romulus gives the order, and the Romans seize the women they need (p. 143). The obelisk stood on the central 'spine' of the Circus Maximus; by putting it and the two temples into a wooded valley, Pietro reproduces the ancient sources' characteristic juxtaposition of scenes from 'pre-urban' Rome with the city-scape of their own time. Similarly, he has equipped his Romans as if they were legionaries of the time of Livy or Plutarch; the segmented armour and the standards are probably inspired by the reliefs on Trajan's Column.

The temple of Neptunus Equester (identified by his trident) is at the top left.

PLATE 13

Jacques-Louis David, 'Les Sabines', in the Louvre in Paris.

The next stage in the story of the Sabine women: their menfolk are ready to do battle to get them back, but it's too late for that now (pp. 143–4). The view is from the south-west, with the Capitol (and a dramatic Tarpeian Rock) on the left. David's source is Plutarch's narrative, where the women's intervention is more energetic than in Ovid, and the starring role is given to Romulus' wife Hersilia. The Romans in the background have taken off their helmets as a sign of peace;

the 'général de cavalerie' to the right is sheathing his sabre. (Note that Romulus' groom wears a Phrygian cap, symbol not only of the Romans' Trojan descent, but of the *liberté* of revolutionary France; the painting dates from 1799.) If Tatius and Romulus look more absurd than heroic, that's as it should be: the women are the heroines here, thanks to whom the children in the foreground can grow up to be the future Romans.

PLATE 14

Benjamin Robert Haydon, 'Marcus Curtius Leaping into the Gulf' (see p. 149), **in the Royal Albert Museum, Exeter.**

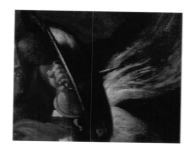

'I congratulate you, my dear friend,' wrote Elizabeth Barrett to Haydon in February 1843, 'upon the Curtius. The Morning Chronicle gives me good news of it as the finest work of art in the exhibition—and my cousin Mr Kenyon, with whom I talked of it yesterday, said that it was a "grand conception"—praised the "serene look (not exaggerated in serenity—)" of the hero; & the wild, plunging turbulence of the horse—& observed that you almost tremble while you look at it lest you should be overwhelmed bodily by man & horse. You may be certain how much pleasure I feel in your success

—moi qui ne suis rien
Pas même Academicien!—

& how, although I cannot see it, I imagine the grandeur of the contrast & antithesis between that calm human will and that violent animal agony!'

Curtius has the features of Haydon himself, who committed suicide in 1846.

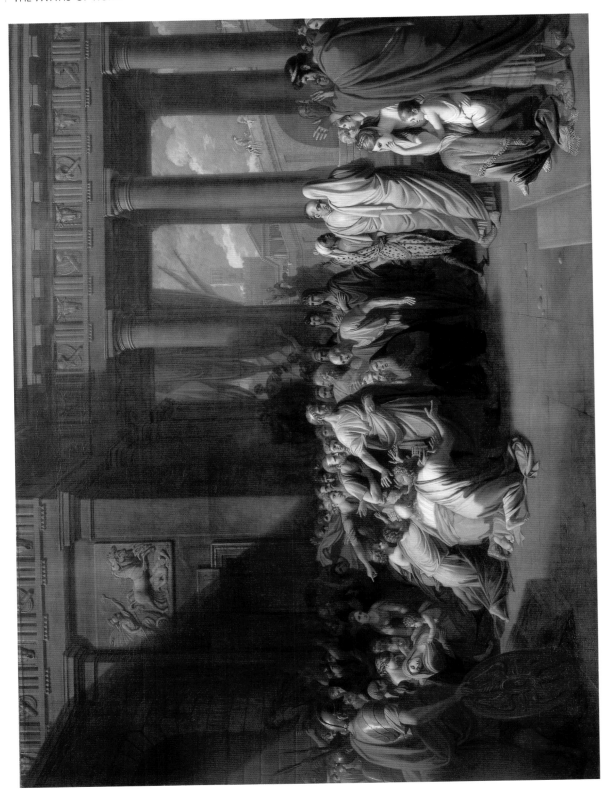

PLATE 15

Benjamin West, 'Departure of Regulus from Rome', in the Royal Collection.

The picture was painted in 1769 for George III, who then appointed West as 'Historical Painter to the King' with a salary of £1,000 per year. (The artist was born in Pennsylvania; see p. 155 for his admiration of George Washington.)

The classic narrative of Regulus' self-sacrifice (pp. 154–8) comes not from Livy, whose history of the First Punic War is lost, but from his Augustan contemporary, the poet Horace. Here is James Michie's translation of the end of *Odes* 3.5:

> They say he drew back from the kiss his true wife
> And little children begged, and like a prisoner
>   Deprived of civil rights
> Bent an austere gaze grimly on the ground,
>
> Until his unexampled admonition
> Had fixed the wavering Senate in their purpose
>   And he could push through crowds
> Of grieving friends, exile- and glory-bound.
>
> And yet he knew what the barbarian torturer
> Had ready for him. Kinsmen blocked his passage,
>   The people held him back,
> But he returned as unconcernedly
>
> As if they were his clients and he'd settled
> Some lengthy lawsuit for them and was going
>   On to Venafrum's fields
> Or to Tarentum, Sparta's colony.

West's grand and somewhat pompous composition is truer to Horace's notion of Regulus—a great noble with country estates—than to the poor farmer of the traditional story.

PLATE 16 (a) **The Sala del Concistoro of the Palazzo Pubblico in Siena, decorated by Domenico Beccafumi, 1529–1535.** The three allegorical scenes in the vault represent Justice, Mutual Goodwill and Patriotism (*patriae amor*). Six rectangles and two octagons, plus eight half-*tondi* at the corners, contain sixteen exemplary scenes from Valerius Maximus.

(*b*) **Beccafumi's version of Valerius Maximus 6.3.2: the tribune Publius Mucius** (p. 194) explains his action to the citizens, while his nine traitor colleagues are burned alive behind him.

has a significance for one generation after another. Such a story may be (in our terms) historical, pseudo-historical or totally fictitious, but if it matters enough to be retold, it can count as a myth. The rape of Lucretia may have been a historical event; the meeting of Antony and Cleopatra certainly was. As for Flora, immortal though she is, she operates as easily in the historical world of men (241 and 173 BC) as in the timelessness of the Elysian Fields.

Gods and goddesses are particularly affected by another misleading modern preconception. Here is Georg Wissowa, in what for most of the twentieth century was the standard work on Roman religion, written in 1902:

> These [Roman] gods are attached to places and things, and naturally lack all personal qualities and individual characteristics; they have no relationship with each other beyond the proximity and similarity of their sphere of activity. Above all, Roman religion has no notion of gods marrying or having offspring, no belief in a world of heroes mediating genealogically between gods and men. Later narratives of such things are without exception the result of free poetic invention or learned inference from Greek models.

Georg Wissowa
Religion und
Kultus . . . 23

Of course (it was assumed), the Romans could have no *real* mythology because they weren't like the Greeks. As Kurt Latte, another great authority on Roman religion, put it in 1926, they were an 'unspeculative and unimaginative people', among whom 'no myth-making imagination winds its tendrils round the gods'. So much for Ovid and Flora.

Absurd though it may seem to define mythology by excluding 'poetic invention' (what did Wissowa think Homer and the Attic tragedians were doing?), this view of Rome as a world without myths has been extraordinarily persistent. It would have been unintelligible to Botticelli, Titian, and Tiepolo.

They knew, and exploited, a world of ancient stories in which the difference between Greeks and Romans was of little significance. Since then, historical sophistication has taught us how far the world of Homer was from the world of Ovid, but that has not been an unmixed blessing. One of its consequences has been the unthinking assumption that the Greeks were somehow 'before' the Romans, more original and more authentic. In fact, the city-states of Athens and Rome were formed about the same time, and in some ways were remarkably similar in their development. Both expelled their autocratic ruling dynasties at the end of the sixth century BC, and if we distinguish them thereafter as Athenian democrats and Roman republicans, the difference is due only to our modern paradigms.

The Romans were not a people without myths. They too had stories to tell about their gods, their forefathers and the achievements of their city. They were indeed profoundly influenced by Greek ideas, but not just in the artificial, antiquarian sense that Wissowa had in mind. We now know, as he could not, that Latin-speakers were familiar with Greek (the language, and therefore also the concepts it expressed) in the early Iron Age, before either Roman or Athenian history begins. This book is an attempt to reinterpret the Roman story-world in the light of that knowledge—and perhaps also to rediscover, on the way, some of the glamour and vividness that inspired the artists.

The order of argument is roughly chronological. Remembering that every story was once told for the first time (and resisting, therefore, the lazy idea that all myths necessarily belong to an unfathomable antiquity), I have tried to arrange the material according to its probable age. In Chapters 2 and 3 the idea is to imagine which of the stories the Romans knew may go back to the archaic world of the eighth, seventh and sixth centuries BC. Chapters 4 to 6 do the same for the fifth and fourth centuries BC, from the expulsion of the Roman kings to the conquest of Italy, and Chapter 7 for the third, down to the defeat of Hannibal. After that we come into the world of texts, of story-telling as literature, whether epic poetry or historical prose. It became also a world of empire, and imperial conquest had a profound effect on the way the Romans thought about themselves. So Chapters 8 and 9, on the second and first centuries BC and the first century AD, look at a new mythic history of power and tyranny, as republican rule collapses and autocracy returns.

My end-point is the reign of Nerva (AD 96–98). That was where Gibbon began, in the first paragraph of *The History of the Decline and Fall of the Roman Empire*:

> In the second century of the Christian era, the empire of Rome comprehended the fairest part of the earth, and the most civilized portion of mankind. The frontiers of that extensive monarchy were guarded by ancient renown and disciplined valour. The gentle, but powerful, influence of laws and manners had gradually cemented the union of the provinces. Their peaceful inhabitants enjoyed and abused the advantages of wealth and luxury. The image of a free constitution was preserved with decent reverence: the Roman senate appeared to possess the sovereign authority, and devolved on the emperors all the executive powers of government. During a happy period of more than four-score years, the public administration was conducted by the virtue and abilities of Nerva, Trajan, Hadrian, and the two Antonines. It is the design of [Gibbon's first three chapters] to describe the prosperous condition of their empire; and afterwards, from the death of Marcus [Aurelius], to deduce the most important circumstances of its decline and fall; a revolution which will ever be remembered, and is still felt, by the nations of the earth.

Edward Gibbon
Decline and Fall
. . . book 1, ch. 1

Our story, unlike Gibbon's, is about a city-state. Once the transition to an imperial monarchy was finally, and painfully, completed, the story-world of Rome was completed too. But it continued to reverberate, centuries and even millennia after the conditions that brought it into being had gone for ever. My final chapter tries to sketch that process, and to show how, even in our own day, the myths of Rome still have the power to move us.

2

LATINS AND GREEKS

EUOIN AND EUBOIANS

Five Greek letters scratched on a vase. That's all—but they are the earliest Greek inscription ever found anywhere, and they come from a site in Latium, the land of the Latins. The discovery was first made public in 1989: at Osteria dell' Osa, about 20 kilometres due east of Rome, where the necropolis of the Iron Age settlement at Gabii was being excavated, tomb no. 482 was found to be marked by a small round vase of local production, less than 6 inches high (13.9 cm), carrying a graffito which could be read as ΕΥΟΙΝ or ΕΥΛΙΝ, *euoin* or *eulin*.

Figure 5

It had been placed on top of the larger jar that contained the remains and the grave-goods, and it had the unusual feature of an aperture deliberately made in the upper part of the body of the vase. According to one school of thought, it was a sacred object with a ritual use: and if the inscription is read as *euoin*, that can only be a variant of the Dionysiac ritual cry *euoi* or the name Euios (for Dionysos) that was derived from it. Dionysos had many names: in Etruscan he was Fufluns, in Latin he was Liber Pater.

The archaeological context of the find is *cultura Laziale* IIB, for which the conventional absolute dating is 830–770 BC; however, recent comparison with parallel sequences from northern Europe, for which tree-ring evidence is available, has suggested a 'high' dating of 950–880 BC. So a conservative estimate for the date of the Gabii graffito would be 'about 800 BC', with the possibility that it could be a century or so earlier even than that.

'About 800 BC' is also the time when prospectors from what would later be called Greece were beginning to find their way back into the sea-lanes and trade routes of the Mediterranean. The Bronze Age palace culture of the Mycenaean

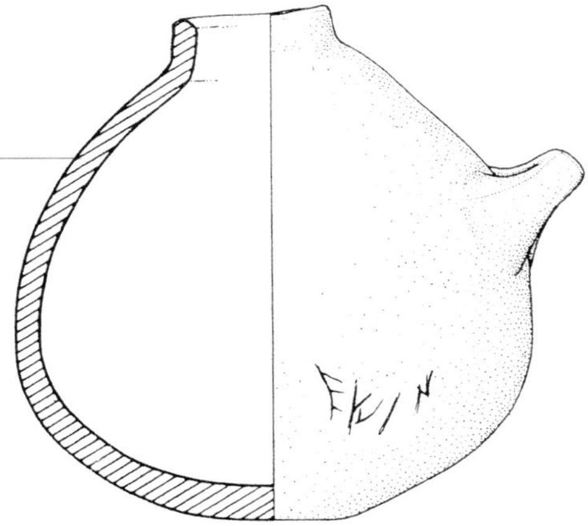

Figure 3
(map: p. xxi)

Figure 5. The Gabii graffito. Greek letters on a pot from Latium (Osteria dell' Osa, tomb 482).

world had collapsed three centuries earlier; now, after generations of weakness and economic stagnation, 'Greek' explorers had become confident enough to compete with the Phoenicians and Cypriots in the search for metals and other raw materials. The material prosperity that followed their success enabled a new sort of culture to develop, for which the first comparatively firm historical date is the foundation of the Olympic games in 776 BC. We call it 'Greek civilisation', but the concept of Greek (or Hellene) as a defining category did not yet exist. In Homer, Agamemnon leads an army of 'Achaeans', 'Argives', 'Danaans', and there is no suggestion that the Trojans spoke a different language. We should try to imagine a similarly unstructured conceptual world when the merchant venturers of Euboia first came into contact with the peoples of western central Italy who spoke early versions of Latin and Etruscan.

The Euboians' first settlement was on Ischia, which they called Pithekoussai, 'Monkey Island'; their sources of metal ore were two days' sail to the north, on Elba and in the *collini metalliferi* of north Etruria. Half way along their coastal route was the outflow of the most important river of peninsular Italy (known variously as Rumon, Albula or Tiberis), which offered an easy route into the interior. About 25 miles upstream was the lowest point at which the river and its flood-plain could be conveniently crossed. This was where an island in the river next to a group of low hills in the flood-plain itself provided a fording-place, and thus a route junction for the Latins to the south and east, the Etruscans to the north and west, and the peoples far upstream in the Apennine highlands. The Euboians must have known this place from year one of their enterprise, whenever that was.

It was, of course, the site of the future Rome, a settlement already growing fast in the ninth century BC. During the phase *cultura Laziale* IIA, about a century earlier than the Gabii inscription, the inhabitants had abandoned their cemetery in the valley to the north of the Palatine and opened a new one a kilometre away on the high ground of the Esquiline, evidently to make room

How Long Ago?

Two quotations, one from a Greek historian, one from a Roman epic poet:

> But it was only—if I may so put it—the day before yesterday that the Greeks came to know the origin and form of the various gods, and whether or not all of them had always existed; for Homer and Hesiod are the poets who composed our theogonies and described the gods for us, giving them their appropriate titles, offices, and powers, and they lived, as I believe, not more than four hundred years ago.

Herodotos was writing about 430 BC, contrasting Greek culture with the immensely older civilisation of Egypt. Modern historians consider his date for Homer and Hesiod at least a century too early.

> Seven hundred years there are, a little more or less,
> Since glorious Rome was founded with august augury.

Ennius was writing about 180 BC, though the dramatic date of these lines may be earlier. (They were quoted by Varro in 37 BC, who commented 'It would be more accurate to say that *now*'.) For modern historians, in any case, the 'foundation' of Rome is not an easy moment to define.

So an early Greek historian put the origins of Greek mythology about 830 BC, and an early Roman poet put the origins of Rome itself about 880 BC, or earlier. Neither date is remotely reliable by modern standards, but the combination of Herodotos' relativism and Ennius' national pride happens to give, in very broad terms, a reasonable result. The community of Rome and the mythology of Greece did indeed take shape at about the same time. When Hesiod was composing his *Theogony*, the Latins were in the prosperous phase IVA of *cultura Laziale*: in archaeological terms, 'exceptional wealth in some of the tombs points to the beginnings of permanent social stratification and the emergence of a dominant aristocracy'. Hesiod might have found a patron there, if he hadn't hated the sea so much.

Figure 6. 'Nestor's cup': a Homeric theme at Pithekoussai (Ischia). The inscription (in Greek, of course) reads from right to left.

for an increased population. By the time of phase IVB, in the second half of the seventh century BC, their settlement would be a recognisable city-state, with an *agora* in the drained valley between the hills (the Roman Forum), and public buildings with terracotta decoration and tiled roofs instead of thatch. By then, at least, the place called itself 'Roma'—an appropriate name, and a Greek one, for *rhome* in Greek means 'strength'.

What archaeologists controversially call the 'proto-urban' period (from the mid-ninth to the mid-seventh century on the traditional chronology) is defined by the detectable origin of cult sites. It was, in every sense, formative—and the formation of the community that would become 'Rome' is contemporary with the formation of 'Greek mythology', the corpus of stories that would soon find its canonical expression in the poems of Homer and Hesiod.

That the Euboians of 'Monkey Island' were already familiar with the material of the *Iliad* before the *Iliad* as we have it was composed, is elegantly proved by the allusion on an inscribed cup from Ischia: 'Nestor had a fine drinking-cup [see *Iliad* 11.632–7], but whoever drinks from *this* cup will soon be struck with desire for fair-crowned Aphrodite.' The merchant venturers who came to trade at that cross-roads community by the Tiber ford had their heads full of the stories Homer and Hesiod knew.

Figure 6

2.2 TROJAN STORIES

The perilous wanderings of Odysseus on his return from Troy were a story whose origins surely belong in that era of exploration in hitherto unknown waters. In the *Odyssey*, probably composed in Ionia (western Asia Minor), they are a traveller's tale with no geographical reference. But Hesiod located them on the western coast of Italy—not surprisingly, since the Boiotian poet lived just across the narrow water from the home port of the Euboians.

Kirke ('Circe') the witch-goddess is the star of book 10 of the *Odyssey*. She is the daughter of the Sun, and though in Homer her island seems to be in the far east, 'by the dancing-places of the early dawn', her father's chariot could easily put her at the other end of the world. For Hesiod, Circe's island was off the coast of 'Tyrrhenia', and her sons were the kings of that land:

> And Kirke, the daughter of Helios son of Hyperion,
> in love with the much-enduring Odysseus, bore
> Agrios and Latinos the blameless and strong
> [and she gave birth also to Telegonos by the will of golden Aphrodite],
> who far, far away in the recesses of the holy islands
> were the rulers of all the famed Tyrrhenians.

Hesiod *Theogony*
1011–1016

'Tyrrhenians' are Etruscans, but since Latinos is their king it is clear that Hesiod did not distinguish them from Latins; what his informants had in mind were the formidable inhabitants (*agrios* means 'wild') of the whole coastline of western central Italy.

The line in square brackets is a later insertion to make Hesiod consistent with the *Telegony*, a late seventh- or sixth-century epic poem by Eugammon of Kyrene extending the story of the *Odyssey* to Odysseus' death:

> Telegonos [Circe's son by Odysseus], while travelling in search of his father, lands on Ithaka and ravages the island; Odysseus comes out to defend his country, but is killed by his son unwittingly. Telegonos, on learning his mistake, transports his father's body with Penelope and Telemachos [his half-brother, son of Penelope] to his mother's island, where Circe makes them immortal, and Telegonos marries Penelope and Telemachos marries Circe.

Photius
Bibliotheca
319a.21

The site of these legendary events was Kirkaion (Latin Circeii, the modern Monte Circeo), a promontory on the coast of Latium which was once effectively an island, cut off by marshes from the mainland proper. It was the main sea-mark for mariners sailing north from Ischia, and it featured an ancient tumulus, later identified as the tomb of Elpenor (as in the *Odyssey* story); however, the plot-summary of the *Telegony* clearly implies an early hero-cult of Odysseus himself at the site.

The Latins and Etruscans got to know these stories—and many others—by word of mouth, long before there were any written texts of Greek epic. The names they used were acoustic approximations, clear evidence of an oral culture. In Etruria, the Ithakan hero was called *ut(h)use*. The Latins called him *Ulixes* (whence the modern 'Ulysses'): that un-Homeric name must derive from the spelling *Olyteus* or *Olys(s)eus* that was used in early Attika, Boiotia and Korinthos (Corinth). The Corinthians were quick to follow the Euboians in maritime trade and exploration in the west, and we shall see in the next chapter how direct their influence was at Rome itself.

Figure 4
(map: p. xxii)

Recent research has demonstrated that eighth-century Euboian (and later Corinthian) exploration into the Adriatic was as significant as that to the west coast of Italy. The key point for both routes—south-west over the open sea to Sicily and the straits of Messina, north-west to the heel of Italy—was Kerkyra ('Corcyra', modern Corfu), identified as the Homeric land of Phaiakia, where Odysseus told the story of his adventures. The north-west route is implied by an un-Homeric tradition about Odysseus, that he left Penelope and Ithaka and found his way across the Adriatic and deep into inland Italy, dying full of honours at Etruscan Cortona, north of Lake Trasimene. It is also implied by the much better-known story of another hero of the Trojan war, Diomedes.

In book 5 of the *Iliad*, Diomedes fights the Trojan hero Aeneas, son of Aphrodite, and is only prevented from killing him by Aphrodite herself, whom he wounds in the hand. After the war, driven from his home in Argos by Aphrodite's anger, Diomedes came to Daunia in eastern Italy (via Corcyra, where he killed a dragon); some versions say he was killed by the local king Daunus, others that he married Daunus' daughter. Traces of this story are detectable around the shores of the Adriatic and all over Apulia and south-eastern Italy—and perhaps in Latium too, via the land routes across the mountains. For the Rutuli of Latin Ardea were a Daunian people, and their king Turnus was the son of a Daunus; the name Ardea means 'heron', and Diomedes' companions were metamorphosed into herons.

Diomedes and Odysseus collaborated in one of the most famous exploits of the Trojan War, the theft of the talisman image of Pallas Athene, the Palladion, from the goddess's temple in Troy. Diomedes took it with him after the war, but was told by an oracle that it would bring him only misfortune until it was returned to the Trojans. Fortunately, he was able to give it to some Trojan refugees who had reached Italy under the leadership of his old enemy, Aphrodite's son Aeneas. Where this happened was disputed—either at the heel of Italy, in Diomedes' own territory, or on the coast of Latium, after Aeneas' people, fleeing from Troy, had made their final landfall. There was also a version which claimed that Aeneas had the Palladion already: what the Greeks stole was only a copy, and Aeneas had rescued the real one from the burning city. Either way, it was thanks to Aeneas that it came to the land of the Latins, and eventually to the temple of Vesta in Rome.

The story of Aeneas' voyage to Latium, and his war with 'Daunian' Turnus when he got there, is told in Virgil's great epic, written to celebrate the hero's alleged descendant, Augustus Caesar. The sequel, presupposed throughout the *Aeneid*, is as follows. After defeating Turnus, Aeneas married Lavinia, daughter of king Latinus, and founded the city of Lavinium (named for his bride); his son founded Alba Longa (a legendary city in the Alban Hills) and peopled it with Trojans; when Rome later destroyed Alba, its nobility joined the victo-

The Palladium

Pallas Athene is the goddess of wisdom, and of arts and crafts, so when Hengler's Circus in Argyll Street closed down in 1909, to be replaced by 'a huge variety theatre, which will not be a music-hall', artistic ambition named the new theatre *The Palladium*. The grand entrance with its Corinthian columns was surmounted by a statuary group representing Art, Science and Literature. But it turned out to be a music-hall anyway.

The Times reported the theatre's opening night (26 December 1910), confident that its readers would recognise classical allusions:

> The venerable image stolen by Odysseus and Diomedes from Troy probably met its fate as firewood on some Greek hearth, when its sanctity had worn off with its paint. [So much for Aeneas, and the temple of Vesta!] It has now risen from its ashes in the shape of a music-hall at Oxford-circus. This is certainly 'the latest thing' in music-halls—beautiful in white and gold and crimson, with palm-courts behind where lady musicians in Pompadour gowns assist the consumption of tea.

Listing the various turns (Miss Topsy Sinden, Miss Nellie Wallace, etc.) with appropriate degrees of approval, the reporter quoted Thomas Hood:

> Then, Pallas, take away thine Owl,
> And let us have a Lark instead.

rious city as Roman patricians; among them were the Iulii, the family of Julius Caesar and thus of his adopted son Augustus; they claimed, and Virgil of course accepts, that the son of Aeneas who founded Alba was also known as Iulus.

But the *Aeneid*, wonderful though it is, represents only one late elaboration of the complex of stories linking Troy and Italy that had been evolving ever since the first contact of Latins and Greeks eight centuries before. Even with the desperately fragmentary evidence that happens to survive, we can see that the tradition of Odysseus in Italy goes back at least as far as Hesiod, that of Diomedes at least as far as Mimnermos, that of Aeneas at least as far as Stesichoros—poets composing about 700, 630 and 580 BC respectively. And when we get to prose literature, already in the fifth century BC the historians Hellanikos and Damastes reported that Aeneas came into Italy from the land of the Molossians and joined with Odysseus in founding Rome. The Molossians lived on the mainland opposite Corcyra, so this story may imply contact via the Adriatic route. According to Aristotle, that area was known as the land of the Graikoi, a people whose self-identification seems to have given the Latins (and through them, all modern western languages) their word *Graecus*, 'Greek'.

Other stories that are known from much later authors may well derive from this archaic context. Rome's neighbour and early rival Tusculum was founded by Telegonos, the eponymous hero of Eugammon's sixth-century sequel to the *Odyssey*. He was a son of Circe and Odysseus, as were Rhomos, Anteias and Ardeias, eponyms of Rome, Antium and Ardea who evidently presuppose a sixth- or fifth-century Latium in which those cities were of equal status. Circe herself founded the Roman chariot-races in honour of her father the Sun, which is why the race-track was called *circus*; the sixth century BC is a likely date for the introduction of the 'Roman Games', and therefore also for the origin of the story. Moreover, there was a tradition that Diomedes founded the Latin city of Lanuvium; it too could be early, though it appears only in a historian of the second century AD.

One might be forgiven for thinking that legendary Italy was somewhat over-populated with wandering heroes in the aftermath of the Trojan War. The multiple traditions gave the mythographers ample opportunity to elaborate. Here is Dionysios of Halikarnassos, explaining why Roman priests, unlike Greek ones, covered their heads while sacrificing:

> They say that when Aeneas, the son of Anchises and Aphrodite, had landed in Italy and wanted to sacrifice to one or other of the gods [in fact, to Circe's father the Sun], after the prayer, while he was preparing the sacrificial rite, he saw one of the Achaeans approaching from a distance—either Odysseus, coming to consult the oracle at Avernus, or Diomedes, arriving as the ally of Daunus. Angered at the coincidence, and wanting to avert the evil omen of an enemy appearing at the ritual, he covered his head and turned his back. When the enemy had passed by, he washed his hands again and finished the sacrifice. When the ritual

Figure 3
(map: p. xxi)

turned out well, he was pleased at what had happened and preserved the same custom for all prayers, and his descendants keep this as one of their liturgical rules.

Dionysius
12.16(22)

This aetiology was sometimes combined with the story of Diomedes handing over the Palladion: Aeneas himself had covered his head and turned his back, so Diomedes entrusted it to a Trojan called Nautes, whose descendants in Rome, the patrician Nautii, were responsible for the cult of Minerva.

The Nautii claimed, indeed, that Nautes had been the priest of Athene at Troy, and had rescued the Palladion from the city himself. So there were at least four versions of how the Palladion came to Rome:

1. Aeneas brought it himself.
2. Nautes brought it himself.
3. Diomedes stole it, but gave it to Aeneas.
4. Diomedes stole it, but gave it to Nautes.

The Nautii were a noble family prominent from the fifth to the early third century BC (consuls allegedly in 488, 475, 458 and 411, certainly in 316 and 287), but totally obscure thereafter; so versions 2 and 4 are not likely to be late inventions. Versions 1 and 3 glorify the patrician Iulii, supposed descendants of Aeneas—an equally ancient family, but one whose prominence later becomes disproportionate in our literary sources thanks to Caesar the dictator and his adopted son Augustus.

There were many patrician houses who, like the Iulii, claimed descent from Troy: the Aemilii, in two versions (Aimilia the daughter of Aeneas, Aimylos the son of Ascanius); the Cloelii, the Geganii and the Sergii, from the Trojans Clonius, Gyas and Sergestus; and the Sulpicii, whose descent from Jupiter via Lavinium must have been through Aeneas. Since three of those families—the Cloelii, Geganii and Sergii—were prominent in the fifth and early fourth centuries BC but of little account in later times, we may make the same inference as for the Nautii, that these claims are likely to be be comparatively early. The Virgilian glamour of the Iulii should not lead us to imagine that Augustus' family was unique.

2.3   ARGONAUTS

The Trojan legend itself wasn't unique, either. Here is the riddling description of Rome given by the prophetess Kassandra in Lykophron's poem of the third century BC:

'[Aeneas] will create the country that is most sung in battles, blessed in its late descendants, a bastion around the tall glens of Kirkaion and the Argo's famous

Lykophron
Alexandra
1271–1280

anchorage, great Aietes, and the waters of the Marsionid lake of Phorke, and the Titonian stream of the hollow that sinks to unseen depths beneath the earth, and the slope of Zosterios, site of the gloomy dwelling-place of the virgin Sibyl, roofed over by a cavernous pit of shelter.'

Circe's island (Kirkaion) we know about already; the lake of Marsyas and Apollo's Sibyl we shall meet later (pp. 68, 49–51). But what are the Argonauts doing here?

Jason and his fellow-adventurers took the Golden Fleece from King Aietes of Kolchis at the eastern end of the Black Sea. Early versions of their voyage home had them escape the pursuing Kolchians by sailing north up the river Tanais and thence by a portage into a river that flowed into outer Ocean; then, sailing west round the edge of the world, they came to the straits of Gibraltar and from there along the north-west coast of the Mediterranean to Italy. A more economical version, relying on a very peculiar notion of the great rivers of Europe, took them up the Danube and down into the Adriatic, then up the Po and down the Rhone into the Mediterranean. The purpose of these geographical expedients was to account for the 'countless manifest signs' of the presence of the Argonauts on the west coast of Italy, from Elba to the bay of Naples. Like the wanderings of Odysseus, the voyage of *Argo* was an analogue for the ninth- and eighth-century exploration of that coast by the Euboians and their successors.

It is Circe who tells Odysseus about 'world-famous *Argo*'. As Aietes' sister, she herself was part of the Argonauts' story. They came to her island, and after that to a bay they called *Hormiai* ('anchorage') next to a harbour they called *Aietes*—which is how Latin Formiae and Caieta got their names. In a different story, Formiae was the land of the Laistrygonian cannibals in *Odyssey* book 10, and Caieta was named after Aeneas' nurse, who died there. But the Argonautic aetiology is likely to be earlier, as the allusion in the *Odyssey* implies.

Figure 3
(map: p. xxi)

Among those who sailed on *Argo* were the Spartan Dioskouroi, 'Zeus's boys' Kastor and Polydeukes, sons of Tyndareus and Leda—or of Leda and Zeus disguised as a swan—and brothers of Helen. Their exploit on the voyage was Polydeukes' defeat of the hostile king Amykos, son of Poseidon, in a boxing match. Wherever they went, cults were founded in their honour, from Dioskourias in Kolchis itself (the modern Suchumi in Georgia) to 'the Kelts who live along the western Ocean'. The existence of such cults was one of the main proofs of the Argonauts' presence in the west.

Figure 7

One example was at Lavinium on the coast of Latium, attested in the sixth century BC by a surviving bronze plaque with the archaic Latin inscription 'to Castor and Podloukes, the *kouroi*'. Kastor is already spelt with a Latin C, and later Polydeukes' name would be further tidied up, as 'Pollux'. By the early fifth century BC, Castor and his brother had a splendid temple in the Roman Forum,

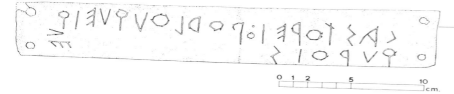

Figure 7. Bronze plaque with dedication to Castor and Pollux ('Podlouques'), from Lavinium. The text reads from right to left: CASTOREI PODLOVQVEIQVE QVROIS.

Figure 8

cited by a Macedonian general two hundred years later ('the Dioskouroi in your *agora*') as evidence of Rome's civilised status. Three of its columns still stand, elegant symbols of eternal Rome: they date from the rebuilding of AD 6, carried out by Tiberius Caesar in the name of himself and his brother Drusus, Dioskouroi to Augustus' Zeus.

The Dioskouroi account for a Spartan element in the mythology of Latium. Along the coast between Circeii and Caieta, the island of Circe and the harbour of Aietes, was the site of Amyklai (Latin Amunclae), founded by companions of Kastor and Polydeukes and named after a town in their native Sparta. It is a reasonable inference, though no source happens to tell us, that Amyklai was the site of the defeat of Amykos in the western version of the Argonauts' adventures.

According to another story, the colonists of this coast were Spartans discontented with the reforms of Lykourgos in their native city. It was they who founded the temple and cult of the goddess Feronia at what later became Tarracina. However, they then moved on up to the Sabine country; so the Sabines were Spartan by origin, which accounted for their frugality and their fondness for war. As we shall see in Chapter 6, the Romans believed there was a substantial Sabine element in their own origins, and noble families who claimed Sabine descent could think of themselves as Spartans. When Roman poets later use the learned epithet 'Oebalian' to describe both Spartans and Sabines, it refers to the

Figure 8. The remains of the temple of Castor and Pollux in the Roman Forum: an illustration (dated 1902) from the Rome of Figure 109 below.

Spartan Oibalos, whose son Tyndareus was the husband of Leda and putative father of the Dioskouroi.

2.4   ARGIVES

Much of the material in this chapter comes from Servius' huge commentary on Virgil, written about AD 400 by a learned schoolmaster working in a long tradition of literary scholarship. His reading put him in touch with parts of the Roman story-world which would otherwise be quite lost to us, and it is perfectly possible—though rarely provable—that the origins of some of the stories he refers to may date back a thousand years or more before his time. Among the many manuscripts of Servius that survive is a small group which result from the work of an erudite reader of the seventh or eighth century AD, possibly in Ireland; this unknown person inserted into his or her text of Servius substantial extra material deriving from a different ancient commentator, normally identified as the fourth-century AD grammarian Aelius Donatus. This augmented text, first edited by Pierre Daniel in 1600, is referred to by modern scholars as 'Servius *auctus*' or 'Servius Danielis'.

A single sentence of Servius *auctus*, stitched into Servius' account of the foundation of Amyklai (Amunclae), informs us that the Spartan companions of Kastor and Polydeukes were accompanied in their enterprise by Glaukos, the son of king Minos of Crete. Elsewhere, Servius describes Glaukos coming to Italy in search of a kingdom, and winning one at Labici in northern Latium. The note is very elliptical, but implies that his father Minos had been there before him; Minos in the west (at least, his death in Sicily) was a tradition known already to Herodotos. At Rome, the patrician Sulpicii Galbae claimed descent from Minos and Pasiphae. The emperor Galba had a family tree set up in the palace with his descent from Jupiter on one side and Pasiphae on the other; his biographer records this as evidence of high nobility, and doesn't seem to find it fanciful. Perhaps if Galba had had seven years in power instead of just seven months, and founded a dynasty like that of the Iulii Caesares, some epic *Glauciad* might have been written, and attracted learned commentators in late antiquity.

Another note in Servius *auctus* explains Virgil's reference to 'the grove of sacred Argiletum' at the site of Rome:

Servius auctus
on Aeneid
8.345

Others say that Danae came to Italy with her two sons Argos and Argeios, whom she bore to Phineus, and occupied the place where Rome is now; and that Argos, ambushed and killed by the Aborigines, gave his name to the place [*Argi letum*, 'death of Argos'].

The prophet Phineus is a character in the tale of the Argonauts, but Danae's arrival in Italy is a different story. She was the daughter of Akrisios king of Argos, impregnated by Zeus in the form of a shower of golden rain, and cast adrift in a chest by her furious father. Where did she and her new-born baby come ashore? According to Pherekydes of Athens (fifth century BC), it was on the island of Seriphos in the Aegean. According to Servius (whose source at least predates Virgil), it was on the coast of Latium: the fisherman who found her took her to the local king, who made her his wife. Together they founded both the capital (Ardea) and the royal dynasty of the Rutuli. So Turnus in the *Aeneid* is not only Daunian, from the Diomedes story, but also Argive, descended from king Akrisios and his primeval ancestor Inachos.

As for Perseus, Danae's son by Zeus, when he grew up he cut off the head of the Gorgon Medusa and destroyed his enemies with her petrifying gaze. Hesiod in the *Theogony* puts the Gorgons in the far west, and since Perseus and Medusa, like Amykos and Polydeukes, was a favourite subject in the art of fourth-century Latium (as we shall see in Chapter 5), it is a reasonable guess that versions of both these episodes were set in Latium itself.

There is no trace of Perseus at Rome. Danae is there in the aetiology of *Argiletum*, but the son that matters in that story is the eponymous Argos. He has a brother called Argeios (Argeus in Servius' Latin), meaning 'Argive'. He too is probably an aetiological eponym, for one of the most ancient of all Roman rituals.

Every year on 14 May the *pontifices* and the Vestal Virgins presided over the hurling of twenty-seven Argives (*Argei*) into the Tiber from the wooden bridge. These were straw figures bound up to resemble men, and they were brought from the twenty-seven 'chapels of the Argives' (*sacraria* or *sacella Argeorum*), the sites of which were carefully listed in a liturgical document, probably of the third century BC, quoted by Varro. These 'Argive places' (*Argea*) were where 'certain distinguished men of the Argives' were buried. How did they come to be in Rome?

Stories did exist of Argives in Latium: Diomedes, of course; Halaesus, who fled to Italy after the murder of Agamemnon, and founded Falerii; or the sons of the seer Amphiaraos, founders of Tibur. Orestes himself (was he Argive or Mycenaean?) brought the cult-image of Artemis to Aricia, and was buried there. But though Orestes' remains ended up in Rome, essentially those tales concerned other cities. The 'Argives' in Rome had to be explained in a different way. One explanation was through Argeios (Latin Argeus) the son of Danae. Another was through Herakles (Latin Hercules)—but that brings us into a whole new cycle of stories.

The poet Stesichoros composed his choral lyrics in the Greek city of Himera, on the north coast of Sicily, in the first half of the sixth century BC. He wrote on a grand scale, his subjects long mythic narratives that rivalled those of Homer himself in their contribution to the development and elaboration of heroic legend. One of his songs, the *Geryoneis*, told of Herakles' tenth labour, the killing of the monstrous Geryoneus in the far west and the bringing of Geryoneus' cattle back across Europe to Argos.

Stesichoros' birthplace, according to some authorities, was near the toe of Italy in a land named after the legendary Arkadians. The territory was called Oinotria, after Oinotros, or Pallantion, after Pallas: Oinotros and Pallas were sons of Lykaon the wolf-man, primeval king of Arkadia. Pallantion was also the name of one of the principal towns in Arkadia itself, in the highlands of the Peloponnese. Stesichoros mentioned the Arkadian Pallantion in his *Geryoneis*, and one version of his biography claimed that he was born there, and driven into exile in Sicily.

All that had a distinct resonance at Rome, thanks to the legend of Euandros (Latin Evander), a man driven into exile from Arkadian Pallantion. The parallel with the Stesichoros story makes it highly likely that Euandros, as well as Pallantion, featured in Stesichoros' song. It was said that Euandros had killed his father, a son of Pallas, for the sake of his mother; a different version said he was a son of Hermes, and left Pallantion voluntarily as the leader of a colonising expedition. His mother was a prophetic nymph—Themis in one version, which makes his name mean 'Goodman the son of Right'—and she accompanied him to the forests of Latium. There he and his followers settled on a hill by the Tiber which they called Pallantion, and introduced the cults of their native gods—Euandros' father Hermes (Latin Mercurius), Pallas' daughter Nike (Latin Victoria), and also Pan, 'to the Arkadians the most ancient and honoured of the gods'.

The Arkadian colony Pallantion became the Latin Palatium, the Palatine hill. A cave in its western slope was the centre of the Roman cult of Pan—the wolf-place, Lupercal, easily associated with Lykaon of Arkadia (Latin *lupus*, Greek *lykos*, a wolf). When the Romans built a temple to Victoria at the end of the fourth century BC, it was at the top of the Palatine slope above the Lupercal, on an archaic cult site which they believed Evander had chosen nine hundred years before. The temple of Mercurius was on the other side of the valley, close to a grove and spring sacred to Bona, 'the good goddess', whom some identified as Mercurius-Hermes' mother Maia (pp. 75–6 below).

All the versions of Evander's story agree that his mother was a prophetess. One of our earliest sources is the Greek scholar Eratosthenes in the third century BC, who was interested in Rome and evidently well informed about it. In one of his works he discussed the various Sibyls, who prophesied through the power

Figure 1
(map: p. xix)

Werewolves

St Augustine attests the belief that humans can be transformed into animals:

> The story goes that [Diomedes] was prevented from returning to his own people by a punishment divinely imposed; and the transformation of his companions into birds is not put forward as a baseless poetic fantasy; it is attested as historical fact. . .
>
> To bolster up this story Varro adduces the equally incredible tales about the notorious witch Circe, who transformed Ulysses' companions into animals, and about the Arcadians who were chosen by lot and swam across a certain lake and were changed into wolves and lived in the desolate parts of that region in the company of wild beasts like themselves. However, if they had not eaten human flesh they used to swim back across the lake after nine years to be turned back into human beings. To crown all, he expressly names a certain Demaenetus, telling a story of how he tasted the sacrifice which the Arcadians made to the god Lycaeus according to their custom, with a boy as a victim, whereupon Demaenetus was transformed into a wolf. Then in the tenth year he was restored to his proper shape; he trained as a boxer and won a prize at the Olympic Games.
>
> This same historian also thinks that the reason for the surname Lycaeus, given to Pan and to Jupiter in Arcadia, can only be this transformation of human beings into wolves, which they supposed could only be effected by divine power. For 'wolf' in Greek is *lykos*, and the name *Lycaeus* [*Lykaios*] is evidently derived from it. Varro also asserts that the Roman *Luperci* took their origin from these mysteries, which were, one might say, the seed from which they developed.

St Augustine goes on to discuss the powers of demons to turn people into animals (Apuleius' *The Golden Ass*, he comments, 'may be either fact or fiction'). His source here is the learned senator Marcus Terentius Varro in his treatise on the genealogy of the Roman people. For Varro, all these stories were factual.

The Arkadian tradition of human sacrifice was begun by Lykaon. It so disgusted Zeus that he turned Lykaon into a wolf and sent the flood to destroy mankind, as described in the first of Ted Hughes' *Tales from Ovid* (1997).

of Apollo. One of them, he said, was the Italian Sibyl, mother of Euandros: 'she dwelt at the *Karmalon* in Rome, and her son founded the cult-place of Pan in Rome, which is called *Luperkon*.' Eratosthenes knew the Latin place-names, and may well have given their etymologies. For *Karmalon* implies a derivation from *carmen*, a song or prophecy, and the Romans identified Evander's mother with their prophetic goddess Carmenta.

In later Latin, the Palatine slope that sheltered the Lupercal was called Cermalus. It overlooked the busy harbour area of Rome and the wide piazza which was known as Cattlemarket (*Forum bouarium*), though by the time the authors who tell us this were writing you could no more buy cattle there than today's Londoners can buy hay in Haymarket. At the north end of Cattlemarket, below the Capitol cliff, was the shrine of Carmenta next to Carmenta's Gate; at the south end was the great altar of Hercules, the Ara Maxima. That topography reflects a story made famous by the poets and historians of the Augustan age, but which originated more than five centuries earlier in Stesichoros' song of Herakles and the cattle of Geryoneus.

Driving the herd on his way back from the far west, Hercules came to Evander's settlement at Pallantion. There he killed Cacus, a monster or a brigand (according to poets and historians respectively), who had been terrorising the community and was rash enough to steal two of Hercules' cows. When Evander's prophetic mother announced that the hero was the son of Jupiter, and himself destined to become a god, the Ara Maxima was set up either by Evander or by Hercules in person; and ever after, the place was called after the cattle. We don't know whether Stesichoros himself put this exploit at the site of Rome, but it is certainly what the Romans themselves believed within a generation or two of the composition of his poem. About 530 BC, a temple at the north end of Cattlemarket was decorated with a terracotta statue-group of the hero being escorted to Olympus.

He who slays a monster (or a brigand) deserves a nymph (or a king's daughter) for his bed—and that, in one narrative idiom or the other, is how the first of the patrician Fabii was conceived. Evander's daughter was Pallantia, and her son by Hercules was called Fovius—whence Favius and then Fabius—because she was made pregnant in the dug-out (*fouea*) where the hero had his riverside camp. Like the Sulpicii with their descent from Minos (also a son of Zeus), the Herculean Fabii could challenge the Iulii, and the other 'Trojan families', in the antiquity of their noble birth.

A much less distinguished patrician house, the Pinarii, evidently claimed to be Arkadians from Evander's colony. Their ancestors were chosen by Hercules to look after his cult at the new altar, but turned up late at the inaugural sacrifice and missed the distribution of the sacrificial meat. 'As for you,' said Hercules (in Greek, naturally), 'you will go hungry', *peinasete*. That shows how old the story was, since it implies that their name was spelt Peinasios; it became Peinarios in the fourth century BC (the 'rhotacising' of intervocalic *s*), and

Figure 9

Figure 9. Acroterion of
Hercules and Minerva
from a sixth-century temple
in the Cattlemarket (*Forum
bouarium*).

Larentia

In due course the Romans built Hercules a temple next to the great altar. The sacristan who looked after it liked playing dice on festival days, and on one occasion when his usual cronies weren't around he got so bored that he played one hand against the other, the left for himself, the right for Hercules. The stake was what he knew Hercules would like, a good dinner and a girl for the night. Hercules won, so the sacristan went out to the market at the Velabrum, just round the corner, to buy the food and wine. While he was there, he hired a local beauty called Acca Larentia. (Some sources call her Fabula, 'Miss Myth'.) That evening he prepared the banquet, and burned most of it on the altar for the god. He and Larentia shared the rest; then he left her in bed in the temple, locked the door and went home.

That night the god enjoyed her thoroughly ('not like a mortal', says Plutarch), and promised her a reward. 'When my sacristan lets you out in the morning,' he said, 'just accost the first man you see.' His name was Tarutius; he was rich; he was smitten; he made Larentia the mistress of his household, and then died, leaving her a wealthy woman. Some years later, in the Velabrum market, she suddenly disappeared. Her will was found, making the Roman People heirs to the fortune the god had provided for her. Now that she had gone back to him, the Romans honoured her as a goddess with a sacrifice at the Velabrum every 23 December, the day called *Larentalia*.

Pinarius, with a long *i* replacing the diphthong, only in the second.

Myths are retold by many different sorts of narrator, and there were some who rejected as naive the story of Herakles the lone hero driving his herd. Yes, he was in Italy, but of course he came with an army, or at least a band of companions from his native Argos, not to mention prisoners and hostages picked up on his campaigns. And that, at last, explains why the *pontifices* and the Vestal Virgins dropped 'Argives' from the bridge every 14 May (p. 25 above).

Here is the account of Lucius Cornelius Epicadus, the learned freedman of Sulla the dictator in the first century BC:

> After killing Geryoneus and driving his cattle through Italy, victorious Hercules built the bridge now called Sublicius for the following purpose: he let fall from it into the river figures in the shape of men, as many as the number of comrades he had lost in the hazards of his journey, so that the flowing current would take them to the sea in place of the bodies of the dead, and as it were restore them to their native lands. From then on the custom of making such figures persisted as part of the sacred rites.

quoted in Macrobius Saturnalia 1.11.47

The more usual story was that when Hercules moved on, the 'Argive chieftains' who had accompanied him stayed behind and settled at the site of Rome. They died and were buried in their new home, and the 'chapels of the Argives' marked their graves. But they were always homesick, as Tiberinus the river-god explains to Ovid:

> 'Thus victor he returned, and with him led
> The oxen which in Spain a prey he made.
> But his companions, most of Greek descent,
> Here fixing hope and home, no further went;
> Yet for their country such a love they have
> That, dying, some would this short mandate leave:
> "My body dead into the Tiber throw,
> Which to the Grecian shore by chance may flow."
> But as the heirs disliked this black command,
> Their corps were buried in the Ausonian land;
> Instead of which (so ran the mandate just)
> Into my stream they men of rushes tossed,
> Which haply might be wafted to the Grecian coast.'

Ovid Fasti 5.649–660

With 'Greek' and 'Grecian', William Massey blurs the point: Ovid is explicit, as his aetiology requires, that these were Argives, and the substitute corpses were to float to Argos.

As for Hercules, he went south to Campania, where the Giants were in rebellion against the gods of Olympus. He defeated them, and they were imprisoned in the earth beneath Vesuvius and what is now the *solfatara* of Pozzuoli.

Figure 3 (map: p. xxi)

That done, he founded two cities, one named after himself, the other after the procession (*pompe*) that he held there to celebrate his victory. They were Herakleion and Pompaia, in Latin Herculaneum and Pompeii—not yet part of Roman myth, but one day they would be, when the Giants took revenge.

2.6 SATURNUS AND LIBER

We have been moving backwards in mythical chronology, from the Trojan War to the voyage of *Argo* to the labours of Herakles. Now we go back further still, from an age of heroes to an age of gods.

In Hesiod's *Theogony*, Kronos is one of the Titans, the children of Ouranos and Gaia (Heaven and Earth); he castrates his father and becomes the ruler of the gods, but is overthrown in turn by his own son Zeus, who makes war on the Titans and throws them into Tartarus. Not everyone was happy with the idea of Zeus' father languishing in hell (some authors have him presiding over the Isles of the Blessed), but the essential outcome of the *coup d'état* was not negotiable. Zeus reigns, and the age of Kronos is over.

The Latins, who called Zeus Jupiter and Kronos Saturnus, had their own story about what happened. Saturnus fled from Jupiter, and the land where he lay hidden (*latebat*) was called Latium. There he ruled, and 'the reign of Saturnus (*Saturnia regna*)' was the Golden Age. Or was it? He was, after all, still the god who devoured his children (as in Hesiod), and whose name was always associated with human sacrifice.

One way of looking at it was to credit Saturnus with the introduction of civilisation. As Evander explains to Aeneas in Dryden's Virgil,

'These woods were first the seat of sylvan powers,
Of nymphs and fauns, and savage men who took
Their birth from trunks of trees and stubborn oak.
Nor laws they knew, nor manners, nor the care
Of labouring oxen, nor the shining share,
Nor arts of gain, nor what they gained to spare.
Their exercise the chase: the running flood
Supplied their thirst; the trees supplied their food.
Then Saturn came, who fled the power of Jove,
Robbed of his realms, and banished from above.
The men dispersed on hills, to towns he brought;
And laws ordained, and civil customs taught;
And Latium called the land where safe he lay
From his unduteous son, and his usurping sway.
With his mild empire, peace and plenty came;
And hence the golden times derived their name.'

Virgil Aeneid
8.314–325

His Latin name Saturnus refers to sowing; the remains of his town of Saturnia could be seen on the slope of the Capitoline hill, where later the Romans built his temple and their public treasury (for he also invented coinage); his origin was proved by the fact that sacrifices at his altar were carried out 'in the Greek manner' with the head uncovered.

On the other hand, you could see Saturnus as the symbol of what men do *before* they are civilised. He was dangerous: the cult statue in the temple had its feet shackled. On this way of thinking, the bringers of civilisation were Evander, who introduced the alphabet, music and agriculture, and Hercules, who abolished the sacrifice of human beings to Saturnus, offering instead (in an alternative aetiology for the *Argei*) symbolic straw figures which were thrown from the bridge into the Tiber. At Hercules' altar too, the sacrifice was 'in the Greek manner'—proof not only of great antiquity (i.e. before Aeneas) but also of the founder's role in civilising the people of Latium.

The Argives left behind by Hercules settled at Saturnia, just across the valley from Arkadian Pallantion—in Roman terms, respectively *Capitolium* and *Palatium*, the Capitoline and Palatine hills, with the valley of the Roman Forum in between. Once again, the multiple legends give a sensation of over-crowding—and it isn't finished yet.

Figure 1
(map: p. xix)

Ovid has a wonderful story in book 6 of the *Fasti*, to explain the cult and temple of Matuta, close to Carmenta's shrine at the north end of the Cattlemarket piazza. Hercules had hardly arrived at the Tiber bank with his herd of cattle when he heard a cry for help. Rushing to the scene, he found a group of Bacchantes attacking a woman with a baby, and chased them off. He recognised her: it was Ino, daughter of Kadmos king of Thebes, with her little son Melikertes. Ino had looked after the infant Dionysos, son of her sister Semele by Zeus, and Hera in revenge had driven her mad. She had taken her baby boy and leapt off the cliff at the Isthmus of Corinth. The nymphs of the sea can take anyone anywhere (if you want those straw figures to go to Argos, just drop them into the Tiber), and mother and son had been delivered to the riverside at Evander's Pallantion. Well, why not?

The queen mother (a prophetess, remember) told Ino that her troubles were over. She would be a goddess, Leukothea in Greek, Matuta in Latin; her son would be a god, Palaemon in Greek, Portunus in Latin. And that is why the temples of Matuta and Portunus were where they were, just across Cattlemarket from the great altar of Hercules. On the other side, by the Aventine, was the Grove of Semele, centre of Rome's Dionysiac cult. As Ovid points out in his introductory prayer, Ino's story is that of Dionysos himself:

> Bacchus, whose hair is bound with berried ivy,
> If her house is your own, direct my song!

Ovid *Fasti*
6.483–484

The essentials of Ovid's light-hearted story may well date back half a millennium before his time. The temple of Matuta was attributed to king Servius

Tullius—in our terms, the mid-sixth century BC. The archaic temple found by the archaeologists, with the statue-group of Herakles' apotheosis on the roof, is in the right place at the right time, about 530 BC, and must be either Matuta's temple or that of Fortuna, which we know was next to it.

Archaeology has also revealed the much grander temple of Matuta at Satricum, which was decorated soon after 500 BC with terracotta groups on the roof representing the battle of the gods and Giants. One of the groups shows Herakles with Pallas Athene (Hercules with Minerva), as in Rome; another shows Dionysos with an unidentified young goddess, no doubt Liber and

Figure 9

Figure 10

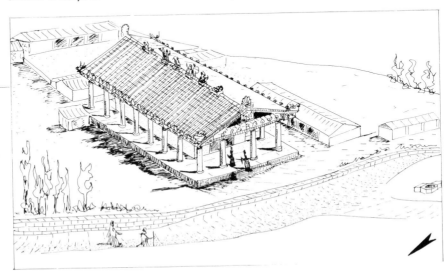

Figure 10. Reconstruction of the archaic temple of Mater Matuta at Satricum, with four of the *acroteria*: from left to right, Dionysos-Liber and a young goddess (Libera?), Juno and Jupiter, Hercules and Minerva, Diana and Apollo.

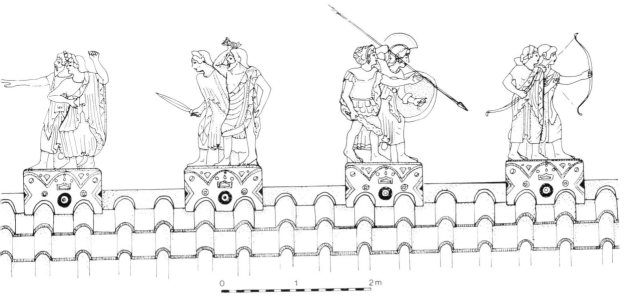

Libera, as in the god's Roman cult (p. 65 below). But the most striking feature of the temple's decoration was the series of terracotta antefixes (more than sixty have survived) showing satyrs dancing with nymphs. Satricum was next to the marsh of *Satyra*, and the very name of the town was probably a Latinisation of the Greek *Satyrikon*, the satyrs' place. Perhaps it featured in the lost story of Dionysos' war against the Etruscans, after which he left the oldest and the youngest of his satyrs behind in Italy to teach the natives viticulture.

Figure 11

The finest wine in Italy was Falernian, from the vineyards on Monte Massico in northern Campania. Dionysos happened to drop in on a farmer there called

Figure 3
(map: p. xxi)

Figure 11. Satyr and nymph dancing: an antefix from the Satricum temple.

Falernus, and in thanks for his hospitality clothed his fields with vines. That happy event took place on Hercules' route into Campania, just a few miles down the road from where the Argonauts anchored, where the followers of the Dioskouroi founded their Spartan town, and where Odysseus and his men met the man-eating Laistrygonians. Looking out from his vineyard on a clear day, Falernus could see Circe's island 40 miles to the west, and 30 miles to the south the Euboians' 'Monkey Island' of Ischia, from where the carriers of the stories we know as 'Greek mythology' first sailed to Latium in the ninth century BC.

We began this chapter with five Greek letters scratched on a vase. Only now, after a bewildering turmoil of stories that link Latium and Rome with Troy, Sparta, Argos, Arkadia and the great cycles of heroic legend, have we finally come round to the god whose ritual may have been alluded to on that pot, in Latium about 800 BC, by the revolutionary medium of the alphabet. The Latins called Dionysos Father Liber. He deserves a chapter to himself—but first we must look at one more Greek traveller to the west (not a hero or a god this time), whose descendants created a great cycle of Roman stories.

3

KINGS (AND AFTER)

THE EXILE'S TREASURE

All those stories of wandering gods and heroes reflect the age of the Mediterranean merchant venturers of the eighth and seventh centuries BC. It was a world of profit and enterprise, of ever-widening horizons, and nowhere was that more in evidence than at 'wealthy Korinthos' (Corinth).

The epithet was proverbial, and there were good reasons for it. The isthmus gave the Corinthians control over all land traffic to and from the Peloponnese, and sea traffic between Asia and Italy that wanted to avoid the stormy and dangerous voyage round Cape Malea. Those advantages were ruthlessly exploited by Corinth's ruling family, the Bacchiadai, until they were over-thrown in a *coup d'état* (allegedly in 657 BC, though it may have been later than that).

Another reason for Corinthian wealth was the crowd-pulling effect of its two great religious institutions. One was the Isthmian Games, a biennial festival rivalling that at Olympia. The other was a famous cult of the eastern love goddess, whom Phoenician travellers would recognise as Astarte (Assyrian Ishtar), but whose local name was Aphrodite. The geographer Strabo explains:

> The temple of Aphrodite was so rich that it owned more than a thousand prostitutes as 'holy slaves', whom both men and women had dedicated to the goddess. It was because of them that the city was crowded and profitable, for sea-captains spent their money easily. That's why the proverb says 'Not for every man is the voyage to Korinthos'.

Strabo
8.6.20 (378)

One of the Bacchiadai was an epic poet, Eumelos, a near contemporary of

Figure 4
(map: p. xxii)

Figure 1
(map: p. xix)

Homer and Hesiod; his story was that Helios the sun-god gave Corinth to his son Aietes, brother of Circe. But the sea god claimed it too, so the Isthmian Games were in honour of Poseidon—Poseidon *Hippios*, to be exact (he was also the god of horses).

The Bacchiadai themselves were descended from Herakles. Two of them in the eighth century BC whose Heraklean descent is emphasised in the sources were the founders of the Corinthian colonies of Corcyra in the Adriatic and Syracuse in Sicily. This involvement in the west is attested archaeologically by the wide spread of Corinthian pottery. In fact, the first securely attested character in Roman history was probably a Corinthian: Kleiklos, 'he who is famed for his fame', buried in the Esquiline cemetery in the mid-seventh century BC with his name scratched on a Corinthian vase. But it was a contemporary of his, a member of the Corinthian ruling house, whose story became that of Rome itself.

Demaratos specialised in commerce with the Etruscans, and became very rich. When he and his fellow-Bacchiadai had to flee from Corinth in 657 BC (or whenever the coup took place), he sailed to Etruria with all his wealth and a crowd of followers, and settled at Tarquinii on the Etruscan coast. He prospered there, and married an Etruscan lady. One source even says he became king, and all are agreed that he called his son Lucumo, which is 'king' in Etruscan. Lucumo in his turn married a local aristocrat, a formidable lady called Tanaquil, skilled in the Etruscan art of divination.

Unable to make his name come true in Tarquinii, Lucumo and his wife loaded up Demaratos' treasure again and set out with their household to look for a kingdom. The road brought them to the ridge of the Janiculum, looking down on the Latin community by the Tiber island. It would be good to know, but we don't, whether it was yet called by the Greek word for 'strength' (p. 16 above), and whether the huge late-seventh-century engineering works had yet been undertaken to drain and restructure the valley between the Palatium and Capitolium and turn it into the Roman Forum, the *agora* of a city-state.

If, just this once, legendary history and modern archaeology are allowed to coincide, it would be preferable to attribute those developments to Lucumo of Tarquinii himself, Latinised as Lucius Tarquinius, king of Rome. For there on the Janiculum, the gods sent him his sign. An eagle snatched his hat off, carried it high into the air, and replaced it on his head. Tanaquil read the omen; they settled, made intelligent use of the ancestral riches, and attained their kingdom. Perhaps it was Demaratos' treasure that paid for the Roman Forum.

Developing his new realm, Lucius Tarquinius remembered the Corinthian cults. Since the Isthmian games were for Poseidon Hippios, there would be games at Rome for the same god, Latinised as Neptunus Equester. He was identified with the local deity Consus, whose altar was where the race-track had to be, in the valley between the Palatine and Aventine. The race-track (*circus*) was called after Circe, daughter of the other divine patron of Corinth, Helios the

Who Came with Demaratos?

Ekphantos of Corinth invented painting: he used a pigment made of powdered earthenware. Some authorities held that he came with Demaratos to Italy. Pliny didn't believe that; but he did accept that Demaratos' followers included three craftsmen called Eucheir, Diopos and Eugrammos, who introduced into Italy the art of modelling in terracotta. Their names mean 'Dextrous', 'Keen-Sighted' and 'Skilled in Drawing'. There was also a tradition, known to Tacitus, that Demaratos taught the Etruscans the alphabet. These culture-hero legends express a historical truth, but put it too late; by the time of Demaratos, the imported skills of writing, painting and ceramics had been familiar in Etruria and Latium for a century or more. They also express a historical *fact*—the dominant Corinthian influence on Etruscan art in the seventh century BC.

sun god. The valley itself was flooded every winter and spring, when the Tiber brought down the melting Apennine snows. One of its slopes was called 'the Fair Shore'; evidently it was thought of as Poseidon-Neptunus' realm, as if it were the sea.

Similarly, it seems that Tarquinius reproduced the famously erotic Corinthian Aphrodite cult. The goddess emerged naked from the sea; where she came ashore there were myrtles growing, all that stood between her and the lustful satyrs. On the slope of the Aventine, just above the flood water of the Roman 'sea', was a myrtle grove with a cult of Fortuna Virilis, the Fortune of Men. Remember the proverb, 'Not for every man is the voyage to Korinthos': in that context, we may read 'the fortune of men' as sexual opportunity. Centuries later, Fortuna Virilis still required the women of Rome, on the first day of Aphrodite's month of April, to make themselves available like the long-forgotten temple prostitutes, wearing only garlands of Aphrodite's myrtle.

Tarquinius and Tanaquil had a son, who inherited the family wealth. He too became king at Rome, but the Romans drove him out and confiscated all the property. For years the younger Tarquinius tried one ally after another to help him win back his realm and his riches, but in vain. Eventually, in the early fifth century BC, he retreated to Kyme (Latin Cumae) in Campania, the oldest Greek city in Italy, now under the autocratic rule of Aristodemos the Effeminate. There he died, having made Aristodemos heir to the ancestral wealth of Demaratos, if only he could get it back from the Romans. The tyrant of Kyme pursued his claim by impounding the ships of a Roman embassy a few years later; but he himself was soon deposed and murdered.

These last events guarantee the historicity of the story of Demaratos' descendants. Greek historians were interested in Aristodemos, and there was evidently an early 'Kymaian chronicle' dealing with his career. So the inheritance and the story of its origin, including the rule of the Tarquinii at Rome, are likely to be authentic early data. Later chronographers were able to date the second Tarquinius' expulsion from Rome to 508/7 BC—or as they put it, twenty-eight years before Xerxes invaded Greece.

The Corinthian inheritance is the factual framework upon which the dramatic tale of the great house of Tarquin was gradually constructed. But there was other early material, from Etruria and from Latium, that contributed to it as well.

3.2 THE ETRUSCAN ANGLE

Aule and Caile Vipinas were Etruscan warriors, brothers from the coastal city of Vulci, but famous far beyond. They lived probably in the first half of the sixth century BC; that at least is the date of a handsome vase dedicated by Aule

at the Apollo temple at Veii. What little we know of their exploits comes from
two sources: Etruscan paintings of the fourth century BC, and Etruscan traditions reported by Romans, from the first century BC onwards.

An Etruscan mirror of the late fourth century BC shows them about to capture   *Figure 12*
a bard or prophet called Cacu; the grape-vine border and the little satyr in the
background suggest that by then they were already a theme for drama. Much
more spectacular is the exploit recorded in the painted tomb (also late fourth
century) of Vel Saties and his family at Vulci.

Figure 12. Etruscan mirror from
Bolsena, late fourth century BC. The
names of Caile Vipinas (left) and Aule
Vipinas (right) appear on the rim, those
of Cacu and his boy assistant Artile in
the design itself; all are written right to
left, as usual in Etruscan.

Figure 13

In the main atrium of the tomb, on either side of the entrance to the central chamber, the wall paintings presented images of heroic slaughter. On the left was Achilles sacrificing the Trojan prisoners to the ghost of Patroklos, as in *Iliad* book 23; round the corner, Eteokles and Polyneikes were killing each other, as in the *Seven Against Thebes*. To the right were Caile Vipinas being

Figure 13. The main chamber of the 'François Tomb' at Vulci, late fourth century BC. Wall-paintings: (1) Eteokles and Polyneikes, (2) Achilles sacrificing the Trojan prisoners; (3) Caile Vipinas, Macstrna, etc; (4) Marce Camitlnas and Cneve Tarchunies Rumach.

freed by Macstrna, who had brought him a sword; Larth Ulthes killing Laris Papathnas Velznach; Rasce killing Pesna Arcmsnas Sveamach; and Aule Vipinas killing Venthical [. . .]plsachs (the inscription is damaged); round the corner, Marce Camitlnas was drawing his sword on Cneve Tarchunies Rumach. All the victims have two names plus an indication of origin: Velznach may be 'from Volsinii' and Sveamach 'from Sovana'; Rumach is certainly 'from Rome'. Two of the victors have one name only, which must imply subordinate or even slave status.

We can guess the story of the main scene from the relative nudity of the figures. Caile and Aule Vipinas and Macstrna and Rasce (their respective servants?) have been captured, stripped and bound. While their captors are asleep, Larth Ulthes has stolen into the camp to rescue them, bringing swords. But the 'round the corner' scene is evidently separate: Marcus Camillus threatening Gnaeus Tarquinius of Rome (to put the names in Latin form) has probably no more to do with the Vipinas brothers than Eteokles and Polyneikes have to do with the *Iliad*.

Figure 14

Figure 14. Wall-paintings in the 'François Tomb' (fig. 13, scenes 3 and 4), as copied by Carlo Ruspi (1862).
(*a*) Scene 3, from left to right: Caile Vipinas (on the back wall), Macstrna, Larth Ulthes, Laris Papathnas Velznach, Pesna Arcmsnas Sveamach, Rasce, Venthical [...]plsachs, Aule Vipinas.
(*b*) Scene 4: Marce Camitlnas and Cneve Tarchunies Rumach.

The brothers themselves were also in Rome at one point, evidently in alliance with the first king Tarquinius; Tuscan Street (*uicus Tuscus*) and the Caelian Hill, named after Caeles Vibenna (the Latin form of the name), were thought to be where their followers settled. 'Max[tarna]' seems to have been with them on that occasion, though the text of our authority is damaged at the crucial point.

According to the learned emperor Claudius, Etruscan sources reported that Mastarna (as he spells it)

*Inscriptiones
Latinae selectae*
212.1.18–23

> was the most faithful companion of Caelius Vivenna [another eccentric spelling] and took part in all his adventures. Susequently, driven out by a change of fortune, he left Etruria with all the remnants of Caelius' army and occupied the Caelian hill, naming it thus after his former leader.

As for Aule Vipinas—Aulus (or Olus) Vibenna in Latin—he too was evidently driven out of his native Vulci. He was then killed 'by his brother's slave', which looks like a disobliging description of Caile's faithful companion Macstrna. Denied burial in his native soil, Aule was secretly interred in Rome, on the hill sacred to Saturnus.

Now, Lucius Tarquinius was determined to build a huge temple to Jupiter on that very hill. Hardly had his engineers started digging the foundations when the head of Aule, perfectly preserved, rolled into view. One late source reports that it carried an Etruscan inscription meaning 'the head of king Olus'. This was a portent, and Etruscans were experts in interpreting portents. Did the king ask the advice of his consort Tanaquil? For this, perhaps, something more formal was necessary.

At any rate, an embassy was sent to consult the leading Etruscan authority. He took their enquiry very seriously, carefully drawing in the dust a plan of Rome and the site of the new temple. 'Now,' he said, pointing with his stick at the spot, 'you say the head was found *here*?' 'No,' replied the ambassadors, who had been warned of this gambit. 'Not *here*, but at Rome, on the Tarpeian hill.' The seer, foiled in his attempt to transfer the omen to his own land, revealed that the place where the head was found was fated to be the head of all Italy. (His son Argus, who had tipped off the embassy, fled to Rome; the seer pursued and killed him, thus providing yet another explanation for Argiletum, 'Killargus Street'.) The hill where the temple of Jupiter was built was called thereafter Capitolium from *caput Oli*, the head of Olus.

All this gives a vivid impression of the wide-open, 'Wild West' nature of Latin and Etruscan society in the sixth century BC. Where did the power and resources come from, to turn village communities into city-states with grand temples and paved squares, to pay the architects and master-craftsmen, to buy the girls who would serve the goddess? If the son of a Corinthian merchant prince could make himself king at Rome, so could the slave-companion of an Etruscan warlord. And that is exactly what Macstrna did, according to Claudius' Etruscan sources.

The Roman tradition knew nothing of a 'King Maxtarna'. But it did know of a king who was born a slave, and it put him precisely at the appropriate place, as successor to the first Tarquinius. Now we have a Latin story, not a Corinthian or Etruscan one.

3.3   THE SLAVE KING

King Tarquinius, making war on his Latin neighbours, captured the town of Corniculum and took as his slave a beautiful girl called Ocrisia. He gave her to queen Tanaquil, who taught her to serve at the royal table and tend the royal hearth, where the first portions of each meal were burned as an offering to the gods who guard the household.

The queen, skilled in divination, perceived one day in the ashes of the hearth sacrifice the shape of a male sexual organ. She stirred the ash, and it stood erect. In another version of the story, it rose spontaneously as Ocrisia herself knelt to make the offering and pour the libation. Tanaquil and the king's soothsayers understood the portent. They told Ocrisia of her high privilege, arrayed her as a bride, and retired. Positioning herself appropriately for the divine orgasm, Ocrisia conceived the destined child.

What god was it who manifested himself in this way? Evidently the Lar, guardian of the household, or Genius, the power of procreation. Learned scholars of a later age believed that Lares and Genii were identical. One author says it was the Seedsowing Gods (*di conserentes*)—but he was a Christian polemicist, keen to emphasise the grotesqueness of this pagan story, and it would suit his argument to imagine an anonymous committee of gods with only one penis between them. Some sources said it was Volcanus, the god of fire—but that doesn't fit very well (the apparition came from the ashes, not the flames), and was probably influenced by a later rationalisation.

Sober historians would have nothing to do with the divine conception story. They claimed that Ocrisia was already pregnant when she was captured, her husband Tullius having been killed in the war, or else that she was married to one of Tarquinius' followers. For them, her son was just an ordinary slave boy until one day he was marked out by a more acceptable portent: flames played round his head without hurting him. Only then, in the historians' version, was he taken up by the royal couple and groomed for the succession.

At any rate, Servius Tullius, as the boy was known (Servius from *seruus*, a slave), did in due course become king. One tradition—quite inconsistent with the historical story of Demaratos' descendants—had it that Tarquinius left no male heirs. But in that case, why was Servius' succession opposed? For opposed it was. The old royal palace, which survived for seven centuries until Nero's fire in AD 64, had a conspicuous upper window next to the Palatine gate. From there, with her husband's corpse on the bed behind her, Tanaquil addressed the anxious crowd and issued false bulletins about the king's health while Servius organised his *coup d'état*. Later, it was through the same bedroom window that the goddess Fortuna came to visit her lover—king Servius, fortune's favourite, the luckiest of men.

What really happened at Rome in the mid-sixth century BC, nobody knows. But a low-born usurper, identified by the Etruscans as Caile Vipinas' liegeman Macstrna, could well have been metamorphosed in the Roman tradition into a divinely conceived slave-boy brought up in the Tarquin palace. For such a ruler, divine conception would be a necessary myth.

Rome was a real prize for the ambitious. It was in its second or third generation as a recognisable city-state (public market-place, public buildings, temples at cult sites), and even in its previous existence as a community of villages it had already outgrown any comparable Latin centre. No doubt that was because of its function as a cross-roads. It is not surprising that a man of Korinthos, son of a merchant prince, had chosen to settle there.

By now the Corinthian commercial influence was waning. The Greek ships that sailed the west coast of Italy in the sixth century BC were more often from the Ionian cities of the eastern Aegean, with the Samians, famous seafarers, conspicuous among them. They brought a cargo of ideas, too. Among those who made their home in sixth-century Italy were the poet and philosopher Xenophanes, from Ionian Kolophon, and the famous Pythagoras, mathematician, mystic and social reformer, who came from Samos. It is probably in that company that Promathion of Samos belongs. Aristotle cites him on the geography of the far west—the river Chremetes beyond the pillars of Herakles, which flows from the Silver Mountain where the Nile rises. But he also wrote on Italy, and Plutarch quotes from him, probably at second or third hand, a very peculiar story about 'Tarchetios the king of the Albans, a most lawless and cruel man'.

The Albans were Latins; Mount Albanus was the site of the great pan-Latin cult centre of Jupiter Latiaris. But 'Tarchetios' is evidently an Etruscan name, akin to Tarchon (legendary founder of Tarquinii) and indeed to Tarquinius. Here is what Promathion of Samos, filtered through Plutarch, says about him:

> In his house there occurred a supernatural manifestation: a phallus arose out of the hearth and remained there for many days. There was in Tyrrhenia [Etruria] an oracle of Tethys [wife of Okeanos], from whom Tarchetios received the response that a virgin must have intercourse with the apparition, for she would bear a child of great fame, pre-eminent in courage, good fortune and strength [*rhome*]. And so Tarchetios told one of his daughters the prophecy, and ordered her to have intercourse with the phallus; but she thought it unworthy of her, and sent in a slave girl to do it.
>
> When he found out, Tarchetios was furious. He seized both the girls to put them to death, but Hestia [Vesta, goddess of the hearth] appeared to him in his sleep and forbade him to kill them. So he chained them and gave them a particular task

of weaving to do, on the understanding that when they had finished it they would be given in marriage. They wove by day, but by night other girls unravelled the weaving on Tarchetios' orders.

When the slave girl gave birth to twins by the phallus, Tarchetios gave them to a certain Teratios ['prodigy expert'?] to destroy them. He took them and put them down close to the river. Then there came a she-wolf which suckled the babies, and birds of all kinds brought morsels of food and fed them, until a herdsman, seeing this with amazement, ventured to approach and pick the children up. So they were rescued, and when they grew up they attacked Tarchetios and overcame him.

Plutarch Romulus 1.3–6

As it stands, the story doesn't work: Tethys promises one son, and the slave girl gives birth to two. But it is easy to guess what has happened. At some point in the six centuries between Promathion and Plutarch, an intermediate source adjusted the story to make it fit the Romans' later foundation-legend of Romulus and Remus.

The prophecy of primeval Tethys has to be justified. The slave girl had one son, and his strength [*rhome*] must imply that the city was named after him. Perhaps already the founder hero was called Romulus, an early adjectival form like *Siculus* for 'Sicilian'. The river where he was exposed must be the Tiber. For Tarchetios had defied the oracle and chosen to treat the baby as a monstrous birth, to be taken a good safe distance and washed away in running water. No doubt he assumed that only his daughter's child could have fulfilled the prophecy. But when a tyrant tries to establish a dynasty, the gods raise up the son of a slave.

If Promathion of Samos does indeed belong in the early fifth century BC (and not everyone accepts that), then the story he picked up must surely have originated in the power politics of sixth-century Rome. A self-imposed ruler, low-born but claiming divine descent, might naturally create a foundation-legend mirroring his own myth, as if to say 'this is how the gods of the Roman hearth (Lar or Genius, and Vesta) have always manifested their divine will'. Tarchetios of Alba was a tyrant overthrown by force; is that what happened to Lucius Tarquinius of Rome? The Promathion story perhaps reflects the reality of conflict more accurately than the Servius Tullius tale of a boy brought up in the palace who needs only a little deception by Tanaquil at the window to get himself accepted in a peaceful transfer of power.

One element of the later tradition may be more or less historical. Servius Tullius set up the citizen assembly organised by age- and property-groups— 'Tullius, who stablished firm the People's freedom,' as a later playwright put it. Various popular measures were attributed to him (debt relief, division of public land); and there was even a story that he was going to abdicate, or abolish the Roman monarchy altogether, and was only prevented when Tanaquil, on her death-bed, made him swear not to. The People loved him, and grieved when he was overthrown and murdered by Tarquinius' arrogant son.

It seems clear enough that the sixth century BC in Rome was a period of strife in which different types of authority were in conflict, the descendants of Demaratos evidently trying to establish a dynasty, Macstrna (if it was he) looking for a personal rule based on the support of the people. And who was 'Gnaeus Tarquinius of Rome', who seems about to be killed by Marce Camitlnas in the Vulci tomb painting? The details are lost, but the general picture is intelligible. The organised norms of a city-state were not yet mature; an older and cruder tradition, of clan chiefs and their 'companions' acting as quasi-feudal warlords, was still powerful.

Figure 14 (p. 43)

That tentative modern view is based on what look like early elements in the confused tradition about the Roman kings. The Romans themselves, as we shall see, evolved a much less messy story; the political issues were interpreted in the light of the long history of the Roman Republic, with its consistent conflict between the many and the few, between popular liberty and aristocratic authority. For them, Servius Tullius was either 'the ignoble reign' or 'the last of the good kings'.

3.4   GODS AND MEN

It was a time of seers and wonder-workers, enterprising holy men who offered salvation in the market-place:

> 'My friends, who dwell in the great town of ——————,
> Who take careful thought for deeds of goodness,
> Respectful havens for strangers, unacquainted with evil,
> Hail! I am a deathless god, no longer mortal,
> As I go about held in honour by all, as is proper,
> Crowned with ribbons and freshly blooming garlands.
> Whenever I come to their flourishing towns,
> By men and women I am honoured; they follow me
> In thousands to ask where the way of advantage lies,
> Some needing prophecies, some asking to hear
> The word of healing for all kinds of ills. . . '

quoted in
Diogenes Laertius
8.64

The greatest of them was Pythagoras, whose groups of ascetic followers established themselves in power in several Greek cities of south Italy in the late sixth century BC. At Kroton, where he lived, they believed he was Apollo; it was known and attested that he could be in two places at once. One of the secret doctrines of his cult was that there were three types of rational living beings: gods, men and Pythagoras. He came from Samos, but some said he was 'Tyrrhenian', which ought to mean Etruscan, and there was even a story that he was a citizen of Rome.

Two hundred years after Pythagoras' own time, when there was a strong revival of interest in his doctrines, Pythian Apollo told the Romans to set up statues to 'the wisest and the bravest of the Greeks'. Their choice for the wisest was Pythagoras, whose bronze statue, with that of the Athenian Alkibiades, stood in front of the Senate house for over two hundred years. The 'citizen of Rome' story may belong to that time (late fourth century), as may the Romans' firm belief that the wisest of their kings, whom we shall meet in a moment, was a Pythagorean. But it is likely enough that there were already Romans among Pythagoras' original disciples in the sixth century BC. And this, according to those later followers, is what they believed:

> All decisions about what to do or what not to do are aimed at being in accord with the divine. This is the principle; all of life is so ordered to follow the god. . . Since god exists and is lord of all, obviously we must ask our lord for what is good; and since everyone gives good things to those they love and delight in, and the opposite to those for whom they feel the opposite, clearly we must do what does delight god. But it is not easy to know what that is, unless you can find out by the god listening to you, or yourself listening to the god, or through some divine technique.

Iamblichus De vita Pythagorica 137–8

Hence the Pythagoreans' interest in divination, as a means of communicating with the divine will.

If you believe that god is lord of all, you're always likely to be in conflict with secular authority. Two stories about king Lucius Tarquinius give us an idea of the tensions that might be involved. We must imagine him throned at the Comitium, with his subjects crowding round in the wide open space of the newly created Roman Forum.

An old, old woman appears, clutching nine scrolls. She has come a long way, and her servants make a fire in a brazier at the edge of the Forum. 'Oracles of the gods, o king! Do you want to know the fates of Rome? Do you want to know how to expiate evil omens? They are yours for three hundred gold pieces.' The king laughs in her face and dismisses her. She goes to the fire, and carefully burns three of the scrolls. 'Six books of prophecy now, o king, and the price is still the same.' Ridiculous! Go away! She goes to the fire, and burns three more. 'Your last chance, o king. Three hundred gold pieces.' The king hesitates, consults his advisers, and pays. The old woman—Amaltheia, the Sibyl of Kyme (Cumae)—hands over the three scrolls, and immediately vanishes.

Figure 15

The second story features a poor farmer's son who made good. Attus Navius was divinely instructed in the arts of augury when he was looking for the finest cluster of grapes to offer to the Lares, who had helped him to find a lost pig. When his gift was recognised, he became the king's adviser—but kings like to have their own way. Lucius Tarquinius had decided to double the number of 'centuries of cavalry' and name the new bodies after himself and his friends. Navius told him he couldn't. Whose authority should prevail? The king

VLTIMA CVMÆI VENIT IAM
CARMINIS AETAS, MAGNVS
ABINTEGRO SAECLORVM
NASCITVR ORDO, IAM RE
DIT ET VIRGO, REDEVNT
SATVRNIA REGNA, IAM
NOVA PROGENIES CÆLO
DEMITTITVR ALTO

SIBYLLA·CVMANA·CVIVS·MEMINIT·VIRGILIVS·ECLOG·IV

summoned Navius to the Comitium to justify his status as a seer.

'All right, prophet,' said Tarquinius. 'I have it in mind to do something; go and consult your gods and tell me whether it can be done.' Navius performed the requisite auguries and reported that what the king had in mind could indeed be done. Tarquinius grinned at the crowd. 'That proves you're a charlatan,' he said. 'My intention is to cut this whetstone in half with a razor. Now let's see if you're right.' Unperturbed, trusting his gods, Navius took the razor and cut the stone in half.

Bronze statues of the Sibyl and of Attus Navius stood at the Comitium. Close by was a sacred enclosure where the stone and razor were buried, and 'Navius' fig-tree', evidence of another of his miracles, was carefully preserved as a guarantee of the freedom of the Roman People. Seers and wonder-workers provide reassuring evidence that royal power is not absolute. Even kings must obey the gods.

The Romans' paradigm of a wise and pious king was Numa Pompilius. He was their lawgiver and the creator of their religious institutions, and his reign was proverbial for peace and tranquillity. He came from Cures, up-country among the frugal Sabines, but what made Numa special was his consort, the nymph Egeria. She was one of the Camenae, whose grove and spring were in the valley between the Aventine and Caelian hills. The Camenae were thought of as goddesses of inspiration (Greek authors called them Muses), and Egeria inspired king Numa, her lover. Anyone who doubted that must have been convinced by Numa's famous dinner party. As the guests sat down to meagre fare in the Sabine king's simple house, the king announced that Egeria was joining them, and suddenly the room was filled with luxurious furniture and sumptuous food and wine.

She taught him how to make gods reveal their knowledge, how to read oracles, how to mollify the divine anger and temper the gods' demands with humanity. On the Aventine, not far from Egeria's grove, was the altar of Jupiter Elicius, where the ritual offering to ward off thunderbolts was made with onions, hair and sardines. That was the result of Numa bargaining in person

Figure 15. Francesco di Stefano, 'Sibilla Cumana' (1482): one of the ten Sibyls in the marble floor of the nave aisles in the cathedral at Siena. She holds the last three books, and the six that Tarquin rejected are just beginning to burn. The whole series of ten Sibyls is taken from Lactantius (*Inst.* 1.6.7-12), who in turn took it from Varro (*Antiquitates divinae*, 47 BC). But this Sibyl is also Virgilian. In her right hand she holds the golden bough with which she escorted Aeneas to the underworld in *Aeneid* 6; in the panel are lines 4-7 of Virgil's fourth *Eclogue*, which Christians believed was a prophecy of the birth of Christ. In Guy Lee's translation (1980):

> Now the last age of Cumae's prophecy has come:
> The great succession of centuries is born afresh.
> Now too returns the Virgin; Saturn's rule returns;
> A new begetting now descends from Heaven's height.

51

Hanging Sibyls

For *The Waste Land* (1922), T.S. Eliot offered his readers a very austere epigraph:

Nam Sibyllam quidem Cumis ego oculis meis vidi in ampulla pendere, et cum illi pueri dicerent: Σίβυλλα τί θέλεις; respondebat illa: ἀποθανεῖν θέλω.

No translation, not even a reference. In fact, this is Trimalchio in Petronius' *Satyricon*, talking to one of his dinner guests: 'Do you remember the story about Ulysses and how the Cyclops twisted his thumb off? I used to read that in Homer when I was a boy. In fact [here begins the Eliot passage], I actually saw the Sibyl at Cumae with my own eyes. She was hanging in a jar, and when the boys asked her "What do you want, Sibyl?", she answered "I want to die".'

It's nonsense, of course, like all Trimalchio's Homeric allusions. Here he has garbled Odysseus' visit to Hades with that of Aeneas and the Cumaean Sibyl in Virgil (*Aeneid* 6), and with Ovid's story that the Sibyl had asked Apollo for as many years as there were grains in a heap of sand, but without also asking for eternal youth.

There was no Sibyl at Cumae in the first century AD. However, it suited Robert Graves to believe there was, and in the first chapter of *I, Claudius* he brings his stammering hero to visit her. There she was, 'more like an ape than a woman, sitting in a cage that hung from the ceiling. . . Her toothless mouth was grinning.' This turns out to be the mummified corpse of the previous Sibyl. The present incumbent, enthroned at ground level, speaks to him in Greek, her voice that of a girl:

'Ten years, fifty days and three,
Clau- Clau- Clau- shall given be
A gift that all desire but he.'

That gives us the date: 30 November, AD 30. In the parallel universe inhabited by characters in novels, Claudius could easily have bumped into Trimalchio's school party at the Sibyl's cave.

with Jupiter at that very spot. The god wanted human sacrifice—'living human heads'. When Numa offered living fish, human hair and onion heads, Jove laughed and the deal was done. As Pythagoras said, find out what delights the god, and do that.

If you didn't want to believe in the literal truth of the Egeria stories, it was easy to attribute good king Numa's wisdom and piety to the teaching of Pythagoras. That idea, particularly attractive to Greek historians of Rome, dates back at least to the Pythagorean revival of the late fourth century BC, and it may be even earlier than that. In Pythagoras' own time, at the end of the sixth century BC, the Romans were much exercised by the nature of kingship, what a good king should and should not be. This was when they threw out the younger Tarquinius ('Tarquin the Proud') and inaugurated the regime which eventually became the Roman Republic. It is quite possible that the story of the pious and frugal Numa, friend of the gods and friend of the People, was created as an ideal of monarchy at a time of furious dissatisfaction with a wealthy and tyrannical ruler.

3.5 THE VULTURES, THE SNAKE AND THE DOG

As we shall see in Chapter 6, the Romans later evolved a long and dramatic history of the Tarquin dynasty and its fall, full of the anachronisms and patriotic fictions inseparable from the foundation-story of a free republic. But even in the fully developed narratives of Livy and Dionysios, written nearly five hundred years after the event, early elements can be identified that may go back to a time when people still had some idea of what really happened in or about 507 BC. As so often, the most revealing stories are those that involve the gods.

Proud king Tarquin had a palace, and next to the palace he had a garden, where he used to feast with his friends. It was a peristyle garden, with a portico of painted wooden columns, and in it there was a tall palm tree, where a pair of eagles had nested and hatched their young. In the palace were the king's wife and two young sons, and also a mute boy called Brutus, apparently an idiot, whom they mocked and abused. His father and brother had been killed by Tarquin.

One day, when the king and his friends were enjoying their banquet in the peristyle, a huge snake slithered out of one of the wooden columns and attacked the diners, driving them out of the garden. In one version of the story, the snake barked like a dog. And then a flock of vultures attacked the nest in the palm tree and destroyed it, killing the young eagles. The parent birds were away hunting; when they returned, the vultures attacked them too and drove them away from the tree.

Anxious, the king decided to consult Apollo at Delphi. He sent his sons, and they took Brutus with them as something to kick on the journey. At the shrine, the young princes presented their rich gifts, and dumb Brutus offered his, a stick of wood. Apollo's answer seemed reassuring. The king's throne would only be threatened when a dog spoke with a human voice. But now the two princes had a question of their own: who would be king after their father? 'He who first kisses his mother will hold the power.' As they hurried out of the temple to get back home, dumb Brutus fell flat on his face.

Tarquin went off to besiege the wealthy city of Ardea, so confident in the security of his throne that he even took his wife with him. Apollo laughed. He knew that Brutus' mute idiocy was feigned, that the wooden stick he had offered at Delphi had a shaft of gold concealed within it, and that when he fell on his face he had kissed Mother Earth. They had treated Brutus like a dog, and now the dog spoke.

We don't know exactly what happened, but the implications of the vultures story are clear enough. The Romans must have destroyed the Tarquins' palace, killed their sons and driven the royal couple themselves into exile when they returned. The fact that the portents are so uncomplimentary—the Romans as carrion birds, Brutus as a barking snake—is the best guarantee that the story is early. It comes not from the Romans' own self-congratulatory tradition, but more probably from a Greek historian sympathetic to the house of Demaratos. Another sign of early date is the quasi-regal power Apollo promises to Brutus. Whatever position of authority he held in the post-revolution regime, it was clearly not the power-sharing consulship of the fully developed Republic.

Nor was the revolution itself the straightforward achievement of political freedom celebrated in the later Roman legend. Another Etruscan warlord, Lars Porsena of Clusium, occupied Rome as soon as Tarquin had left, and imposed humiliating terms on the Romans. He withdrew only when his army was defeated in an attack on the Latin city of Aricia. The Latins were victorious with the help of an army from Greek Kyme under Aristodemos the Effeminate, the autocrat with whom Tarquin eventually took refuge (p. 40 above) and whose story brought these events into the range of reliable Greek historiography.

Survivors from the Etruscan army took refuge in Rome. The place where they settled became known as 'Tuscan Street'—unless it was the followers of Caile and Aule Vipinas a generation earlier who had given it that name. Either way, it was a reminder of the Etruscan warriors who were always interested in controlling the Tiber crossing. The citizens had won their freedom, but keeping it wouldn't be easy.

What Counts as Truth

In Cicero's dialogue *De republica*, Scipio denounces the common view that Numa was a Pythagorean as 'not only an invention, but an ignorant and absurd invention', clearly disproved by chronological records. 'Good heavens,' replies Manilius, 'What a blunder! And believed for so long! Still, I'm not sorry that we Romans were educated not in arts imported from overseas but in the genuine virtues of home.' Livy took a similar line in his *History*; he preferred to think of Numa's wisdom coming from the austere and unbending discipline of the ancient Sabines.

For Plutarch, in his biography of Numa, it wasn't so easy. He knew the chronological arguments all right—but on the other hand it's hard to be exact, the dates may not be reliable, we don't want to argue like opinionated young men on such a disputed question, and so on. As a Greek and a philosopher, he felt strongly that somehow it *had* to be true: 'so we may well excuse those who aspire to link Numa with Pythagoras on the evidence of so many resemblances.'

Another Ciceronian dialogue, *De divinatione*, brings in the story of Attus Navius and the whetstone as evidence for the divine power of augury. Quintus in book 1 is impatient with the sceptics: 'Let's deny it all, let's burn the annals, let's say it's an invention—anything at all rather than admit that the gods care about human affairs!' But Marcus in book 2 will have none of it: 'Invented stories should have no place in philosophy.' Whose side are we meant to be on, the traditional believer's or the sceptical rationalist's? It's up to us, says Cicero at the end of the dialogue. He has simply set out the case for each view, leaving the listeners free to make their judgement.

Readers of this book, interested as much in story-telling as in real history, may perhaps have some sympathy with Quintus and Plutarch.

THE BARONS' STORIES

The territory of Rome in the late sixth century BC was divided up into districts called *tribus*—not kin-groups, as the modern sense of 'tribe' would suggest, but geographically defined. There were twenty of them, four in the city, sixteen in the country, and since the 'rural tribes' all have family names (as for instance *tribus Fabia* from the Fabii), the natural assumption is that the dominant landowner gave his name to each area. Later tribes, added as Roman territory expanded, were given topographical names, but the original sixteen preserved as a kind of fossil the names of the territorial magnates of Rome in the last years of the monarchy.

Here they are in alphabetical order:

Aemilia	Menenia
Camilia	Papiria
Claudia	Pollia
Cornelia	Pupinia
Fabia	Romilia
Galeria	Sergia
Horatia	Voltinia
Lemonia	Voturia

Six of the sixteen families evidently died out: nothing more is known of the Camilii, Galerii, Lemonii, Pollii, Pupinii or Voltinii. By contrast, the Aemilii, the Claudii, the Cornelii and the Fabii lasted triumphantly throughout the history of the Republic, and beyond; five and a half centuries later, the Claudii even provided an unexpected emperor.

As we have seen (p. 28 above), the Fabii claimed to be descended from Hercules. The Aemilii went back to Aeneas, who had a daughter Aimylia and a grandson Aimylos, and to Numa and Pythagoras, each of whom had a son nicknamed *aimylos* (Greek for 'graceful'), which the Aemilii translated as *lepidus* and used as a surname. As for the Claudii, they came from the Sabine country. They knew that Attus Clausus had brought his family and five thousand dependants to settle on the border land north of the river Anio, but when the migration had taken place was disputed. Some authorities said it was soon after the foundation of Rome, in Romulus' time; others put it in the sixth year after the expulsion of the Tarquins.

Two early stories that happen to survive in the literature may have begun life as family myths of the Claudii and the Cornelii. The first was used by the Alexandrian scholar-poet Kallimachos in the third century BC, as an example of pan-Hellenic virtue; it is known today only from a commentator's summary which quotes the first line of the poem. The Romans are being besieged. One of the defenders leaps from the wall and kills the enemy commander, at the cost of a wound in the thigh. When afterwards he complains about his limp, his mother rebukes him: every step he takes should be a reminder of his valour. Since the Greek poet didn't understand Roman nomenclature, the hero is called simply 'Gaius the Roman'. But *claudus* is Latin for 'lame', so perhaps his family name was Claudius.

The other story is told by various authors of the first century BC and later, but its origin goes back half a millennium before that, to a time when Rome's Sabine neighbours were also her rivals. A heifer of wondrous size and perfection is born on a Sabine farm. A prophet tells the farmer that it is sent by the gods, and that whoever sacrifices it at the great temple of Diana, on the Aventine south of Rome, will guarantee for his people rule over Italy. The farmer's slave overhears the prophecy and tells the king of Rome, Servius Tullius, who passes on the message to the priest in charge of the temple. When the Sabine turns up at the Aventine with the miraculous heifer, the priest tells him first to wash in the Tiber, and while he is doing so sacrifices the beast himself. The huge horns (*cornua*) were set up on the temple itself, and no doubt that is the reason why the cunning priest was called Cornelius.

Papirii, Sergii and Veturii also had long histories, if less distinguished ones than the 'big four'; Horatii, Romulii and Menenii, on the other hand, are known only from the suspect magistrate lists of the fifth and early fourth centuries BC. But all six families had their legendary ancestors. Sergestus, the proto-Sergius, came from Troy with Aeneas. Mamurius Veturius was the craftsman who copied the shield that fell from heaven (p. 78 below). Romulius Denter was the deputy of Romulus the founder-king. Sextus Papirius collected and codified the laws of the kings. Menenius Agrippa was the wise patrician who calmed rebellious plebeians with the parable of the belly and the limbs: if the limbs go on strike against the belly, the whole body dies.

Most elaborate of all, however, are the stories of the Horatii. There are three of them, each with its exemplary hero and each leaving a visible reminder for posterity. Since the family disappears from the historical record in the early fourth century BC, we can be sure that all three stories date back a long way.

The first belongs to the war of Rome against her legendary mother-city Alba Longa. (The conquest of Alba, founded by Aeneas' son Ascanius, was a necessary link in the story of Rome's Trojan ancestry.) There were triplets in each of the opposing armies, the Horatii for Rome, the Curiatii for Alba, and the issue was decided by matching them against each other. At first the Albans got the better of it, killing two of the Romans but receiving wounds in the process. The surviving Horatius was unhurt and ran from his opponents, whose injuries slowed them up at different rates. When they were sufficiently separated, he turned and killed them one by one.

He stripped the bodies and returned in triumph to Rome, where he met his sister at the gate. She was engaged to one of the Curiatii, and cried out in grief as she saw her lover's bloodstained cloak. Horatius killed her on the spot. His father refused to condemn the act, and by a ritual purification the hero was cleansed of the pollution of kin-murder. The wooden yoke he had to pass under was preserved as the *tigillum sororium* (Sister's Beam); the weapons of the defeated Albans hung from a pillar in the Forum (*pila Horatia* can mean both 'Horatian spears' and 'Horatian pillar'); and the battlefield itself, five appropriately spaced tombs in half a mile of green grass near the fifth milestone of the Via Appia, was still known centuries later as the Field of the Horatii.

The second Horatian story is about the great temple of Jupiter Optimus Maximus on the Capitol. The temple was built by the Tarquins, but they were expelled before it was completed and dedicated. That was done by Marcus Horatius, presumably as chief magistrate of the post-revolution regime; his name was there on the inscription for over four hundred years, until the temple was burned to the ground in the civil war of 83 BC. The dedicator of a temple must be free of any ill-omened connection with grief or mourning. Marcus Horatius' son was away fighting, across the Tiber in a Roman campaign against Veii. Marcus was just carrying out the dedication ritual when a messenger announced that his son was dead. 'That is nothing to me,' he said. 'Cast out the body; I will not grieve or mourn.' So Jupiter's temple escaped the contagion of death.

The sacred grove of 'the hero Horatius', across the Tiber in the direction of Veii, may be evidence for the death of the warrior son. A later version of the story, claiming that the report of his death was a malicious falsehood, probably belongs to a time when it was assumed that Horatius must have been a power-sharing consul, with a jealous colleague.

The third Horatian story is about a man called Cocles. The name is old Latin for 'born with one eye', but that seems to have no bearing on his exploit; it must have been the real name of a historical character. The story evidently predates the building of Rome's great circuit wall in the early fourth century BC. Cocles' Rome was defended on one side only by the river, over which there was just one narrow bridge, the Pons Sublicius. When Rome was threatened from the Etruscan side, the bridge had to be held or broken.

Here is the earliest extant form of the story, told by Polybios as one of the exemplary tales that inspired the young Romans of his day to lay down their lives for their country:

> The story goes that while Horatius Cocles was engaged with two of the enemy at the far end of the bridge over the Tiber which gives entrance to the city on the west, he saw a huge body of reinforcements approaching. Fearing that they would succeed in forcing the passage and entering the city, he turned round and shouted to those behind him to retire at once and make haste to break down the bridge. His comrades obeyed, and all the time that they were demolishing it he stood his ground. He suffered many wounds, but he held back the enemy's attack and astounded them not so much by his physical strength as by his endurance and courage.

Once the bridge was cut the enemy's advance was halted, whereupon Cocles threw himself into the river still wearing his armour and weapons. He deliberately sacrificed himself because he valued the safety of his country and the glory which would later attach to his name more than his present existence and the years of life that remained to him. This is a typical example, it seems to me, of the spirit of emulation and the ambition to perform deeds of gallantry which the customs of the Romans help to implant in their young men.

Polybios 6.55

If you jump in a deep river in full armour, of course you drown. But all the other versions of the story have Cocles miraculously saved by the gods; he comes safe to shore, still with his arms, and is rewarded with a statue in the Comitium and as much land as he can plough round in a day. Though our sources don't spell it out, that land must be the *tribus Horatia*.

The Etruscan attack was foiled, and Rome was saved. Polybios doesn't specify the occasion, but from Livy onwards all accounts agree that it was Lars Porsena's army coming to reimpose the rule of Tarquin. Virgil puts the scene on the shield Volcanus makes for Aeneas:

> There was Porsenna, too, demanding that Tarquin
> Should be taken back, and laying siege to Rome
> While Aeneas's descendants threw themselves
> Against the attackers for the sake of liberty.
> You might have seen Porsenna then depicted
> Menacing them in fury as he saw
> Cocles cutting the bridge down . . .

Virgil *Aeneid* 8.646–650

A story to account for a noble family's broad acres, and the district that took its name from them, has been turned into an exemplary tale for the whole community, the heroic defence of *libertas*.

The kings were gone, and would not return for five hundred years. But liberty couldn't be taken for granted. The Romans would have to defend it, and they would need the help of their gods.

'Even the ranks of Tuscany
Could scarce forebear to cheer.'

From the middle of the nineteenth to the middle of the twentieth century, 'How Horatius kept the bridge' was the one Roman story every English-speaking person knew. As the first of Macaulay's *Lays of Ancient Rome* (1842), it was used just as the Romans used it, a lesson in bravery and patriotism to be learned by generations of schoolchildren.

Macaulay's brilliant adaptation of the historians' narratives to ballad form successfully concealed the erudition on which it was based. The famous opening, for example,

> Lars Porsena of Clusium
>> By the Nine Gods he swore
> That the great house of Tarquin
>> Should suffer wrong no more,

forcefully dramatising a banal sentence of Dionysios, also alludes to Etruscan writings cited by the elder Pliny, according to which there are nine gods who send thunderbolts. But Macaulay oddly misunderstood Rome's defensive problem.

> They held a council standing
>> Before the River-Gate;
> Short time there was, ye well may guess,
>> For musing or debate.
> Out spake the Consul roundly:
>> 'The bridge must straight go down;
> For, since Janiculum is lost,
>> Nought else can save the town.'

The River-gate implies a wall and a fortified bridge, and it must have an officer in charge:

> Then out spake brave Horatius,
>> The Captain of the Gate:
> 'To every man upon this earth
>> Death cometh soon or late.

And how can man die better
Than facing fearful odds
For the ashes of his fathers,
And the temples of his Gods?'

But the Gate and its Captain are just the result of an over-translation. According to Livy, Cocles 'happened to be on guard at the bridge'—a soldier, not an officer, with no wall or gate behind him.

The other oddity is not Macaulay's fault. The whole point of Cocles' exploit was that he faced the enemy *alone*. But Macaulay, true to his sources, makes Horatius go on:

'Hew down the bridge, Sir Consul,
With all the speed ye may;
I, with two more to help me,
Will keep the foe in play.
In yon strait path a thousand
May well be stopped by three.
Now who will stand on either hand
And keep the bridge with me?'

Spurius Larcius and Titus Herminius duly volunteer, and share the first part of the defence, as Livy, Dionysios and Plutarch all report. But why? They withdraw before long, to leave the hero where he has to be. Only one man can speak the great last words before the jump:

'Oh Tiber! father Tiber!
To whom the Romans pray,
A Roman's life, a Roman's arms,
Take thou in charge this day!'

Larcius and Herminius may be historical characters; at any rate, when the magistrate-list was created, the two consulships for the fourth year of the Republic were attributed to them. But in the story they are lay figures, contributing only an unhelpful complication. Why should it matter so much to make Horatius one of three?

Hanging on the corner pilaster of the portico on the north side of the Roman Forum were three ancient spears, immemorially known as the *pila Horatia*. Usually, they were thought to be the spoils of the battle of the triplets. But it looks as if some late-republican historian, used by all three of Macaulay's narrative sources, chose to see them as evidence for the story of Cocles, and stitched in the two brave allies to account for them.

4

THE GOD OF LIBERTY AND LICENCE

4.1 **A STORY IN THE CALENDAR**

September, October, November, December: 'seventh', 'eighth', 'ninth', 'tenth'. July and August were 'fifth' and 'sixth' (Quintilis and Sextilis) until they were renamed in honour of Julius Caesar and Augustus. The early Roman calendar began the year with March, the month of Mars, and ended it with February, the month of cleansing.

The creation of the calendar, as a list of religious festivals, was naturally attributed to Numa, but modern scholars date it to the sixth or fifth century BC (it may even belong to the fourth). Naturally, the surviving fragments of actual calendars are much later than that, but the essentials of the archaic structure are detectable in what the later evidence preserves.

All but one of these fragmentary calendars are of the Julian year, as revised by the dictator Caesar in 46 BC. The exception, known as the *Fasti Antiates maiores*, was found at the Latin coastal town of Antium (Anzio) in 1915, painted on wall-plaster, of which about three hundred small pieces survive. The date of the Antium calendar can be inferred from the annual magistrate-list which accompanied it: after 84 BC (the latest surviving fragment) and not later than 67 BC (the last year for which there was room). So those pieces of plaster are what's left of the one known example of the calendar of the Roman Republic.

By the time the Antium calendar was put up, the start of the Roman civic year had been moved from March to January, and Plate 6 therefore shows the first four months of the year as it was in the first century BC. But the sequence

Colour plate 6

of festivals from February into March can still show us how the creators of the calendar, whoever they were and whenever they did it, conceived the end of *their* year, and the beginning of the next. And that is why the calendar matters for our purposes, because the sequence implies a story.

Terminus was the god of limits and endings, thought of as an unmovable boundary-stone. His festival on 23 February, the *Termi[nalia]*, would be appropriate as the last of the year—but it isn't. The following day is *Regi[fugium]*. When Ovid gets to that point in his calendar poem, he says 'Now I must speak of the flight of the king (*regis fuga*)', and when he has told his story he ends, as he must, by explaining the name of the day:

Ovid *Fasti*
2.851–852

> Tarquinius flees [*fugit*] with his offspring. A consul undertakes the government for a year. That day was the last of kingly rule [*regnis*].

Regifugium meant 'Kingsflight'.

The gods dislike sudden change, so when the Tarquins were banished the Romans appointed a quasi-king, the *rex sacrorum*, to look after the real king's religious functions. He was not allowed to hold political office, or even to address the People, and every year on 24 February he re-enacted the flight of the real king by running out of the Forum as fast as he could as soon as he had carried out the necessary sacrifice. The *Regifugium* ceremony was an annual reminder of political revolution.

Colour plate 6

Now look again at the calendar. The sequence of named days continues: 27 February, *Equir[ria]*; 14 March, *Equir[ria]*; 17 March, *Liber[alia]*; 19 March, *Quin[quatrus]*. The *Equirria* were chariot-races in honour of Mars, held whenever possible in the Field of Mars, the Campus Martius. Often it was not possible, since at that time of year the Tiber water is at its height and the Campus was frequently flooded. When that happened, the races were held on the Caelian. But why schedule them in the Campus at that time of year in the first place? Another oddity is that the *Regifugium* and the second *Equirria* (24 February, 14 March) are the only festivals in the whole archaic calendar which took place on an even date. There was evidently something special about that sequence.

In the story as we have it in Livy and Dionysios, nearly half a millennium after the event, the first thing the Romans did after the expulsion of the Tarquins was to seize and plunder the tyrant's property. The fertile land 'between the city and the Tiber' was made public and consecrated to Mars, thus becoming the Campus Martius. (Dionysios says it was *re*-consecrated, having belonged to Mars before the Tarquins took it.) That is very likely to be historical—and if so, it may be the reason why the calendar shows *Equirria* horse-races in the god's honour.

What matters more is the calendar's next item, the *Liberalia* on 17 March. For *liber* means 'free', and *Liber pater*, Father Liber, was the Latin name for Dionysos. His festival comes in the middle of the five-day sequence from the Ides of March to *Quinquatrus*, a day in honour of Mars and Minerva. That is,

Liber is embedded into the celebration of the god who presided over the original first month of the Roman year. Not only that, but his cult was instituted soon after the expulsion of the Tarquins, which must be why his festival comes after the *Regifugium* in the calendar.

Liber's cult at Rome was shared with the goddess of the harvest as 'Ceres, Liber and Libera', and located at a splendid archaic temple on the slope of the Aventine. It must have been similar in date and style to the Matuta temple (p. 34 above), and though its terracotta statuary and reliefs have not survived, we do know who made them—Damophilos and Gorgasos, named on a Greek inscription that was evidently preserved when the building was restored.

Father Liber was the god of ecstasy, of freedom from social inhibitions, of wine, sex and orgiastic ritual. Those may seem very un-Roman characteristics, and it is true that from the second century BC onwards, when the Roman state was refashioning its image of itself in the new guise of imperial power, Liber's anarchic influence had to be strictly controlled. But that was a late development. In the formative centuries of Rome, the god called 'Free' was fundamental to the life of the community. His festival, as the calendar sequence shows, inaugurates the free state, the republic of the Roman People.

4.2   FREEDOM AND THE REPUBLIC

Apollo promised rule, *arche*, to whoever fulfilled his oracle (p. 54 above). But what sort of rule was it? By the time the Romans started writing their own history, three centuries after the expulsion of the king, Brutus had become one of the first pair of consuls, sharing power with a colleague. Of course: by then, the consulship was the institution that defined the Republic, and it was natural to read it back into the Republic's origins. But whoever created the 'first to kiss his mother' story certainly didn't have power-sharing in mind; and in any case it is highly unlikely that the chief magistracy of the developed Republic was created at once in the chaotic circumstances of post-Tarquinian Rome.

In the developed version of the Roman liberation myth, Brutus' story ends when the Tarquins enlist the aid of Etruscan Veii in a war against Rome: Brutus and Arruns Tarquinius kill each other in single combat. The battle was inconclusive, but a divine voice in the wood where it took place announced that the Veientes had lost, because their casualties exceeded the Romans' by one.

For more than a decade Tarquinius schemed to return. Eventually, with the help of his son-in-law Octavius Mamilius of Tusculum, he amassed an alliance of Latin communities against Rome and forced a military showdown at Lake Regillus. That was a desperately hard-fought battle, eventually won by the Romans with divine help. Two young horsemen fought heroically on the Roman side; they were nowhere to be found when the Roman commander

Colour plate 7

Figure 8 (p. 23)

wanted to reward them, but were seen in the Forum at Rome, watering their weary horses at Juturna's spring, long before the news of the victory arrived. The Romans recognised Castor and Pollux, the Spartan Dioskouroi, and built them a temple next to the spring.

Give or take the gods, those two wars are likely to be historical. As we saw in the last chapter, these great events, like Tarquin's death at the court of Aristodemos soon after Lake Regillus, were of interest to Greek historians and thus reliably reported. But it would be more than a hundred years before events in Roman history next impinged on the consciousness of Greek authors. That was when the Romans sent a golden bowl to Delphi in thanksgiving for the conquest of Veii, and when a few years later, in 387 BC, their city was sacked by the Gauls. The intervening century is a dark age; the detailed but wholly anachronistic narratives of Livy and Dionysios allow us to infer only the most general and uncertain outline of a period of constant defensive warfare (on disputed frontiers very close to the city), economic decline (detectable in the archaeological record), and consequent on-going disputes between rich and poor within the citizen body (formalised in the tradition as 'the struggle of the orders').

Yet this is the period in which the Roman Republic took shape. From those three or four generations of struggle and hardship emerged the formidable community that would conquer and destroy Veii, survive and rebuild after the Gallic sack, and begin, by the end of the fourth century BC, that astonishing process of military expansion that became, in due course, the Roman Empire.

How could the power vacuum left by Tarquinius be filled? There might be a return to the old style of feuding warlords (Macstrna and all that), which the tyrant's authority had hitherto controlled. Lars Porsena, with his short-lived control of Rome, may be one example. Another may be Attus Clausus, who came with his clan and his followers from the Sabine country and settled in Rome. Yet another may be Poplios Valesios, whose 'companions' made a dedi-

Figure 16

cation to Mars at Satricum about 500 BC.

Two famous stories in the later tradition seem to originate from some such world of semi-feudal *condottieri*. The Fabian clan, who claimed to be descended from Hercules (p. 28 above), made war on Veii on their own account, and were almost wiped out at the River Cremera; and Gnaeus Marcius, better known to moderns as Coriolanus, put himself at the head of a Volscian army that would have taken Rome if he had been able to ignore the pleas of his wife and mother.

On the other hand, the expulsion of the king might result in the establishment of constitutional government in an ordered city-state. That is what the Romans' own later tradition would have us believe:

> My task from now on [wrote Livy] will be to trace the history in peace and war of a free nation, governed by annually elected officers of state and subject not to the caprice of individual men, but to the overriding authority of law.

Livy 2.1.1

In this scenario, Poplios Valesios and Attus Clausus are metamorphosed into Publius Valerius and Appius Claudius, patrician senators respectively liberal and conservative in their policies. That's a bit like saying that King Lear lived in Buckingham Palace. But the pseudo-historical tradition does preserve some items that must reflect early constitutional ideas of citizenship and the rule of law.

The system whereby Romans were enrolled in local areas (called 'tribes', p. 56 above), and in property-classes that defined both military responsibility and political privilege, was confidently attributed to Servius Tullius, and there are good reasons to believe that the essentials of it may indeed date back to the sixth century BC. The 'secession' of the plebeians, which resulted in the institution of tribunes—to provide as a right the protection otherwise obtainable only by some great man's patronage—was firmly placed in the year after the death of Tarquinius; it may well be, as Sallust believed, that removal of the external threat which had forced co-operation on all classes at Rome resulted in economic exploitation and a violent reaction from below. But the best evidence of all is the Romans' first law code, the 'Twelve Tables', of which many clauses survive in later texts. The tradition dates it to 450–449 BC, credible enough for a document that presupposed the Tiber itself as the boundary of Roman jurisdiction.

One way or another, those two rival political systems, and the tensions they created between them, defined the Roman Republic from first to last. They both presupposed *libertas*, freedom, but of two different kinds: freedom *to*, and freedom *from*. The absence of the king offered a quasi-feudal aristocracy—the warlords and clan leaders and their descendants, self-defined as 'patricians'—freedom to pursue power and glory on their own terms, and to treat their dependants, retainers and tenant farmers as if they were serfs. But it also enabled a citizen body to stand up for its own rights and claim freedom from exploitation and arbitrary jurisdiction in return for defending the common good as a disciplined citizen army. The assimilation of the two systems into a single polity was a slow and painful process. What Livy says was there from

Figure 16. Inscription from Satricum, on a block reused in the construction of the early fifth-century temple of Mater Matuta (fig. 10). The text reads [...]IEI STETERAI POPLIOSIO VALESIOSIO SVODALES MAMARTEI: 'The companions of Poplios Valesios set this up(?) to Mars.'

the start—'the overriding authority of law'—took at least two centuries to achieve.

It is likely that the god of freedom, Father Liber, was associated with the process throughout those two centuries, though it is only at the beginning and end of the period that we can see how.

Colour plate 6

The archaic calendar records Liber's festival immediately after 'Kingsflight' and the horse-races in the redeemed Campus Martius. A later development, marked by an addition in red, inserted the festival of Anna Perenna, goddess of the year (*annus*), on 15 March, just two days before the *Liberalia*. That was the day the magistrates entered office in the republican constitution as it eventually evolved in the fourth century BC. The choice of that date as the start of the civic year indicates clearly enough the importance and significance of Liber, whose festival two days later was when Roman boys put on their adult togas and became full citizens.

At Rome Liber shared his cult with Ceres and Libera. The very fact of a triad of divinities looks like an ideological statement. The grand temple of Jupiter Optimus Maximus on the Capitol, supposedly begun by the first Tarquinius and ready to be dedicated by the second at the time of his expulsion, was a triple cult of Jupiter, Juno and Minerva—the ruler of gods and men, with his wife and daughter. The Aventine triad of Ceres, Liber and Libera sent a very different message, of bread and wine, liberty and law. For Ceres and Libera were Demeter and Persephone, the goddesses who gave men laws (*Thesmophoroi*).

One strand of the tradition dates the dedication of the Aventine temple in the same year as the creation of plebeian institutions. Certainly it was in that temple that the *plebiscita*, resolutions of the plebeian assembly, were kept, as were senatorial decrees, once the Senate had evolved as a deliberative body in the second half of the fourth century BC.

By that time the plebeians had achieved political equality. They had the right to one of the two annual consulships, the new supreme magistracy introduced (the tradition says reintroduced) in 366 BC, and their *plebiscita* were authorised in 339 BC as laws binding on the whole community. Their economic emancipation was achieved by a law passed in either 326 or 313 BC, outlawing the enslavement of free citizens for debt—and that is where we meet Father Liber again.

Among his servants is the satyr Marsyas, who is such a virtuoso pipe-player that he once challenged Apollo to a music competition; the winner, it was agreed, could do what he liked with the loser. It was a bitterly disputed contest. Marsyas won the first round, and only lost the second because Apollo sang to his lyre, which the pipe-player claimed was unfair. But Apollo got the verdict, and Marsyas was chained up to await his fate. The Phrygians say that Apollo had him hung from a pine tree and flayed alive. But no: Father Liber freed him and brought him to Italy, where he founded the Marsic people and built a city which is now submerged in 'Marsyas' Lake' (p. 22 above). He is a master of

Figure 17. Marsyas statue from Paestum. The leg-irons are a reminder of Liber's gift of freedom.

augury, and the great plebeian family of the Marcii, famous for their seers, take their name from him.

If Apollo had been a Roman, he would have been an arrogant patrician. So the plebeians, now free from the threat of enslavement, put up in the Comitium a bronze statue of Marsyas, unshackled but with the irons still on his ankles. Replicas were set up also in the colonial foundations which Rome settled on the lands of her defeated subjects in Italy, and the one from Paestum, founded in 273 BC, happens to survive. Throughout the history of Rome's empire, in each city Marsyas stood in the public square with his right hand raised, as a symbol of *libertas*, the quality of his master Liber.

Figure 18. The Marsyas statue in the Roman Forum, on a *denarius* of L(ucius Marcius) CENSOR(inus), 82 BC; right arm raised, wine skin over left shoulder.

Figure 17

Figure 18

4.3   **ATHENS IN ROME**

Two great events occurred in or about 338 BC. In Greece, at the battle of Chaeronea Philip II of Macedon effectively ended Athens' independence and her status as a great power; in Italy, Rome established final control over her Latin neighbours, incorporated most of them into her citizen body, and set up a system of alliances which provided her with the manpower to conquer the whole of peninsular Italy in the next seventy years.

In retrospect, we moderns see this date as a turning point, the end of one era and the start of another. But that wasn't clear at the time. For the Romans of the late fourth century, full of energy and self-confidence, the Athenian empire was an example and an inspiration.

> '[Their] daring will outrun its own resources; they will take risks against their better judgement, and still, in the midst of danger, remain confident. . . If they win a victory, they follow it up at once, and if they suffer a defeat, they scarcely fall back at all. As for their bodies, they regard them as expendable for their city's sake, as though they were not their own. . .'

Thucydides
1.70.3–6

That was the Athens of a hundred years before, as analysed by the Korinthians in Thucydides book I. And the man who best symbolised their restless, aggressive character was Alkibiades, the extravagant and charismatic aristocrat who led the Athenian democracy into its greatest imperial adventure:

> 'It is not possible for us to calculate, like housekeepers, exactly how much empire we want to have. The fact is that we have reached a stage where we are forced to plan new conquests and forced to hold on to what we have got, because there is a danger that we ourselves may fall under the power of others unless others are in our power. . .'

Thucydides
6.18.3

When Rome consulted Delphi at the time of the Samnite wars, perhaps after the disaster of the Caudine Forks in 321 BC, Apollo told them to set up in a conspicuous place images of the wisest and the bravest of the Greeks. They obeyed; and the statues they put up in the Comitium were of Pythagoras (p. 49 above) and Alkibiades.

Those statues, like that of Marsyas, were evidently part of a substantial remodelling of the Comitium and the adjacent Forum piazza begun by one of the consuls of 338 BC, Gaius Maenius. The political centre of Rome was to reflect the political nature of the Republic in an architectural form that would be internationally recognisable. Although the literary and archaeological evidence is desperately controversial, it seems likely that what Maenius and his successors created was a circular *ekklesiasterion* for the voting assemblies of a sovereign people, and next to it a *bouleuterion* for the council of elders—the Senate, now formally integrated into the constitution. Alkibiades was to watch over a familiar process, in a familiar setting.

A Report from Latium

When Aristotle died in 322 BC, Theophrastos of Eresos succeeded him as head of the Lyceum in Athens. He was a naturalist, among many other things, and his surviving work on plants incorporates a detailed report on the trees of Corsica and Latium from a research student who had evidently been talking to Roman citizens at the 'coastguard colony' of Circeii, founded in 393 BC:

> The largest trees by far are said to be those in Corsica. For though splendid pine and fir grow to a great size in Latium, better and bigger than those in south Italy, they are nothing to those in Corsica. It is said that the Romans once sailed with a fleet of twenty ships intending to found a city there, . . . but the whole island is thickly wooded, like a wild forest, so they gave up the idea of founding a city. However, some of them went inland and cleared a huge number of trees from a small area, enough to make a fifty-sail raft (though it broke up in the open sea). Anyway, whether because of its uncultivated state or because of its soil and climate, Corsica far excels the rest.
>
> The country of the Latins is all well-watered. The lowland part contains laurel, myrtle, and beech of an astonishing size—for they cut timbers from it long enough for the whole length of the keel of Tyrrhenian ships. The hill country produces pine and fir. The place called Kirkaion is said to be a high promontory, thickly wooded and producing oak, laurel in abundance, and myrtle. The inhabitants say Kirke lived there, and they show the tomb of Elpenor, on which grow myrtles like those used for garlands, though the other myrtles are big trees. They also say that Kirkaion was once an island about eighty stades [over 15 km] in circumference, but now rivers have silted it up and it is part of the mainland.

The abortive attempt to colonise Corsica is unknown to the later historiographical tradition. This tiny piece of contemporary evidence gives us a precious glimpse of the Romans of the late fourth century BC—boldly enterprising, not in the least afraid of the sea and thoroughly familiar with Homer.

Parallels with Athens, real and imaginary, are frequent in the story of the early Republic as it eventually evolved. First and most important is the historical fact that the Romans expelled their family of tyrants just after the Athenians expelled theirs. (Greek chronological research gave the dates as 511/10 BC for Athens and 508/7 BC for Rome, and there is no reason to doubt their accuracy.) Since the Romans were importing large quantities of Athenian painted pottery at that time, it is quite possible that they imported the idea of a free city as well.

In each case, the exiled despot found powerful allies who tried to reinstate him by force—for Hippias the Spartans and the Persians, for Tarquinius the Etruscans and the Latins. So when the Romans told their own story, of course they borrowed motifs from the Athenian one. The voice in the wood (p. 65 above) was that of Faunus or Silvanus, Roman analogies for Pan, because Pan had told the Athenians he would be on their side at Marathon. The developed version of the story of Lars Porsena has him march on Rome to restore Tarquinius, because Kleomenes of Sparta had marched on Athens to restore Hippias; and he supposedly abandoned the project, impressed by the Romans' heroism, because the Spartans had abandoned their invasion, impressed—so Herodotos says—by the evils of tyranny.

The man we know as Marcius Coriolanus, who threatened Rome in or about 488 BC, was probably an old-style warlord with no particular loyalty to a city-state. But that may not have been understood when the story of the early Republic was taking shape. Again, Athenian history offered a way of making sense of the event. Coriolanus must have been like his contemporary Themistokles, a hero of his country's wars driven into exile for political reasons by an ungrateful people.

In the seventh and sixth centuries BC, the creation of narrative had been conditioned by heroic epic, with the results detected in Chapter 2 above. By the fourth century the predominant narrative mode was historiography, and its great exponents—Herodotos, Thucydides, Ephoros, Theopompos—gave as much attention to the Persian Wars and the Athenian empire as the old epic tradition had given to the Argonauts and the tale of Troy.

Moreover, a new departure in Athenian historiography may have had a particular effect on Rome. Kleidemos, writing probably in the 340s BC, was the first to create a history of Athens itself from its origins down to his own time. By exploiting the festival calendar, the aetiological explanation of rituals, the topography of the city, and all the antiquarian material he could find in his capacity as an 'exegete' of religious custom and institutions, Kleidemos rationalised the mythic stories into what looked like history—and was publicly honoured for it by the Athenian people. As we shall see in Chapter 6, though the evidence is very uncertain, there is reason to think that Kleidemos had Roman readers in the late fourth century BC.

At any rate, it's easy to see how the story of the free city of Rome and its early struggles repeatedly echoed the Athenian experience. Not all of it was anachronism. The achievement of the free state by the expulsion of the tyrant and his family did indeed repeat what had happened in Athens; and when the Romans resolved to formalise the rules of their community with a written law code, it was predictably to Athens (as well as to the Greek cities of southern Italy) that they turned for guidance. Even in the fragments of the Twelve Tables that happen to survive, the influence of Solon's Athenian law code is clear enough.

So it may be significant that the *Quinquatrus* festival of Mars on 19 March, part of the sequence of significant dates at the start of the Roman civic year, features a red-letter addition to the ancient calendar: a sacrifice to Minerva, who as Pallas Athene was the patron goddess of Athens. On that day, which the Romans believed was Minerva's birthday (two days after the festival of Father Liber), they dedicated a temple to her on the Aventine, just above the temple of Ceres, Liber and Libera.

Colour plate 6

It may also be significant that the nearest parallel for the combination Ceres-Liber-Libera is the presence of Iacchos along with Demeter and Kore at the great Athenian cult centre of Eleusis. The Athenians called Iacchos the son of Semele, and identified him as Dionysos. Demeter and Kore themselves, the law-giving goddesses, were particularly associated with Athens, and with the Athenian *Thesmophoria* festival. Moreover, Dionysos had a cult centre in Athens which was set up, like that of Liber, just a few years after the expulsion of the tyrants; and the name under which he was worshipped exactly parallels that of the Roman god of freedom.

This is Dionysos Eleuthereus, named after the village of Eleutherai on the border between Attica and Boeotia. His festival became the City Dionysia, and from 502/1 onwards it featured competitions in the newly developed dramatic forms known as tragedy and satyr-play. As an expert on Dionysiac religion points out,

> various factors may have favoured Eleuthereus as patron of drama: the spring weather in which his festival was celebrated, the presence by his sanctuary of a slope capable of seating large numbers, and the political development of Athens in the sixth century. . . [It has] been persuasively argued that the establishment of the festival 'fits perfectly into the context of the years following the establishment of the Kleisthenic system of government', and may have conveyed a message of political liberation in the civic cult of Dionysos 'Eleuthereus' to celebrate the overthrow of the tyrants.

Richard Seaford
Reciprocity and
Ritual 243–4

Greek *eleutheros*, like Latin *liber*, means 'free'. Liber's festival too was in the spring, his cult centre on a slope (the Aventine) overlooking an open space (the Circus Maximus valley); and the placing of his festival in the Roman calendar seems to imply that same message of political liberation. And Liber too was a god of drama—how early, we don't know, but certainly by the late third century BC, which is when Roman literary evidence first becomes available.

Perhaps the free god of Rome imitated the free god of Athens right from the start.

4.4   THE WILDERNESS VALLEY

Figure 1
(map: p. xix)

The temple of Ceres, Liber and Libera was situated 'at the end of the Circus Maximus, right above the starting-boxes'. So writes Dionysios of Halikarnassos in the late first century BC. He knew the Circus as a huge 150,000-seat chariot-racing arena, over 600 metres long and with triple-tiered terraces of seats all round, 'one of the finest and most wonderful buildings in Rome'. But that was something new in his time, the creation of Julius Caesar. Four and a half centuries earlier, when the temple was built, Liber had looked out across an open valley, flooded each winter and spring, dotted with cult sites among the trees on either side.

It was a long valley, running roughly east to west, dividing Rome proper (the Caelian and the Palatine, to the north) from the Aventine and its hinterland. The valley, and everything to the south of it, was outside the *pomerium*, the ritual boundary of the city, and equally outside the conventions and disciplines of the city-state. Conceptually, it was where the wild things were.

Five sacred groves defined its nature. The first was on the south side, close to where the stream debouched into the Tiber. This was the grove of Stimula, the centre of Rome's Bacchic cult. Some called it the grove of Semele, after the mother of Dionysos in the Theban story (p. 33 above for her sister Ino, who became the goddess Matuta). But Dionysos had many mothers in many different stories. In one he was the son of Thyone, whose name means 'stirrer-up' in Greek; that explained why frenzied Bacchants were called *Thyades*.

Some mythographers said that Semele and Thyone were one and the same. The mortal Semele became the goddess Thyone after Dionysos, with help from Hermes (who knows the way), went down to Hades, brought her back and made her immortal. One of Liber Pater's neighbours on the northern slopes of the Aventine was Summanus, god of the night and lord of the dead. Another was Mercurius (Hermes), whose cult Evander's Arkadians had set up, and whose temple, like that of Liber himself, dated back to the first years of the Republic. As we shall see, among the wooded clefts in that valley was at least one that functioned as a route to the underworld.

As Semele-Thyone, Stimula goaded the women who worshipped Liber into the orgiastic frenzy the god required. The maenads of Rome ran wild on the hillside as far as the second sacred grove, a copse of myrtles. The goddess of that grove had many names—Myrtea, Fortuna Virilis, Venus Verticordia—but the one that expressed her role in this context was Murcia, from the old Latin word *murcidus*, 'inactive'. Stimula got you going, Murcia slowed you down. When the valley was used for chariot-races, up one side and down the other, the place where the drivers slowed for the turn was opposite Murcia. So too with the maenads; by the time they reached the myrtle grove, the bacchic stimulation was wearing off.

Satyrs like to take advantage of exhausted maenads, and these are the very myrtles where the satyrs spied on naked Venus (p. 40 above). That was the mythological analogue for something that happened there in real life, every year on the first day of April: the women of Rome showed themselves naked—but wearing myrtle crowns—for the ritual bath and what was expected to follow it. The myrtle is sacred to the goddess of sex.

A few hundred yards further up the valley bring us to our third sacred grove—still on the south side, and below an outcrop called The Rock (*saxum*). Here the myrtle is banned. The trees are poplar and evergreen oak, and the goddess of the grove is mysteriously reclusive. Some say she is a dryad (they are retiring creatures), others that she was once a queen of ancient Latium, so modest that she was never seen by men. Here, at her sacred grotto, the women of Rome meet on 1 May for an all-night session of music and dance and secret ritual. They drink the wine that in everyday life they are expected to abstain from, but they call it milk, and the wine-jar a honey-pot; no men are admitted, but a cynical satirist notes that they are eager for sex when the ritual is over. (He calls them 'maenads of Priapus', and describes their dancing as erotically orgiastic.) This is the grove of the Good Goddess.

Her mysterious nature was a challenge to the story-tellers. One way of making sense of it was to bring in her cultic neighbours and identify her as Maia, the mother of Mercurius, or as Semele or Persephone, 'the mother of Dionysos who may not be named'. But in the books of the Roman priests she was called Fauna, and she shared her myth, as she shared her grove, with Faunus.

Who or what was Faunus? Some called him a son of Circe, and one of his stamping-grounds was indeed this wild valley where Circe founded the chariot-race games that bore her name (*ludi circenses*). But he and Fauna as a pair belong in two quite different types of story—one where she is a queen (or a princess), and one where she is a nymph.

Rationalising mythographers believed in a primeval dynasty of kings of Latium, which provided the background for some of the stories we looked at in Chapter 2. First there was Janus, who received Saturnus when he was in flight from usurping Jupiter. Then came the reign of Saturnus himself (pp. 32–3 above), followed by those of his son Picus, his grandson Faunus, and his great-grandson Latinus. Picus was the husband of Circe, who turned him into a woodpecker; Faunus generously welcomed Evander's colony from Arkadia and Marsyas' messengers from Phrygia; Latinus betrothed his daughter to the Trojan Aeneas. All but Latinus were deified at their deaths. Since Picus and Faunus had been skilled prophets, Picus the woodpecker became a bird signif-icant in augury, while Faunus' cult provided oracles.

In this quasi-historical mode of story-telling, Fauna too must be a mortal subsequently deified. She was the sister, or wife, or daughter of Faunus; she too was a seer, prophesying for women as he did for men; she was proverbially chaste, and never left the women's quarters. However, it was also said that she drank in secret, so her husband beat her to death with myrtle-branches (hence the taboo), but then repented of his act and made her a goddess. According to an even darker story, Faunus lusted after his daughter, made her drunk, beat her with myrtle rods when she still resisted, and finally forced himself on her in the form of a snake.

With Faunus as a snake, and Picus as a woodpecker, the rationalising mode has gone beyond its limit. Those features bring us close to the other and older way of thinking about Picus and Faunus, which made no pretence that they were ever human. On the contrary, they were gods or demigods of the wild country, satyr-like and horned like Pan. As Lucretius says (in C.H. Sisson's translation),

> These are places the nymphs and satyrs inhabit
> Or so the inhabitants say, and they speak of fauns
> Whose noises in the night and boisterous play
> Break up, so they say, the most silent nights.
> And they hear the sound of strings, and sweet complaints
> Pour forth from pipes as the players' fingers touch them;
> For the country people this is the sound of Pan,
> Shaking the crown of pine on his half-wild head
> As he runs his curved lip over the open reeds
> And pours out woodland songs.

Lucretius De rerum
natura
4.580–589

Figure 19

Faunus could be thought of as an individual, or as one of a race of creatures called fauns. *Fauni* and *faunae* were like satyrs and nymphs, with one extra characteristic: they were 'speakers'. In times of crisis divine powers may speak directly to mortals. If the voice comes from a temple, it is that of the god or goddess who lives there. But if, as often happened, it comes from the wild country or the depths of a wood, that is a faun, or Faunus himself.

When not being prophetic, fauns are as lecherous as satyrs. Faunus pursues the fleeing nymphs, and there is nothing he likes better than an unsuspecting female in his grotto. Occasionally he is too ambitious and gets his come-uppance, as when he crept up on Omphale the queen of Lydia, asleep in a cave in the grove of Bacchus, only to discover in the dark that she and her lover Hercules had been cross-dressing.

Figure 20

Figure 19. Copy of Praxiteles' 'Resting satyr' in the Capitoline Museum, Rome (Palazzo Nuovo, Sala del Gladiatore), presented by Pope Benedict XIV in 1753. This is the eponymous statue of Nathaniel Hawthorne's *The Marble Faun* (1859): 'Only a sculptor of the finest imagination, the most delicate taste, the sweetest feeling, and the rarest artistic skill—in a word, a sculptor and a poet, too—could have first dreamed of a faun in this guise, and then have succeeded in imprisoning the sportive and frisky thing in marble. Neither man nor animal, and yet no monster, but a being in whom both races meet on friendly ground.' The photograph shows the statue as Hawthorne saw it, still wearing its pre-1870 papal fig-leaf.

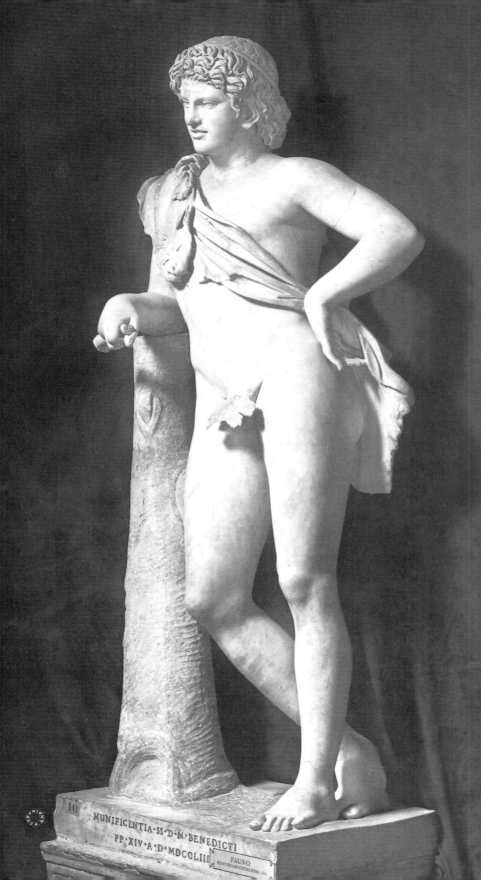

MUNIFICENTIA·SS·D·N·BENEDICTI
PP·XIV·A·D·MDCCLIII   FAUNO

Figure 20. Francesco Primaticcio, 'Hercules surprised with Omphale', c. 1540. This is the farcical conclusion of Ovid's story of Faunus, Omphale and Hercules: Faunus, groping in the dark, 'his swollen penis harder than his horn' (Ovid *Fasti* 2.346), has just put his hand up Omphale's dress, and Hercules (who is wearing it) has just kicked him off the bed. 'The sudden noise awaked the Lydian queen, Who called for lights, which showed the comic scene' (Massey 1757.80). Omphale, of course, is wearing Hercules' lionskin.

Precisely here, below the Aventine, in the grove of his dryad consort, is the spring where Roman Faunus likes to drink. One day, in the time of good king Numa, he and Picus came as usual in the heat of the afternoon. They found vessels there brimming with wine, drank it at their leisure, and fell asleep unaware that the king had set an ambush; there were twelve young men hiding in the grotto, who now rushed out and bound them fast. Numa had done this on the advice of his own nymph-consort, Egeria, whose grove and spring were just across the valley. Numa wanted to know how to deal with Jupiter's thunderbolts, and refused to release Picus and Faunus until they had told him how to bring Jupiter himself down from heaven. So they did, and Jupiter came. This was the occasion of Numa's bargain with Jupiter about the sardines (pp. 51–3 above). Jupiter laughed, and promised Numa a pledge. At dawn the next day a bronze shield fell from heaven next to Egeria's spring, and a voice was heard: 'As long as your city keeps this, it will be the most powerful of all.'

We have visited three sacred groves on the south side of the wild valley, those of Stimula, Murcia and the Good Goddess. On the north side were Egeria's, below the Caelian, and one other, down at the other end below the Palatine, opposite Stimula and Liber's temple—the grove and grotto of Pan. Dionysios tries to describe it for us, though in his day it was all built up and hard to make out:

In ancient times, it is said, there was a large cave below the hill, roofed over with

78

a dense thicket and with springs at the bottom beneath the rocks, and the dell adjoining the cliff was shaded by thick, tall trees.

Dionysios
1.32.4

Here Evander's colonists set up an altar to their ancestral god, Pan Lykaios from Mount Lykaion in Arkadia, and the Romans adapted the name as *Lupercal*. From here, once a year in the 'purification month' of February, the young men of the Roman elite, drunk and naked, ran around in licensed horseplay, striking whoever they met with strips of freshly cut goatskin.

It was never clear to the Romans whether or not Pan and Faunus were

Figure 21. Bronze mirror, fourth century BC. The twin Lares are being suckled by a she-wolf and protected by a lion; Pan (left, with goatskin cape) and Quirinus (right, with spear) look on; behind are the twins' parents, Mercurius and Lara (or Larunda), 'the silent goddess'.

Figure 21

identical. Silvanus, too, was not easy to distinguish from either of them. The names evidently represented different ways of conceptualising the dangerous and unpredictable power—or powers—that live in the wild. No stories of Pan in Rome happen to survive, but we do have a fourth-century BC image of him, with his calendar neighbour Quirinus (15 and 17 February, pp. 114–15 below), witnessing the conclusion of someone else's story. What they are looking at is the miraculous birth of the citizen body's divine protectors, the Guardian Lares.

The mother of the Lares was a nymph, daughter of the river Almo. She offended Jupiter (how, we shall see in the next chapter), and he banished her to the underworld. Her escort, Mercurius, raped her in a wood on the way. It was probably the wood Faunus shared with the Good Goddess: one of her names was Hekate (so perhaps her grotto led to the world below), and the twin Lares who were conceived there had their annual sacrifice at her festival, on the first day of Mercurius' month.

Colour plate 6

Even in the underworld, children conceived in May are born in February. At Rome, for nine days in that month the worlds of the dead and the living were very close, an uneasy period which ended when offerings were made for the dead on 21 February. The day was called *Feralia*, and was sacred to the Silent Goddess, the mother of the Lares. In this scene, she has brought her twins to the world of light, and though she must return to the dark, they will be suckled and protected by wild beasts (*ferae*, whence *Feralia*), and grow up to be the city's guardian gods. One day, at a desperate moment far in the future, these children of the wild will drive Hannibal from the gates of Rome.

4.5   FUN AND GAMES

This tour of the 'valley of the Circus Maximus', about half a mile up one side and the same distance down the other, has brought us into a conceptual landscape of woods, caves and springs, the haunt of wild, licentious creatures, nymphs and satyrs, Faunus and Pan. And we have found real-life people, Roman citizens, behaving in the same Dionysiac way—the naked Luperci on 15 February, the maenads of Liber on 17 March, the myrtle-crowned ladies on 1 April, the secret orgiasts of the Good Goddess on 1 May. Solemn anthropologists may recognise rites of spring, a community facilitating the conception of its next crop of children. The Romans just called it 'games'.

Like 'play' in English, the verb *ludere* (Greek *paizein*) and the nouns *ludus* and *lusus* (Greek *paignion* and *paidia*) could be used for a wide range of activities, dance, music and sex prominent among them. They were the words you would use for what nymphs and satyrs do, and the celebrants of those deliberately licentious festivals, who imitated what nymphs and satyrs do. Also like 'play' in English, the sense of the words included the imitation itself, and thus, by a natural extension, the mimetic performances that we call drama. Liber presided over that too: as a later playwright put it, free speech prevailed at the *Liberalia* games.

So we return, from a different angle, to the analogy of Father Liber with Dionysos Eleuthereus, god of freedom and patron of the dramatic festivals of Athens (p. 73 above). All the main genres of Attic drama were derived in one way or another from Dionysiac ritual, which was itself mimetic. According to Aristotle, comedy originated with 'the leaders of the phallic songs which still survive today [late fourth century bc] as traditional institutions in many of our cities'. Such songs were sung as the sacred phallos was borne in procession to where the performances were to be held. They continued to 'survive' (our best evidence is from Delos), and like other aspects of Dionysiac worship they were equally familiar in Latium.

Here is Varro's description from the mid-first century bc, reported by the indignant St Augustine five centuries later:

> Varro tells us about some of the rites of Liber which were celebrated at the cross-roads in Italy with such obscene licence that the male organs were made the objects of worship in honour of this divinity. And this was not done in secret, so that some degree of modesty might be retained; it was performed as a public display in an exultation of debauchery. During the festival of Liber this obscene organ was mounted, with great honour, on carts, and exhibited first at the cross-roads in the country, and afterwards conveyed to the city. In the town of Lavinium a whole month was consecrated to Liber, during which time everyone used the most indecent language, until the time when that organ was conveyed across the forum and brought to its final resting-place.
>
> It was obligatory for the most respected mother of a family to place a crown on this disreputable organ in full view of the public. This was how Liber had to be placated to ensure successful germination of seeds; this was how evil spells had to be averted from the fields. A matron had to be compelled to perform an act in public, which even a harlot ought not to have been allowed to perform in the theatre if there were matrons in the audience.

Augustine *City of God* 7.21

Lavinium, founded by Aeneas, should be a good parallel for early-republican Rome, and we might well imagine such a procession from Liber's temple 'in the country' to the Roman Forum for the *Liberalia* games on 17 March. But since Varro was writing 130 years after Rome's Liber cult had been purged of all orgiastic elements, even his evidence can't tell us for certain what we want to know.

Similarly tantalising is Ovid's account of Anna Perenna, whose festival was on the Ides of March, just two days before the *Liberalia*. Her sacred grove was by the Tiber a mile upstream of Rome. Was she a nymph? Was she the wandering Argive princess Io? Was she Themis, who some said was the mother of Evander? No, says Ovid: she was a little old lady who supplied cakes to the plebeians on the Sacred Mount at the time of the great secession of 494 bc. Out

Colour plate 6

Dionysiac Drama: Athens and the West

The first theorists of drama, Aristotle and Theophrastos in the fourth century BC, divided plays into four types: comedy, tragedy, 'the satyrs', and mime.

1. *Comedy*. The first classic author in this form was Epicharmos of Syracuse, a pupil of Pythagoras active as a playwright about 500–480 BC; his subjects were mythological (*Amykos*, *Odysseus the Deserter*, *Herakles and the Girdle*, etc.), and two at least were Dionysiac (*Bacchai*, *Dionysoi*). The Romans must have known his work, as they knew that of his fellow-Sicilian Stesichoros a century earlier (pp. 26–8 above). Athenian comedy, which developed slightly later, used invented characters and plots for the most part; however, mythological burlesque became popular in the fourth century BC, and Plautus' *Amphitruo* was adapted from one or more such comedies.

2, 3. *Tragedy and 'the satyrs'*. These forms evolved in the late sixth century BC in Athens, with mythological themes treated seriously in tragedy, playfully and boisterously by the satyrs. At the Athenian City Dionysia (the festival of Dionysos Eleuthereus), each competing poet offered three tragedies plus a satyr play. According to Aristotle, tragedy developed from the Dionysiac dithyramb; it is likely that when tragedy's subject matter expanded beyond the mythology of Dionysos himself, satyr play was invented to keep the Dionysiac element in a quasi-tragic format.

4. *Mime*. 'Imitation involving events both permitted and forbidden' (Theophrastos), dramatic but not necessarily in verse, subject matter usually from everyday life; the first classic author in this form was another Sicilian, Sophron of Syracuse in the fifth century BC. But mime also included cabaret-like musical performances, like the erotic ballet of Dionysos and Ariadne presented by a Syracusan troupe in Xenophon's *Symposion*. Unlike the other forms, mime featured female performers, and masks were not normally used.

The dramatic festivals of fifth-century Athens, for which practically all our surviving texts of 'Greek drama' were written, kept these forms strictly separate, and did not admit mime at all. But show business never stands still, and the restrictive conventions could not be maintained. (In other places they may never have applied at all.) Music and dance were essential in all four genres, but in comedy, tragedy and satyr play they were originally provided by an amateur chorus of young citizens. Ambitious composers and choreographers needed professional performers, and progressively the traditional chorus became obsolete.

'The satyrs' were detached from the Athenian tragic-tetralogy format, and resumed their natural affinity with mime. Both forms were familiar outside the theatre as part of Dionysiac ritual, as we know from Plato in the mid-fourth century BC. He refers to Bacchic dancing at rituals of purification and initiation, 'where the dancers "imitate" (as the saying is) drunken persons, calling them nymphs, Pans, Silenoi and satyrs'. His parenthesis shows that imitation (*mimesis*) is a technical term: mime is the mode for imitating nymphs and satyrs.

Even tragedy could not remain aloof. The Athenian tragic poet Gnesippos in the late fifth century was also 'a *paignion*-writer of the cheerful muse'—and *paignion* ('play' in both senses) was a form of mime. A century and a half later, in Tarentum in south Italy, Rhinthon pioneered a whole genre of 'cheerful tragedy', and a century later again, Plautus could play with the idea of 'tragicomedy' and know his audience would not be baffled.

We must bear in mind this constant generic flux and creative innovation when we try to imagine how Dionysiac drama and the Greek performing arts affected the Romans and their neighbours. Colour plate 8 offers a revealing insight, from the inland Etruscan city of Clusium (about 150 years after Lars Porsena had ruled there): on two red-figure cups of local manufacture, wholly Greek in style and iconography, showgirls (*mimae*) appear, first with a dancing satyr, and then playing a burlesque version of Leda and the swan, taken from Euripides.

At Rome, too, the stage performances were 'seriousness mixed with laughter'. That was how the Sibyl herself saw it, advising Augustus three hundred years later. The Romans of that time believed that their own drama had been introduced from Etruria in the fourth century BC, and that it was entirely independent of Greek models. They may or may not have been right on the first point; they were certainly wrong on the second.

of gratitude they made her a goddess; but she stayed in the supply business, and when Mars asked her to procure Minerva for him, she said she would.

> As he more instant grew, 'Well, now,' she cried,
> 'Pallas at last consents to be your bride.
> She does at last to my entreaties yield;
> Come, god of war, and joyful take the field.'
> With eager haste he went to press the bed
> Where Anna, like a bride, with muffled head,
> Was laid; but when just ready for th'embrace,
> How great was the deluded god's disgrace,
> At seeing Anna's old and ugly face!
> The new-made goddess grinned at the deceit,
> And Venus tittered when she heard the cheat.

Ovid *Fasti*
3.687–696

It is as certain as it can be that Ovid's source was a stage farce, and we happen to know that the playwright Decimus Laberius in the mid-first century BC wrote a mime entitled *Anna Peranna*. But was the story only invented then? Ovid calls it an old joke, and it may well have been a traditional plot for stage perform-ances at the *Liberalia*. The combination of Mars and Minerva, close to Liber in the archaic calendar (pp. 64–5 above), suggests an early date. So too, perhaps, does the implied starring role of the patron goddess of Athens. But once again, we cannot know.

These two passages—Varro on Liber's phallic ritual, and Ovid on the comic myth of Anna Perenna—are just two particularly conspicuous examples of a general methodological difficulty. The chronological context of this chapter has been essentially the fifth and fourth centuries BC, from the expulsion of the Tarquins in 508/7 to (say) the erection of the Pythagoras and Alkibiades statues about 320. Chapters 2 and 3 focused on an even earlier period, from the eighth century BC to the sixth. But our evidence for the thought-world of archaic and early-republican Rome is almost entirely drawn from literary texts composed centuries later in a vastly different type of society.

From Cicero in the first century BC to Augustine in the fifth century AD, the literary tradition is extensive, varied and wonderfully informative. But those authors could have no first-hand insight into the world of their distant ancestors. Nor second-hand either, for though they had access to earlier texts which are lost to us, even the pioneering authors of Latin literature were writing no earlier than the second half of the third century BC. So we have to try to identify, among the myriad data provided by the literary texts, material which may have originated centuries earlier, stories (or accounts of rituals) which look as if they were already old when the authors whose texts survive reported them. Effectively, it is an attempt to think ourselves back, through literature, into a world before literature.

It's not an entirely hopeless quest. Even the literary sources preserve some memory of the conditions of an oral culture, and the way stories were created and recycled before there were texts to preserve them. We can still just catch sight of some unfamiliar figures—a hymn-singer at a sacrifice praising a god or hero, a prophet-bard frightening the Forum crowd with tales of the gods' punitive power, a freelance praise-singer flattering the family at a banquet or funeral, an itinerant story-teller collecting coppers from a circle of listeners in the tavern or the market-place, a fast-talking stage entertainer telling the audience what Juno said to Jupiter. Some of their material must have survived into our literary sources. How much, and which bits, we can only guess.

What we need is a standard against which our guesswork can be checked, a contemporary insight into pre-literary Rome independent of later sources. And now at last, for the late fourth century BC, such a thing becomes available.

5

WHAT NOVIUS KNEW

THE WORKPLACE

Novius Plautius was a master craftsman. He worked in Rome about 340 BC, at a time when there may still have been old people alive whose grandparents had been born under the rule of king Tarquin. Novius himself wasn't born in Rome—his given name is Oscan, not Latin—but he had become a Roman by the time he created the masterpiece by which we know him. Rome was now a good place for the talented and ambitious; a lot had happened since the end of the monarchy.

After their expulsion of Tarquinius and the brief occupation of their city by Lars Porsena, the Romans faced and defeated a coalition of their Latin neighbours at the battle where Castor and Pollux fought on their side (pp. 65–6 above). Rome and the Latins made a peace treaty, inscribed on a bronze column in the Roman Forum: it carried the name of Spurius Cassius, the first reliably attested spokesman for the free community of Rome. But Romans and Latins alike were already being hemmed in to east and south by aggressive mountain peoples, with whom warfare recurred, constantly and exhaustingly, for well over a hundred years.

External pressure exacerbated the internal tension between the rival ideals of hereditary 'patrician' kin-group authority and the disciplines of a constitutional citizen body (pp. 66–7 above). Two fundamental innovations were achieved during the obscure years of conflict in the fifth century BC: the written code of laws (p. 67 above), and the institution of a popular assembly and elected tribunes to protect the interests of the people against overbearing executive authority. Gradually, over the years, the plebeians' self-help organisation came

Figure 22. The *emissarium* of the Alban lake: 2234 m long, 2 m high, 1.20 m wide. When the lake had risen inexplicably, the Romans consulted Delphic Apollo, who replied: 'Roman, let not the water be confined within the lake of Alba, neither let it flow by its own channel to the sea.'

Figure 22

Figure 61

to be the main legislative authority of the Roman republic.

Two events early in the fourth century BC indicated how formidable that republic had become. The first was a triumph of engineering, the digging of an outflow tunnel a mile and a half long through the crater wall of the Alban Mount, to control the waters of the lake and use the surplus to irrigate Roman fields in the plain between the hills and the Tiber. The second was an astonishing—and ruthless—military achievement, the defeat and destruction of Veii, Rome's nearest rival to the north, after a long war and a long siege. The population of Veii was killed or enslaved; their lands increased Rome's territory by at least half.

It was only a few years later that Rome itself was stormed and captured by a large war-band of Celtic Gauls, who occupied the city for seven months, comprehensively sacked it, and withdrew only on payment of a huge weight of gold. The double impact of victory and humiliation acted as an unexpected catalyst of the Romans' internal strife. Weakened by the disaster, the patricians made a crucial concession. Much of the territory of Veii was distributed in small-holdings to the Roman citizen body, which was thus effectively emancipated from the quasi-feudal economic dominance of the clan leaders.

Within twenty years the new situation was reflected in political terms, with the introduction of a power-sharing executive. There were to be two annual 'consuls' (the word implies shared authority), of whom, as the scheme finally evolved, only one could come from the old self-defined group of 'patrician' clans. Political leadership was now a career open to talent, and suddenly Rome became attractive to able and ambitious men from elsewhere. The Plautii from Tibur did very well in the new system, with six 'plebeian' consulships in thirty years. It is likely that one of those consuls—perhaps the first, conqueror of the Hernici in 358 BC—was the patron of Novius Plautius the master craftsman.

Rome offered not only opportunity, but physical security as well. By a herculean effort of communal will in the 370s BC the Romans created an enormous city wall 11 kilometres long (p. 142 below), enclosing an area nearly

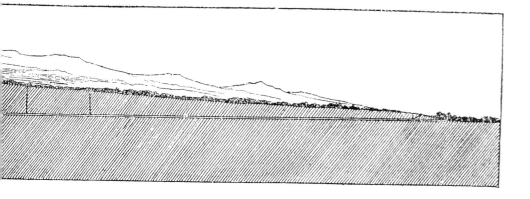

twice the size of Veii. The capture of Veii provided the means—hundreds of thousands of huge tufa blocks from the quarries at Grotta Oscura—and the experience of the Gallic sack provided the motivation. From now on, the walls of lofty Rome (in Virgil's phrase) symbolised a renewed and formidable city. Within forty years of the Gallic catastrophe she had not only reasserted her authority over her Latin neighbours, and extended it into Campania, but also imposed a lasting political settlement which confirmed her as the dominant power in central Italy.

Military success was good for business. It was a lady from the ancient Latin city of Praeneste, until recently a dangerous rival of Rome, who came to Novius Plautius' workshop with the commission (for her daughter's wedding present) that gave him his place in history.

5.2   THE FICORONI *CISTA*

What Novius made for Dindia Macolnia was found near Palestrina in 1738, in the Praenestine necropolis where it had no doubt been buried with her daughter two thousand years before. It was bought by Francesco de' Ficoroni and presented by him to the Museo Kircheriano in Rome, where in the winter of 1901–2 it inspired one of E.M. Forster's first essays. In 1914 it passed to its present home, the Villa Giulia museum. It's a *cista*, a cylindrical bronze casket, standing about 30 inches high (74 cm).

Figure 23

Look first at the feet. Each one is a lion's paw (conventional enough)—but a lion's paw on a squashed frog. That combination is characteristic of the whole sophisticated story-world of fourth-century BC Rome and Latium, as revealed in the work of Novius Plautius and his anonymous colleagues—the predictable juxtaposed with the unexpected, heroism with humour, epic with farce.

What we're *meant* to look at first, of course, is the conspicuous group that

False Light on a Dark Age

The sack of the city by the Gauls was probably the earliest event the Romans could date reliably from internal records. That isn't surprising: reliable records are a characteristic of constitutionally organised administrations, and Rome achieved that status only in the fourth century BC.

The alleged chronology of the first century or so of the Republic was highly controversial. A certain 'Clodius'—probably the historian Claudius Quadrigarius, early in the first century BC—wrote an essay entitled *Chronology: a Critical Enquiry*, in which he insisted that genuine ancient records had disappeared in the disaster. Livy too tells us that 'whatever public and private records there were'—including the chronicle of the *pontifex maximus*—'mostly perished in the burning city'.

Now, it's clear from the archaeological remains that the Gauls didn't burn the city at all—and there's certainly no reason to think they were interested in destroying archives. So according to the leading modern authority on early Rome, Clodius and Livy provide merely 'a false solution to a non-existent problem'. But that's only half true. The solution was false, but the problem must have been real, or why would they need an explanation anyway? It only makes sense if there were no early records available. In particular, the need for Clodius' 'critical enquiry' into chronology must imply that (despite modern assertions) there was no official year-by-year list of magistrates for the early Republic.

Of course there were *some* early documents, including conspicuous public items like Spurius Cassius' Latin treaty and the 'twelve tables' of the law code. Other information could be found by careful research in temple deposits and family archives. But it would take a serious effort of historical interpretation to put such data into a coherent chronological framework, and create for the early Republic an equivalent to the consular lists that were kept from 367 BC onwards.

That work of reconstruction was evidently carried out in the second and first centuries BC, and its results were used both by historians (Diodoros, Livy, Dionysios) and by those who were responsible for inscribing on the triumphal arch of Caesar Augustus in the Forum a list of all the magistrates of the Republic from the expulsion of Tarquin to Augustus' own day. It was a great monument (and Mommsen's first edition of the fragments of it was a great monument of scholarship), but that doesn't alter the likelihood that for the first 140 years or so it was based on fallible hypotheses.

The Romans were well aware of one possible source of error, the insertion of false ancestors by ambitious families. But they were blind to a greater one, that the early list had been reconstructed on a false premise. For it was assumed that the consulship was the original magistracy of the Republic, and therefore the names that were found had to be arranged in annual pairs. It was a natural assumption to make, but it was wrong—and the result is that now we cannot use the names listed before 367 BC as reliable historical evidence.

Figure 23. What Novius made: the Ficoroni *cista*.

Figure 24

forms the handle. (The three figures stand on, and are fastened through, the plate bearing the artist's signature.) In the centre is the young Liber, his mantle draped over his shoulder; he wears a necklace with the gold locket or *bulla* which was the sign of a free-born Roman boy. The supporting figures are satyrs with fawnskins (*nebrides*) knotted round their necks. Ithyphallic, though not in the comic mode, and with conspicuously animal ears, their stance conveys a formidable sexy nonchalance.

The lid shows a hunting scene. The plates that attach the feet show three male figures, the central one winged, the one on the right recognisable as the

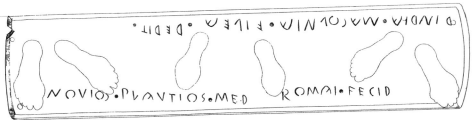

Figure 24. Inscription on the Ficoroni *cista*: NOVIOS PLAVTIOS MED ROMAI FECID / DINDIA MACOLNIA FILEAI DEDIT, 'Novius Plautius made me at Rome, Dindia Macolnia gave (me) to her daughter'. The customer's name is also scratched on the inside of one of the feet: MAQVOLNA, written right to left (*CIL* I² 562).

young Hercules with his club. The body of the casket has an upper frieze with an elaborate repeating floral design around female faces or masks, and a lower frieze with heraldic sphinxes. Between them unfolds a complex mythological scene. Where does it start? On the cylinder, you can begin anywhere and just keep going round. But there is one point where two of the figures have their backs to each other, so it makes sense to 'unroll' the scene from there.

Figure 25

A bearded man, naked, sits on a large amphora holding a spear. Another bearded man, winged this time and with a mantle, rests his foot on a rock, his elbow on his knee, his chin on his hand. In front of them, a naked young man binds a naked mature man to a tree. The binder and the bound are both boxers, their hands and wrists still strapped up for the fight. The young man has won, and winged Victoria flies towards him, holding out a crown and the ribbons to tie on it.

We know this story. The beaten boxer is Amykos (p. 22 above), who challenged any seafarers who wanted to get water from his spring. The victor is Pollux (Polydeukes), and the Argonauts are now able to fill their jars. Minerva (Pallas Athene) looks on with approval, while the other two spectators—again, one seated and one standing—may be Jason and Hercules. The latter's physique seems unmistakable, and it matters not at all that in the standard Greek account of the voyage of *Argo* Herakles leaves the ship before the encounter with Amykos. The version Novius knew pre-dates Apollonios Rhodios by about a

Figure 25. The Ficoroni *cista* 'unrolled': one scene is centred on the binding of Amykos, the other on the mocking old satyr.

century, and probably sited the Amykos episode on the coast between Latium and Campania (p. 23 above).

The Latin version of the story involved the moon-goddess Losna, or *Luna* in the spelling we're accustomed to. A bronze mirror that was found with the Ficoroni *cista*—though clearly not by the same artist—shows her between Pollux and Amykos in what must be the challenge scene. To the right stands a pillar with a large egg-shaped object on top. What that meant was no doubt obvious in the fourth century BC, but not now, since Novius Plautius' world is one we only partially understand.

Figure 26

For instance (to go back to the *cista*), who is the winged figure with the beard? Perhaps he is Mopsos the prophet, who sailed with the *Argo*; contemporary Etruscan art sometimes portrays prophets with wings (p. 151 below). Look at him again, and ask yourself what *he* is looking at. Not, after all, at the binding of Amykos, but at something very surprising at the bottom of the tree. There, tilted up to face him, its lips slightly parted as if in speech, is a small human head.

Figure 64

Again, contemporary art from neighbouring Etruria provides a parallel for this diagonal dialogue of disembodied head with privileged mortal, and explains it as communication from the supernatural world. Mopsos (if it is he) is being told of what is to come—perhaps the foundation of the city of Amunclae, or the dedication of the temple to Castor and Pollux in the Roman Forum (pp. 22–3 above). A whole heroic enterprise is presupposed in the details of Novius Plautius' composition.

The startlingly literal imagery of the speaking head is characteristic of Novius' world, with its casual interpenetration of the natural and the supernatural. An even more surprising example can be seen on a bronze mirror in New York—no provenance, but probably from Praeneste—showing Jupiter seated on an altar, from the base of which emerges a prominent set of male genitals. (The scene probably refers to the wedding night, since the other figures

Figure 27

Figure 26. Bronze mirror found with the Ficoroni *cista*: Poloces (Pollux), Losna (Luna), Amuces (Amykos).

are Juno, who was in charge of the bride's girdle, and Hercules, whose knot fastened the girdle and had to be untied by the bridegroom.) That apparition is like the penis in the hearth that begot king Servius on Tanaquil's maidservant, just as the talking head in Novius' Amykos scene is reminiscent of the voice in the wood that gave Brutus' army the victory (above, pp. 45 and 65). The gods move in mysterious ways, but the artist's job is to make them visible.

Figure 25 The rest of Novius' composition illustrates the point. Moving rightwards from the beached *Argo*'s towering stern, we see twelve figures. Ten of them are Argonauts, relaxing in various ways. The other two are immortals.

Figure 27. Praenestine mirror showing Jupiter (IOVEI) with Juno, Hercules, and disembodied genitalia.

Below the fountain which caused the whole dispute sits a grinning, fat old satyr with what looks like Hercules' lionskin round his shoulders, cheerfully mocking the young man working out at the punch-bag. E.M. Forster thought he was Pan, and put this in his mind: 'Work is at all times unseemly, and why this pother over water when the one thing needful is wine?' In fact, it probably *was* wine. A century or so before Novius Plautius' time, Sophokles had used the Amykos story for a satyr play; what better reward could the satyr-chorus have had than their master Dionysos turning the fountain's water into wine? In which case Novius has given us an epic story with a touch of farce.

From the fat satyr, move upwards to the right, past the drinking Argonaut and the one holding the amphora. There, sprawled at his ease, is the young Liber himself, the Latin Dionysos with the *bulla* round his neck, as if he had just stepped down into the scene from his place on the handle of the lid. The two ribbons he waves so nonchalantly must be *lemnisci*, the coloured streamers used to decorate crowns and garlands. The one which winged Victoria is bringing to Pollux in the binding scene will go on the victor's laurel wreath; what Liber has in mind is more likely the crown of roses worn at drinking-parties.

None of the mortal characters seems aware of the presence of Minerva, Victoria, Liber or the old satyr. But we can see them, and they show us both the duties and the rewards of virtue. There is no point asking which is more

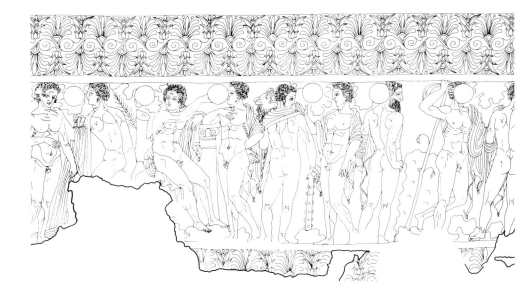

Figure 28. Narrative frieze on a *cista* in the Walters Art Gallery, Baltimore: Bacchic dance with the killing of Medusa.

important, the stern war-goddess or the easy-going god of licence. They are both present, like the lion's paw and the frog, and their respective spheres are seamlessly interdependent. And that is not just one artist's vision. The other bronzes that survive from late fourth-century Latium reveal the same sophisticated thought-world, often emphasising the erotic element hinted at by Novius Plautius' able-bodied satyrs, supporting Liber on the handle.

5.3   **GODS, GODDESSES AND GORGEOUS GIRLS**

On a *cista* now in Baltimore, a Bacchic dance merges into a scene of heroic myth. Perseus, armed with an odd version of his famous sickle-sword (*harpe*),

Figure 28

Figure 29. Narrative frieze on a *cista* in the Museo di Palestrina: Perseus holds up the Gorgon's head. Left to right: ten heroes, relaxing in various ways; unidentified figure making apotropaic gesture (to avoid being turned to stone); Jupiter, crowned, holding thunderbolt, with eagle; Perseus, in winged helmet and sandals; Minerva, winged; Mercurius, with *caduceus*.

97

has just cut off the head of the Gorgon Medusa. One of her sister-Gorgons pursues him, but she herself falls back dead, with the miraculous horse-god Pegasus being born amid the snakes from the wound. The ribbons for this victorious hero are brought by a bird—evidently a dove, though one of the rings for the chain attached to the *cista* has half obscured it. Perseus is welcomed back by Mercurius, whose identity is confirmed by another version of the same scene, on a *cista* in Palestrina where Jupiter and Minerva are the main welcoming party.

These were not foreign stories. Perseus, whose mother founded Ardea, was a Latin hero as well as an Argive one (p. 25 above). Pegasus appears with Jupiter's eagle and thunderbolt on Roman bronze currency bars in the third century BC, and alone or with Hercules on contemporary Roman bronze coinage. As for Minerva, who is omnipresent in the scenes of heroism on the *cistae*, as the daughter of Jupiter she occupied one of the three shrines in the great temple on the Capitol. On her shield and at her breast, the warrior goddess displays the Gorgon's head, the gift of Perseus.

What led us into the Perseus-Medusa story on the Baltimore *cista* was a Bacchic dance, led by a girl veiled from head to foot and carrying a *thyrsus*. Behind her, a young satyr with a lionskin has a large amphora on his shoulder. Behind him are two half-naked girl musicians and a hairy character, also carrying a *thyrsus*, who wears a distinctive ivy-leaf crown or cap. In fact, he is a performer in a hairy suit, as we can see more clearly in a splendid pair of contemporary bronze mirrors. The first shows a drinking party, the second a bedroom scene. The lady is ready for her man, but he has passed out; so Pan, with the help of a girl piper and a couple of revellers costumed as hairy satyrs, tries to wake him up and shows him what to do.

This sexual frankness is one of the most striking features of the world of Novius Plautius. The coupling of young men and women, necessary for the future of the community, is presided over by Liber. That seems to be illustrated on a fine *cista* now in Karlsruhe. The scene is almost, but not quite, symmetrical, centred on the fountain-house between the columns and the five beautiful

Figure 29

Figure 30

Figure 28 (pp. 96–7)

Figures 31–32 (pp. 99–100)

Figure 33. Narrative frieze on a *cista* in the Badisches Landesmuseum, Karlsruhe. Liber and Libera(?) preside over the selection of brides.

Figure 30. Five-pound bronze ingot, c. 280–240 BC: on one side, an eagle clutching a thunderbolt; on the other, Pegasus and the legend ROMANOM. 'Pegasus dwells in the house of Zeus and brings to wise Zeus the thunder and lightning' (Hesiod Theogony 285–6).

Figure 31. Bronze mirror in the Walters Art Gallery, Baltimore. At an elaborate couch sit a girl musician and a young man blowing a conch shell; the horns in his hair identify him as Pan. Behind is a bearded figure in a hairy suit (see his left arm for the sleeve), wearing an ivy-leaf crown or cap and with a *thyrsus* in the crook of his arm [compare fig. 28, on the left]; sprawled in front of him, a young man totally drunk. A wreathed amphora stands to the right of the couch.

Figure 33

girls there, of whom four are wearing only their jewellery. On each side, a satyr escorts a divinity—to the left, Liber himself; to the right, presumably his consort Libera (pp. 34–5, 65 above). Asymmetrically behind Liber are two young men, naked but for loose mantles, one of them carrying a spear. Such figures are not uncommon on *cista* scenes, but here their evident interest in what's going on shows that they are more than mere observers. No doubt each is hoping to choose one of the girls.

Figure 34

A mirror in Berlin shows two girls washing in the company of a young man who holds an oil-bottle and strigil, evidently after physical exercise. The lid handle of a *cista* in the British Museum shows a man and a girl, both naked,

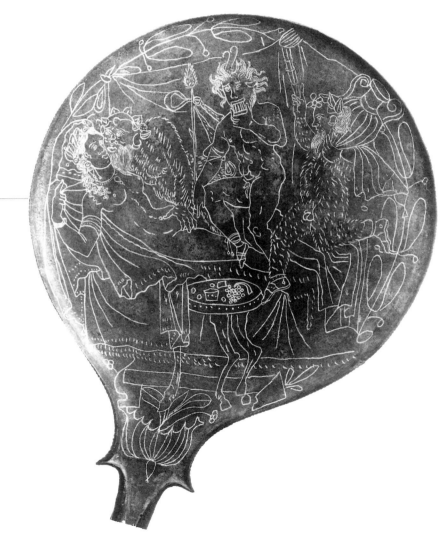

Figure 32. Bronze mirror in the Museo Nazionale di Villa Giulia, Rome. A young woman lies on a bed, naked but with elaborate jewellery and coiffure, holding open with her right hand the mantle that could have covered her. Pan, identified by his pipes and stylised horns, leaps across the bed and points at her groin. The hairy-suited bearded figure with the ivy crown and *thyrsus* (see fig. 31), is pawing her body; another in the same costume gallops across carrying a torch and an amphora.

though she is wearing jewellery; this time she has the oil-bottle and he the strigil. *Figure 35*
This pose, though normally without the detail, is a favourite design for *cista-*
lid handles. Sometimes the pair are a young man and a young woman,
sometimes they are a satyr and a nymph; only in the latter case is the male's *Figure 36 (p. 103)*
sexual arousal made explicit.

Another frequent lid-handle design is a pair of wrestlers, a young woman *Figure 37 (p. 104)*
and a young man. So what the strigil and oil-bottle indicate was evidently a
stylised form of physical courtship in which the pairing of the young people

Figure 35. Lid-handle of a *cista* in the British Museum: girl with oil-bottle, man with strigil.

Figure 38 (p. 105)

Figure 39 (p. 105)

might also be expressed in mythic terms as that of a satyr and a nymph. Even later Romans knew that there had once been an archaic custom of marriage by capture, of which the one surviving trace was the ritual parting of the bride's hair with a spear. Perhaps a wrestling match under Liber's genial patronage was one of the forms it took in Novius Plautius' day. That seems to be implied by a *cista* in Berlin, where a forcible abduction is taking place in the presence of other more formally posed couples, all under a conspicuous ivy-leaf border.

The fourth standard design for a *cista*-lid handle was a female acrobat bent over backwards. Here too there is a strong erotic element—she presents her

body to be handled every time the *cista* is opened—but the context is one of performance and entertainment. Several of the surviving *cistae* show narrative scenes accompanied by piping or dancing satyrs with young women who seem to be *mimae*, or showgirls. The natural inference is that the scenes are to be imagined as being performed; one of them, indeed, is recognisably a burlesque version of Euripides' *Iphigeneia at Aulis*.

In fact, many of the scenes represented on *cistae* and mirrors are illustrations of familiar Greek myths—the judgement of Paris, Hercules and the Amazons, the battle of the gods and Giants, and so forth. But there are also many where

Figure 36. Lid-handle of a *cista* in the British Museum: nymph and satyr, the latter identified by his tail and pointed ears.

103

the subject is not one we can recognise, and they are the ones which best illustrate the particular quality of Novius Plautius' fourth-century BC story-world.

Figure 40 (p. 106) Consider for instance a scene known from two *cistae* in Palestrina. Reading from the right, we have two girls at the fountain, with a satyr piping beneath; a young man with a spear, as on the Karlsruhe *cista*; a young woman heavily veiled, like the one leading the Bacchic dance on the Baltimore *cista*; a bound naked prisoner kneeling before a man with a staff; a warrior and his horse; and a winged naked female with a parasol, evidently in conversation with a tall mature woman. Venus' dove, Minerva's owl and a huge table-like flower mark out the central scene. Perhaps the man who leans on his staff with that air of authority is the father of the veiled young woman. Does she have to decide the prisoner's fate? Is the tall lady her mother? Is the warrior in love with her?

We don't know what the story is, but we can see how casually, in this world, supernatural beings take their part in the human drama. And it probably *is* a drama, for performance, as the piping satyr suggests. Did the two girls at the basin play the heroine and the winged goddess? We can never know—but the fluidity of role-play and real life is startlingly illustrated by a scene on another Figure 41 (p. 106) *cista* from the same site, where the satyr under the basin is making free with one of the girls, who in this scene are both wearing wings.

Figure 37. Lid-handle of a *cista* in the Nationalmuseet, Copenhagen: wrestling couple.

Figure 38. Narrative frieze on a *cista* in the Staatliche Museen, Berlin: marriage by capture? (To the right, winged Victoria hangs a boar's head hunting trophy on a tree.)

Figure 39. Lid-handle of a *cista* in the Pierpont Morgan Library, New York: acrobat. For the scene on the body of the *cista*, see fig. 46 below.

Figure 40. Narrative
frieze on a *cista* in the
Museo Archeologico,
Palestrina: unknown story,
with piping satyr and
naked girls (right). Another
example found at the
same time, in the
Colombella necropolis at
Palestrina in 1859, is
much more sketchily
drawn and omits the
young man with the spear
and sword-belt.

Figure 41. Groping satyr:
one side of a rectangular
cista in the Museo
Nazionale di Villa Giulia,
Rome, found in the
Colombella necropolis at
Palestrina in 1866.

.4 NAMING NAMES

Like their Etruscan colleagues, the Latin bronze-engravers quite often included written inscriptions on their work, naming the characters portrayed there. Let's see what they can tell us about the world of pre-literary Latium and Rome.

First, a mirror signed by the engraver Vibi(u)s P(h)ilip(p)us. A little Pan

Figure 42

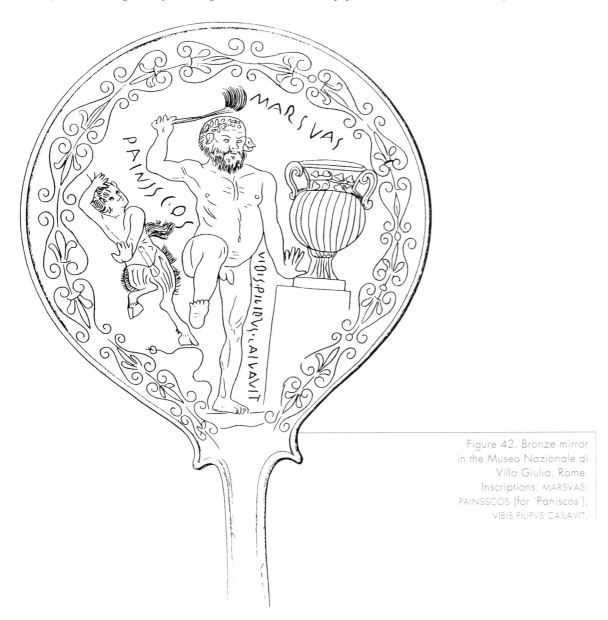

Figure 42. Bronze mirror in the Museo Nazionale di Villa Giulia, Rome. Inscriptions: MARSVAS; PAINSSCOS (for 'Paniscos'); VIBIS PILIPVS CAILAVIT.

(*paniskos* in Greek), goat-legged and ithyphallic, imitates the stamping dance of Marsyas the satyr before a huge amphora decorated with ivy leaves. Marsyas is the servant of Liber, and his statue stands in the Roman Forum as a symbol of liberty (p. 69 above). But here he is evidently a performer, waving his own detachable tail. Is this drama, or ritual? And is the distinction a real one?

Next, a scene on the lid of a *cista* in Berlin: two three-horse chariots (*trigae*) driven by female figures named as Venus and Aucena. A naked girl holds up Venus' chariot, while Aucena's is in hot pursuit of a naked young man. Above, a laurel branch implies victory. We know who Venus is, of course; but 'Aucena' is evidently a family name, known from the seventh century BC (Avile *Aukana*, at Veii) to the fifth century AD (Flavius Anicius *Auchenius* Bassus, consul in 408). Perhaps she is the lady for whose marriage the *cista* was made, defeating even a goddess in the contest to win her man.

Figure 43

Figure 43. Aucena's chariot race: lid of a *cista* in the Staatliche Museen, Berlin.

Figure 44

The main scene on Aucena's *cista* is a fountain-house between two columns, as on the Karlsruhe example. This time, the visitors at each side are not satyrs but Amazons, mounted and armed; they are named as Oinumama and Casenter, and behind Oinumama are Ajax, carrying shield and spear, and Crisida, carrying a cup. Inside the fountain-house are two men, Alses and

Figure 44. Narrative
frieze on the same *cista*: a
local version of the
judgement of Paris,
witnessed by women
warriors.

Alixentr, and three girls, Ateleta, Alsir and Helena. It looks as if Alixentr has chosen Ateleta (he hands her a twig from his laurel staff), and the other two girls are not pleased.

Ajax and Crisida—i.e. Chryseis, daughter of the Trojan priest of Apollo— are characters from Homeric legend. So too is Alixentr, if he is Alexandros, otherwise known as Paris, who famously chose one of three competing beauties in a different contest. The Amazons have vaguely Greek names, recalling Kassandra and Oinomaos; Ateleta could be Atalanta, so often a winner, and Helena might be Helen of Troy. That leaves Alses and Alsir—brother and sister?—whose names are unknown to fame. Are they contemporary figures, as Aucena may be? What will be the result of Alses' conversation with Oinumama? Why are Crisida and Ajax so unhappy? What are the two faces, or masks, that interrupt the upper border? Nobody knows.

Helena and Crisida—spelt Creisita this time—are the girls at the fountain in a scene on a *cista* in Rome. To the right, Ac(h)il(l)es, followed by Simos (his servant?) and Orestes; to the left, Seci Lucus, followed by a figure whose name is lost and an old man called Tondrus (Tyndareus?). It is not known who Seci Lucus is, but his name sounds Latin; a face, or mask, interrupts the border just above his head, and there seems to be a window behind him. (Sometimes a window may indicate a stage building, but one would expect to see something through it.) Here too it's impossible to know what's going on, but it does look as if a figure from contemporary Latium is taking part on equal terms in a story of heroes and heroines.

Figure 45

So too on a splendid *cista* in New York, featuring a young man called Soresios. His name should mean 'man of Sora', so he probably needed the sword and two spears he carries; for Sora was a stronghold in the Apennine foothills that was disputed between the Romans and the Samnites for forty years before a Latin colony was established there in 303 BC. In a near-symmetrical composition, he stands with Acmemeno opposite Aiax Ilios and Ladumeda—that is,

Figure 46

in the same story, whatever it was, as Agamemnon, 'little Ajax' the son of Oileus, and Laodameia.

There are two pairs of horses, one looking out of the stable window; there is a man called Istor, whose name means 'judge' in Greek; there is a prominent column with a notice on it (*leces* for *leges*, 'the laws'?); and there are two women enclosing the main scene, one called 'glory' in Greek (*doxa*), the other called 'praise' in Latin (*lauis = laus*). Ladumeda is leaning on a pillar decorated with a satyr mask, and holding a string attached to the horn of a spotted deer. The key is lost, but Soresios was evidently involved in a complex myth. And outside the main story, engrossed in each other, a naked young woman and a young satyr called Silanus dance closely together.

What the garbled names and unexpected juxtapositions seem to imply is an imaginative mythic world in which the characters of Greek heroic legend, known not from texts but from oral story, might be combined in quite uncanonical ways, perhaps in a Dionysiac performance tradition which was at least intermittently erotic.

Figure 47

Ajax seems to have been a favourite character. He appears on a mirror scene with a nymph called Telis helping him into or out of his armour, while Alcumena plays the lyre and a little fat satyr enjoys a drink. And on a *cista* in the Vatican, too badly drawn to deserve illustration, he is being handed his helmet by 'Iuentus', who is probably *Iuuentas*, the goddess of Youth; at the other side of the scene, winged Victoria is doing the same for Ac(h)il(l)es, while 'Mircurios' holds a balance, evidently weighing the fates of the two heroes in the scale. Famously, Ajax failed to win the contest for Achilles' armour. Perhaps, like other 'losers' of Greek myth (Kronos, Marsyas, Aeneas), he found a compensating success story in the land of the Latins.

Figure 47. Ajax and Telis: bronze mirror in the British Museum.

Figure 48

Figure 48. Jupiter and Aeneas: narrative frieze on a *cista* in the Staatliche Museen, Berlin.

Figure 49

Aeneas himself is not named on any of the surviving bronzes, but he is recognisable on a *cista* in Berlin. Old now, and a bit overweight, but resplendent in his patterned tights and holding a magnificent eagle-topped sceptre, he awaits the arrival of Jupiter's *quadriga*. The god has come to claim the year's vintage of the wine of Latium. This is a story we happen to know: the Rutulians of Ardea, in their war against Aeneas' Trojans, promised the vintage to the Etruscan tyrant Mezentius in exchange for his support; Aeneas vowed it to Jupiter, and won the war. Now a priest and two acolytes stand ready to serve the god, and Aeneas' son Ascanius, ancestor of the royal dynasty of Alba, springs forward to control his horses. The richly dressed young man following the chariot is unidentified, but the two boys riding the outer horses may be the Dioskouroi.

Castor and Pollux more usually feature on the bronzes as grown men, for instance on a *cista* in Lyon, where they seem to be discussing the challenge of a grotesque figure sporting the scimitar of Perseus and the lionskin and club of Hercules. He is identified as 'the father of the Pygmies' (*pater poimilionum*), and since the Pygmies lived by the river Okeanos, perhaps he has run into Castor and Pollux in their role as Argonauts. Behind him, Minerva, in a very formal pose, is being greeted by winged Victoria and a young man with his wife and two small sons. They, unfortunately, have no inscriptions to identify them.

Once again, the unfamiliar story reminds us how little the mythic world of Novius Plautius' time corresponds to that of the Rome we know from our literary sources, three or four centuries later. But not everything is unfamiliar. We can recognise Minerva and Victoria, as we could recognise Jupiter in his chariot. Indeed, the two goddesses are very frequently present in the various scenes of strife and heroism depicted on the bronzes: of the eighty-five surviving *cistae* with authentic scenes, Minerva appears on fifteen and Victoria on seventeen. That's not surprising; the victory goddess had come with Evander

Figure 49. The father of the Pygmies: narrative frieze on a *cista* in the Musée des Beaux Arts, Lyon.

Figure 50

Figure 50. Liber, Minerva and Mars: narrative frieze on a *cista* in the Staatliche Museen, Berlin. Inscriptions: IVNO, IOVOS, MERCVRIS, HERCLE, APOLO, LEIBER, VICTORIA, MENERVA (retrograde), MARS, DIAMA (sic, retrograde), FORTVNA.

from Arkadia (p. 26 above), while Minerva, her childhood companion, shared with Jupiter and Juno the great temple created by Tarquinius on the Capitol. What *is* surprising is the absence of Mars.

He is named once, on a superb inscribed *cista* in Berlin. The gods are all identified, and mostly recognisable anyway: Juno with Jupiter; Mercury with Hercules, and a dog; Apollo and Liber, apparently not on friendly terms (remember Marsyas); on the far side, Diana and Fortuna. Most conspicuous is winged Victoria, holding up a garland apparently of ivy. Next to her is a shield and helmet on a pile of rocks. They belong to Minerva, who is applying ambrosial ointment to the lips of the young Mars. Naked, but equipped with miniature helmet, shield and spear, he kneels over a huge container-jar evidently filled with boiling or fermenting liquid. Behind Minerva's head, a little Victoria flies in with ribbons for him. Above, the three-headed dog Cerberus breaks the floral decoration at this point only, marking the significance of the scene.

Whatever is happening is clearly Liber's business (keep away, Apollo!). Fortuna's beribboned staff looks like a Bacchic *thyrsus*; the liquid in the jar may well be new wine; Victoria's ivy-garland, much too big for Mars, may be

Figure 42 (p. 107)

to crown the jar itself, as in the scene of Marsyas' dance. As we saw in the last chapter (pp. 64–5 above), Liber, Mars and Minerva all belong together in the archaic Roman calendar.

It's important to remember that Roman Mars was the farmer's god, protecting his cornfields, his vineyards and his flocks. He could be thought of as Silvanus, god of the forest, or as the father of Faunus, god of the wild. But myth and ritual adapt to new circumstances, and in Novius Plautius' time Rome was already beginning her great career of military conquest. What we see on the Berlin *cista* may be part of the Romans' readjustment of their view of themselves. As the glory of empire passes from Athens to Rome (p. 70 above), the warrior goddess Pallas Athene anoints her successor. From now on Mars is a war-god—and he has that role with the blessing of Liber, who stands for Roman freedom.

5.5 THE TWINS

What Novius knew was a whole repertoire of stories, some of them familiar to us as 'Greek mythology', others no longer recognisable because we have no texts to tell us about Seci Lucus, Ladumeda and the rest. Not that 'Greek mythology' is a concept Novius would have been familiar with. I imagine he didn't think of Amykos and Ajax as particularly Greek, any more than we think of Cinderella as Italian or Snow White as German; they were simply characters in stories everybody knew. And it seems that one of the ways he knew the stories was via a Dionysiac performance tradition which mixed hero-tales with erotic farce (the lion's paw and the frog).

One story which did happen to survive into a literary text is featured on a mirror we have seen already, used in advance in the last chapter to illustrate

Figure 21

the creatures of the wild (p. 79 above). Let's look at it again.

The key to its meaning is the calendar, and the three successive festivals of *Lupercalia*, *Quirinalia* and *Feralia* on 15, 17 and 21 February. On the left, the god of the *Lupercalia* with his goatskin and shepherd's staff; on the right, Quirinus with the spear that gives him his name; in the centre, a wolf and a lion, wild beasts (*ferae*) respectively suckling and protecting the twin Lares, guardian gods of Rome; above, the twins' parents Mercurius and the Silent Goddess, the latter of whom was honoured at the *Feralia*.

Serious matters are at stake here. The *Lupercalia* was among other things the cleansing of the Roman citizen body at the end of the archaic year.

Figure 51

Quirinus—whose iconography is confirmed by a later coin-type—personifies the citizen body itself, the *Quirites*. He was a god of particular significance in Novius Plautius' time, when the incorporation of many Latin communities after 338 BC enormously extended the Roman citizenship. The city itself expanded to accommodate an influx of new citizens, and it seems that the Quirinal hill, named after the god, was settled as a new quarter at just this time. A splendid new temple of Quirinus was built there, vowed in 325 BC and dedicated nearly thirty years later.

Figure 51. Obverse of *denarius* struck by Gaius Memmius in about 56 BC: legends QVIRINVS and C. MEMMI. C.F. Quirinus has the beard, moustache and strong hair of the figure on the right in fig. 21 (p. 79 above).

The Lares are the protectors of Rome, and they are twins because authority in Rome was now shared between two consuls. The historic compromise of 367 BC was symbolised at the new Quirinus temple by two myrtle trees planted

Figure 52. Bell-krater by the 'Brooklyn-Budapest Painter', Lucania c.390–380 BC: a burlesque Mercurius (Hermes) receives offerings from a woman and a running satyr.

115

Figure 53. Mercurius, as played by an actor wearing a prosthetic phallus, on a wall-painting from Pompeii.

in the precinct, one called 'patrician', the other 'plebeian'. Quirinus' gesture on the mirror is that of a new Rome conscious of the reason for its confidence and prosperity. What subject could be more serious than the turning-point of Roman history?

Figure 21

But turn back again to p. 79, and look at nonchalant Mercurius. *He* doesn't seem to be taking it very seriously—and that's because his part of the story belongs in the cheerfully sexy, traditionally Dionysiac world of dancing Marsyas and naked Cressida (above, pp. 107, 110). Two images of Mercurius, four centuries apart, give us an idea of his role. The first is a vase-painting from Lucania in southern Italy, about fifty years before Novius Plautius' time; the second is a wall-painting from Pompeii, about fifty years after Ovid told the old story of the Silent Goddess in book 2 of the *Fasti*.

Figures 42, 45

Figure 52

Figure 53

The mother of the Lares was called Larunda. However, the story Ovid tells shortens it to Lara, which in turn was supposedly corrupted from Lala, 'the talker' (Greek *lalein*, to chat). Lara is a nymph, daughter of the river Almo, and her story is best thought of as a performance scenario for the showgirls we have seen on the *cista* engravings.

Scene one: the girls dance, as the nymphs of Latium. One of them is Juturna, beautiful but shy; another is Lara, beautiful but loquacious. 'That tongue will get you into trouble one day,' says her father the river-god, but Lara just laughs and talks on. Scene two: enter Jupiter in a bad mood, with Mercurius in attendance. The girls scatter; Juturna escapes unnoticed, the others return at Jupiter's summons, and he harangues them. He wants Juturna, but she keeps evading him:

> 'Your sister-nymph much wrongs herself, alas,
> By striving to avoid a god's embrace. . .
> Then all assist my pleasure to obtain,
> Which will be vastly to your sister's gain;
> If e'er she to the river's bank should run,
> When my pursuits she does unkindly shun,
> Prevent her plunging in the crystal flood,
> And by that favour gratify a god!'

Ovid Fasti
2.591–596

Yes, sir, they say. Mercurius, who has had his eye on Lara, follows his master off stage. Scene three: Lara to Juturna, warning her to keep out of sight; Lara to Juno, reporting Jupiter's plan ('What you married ladies have to put up with. . .'). Scene four: re-enter Jupiter and Mercurius. Jupiter, in a comically furious rage, siezes Lara and pulls out her tongue. No pain, of course; this is a pantomime played for laughs, as the astonished fast-talking nymph opens and shuts her mouth and no words come. 'Take her to the underworld,' snarls Jupiter, and Mercurius obeys with particular pleasure. Scene five: a sacred grove, where he has his way with her.

> Twins consequent to that embrace there came,
> And from their mother Lares was their name;
> Our streets by day these careful guardians keep,
> And watchfully defend us while we sleep.

Ovid Fasti
2.615–616

The Lares are born in February, and their mother, the Silent Goddess, brings them to the world above. On 21 February (*Feralia*), she leaves them to be looked after by the beasts of the wild. And that is what Pan and Quirinus witness on the mirror, in the name of the Roman People.

Another witness is Minerva's owl. But the Berlin *cista* (p. 113 above) seemed to show Minerva anointing her successor as patron of Rome's military conquests. In the fast-changing world of Novius Plautius, the story on the mirror may already have given rise to the far more famous narrative in which the twins suckled by the she-wolf are the sons of Mars. Perhaps the newly dominant Rome of the late fourth century BC felt the need of national symbols with a more dignified origin, the union not of lecherous Mercurius and a talkative nymph but of the war-god himself and a priestess of Vesta.

After so much conjectural discussion of the myths of an oral society, we have now reached the point where the first signs can be detected of the great heroic stories of the Roman historical tradition. The tradition itself began a century later, with the literary drama, epic poetry and historiography of the late third century BC; but the stories the playwrights, poets and historians then wrote down had been created three generations before, in the excitement of Rome's expansion as the leading power in Italy.

6

HISTORY AND MYTH

THE CRUCIBLE

Half way through the book (five chapters out of ten), we are also half way through the story—very roughly four centuries each way between the formation of the city-state called 'Strength' (*Rhome*) and Gibbon's starting point for *The Decline and Fall*.

Let's put ourselves in 296 BC. The Romans have been at war with the Samnites to the south more or less continuously for the last thirty years, and with the Etruscans to the north for the last fifteen. Already they have changed the face of central Italy, with eleven new colonies of Latin and Roman settlers— each of them a miniature Rome—founded in the past thirty years from Narnia in Umbria to Luceria in Apulia, and newly engineered military roads imposed on the landscape to serve them. The first of the Roman aqueducts is already in service, evidence for the sudden growth of the city's population, which is now causing serious unrest among the urban poor.

The Romans know success is precarious, and the gods must be honoured. Two splendid new temple complexes are nearing completion—one for Quirinus, god of the citizen body, on the hill named after him, where much of the city's expansion is taking place; and one for Victoria on the Palatine, immediately above the grove and grotto of Arkadian Pan, looking out over the altar of Hercules and replacing (so the Romans say) Evander's own temple to the goddess of victory.

It is a changing world. At the altar of Hercules itself, the traditional cult superintendents were replaced by public slaves sixteen years ago. Hercules appeared in person to curse the Roman censor responsible, but for the moment Appius Claudius has survived; indeed, he is consul this very year, in command

The Death of Diomedes

In 314 BC the Romans colonised a Daunian stronghold dominating the north Apulian plain. The *tavoliere di Puglia* is ideal country for cavalry; when Diomedes built his city in the plain, he called it Argos Horsetown. A force of fast light cavalry was the latest addition to Rome's military power in the late fourth century BC, organised in three regiments called *Titienses*, *Ramnes* and *Luceres*. The *Luceres* were named after Lucerus, legendary king of Latin Ardea, which claimed an ancestral connection with Daunia. So the new colony was called Luceria.

Apulia had been won for the Romans by Gaius Iunius Bubulcus as consul in 317 BC, and it's likely—though the names are not recorded—that he headed the commission sent to found the settlement and mark out the colonists' holdings. The land of Diomedes had new masters now.

Like Rome, the colony had a talismanic statue of Minerva, brought from Troy—perhaps the very one Diomedes stole, with no need for any complicated 'gift to Aeneas' story (p. 18 above). Certainly the myth of the Argive hero had to be accommodated to the new events. 'Some say,' noted a commentator on the *Iliad*, 'that Diomedes was killed in a hunting accident by Iunius the son of Daunos.' Riding fast horses can be a dangerous business. Since Diomedes was married to Daunos' daughter, it's a safe bet that Iunius inherited his kingdom.

of a Roman army in Etruria, and the goddess Bellona has given him victory in return for the promise of a temple.

Appius the consul is the man who had the aqueduct built, and the great road south to Capua. He is also a symbol of change in another way: he writes books. The Romans are becoming used to the art of writing, not just on bronze or stone to make a law or treaty permanent, but also on papyrus, in rolls that can be kept in a library or an archive. Where once the procedures of jurisdiction were only to be discovered by applying to a *pontifex*, now they are available for any citizen to consult for himself, along with the official calendar of days on which legal business is allowed. That democratic reform was carried out a few years ago, in the teeth of aristocratic opposition, by a professional scribe under the patronage of Appius himself.

'Every man,' says Appius, 'is the maker of his own fortune'—but to be so he needs information, and Rome is no longer content to let such matters be the secret possession of the *pontifices*. She is following the precedent of Athens, where Kleidemos the historian has recently published the arcane lore of the 'exegetes'.

Four years ago the Roman colleges of pontiffs and augurs were thoroughly reformed; membership of those priesthoods is now jointly patrician and plebeian, with a built-in plebeian majority. From now on arcane knowledge will be written down; there will be records kept, an archive built up. Rome is becoming a literate society. A century on, Roman authors will write their city's history, in heroic verse and historical prose. Three centuries on, a Roman poet will look back at 'the pontiffs' books and the prophets' ancient scrolls' as the beginning of Latin literature.

But now, in Appius Claudius' consulship, Rome needs as never before her interpreters of the will and favour of the gods. Her enemies have joined forces, and the new Samnite–Etruscan coalition is negotiating with the Gauls for an overwhelming combined effort to wipe out Rome for ever. The Romans anxiously remember their grandparents' stories of the Gauls who sacked the city in 387 BC. The gods have sent terrifying portents, and the prophets—for there are now experts on prophecy in the college of augurs—demand equally terrifying expiation.

In this year of crisis the curule aediles are the brothers Gnaeus and Quintus Ogulnius, the same men who as tribunes of the *plebs* forced through the reform of the priestly colleges. Now, they have imposed huge fines on illegal money-lenders; profiteers must be made to contribute to the common good, and the aediles are spending the money where it matters, on the gods whose favour Rome desperately needs.

Mars, the newly anointed god of Roman warfare, has a temple between the first and second milestones outside the Porta Capena; now there will be a processional way from the gate to the temple, paved in squared stone. Every year on 15 July, in a ceremony established eight years ago, the Roman cavalry will parade along it from the Mars temple to the city, ending at the temple of the divine riders Castor and Pollux in the Roman Forum.

At the great temple of Jupiter on the Capitol there will be silver serving-vessels, and bronze thresholds where the feet of the pious have worn away the stone. On the roof of the Capitol temple there has stood for two centuries a terracotta statue group of Jupiter in a four-horse chariot; it symbolised Rome's rivalry with Etruscan Veii, but now that Veii is conquered and absorbed, a new bronze chariot-group will replace it, and perhaps Jupiter will give Rome supremacy over all the rest of Etruria as well.

Figure 54

Figure 55

The last of the aediles' dedications will be another bronze statue group, to be placed beneath the Ruminal fig-tree in Pan's grove at the Lupercal. It will

Figure 54. Didrachm, 225–212 BC: obverse, head of Janus with laurel wreaths; reverse, Jupiter in a *quadriga* driven by Victoria, sceptre in his left hand and thunderbolt in his right. See pp. 161–3 below for Janus. The reverse design no doubt represents the bronze *quadriga* on the Capitol temple, dedicated by the Ogulnii in 296 BC.

stand at the bottom of the newly engineered paved street that zig-zags up the western cliff of the Palatine to the almost-completed temple of Victoria. The old Palatine gate at this point is called Porta Romana, and the aediles' statue group will be of Rome's founders, the infant twins suckled by the she-wolf.

In 296 BC, this is a new story. A great deal has happened since a low-born warlord justified his rule with the legend of a founder-hero fathered on a slave girl by a divine apparition. For Rome as it is now, something more complex is being evolved. Twin founders are appropriate for a city that owes its success to the power-sharing partnership of patricians and plebeians; the myth of the Lares (above, pp. 80, 117) can be adapted to accommodate them, and in this world of war they must be the sons of Mars.

Figure 21 (p. 79)

Figure 14 (p. 43)

The bronze-workers of Rome—colleagues and successors of Novius Plautius—have already begun to represent Rome's past in visual form. A statue of Lucius Brutus the liberator, with sword drawn, stands on the Capitol; a statue of Marcus Camillus, who killed Gnaeus Tarquinius in the story known to the Etruscans of Vulci (pp. 42–3 above), stands on the new speakers' platform in the Comitium. For the Romans in 296 BC, these archaic heroes represent prominent contemporary families, respectively plebeian and patrician: they are now Lucius *Iunius* Brutus and Marcus *Furius* Camillus. How that came about

Figure 55. Didrachm, 269–266 BC: obverse, head of Hercules with diadem; reverse, she-wolf and twins. The consuls of 269 BC were C. Fabius Pictor, whose family claimed descent from Hercules (p. 28 above), and Q. Ogulnius, who as aedile in 296 had set up the bronze she-wolf and twins at the Ficus Ruminalis.

(to revert to the perspective of AD 2004), this chapter will attempt to show.

The aediles' pious work was not in vain. The gods did protect Rome, but it was a close thing. At Sentinum in Umbria the following year the Romans faced the combined armies of the Gauls, Samnites and Etruscans, and would have been defeated and destroyed but for the self-sacrifice of the plebeian consul, Publius Decius Mus. 'Jupiter, Juno, Father Mars, Quirinus, Bellona, Lares. . .': it was the new plebeian *pontifex maximus* who dictated to the consul the prayer-formula dedicating himself and the enemy forces to Earth and the spirits of the dead. There were more wars to follow, and plague and famine too, but Rome survived, and overcame her rivals to become the dominant power in Italy.

The conquest of Italy ended as a rematch between Achilles and the Trojans, with a different outcome this time. So it least it may have seemed to Achilles' descendant, Pyrrhos king of the Molossians (on the borders of present-day Greece and Albania), who in the well-informed opinion of Hannibal was second only to Alexander the Great as a military leader. Brought across by the Tarentines in 280 BC to halt the Roman advance into south Italy, he inflicted a serious defeat on the 'Trojan colonists' of Rome, and followed it up with a diplomatic initiative, offering peace and alliance in return for a Roman withdrawal into Latium.

While the proposal was being debated, the aged Appius Claudius was brought to the Senate house by his sons. He was blind now (the vengeance of Hercules had come late), but his message was clear: the Romans would talk to Pyrrhos only when he had left Italy. Five years later Pyrrhos did so, leaving all Italy south of the Apennines in Roman control. One of the consuls of 268 BC dedicated a temple to Tellus, Mother Earth, and had a map of Italy painted on the wall. What the gods had promised, stubborn resolve had brought about.

The seventy years from the settlement of Latium in 338 BC—from the time of Novius Plautius to that of his grandsons, if he had any—were formative for Rome. I think it was in this period, partly as a result of the innovative histories of Kleidemos and his successors in Athens, that the great quasi-historical

Talismans

From time to time, the gods vouchsafe to mortals some tangible proof of their favour, some sacred object which will count as a pledge of divinely guaranteed prosperity.

As we have seen already, the Romans had several such talismans—the Trojan Palladion (p. 18 above), in the temple of Vesta; the shield that fell from heaven (p. 78 above), in the shrine of Mars in the Regia; the head of Aulus of Vulci (p. 44 above), buried in a secret chamber on the Capitol; the horns of the prodigious heifer (p. 57 above), attached to the temple of Diana on the Aventine.

The learned 'Servius *auctus*' (p. 24 above) lists five more, though the first has been garbled in the transmission of his text. They are:

1. The '*aius*' of the Great Mother. Perhaps the word was *lapis*, referring to the stone embodying the goddess's power that was brought to Rome from the Mother's cult centre at Pessinus in Asia Minor in 204 BC. Whatever it was, it must have been kept in the Great Mother's temple on the Palatine.

2. The sceptre of Priam, and 3. the veil of Iliona. Since Iliona was Priam's eldest daughter, both of these must symbolise, like the Palladion, the transfer of Troy's power to Rome. But we have no further information about either object; in Virgil, Iliona's sceptre is one of Aeneas' diplomatic gifts to Dido.

4. The ashes of Orestes. When Orestes and Iphigeneia escaped from the land of the Taurians at the end of Euripides' play, they brought with them the cult-image of Artemis Tauropolos. They took it to Latium, to the woods round the deep volcanic lake known as 'Diana's mirror' in the territory of Aricia, that

numinous place immortalised in the opening passage of Sir James Frazer's *The Golden Bough*; and there they founded the cult of 'Diana in the Wood'. Orestes died and was buried there, and when the Romans subjected the Latins in 338 BC his remains were taken to Rome and reburied in front of the temple of Saturnus. For Delphic Apollo had promised success in war to the city that held Orestes' bones.

5. The Veian terracotta chariot. For the roof of his great new Jupiter temple on the Capitol, King Tarquin ordered a large terracotta statue-group of the god in a four-horse chariot from the only workshop capable of producing it, in Etruscan Veii. Unaccountably, it swelled up in the oven during firing, and the soothsayers declared it a prodigy: the city that owned it would be pre-eminent. Meanwhile, Tarquin had been expelled, and the Veientes declined to deliver it to the new regime at Rome. But the gods declared their will: at a chariot-race in Veii, the winning *quadriga* didn't stop at the finishing line but galloped all the way to Rome, fording the Tiber, throwing out the hapless charioteer at the foot of the Capitol, and then dashing up to the new temple and circling it three times. So the Romans went to war with Veii (it was the war in which young Horatius became a dead hero, p. 58 above), and the terracotta chariot was brought to Rome and placed on the temple roof. A century later, Rome conquered Veii and confiscated all her land; a century later again, in 296 BC, with a new and greater war with the Etruscans looming, the aediles replaced the old terracotta group with a new one of gleaming bronze.

Roman myths were first moulded into the form that literature would make canonical. We shall look at three of them, stories of events that were literally epoch-making, since the Romans came to use them as dating-eras—the foundation of the city, its liberation from the kings and its capture by the Gauls in 387 BC. But we shall look at them in reverse order, the order (I think) of their creation and development.

6.2   CAMILLUS

The Etruscan city of Veii was protected by Queen Juno in her temple on the citadel. But nothing is for ever, and the commitment of Juno and the city's other gods was mysteriously dependent on the waters of the Alban lake in Latium, 30 miles away: only while the overflow ran down to the sea would Veii still be safe. So at least it was written in the Etruscan Books of Fate, a secret known only to the *haruspices*.

By our reckoning, it was probably in 393 BC that the secret became known. The Romans' assault on Veii had got bogged down in a long and fruitless siege. By chance (but what is 'chance' when the gods have their agenda?), an old *haruspex* revealed the secret in the hearing of a Roman soldier, who on his own initiative captured the old man and took him to headquarters. At Rome the patrician authorities were unimpressed, until an embassy to the Delphic oracle confirmed it. Only then was the outflow channel from the Alban lake constructed (p. 88 above), bringing the surplus water to the Tiber.

Figure 22

At that point the Veientes sued for peace, but were contemptuously rejected. As they left the council chamber the senior ambassador, himself a *haruspex*, turned at the door and spoke one last time:

> 'A fine and magnanimous decree you have passed, Romans, you who lay claim to the leadership over your neighbours on the ground of valour, when you disdain to accept the submission of a city neither small nor undistinguished which offers to lay down its arms and surrender itself to you, but wish to destroy it root and branch, neither fearing the wrath of the gods nor regarding the indignation of men! In return for this, avenging justice shall come upon you from the gods, punishing you in like manner. For after robbing the Veientes of their country you shall ere long lose your own.'

Dionysios
12.13.2–3

The patricians took no notice. Nor, it seems, did they remember Delphic Apollo when they made their vows to the gods for victory over Veii.

It's likely that this first version of the story was told in the 370s BC, as part of the plebeians' demand for power-sharing. Certainly the patricians in power don't come out of it well. Credit for the victory goes to the common soldiers of Rome (plebeians, of course), who were sensitive to divine messages and quick to act on them. That was how Veii's secret had first been discovered, and that was how the city itself was taken.

For Queen Juno's temple was now undermined by Roman sappers, patiently tunnelling beneath the citadel. When they were ready to break out, a sacrifice was in progress above their heads. The *haruspex* examined the entrails of the sacrificial beast, and announced excellent omens to the king of Veii. 'He shall be victorious, who completes this sacrifice!' The soldiers at the head of the tunnel burst out, seized the entrails and carried them back to be burned on a Roman altar; the rest of them occupied the citadel.

The city fell, and was sacked. When the Romans came to strip the temple of Queen Juno, it was not the patrician commander but one of the soldiers who thought to ask the goddess's permission. 'Juno,' he said, 'do you want to go to Rome?' Queen Juno nodded, or even spoke her assent. Without sacrilege, the statue was taken to Rome. The goddess was rehoused in a fine new temple on the Aventine, the plebeians' hill.

The patricians' contribution was wholly negative. Marcus Furius, the commander, offended the gods by harnessing four white horses to his triumphal chariot, as if he were Jupiter or the sun-god. Then, when the booty had already been distributed, he remembered that he owed a tithe of it to Delphic Apollo, and the ordinary citizens had to find the money. The plebeian tribunes prosecuted him, and he went into exile at Ardea.

And so it went on. Even when the gods gave Rome a clear message, the patricians ignored it. From the sacred grove by the temple of Vesta a supernatural voice spoke to a plebeian called Marcus Caedicius. 'Tell the magistrates they must see to the city's defences. The Gauls are coming.' He duly reported it, and the magistrates just laughed at him. When the Gauls did come, as far as Clusium, 90 miles to the north, the Romans sent a fact-finding embassy, three patricians of the Fabian house. Supposedly neutral, they rashly joined in the fighting on behalf of Clusium, thus simultaneously putting the Romans in the wrong and provoking the Gauls' anger against Rome itself.

That was bad enough, but the patricians couldn't even defend the city. As the Gallic horde approached, the army was drawn up 11 miles north of Rome, where the little river Allia flows into the Tiber. Incompetent generalship resulted in utter defeat. The demoralised survivors fled to Veii, and ever afterwards 'the day of the Allia', 18 July, was the blackest date in the Roman calendar.

Rome was defenceless; perhaps the Capitol could be held, but that was all. Her citizens took what they could, and fled. Among the stream of refugees were the priest of Quirinus and the Vestal Virgins, carrying the sacred vessels and a brazier with the fire that must never die. A plebeian, Lucius Albinius, was escaping with his family in a cart. He stopped; his wife and children got out, and he drove the Vestals and their precious burden to safety.

Meanwhile, the Gauls occupied the deserted city and ransacked it at their leisure. Eventually they turned their attention to the Capitol, where a Roman force was holding out under the same patrician who had lost the battle of the

Allia, and had fled that stricken field. He was no more effective defending a citadel. The Gauls took the Capitol the way the Romans had taken Veii—by tunnels, into the temple of Jupiter Optimus Maximus himself. Even then the humiliation was not complete. When the gold was being weighed out to pay the ransom for the Gauls to leave, Brennus the Gallic chieftain threw his sword on to the scale. The Roman commander protested in vain. 'The vanquished must suffer,' said Brennus with contempt.

The litany of patrician failure is redeemed only by tales of honest and god-fearing plebeians. About twenty years after the catastrophe (the exact chronology is uncertain), the patricians lost their monopoly of power. But they were tenacious, and fought back. A prominent part in the rearguard action was played by the Furii, the family of the commander in the Veii campaign who had offended the gods with his white horses. What happened to the real Marcus Furius is not known. Historical fact has been smothered under the legend of Marcus Furius Camillus, the greatest of all generals, Rome's destined leader.

Figure 14

The myth-makers seem to have taken the name, and no doubt the aura, of an existing exemplary hero (Marcus Camillus, p. 43 above), grafted it on to Marcus Furius the patrician commander, and deployed this new champion in a radical retelling of the interlocking stories of Veii and the Gallic sack.

First, Camillus was not just one of a college of elected military tribunes; he was in sole command, as dictator. Next, Camillus was deeply devoted to the gods. His very name (*camillus* means 'altar-boy') was a reminder that the patricians still claimed exclusive control of religious ritual. Before the final assault on Veii, Camillus made two personal and very public vows: to Queen Juno, to give her a new temple at Rome if she would leave Veii, and to Delphic Apollo, to give him a tithe of all the spoil of victory. At the fall of the city, he prayed again: if so complete a conquest went beyond what was proper for mortals, let the anger of the gods fall on him, Camillus, and not on Rome. As he turned, he tripped and fell; but the gods required more than that.

Camillus' young son died, and as he was grieving he himself was prosecuted by demagogues on a petty trumped-up charge about the division of the spoil. He withdrew into exile, with one last prayer to the gods: if he was innocent, as they knew he was, let them make his ungrateful countrymen soon want him back!

Meanwhile, Juno sent the Romans a warning: 'The Capitol must be defended.' So when the gods brought the Gauls against them, at least the Romans knew what they had to do. Arms, provisions and a thousand able-bodied men with their wives and children were installed on the Capitol, under the command of a patrician officer, Marcus Manlius. The rest of the city was abandoned.

In this telling of the story, the patricians are exemplary. Those of them who were too old to defend the Capitol were also too proud to abandon their homes. They gathered in the Forum, eighty old men in the robes and insignia of their priesthoods and the magistracies or triumphs they had held, seated on ivory chairs as if they were representing the ancestors at a noble funeral. The *pontifex maximus* took them through the solemn ritual of *deuotio*, as they vowed their lives to the gods of the dead. Then each man returned to his house and sat in his robes in the *atrium* with the doors open, waiting for the barbarians. When the Gauls came, nervous at first in the deserted city, the silent figures filled them with superstitious awe. The spell was broken at the house of Marcus Papirius. When a Gallic warrior touched his beard, the old man struck him with his staff, and was immediately killed. The others too were butchered, the sacrifice to the infernal gods duly completed.

That was in July. Throughout the summer and autumn the Capitol was under siege. But the gods must still be honoured, and patricians must show the way. When the day came for a necessary sacrifice at the temple of Vesta, the *pontifex* Fabius Dorsuo walked down from the Capitol in his priestly robes, carrying the sacred utensils. He passed unscathed through the awe-struck Gauls, performed the sacrifice, and walked back the same way. The gods protect traditional piety and courage.

Meanwhile, the Romans who had fled from the Allia to Veii sent a message to the exiled Camillus at Ardea. The magnanimous hero agreed to command them, but only if appointed dictator in due form; and the magistrates who could do that were besieged on the Capitol. So a brave volunteer from the Veii troops made his way to Rome by night and climbed the precipitous cliff at the south end of the Capitol. The magistrates heard his report and appointed Camillus dictator; the messenger climbed down again and was gone before dawn.

But the Gauls found his tracks, and the next night they climbed the cliff themselves. However, in this version of the story the Gauls never took the Capitol at all, thanks to Juno and the patrician commander. Her sacred geese raised the alarm, and Marcus Manlius got to the cliff just in time to cut off the arm of the leading Gaul and hurl the next one down on top of the rest with one thrust of his shield.

All that remained now was the happy ending. The humiliating ransom, and Brennus' contemptuous comment, could not be denied. But they could be subverted. In this version, hardly has the sword hit the scale when the gods bring Camillus into the Forum at the head of the relief force to put the Gauls to flight. Rome is saved; the patrician hero is the city's second founder.

In the cold light of history, we can be certain that that didn't happen. What the real Marcus Furius did after the fall of Veii is now unknowable; the real Marcus Manlius 'Capitolinus' was executed for treason five years after the Gauls left. The story of the patricians who saved Rome was evidently an exercise in wishful thinking, and it is even possible to guess when it was created.

Marcus Furius had a son (Lucius) who was consul in 349 BC, and a grandson (also Lucius, and the nephew of his namesake) who was consul in 338 and 325 BC. One or other of them, we don't know which, was appointed dictator during the patrician 'backlash' of the 340s, in a year when both consuls were patricians. His deputy was a Manlius Capitolinus; one of the consuls was a Fabius

Dorsuo; and in his dictatorship he vowed a temple on the Capitol to 'Juno the Warner' (*Moneta*). When the temple was dedicated the following year, the aediles in charge of the games will certainly have made sure that the people knew, in appropriately dramatic detail, what Juno had done to deserve her *second* splendid new home. Those Romans who remembered what had really happened forty-six years before were no doubt happy to go along with an exemplary story of patrician piety and heroism. It was a story that *ought* to be true.

<table>
<tr><td>6.3</td><td></td></tr>
</table>

6.3   DYNASTY AND LIBERTY

Patricians like the Furii, Manlii and Fabii were now sharing power with men who were far from being their social equals. The plebeian consul of 325 BC was Decimus Iunius 'Scaeva', which means 'left-handed' and therefore 'clumsy'; his cousin, consul in 317, 313 and 311 BC, was Gaius Iunius 'Bubulcus', which means 'ploughman' or 'ox-driver'. Soon both men would have an even more uncomplimentary nickname—'Brutus', meaning 'dumb' or 'stupid'—but it was one which they and their descendants would bear with pride. For it was the name of the Liberator (pp. 53–4 above); by the late fourth century BC, the plebeian Iunii had successfully claimed the founder of the Roman Republic himself.

The old story of how 'dumb Lucius' led the revolt that expelled king Tarquin was no longer adequate. The Republic as it had now developed needed a more nuanced origin. What defined it was the consulship, a plebeian and a patrician in equal authority each year. If Lucius Iunius Brutus inaugurated that, he must have had a colleague—and that was indeed the outcome of the newly elaborated liberation story. It began with the very origins of the Tarquin dynasty, and marked its whole murderous course in dramatic detail.

Figure 56

First, we must understand that Demaratos of Corinth had *two* sons by his Etruscan wife (p. 38 above). The elder, Arruns, died young, leaving his wife pregnant. Demaratos himself died of grief soon after, unaware of his grandson in the womb. So all the wealth went to the younger son, Lucumo, and we have an elder but impoverished branch of the family to be exploited later in the plot.

Lucumo is Lucius Tarquinius. He goes to Rome with Tanaquil in the reign of Ancus Marcius. He makes himself essential to the king, who appoints him guardian of his two sons. When Ancus dies, Tarquinius gets the boys sent out of the way and becomes king himself. Two neighbouring towns, Collatia and Corniculum, fall to King Tarquinius in his campaign against the Latins. From Corniculum he takes the beautiful Ocrisia to serve in the palace. At Collatia he puts his nephew in command of the town. This is Arruns son of Arruns, nicknamed Egerius (from *egere*, to be in want), the boy who was born too late; now, from the fiefdom entrusted to him, he takes the name Collatinus.

Ocrisia gives birth to a son, Servius Tullius, who is marked out for his destiny by the portentous fire playing round his head. The years pass (but don't ask

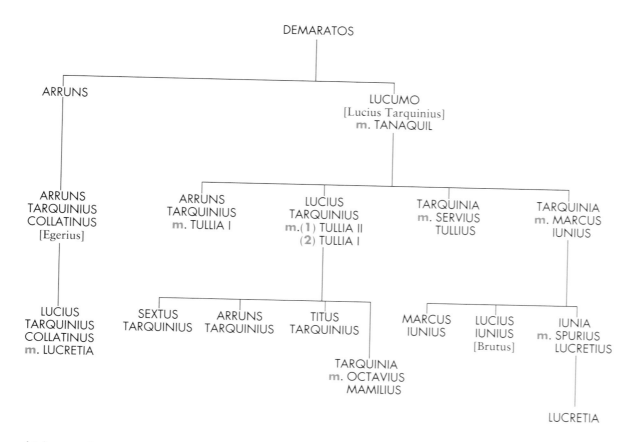

DEMARATOS

ARRUNS

LUCUMO
[Lucius Tarquinius]
m. TANAQUIL

ARRUNS
TARQUINIUS
COLLATINUS
[Egerius]

ARRUNS
TARQUINIUS
m. TULLIA I

LUCIUS
TARQUINIUS
m.(**1**) TULLIA II
(**2**) TULLIA I

TARQUINIA
m. SERVIUS
TULLIUS

TARQUINIA
m. MARCUS
IUNIUS

LUCIUS
TARQUINIUS
COLLATINUS
m. LUCRETIA

SEXTUS
TARQUINIUS

ARRUNS
TARQUINIUS

TITUS
TARQUINIUS

MARCUS
IUNIUS

LUCIUS
IUNIUS
[Brutus]

IUNIA
m. SPURIUS
LUCRETIUS

TARQUINIA
m. OCTAVIUS
MAMILIUS

LUCRETIA

Figure 56. The Tarquin dynasty, as developed (a) to account for Tarquinius Collatinus and (b) to make Brutus a close kinsman of Lucretia.

which years they were). Servius grows up, fights in the king's wars, marries the king's daughter. One of the king's daughters, that is: the other is married to a prominent citizen called Marcus Iunius. Both couples have children, who will star in later episodes.

Tarquinius also has two sons, much younger than their sisters. How old is Tanaquil by now? Some authorities give Tarquinius a second wife, Gegania—one of various Geganiae who turn up inexplicably in the tradition, no doubt remnants of lost stories celebrating that ancient patrician family. But Tanaquil cannot be supplanted, for she has her famous role to play in the transition of power (pp. 45–6 above).

The sons of Ancus Marcius plot to regain their father's kingdom (don't ask what they've been doing all this time). They succeed at least in killing Tarquinius. But with Tanaquil's help at the window, Servius Tullius establishes himself in power. To secure his position, he marries his two daughters to the late king's two sons. (Our sources make no comment about these uncle–niece marriages.) Both pairs are ill-matched: the younger Tullia is fiercely ambitious, the opposite of her husband Arruns; the elder Tullia is mild and gentle, the opposite of her husband Lucius. The two ruthless ones get together, murder their respective spouses, and marry.

The years pass. Now Tullia acts Lady Macbeth:

> '. . . Why
> Did my dear sister and your brother die
> If here we stop, and lead a private life?
> For higher purpose sure we're man and wife.
> If here we stop, nor act what we conceived,
> My husband and your spouse might still have lived.
> My dowry is my father's head, and crown;
> Then be a man, and claim them as your own.
> Bold wickedness to act's a royal thing.
> Kill but my father, and you'll be a king.'

Ovid *Fasti*
6.589–595

Tarquinius makes his preparations, then marches into the Forum with an armed escort and usurps the royal throne. When Servius appears, indignantly protesting, Tarquinius hurls him bodily down the steps into the Comitium. The old man limps away towards his house on the Esquiline. Tullia comes, hails her husband as king, and urges him to send assassins after her father.

> Beneath the *Esquiliae* where his palace stood,
> Was Servius slain, and wallowed in his blood.
> His daughter in her coach, with cruel pride,
> To take possession of the palace hied.
> Soon as her father's corpse the coachman saw,
> He stopped amazed, and would no further go.
> 'Drive on,' she cried, 'if you'd my favour gain,
> And force the crashing wheels across his brain!'

Ovid *Fasti*
6.601–608

That's why it's called Wicked Street (*uicus sceleratus*)—and why the affronted household gods and the avenging Furies will see to it that Tullia comes to a bad end.

The second Tarquin is harsh, haughty and tyrannical. He surrounds himself with a bodyguard, imposes forced labour and cruel punishments on the citizens, and systematically eliminates all those prominent enough to be a threat to his power. Among the victims are Marcus Iunius, the king's brother-in-law, and his son of the same name. The second son, Lucius Iunius, is the apparently mute idiot whom the king installs in the palace as a laughing-stock. This is the boy they call Brutus.

Meanwhile, Tarquinius is making himself master of the whole of Latium. He marries his daughter to Octavius Mamilius, a descendant of Circe and Ulysses and ruler of Tusculum. He instals his eldest son Sextus as his viceroy at Gabii, which he has treacherously captured. Not far away is Collatia, home of the impoverished elder branch of the family; there live Sextus' cousin Lucius Collatinus and his wife, the beautiful and virtuous Lucretia. Now Tarquinius attacks the coastal city of Ardea, and lays siege to it.

Sextus Tarquinius lusts after Lucretia. While Collatinus is in camp at Ardea, Sextus comes to Collatia and is received by his cousin's wife with unsuspecting courtesy. That night, he comes to her bedroom. 'You have a choice, Lucretia,' he says. 'Submit to me now and I will marry you; you will be queen when my father dies. Refuse me, and I will kill you, kill a slave, and say I found you in bed with him.' Chaste Lucretia yields. Next day she summons her menfolk, tells them what has happened, and stabs herself through the heart.

Colour plate 4

Dumb Lucius is present. (Why? Well, it turns out that he is Lucretia's uncle.) While her father and husband are helpless with grief, Lucius Iunius Brutus draws the knife out of Lucretia's breast and swears vengeance on Tarquinius and all his kin. The Romans rise against the tyrant and gain their liberty.

Colour plate 9

What the Romans do with their liberty is elect consuls, Lucius Iunius Brutus and Lucius Tarquinius Collatinus. That, no doubt, is what the whole elaborate story of the Tarquin dynasty was created to achieve—a constitutionally necessary colleague for Brutus, equally symbolic of the Liberation, as Lucretia's husband, and yet easily dispensable, so as not to dilute the hero's glory.

The Athenian paradigm (pp. 72–3 above) provided a way of getting rid of Collatinus. Just as in the free state of Athens the archon Hipparchos of Kollutos was banished because he was related to the tyrant, so in the first year of the Roman Republic the consul Tarquinius of Collatia went into voluntary exile because he was related to the tyrant. Blameless though he was, he bore the name of Tarquin, and that was too much for the Romans.

Meanwhile, the defence of the infant Republic rests with Brutus. Tarquinius' agents plot a counter-coup; Brutus' sons are involved in the conspiracy. Brutus has them arrested, flogged and executed, grimly watching the whole process as his duty demands. And that is why there was no one to bear the Liberator's name in subsequent generations, till Scaeva and Bubulcus were consuls nearly two centuries later.

Figures 57, 58

Tarquinius' next attempt is an alliance with Veii and a full-scale war on Rome. As the two armies meet, anger and hatred bring Brutus and the king's son Arruns Tarquinius in sight of each other. Galloping headlong, each kills his enemy and is killed by him. After Brutus' death, the married women of Rome mourn a whole year for the avenger of their honour.

Ideally, what should have happened was the killing of Tarquinius himself, and of his son Sextus, the rapist. But no: the great dynastic myth was denied its proper culmination by the inconvenience of real events; Tarquinius lived to fight again (pp. 65–6 above).

One consul exiled, the other dead: the story still left room for families other than the plebeian Iunii to place an ancestor as consul in Year One of the Republic. The Horatii had a strong contender in Marcus Horatius, the stern

Figure 57. Jacques-Louis David, study for a projected painting (never realised) of the execution of the sons of Brutus: 1787.

Colour plate 9

old man who dedicated the temple of Jupiter Optimus Maximus (p. 58 above); the Lucretii, family of the story's tragic heroine, put forward her father, Spurius Lucretius. But the Horatii and Lucretii were yesterday's men—patrician families whose tradition of power did not survive the reform of 367 BC. The patrician Valerii on the other hand, powerful throughout the Republic and beyond, were able eventually to install Publius Valerius, 'the People's friend', as a hero of the Liberation rivalling Brutus himself.

Valerius figured also in the story of Year Two, when Lars Porsena came to Rome (p. 54 above). As with Brennus and the Gauls, the fourth-century myth-makers chose not to recall that Porsena took the city. In this story the Etruscan warlord is a chivalrous king, in alliance with Tarquinius (the exile's third attempt to regain his power), but only until he recognises the superior virtues of the free Romans; then he abandons Tarquin and takes his army elsewhere.

What made him change his mind were two heroes and a heroine—as a late historian puts it, 'those three prodigies and marvels of the Roman name, Horatius, Mucius and Cloelia, who if they were not in the annals of history would today seem legendary'. The first exploit was the old Horatian story of Cocles at the bridge (pp. 58–9 above), now retold with Porsena's army as the Etruscan host

Figure 58. (a) Detail of fig. 57. (b) Bronze portrait bust of a Roman, c.300 BC. Capitoline Museums, Rome: Palazzo dei conservatori, Sala dei trionfi. Given to the Museum by Cardinal Pio da Carpi in 1564, and traditionally (but with no good reason) identified as Lucius Brutus. Jacques-Louis David studied in Rome from 1775 to 1780.

Lucrece

Now mote I seyn the exilynge of kynges
Of Rome, for here horrible doinges,
And of the laste king Tarquinius,
As seyth Ovyde and Titus Lyvius.
But for that cause telle I nat this storye,
But for to preyse and drawe to memorye
The verray wif, the verray trewe Lucresse,
That, for hyre wifhod and hire stedefastnesse,
Nat only that these payens hire comende,
But he that cleped is in our legende
The grete Austyn, hath gret compassioun
Of this Lucresse, that starf at Rome toun.

Chaucer, The Legende of Good Women 1680–91

'Ovyde and Titus Lyvius' were also the main source for Shakespeare's *Lucrece*, and for a long sequence of plays and operas on the subject from the sixteenth century to the twentieth. But Chaucer cites 'grete Austyn' too—St Augustine, who questioned Lucretia's choice of suicide, and even wondered whether, 'although the young man attacked her violently, she was so enticed by her own desire that she consented to the act', and punished herself for it.

Benjamin Britten's 'chamber opera' *The Rape of Lucretia* (1946) is loosely based on *Le viol de Lucrèce* by André Obey (1931: translated by Thornton Wilder as *Lucrece*, 1933). That was already a long way from Livy and Ovid, and Ronald Duncan's libretto strays even further from the Roman story. His Iunius (i.e. Brutus) is a power-hungry cynic:

'Women are chaste when they are not tempted.
Lucretia's beautiful but she's not chaste.
Women are all whores by nature.'

And his Lucretia seems to agree, as she sends for Collatinus the morning after:

'Give him this orchid.
Tell him I have found
Its purity
Apt; and that its petals contain
Women's pleasure and women's pain,
And all of Lucretia's shame.
Give him this orchid
And tell him that a Roman harlot sent it.'

Augustine would have been gratified to see the twentieth century's preoccupation with female sexuality undermining, just as his Christian argument had done, the Roman story of a noble suicide.

What happened to Sextus?

According to Livy, when the Tarquins were expelled Sextus the rapist went back to his own kingdom at Gabii, where he was killed in revenge for his bloodthirsty and avaricious rule. Given Dante's admiration for Livy ('Livio che non erra'), that must be the reason for Sextus' immersion with other violent rulers in the river of boiling blood in the seventh circle of Hell:

> La divina giustizia di qua punge
> quell' Attila che fu flagello in terra,
> e Pirro e Sesto. . .

Modern Dante scholarship is surely wrong to see this as a reference to the 'pirate' Sextus Pompeius, son of Pompey the Great.

Dionysios, on the other hand, has Sextus accompany his father in all the Tarquins' efforts to regain power, culminating in the great battle of Lake Regillus, where he commands the left wing. When he sees all is lost, he rushes on the Roman lines 'like a wild beast' and kills as many as he can before being surrounded finally and overwhelmed. So defiant a death didn't seem right to Macaulay, who made Sextus turn and run, with a very different simile:

> And in the back false Sextus
>   Felt the good Roman steel,
> And wriggling in the dust he died
>   Like a worm beneath the wheel.

But Macaulay's Sextus had had his morale undermined from the start, in a wonderful scene unknown to any ancient source [Figure 59]:

> Their leader was false Sextus,
>   Who wrought the deed of shame:
> With restless pace and haggard face
>   To his last field he came.
> Men said he saw strange visions
>   Which none beside might see,
> And that strange sounds were in his ears
>   Which none might hear but he.
> A woman tall and stately,
>   But pale as are the dead,
> Oft through the watches of the night
>   Sat spinning by his bed.
> And as she plied the distaff,
>   In a sweet voice and low,
> She sang of great old houses
>   And fights fought long ago.
> So spun she, and so sang she,
>   Until the east was grey,
> Then pointed to her bleeding breast,
>   And shrieked, and fled away.

Figure 59. Illustration of Sextus' dream from 'The Battle of the Lake Regillus', in Macaulay's *Lays of Ancient Rome*.

foiled by the hero's stubborn resistance.

Then follows Cloelia, one of a group of girls sent across the Tiber to Porsena's camp as hostages. She gets free, finds a horse and fords the river back to Rome. In another version, she leads a mass break-out, and they all swim across. Honourable Valerius sends them back; magnanimous Porsena frees them, with an admiring gift for courageous Cloelia. And that was why a bronze statue of a girl on horseback stood opposite the temple of Jupiter Stator on the Sacred Way.

Colour plate 10

The third exemplary exploit is that of a young patrician who makes his way into Porsena's camp in the guise of a deserter. He reaches the king's tribunal, sees a man richly dressed surrounded by soldiers, draws a hidden dagger and kills him. But it was Porsena's chamberlain, paying the troops. Captured and brought before the king, who is at a sacrifice, he boldly pretends that he is only one of three hundred young Romans who are sworn to kill him. Porsena is shaken, and would have him tortured to reveal more; but he thrusts his right hand into the flames on the altar to show how little the threat of pain can move him.

Like Horatius Cocles and Cloelia, the steadfast young man was cast as a patrician. What his name was in the original story we don't know; by the time our sources were writing he had been claimed by the plebeian Mucii, who used the surname Scaevola, 'left-handed'. That was a century or so after Iunius Scaeva and his cousin had claimed Brutus. The similarity of the names Scaeva and Scaevola may be an accident; more important is the myth-making context, as the new plebeian 'aristocracy' wove itself into the fabric of Rome's heroic past.

The equality of plebeians and patricians was a political fact, and myths had to reflect political facts, not just for the foundation of the Republic but in the origins of the city itself. Hence the new story of the twins.

6.4 THE FOUNDATION LEGEND

Aeneas had two daughters, one who came with him from Troy to Latium, and another born to him by a Latin princess. After Aeneas' death, they served as Vestal Virgins under King Amulius of Alba Longa. One night the younger, Ilia, had a strange and disturbing dream. She was taken by a man of supernatural beauty along a river bank shaded with willows. Afterwards, alone and frightened, lost in an unfamiliar place, she tried in vain to find her sister. Then she saw her father, who spoke to her like an oracle:

Ennius Annales
44–45 Sk

> 'Sorrows, my daughter, you must first endure;
> Then from the river fortune will return.'

He disappeared, and all her pleading could not bring him back. She cried aloud, and woke in tears.

Colour plate 11

The god was Mars. He left her pregnant with twins, and thus doomed to execution as an errant Vestal. At Amulius' order, after the birth Ilia was

The Ravishing of Rhea Silvia

Rubens' painting of Mars and the Vestal in the Liechtenstein collection (Colour plate 11) has, as Elizabeth McGrath points out, 'a distinctly Ovidian flavour'. Ovid opens book 3 of the *Fasti* with a request to Mars to lay down his shield and spear, and take off his helmet; the *putto* on the left is just completing that stage in the proceedings. 'Be like Pallas,' urges Ovid; and there on the right is Pallas—i.e. the Palladion in Vesta's temple—with her shield ostentatiously held aside. 'You'll find something to do without your weapons; after all, you were unarmed when the Roman priestess caught you.' Ovid's phraseology suggests the initiative came from her ('so you could give this city mighty seed'), and Rubens' scene is compatible with that: as Professor McGrath puts it, 'Rhea's apprehension seems to be modified at least by a hint of desire'.

Ovid then retells Ennius' story of the Vestal's impregnation as she lay asleep on the river bank. That's not what Rubens shows, but he does allude to Ovid's version of the Vestal's dream.

> 'Lo! as I made the sacred fire my care,
> Methought my fillet dropped from off my hair;
> Soon was it burnt by the devouring flame,
> And, strange! two palm-trees from its ashes came . . .'

(She has conceived the twins—and the palm is of course the symbol of victory.) By setting his scene at the altar of Vesta, Rubens can emphasise the sacred fire; and he also shows the Vestal's woollen fillet slipping off her hair.

With the little phrase *aperto pectore* mischievous Ovid has Silvia bare her breasts before falling asleep, a honey-trap for any passing god. What happens next is an Ovidian *tour de force*, as Mars sees her, desires her, and possesses her, all in one line of verse: 'Mars uidet hanc, uisamque cupit, potiturque cupita.' And that, surely, is what Rubens expresses in his image of the impetuous god.

All three of Ovid's verbs are represented, from seeing (*uidere*), as the two principal characters look into each other's eyes, to possessing (*potiri*), as Mars lays his hand on the Vestal's arm. The middle term is desiring (*cupire*), and there in the centre is Cupido himself, identified by his quiver of arrows, helpfully pulling off the god's cloak and the Vestal's mantle. If Cupid, as Professor McGrath drily observes, 'has to work more seriously (and quickly) than is usual in Rubensian love scenes', that's because he's working for Ovid too.

drowned; but her father's prophecy was true, for she became the wife of the river-god Anio. The twin babies were set adrift on the swollen Tiber, in a basket which was washed ashore at the fig-tree by the Lupercal grotto. There they were suckled by a she-wolf—just like the twin Lares (pp. 79–80 above), whose myth they have borrowed—and rescued and brought up by the swineherd Faustulus and his wife Acca Larentia.

Figure 21
Figure 60

Figure 60. Reverse of *denarius* struck by Sextus Pompeius(?), 137 BC: the she-wolf suckling the twins by the Ficus Ruminalis, with Faustulus looking on. Legends: FOSTLVUS (i.e. Faustulus), SEX. PO (half worn away on the right).

So ran the first version of the story, as expounded by Ennius' epic poem in the early second century BC. But already by then historians were telling the story too, and historians preferred to avoid miraculous events. It wasn't difficult to rationalise the she-wolf story, since *lupa* in Latin also meant 'whore', and there was the tomb of Acca Larentia (p. 30 above), in the Velabrum market-place just next to the Lupercal. In sober history, therefore, she must have been the twins' wet-nurse and foster-mother.

The historians also knew that the founders couldn't be Aeneas' grandsons. Eratosthenes of Kyrene had dated the fall of Troy, and Timaios of Tauromenium had dated the foundation of Rome, and the two dates were 371 years apart. How do you fill a gap of fourteen generations?

According to the historians, Aeneas' son Ascanius founded Alba Longa, and after him his descendants ruled it in turn: Silvius, Aeneas, Latinus, Alba, Epitus, Capys, Calpetus, Tiberius, Agrippa, Aremulus, Aventinus, Proca. (Some of the names differ slightly according to different authorities.) Proca had two sons, Numitor and Amulius, of whom Numitor, the elder, was cheated out of the succession by his brother. Amulius also had Numitor's son killed, and made Numitor's daughter Silvia, or Rhea Silvia, a Vestal Virgin in order to prevent the birth of a male heir. In this revised version it was she who bore the twins to Mars, and when they grew up they killed Amulius and restored their grandfather to the throne of Alba.

The twins were Remus and Romulus (to put the names in the proper order), the latter probably the name of the slave girl's wonder-child in the old story (pp. 46–7 above). Romulus meant 'forceful', from the city's name of *rhome*, strength; Remus meant 'cautious', from *remorari*, to hold back. Together, they represented not only the sharing of power in the double magistracy of the consulship, but also the complementary patrician and plebeian virtues to which Rome owed her spectacular success.

In the original version of the story, they founded the city together. That fact is clear even from our literary sources of centuries later. The statue group at the Lupercal was the precinct of a shrine to the founder-heroes, where hymns were sung to both the twins together. However, the story was adjusted at a very early stage in its evolution, perhaps as a result of the desperate crisis that ended with the battle of Sentinum in 295 BC.

The twins grew up in Faustulus' hut, and by the time they were eighteen they were the joint-leaders of the herdsmen's community. They resolved to found a city, which they would rule together; but where would it be, and would it be called *Roma* or *Remora*? They left the decision to the gods, whose will was divined by augury. Before dawn, the twins each took up a separate observation post and watched for the birds. Remus, our earliest source seems to say, vowed himself as a sacrifice (*se deuouet*), perhaps as a bargain with the gods in return for their favour. What happened was that Remus received the earlier sign and Romulus the greater—twelve birds in the well-omened quarter of the sky. Forceful Romulus claimed victory; cautious Remus yielded.

Romulus' confidence and speed of action were essential to the story, as recognised by Remus in a remarkable prophecy. 'In this city,' he said, 'many things rashly hoped for and taken for granted will turn out very successfully.' Bold self-confidence or even rashness was what had won Rome her supremacy in Italy, and no arm more embodied that Romulean characteristic than the newly instituted fast light cavalry, the *celeres*. Though a fourth-century innovation, these dashing young hussars claimed to have been founded by Romulus, who appointed their first commander and named him Celer, 'Fast'.

In historical time, the cavalrymen were particularly associated with Quintus Fabius Maximus, patrician joint-commander at the battle of Sentinum. Fabius had made his reputation thirty years before, in 325 BC, when as Master of Horse he had seized the opportunity to rout a Samnite army with a headlong cavalry charge, even though under orders from the commander-in-chief not to attack. From then on his career was one successful campaign after another. In 295 BC, as often in his later years, Fabius shared command with the plebeian Publius Decius Mus; they worked together as if they had one heart and one mind.

What happened to Remus in the story is what happened to Decius in the battle: he acted out of character, and had to die for the common good.

Romulus marked the line for the walls of his city by ploughing a furrow and lifting the ploughshare where the gates would be. In historical time, that was the ritual procedure used by the Romans for their colonial foundations; it was necessary to establish the sacred inviolability of the walls. To enter a Roman city or military camp over the walls instead of by the gate was sacrilege as well as treason. Romulus' men were digging the ditch (or building the wall, in another version), with Celer in charge of the work. Remus let his disappointment get the better of his caution, and jumped over the sacred defences. True to his duty (and his name), Celer killed him with a single blow of his spade. On this one occasion Remus had acted too fast for his own good.

So too Publius Decius at Sentinum was too quick to lead his cavalry against the Gauls. That sort of charge was what had made Fabius' reputation in 325 BC, but Decius couldn't pull it off. Surprised by a counter-attack, he could only regain the initiative by the desperate expedient of a formal self-sacrifice, vowing both himself and the enemy to the powers of the underworld, and then advancing deliberately to be killed. The battle was won, Rome was saved, and the following year the new temple of Victoria was dedicated on the Palatine.

Now that the site of the temple has been excavated, we know that below the altar in front of it was a grave sealed by a single slab of Monteverde tufa. It is possible (no one can be sure) that the human sacrifice demanded by the prophets in 296 BC was buried here. For Rome to survive, the gods required a death. The college of augurs understood that, and so did the consul in his desperate battle. The myth must reflect it too; the death of Remus was necessary, a foundation sacrifice for Rome's protective walls.

So the twin founders became one founder. And that was not the last twist in the story. For this was a time of rapid change and dangerous tensions, when those who hated and feared the Romans had every motive for adding their own negative spin. The Vestal Virgin bears the twins to a secret lover; they are suckled not by a she-wolf but by a prostitute; the birds they watch for at the augury contest are carrion-eating vultures; the death of Remus is simply murder—and worse than murder, fratricide. It is an index both of the unpredictable evolution of myth and of the tragic outcome of the Roman Republic that when Titus Livius began his great history of Rome, after more than fifteen years of constant civil war, the story most Romans accepted was that Romulus killed his twin brother with his own hand.

Figure 61

Now, having built his walls, Romulus needed men to defend them. In the historical time of the fourth century BC, it was a generation or so after the Romans had built their great new walls that the city started to attract large numbers of hopeful immigrants. In the myth it was more immediate: Romulus established a sacred refuge on the Capitol, the *asylum* 'between the two groves',

Figure 61. The most extensive surviving remains of the city wall of Rome of the fourth century BC (pp. 88–9 above), on the high ground to the north-east of the city, beyond the Viminal hill; in modern Rome, it is in Piazza dei Cinquecento, in front of the Termini railway station.

and anyone who came there was accepted as a citizen with no questions asked. The story implies a confidently egalitarian society, easily reinterpreted by ill-wishers as a den of outlaws, criminals and runaway slaves.

Having got his men, Romulus needed women. But when he applied to the neighbouring communities for *conubium* (lawful marriage), he was rejected with contempt. Mars told his son to use force instead: warfare was what would make Rome great. Consus, the god of counsel, suggested a way. Romulus invited the neighbours to a show, and when they came with their families from the Latin towns of Caenina, Antemnae, Crustumerium and Fidenae, the Romans at a given signal seized the young women and chased the unarmed menfolk back home.

In Roman terms, it was a traditional marriage by capture, at the traditional site. For Consus was also Neptunus Equester, lord of the chariot-races and of the 'sea-shore' (pp. 38–40 above) where the ritual bathing of the women of Rome provided an annual opportunity for taking a wife. That was why Romulus held his games on the day of the *Consualia* (21 August), in the valley of the wild things between Palatine and Aventine, where in historical time the chariots raced in the Circus Maximus.

Of course the Latins made war to get their daughters back, but they were defeated and incorporated into the community of Roman citizens. In historical time, that was what happened in 338 BC. In 290 BC, the lowland Sabines of Cures, 30 miles up the Tiber valley, were also incorporated into the Roman citizenship, and the myth was duly extended to include them. The whole purpose of the story was to read back into the origins of Rome the new common status of Romans, Latins and Sabines.

That 'blending of peoples' was of course Romulus' sole motive from the start, and the behaviour of his men towards the captured girls was entirely proper. Or so we are told, by authors who sound just a little defensive. For of course the pejorative interpretation was all too easy—the Roman outlaws got their women by rape—and here too it came to influence the Romans' own perception. Both Cicero and Virgil thought Romulus' action a little uncivilised, and ever afterwards this most famous of Roman myths was known as 'the Rape of the Sabine Women'.

Colour plate 12
Figure 62 (b)

The Sabine version of the story had a sequel. They too made war on Rome to get their daughters back, under the command of Titus Tatius the king of Cures. His campaign got off to a good start when Romulus' citadel on the Capitol fell into his hands without a blow being struck. That set up a symmetrical scenario: Sabines on the Capitol, Romans on the Palatine, and a battleground valley between them which would one day be the Roman Forum. The battle that duly took place there is narrated by the historians with constant reference to the topographical features of the Forum, in just the same way that Kleidemos, the pioneering myth-historian of Athens, pointed out the exact sites in his city where the Amazons fought and fell.

This way and that the battle raged, with no result. They would have resumed next day, but for an unexpected intervention. The Sabine women

Colour plate 13

143

Figure 62. *Denarii* of Lucius Titurius Sabinus, 89 BC. Obverse of both (*a*): head of Titus Tatius, inscribed SABIN[VS] and TA[TIVS], the latter in monogram. Reverses: (*b*) two Romans, each carrying off a girl, (*c*) Tarpeia between two warriors with shields, both with the legend L. TITVRI.

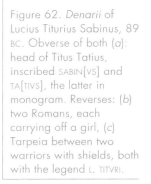

loosed their flowing hair,
And mournful all in funeral robes appear,
And just before the battle was begun
Between their angry sires and husbands run.
Bathed all in tears, and with dishevelled hair,
Each at her breast a tender infant bare.
There they in sad and suppliant posture stood,
To stop the effusion of much kindred blood.
The infants seemed as if they grieved, implored
They might not suffer by the cruel sword;
Their cries instead of words prevailing spoke,
And warded off the dire impending stroke.
The men on either side their arms let fall,
And did each other sons and fathers call;
Their wives and daughters they with joy embrace,
And on their shields bear home their infant race.

Ovid Fasti
3.219–228

So the two sides were reconciled, and made a treaty which merged their two peoples into one. The Sabines would move to Rome, the combined citizen body would be called *Quirites*, as if from Cures, and Tatius and Romulus would be joint kings.

That expressed the historical reality of 290 BC, when the Sabines of Cures were enfranchised. Tatius' Sabines occupied the hill that was now called Quirinal; so too, in historical time, did Rome's new citizens, filling up the once exposed high ground that was now safe behind the walls. The actual derivation of 'Quirinal' was from the great new temple of Quirinus that had been dedicated there in 293 BC.

As with Remus and the twin founders (pp. 140–1 above), so too in the case of Titus Tatius and Romulus there are clear traces of a 'first state' of the myth which emphasised power-sharing. There were old statues of Tatius and

Tarpeia

The Tarpeian Rock, from which criminals and traitors were hurled to their death, was a vertical cliff on the side of the Capitol facing the Forum. Some said it was named after its first victim—either Lucius Tarpeius, who opposed Romulus over the rape of the Sabine women, or Spurius Tarpeius, who was in command of the Capitol when Titus Tatius captured it. But the usual derivation was from Tarpeia, a Vestal Virgin whose tomb stood on the hill not far from the cliff-top. She was probably a real person (her family is known to have existed in the early Republic), though why public offerings were made every year at her tomb is not recorded.

The Greek historian Antigonos in the third century BC said she was Titus Tatius' daughter, forcibly 'married' to Romulus after the rape. That was why she opened the Capitol gate to her father's men—and no doubt she had a leading role in the ensuing battle, when the Sabine women ran out to separate their fathers and husbands. We know there was a famous statue of Tarpeia, and to judge by Titurius Sabinus' coin-type [fig. 62(c)] it showed her with arms outstretched between two warriors with shields.

But statues can be interpreted in more than one way. The earliest Roman historians made her a traitor—the commander of the Capitol, or more plausibly the commanding officer's daughter, who was bribed by Tatius to let the Sabines in. A more romantic version made her a Vestal who fell in love with the Sabine king and opened the gate to him for that reason. Either way, she died at Tatius' order, crushed by the shields the Sabines hurled on her. *That* was what the iconography meant, and her tomb near the place where traitors were executed. But in that case why the public honours? The historian Piso in the late second century BC made a heroic attempt to keep the story but save Tarpeia's reputation. He claimed her 'betrayal' was a trick to get the Sabines to give her their shields; they did, but not in the way she intended.

'The punishment of Tarpeia' featured on the great historical frieze in the Basilica of Paullus next to the Roman Forum [fig. 63]. (It is one of the very few recognisable scenes that can be reconstructed from the debris of that important monument.) The symmetrical iconography is preserved, but beyond the two men piling the shields are two cloaked and bearded warriors observing the scene. The one on the left wears boots; the one on the right, at a slight distance, is barefoot, and his helmet

Figure 63. Frieze from the Basilica Paulli (panel 3.177, Tarpeia); late first century BC. The frieze is 0.72 m high, and was originally about 184 m long, running round the central nave of the Basilica above the columns. It was made of thin slabs of Pentelic marble let into the Italian marble of the architecture; they shattered into small pieces when the building was destroyed about AD 400, and most of them went into lime kilns. The surviving fragments, about 9% of the original extent, were excavated between 1898 and 1940.

has a flowing crest. One of them must be Titus Tatius, but who is the other? And why does the episode immediately following this one feature five women in what looks like a bridal scene?

The Basilica was the family monument of the patrician Aemilii, who claimed an Aemilia as the mother of Romulus, so there may have been some particular variants in their version of early Roman history. But variants were normal. It so happens that we have plentiful evidence for the Tarpeia story, and the fertile variety of myth-creation that it attests is probably typical of how the Roman story-world developed.

Romulus on the Capitol; alleged 'laws of Romulus and Tatius' were cited in legal handbooks; one of the three constituent regiments of the new Roman cavalry was called 'Titus' men'; and the annals of the new pontifical college listed the cults which King Tatius founded in Rome.

But soon Tatius was mythically superfluous. The new citizens became integrated (partly no doubt under the pressure of the common struggle against Pyrrhos), and the inhabitants of the Quirinal evidently preferred to define themselves by topography rather than ethnic origin. So Tatius was removed; it was said that some of his friends and relatives had been involved in the murder of ambassadors from Lavinium, and when he went to Lavinium he was killed in revenge. He was buried in a laurel grove, where annual offerings were made at his tomb. But it was on the Aventine, not the Quirinal; Romulus himself was about to take over the Quirinal, in a most spectacular way.

Now once more sole ruler, Romulus reigned gloriously until it pleased the gods to claim him back. It was a summer morning. Romulus was addressing an assembly of the citizens at Goat's Marsh, in the meadows that would one day be the Campus Martius. Suddenly there was total darkness, thunder, a tempestuous wind. The people fled in terror, and when the light returned and they reassembled, Romulus was gone.

His father Mars had come down from heaven in a four-horse chariot and carried him away. But the people didn't know that; they thought he had been murdered, by the senators or by the new citizens. (In historical time, internal strife in Rome culminated in a secession of the *plebs* in 287 BC.) Their suspicions were only put to rest when they heard what happened to Iulius Proculus. (In historical time, the Iulii were an old patrician family; one of them was consul in 267 BC.) Proculus was on the Quirinal at dawn when Romulus himself appeared before him, taller and more splendid than in life. 'Go,' said the vision, 'and bid the Romans cease from strife and cultivate the arts of war. It is the gods' will that Rome should conquer. As for me, I am now Quirinus. Let them build a temple at this spot and worship me.' Proculus reported what he had seen and heard, and the Roman People did as their founder told them.

A dynamic myth for a dynamic people, the Romulus story reflects fast-changing perceptions and priorities in a dangerous time. Nobody now knows how it was created and developed, but I think the best guess is that it was done by drama. The visual evidence we looked at in the last chapter presupposes a lively culture of mythological performance in Rome and Latium in the late fourth century BC, and that culture could be guided, for the Roman People's entertainment and education, by the People's own elected representatives. For every year the aediles organised the public games—the *ludi Romani* in September, the *ludi plebeii* in November, the *ludi* of Liber and Ceres in March and April—and what they commissioned was what filled the minds and memories of the citizen body.

Camillus defying the Gallic chieftain, Lucretia drawing her hidden dagger,

Romulus giving the signal to seize the women—most of the dramatic stories in this chapter were probably dramatic in the literal sense, created for public performance. No doubt plebeian and patrician aediles had their respective angles on the presentation of the past, and the two great autumn celebrations of parallel 'Roman' and 'plebeian' games for Jupiter must have offered a constant opportunity for contested versions of the national myth. For a while, the plebeians needed Remus, the new citizens needed Titus Tatius. But what is most striking is the way internal rivalries were subordinated in the end to the good of the community as a whole.

That final scene in the Romulus story sums it up. The factious Romans accepted Iulius Proculus' report 'as if they were inspired by the gods'. In historical time, by a brilliant exercise of lateral thinking, the new temple of the citizen-god Quirinus, dedicated in 293 BC on the newly built-up hill called 'Quirinal', was now the shrine of Rome's deified founder-hero. Concord had been achieved. The next time the Romulus myth had to be revisited, the Republic would be in deep trouble.

7

FACING BOTH WAYS

WHAT THE GODS DEMAND

One year (Livy says it was 362 BC), a huge chasm opened in the Roman Forum. Ever wider it yawned, threatening to engulf the city. The *haruspices* were consulted. They said the gods of the underworld were claiming an unpaid vow: the Romans must cast into the chasm their most valuable possession, the thing that made them strong. What could that be? The citizens were at a loss.

Then young Marcus Curtius spoke up. What made the Romans strong was valour in arms; what could be more precious than that? He fetched his horse and mounted, fully armed and wearing the decorations he had won in battle. Facing the Capitol, he prayed to the gods above and the gods below. Then he dug in his spurs and rode headlong over the edge and into the abyss. The citizens threw in their own offerings—jewellery, first-fruits of the harvest, whatever was precious to them—and the chasm closed. The *lacus Curtius* marked the spot— an unpaved area in the Roman Forum, with a pool, an altar and a shady olive-tree.

Colour plate 14

Another year (no date given this time), a Roman commander called Genucius Cipus brought his victorious army back to the city gate, and discovered that horns had grown on his forehead. The *haruspex* told him that if he entered the city he would become king. Cipus called a citizen assembly outside the gate. Covering his brow with a laurel wreath, he told the Romans they were in danger of losing their liberty: they must kill the man with horns if he passed through the gate. 'Where is he?', they cried. Cipus took off his laurel wreath. 'Here he is', he said, and turned away to his lifelong exile. In memory of his sacrifice, they decorated the gate with a bronze head of a horned man.

Yet another year (the date was disputed), a praetor called Aelius Paetus was dispensing justice from his curule chair in the Forum when a woodpecker perched on his head, and wouldn't move. The *haruspices* announced an ambiguous omen. If Aelius killed the bird it would be beneficial for the Republic but disastrous for himself and his family; and *vice versa* if he did not. Aelius took the bird and wrung its neck. Soon afterwards, he and more than a dozen of his kinsmen were killed in battle.

During the war that gave Rome final dominance in Latium, the consuls of 340 BC were encamped facing the Latins at Capua. To each of them the same vision came in the night. An august figure of greater than human form announced that the commander of one side, and the army of the other, were owed to Mother Earth and the spirits of the dead. Whichever commander would vow to those deities both himself and the forces of the enemy, his side would have the victory. The *haruspices* confirmed that that was the gods' will.

Which of the consuls would have that dreadful duty? Again the *haruspices* gave the answer. The entrails of Publius Decius' sacrificial beast signified good fortune, but death to himself. When battle was joined, and the Romans were forced to give ground, Decius ordered the *pontifex maximus* to dictate to him the formulaic prayer, donned his sacrificial robe over his armour and spurred his horse into the enemy ranks. He was killed, but the Latins were overcome by an uncanny terror. The Romans regained the initiative, and Decius' colleague led them to victory.

It was Decius' son, forty-five years later at the battle of Sentinum (p. 123 above) who repeated his father's self-sacrifice and saved Rome from defeat by an even more formidable enemy.

Figure 64

Notice how prominent in these stories the *haruspices* are as interpreters of the gods' will. That form of divination was an Etruscan speciality; by the third century BC the Etruscans were under Roman control and their skills available for the benefit of Rome. Two datable stories show how influential they had become.

Before the battle of Sentinum in 295 BC, the Roman augurs had been faced with an eerie portent, first blood, then milk and honey, appearing on the altar of Jupiter. Their interpretation was to require a human sacrifice, after which prosperity would come. It seems that the dreadful deed was carried out (p. 142 above), and the crucial battle was indeed a Roman victory. But then came three years of plague and famine, which ended only when the cult of Aesculapius was brought from Epidauros and established on the Tiber island (the god's own sacred snake chose the spot). An Etruscan diviner—he must have been a *haruspex*—gave the answer. Blood on the altar was the victory itself, celebrated with the proper thanksgiving sacrifices; honey was the plague, for that's what sick people eat; and milk was the famine, for that's all there is when the crops fail.

The second story dates from a similar context in 276 BC. Rome was suffering

Figure 64. Etruscan mirror from Vulci, late fourth century BC. Kalchas, the prophet of the Achaeans in the *Iliad*, is portrayed as an Etruscan *haruspex*, inspecting the liver of a sacrificial beast. He is winged, like Mopsos on Novius Plautius' masterpiece (fig. 25 above).

an epidemic of miscarriages and still-births. The ritual solution was to introduce a new element into the *Lupercalia* on 15 February: from now on the young women of Rome were to offer themselves for flagellation by the naked Luperci with their goatskin lashes (p. 79 above). The innovation was explained by a creative elaboration of the foundation story.

Here is Ovid, in Massey's eighteenth-century version:

> New-married wife, would'st thou a mother be,
> When charms and drugs are of no force to thee?
> The lashes of prolific hands receive,
> Which the Luperci in their ramblings give;
> Before the sun shall run his annual round
> A happy sire thy husband shall be found.

Ovid *Fasti* 2.425–428

After the rape of the Sabine women, Romulus and the Romans waited in vain for the birth of children. In despair they went to the grove of Juno Lucina, goddess of childbirth:

> By the Esquilian hill, there long had stood
> A thick, uncut, and venerable wood;
> Great Juno claimed the honours of the place,
> Famed for devotion in those early days.
> Thither the husbands with their wives repair
> And on their knees put up a fervent prayer.
> With sudden noise the grove all trembling shook,
> And thus in phrase obscure the goddess spoke:
> *Let a shagged goat ascend the Italian dames,*
> *And wantonly augment their amorous flames.*
> At this they all were struck with wild amaze,
> A strange command, in such a dubious phrase.
> An augur's called (by time his name is lost),
> A stranger banished from the Tuscan coast;
> He kills a goat, and of his shaggy hide
> Long thongs he cuts, and lashes every bride.

Ovid Fasti
2.435–446

The last phrase is a mistranslation. What Ovid says is that at his instruction the young women offered their backs to be *cut* by the thongs. That was essential for the goddess's command to be fulfilled, for what she had ordered, obscured in Massey's italicised couplet, was that 'the sacred goat must *enter* the women'. That is, the powers of fertility—Pan, Faunus, or their human counterparts, the Luperci themselves—must literally penetrate them. What the Etruscan expert devises technically fulfils her demand, but only if the goatskin cuts the flesh. An orgiastic solution is replaced by a painfully metaphorical one.

In Romulus' time, an Etruscan 'augur' must be an exile; in the historical time of 276 BC he was no doubt one of the newly engaged *haruspices*, bringing his expertise to bear on a Roman crisis, just as his colleagues were imagined as doing in the stories of Marcus Curtius, Genucius Cipus, Aelius Paetus and Publius Decius. Whatever the dramatic date of the alleged events, from the rape of the Sabines to the Latin war, the creation of these stories belongs in a third-century context.

It was a world where the rivalry of patrician and plebeian, so conspicuous in the previous chapter, was no longer an issue. All four heroes of the stories of self-sacrifice happen to belong to plebeian families, but that's not what was important about them. Three of them were magistrates in office, and the fourth (Marcus Curtius) a young cavalryman. For a while at least, the old tensions seem to have become obsolete; these are stories about what it is to be a *Roman*.

What we may now call the Roman virtues were well displayed in the lives of two of the leading statesmen and commanders of the 280s and 270s BC, Gaius Fabricius and Manius Curius. Even after five consulships and five triumphs between them, each lived modestly on his small farm; they symbolised what later Romans honoured as the true ethic of the Republic, duty to the community for no personal gain.

When Fabricius was consul during the war against Pyrrhos (p. 123 above), he was approached in secret by the king's physician, with an offer to poison Pyrrhos. He and his colleague wrote to the king:

> Your friend Nicias came to us asking for a reward if he should kill you secretly. We told him we had no such wish, and he could expect no advantage from such an action. At the same time it seemed right to inform you, lest other states should think it was done by our will, if any such thing should happen, and because we do not care to fight with bribes or rewards or treachery.

Aulus Gellius
3.8.8

It was important what other states thought. The Greek city of Lokroi in the toe of Italy struck coins at this time honouring 'Roman Honesty', and a contemporary Greek historian derived the name of Rome from that of a granddaughter of Aeneas who founded a temple to Honesty on the Palatine. The Greek word was *pistis*, translating the Latin *fides*; and there was indeed a temple of Fides Publica, founded (on the Capitol, not the Palatine) in the year 257 BC. Public Honesty was worshipped as a goddess in third-century Rome.

In his first consulship (282 BC), Fabricius had been trying to help Thurii, another south-Italian Greek city in alliance with Rome, which was being fiercely besieged by the Lucanians and Bruttians. The Romans were hesitant, until a huge young man urged them to take courage; he picked up a scaling-ladder, ran right through the enemy lines to their camp, and climbed the rampart. In a huge voice he shouted that he had taken a step (*gradus*) to victory; the Romans followed to attack the camp, drawing the enemy off from the siege; in the desperate fight that followed, the huge young man was seen cutting down the enemy troops single-handed. After the victory Fabricius wanted to decorate him for his valour, but he was nowhere to be found. Then the Romans knew who had been fighting for them—Mars himself, *Gradiuus*, as the infantry called him, the god who makes you stand firm or step forward in the battle line.

Now, gods don't appear in person for just anyone. It must have been because Fabricius was the man he was; for the gods love men of virtue.

His friend and fellow-paradigm Manius Curius, 'whom none could overcome by steel nor gold', won the hard-fought final battle of the war against Pyrrhos, after which the king left Italy for good. Manius celebrated his third and last triumph, and the booty paid for a great benefit to the citizens, a new aqueduct to bring in the waters of the Anio to Rome. The victor retired to his little farmhouse in the Sabine country. An embassy from the Samnites came to him there, to pay their repects to the man who had defeated them. They found him roasting turnips for his supper. They had brought him a gift of gold as a mark of honour, but Manius laughed and pointed at his earthenware crockery. 'I don't need gold,' he said; 'but those who possess it obey my orders.'

The turnips turn up again in satirical authors as what Romulus eats in heaven—a nice indication of the way the Romans of more luxurious times had to disguise in irony their shamefaced admiration of the frugal and self-denying heroes who had made their city great.

Another third-century exemplar was Atilius 'Serranus', so called because he was summoned to the consulship while sowing his fields, probably in 245 BC. So powerful was that idea, of the small farmer called to serve his country in high office, that it was read back into the distant history of the Republic. By the time Livy was writing, the classic case was that of Quinctius Cincinnatus in 458 BC:

> Now I would solicit the particular attention of those numerous people who imagine that money is everything in this world, and that rank and ability are inseparable from wealth: let them observe that Cincinnatus, the one man in whom Rome reposed all her hope of survival, was at that moment working a little three-acre farm (now known as the Quinctian meadows) west of the Tiber, just opposite the spot where the shipyards are today. A mission from the city found him at work on his land—digging a ditch, maybe, or ploughing. Greetings were exchanged, and he was asked—with a prayer for the gods' blessing on himself and his country—
>
> *Livy 3.26.7–9*   to put on his toga and hear the Senate's instructions.

Wholly anachronistic for the fifth century BC (when the Senate didn't yet exist), the Cincinnatus story has arrogated to an ancient patrician family the credit that belongs to the honest turnip-eaters of two centuries later.

When the Republic takes a man away from his farm, it has an obligation to look after his family. So it happened that the wife and children of Marcus Atilius Regulus, consul during the first great war against Carthage, were supported at public expense. Farmer Regulus won a naval victory off the south coast of Sicily in 256 BC, then landed his army in the territory of Carthage itself and defeated its defenders on land as well. The Carthaginians asked for terms, but what Regulus demanded was so harsh that they fought on in despair. Against all the odds, and thanks to a brilliant general hired from Sparta, the Carthaginians succeeded in inflicting a catastrophic defeat on the Roman invaders. Regulus was captured, the victim of his own self-confidence. According to Greek historians, his wife and sons reacted by systematically torturing two young Carthaginian prisoners, one of whom died as a result of their pitiless mistreatment before the tribunes of the *plebs* were alerted and put a stop to the abuse.

The Romans themselves had quite a different story, presenting Regulus as

The Cincinnatus of the West

In June 1775, the Congress of the thirteen American colonies that were resisting the taxes and tyranny of the mother country created a 'Continental Army' to achieve their independence, and elected George Washington of Virginia as its commander in chief. It was an army of citizens, unlike the paid professionals it fought, and it would be disbanded when its aim had been achieved. The same applied to its General: Washington made it clear that he would not serve for pay, and that he would resign when independence was won.

There is a story, which may be *ben trovato*, that during the war George III asked Benjamin West (see Colour plate 15) what General Washington would do if he won. 'I think he will return to his farm,' said West. 'If he does that', the King replied, 'he will be the greatest man in the world.' And that was indeed what he did.

Before their disbandment in 1783, the officers of the victorious revolutionary army founded a society to perpetuate the ideals they had fought for. They called it The Society of the Cincinnati, after Livy's idealised portrait of the citizen called from his plough to serve his country and returning to it when the job was done. That same year Sir Joseph Banks, the President of the Royal Society, wrote to his friend Benjamin Franklin:

> General Washington has we are told Cincinnatus like return'd to cultivate his garden now the emancipated States have no farther occasion for his sword.

(The Voltairean phrase was hardly fair, either for Washington or for Cincinnatus: what mattered was to cultivate one's *fields*, and at Mount Vernon Washington took agriculture very seriously.) In 1790 the first Governor of the Northwest Territory named the settlement by the Ohio River 'Cincinnati'— farmers who had been soldiers and were now farmers again.

Houdon's statue of Washington in the State Capitol of Virginia [fig. 65] expresses the ideal with elegant economy. Washington still has his uniform coat on, but he holds a civilian walking stick; his sword is hung on the fasces, symbol of the states in whose defence he used it; and the fasces themselves rest on a ploughshare.

The Parisian sculptor completed that great image in 1788. In the next twenty

years his fellow-countrymen both imitated the American Revolution and betrayed its ideals by creating an emperor. So in 1814 Byron reproached Bonaparte for not resigning the power the people had entrusted to him ('But thou forsooth must be a king. . .'), and found but a single antidote to the resulting disillusion:

> Where may the wearied eye repose
>> When gazing on the Great;
> Where neither guilty glory glows
>> Nor despicable state?
> Yes—one—the first—the last—the best—
> The Cincinnatus of the West,
>> Whom envy dared not hate,
> Bequeath'd the name of Washington
> To make man blush there was but one!

Two centuries later the score is still the same.

Figure 65. Jean-Antoine Houdon, 'George Washington', in the State Capitol of Virginia (Richmond). The ploughshare is behind Washington's feet; the fasces tip forward slightly because they are resting on it. The hilt of Washington's sword is visible to the right.

the supreme exemplar of Roman honesty. Some years after his capture, the Carthaginians sent him to Rome to achieve the release of their prisoners (or even, in some versions of the story, to urge an end to the war), on the understanding that if he were successful he would stay in Rome a free man; if not, he was on oath to return to captivity. Regulus openly advised the Romans to reject the proposals, free no prisoners and fight on to victory. Then he returned, knowing that his captors would inflict on him every refinement of cruelty before death could release him from their torture. And that did indeed happen.

Colour plate 15

His friends and family begged Regulus not to go, but he had given his oath and would not break it. He was true to the honesty of Rome, to the winged goddess Fides Publica whose temple stood on the Capitol. Two centuries later, in a world that felt it had forgotten honesty, Regulus would serve as the culminating example in Cicero's treatise *On Duties*.

7.3   JANUS AND HIS FRIENDS

Besides Fides Publica, we know of a dozen or so gods and goddesses for whom the Romans founded new temples in the mid-third century BC:

Consus (272)	Tellus (268)
Vortumnus (264)	Pales (267)
Janus (262)	Tempestates (259)
Fons (231)	Spes (241)
Volcanus (exact date unknown)	Juturna (241)
	Flora (241 or 238)
	Feronia (exact date unknown)
	Nymphae (exact date unknown)

Each temple implies a new cult, a new commitment to regular sacrifices, a new public investment. The Romans of this period prided themselves on their devotion to the gods, and their choice of which gods to honour should tell us something about their view of the divine world.

Spes ('Hope') is self-evident, a fitting companion to Fides Publica and dedicated at the same time; so too is *Tellus*, Mother Earth and the land of Italy (p. 123 above); so too are the *Tempestates*, storm-gods honoured during a difficult naval war around Corsica. Consus is the god of good counsel who presided over Romulus' abduction of brides (p. 143 above). But the most interesting aspect of this list is the almost total absence of the great Olympians. Only Volcanus, the limping smith, cuckolded husband of Venus and subject of the great gods' laughter, represents the Homeric pantheon here. The Romans laughed at him too—they said Venus needed a sleeping draught before her wedding night—but they also knew how dangerous he was.

One day in 241 BC, the *pontifex maximus* Lucius Metellus was on his way from Rome to Tusculum when two ravens flew at him as if to make him stop. Recognising a divine warning, Metellus turned back to Rome. That night a disastrous fire broke out in the area round the Forum. The temple of Vesta was well alight, and the Virgins had had to flee, leaving the sacred objects behind them. Despite the rule that no man should enter, Metellus fought his way into the blazing building to rescue the talismans of Rome. Perhaps that was when the Romans gave the fire-god his temple.

The rest of the list contains some unfamiliar names. Pales is the goddess of herdsmen; she appeared to Marcus Regulus in his first consulship and promised him victory over the Sallentines in the heel of Italy. Her festival was the *Parilia* on 21 April; on that day Romulus, who had been brought up by the herdsman Faustulus, founded the city of Rome. She is a farmer's goddess, at home in the woods and hills with Faunus, Silvanus and the nymphs, an appropriate deity for the time when

Colour plate 6

> in days of old
> Brave Romans turned the glebe, and penned the fold;
> When senators came from the furrowed field
> Which their hard hands industriously had tilled,
> And could with equal lustre grace the bar
> Or bear the ensigns of victorious war.

Ovid Fasti
3.779–782

The nymphs themselves, those shy divinities of woods and streams, had their collective cult at a temple in the Campus Martius. Among their number were Feronia, Juturna and Flora—but those three were also goddesses in their own right.

Feronia was worshipped in the Sabine country, where she had a sacred grove, and at Tarracina on the border of Latium and Campania. At Rome she was honoured by ex-slaves as the goddess who gave them their freedom; when threatening portents had to be exorcised, the matrons took their offerings to queen Juno on the Aventine, the freedwomen to Feronia in the Campus Martius.

No stories survive for Pales and Feronia, though we may be sure they once existed. On Flora and Juturna we are better informed. As we saw in the first chapter from Ovid and Botticelli, Flora was a nymph of the Elysian Fields, promoted to full goddess status by the god of the West Wind, who ravished and married her. Juturna was promoted too, but with no subsequent marriage because her rapist was Jupiter. She was the nymph of a healing spring in the territory of Lavinium, but grateful Jupiter gave her a wider scope, and the Romans claimed her for the spring in the Roman Forum where Castor and Pollux were seen watering their sweating horses the day of the battle of Lake Regillus (p. 66 above).

Divine-rape stories are appropriate to the erotic nature of nymphs. Flora's new temple was celebrated with famously sexy shows at the *ludi Florales* (pp. 6–9 above), and her myth duly emphasised that side of her nature. For Ovid makes it clear that the nymphs of the Elysian Fields were part of the posthumous reward that men could expect for good behaviour in this life; in mythological terms, they were as available as the showgirls who performed at Flora's games. The new temple was next to that of Liber, with whom Flora has much in common (as Ovid observes, sex, wine and flowers all belong together), and some even said that Liber was Flora's son.

A remarkable story—the birth of Mars, no less—accounts for Flora's cult in Rome. One day Juno passed through the Elysian Fields, furious with Jupiter and keen to become pregnant without any help from him. Flora's herb-garden provided the answer. Flora touched Juno's bosom with a magic flower, and Juno conceived. So Mars was born; and in gratitude for his conception he promised Flora a place in Romulus' city.

Flora was the goddess of spring flowers; the goddess of autumn fruits was Pomona. She too was a promoted nymph, and the grateful god to whom she eventually submitted was Vortumnus, the shape-shifter, brought from Etruscan Volsinii by a victorious Roman consul in 264 BC. She too must have had a temple (she certainly had her own specialist priest), but alas, no information about it has survived. Pomona is an attractive character, devoted to her country garden:

> This was her love, her passion. Venus' charms
> Meant nothing; yet for fear of rustic force
> She walled her garden in to keep away
> The sex she shunned. What tricks did they not try,
> The quick young light-foot Satyrs, and the Pans
> Who wreathe their horns with pine, and that old rake
> Silenus, ever younger than his years,
> And he, the god whose scythe or lusty loins
> Scare thieves away—what did they not all try
> To win her love?

Ovid
Metamorphoses
14.634–641

Flora had trouble with Priapus too, and only avoided his urgent attentions by taking refuge in her laurel grove. Now the desirable nymphs are married ladies, goddesses with temples of their own. But Flora, at least, remembers her frisky past.

Yearning males with big erections are an age-old theme of comedy, and no doubt featured as such at Flora's games. Two Ovidian examples we have already looked at—Priapus' pursuit of Lotis and Faunus' of Omphale (pp. 3–5, 76–8 above)—and the early stage of Jupiter's pursuit of Juturna, which gave rise to the story of Lara the silent goddess (pp. 116–17 above), belongs in the same category of comic frustration, though of course the father of gods and men must get his way in the end.

There's a nice variation on the same scenario in Ovid's story of Cranae, a nymph of the Tiber valley who preferred hunting to sex.

> When her some youth would amorously caress
> This answer she returned to his address:
> 'Be not immodest in this open field,
> Go to some private grot—and there I'll yield.'
> Away he fondly goes, she lags behind
> And hides in bushes, which he ne'er can find.

Ovid *Fasti*
6.113–118

But now she is desired by a less gullible suitor, the god Janus:

> 'To some remote and private cave repair,'
> (Her usual trick) said she, 'I'll meet you there.'
> She followed, but in vain she strove to hide;
> The god, who sees behind, her steps descried.
> To strive to hide was vain; the nymph he seized
> Beneath a hill, and his rude passion pleased.

Ovid *Fasti*
6.121–126

Cranae the nymph becomes Carna the goddess, with a temple on the Caelian. She looks after the body's organs and flesh (Latin *caro, carnis*, feminine), particularly the vulnerable flesh of children. So if, as may happen, your baby is attacked by witches in the form of blood-sucking birds, Carna will come to the rescue with the magic whitethorn given to her by Janus.

The god with two faces could be thought of in various ways. In the quasi-historical mode, he was the ruler of primeval Latium, welcoming Saturnus as he arrived in flight from Jupiter (p. 32 above), his own citadel on the Janiculum sharing authority with that of Saturnus on the Capitol. Philosophical allegory could present him as the overseer of time or the father of the universe, his two faces looking simultaneously on the past and the future, chaos and civilisation, the world of gods and the world of men. A less rarefied mythology saw him as the doorkeeper of heaven, controlling access from mortals to the gods; that was why the Romans always named him first in their prayers.

On earth too he was a doorkeeper. His shrine in the Roman Forum was a passage with gates, which were closed only on the rare occasions when Rome was totally at peace. That happened in the reign of good king Numa, and again in 235 BC—or perhaps the custom of 'closing Janus' was a third-century innovation, and the Numa story was created then as a legendary precedent.

This gate-like shrine was once a real gate, the Porta Ianualis, one of the entrances to Romulus' Palatine community. So at least some Romans thought, and there was a story to prove it. Tatius and his Sabines had taken the Capitol (p. 145 above), but if they were to rescue their daughters they still had to get through Romulus' city wall. Juno helped them, taking away the bolts from the gate. Janus noticed (it was his gate), but didn't want to offend Juno by putting them back. So with the help of the nymphs, whose springs were nearby, he caused a flood of boiling water to keep the Sabines out till Romulus was ready to do battle.

Janus was on intimate terms with the nymphs of Rome. Besides Cranae the huntress (according to Ovid the god of gates made her the goddess of hinges), Janus' sexual partners included Camasene (she bore him the warrior Tiberis, after whom the Tiber was named), Venilia of the Palatine (she bore him the nymph Canens, beloved wife of Picus), and finally Juturna, daughter of the river-god Volturnus (she bore him Fons, the god of spring water).

There must have been a story for each of these love-affairs, but passing references are all we have in our surviving sources. Here for instance is Arnobius about AD 300, mocking the pagans for their inconsistent theology:

> So let us [Christians] too begin solemnly with Father Janus. Some of you say he is the world, some the year, some the sun. But if we accept that as true, we must understand as a consequence that the Janus who they say was the son of Caelus and Hecate, the first king in Italy, the founder of Janiculum, the father of Fons, the son-in-law of Volturnus, the husband of Juturna, never existed. Thus by your own doing the name of the god whom you put first in all your prayers, who you believe opens the way for you to the hearing of the gods, is wiped out.

Arnobius 3.29

Five and a half centuries earlier, when the Romans founded temple cults for Janus, Juturna and Fons in 262, 241 and 231 BC, we can be sure that the nature of their power and beneficence was understood by the citizens at various levels, from philosophical allegory to the spectacle of sexy nymphs and randy gods in live performance at the theatre games. Thanks to Novius Plautius and his colleagues, whose work was illustrated in Chapter 5, we can just begin to visualise the sort of story-world that the Roman Games, the Plebeian Games, the Games of Liber and the newly founded Games of Flora were able to put on stage at the Roman festivals.

Figure 66. Roman bronze *as*, 280–276 BC. Obverse: head of Janus, beardless. Reverse: head of Mercurius.

As it happens, Janus does not feature on any surviving *cista* or mirror from the fourth century BC. But he is conspicuously present in the third century on a different sort of bronze—not private luxury ware but the currency of the Republic itself. The main denomination (*as*) of the very first issue of Roman bronze coins, some time in the years 280–276 BC, has a beardless Janus on one side and Mercurius in his winged helmet on the other. The same combination appears in an *as* issue of 241–35 BC, and then, from 225 to 214 BC, the beardless Janus, now with a laurel wreath in his hair, was used for all Roman gold and silver coin types, a sequence known as *quadrigati* from the reverse image of Jupiter's four-horse chariot (p. 122 above).

Figure 66

Figure 54 (p. 122)

Meanwhile, a bearded Janus, with a ship's prow on the reverse, was introduced for the bronze *as* about 220 BC and issued regularly thereafter for nearly

Figure 67

140 years. It was *the* Roman bronze coin (gamblers called 'heads' or 'ships'), and it circulated long after its final issue; small wonder some people thought Janus invented coinage. No doubt constant use of this venerable image predisposed the Romans to think of Janus as a survivor from deep antiquity (as the god himself observes to Ovid, 'I'm an item from the past'). But the young Janus and his friends the nymphs were not forgotten. A moneyer of about 114 BC used the beardless third-century image on his silver *denarii*—perhaps in memory of a divine ancestor, since his name was Fonteius, and the son of Janus and Juturna was Fons.

Figure 67. Roman bronze *as*, 225–217 BC. Obverse: head of Janus, bearded. Reverse: prow of ship.

Figure 68. Obverse of *denarius* struck by Gaius Fonteius, *c.*114 BC (the reverse carries the legend C. FONT.): beardless Janus, as on the third-century coins illustrated in figs 54 and 66.

Figure 68

The Olympian gods were not wholly out of sight or out of mind. Jupiter's sister Vesta, normally the most retiring of them, gave a spectacular demonstration of her power at the trial of one of her Vestal Virgins in about 230 BC.

Tuccia was accused of unchastity, and her prosecutor must have had a plausible case, for the college of *pontifices* found her guilty. But the evidence was false, and Tuccia demanded the right to prove her innocence. The *pontifices* permitted her to go to the Tiber and fill a sieve with water. She prayed to the goddess, and then, with the awe-struck citizens looking on, she carried the water in the sieve back to the *pontifices* without losing a drop. They looked for the prosecutor, but he was never seen again, alive or dead.

It must have been about the same time, or a few years earlier, that Jupiter entered the bedroom of a Roman lady at siesta time in the guise of a huge snake. Her name was Pomponia, the wife of a patrician called Publius Scipio; she died giving birth to the son she conceived that afternoon.

Young Scipio was unusual. He spent much time in Jupiter's temple, and it was noticed that even when he went there at night, the dogs didn't bark. He soon acquired—or created, according to sceptical historians—the reputation of a man whose judgements had divine authority.

Jupiter, meanwhile, was watching the new leader of the Carthaginian forces in Spain. As a boy, Hannibal had sworn lifelong enmity against the Romans, and in 218 BC he provoked war by capturing Saguntum, a Spanish city in alliance with Rome. Jupiter summoned him in a dream to the council of the gods, and commanded him to take the war into Italy. 'I will give you a guide,' he said. Still in his dream, Hannibal led out his army in the company of a young man of more than human size, who warned him on no account to look back. But he did—and what he saw was darkness and thunderstorms, and a huge, hideous reptilian monster destroying everything in its path. 'What is *that*?', he asked in horror. 'That,' said his guide, 'is the devastation of Italy, something only the Fates should know about. March on!'

That story was told by a Greek historian. A Roman might have been less indulgent to the Carthaginian, whose strategy was quite deliberate: to get into Italy and do as much damage as he could, to persuade Rome's allies to desert her. And he was a military genius. He did indeed get his army into Italy, across the Alps and then across the Apennines, and he destroyed two Roman armies in successive years, at Lake Trasimene in 217 BC and even more catastrophically at Cannae in 216.

The Romans lost fifteen thousand men at Trasimene. Characteristically, their first thought was for the gods. Work began urgently on the building of two new temples next to each other on the Capitol. One was for the goddess Mens ('Mind', 'Intelligence'); the other was for Venus Erucina, the Phoenician fertility goddess whose ancient cult-centre at Eryx at the western tip of Sicily was famous for the ready availability of sex. Not that the Romans thought of her as Phoenician: on the contrary, they were keen to claim her from the Carthaginians. Since the Eryx cult had been founded by Aeneas for his goddess mother, she was really an ancestress of Rome. Together, the twin temples of Mens and Venus represented human libido rationally directed. The Republic needed to replace those lost citizens.

Then came Cannae. Forty-eight thousand dead, about half of them Roman citizens, the rest allies. How could Rome survive such losses? Some of the refugees were sure she couldn't. A group of young aristocrats were planning to head for the sea, commandeer some ships, and sail off to offer themselves as mercenaries to whatever Hellenistic kingdom could offer them work. But their scheme was foiled by young Scipio, only nineteen but already (as Livy puts it) Rome's destined leader. 'Let those who want to save the Republic follow me!', he cried, and with a few followers burst in on the conspirators and forced them at sword-point to swear they would not abandon the Roman People. But what rational reason was there to think that the Republic *could* be saved?

Two generations later, the conspicuously rational Polybios of Megalopolis wrote his great *History* to explain to his fellow-Greeks

> by what means, and under what system of government, the Romans succeeded in less than fifty-three years [220–167 BC] in bringing under their rule almost the whole of the inhabited world, an achievement which is without parallel in human history.

Polybios 1.1.5

He meant 'system of government' (*politeia*) in the broadest sense; and he chose to put his book-length analysis of Roman political, military and social institutions at precisely this point in his narrative, when Hannibal seemed to have defeated Rome, in order to show his readers why he hadn't, and why he never could.

Polybios' digression begins with the Roman constitution. He defines it not as any one of the three classic forms, but as a mixture, comprising elements of democracy (the People), aristocracy (the Senate) and monarchy (the consuls). The way the three elements checked and balanced each other resulted, he thought, in a stability which none of them alone could ever achieve. The Polybian mixed constitution was to have a long and distinguished career in political thought (it was, as John Adams put it, 'in the contemplation of those who framed the American constitution'), but it is obvious that it fits the data only very imperfectly. The consulship was shared power, temporary power, devised precisely as *non*-monarchy.

When Roman authors refer to republican politics, they take for granted a bipolar model—*plebs* and *patres*, the People and the Senate, the many and the few. The survival of the Republic depended on each side not pursuing its interests at too great a cost to those of the other. That was why the Romans

The Sword and Shield of Rome

While the destined leader was still too young to command, two men of very different character bore the brunt of Rome's struggle against Hannibal. The Romans called them the sword and the shield.

Marcus Claudius Marcellus was daring and valiant—'such a one,' wrote Plutarch, 'as Homer calls "lofty in heart, in courage fierce, in war delighting".' In his first consulship, five years before Cannae, he had been the first Roman commander to cross the river Po into the land of the Gauls; he killed the Gallic king Virdomarus in single combat, an exploit celebrated in a play by Gnaeus Naevius. (It was a play with a text, to be read by future generations, for Naevius was one of the pioneers of Roman literature.) Against the Carthaginians, Marcellus' main campaigns were in Sicily, where he captured Syracuse in 211 BC after a long siege. At the fall of the city one of his soldiers killed the great mathematician Archimedes (the man who said 'Eureka!' and 'Give me a place to stand and I'll move the Earth'); there were various stories of how it happened, but all agree that 'Marcellus was much concerned at his death, and turned his face away from his murderer as if from an impious and execrable person'.

Quintus Fabius Maximus was an older man, already nearly fifty at the time of Cannae. He was slow, patient and cautious, most unlike his dashing great-grand-father (p. 141 above); his strategy was one of attrition, avoiding pitched battles and waiting for Hannibal to wear himself out. It wasn't popular, but it worked. Marcellus got himself killed in an ambush in 208, but Fabius lived on to be immortalised in Ennius' epic poem (and Virgil's too) as 'the one man who rescued us by delaying'. His 'Fabian policy' lives on too, in the English language. In 1884, the Fabian Society was founded by a group of English socialists who preferred a long-term strategy against capitalism, without recourse to revolution.

deified such concepts as Concord, Hope, and Public Honesty. It's one of many reasons why it was appropriate that Rome's standard image on her bronze coinage was the god who faces both ways.

Polybios is well aware that the Roman Republic was a very particular type of political community. He also knows that the factors that made it so went back a long way and were too complex to be easily understood. (He did try to explain them, but that part of his treatment is lost.) He knows too that a community's customs and laws are the best index of its moral qualities, and he makes excellent explanatory use of his Roman examples.

Unlike the Carthaginians with their paid professionals (here too one thinks of the American Revolution), every Roman soldier was a citizen defending his home and children, and he would fight for them to the end. But something more was needed. Polybios draws his readers' attention to the Roman custom for aristocratic funerals.

The body was brought, at the head of a long procession, into the Roman Forum. The procession included men impersonating the dead man's ancestors, each wearing the appropriate portrait mask, dressed in the appropriate magisterial regalia, accompanied by the appropriate lictors. When the procession reached the Forum, they sat on ivory chairs in the Comitium while the dead man's son, or other close relative, delivered the oration from the Rostra to the huge crowd of citizens thronging the piazza. He related not only what the dead man himself had achieved in his lifetime, but also the achievements of each of his ancestors in turn, the men whose living images were sitting listening to his eulogy. 'Who could remain unmoved,' asks Polybios, 'at the sight of the images of all these men who have won renown in their time, now gathered together as if alive and breathing? What spectacle could be more glorious than this?'

As he goes on to explain, it is all done for a purpose:

> The most important consequence of the ceremony is that it inspires young men to endure the extremes of suffering for the common good in the hope of winning the glory that waits upon the brave. And what I have just said is attested by the facts. Many Romans have volunteered to engage in single combat so as to decide a whole battle, and not a few have chosen certain death, some in war to save the lives of their countrymen, others in times of peace to ensure the safety of the Republic. Besides this, there have been instances of men in office who have put their own sons to death, contrary to every law or custom, because they valued the interest of their country more dearly than natural ties to their own flesh and blood. Many stories of this kind can be told of many men in Roman history, but one in particular will serve as an example and a proof of my contention.

Polybios
6.54.3–6

And the example he gives is the story of Horatius Cocles at the bridge (pp. 58–9 above).

Thus far Polybios. What he omits, but we know from other sources, is that the procession that brought everyone to the Forum was a carnival of music, dance and comedy. The men who played the ancestors were sometimes actors whose impersonations—at this stage in the proceedings—could be comic or satirical; and if they played them straight, dancing satyrs mocked them from behind. It is a characteristic example of the Republic's facing-both-ways culture, a disrespectful revel leading directly into a solemn pageant of patriotic self-definition.

The final item in Polybios' account of what made the Roman people indomitable is one that he himself found very surprising. They believed in their gods. A rationalist himself, he could only suppose it to be deliberate policy, adopted by a wise ruling class to keep an unruly people disciplined. What made him think that was the *theatrical* nature of Roman religion. The word he uses is 'tragedy', but in a sense not easily caught in translation:

> It is impossible to exaggerate the extent to which this matter is turned into tragedy and brought both into their private lives and into the business of their city. . . Since every populace is fickle and full of lawless desires, unreasoning anger and violent passion, the only way of controlling it is by hidden terrors and other such tragedy.

Polybios
6.56.8 and 11

He may be using the word as a metaphor (a bit like describing church music as 'operatic'), but it's also possible that he had real theatrical tragedy in mind. The particular 'hidden terrors' he refers to are the myths of divine punishment in Hades; and we know from Cicero that the Furies pursuing sinners with their blazing torches were a familiar sight on the Roman stage.

As we saw with Flora (p. 160 above), the stage could also present, in comic and erotic mode, the pleasures of the virtuous dead in Elysium; but that would be too frivolous for Polybios' argument here. More relevant to his theme is something we know from Plautus, that it was normal in Roman 'tragedy' to have gods and goddesses on stage announcing to the audience the good deeds they have done on Rome's behalf. What the funeral orator does for the deeds of men, the actor at the theatre games does for the benefactions of the gods.

What it all means is best illustrated by Polybios' comment about the funeral pageant:

> By this constant renewal of the good report of brave men, the fame of those who have performed any noble deed is made immortal, and the renown of those who have served their country well becomes a matter of common knowledge and a heritage for posterity.

Polybios
6.54.2

The Romans of the Republic articulated their moral values in narrative stories. Regular public spectacles gave the citizens all they needed to know about how to behave in the world of men and what to expect from the world of gods. And that is why the Republic didn't collapse after the catastrophic defeats of 217–216 BC. Polybios, the pragmatic outsider, gives us the answer. What made the Romans fight on was their myths.

APOLLO'S AUTHORITY

Immediately after Cannae, the Romans sent to Delphi to ask what they should do. The envoy was Quintus Fabius Pictor, who was probably already at work on the first-ever history of Rome, written in Greek for an international audience. The question he had to put to the oracle was this: 'With what prayers and supplications can we please the gods, and what will be the outcome of such great disasters?'

In due course Fabius returned, bearing Apollo's list of the gods and goddesses to whom supplications had to be made, Apollo's promise of success and victory if that was done, Apollo's request for a gift from the booty, and Apollo's instruction 'to keep all licentiousness away from you'.

We don't know who was on Apollo's list of supplicable gods, but it probably didn't include Pan, Flora or Venus of Eryx. Probably not Liber either, if iconography truly represents their relationship (p. 113 above). It seems from the last item in his response that Apollo had sympathy for only one side of Rome's Janus-faced theology. And no doubt there were those in Rome itself who were uneasy about the god of freedom and his uninhibited friends.

Figure 50

Three years pass. The long military stalemate is affecting morale in Rome. The self-styled prophets and holy men who can be found in the market-place of any city of the ancient world are doing good trade with the anxious citizens in the Roman Forum. The aediles have nothing against them, but certain 'respectable citizens', choosing to regard these prayers and sacrifices as somehow un-Roman and contrary to the war effort, complain to the Senate that the aediles aren't doing their job. The Senate instructs the urban praetor to 'free the people from these superstitions', and he immediately confiscates all books of prophecy, prayers or sacrificial ritual.

The following year, the new praetor announced that two prophecies by the famous seer Gnaeus Marcius had been found among this material. The first was as follows:

> Thou who art sprung from Trojan blood, beware
> The stream of Canna. Let not aliens born
> Force thee to battle on the fatal plain
> Of Diomed. But thou wilt give no heed
> To this my counsel until all the plain
> Be watered by thy blood, and mighty hosts
> The stream shall bear into the boundless deep
> From off the fruitful earth. Thy flesh shall be
> Food for the fish and birds and beasts that roam
> The earth. For so hath Jupiter told me.

quoted in Livy 25.12.5–6

Such a clear prophecy of Cannae had to be genuine. So the advice in the second prophecy was taken seriously:

If, Romans, ye would drive the foemen forth,
Who come from far to mar your land, I urge
That to Apollo games be vowed, and held
Each year with graciousness. The people shall
Contribute part from public funds, then each
Privately for himself and family.
Your praetor, who does justice for the *plebs*
And people, shall have charge. Then let there be
Ten chosen who shall offer sacrifice
In Grecian fashion. This if ye will do,
Then shall ye evermore rejoice and all
Your state shall prosper; yea, the god shall bring
Your foes to nought, who now eat up your land.

quoted in Livy
25.12.9–10

So the *ludi Apollinares* were founded, the only annual games to be organised not by the aediles, whose responsibility it should have been, but by the urban praetor, with all the authority of his office. Give the people what they need, but make them contribute to the cost, and keep them under control.

The events of the following year (211 BC) were not good for Apollo's credibility. Far from being driven from Italy, Hannibal made a rapid march north from Campania and encamped his army about four miles from the walls of Rome. There was panic in the city: women thronged the temples, sweeping the altars with their hair in desperate supplication. Hannibal took two thousand cavalry and rode up to the Porta Collina to inspect the defences; the following day he brought out his army and formed it into line of battle. The consuls mustered what forces they had. Every man took an oath that he would return to the city that day only with his arms. Then they marched out to meet Hannibal's challenge.

There are three versions of what happened next. The first, in Polybios, is no doubt what really happened. Hannibal could see that Rome was competently defended, and calculated that the risks of an attack on those great walls would not be justified; so he withdrew, taking his army back into south Italy where it could do more damage at less cost.

The second version is what the Romans believed took place. Battle was about to be joined when a torrential downpour of rain and hail drove both sides back to shelter. The following day the same thing happened. Hannibal offered battle, the consuls accepted; a furious hailstorm kept them apart, but once the armies had withdrawn the blue sky returned. The message was clear to both sides: the gods were protecting Rome. Warned by Juno, Hannibal retreated. They said he cried in despair 'Oh, Cannae, Cannae!'

The third version is set during the newly founded games of Apollo. On wooden seats that form a temporary theatre, in the Circus Flaminius piazza in front of Apollo's temple, the citizens are watching a veteran mime-actor dancing to the music of a piper. Somebody comes with the news that Hannibal is ready to attack; the citizens rush off to arm themselves; they fight, and win; then they come back to the theatre, anxious that the disruption of the show may have angered the gods. But there are the old man and the piper, still doing their turn. The games were not interrupted, there has been no sacrilege. Which is why the *parasiti Apollinis*, an honorific guild of mime-actors, have as their motto 'It's all right, the old man's dancing'.

Mime-actors are not the companions one would expect for the god who warned the Romans against licentiousness. But perhaps it took more than just a hint from Delphi to make the Romans rethink their traditional relationship with the gods of pleasure and sex.

The one play that we happen to know was created for the Games of Apollo offers a scenario which is licentious in the highest degree. It provided an explanation for the festival on the *Nonae Caprotinae* (7 July), when the slave-girls, wearing their mistresses' dresses, sacrificed to Juno Caprotina and made themselves available as sexual partners. (The Games of Apollo on 13 July were later extended several days back, and at some point incorporated the *Nonae Caprotinae*; it must have been helpful to the urban praetor to bring that festival directly under his control.)

The play is set in the immediate aftermath of the Gallic occupation. It presupposes Romulus' abduction of the Latin, not the Sabine, women (p. 143 above). We know nothing of the dramatic genre to which it belonged. The following imaginative reconstruction—based on the plot-summaries in our sources—assumes that some at least of the performance conventions detectable in the fourth century BC visual evidence still applied a century later.

A substantial stage and banks of wooden seating enclose the eastern end of the Circus Flaminius piazza as a temporary theatre in front of Apollo's temple. The stage building is in the form of a battered city wall with an open gate, mimicking the real city wall of Rome and Carmenta's Gate about 100 metres behind. In front of the stage is an altar, overshadowed by a large fig-tree. Between that and the podium of the Apollo temple itself (where the urban praetor and his guests occupy the seats of honour), the paving of the piazza forms a broad *orchestra* with plenty of room for dancers.

The piper plays an aubade, then breaks into a cheerful dance tune as the female chorus runs out of the gate in the 'city wall' and down into the *orchestra*. They are slave-girls, as shown by the short shifts they wear, and they dance up to the altar singing a hymn of thanksgiving to Juno Caprotina, now that the Gauls have gone away. When their dance is done, a man in a consul's toga comes out on to the stage in an attitude of despair. In dialogue with the leader of the girls' chorus (her name is Tutula, though some sources call her Philotis or Rhetana), he explains that after the occupation Rome is desperately weakened; even the city gates cannot be barred. And the Latins have rebelled;

The Slave-Girls' Holiday

Only one of the 36 Kalends, Nones and Ides of the months of the Roman calendar had a title of its own—the 'Caprotine Nones' (*Nonae Caprotinae*, 7 July), named after Juno Caprotina.

On that day the slave-girls of Rome, dressed in clothes borrowed from their mistresses, joined the free citizen women in a sacrifice to Juno, the goddess of childbirth and human fertility. This took place at an ancient fig-tree (*caprificus*) in the Campus Martius, on which sheets were hung for privacy as the women employed branches of the tree and its milky sap in ritual mimicry of sexual insemination. Then there was a feast, after which the citizen women presumably went home to their husbands. But the slave-girls continued to enjoy their holiday, running about, playing at mock fights, calling out to the watching men and joking with them. They were dressed as free women, but available as free women would not be; and for Juno's purposes, the more sex there was, the better. No doubt couples retreated at first behind the sheets hung on the boughs of the tree, but once darkness fell there would be no need for that.

The most helpful commentary on this erotic cult is a letter written by King Philip V of Macedon in 214 BC to the city of Larisa in Thessaly. He urges the authorities there to be generous in granting citizenship—like the Romans, 'who when they manumit their slaves admit them to the citizen body and grant them a share in the magistracies, and in this way have not only enlarged their country but have sent out colonies to nearly seventy places'. Manpower was the secret of Rome's success.

How many chattel slaves were owned by Romans in the early Republic? We have no idea. But they were a resource to be exploited for the common good. If a man had a nubile slave-girl and chose not to make her pregnant, that was a waste. The *Nonae Caprotinae* ritual was evidently intended to maximise output, to ensure a harvest of slave children the following April, many of whom might in due course be manumitted, and thus to keep the Republic well supplied with potential citizens.

they want vengeance for the women Romulus stole; their leader has demanded the Romans' wives and daughters immediately, and Rome has no way of denying him. Shocked, the girls return through the gate, Tutula engaging the consul with respectful but urgent advice.

Horns and trumpets, shouts of triumph, marching feet—enter the male chorus from the main piazza to the right, full of macho swagger. They are the Latins, under their leader Postumus Livius of Fidenae. The Romans peer over the top of their 'city wall', the men anxious, the women hysterical. Contemptuously, Livius calls the consul down.

The two men face each other across the stage. Livius demands the Romans' women, the consul appeals in vain for decency. There can only be one outcome. Defeated, the consul summons the women by name. They come out one by one, wrapped in fine coloured togas drawn up over the head and face (the toga was worn by citizens of both sexes in the early Republic). As each woman steps down into the *orchestra*, and the grinning Latin chosen by Livius takes firm hold of her, a different Roman among the watchers on the wall gives an anguished cry. The scene is played slowly, building up the sexual tension as the Latins, torn between desire and discipline, impatiently await Livius' signal. The last lady is for Livius himself. He orders the consul back inside and turns to the *orchestra*. 'Now!'

What follows is frenetic choreography, exploiting in the first phase the fact that a toga is only a large wrap, easily removed. The girls must end up naked, their togas spread high over the fig-tree by the altar. (If we hadn't recognised them before, we now see that they are Tutula and the slave-girls: the wives and daughters have kept their honour.) The Latins take their pleasure for as long as their energy lasts, in an elaborate sex-mime with its own comic development. In the first bout, the men are ruthless and the women scream; in the second, the men ask first and the women allow themselves to be cajoled; in the third, the men are reluctant and the women enthusiastic. It ends as the plot requires, with all the dancers prostrate and exhausted. The piper plays a nocturne.

Eventually, Tutula looks up. Cautiously, she makes her way through the sleeping bodies to the front of the stage. Taking a torch, she waves it towards the 'city wall'; the spread togas shield the light from the Latins. Suddenly the silence is broken as the Romans burst out from the gate with drawn swords. The bleary-eyed Latins flee as best they can, but we know they won't get far. While the Romans' shouts of triumph sound from off to the right, we enjoy our last look at the naked girls as they dance joyfully to the altar and collect their togas from the fig-tree.

They are all dressed and respectfully attentive when the consul comes out on stage to make his closing speech. In recognition of their bravery, every year henceforth on the *Nonae Caprotinae* the slave-girls shall have the right to wear their mistresses' clothes and take part in the sacrifice to Juno Caprotina as if they were free women.

'Keep all licentiousness away from you'? Whatever Delphi might say, the Romans understood that sexy fun (*liberior iocus*, in Ovid's phrase) could have a patriotic purpose. The people in the audience had just had their enemy at the gates in cold reality, despite Apollo's promises. Why should they be told to restrict their entertainments to the 'Grecian fashion'? Apollo's authority could try to control such spectacles, by extending the *ludi Apollinares* to cover the slave-girls' holiday festival; but it could not abolish them.

7.6 WELCOMING THE MOTHER

The year Hannibal appeared at the gates of Rome, the two Roman commanders in Spain were killed. They were brothers, Publius Scipio and Gnaeus Scipio, and each of them left a son. Publius' son we have already met—if he *was* Publius' son, and not Jupiter's. That same year, on a wave of popular enthusiasm, he was elected to the Spanish command at the age of only twenty-six. Gnaeus' son was just a boy of about thirteen, but he too had a future destiny.

Young Scipio's first exploit in Spain was the capture of New Carthage (Cartagena), achieved with the miraculous help of Neptunus: the god lowered the water of the lagoon that defended the city on the north side, to allow the Romans passage through. While Scipio was seeing to prisoners and hostages, a particularly beautiful girl was brought to him. He sent for her fiancé, freed her and provided a dowry—little knowing how many moralising paintings of 'The Continence of Scipio' would hang in the galleries of Europe two thousand years later.

His divine charisma didn't let him down, and after four years' successful campaigning in Spain he returned to Rome to be elected consul at the age of only thirty. It was in his year of office, as if by chance, that the gods finally told the Romans how to get Hannibal and his army out of Italy.

The relevant priests were consulting the Sibyl's books about something quite different—routine prodigies, rain of stones, that sort of thing—when they came across this:

> If ever foreign foe should carry war
> Into the land of Italy, from Italy
> He can be driven out and overcome
> If the Idaean Mother shall be brought
> From Pessinus to Rome.

quoted in Livy
29.10.5

For twelve years already Hannibal had been defiantly at large, and all the time the answer had been there in the scrolls of the old prophetess.

Pessinus was in Phrygia, in the lands of king Attalus of Pergamum. The Roman ambassadors called at Delphi on the way, to make sure Apollo wasn't offended. From Pergamum the king himself conducted them to Pessinus, where he handed over the sacred stone that had fallen from heaven charged with the godhead of the Great Idaean Mother of the Gods (p. 124 above). A ship was constructed to carry the precious cargo, and the ambassadors began their long voyage home. One of their number went ahead to tell the Romans that the goddess was on her way, and to report Apollo's requirement, that the best man among the citizens must be chosen to receive her.

The man the Senate chose was just twenty years old. He was Publius Scipio Nasica, the other young Scipio orphaned in 211 BC, first cousin of the charismatic consul. The criterion was evidently moral character rather than proved achievement; perhaps Apollo was still worried about licentiousness.

It's possible, though the evidence is ambiguous, that Apollo asked for the married women to choose the chastest of their number for the same duty, and that the choice fell on Quinta Claudia. But the best-known version of Claudia's story tells it in quite a different way. Here is Massey's eighteenth-century Ovid again, reporting the Mother's arrival at the mouth of the Tiber:

> Hither to welcome the great goddess come
> Knights, senators and mob in crowds from Rome;
> With them the ladies mixed a splendid train,
> Led on by those who watch in Vesta's fane.
> Toiling with ropes, the men did all they could
> To hale the vessel up the adverse flood.
> A droughty season had the river dried;
> High were the banks of sand, and low the tide.
> To drag the ship along, they pull and strain,
> But all their labour, all their toil is vain;
> With cheering voice they help the working hands,
> But like a solid rock unmoved she stands.
>   Astonished at this strange unusual sight,
> The men were put into a panic fright;
> But Claudia Quinta happened to be there,
> A lady great by birth as well as fair,
> And really chaste; though false yet common fame
> Had long deprived her of her better name.
> Pleased with a gay and over-curious dress,
> Which might a kind of wantonness express,
> To censure prone, the rigid of her sex
> Of levity her conduct freely tax.
> Too readily, 'tis true, most lend an ear
> To false reports injurious to the fair;
> But she that's of a chaste and honest mind
> May give ill-grounded censure to the wind.
>   But now as Claudia, singly from the rest

Figure 69. Quinta Claudia pulls the ship carrying the Great Mother: altar in the Musei Capitolini in Rome, first or second century AD. The inscription reads: 'To the Mother of the Gods and the Saviour Ship Claudia Syntheche gave this [altar] having undertaken a vow' (the word for 'saviour' is repeated).

Of all the ladies, to the river pressed,
With both her hands she scoops the limpid waves,
And o'er her head she thrice the water heaves,
And thrice her arms she stretches to the skies
With solemn aspect and uplifted eyes,
Then to the sacred image turned her head,
And falling on her knees this prayer made:
'Great mother of the gods! whom I revere,
On certain terms my just petition hear.
'Tis said I am unchaste. Thy sentence give;
If thou condemn'st me, I'm unfit to live;
But if I'm guiltless, goddess, deign to show

Some sign, that all my innocence may know.
If chaste, let not the ship unmoving stand,
But as I draw it, follow my chaste hand.'
    She said, and gave the ship a gentle hale,
When to the great amazement of them all
The ship began along the stream to glide
And took her course as Claudia was her guide.
A general pleasure followed the surprise.
And shouts of gladness rend the echoing skies.

Figure 69

Ovid Fasti
4.293–328

That was in 204 BC, the year Scipio invaded Africa. In 203 the Carthaginians recalled Hannibal to defend their homeland. The Sibyl had been right.

For the Great Idaean Mother of the Gods (Cybele was one of her many names), a splendid new temple was constructed next to the temple of Victoria on the Palatine. A new programme of annual games was set up in her honour, called *ludi Megalenses* from *megale meter*, the Greek for 'Great Mother'. Ovid tells us that his story of Quinta Claudia's miracle came from a play; it must have been a patriotic comedy for the new theatrical festival, with Claudia played as a chic young lady quite prepared to answer back to the strict old men.

The Mother herself was a good example of the way Roman culture still looked both ways. She brought with her an exotic cult of noisy processions and garishly dressed eunuch priests, though the aediles kept the more alien features out of her public games. But she was also a sort of ancestress. She was called the *Idaean* Mother after Mount Ida, the place where Aeneas was born and where he gathered the Trojan survivors before setting out to the West. Like Aeneas, Roman generals would pray to her for victory, for in that department she had been spectacularly successful.

One of the Scipio cousins received her at Ostia on behalf of the Roman people, and two years later the other defeated Hannibal at Zama (the first time since Cannae that a Roman commander had faced him in open battle). Victorious Scipio was known thenceforth as 'Africanus'. They said in Rome that he was a son of Jupiter—and now the world might well believe it.

8

POWER AND THE PEOPLE

NEW WAYS

For Rome, everything was changed by the Hannibalic experience, 'when all the world' (as Lucretius put it many years later), 'shaken by the tremorous turmoil of war, shuddered and reeled beneath the high waste of heaven, in doubt to which people's sway must fall all human power by land and sea'. Scipio's victory settled the issue: Rome, not Carthage, would be the super-power.

A mere five years after Zama, at Dogsheads (Kunoskephalai) in Thessaly, the Romans defeated Philip V of Macedon in a pitched battle. At the Isthmian Games the following year (196 BC), the Roman commander, Titus Flamininus, proclaimed to a wildly enthusiastic audience that the Greek cities were now free from the tribute and garrisons that the Macedonian kings had imposed on them more than a century before. At Delphi, Flamininus made offerings not only to Apollo but also to the Romans' own Castor and Pollux:

> On your ambrosial locks, O son of Leto,
>   The Aeneads' great chief has placed his gift,
> This wreath of gleaming gold. Archer Apollo,
>   Grant godlike Titus glory for his might.
>
> Hail, boys of Zeus, delighting in swift horses!
>   Hail, Spartan princes, sons of Tyndareus!
> This splendid gift Aenead Titus brings you,
>   He who wrought freedom for the sons of Greece.

quoted in Plutarch
Titus Flamininus
12.6–7

The descendants of Aeneas had humbled the successors of Alexander the Great.
   Alexander's Asiatic empire, in modern terms from Turkey to Afghanistan,

was loosely controlled by the Seleucid dynasty at Antioch. The present king, Antiochus III (who also called himself 'the Great'), now tried to expand his empire into Europe. In 191 BC the Romans threw him out of Greece; the following year, under Lucius Scipio, Africanus' brother, they crossed into Asia and defeated Antiochus at Magnesia. The great king's ambassador humbly besought the Romans to show magnanimity:

Livy
37.45.8–9

> 'This victory has made you masters of the world. It now behoves you to put aside quarrels with mortals and act like gods in taking thought for the welfare of the human race.'

Africanus himself replied on his brother's behalf. He fixed the king's western border at the Taurus mountains, and went on to observe:

Livy
37.45.11–12

> 'We Romans have what was in the gods' power to give us. Our attitudes are controlled by our own minds, and we keep them unchanged whatever fortune brings. Success has never exalted them, nor adversity brought them low.'

Fine words, but that was not how it turned out.

Rome had inherited Carthage's empire: Sicily, Sardinia, Corsica and eastern and southern Spain were now provinces of the Roman People. The defeated kingdoms of the Greek East were not yet directly ruled by Rome, but those victories brought in huge amounts of precious metal and luxury goods as booty. Rome had become very rich very fast, and there was real fear that the effects would destroy her.

The spokesman of that fear was Marcus Cato, himself a legendary figure, but as different as could be from his enemies Scipio Africanus 'son of Jupiter' and 'godlike' Titus Flamininus:

Livy
37.40.4

> There was such force of character and such a wealth of natural endowments in this man that it was evident that he would have made his own fortune, whatever the station in which he had been born.

In fact he was a 'new man', brought up in the Sabine countryside not far from Manius Curius' cottage, which he used often to visit, remembering the story of the Samnite ambassadors (p. 154 above). Livy's character-sketch continues:

Livy
39.40.9–11

> He was dogged in the prosecution of his quarrels; indeed one would be hard put to it to say whether the nobility was more concerned to crush him or he to vex the nobility. There was no question about the harshness of his disposition, the bitterness and unbridled freedom of his language; but his character was proof against the assault of appetites; he was marked by a rigid integrity and a contempt for popularity and riches. In the austerity of his life, in his endurance of hardship and danger, he showed himself a man of iron constitution.

In 184 BC this paragon put his old-fashioned frugality and moral rigour into practice, in the magistracy which defined him for posterity as 'Cato the censor'. How necessary his harsh regime was thought to be is shown by the inscription

High-Class Robbers

'It's not easy,' said Cato, 'to save a city where a fish costs more than a ploughing-ox.' Exotic fish were the ancient world's gourmet food *par excellence*; at Rome you could buy them at the Macellum, otherwise known as the Forum Cuppedinis ('delicacy market'), in the district north-east of the Sacra Via that was called Corneta ('cornel grove').

'Macellum' was a loan-word from Greek (*makellon*, an enclosure), but both names had a different derivation in a story that can be dated to 179 BC. The censors of that year redeveloped the area with a basilica and a new fish-market behind it. It was said that they had created the space for their market by confiscating and demolishing the house of two condemned criminals, notorious robbers called Equitius Cuppes (or Cuppedo) and Romanius Macellus. So the new market was called Cuppedinis or Macellum after them.

Equitii and Romanii were real Roman families, but the story wasn't aimed at them. If these robbers had such a big house in such an up-market part of town, they must have been high-status citizens, in fact Roman knights—*equites Romani*.

As aetiological stories go, this one is pretty unsophisticated. But the author who reports it is the sober and learned Varro; it featured in his *Antiquitates humanae*, written probably in the 50s BC. So it took only four or five generations for a transparently invented legend to become acceptable history.

on the statue of him set up at the temple of Public Health (*Salus*): 'elected censor when the Republic was falling into bad ways, he set it upright again with good guidance and sound moral discipline.'

Cato was particularly hostile to Greek influence on Roman life. 'Theirs is an utterly vile and unruly race,' he wrote to his son. 'Consider this as spoken by a prophet: when that race gives us its literature it will corrupt everything.' Since the current slang for extravagant self-indulgence was *pergraecari*—'Greeking it up', in Erich Segal's rendering—Cato's prejudice was all part of his crusade against luxury. He wasn't alone in his anti-Hellenism, and it had some far-reaching consequences.

Two years before Cato's censorship, the consuls had conducted a ruthless police action against the cult of Liber at the grove of Stimula (p. 74 above). They claimed it had been perverted by an obscure Greek 'sacrificer and prophet' introducing secret initiations as a cover for sexual abuse and other crimes. The citizens were harangued on the need to worship their ancestral gods, and not 'those who with goads [*stimuli*] implanted, so to say, by the Furies have spurred minds enslaved by debased and alien rites to perform every kind of crime and lustful deed'. The magistrates acted against the *Bacchae* and *Bacchanalia* (only those Greek terms used) as if they were a conspiracy against the Republic itself. In an atmosphere of terror and panic, thousands of people were arrested and imprisoned; most of them were executed.

Wine, sex and play-acting had always been part of Liber's cult. What was new was the determination of the Senate and magistrates to brand as un-Roman, and then stamp out, an institution that was not only popular but actually symbolic of the People's liberty. Now there was no military threat to make social cohesion necessary, a more rigorous discipline could be imposed from above. No more satyrs, nymphs and maenads; Marsyas was back under the authority of Apollo.

A similar action five years later—but with no loss of life this time—announced the rejection of Numa's teacher Pythagoras (pp. 53 and 55 above). The old king's tomb had come to light on the Janiculum. His coffin was empty, but another stone chest contained some ancient volumes, seven (or twelve) of pontifical law and seven (or twelve) of Pythagorean philosophy. The urban praetor was informed. He declared that they were 'destructive of religion', and should be neither read nor preserved. With the Senate's approval, he had the books publicly burned in the Comitium.

On the very site where Tarquinius Priscus had bought what was left of the Sibyl's books (p. 50 above), the authorities of republican Rome destroyed as subversive what purported to be first-hand evidence for the influence of 'the wisest of the Greeks' (p. 49 above) on the wisest of the Romans. Rome was reinventing herself. The Senate and magistrates would decide what was good for the citizens, and that didn't include taking as gospel what some Greek had written. We can be sure that Cato approved.

Figure 70

Figure 15

However, there were some Greeks whom not even Cato could keep out of Rome—like the nine Muses, and Homer. The Muses came as a choir, in bronze or marble, we don't know which, as booty from Ambrakia in north-west Greece. With Hercules as their accompanist on the lyre, they graced the new temple of Hercules and the Muses put up by Marcus Fulvius Nobilior after his triumph in 187 BC. As for Homer, he appeared from Acheron to announce in a dream to the poet Quintus Ennius that his soul had entered into Ennius himself.

Figure 71

Ennius came from a small town in the heel of Italy, not far from Greek Tarentum and the new Latin colony of Brundisium. He said he had three hearts—Greek, Latin and his native Oscan—and it was out of that fertile mix of cultures that this reincarnation of Homer created the Latin epic tradition.

Not that he was the first to write epic in Latin. That distinction belonged to Gnaeus Naevius, who had completed his long poem *The Punic War* just before Ennius came to Rome in 203 BC. (It included the voyage of Aeneas from Troy, and his meeting with Dido at the foundation of Carthage.) But Naevius' poem was in the archaic metre the Romans named after king Saturnus—'verses in which the Fauns and prophets sang', as Ennius contemptuously put it. *He* would use Homer's metre, the hexameter, and take his inspiration from the Muses—'you who tread great Olympus in your dance'.

Ennius was granted Roman citizenship in 184 BC. He called his epic *Annales*, 'yearly records', for its subject was not the wrath of Achilles or the return of Ulysses, but the whole long history of Rome. For the first time ever, the Roman

Figure 70. Giulio Romano and/or Polidoro da Caravaggio, 'Discovery of the Tomb of Numa Pompilius', 1523–4; painted for the *salone* of the Villa Lante (seen in the background), on the Gianicolo close to the site of the event itself; now in the Palazzo Zuccari.

Figure 71. Reverse images of *denarii* struck by Quintus Pomponius Musa, c.66 BC, evidently representing the statues in the temple of Hercules and the Muses: HERCVLES MVSARVM (centre), surrounded by (clockwise from the top) Calliope, Clio, Erato, Euterpe, Melpomene, Polyhymnia, Terpsichore, Thalia and Urania.

People had an accessible narrative of its own past. Yes, there were already prose historians, but they were senators writing in Greek, to explain Rome to foreigners. What an epic on Ennius' Homeric scale provided was a repertoire for public recitations. Just as the rhapsode of the tale of Troy might ask his Muse

'Begin from where godlike Achilles first
Quarrelled with Agamemnon, king of men',

Homer *Iliad*
1.6–7

so now his equivalent at the Roman games could start

'Tell, Muse, what each commander of the Romans
Achieved in battle in king Philip's war'.

Ennius *Annales*
322–323 Sk

For this heroic story came right up to date, to the audience's own time.

Ennius was a Hellenising modernist, but his story of Rome was everything an old-fashioned patriot like Cato could have asked for. One of his lines became proverbial:

Old ways, and men, make strong the Roman state.

Ennius *Annales*
156 Sk

For Cicero, over a century later, that had the laconic authority of an oracle.

Meanwhile, old ways were being forgotten. In 171 BC, in a stand-off with the new ruler of Macedon, the Romans offered a truce merely to give time for

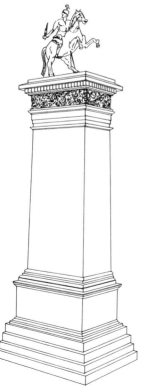

their war preparations, while encouraging king Perseus to hope for peace. When the ambassadors boasted of this deceit in their report to the Senate, some of the older members grumbled that this 'new cleverness' was not the Roman way of doing things; what had happened to Roman honesty (p. 153 above), the moral standards of the time when Fabricius warned king Pyrrhos of the assassin's plot?

But they were in a minority. The Senate approved, the war went ahead and Rome won another famous victory, which was followed by the capture of the king of Macedon himself.

That was announced by Castor and Pollux in person, materialising, as the recipient of their epiphany reported to a sceptical Senate, in the country of their own Spartan Sabines (p. 23 above). They met Lucius Domitius on the road, and touched his cheeks to make his beard red.

Aemilius Paullus, the victorious commander, returned to Rome in magnificent state; the royal galley, sumptuous with purple hangings, rowed him slowly up the Tiber with sixteen banks of oars.

Figure 72. Reconstruction of the monument of Aemilius Paullus at Delphi. 'At Delphi, he saw a tall square pillar composed of white marble stones, on which a golden statue of Perseus was intended to stand, and gave orders that his own statue should be set there, for it was meet that the conquered should make way for their conquerors' (Plutarch *Aemilius Paullus* 28.4, trans. Bernadotte Perrin). The upper plinth survives, with the sculptured frieze and the cuttings for where the horse's hind hooves were anchored; also the inscription from the base, in the conqueror's language: L. AIMILVS L.F. INPERATOR DE REGE PERSE MACEDONIBVSQVE CEPET.

His triumphal procession took three days to display all the captured wealth, and on the third day Perseus and the royal children walked as captives before Aemilius' chariot. It was a defining moment, for Rome and for the world.

Aemilius Paullus had a son, who was also, by adoption, the grandson of Scipio Africanus. His very name was a reminder of Rome's two greatest conquerors. This young man became a close friend of the Greek historian Polybios, whose character-sketch of him is a well informed first-hand portrait of both a man and a society:

Figure 73

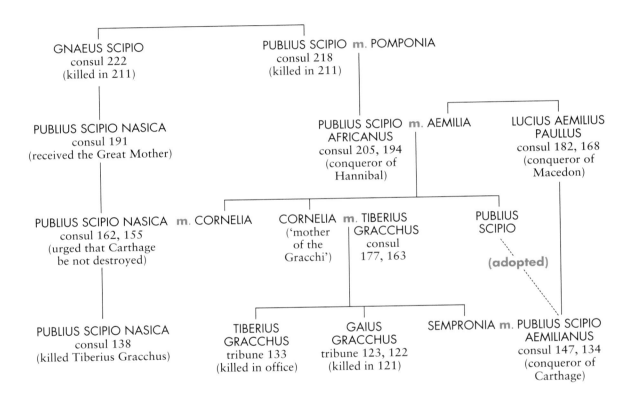

Figure 73. Simplified stemma of the Scipios (family name Cornelius), showing their relationship with Aemilius Paullus and with the Gracchi (family name Sempronius).

The first manifestation of Scipio's desire to lead a noble life was to gain a reputation for self-discipline, and in this respect to rise above the standards observed by his contemporaries. This is a high and normally a difficult aspiration, but at that time it was easy enough because of the deterioration of morals among the great majority.

Some young men squandered their energies on love affairs with boys, others with courtesans, and others again upon musical entertainments and banquets and the extravagant expenses that go with them, for in the course of the war against Perseus and the Macedonians they had quickly acquired the luxurious habits of the Greeks in this direction. . . The reason was first of all the belief that after the destruction of the Macedonian kingdom the universal supremacy of Rome had been established beyond dispute, and secondly the fact that after the riches of Macedon had been transported to Rome there followed a prodigious display of wealth and splendour both in public life and in private.

Scipio, by contrast, set himself to follow the opposite path. He disciplined all his appetites, and by dint of laying down for himself a consistent and undeviating system of conduct, he built up within the space of five years a reputation in the eyes of the whole people for moderation and self-control.

Polybios 31.25.2–8

Twenty-one years after his father's triumph, Scipio Aemilianus stood with Polybios watching a city burn. The city was Carthage, and the decision to destroy it had been taken after a bitter policy debate at Rome. Carthage was no military threat, but one day she might be. Old Cato insisted, in a phrase destined for the dictionary of quotations, that Carthage must be destroyed; Scipio Nasica on the other hand (son of the young man who had received the Great Mother) wanted Carthage spared for the very reason that she *might* be a threat, to keep the Romans from luxurious complacency. Predictably, the short-term interests won. A war was provoked, the young Scipio was promoted to finish it off, and now he was watching seven hundred years of proud history go up in flames.

'It's a wonderful sight, Polybios,' he said, 'and yet I have a fear and foreboding, I don't know why, that one day someone will give the same order about my own city.' And he quoted the words of doomed Hector:

> 'The day will come when sacred Troy shall perish,
> And Priam and his people.'

Homer Iliad 6.448–449

The Bronze Beards

The Domitii were among the early plebeian nobility, with consuls in 332 and 283 BC. At that time they called themselves Domitii Calvini ('bald'); the great sequence of Domitii Ahenobarbi ('bronze-beard') began with Gnaeus Domitius son of Lucius, who was consul in 192 BC, and continued with consulships in each of the next eight generations—162, 122, 96, 54, 32, 16 BC, AD 32, 55. The story of the reddening of Lucius' beard by Castor and Pollux (p. 185 above) was probably created at the time of the 168 BC epiphany, and retrojected to that of the Lake Regillus battle (pp. 65–6 above) in order to give a newly prominent branch of the family a dignified antiquity.

The last of the Ahenobarbus consuls listed above no longer carried the family name, having been adopted five years earlier by a patrician Claudius. He was, in fact, the emperor Nero.

THE CATASTROPHE

Who shall have power, the many or the few? The Roman Republic's pragmatic answer had always been 'both, within limits'. But now the world had changed. Rome's meteoric rise to sole super-power status had brought with it a new intolerance, xenophobic in external affairs, authoritarian at home. The suppression of the 'Bacchanals' in 186 BC, condemning a traditionally orgiastic cult as alien and subversive, was a violent sign of the times.

Not that the puritanical control-freaks had it all their own way. In 173 BC (p. 9 above) the games of Flora, hitherto dependent on the budget of each year's plebeian aediles, were made part of the regular annual programme of public *ludi*. That was a reminder of the issue that had paid for Flora's games in the first place, the encroachment of big private estates on to land that belonged to the community. Now it was happening again, as part of the sudden enrichment of Rome's elite; the small farmers who rented the public land were being forced off it.

One of the consuls of 140 BC tried to bring in legislation to stop the abuse, but there was so much opposition in the Senate that he withdrew it. They called him 'Laelius the Wise', for avoiding reform.

Then came Tiberius Gracchus. A serious young man, grandson of Scipio Africanus on his mother's side (p. 186 above), he was elected tribune in 133 BC. With huge popular backing, and in the teeth of fierce opposition from most of the Senate, he got a law passed restricting possession of public land to the limit set in 366 BC; everything above that was confiscated and assigned to poor citizens in a huge redistribution programme. His opponents had used one of his tribunician colleagues to veto the proposal, but Gracchus overcame that tactic with an argument that went to the heart of the matter: was it right for a tribune, whose office was for the protection of the People's interests, to oppose those interests? The citizens' assembly thought not, and voted the vetoer out of office.

Figure 73

Now Gracchus was standing for re-election. It was very unusual for a tribune to hold office two years running, but not unprecedented. The majority in the Senate, however, regarded it as an assault on liberty. Totally irreconcilable views of what the Republic was were now in conflict, and the result was a catastrophe. The depth of the ideological schism which destroyed the Republic can be seen from these two partisan accounts of what happened next:

> During his tribunate Tiberius Gracchus got control of the People's favour by lavish bribes. The Republic was helpless under his power. Openly and repeatedly he urged that the Senate should be done away with, and all political business handled by the *plebs*. The Senate, convened by the consul Mucius Scaevola in the temple of Public Honesty, was discussing what could be done in such a crisis. All the

senators wanted the consul to defend the Republic by force of arms, but Scaevola refused to resort to force. Then Scipio Nasica spoke. 'Since the consul, in observing the rule of law, is effectively bringing about the collapse of Roman authority and all the laws with it, I, a private citizen, offer myself as leader to carry out your will.' Then he wrapped the fold of his toga round his left arm, raised his right and cried out 'Follow me, if you want the Republic saved!'. With that he dispelled the hesitation of the honest citizens, and forced Gracchus and his criminal faction to pay the penalty they deserved.

Valerius Maximus
3.2.17

As soon as Gracchus notices that the People are wavering, in their fear that the Senate's authority may move him to abandon his project, he calls a public meeting. Meanwhile, *he* [Nasica] comes flying out of the temple of Jupiter, brimming over with murderous intent. Sweating, eyes blazing, his toga twisted up, several others following him, faster and faster he comes. As Gracchus' herald is calling the People's attention, this madman plants his heel on a bench, breaks off one of the legs with his hand, and tells his followers to do the same. As Gracchus is beginning a prayer to the gods, they attack, rushing in from all sides. Someone from the People shouts 'Run, Tiberius! Can't you see? Look behind you!', and the fickle crowd starts to escape, suddenly terrified. But *he* swings his arm, with crime on his slavering lips and cruelty in his heaving lungs. Gracchus doesn't know what's happening, doesn't move from where he stands. *He* strikes his temple, and Gracchus falls without a sound; no cry demeans his noble character. Spattered with a brave man's grievous blood, *he* looks round as if he had performed a hero's exploit, and with a laugh holds out his murderous hand to be congratulated.

Rhetorica ad
Herennium
4.55.68

Figure 74. Statue base in Pentelic marble from Rome, late second century BC. Both inscriptions have been re-cut: 'Cornelia, daughter of Africanus, [mother] of the Gracchi' (late first century BC); 'the work of Tisicrates' (late second century AD).

Cornelia

Cornelia was the daughter of Scipio Africanus. She was about ten when her famous father died, and about seventeen when she was married to a distinguished senator called Tiberius Gracchus. She bore him twelve children, of whom three survived, two boys and a girl. After his death she didn't remarry—not even when the king of Egypt proposed to her—but devoted her life to her children's education. On one occasion a wealthy lady from Campania, who was a guest in her house, showed Cornelia her splendid jewellery. Cornelia made no comment till her children came in from school. 'These are my jewels,' she said.

Her daughter was married to Scipio Aemilianus, the destroyer of Carthage and Cornelia's nephew by adoption [fig. 73]. Her sons had the benefit of the best tutors and of Cornelia's own instruction, growing up with a combination of Greek culture and the traditional Roman will to succeed. 'How long,' she asked them, 'shall I be known as Scipio's daughter, rather than the mother of the Gracchi?' She soon got her wish.

Cornelia was about sixty when her eldest son, as tribune of the people, was beaten to death by the senators. Scipio Aemilianus approved of the killing of his brother-in-law. He quoted Homer: 'So perish whoso else may do such deeds.' Soon afterwards he was found dead, and the Roman People were not sorry. Nobody knows whether the death was natural or not, but at the time some suspected his wife (it was not a happy marriage), or even her mother, Cornelia herself.

Both sides in the Gracchan crisis claimed that Scipio's daughter agreed with them. Extracts happen to survive from alleged letters of Cornelia to her younger son, pleading with him not to 'throw the state into turmoil and confusion' by seeking the tribunate; the phraseology betrays their tendentious origin. The Roman People knew where she stood: after her death, at a time when the oligarchic stranglehold was temporarily loosened, they put up a bronze statue to her, with the simple inscription 'Cornelia, mother of the Gracchi'.

But even that was censored. When the marble statue-base was discovered in 1878, it became clear that the original inscription had been chiselled out; the new one [fig. 74] emphasises her descent from Scipio, and pointedly omits the word 'mother'.

A fateful line had been crossed. Never before had the Republic's political strife gone so far as murder. And it was not just a single assassination but a deliberate act of terror. About three hundred of Gracchus' supporters—Roman citizens, of course—were beaten to death, and their bodies, with that of Gracchus himself, thrown into the Tiber as if they were self-evidently traitors to the Republic. Other citizens were arrested later and put to death without trial.

For the Roman People, it was sacrilege as well as murder. Their ancestors 360 years before had forced the concession from the patricians that the tribunes of the *plebs* were sacrosanct. Lay a finger on one of them and your life was forfeit to Ceres, the archaic goddess of law (p. 68 above). A newly dominant oligarchy had shown how much they cared about that. When the Sibylline books told the consuls to appease 'ancient Ceres', they sent a deputation to make offerings at her cult site in Sicily, ignoring the old plebeian temple of Ceres, Liber and Libera below the Aventine. (Liber was already tamed, his worshippers policed by the urban praetor.) Now law and liberty were merely a matter of what the Senate decided.

Twelve years later that principle was made explicit, to justify the death of another popular hero. The crime of Gaius Gracchus, Tiberius' younger brother, was to have passed a law as tribune guaranteeing grain distribution to the urban populace at a fixed price, using public revenues to subsidise the cost. This time, the Senate waited till he was out of office. Then it passed a resolution 'that the consul should see to it that the Republic be not harmed'. The Senate was not a legislative body, its resolutions were not legally binding; this was effectively a unilateral declaration of martial law against a popular ex-tribune of whose policies the Senate disapproved. The consul of 121 BC raised a military force, including a contingent of Cretan archers, and announced that whoever should bring him Gracchus' head would have its weight in gold. Again, the corpses of citizens were thrown into the Tiber, three thousand of them this time. In a move reminiscent of Orwell's *1984*, the Senate ordered a temple of Concordia to be built in the Forum.

The first Roman historians—senators, writing at the time of the Hannibalic War—had drawn attention to two occasions in the early Republic when demagogues aiming at tyranny had been put to death. The first was Spurius Cassius in 486 BC, the second Spurius Maelius in 440 BC, and in each case (so they said) the People had been willing to accept the Senate's judgement. That was quite anachronistic, since the Senate in the sense they understood it had not yet been created in the fifth century BC; but they were writing at the end of the third century, in Greek for an international readership, and they wanted to show that the Roman constitution was a stable aristocracy which had the trust of the People.

Now, however, following old Cato's revolutionary example, senatorial historians were writing in Latin, for an internal audience that had to be persuaded of the merits of the new hard-line Roman oligarchy. As they now told it, the sedition of Cassius had consisted of bribing the people with land distribution (one version even made him a tribune of the *plebs*), and that of Maelius had been the supply of cheap corn. History teaches by example, and these would be the 'historical' precedents for the killing of the Gracchi. Political myths too were a part of the Roman story-world.

But the Roman People were not persuaded. They saw the new Concordia temple as a monument to Discord, honouring the slaughter of citizens. They put up their own shrines, statues of the martyred brothers at the places where they died, and brought offerings and made sacrifice as if to gods. Cornelia approved. 'My dead have worthy tombs,' she said, for all that their bodies were unburied, washed out to sea like the refuse of the city.

The old lady didn't come to Rome much, but guests were always welcome at her country house, where her table talk was a historical education in itself. She used to speak of her father, Scipio Africanus—and also of her sons, what they did and what happened to them, as if they were men of the early days of Rome. For that was what she had brought them up to be.

8.3   SALLUST, CICERO AND CIVIL WAR

This book is not a political history of Rome. But myth and history interconnect, and never more so than in this chapter and the next, where the real protagonists of real events become mythic figures in their own right, and some of them even gods. One way to make sense of an immensely complex story is to try to see it through the eyes of the Roman People.

Here they are in 111 BC, listening in indignation as their tribune describes the aristocratic clique who now control Rome:

> 'They killed Tiberius Gracchus because they said he was going to make himself king, and they punished the Roman *plebs* afterwards. After the slaughter of Gaius Gracchus and [his ally] Marcus Fulvius, many plebeians again were killed in prison. And it wasn't the law that ended either massacre, but just their own inclination. All right, let's say that giving the plebeians back their property is the same as aiming at kingship! Let's call any action legal that can only be avenged by spilling more citizen blood! . . .
>
> Who are these people who have taken over the Republic? Criminals with blood on their hands, insanely avaricious, utterly guilty but utterly arrogant, men who use honesty, reputation, loyalty—everything, good or bad—for profit. They've killed your tribunes, they've set up unjust tribunals, and they've strengthened their own position by slaughtering *you*!'

Sallust Jugurthine War 31.7–8 and 12–13

The historian who gave the tribune that speech was Gaius Sallustius, whom the English-speaking world calls 'Sallust'. He had been a tribune of the *plebs*

Nine Tribunes' Pyre

Somewhere near the Circus Maximus, probably on the Aventine side, was a place marked with white stones called 'Nine Tribunes' Pyre'. It was where the People had cremated nine plebeian tribunes treacherously murdered by the patricians in the early Republic.

The oligarchs of the second century BC didn't like that story, so senatorial historians invented other explanations. One version made them *military* tribunes, heroically fallen in battle against the Volsci. Another, inspired by the events of 133 BC, kept the political context but reversed the moral. According to this version, when Spurius Cassius was plotting to become tyrant in 486, nine out of the ten tribunes of the *plebs* supported him, and planned to stay in office; the tenth, Publius Mucius, protected the 'common liberty' by burning them all alive [Colour plate 16]; thereafter, that was the penalty for tribunes who failed to get successors elected.

The contemporary message was clear. To stay in office as tribune, as Tiberius Gracchus was proposing to do by standing for re-election, was treason punishable by death; and Publius Mucius the tribune had taken just the sort of decisive action which Publius Mucius (Scaevola) the consul had refused to take against Gracchus. Learn the lesson, citizens. . .

himself, at a moment of acute political tension; indeed, he had seen the enraged populace burn down the Senate house.

Sallust's testimony is important for us, because otherwise we see the tragic history of the fall of the Republic from the opposite point of view, in the works of Cicero, whose experience was quite different.

Marcus Cicero was a great man. Thanks to the survival of his speeches, his correspondence, and especially his philosophical dialogues, it is to him above all that we owe the civilised values of liberal humanism that have made Western culture what it is. He was also—when it came to the crunch—a brave man, who gave his life for the Roman Republic. But the fact remains that the turning point of his political career (pp. 203–4 below) was when he put down an attempted *coup d'état* by employing the same tactic the Senate had used against Gaius Gracchus—a resolution giving the consul *carte blanche*, in order to justify the execution of Roman citizens without trial.

Cicero's ideal republic, as sketched in his dialogue *On the Laws*, was one governed by a morally exemplary Senate whose resolutions would have the force of law, respected and obeyed by a disciplined populace. He did allow tribunes of the *plebs*, but the dialogue form enabled him to qualify the concession by making the other two interlocutors argue for the abolition of the tribunate as a necessarily seditious institution.

The rival notions of what the Republic was—or should be—were defined in Greek as *demokratia* and *aristokratia*. Latin had no equivalent abstract nouns: Romans referred not to the concepts but to the individuals who believed in them, respectively *populares* (from *populus*, Greek *demos*, 'the people') and *optimates* (from *optimi*, Greek *aristoi*, 'the best'). The Greek terms are both problematic in modern English—'democracy' because it is now necessarily a term of approval, 'aristocracy' because its meaning is now restricted to 'noble birth'. What the *optimates* laid claim to was not just social pre-eminence but moral excellence.

That claim wasn't easy to substantiate. Even Cicero admitted that his ideal republic didn't quite correspond to the contemporary reality. As for Sallust, he had a clear view about the moral corruption of the Roman elite: it was a result of Rome's new position as a world power. Once the destruction of Carthage removed the last chance of any external threat,

> growing love of money, and the lust for power which followed it, engendered every kind of evil. Avarice destroyed honour, integrity, and every other virtue, and instead taught men to be proud and cruel, to neglect religion, and to hold nothing too sacred to sell. . . One small group of oligarchs had everything in its control alike in peace and war—the treasury, the provinces, public offices, all distinctions and triumphs. The people were burdened with military service and poverty, while the spoils of war were snatched by the generals and shared with a handful of friends.

Sallust Catiline 10.3–4, Jugurthine War 41.7

Sallust never dignified the oligarchy with the flattering title of *optimates*. For him the struggle was between the People and the Senate, or the People and the nobility. As a historian he was pointedly neutral, but at least we can hear the *popularis* case through the speeches of his characters.

It was clear to Sallust that this murderous party strife—something quite unprecedented in Roman experience—had led directly to the civil wars that were still raging as he wrote. When political disputes were settled by violence, it was only a matter of time before armies were used. That moment had come in 88 BC, two years before Sallust was born and when Cicero was eighteen. The gods marked it with a terrifying portent. Out of a cloudless sky came the sound of a trumpet, loud and shrill and mournful. The *haruspices* said it marked the passing of an age.

By then Rome had an eastern empire. Greece (since 145 BC) and western Asia Minor (since 129) were now Roman provinces; but both were lost to the forces of king Mithridates of Pontus in 88. The Romans had only just survived the invasion of the German Cimbri and Teutoni into north Italy in 102–1, and the revolt of their own Italian allies in 90–89. The commanders who brought Rome victory in those two wars were respectively Gaius Marius, scourge of the nobility and hero of the People, and Lucius Sulla, a ruthless aristocrat. Which of them should now command against Mithridates? Sulla was consul in 88, but amid rioting the tribune Sulpicius proposed, and the People enthusiastically endorsed, a law giving the command to Marius.

Sulla left Rome. He went to Campania, where the last of the allied rebels were being besieged. He marched the army north and took the city by force. There were battles in the streets,

Appian *Civil Wars*
1.58.259

> the first regularly fought in Rome with bugle and standards in full military fashion, no longer like a mere faction fight. To such extremity of evil had the recklessness of party strife progressed among them.

Sulpicius was killed, Marius exiled. Sulla abolished the powers of the tribunate, then left to deal with Mithridates. Five years later he returned, renewed the civil war, and after a final victory at the gates of Rome enforced his will as permanent dictator.

At the south-west corner of the Campus Martius was a large open area called the Villa Publica. Every Roman citizen knew it as the place where his citizenship was defined every five years, when he made his sworn declaration to the censors; it was also where he queued to obtain the citizen's privilege of the subsidised grain ration introduced by Gaius Gracchus. Into this symbolic space, surrounded by his soldiers, Sulla brought seven thousand Roman citizens who had surrendered to him after the battle of the Colline Gate. Then he walked to the nearby temple of Bellona the war-goddess, where the Senate had been summoned. As the meeting began, so did the killing. The only person unmoved by the screams was the Dictator. 'Pay no attention,' he told the horrified senators. 'It's just a few traitors whom I have ordered to be dealt with.'

The Third Founder

About 114 BC the Cimbri and the Teutoni left their sea-girt territory in northern Jutland and headed south, a huge wagon train with thousands of fighting men and their families, looking for rich lands to conquer and settle. For twelve years they roamed round Europe, plundering as they went, defeating whatever armies the anxious Romans sent out against them (113, 109, 107 and 105 BC). At last they decided to invade Italy, the Teutoni from Provence, the Cimbri over the Alps by the Brenner Pass.

The defeated Roman generals were all aristocrats. Their failure, and the unsatisfactory conduct of the war against Jugurtha in north Africa, weakened for the first time the political dominance the Roman oligarchy had enjoyed since the killing of Tiberius Gracchus. In 108 BC, in what Sallust called 'the first challenge to the arrogance of the nobility', the People elected to the consulship an ex-tribune of humble origin but outstanding military competence. He was Gaius Marius of Arpinum, and his election speech in Sallust is one of the historian's great *popularis* set-pieces.

Marius was re-elected again and again—the soothsayer who had predicted a great destiny for him turned out, improbably, to have got it right. In his fourth consulship he destroyed the Teutoni at Aix-en-Provence, while his aristocratic colleague fled before the Cimbri and lost all the territory between the Alps and the Po. In his fifth consulship the two of them together destroyed the Cimbri at the great battle of the Raudian Fields; the exact site isn't known, but what matters is that it was in Italy. If Marius had failed, the horde could have swept south and taken Rome as Brennus and his Gauls had done nearly three centuries before.

So if Camillus had been the second founder of Rome, Marius was the third. So said the Roman People, pouring libations to their hero as if to a god.

After that, alas, it was downhill all the way. Marius' sixth and seventh consulships, in 100 and 86 BC, were marked by political atrocities which showed that *populares* too were capable of brutal murder. His Greek biographer put it down to his lack of education. 'If Marius could have been persuaded to sacrifice to the Greek Muses and Graces, he would not have put the ugliest crown possible upon a most illustrious career, nor have been driven by the blasts of passion, ill-timed ambition and insatiable greed upon the shore of a most cruel and savage old age.'

After that, he put up his lists, introducing a new word, 'proscription', into the vocabulary of power politics. Anyone whose name was on the list was condemned to death, and his killer would be rewarded. The first list had eighty names, the next day 220 more were added, and so on; the final total was 4,700. Particularly prominent victims were tortured to death in public as an example to the citizens. Others were just killed in the street, their heads severed and taken to Sulla as proof to claim the prize money. He had the heads set up in the Forum, on the Rostra, even in the public atrium of his own house—wherever there were citizens to see the ghastly trophies and learn the lesson of fear.

Marius, the People's hero and the saviour of Rome, had died five years before. Sulla had his ashes thrown in the river, and dismantled the monuments on the Capitol that the grateful People had set up for his victories over the Cimbri and Teutoni. It was as if he had never been.

Having sorted out the constitution on optimate lines—the tribunate emasculated, only senators to sit on juries—Sulla then resigned his dictatorship. 80 BC was the first year of the restored Republic, with Sulla as one of the consuls. In the Forum, the rotting heads were taken down (though their memory would last a lifetime) and the lawcourts were again in session.

In that year Marcus Cicero took on his first public case: at twenty-six, he defended a man who had been framed for murder by one of Sulla's freedmen. Of course (he said) Sulla knew nothing of it. Of course every right-thinking citizen approved of the present political situation, the victorious cause of the nobility. He was glad that the power struggle between the lower orders and their betters had resulted in everyone having their proper rank and honour restored. He understood that severe measures had to be taken against those who had defied reason. But if the result was a moral chaos where any jumped-up hanger-on of the winning side could get rich by having an innocent man condemned, the winning side would not keep their power long. The nobility must be 'watchful and upright, strong and merciful'. If not, they would have to give way to people who did have those virtues.

Throughout his career, Cicero stood for law and ethics against force and violence. He was indeed an optimate, a believer in *aristokratia*, but when the oligarchy was indefensibly corrupt, as it was between the middle 70s and the middle 60s BC, he threw his weight behind the *popularis* reformers because that was where the moral high ground lay.

So now he ended his courageous speech with a plea for the wounds of the Republic to be healed, addressing the senators on the jury-benches but aware too of the citizens in the Roman Forum, crowding round to hear his peroration. His message was a simple one, that barbarous behaviour damaged the Roman People:

> Gentlemen of the jury, drive that cruelty out of our city, let it not survive in this Republic! The evil it brings with it is not just that so many citizens have been foully

done away with; it is also that moderate people, habituated to disasters, have lost their sense of pity. For when we hourly see or hear of some atrocity, the habit of outrage causes even the mildest of us to lose every sense of human sympathy.

Cicero Pro Roscio Amerino 154

A bleak message for a bleak time. In the long run it proved all too accurate, as the power struggle, and its brutalising effects, in due course brought back civil war and more proscriptions. Thirty-seven years on, there would be severed heads on the Rostra again, with Cicero's prominent among them. And next time it would be not the nobility but the People's own champions who put them there.

8.4   THE PEOPLE'S HISTORIAN

Within eight years of Sulla's death, when the 'aristocracy' he put in power had proved itself unworthy to rule unchecked, the People's tribunes got their powers back. One of the *popularis* agitators who fought for that outcome was a historian, Licinius Macer, who provided a new narrative of Rome's story from the People's perspective. His work has not survived, but we know his politics from the tribune's speech Sallust gave him, and we can gauge his influence on the Roman historical tradition from the way the extant historians used him alongside their optimate source texts to produce a political history of the early Republic polarised by just the same issues as post-Sullan Rome.

There was no divine providence in Licinius' history. Even the foundation story itself was driven by the all too recognisably human motives of lust, betrayal and murderous political strife.

As Licinius told it, Rhea Silvia was indeed ravished in the grove of Mars, but the armed figure who overpowered her in the misty dawn light was her uncle Amulius. When the twins were abandoned, it was not a she-wolf that found and suckled them, but a shepherdess called Lykaina (Greek for 'she-wolf'); this one example of human kindness was evidently an ancestress of the plebeian Licinii, and thus of the historian himself.

The twins quarrelled over who should rule; their respective followers fought it out like the political thugs of contemporary Rome, and Remus was killed in the fighting. In despair at the triumph of ruthless violence, Faustulus the herdsman, who had brought up the twins, rushed unarmed into the riot to find his own death.

So Romulus was king, until he too was killed. The sudden darkness that fell when he was addressing the People was not supernatural, but an eclipse of the sun. The senators took the opportunity they had been waiting for: they murdered Romulus, then quickly cut up his body and hid the pieces under their togas, so that when the light returned there was no trace of the king. As for Iulius Proculus' story of the appearance of the deified Romulus (p. 147 above), that was just a lie, the Senate's cynical manipulation of the Roman People. Right from the beginning, that was how it had been.

Licinius' reading of Romulus' death could be given an optimate spin by alleging that Romulus had become tyrannical, surrounding himself with a bodyguard, and that the senators' action was a heroic vindication of freedom, like the killing of Tiberius Gracchus. In 67 BC, when the People were about to vote a special five-year military command to their new hero Pompeius ('Pompey the Great'), one of the consuls was nearly torn to pieces by the crowd when he said that if Pompey emulated Romulus he would not escape Romulus' fate. Licinius had made the old legend frighteningly topical.

We don't know how Licinius dealt with the foundation of the Republic, but it's clear that what mattered most to him was the exploitation of the poor by the arrogant patricians. In the narratives of both Livy and Dionysios, the first act of the 'struggle of the orders' begins in 495 BC, when a dreadful figure stumbles into the Roman Forum. Filthy, emaciated, his back a mass of recent scars, he tells his story to the People. He is a Roman citizen, a veteran of the Republic's wars who fell into debt when his farm was destroyed by the Sabines; after all he owned had gone to pay the interest, he himself was seized by the creditor and subjected to a regime of hard labour, imprisonment and frequent floggings. Popular indignation and senatorial intransigence lead to the secession of the *plebs* the following year, which in turn results in the establishment of the tribunate.

Not surprisingly, a Licinius is named as a member of the founding college of tribunes. Licinius Macer was well known for writing up his own ancestors; he also claimed that a Licinius had been the first plebeian consul in 366 BC, but that didn't make it into the canonical version.

More important, the issue of rural hardship as a result of war was an urgent issue in Licinius Macer's own time. Many small farmers had had their land ruined in the war of the allies, or in the Sullan civil war, or in the slave-revolt of Spartacus, who from 73 to 71 BC had a force of up to seventy thousand men at large in Italy. And there is good evidence that the creditors were just as brutal, and redress just as hard to come by, as in that dramatic fifth-century scene from Licinius' history. He too, like his optimate predecessors, made the past an exemplary mirror for the present.

Two centuries before (pp. 153–4 above), the Romans had prided themselves on being a race of small farmers, tough and self-sufficient. Now the small farmers were fleeing to the city, or facing the prospect, if they stayed on the land, of permanent debt-servitude to the big landowners. For desperate peasants far from the main road, the news that filtered through on market days was not encouraging. Yes, the tribunes had got their powers back; but now their main ally was away fighting in the East (Pompey 'the Great', sorting out Sulla's unfinished business with Mithridates), and an optimate backlash was hindering the reformers' programme.

Spartacus

For us, Spartacus is one of the most powerful of Roman myths. The Romans themselves, however, admired him only in the way they admired Hannibal, with the respect and fear due to a dangerous enemy. He could not become a hero until the institution of slavery began to be questioned.

It was Montesquieu in the 1730s who declared that Spartacus' insurrection was 'the most legitimate war that has ever been waged'. According to Karl Marx in 1861, Spartacus was 'a real representative of the proletariat of ancient times'. The revolutionaries who broke away from the German Socialist Party in 1917 called themselves the *Spartakusbund*, and the murder of Rosa Luxemburg and Karl Liebknecht in the attempted revolution of 1919 confirmed Spartacus as a Communist symbol. Stalin announced in 1933 that 'the great slave-uprisings of the declining Roman republic annihilated the slave-owner class and the slave-owner society', and until the Twentieth Party Congress in 1956 any Soviet scholar who queried that piece of historical wishful thinking did so at the risk of his life.

Arthur Koestler, who left the Party in 1938, wrote his Spartacus novel *The Gladiators* the following year as a disillusioned analysis of failed revolution:

> The democratic opposition of Rome had been defeated because of the incapacity of its leaders; the refugees had destroyed themselves with inner discord. The opponents' weakness, not its own strength, had once again—and how often before!—saved the doddering regime which had lived beyond its time. And how many times more in the course of centuries to come will the pitiable spectacle be repeated?

It looked quite different to the American novelist Howard Fast, who was still a loyal Party member when he wrote *Spartacus* in 1951:

> The heroes of this story cherished freedom and human dignity, and lived nobly and well. I wrote it so that those who read it, my children and others, may take strength for our own troubled future and that they may struggle against oppression and wrong—so that the dream of Spartacus may come to be in our own time.

And that was certainly the message of Stanley Kubrick's great movie (1960), which was based on Fast's novel.

Spartacus did not, in fact, end up crucified. He died fighting in the last battle, and his body was never found. But the crucifixions themselves were all too factual—six thousand of them, one every twenty-two paces along the great main road from Capua to Rome, each hanging corpse a reminder of the price to be paid for challenging authority.

It is even possible that some of the crucified were Roman citizens. The most reliable account of the insurrection clearly states that 'free men from the countryside'—turnip-eaters in the old Roman tradition—chose to throw in their lot with the rebel slaves. No one knows how many made that desperate choice. That any did so is ominous enough, evidence of deprivation and despair that proves the Marxist reading at least partly true.

Figure 75

Marius' nephew, a bold and brilliant young senator called Gaius Iulius Caesar, had replaced the old hero's battle trophies on the Capitol, and then, as president of the murder court, encouraged the prosecution of those who had killed proscription victims. That was a welcome defiance of Sulla's ghost, and Sulla's heirs. But since Caesar was a patrician, ineligible for the tribunate, he would have to fight his way to the consulship to make any serious impact—and surely the optimate establishment would stop him before he could get that far?

By the end of 64 BC, having comprehensively defeated Mithridates, Pompey was organising no fewer than three eastern kingdoms—Bithynia, Pontus and Syria—as tribute-paying Roman provinces. The revenues of the Roman treasury would be more than doubled. Now that it was financially responsible to do so, the tribunes of 63 BC, with the help of Caesar and other well-wishers, brought forward a carefully planned legislative programme of debt relief and land redistribution. It failed. The oratory of Cicero, now consul, swayed the city voters against the tribunes' bills, and all over Italy the rural poor drew the inevitable conclusion. They would get no justice by relying on politics.

These were the turnip-eaters, the frugal farmers who once had defined the Republic. Now they rose in arms—not, they insisted, against the Republic itself, but against the brutal faction of the rich and powerful which seemed to have hijacked it. The precedent they quoted was the armed secession of the *plebs* against the patricians in the early years of the Republic. Licinius Macer's history had taught them that.

Figure 75. Marius, Caesar and Octavius.

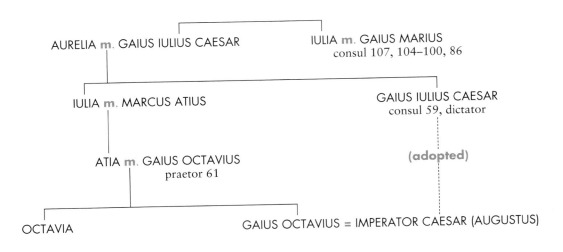

The best organised of the risings was in north Etruria (modern Tuscany), and it had a formidable commander. Lucius Catilina ('Catiline') was a ruthless and ambitious aristocrat with a sinister past. Having failed three times to get himself elected consul, in the autumn of 63 BC he declared himself 'the leader and standard-bearer of the oppressed' and fled his creditors in Rome to put himself in command of the Etruscan insurrection. 'Standard-bearer' was no mere figure of speech: he took with him not only the *fasces* of military command but also a standard with a silver eagle, which had once been carried in Marius' war against the Cimbri.

This civil war was short but bloody. Of Catiline's eight or ten thousand men, only a quarter had proper weapons. But they fought the government forces with desperation, and not one was taken prisoner. Three thousand were killed; Catiline's head was taken back to Rome.

His friends in the city were to have mounted a coup, but they were betrayed, arrested, and put to death without trial. Caesar, who argued against the executions, was surrounded by Cicero's bodyguards with drawn swords. They looked to the consul for the signal to strike, but Cicero shook his head, and Caesar escaped. Despite what he had just done, Cicero believed in the rule of law. But the very fact that a political opponent could have been killed at the consul's nod shows all too clearly what the Republic had become.

.5   CAESAR AND SON

Since it is the purpose of this chapter to look at the fall of the Republic from the People's point of view, we need to beware of the literary influence of Cicero. The survival of his political and forensic speeches, and later of his correspondence and his philosophical dialogues as well, means that we are uniquely well informed about this period—but also that we inevitably see it through Cicero's eyes. He always believed that his decisive action as consul in 63 BC had saved the Republic, and that Catiline and the conspirators were self-evidently enemies of the state. It takes a conscious effort to remember that there was another way of looking at it.

One man who made that effort was E.S. Beesly, scholar and socialist. He was writing in 1865 in the second issue of *The Fortnightly Review*, a journal founded with the aim of 'aiding Progress' by a group which included Walter Bagehot, George Eliot, T.H. Huxley and Antony Trollope:

> The little army of Catiline died round their leader like the Spartan Three Hundred round Leonidas at Thermopylae. Even Sallust cannot withhold his admiration, and rises into a genuine enthusiasm as he describes the closing scene. 'All wounded in front; not a man taken alive; Catiline himself gasping out his life ringed round with the corpses of his foemen.' The world has generally a generous word for the

memory of a brave man dying for his cause, be that cause what it will. But for Catiline none. The execrations of nineteen centuries lie piled on the grave of the successor of the Gracchi and the forerunner of Caesar. It is not good to make a literary man your enemy.

You can be an admirer of Cicero and still feel that there is truth in that.

Caesar was now openly the leader of the People's cause. Elected *pontifex maximus*, he was their spokesman for the gods; on earth too, when he became consul in 59 BC against furious optimate opposition, it seemed that the People's cause had triumphed. 'Groan all you like,' he taunted his opponents in the Senate; 'now that I've got what I wanted, I'll trample all over you.' The tomb of Catiline was decked with flowers. The land distribution programme was voted through. Caesar was given a special command for a war of conquest in Gaul.

Figure 75 (p. 202)

Caesar's niece was married to a senator called Octavius. They had two children, a girl and a boy, and they lived at Velitrae, 20 miles or so down the Via Appia. Little Gaius Octavius was three when the family came to Rome for the ceremonial first day of Caesar's consulship. As the solemn procession of senators made its way to the altar of Jupiter Best and Greatest on the Capitol, Caesar and Cicero happened to be in conversation. Cicero had had a strange dream the night before. He had seen a young boy let down from heaven on a golden chain, and Jupiter presenting the boy with a whip. Suddenly Cicero caught sight of Caesar's great-nephew trotting beside him. 'Why, that's the boy I saw!'

So at least the story was told later, and there were others like it. What is certain is that Caesar took a great interest in the boy's education, and provided in his will that if—as turned out to be the case—he died without a son of his own, Gaius Octavius should be his heir and bear his name. Cicero would live just long enough to see how the young Caesar used his whip.

When little Octavius was four, the People sent Cicero into exile for putting citizens to death without trial. When he was five, the *optimates* regained the political initiative and got Cicero recalled. He was ten when the radical *popularis* Publius Clodius was murdered, the People burned down the Senate house as his funeral pyre, and Pompey, once the darling of the *populares*, was elected 'sole consul' to restore order.

Octavius was a boy of twelve when Caesar—who had conquered, lost and reconquered the whole of what is now France and Belgium, and taken Roman legions across the Rhine into Germany and across the Channel into Britain—was proposing to come back directly from his military command to a second consulship. The *optimates* wouldn't have it. The tribunes who put Caesar's case were threatened with execution by senatorial decree, and fled the city. Pompey was entrusted with the defence of the Republic. Caesar declared that he would defend himself against his enemies' insults, restore the plebeian tribunes to the dignity they deserved and liberate the Roman People from the domination of an oligarchic faction. The next time Gaius Octavius saw his great-uncle, the world would be at war.

The Rubicon is a small river, and it was a small bridge that took the Roman road over it, out of Caesar's provincial jurisdiction into Italy. When he reached it, Caesar stopped the carriage and got out. 'We can still go back,' he said to the group of officers who were with him. 'But once over that little bridge, every-thing will have to be done by force of arms. If we don't cross it, this is the beginning of disaster for me. If we do, it's the beginning of disaster for the world. But what a story we shall leave for posterity!'

As one version of the story told it later, they suddenly saw a figure of super-human size and shape sitting nearby, playing on a reed pipe. When some of the soldiers ran up to listen, it snatched a bugle from one of them, sprang forward to the river, and blew a mighty blast before crossing to the other side. Caesar threw off his hesitation. 'Let us go,' he said, 'where the portents of the gods and the villainy of our enemies call us. The die is cast!'

The first stage of the war was a duel between Rome's two greatest commanders. Pompey had extended the empire of the Roman People to the Euphrates, Caesar to the Atlantic. Only recently they had been allies against the senatorial establishment, bound by a marriage. But now the woman they both loved was dead, and Pompey had thrown in his lot with the oligarchs. The decisive encounter was in Thessaly in 48 BC. 'Strike at the face,' said Caesar to the men facing Pompey's cavalry. 'Those fancy aristocrats won't want their looks spoiled.' When it was all over, and six thousand Roman dead lay on the field of Pharsalus, it was not Pompey whom Caesar blamed. '*They* wanted this,' he said.

Pompey fled to Egypt, and was murdered as he stepped off the boat. The assassins took his head, expecting a reward from Caesar (who wept when they presented it, and had them executed). Meanwhile, on the shore

The vast trunk headless lies without a name.

That sombre epitaph for Pompey 'the Great' comes from the history of Asinius Pollio, who had served as an officer under Caesar in the civil war, and then, like Licinius Macer, as a tribune of the *plebs*. His vivid eye-witness accounts— for instance, the Rubicon and Pharsalus scenes—did much to create this part of Caesar's myth. As with Licinius, we know his work only from its traces in other authors, one of whom tells us that he aimed to write 'like a citizen'.

The second stage of the war (also witnessed by Pollio) presented a much starker ideological polarity: Caesar against the Republic. For so it was presented, once the *optimates* were free of Pompey's ambiguous support. Their leaders now were a Scipio and a Cato, the latter the great-grandson of Cato the Censor. We have already met Marcus Cato 'the younger' in Chapter 1, at the games of Flora (p. 6 above), leaving the audience to enjoy the strip show they were ashamed to call for in his presence. Cato was a man of conspicuous self-control and unbending principle, the moral conscience of politics. Even the Roman People reluctantly admired him, though his view of the Republic was not theirs.

This time, in 46 BC, the decisive encounter was at Thapsus in North Africa. Which of them won—Caesar, victorious in the battle, or Cato, who killed himself rather than outlive the Republic as he conceived it? It was Caesar's policy to pardon those who fought against him and survived; but 'the harsh spirit of Cato' (Pollio's phrase) could not accept the victor's clemency. For ever afterwards, Cato's stern virtue would be a challenge to Caesar's fame.

Figure 76

Marcus Brutus, Cato's nephew and son-in-law, *did* accept Caesar's clemency. His mother Servilia had been Caesar's mistress long before, and Caesar loved him like a son. But that mattered less to him than the stories of his ancestors—Lucius Brutus, who drove out Tarquin, and on his mother's side Servilius Ahala, who had killed a would-be tyrant. Once the civil war was over, Caesar dispensed with a bodyguard. 'It matters more to the Republic than to me that I should stay alive,' he said. 'There will be worse civil wars in future if anything happens to me.'

Figure 76. *Denarii* struck by Marcus Brutus in 54 BC. (*a*) Obverse, head of the goddess LIBERTAS; reverse, Lucius BRVTVS with two lictors and an attendant. (*b*) Portrait heads of Brutus' ancestors: obverse, Lucius BRVTVS; reverse, Servilius AHALA.

The Ides of March are come. Caesar falls with twenty-three wounds, one of them mortal. You too, Brutus? Fifty years later Ovid was reluctant to tell the story, but the goddess Vesta encouraged him:

'Fear not to mention the atrocious deed.
His murderers thought they saw the hero bleed,
But that was all appearance; as he lay,
I came, and snatched his fleeting soul away.
He was my sacred priest, to me the crime
Was really done, which was designed to him.
But now, in the celestial choir above,
He lives immortal near the throne of Jove. . .'

Ovid Fasti
3.699–703

The People riot at the funeral ('We will be revenged!'), and set up a hero-shrine as they had done for the Gracchi. Young Octavius, named in the will as Caesar's heir and adopted son, comes to claim his inheritance, his new name and his duty of vengeance. He is eighteen years old. At the games he celebrates for his father's victories—in the month now called 'July'—a comet blazes in the sky, the visible sign of Caesar as a god.

The assassins under Brutus and Cassius gather their forces in the East. Cicero, a brave man in a lost cause, tries to guide the restored Republic by the rule of law, as moderate *optimates* like himself understand it. Young Caesar sees it differently, and marches on Rome 'to free the Republic from the tyranny of a faction'; he becomes consul at nineteen. Six vultures are seen at the election, and twelve more when he addresses his father's veterans, combining the auguries of both Remus and Romulus. The eldest of the college of *haruspices* announces to the People that the age of kings is returning: they will all be slaves, and only he will escape it. As he falls silent, the gods send him his death.

Two months after his twentieth birthday, young Caesar is given supreme power by vote of the People, as Triumvir with Marcus Lepidus and Marcus Antonius ('Antony') in a joint dictatorship. Clemency is declared officially obsolete. 'The malice of those who have conspired against us, at whose hands Caesar suffered, cannot be mollified by kindness.' So the People's champions bring back the horrors of the age of Sulla—proscription lists, severed heads, murder rewarded by the state.

Among the grim trophies on the Rostra in December 43 BC were the head and hands of Cicero. Livy reports, and we can believe him, that the weeping citizens couldn't bear to look at them.

.6   APOLLO'S AGENT

In the victor's myth, the war against Brutus and Cassius was both just and pious: Caesar avenged his father and punished those who had killed Vesta's

Figure 77

priest, the *pontifex maximus*. The new god, Divus Iulius, was manifest in person at the final battle, grander and fiercer than in life as he pursued his murderers across the plains of Philippi. Brutus was a parricide, his death a matter for celebration in the public calendar.

The reality was messier. Brutus had struck for liberty, and fought for what he saw as the Republic. Those of his allies who survived fled to join Pompey's son Sextus, who held Sicily. There was rioting in the streets of Rome and civil war in Italy, in the name of freedom and the Republic. On the fourth anniversary of the Ides of March Caesar put to death three hundred senators and knights before the altar of Divus Iulius at Perugia. Or so it was believed, in a time of famine and despair. Sextus Pompey controlled the seas, and cut off the corn supply. Where were the gods? The new *pontifex maximus* was Lepidus,

Figure 77. *Denarius* struck by Brutus' legate Lucius Plaetorius Cestianus in Macedonia before the battle of Philippi. Obverse: head of Brutus, bearded, with the legends BRVTVS IMP(erator) and L. PLAET. CEST. Reverse: cap of liberty (*pilleus*) between two daggers, with the legend EID. MAR. ('Ides of March'). 'The men who fell at Philippi,' wrote Sir Ronald Syme in *The Roman Revolution* (1939), 'fought for a principle, a tradition, and a class—narrow, imperfect and outworn, but for all that the soul and spirit of Rome.' However, assassination of political opponents was a rather recent tradition at Rome; and there were other ways of defining the Republic's soul and spirit.

far away in Africa. 'Impious Caesar'—he was twenty-three and had not yet learned wisdom—masqueraded as Apollo while the People starved.

Apollo, of all gods! The People called him Apollo the Torturer, remembering Marsyas, the symbol of their liberty (p. 69 above). In distant Asia Minor Antony, the other victor of Philippi, was received by the Greeks in a Dionysiac procession of satyrs and bacchants. But the new master of Rome had no time for Liber Pater and his anarchic followers.

The People remembered Remus too. Thirty years earlier, Licinius Macer had had Remus killed in a political riot, by an unknown hand. Now, that was too easy an answer. With constant civil war, citizen fighting citizen, brother fighting brother, the death of Remus made sense only as a fratricide. A young poet who had fought and fled at Philippi imagined himself indignantly haranguing the citizen body. Why are they rushing again into civil war? What is it that drives them to such a crime? He demands an answer, but they stare back stupefied, saying nothing.

> That's how it is. What hounds the Romans is bitter fate
> And the crime of a brother's murder,

Ever since the blood of innocent Remus flowed into the earth,
A curse to his descendants.

Horace *Epodes*
7.17–20

But Caesar was lucky as well as ruthless. Helped by his boyhood friend Marcus Agrippa, who turned out to be a formidably effective military commander, he defeated Sextus Pompey in a difficult campaign which also saw Lepidus stripped of his triumviral power. Now the Roman world was divided between Caesar in the West and Antony in the East. Antony had married Caesar's sister Octavia, but she could not compete with Kleopatra, monarch of the last remaining Hellenistic kingdom and Antony's partner in both politics and love.

Kleopatra's capital Alexandria was the greatest city in the world, unrivalled in elegance and size and wealth and luxury. It boasted the tomb of Alexander the Great, and it was said that Caesar the dictator had even contemplated making it the capital of Rome's world empire. When Antony formally transferred provinces of the Roman People—Cyprus, Syria, Kyrene—into the authority of Kleopatra and her son, it began to look from Rome like a dangerous rival power. The triumvirate expired at the end of 33 BC, leaving Caesar and Antony with no constitutional basis for the power they each held. Something had to happen.

Antony divorced Octavia and organised his forces for an invasion of Italy; the queen of Egypt looked forward to holding court on the Capitol. Caesar was authorised as war leader by the whole population of Italy swearing personal allegiance to him. Rome declared war on Kleopatra.

The decisive engagement was fought at sea, off the eastern Adriatic coast at Actium, on 2 September 31 BC. Caesar was now consul, representing the Republic—People, Senate, Italy—against the alien forces of the East. Apollo the archer watched from his temple on the promontory. Kleopatra fled, followed by Antony, to make a last stand in Alexandria.

The following year, on the first day of the month not yet called August, Egypt was brought into the power of the Roman People. Annual thanksgiving sacrifices were instituted at the temple of Hope (*Spes*) 'because on this day Imperator Caesar, son of Divus Iulius, freed the Republic from dreadful danger'.

The civil wars were over; the Republic was saved; the wealth of Egypt enriched the treasury of the Roman People. And it was *their* victory. They gave Caesar power by law to appoint a Prefect to govern the new province in their name; there would be no senatorial proconsul in charge of Egypt, and no senator would even be allowed to visit it except by special permission.

Just over a century had passed since the senatorial oligarchy laid claim to its own interpretation of the Republic by assassinating a tribune of the *plebs*. Divus Iulius had gone to war to defend the tribunes' rights, and the *optimates* had killed him too. Now Caesar was the champion of popular liberty, restoring law and justice to the Roman People. As a patrician, he could not be elected tribune, but the People gave him by law the tribunes' sacrosanctity and the tribunes' powers.

Figure 78

209

'Finish, good lady; the bright day is done'

Kleopatra was Greek, or at least Macedonian. (Whether that counted as Greek was, and is, a controversial question.) She was the great-great-great-great-great-great-great-granddaughter of Ptolemaios son of Lagos ('Ptolemy'), the friend and companion of Alexander. When the great conqueror died and his empire fragmented, Ptolemy took Egypt, and hijacked the coffin of Alexander himself. Glorious Alexandria would provide his tomb, and inherit his power.

By the time Kleopatra became queen in 51 BC (she was seventeen), all the other 'successor-kingdoms' of Alexander's empire had become Roman provinces—Macedonia itself in 146, Pergamum in 129, Bithynia in 74, Syria and Pontus both in 63, Cyprus in 58. So the fall of Alexandria in 30 BC, and her own death, marked the end of a historic era. Two centuries later, a Syrian-Greek essayist called Loukianos ('Lucian') could refer without any sense of paradox to 'the whole history of the world, from the time when it first emerged from Chaos down to the days of Kleopatra of Egypt'. That was the end of history; what followed was just the Roman Empire.

Lucian was describing the potential repertoire of the mime-dancer, a form of spectacle in which the theatre-mad Alexandrians of Kleopatra's time were pre-eminent. A single virtuoso performer danced all the main roles, with supporting singers or actors to provide narrative or dialogue as necessary. How Kleopatra's own tragedy was staged may perhaps be detectable from the final narrative of Plutarch's *Life of Antony*.

Once Antony has fallen on his sword, 'a Roman by a Roman valiantly vanquish'd', Greek Plutarch turns to his Alexandrian sources (including at least one eye-witness account) to follow the fortunes of the queen and her two waiting-women, barricaded in the monumental tomb. Essentially, through Sir Thomas North's translation, it is Act 5 of *Antony and Cleopatra*—sometimes word for word, as in Charmion's proud dying speech:

> 'What work is here! Charmian, is this well done?'
> 'It is well done, and fitting for a princess
> Descended of so many royal kings.'

It's striking that the lines are given to a servant, and that there is no dying speech for the queen herself. (Shakespeare had to write his own.) That, I suggest, is because Plutarch's source knew the story from the stage, in a format where the words were secondary and the queen's death was *danced*.

'It is his profession,' wrote Lucian of the mime-dancer, 'to show forth human character and passion in all their variety; to depict love and anger, frenzy and grief, each in its due measure. Wondrous art!' The story of the last queen was worthy of that tragic ballet. In the Alexandrian theatre at least, no 'squeaking Cleopatra' boy'd her greatness.

Figure 78. Two coin issues of 28 BC. (a) Aureus (= 25 denarii). Obverse: head of Caesar with laurel wreath; legend IMP. CAESAR DIVI F. COS. VI ('Imperator Caesar, son of Divus [Iulius], consul for the sixth time'). Reverse: Caesar wearing a toga, seated on a curule chair, holding a scroll and with a box of scrolls at his feet; legend LEGES ET IVRA P.R. RESTITVIT ('restored laws and justice to the Roman People').
(b) Cistophorus (tetradrachm) from the Roman province of Asia. Obverse: head of Caesar with laurel wreath; legend IMP. CAESAR DIVI F. COS. VI LIBERTATIS P.R. VINDEX ('Imperator Caesar, son of Divus [Iulius], consul for the sixth time, champion of the liberty of the Roman People'). Reverse: Peace (PAX) and Bacchic cista, within laurel wreath.

Caesar's triumph took place on 13–15 August 29 BC, followed on 18 August by the dedication of the new temple to Divus Iulius. Caesar and his friend Agrippa—a plebeian, loved by the People and resented by the aristocracy—had already been elected as consuls for the first year (28 BC) of the restored constitution. The Senate and People marked the saving of the Republic by erecting in Caesar's honour a huge triumphal arch adjoining the new temple, and inscribing on it the names of every Roman who had ever celebrated a triumph, and every Roman who had ever held the consulship.

'The citizens gloried in your triumph and your victory, Imperator Caesar.' So wrote a practical man, an engineer who knew about artillery and aqueducts, the nearest we can get to the voice of the People. 'Freed from fear, the Roman People and the Senate were guided by your majestic thoughts and policies.'

What they did with that guidance is best described by Caesar himself, recording with pride at the end of his life one of the two culminating moments of his extraordinary career:

Figure 79

Figure 80

Figure 79. Reconstruction of the 29 BC triumphal arch by Guglielmo Gatti, showing the probable arrangement of the lists of triumphs (on the pilasters) and of consulships (the panels on the wall). The foundations, and a few architectural fragments, are all that remain of the arch, but we know from literary and numismatic evidence that it was decorated with trophies (notably ships' prows from the victory at Actium), that the central attic carried a bronze *quadriga*, and that on the two side attics bronze figures of Parthians handing back standards were added after Augustus' diplomatic settlement with Parthia in 19 BC.

Figure 81

Augustus *Res gestae* 34

In my sixth and seventh consulships [28–27 BC], after I had extinguished the civil wars, and at a time when with universal consent I was in complete control of affairs, I transferred the Republic from my power to the dominion of the Senate and the Roman People. For this service of mine I was named Augustus by decree of the Senate, and the doorposts of my house were publicly wreathed with laurel, and a civic crown was fixed over my door and a golden shield was set in the Curia Iulia, which, as attested by the inscription thereon, was given me by the Senate and the Roman People on account of my courage, clemency, justice and piety. After that time I excelled all in authority, although I possessed no more official power than others who were my colleagues in each magistracy.

It was conceived as a restoration of the *old* Republic, before politics had been turned into murder. The sovereign People elected their magistrates and passed their legislation, and peace and civil concord returned to Rome.

If the price of that was one man excelling all in authority, it was a price worth

Figure 82

paying. The poet Horace no doubt spoke for most Romans when he said 'I shall not fear riot or violent death while Caesar holds the world'. The 'civic crown' of oak leaves that was fastened over his door was the Republic's decoration for saving the lives of citizens.

The young Octavius who became Caesar at eighteen was now, at thirty-five, Caesar Augustus. Great men in the past had taken honorific names—Pompeius 'Magnus', Fabius 'Maximus'—but this, as Ovid says, was something different:

Ovid Fasti
1.607–614

> All these with titles merely human shine,
> But, Caesar, Jove's high name is joined to thine.
> *Augustus* is a word that does denote
> Whate'er majestic or divine is thought.
> All sacrifices are 'august' decreed,
> And temples, where those sacrifices bleed;
> On the same root our augury depends,
> And whatsoe'er Jove by his power defends.
> May he preserve thee, Caesar, to our states,
> And may oak garlands ever guard thy gates!

Figure 82. Bronze *sestertius* of about 16 BC. Obverse: oak-leaf crown flanked by laurel branches; legend OB CIVIS SERVATOS ('because of the saving of citizens'). Reverse: S.C for *senatus consulto* ('by decree of the Senate'), surrounded by the moneyer's name, TI(berius) SEMPRONIVS GRACCVS, and his office, IIIVIR AAAFF for 'triumuir aere argento auro flando feriundo' ('member of the Board of Three for casting and striking bronze, silver and gold'). The mint of Rome, closed during the civil wars, reopened in 23 BC. These mass-circulation issues conspicuously advertised the Senate's responsibility for bronze coinage—and in this case also the achievement of political harmony, the moneyer being a descendant of the man the senators had killed four generations before. Now the Senate acts with Augustus to protect the citizens of Rome.

The People had set up shrines to the martyred Gracchi, and their altar to the elder Caesar was now the centre of a great public cult, with its temple of Divus Iulius dominating the Forum. They took it for granted that the son of Divus Iulius too was in some sense divine, and that when his work on earth was done, like Romulus he would become a god.

At the historic meeting in January 27 BC, some senators had proposed that Caesar be given the name Romulus, as the new founder of Rome. But that was much too sensitive now that civil war had created an alternative Romulus, tyrannical and fratricidal (pp. 200 and 208 above); indeed, the proposer of the successful resolution was himself alleged to have had his brother killed during the proscriptions. 'Augustus' was a much subtler suggestion, alluding to the

foundation story only indirectly via a famous line in Ennius' epic poem: 'Since glorious Rome was founded with august augury.' The gods had sent the birds as a sign of their favour, not only to Romulus in the mythic past but to Caesar as well, when he came to free the Roman People from its oppressors (p. 207 above).

So the return to the old Republic was a re-foundation of Rome. More than that, it was a new Golden Age, presided over this time by Apollo. The god's magnificent new temple, next to Augustus' house on the Palatine, dominated the Roman skyline with its bright marble pediment and the bronze four-horse chariot above it. It looked down on a significantly empty space, where once the historic temple of Ceres, Liber and Libera had stood, with Flora's temple next to it. Both had been burned to the ground in the same year that Apollo gave Caesar the victory at Actium. On his return, Caesar piously restored no fewer than eighty-two temples, 'neglecting none that required restoration at that time'. Those of Liber and Flora were not among them. The new age would be a puritanical one, keeping away licentiousness just as Apollo had ordered nearly two centuries before (p. 169 above).

.7 THE FATHER OF HIS COUNTRY

Two poets express the moral seriousness of the time. Quintus Horatius Flaccus ('Horace'), whose lyric inspiration came from Liber, Faunus and the nymphs, turned to the high Pindaric style for his long sacerdotal meditation on piety, patriotism and the Roman virtues. *Dulce et decorum est pro patria mori. . .* 'The old lie', Wilfred Owen called it—but you can't blame Horace for the Somme, and his readers in the 20s BC knew what he meant. It's good to die defending your country, not fighting fellow-citizens in civil war. His question was, do we still have the stomach for it? Have we forgotten the shield that fell from heaven, and Vesta's eternal flame? Luxury, self-indulgence and neglect of the gods had brought the Romans a long way from the days of steadfast Regulus and the farmer-soldiers who conquered Hannibal:

> Time corrupts all. What has it not made worse?
> Our grandfathers sired sickly children; theirs
> Were weaker still—ourselves; and now our curse
> Must be to breed even more degenerate heirs.

Horace Odes 3.6.45–48

Meanwhile, his friend Publius Vergilius Maro ('Virgil') was writing the epic poem which would make Rome, and Caesar Augustus, immortal. Homeric in conception, an *Odyssey* and an *Iliad* combined in twelve books, Virgil's *Aeneid* tells the tale of pious Aeneas, ancestor of the house of Caesar, bringing his people and his gods from fallen Troy to the land of the Latins. In Book 8, having admired, with Evander at Pallantion, the hills and valleys that will one day be

Poets and Prophets

Virgil was confident that his great epic would live 'as long as Aeneas' descendants dwell beside the Capitol's unshaken rock'. Horace too was sure of posterity's fame 'as long as the *pontifex* with the silent Vestal goes up to the Capitol'. They were conscious of being not only poets but prophets (*uates*), with a public role, using their god-given talent to inspire as well as entertain.

The *uates* is privileged to narrate what happens in heaven and the underworld. So in the first and sixth books of the *Aeneid*, first Jupiter himself and then the dead Anchises prophesy the Romans' greatness. 'I have given them,' says the father of gods and men, 'empire without limit.' And they will be a very particular kind of people, as Anchises in Elysium reveals:

> 'Others, I have no doubt, will do better
> At making breathing figures out of metal
> Or giving lumps of marble living faces;
> They will be better orators, better astronomers;
> But you, Roman, remember, you are to rule
> The nations of the world: your arts will be
> To bring the ways of peace, be merciful
> To the defeated and smash the proud completely.'

That Rome was destined for world empire, and that her very nature was defined by contrast with the Greeks (for they of course are Anchises' 'others'), were familiar ideas during the period covered in this chapter—but before that they would have seemed very strange indeed.

Think of Novius Plautius, with his elegant mastery of an art and culture common to both Greeks and Latins, in his Roman workshop three hundred years before—what would *he* have made of Virgil's disparagement of craftsmanship in bronze? How would *he* have reacted to Horace's view that before the wars with Carthage the Romans were uncultured peasants?

> When Greece was captured, it took the fierce victor captive and brought the arts into rustic Latium. . . For it was only late that the Roman applied his intelligence to Greek pages, and in the peace after the Punic Wars began to ask what use Sophokles and Thespis and Aeschylus could be.

'Greek *pages*' gives the game away. Horace's idea of culture is defined by books and literature. Novius Plautius knew Sophokles all right (p. 95 above), but he probably didn't have a text; and if Horace could have seen the Ficoroni *cista*, he would have been utterly astonished by its inscription. By his time, all those marvellous bronzes had long been buried with their owners in the earth, waiting for the treasure-hunter and the archaeologist.

Horace was right to describe his poetry as 'a monument more lasting than bronze'. What he and Virgil represent is literary culture at its most authoritative. Their texts would be what school-children learned for over four hundred years, stamped on the memory of every literate person; and long after that they would be copied and re-copied by scribes and printers century after century, to be read by people who will never see the Vestal and the *pontifex* go up to the Capitol. The ideology they transmit defines what the world knows of Rome. But there was also a Rome of which they knew nothing, because it existed before their literary culture came into being. That is why books like this one are necessary.

Rome, Aeneas receives Rome's future history as a gift from his mother Venus. It is on the shield made for him by Volcanus, who knows what is to come: Ascanius' descendants, the kings of Alba; the she-wolf and the twins, the rape of the Sabine women and the treaty with Tatius; Porsenna, Horatius Cocles, Cloelia; the Gauls' assault on the Capitol; the Salii, priests of Mars, and the naked Luperci; the underworld, with Catiline hanging in Hell and Cato administering justice to the righteous; and in the centre is Caesar Augustus, his father's star on his forehead, leading the Senate and People to victory at Actium, and reviewing the subject nations of the world before the gleaming temple of Apollo.

> Such were the scenes Aeneas wondered at
> Upon this shield that was his mother's gift
> And Vulcan's handiwork; of the events
> He knew nothing, but what was represented
> Gave him great pleasure as upon his shoulder
> He took the fame and fates of his descendants.

Virgil Aeneid
8.729–731

As Aeneas shouldered the burden of Rome's future, so his descendant, at the other end of prophetic time, took on that of Rome's past. All the consuls and censors of the Republic, all the triumphs from Year One of the city, were listed on his triumphal arch in 29 BC. The huge Forum Augustum, begun probably in

Figure 80

Figure 83

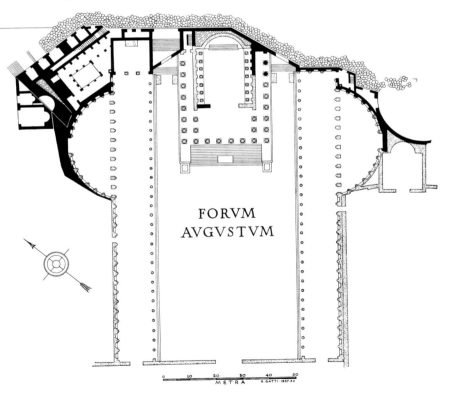

Figure 83. The Forum Augustum and the temple of Mars Ultor, reconstruction drawing by Guglielmo Gatti. Each of the two apses has a central niche with two columns, flanked by seven subsidiary niches on either side. That to the left, on the north-west side, was for Aeneas, no doubt with the fourteen kings of Alba from Ascanius to Numitor (p. 140 above); that to the right, on the south-east side, was for Romulus. If the reconstruction of the unexcavated part is accurate, there were sixteen niches south of each apse, plus two north of Aeneas' and four north of Romulus'—i.e., room for eighteen Julian ancestors on one side, and thirty-four war leaders on the other.

FORVM
AVGVSTVM

19 BC, featured two parallel rows of honorific statues, each with a panel beneath it recording the exploits of the man portrayed—on one side were Augustus' Julian ancestors, going back to Aeneas; on the other, the military commanders from Romulus onwards who had made the empire of the Roman People great. 'It is against their example,' he told the citizens, 'that you should judge both me, while I live, and the leading men of future ages.'

Similarly annotated statues adorned the splendid new Pantheon temple built by Agrippa in 25 BC. Here there were exemplary figures of a different kind, such as the pious plebeian who had looked after the Vestal Virgins in the flight from the Gauls (p. 127 above). How to do right by the gods was a matter of importance to the Roman People, who desperately wanted Augustus to be *pontifex maximus*. That couldn't happen while the present incumbent, the disgraced ex-Triumvir Lepidus, was still alive, but the new 'temple of all the gods', with twin statues of Augustus and Agrippa in the porch, helped to reassure an anxious populace. So too did the unprecedented insertion of Augustus into the public festival calendar.

Figure 84. Calendar from the Sabine city of Amiternum: the top half of the panel showing the months from July to December (compare Colour plate 6). The three 'large-letter' items at 11–13 October are MED for *Meditrinalia*, an ancient festival to do with the wine vintage, AVG for *Augustalia*, introduced on Augustus' return from the East in 19 BC, and FONT for *Fontinalia*, the festival of Fons, son of Janus (p. 162 above). The annotation for the *Augustalia* reads: 'Holiday by decree of the Senate, because on this day Imperator Caesar Augustus entered the city from the overseas provinces, and an altar was set up to Fortuna the Bringer-Back [*Fortuna Redux*].'

Figure 85. Cross-roads altar, 7 BC. To the left, the *Genius* of Augustus, wearing a toga and with head veiled; to the right, the Lares, each with a drinking-horn, and between them two laurel branches, as at the door of Augustus' house. The first line of the inscription (*ILS* 3613) has the dedication 'To the Augustan Lares...', presumably followed by '...and the *Genius* of Augustus' in the damaged part (the G is just detectable); then follow the names of the four *magistri* of the *uicus*, of which Q. Rubrius Pollio and L. Aufidius Felix are still legible. The bottom line announces that they were the first *magistri* of the *uicus* to enter office on the Kalends of August—i.e. the first in Augustus' new arrangement, of which the new altar is itself a sign.

When Lepidus eventually died in 13 BC, a huge and enthusiastic electorate voted Augustus into office as the chief religious authority of Rome. The archive of the *pontifices*, attesting the gods' interventions in mortal affairs (p. 121 above), was expanded and published in a huge new eighty-book edition going back to Aeneas. The Sibylline books were also edited, in this case for expurgation rather than expansion (two thousand less 'reliably' prophetic volumes were publicly burned in the Forum), and transferred from Jupiter's temple on the Capitol to Apollo's temple on the Palatine. Like the civil and the military, so too the sacred history of Rome was incorporated into the Augustan present.

Virgil's Jupiter had prophesied a new Rome free from fratricidal strife, where the deified Romulus and his brother Remus together would give justice to the People; the allusion to Augustus and his constant partner Agrippa was unmis-

Figure 86. Domestic shrine in one of the wealthiest houses in Pompeii ('the house of the Vettii'): the togate *Genius* stands between the two Lares with their drinking-horns. (The snake represents the *genius* of the place.)

221

takable. But Agrippa died in 12 BC, on campaign, having done more than anyone to help Augustus 'bring the world under the empire of the Roman People'. By then Virgil was dead too, and Augustus was fifty years old, no longer the wondrous youth of the *Eclogues* and the *Georgics*. It was time for a more paternal image.

In 8 BC Augustus held a census of the Roman People. It was a ritual cleansing of the citizen body, as a bull, a ram and a boar were led three times round the assembled citizens in the Campus Martius and brought to the altar of Mars for sacrifice. It had last been done twenty years before, in the year law and justice were restored (p. 211 above). Then, Caesar and Agrippa had presided together, and made the prayer for the safety and prosperity of the Roman People. This time, Caesar Augustus did it alone.

As part of his census, Augustus organised the city of Rome into fourteen administrative districts (*regiones*), each the responsibility of an aedile or a tribune of the *plebs*, and 265 local parishes (*uici*), each centred on a shrine of the Lares at the main crossroads. Lara's twins, protectors of Rome (pp. 114–17 above), were now 'the Augustan Lares' (*Lares Augusti*), and they shared their

Figure 85

Figure 86

new altars with Augustus' *Genius*. The combination was familiar from domestic cult, where the Lares were protectors of the house and the *Genius* the personal 'guardian angel' of the head of the household. On the streets of Rome the citizens already thought of Augustus as their tribune, with his powers annually renewed, as the guarantor of their corn supply, and as the proconsular commander whose praetorian cohorts kept the city safe; now the reorganisation of their civic life encouraged them to think of him as their *paterfamilias* as well.

They were the sovereign People, with strong opinions and sometimes violent enthusiasms; he was the leading citizen (*princeps*), who had to carry them with him as he reconstructed Rome. He was in constant dialogue with them by edict and in public speeches, often explaining, sometimes rebuking, always reminding them of the seriousness of what he was trying to do:

> May it be granted to me to establish the Republic safe and sound on a firm footing, and to achieve the reward I seek for that—but only on this condition, that I am called the author of the best possible constitution [*status ciuitatis*], and carry with me when I die the hope that the foundations I lay for the Republic will remain in their place.

Suetonius Divus
Augustus 28.2

It was a heavy responsibility, and he looked forward to when the task would be done, the Republic could govern itself and he could retire. By 2 BC, when he was sixty, he may have thought the time had come.

It was a special year. Augustus was consul for only the second time in over twenty years. On 17 March he would oversee the coming-of-age of his second son and heir. On 12 May the great temple of Mars the Avenger, which he had vowed forty years before in the year of Philippi, would at last be dedicated in the Forum Augustum. Spectacular shows were going to be put on, with a naval battle in an artificial lake across the Tiber, 260 lions hunted in the Circus Maximus, and thirty-six crocodiles in the flooded piazza of the Circus Flaminius. But before any of these great events took place, the plebeians of Rome sent a formal embassy to Augustus' seaside home at Antium, asking him to accept the title Father of his Country (*pater patriae*).

Augustus politely declined to accept such an honour unless it was unanimous, so the People and the Senate together planned a symbolic event. 5 February was the festival of the cult of Concordia on the Capitol, founded after the disaster at Cannae, when People and Senate really were as one. This year, after the sacrifice a show was put on in the Forum, with a huge audience of all ranks of society wearing laurel wreaths; when Augustus arrived, they hailed him as *pater patriae*. Then a Senate meeting was called. Augustus' consular colleague presided, and called on one of the senior members to speak for all of them. This was Marcus Messalla Corvinus, who had fought with Cassius at Philippi.

The normal way to begin the session was with the prayer 'Good fortune and blessings be on the Senate and People of Rome'. Messalla, however, had a different formula:

> 'Good fortune and blessings be on you and your house, Caesar Augustus—for in our view that is a prayer for the lasting happiness and prosperity of this Republic. The Senate joins with the People of Rome in saluting you together as Father of our Country.'

Augustus had tears in his eyes as he replied:

> 'Now that I have achieved all I prayed for, members of the Senate, I have only this to ask of the immortal gods, that I may be permitted to extend this consensus of yours to the very end of my life.'

Suetonius Divus Augustus 58.2

Here was the achievement of concord, the end of the long nightmare of civil strife, if only the gods would allow it to last.

This long, action-packed chapter has covered exactly two hundred years (202–2 BC). It has dealt only in passing with the Romans' two great achievements during those two centuries—their world empire and their literature—and has focused instead on the internal conflict between the many and the few, the People and the Senate.

Figure 87

The Senate's wise and patient leadership in the war with Hannibal gave it a moral authority which was soon corrupted by the power and wealth of empire. 'Saving the Republic' came to mean assassinating a tribune of the *plebs* when the sovereign People acted against the interests of the rich. Polarised politics became civil war, with new barbarities inflicted on the People by Sulla. The *populares* fought back; their champion became dictator, and was murdered by

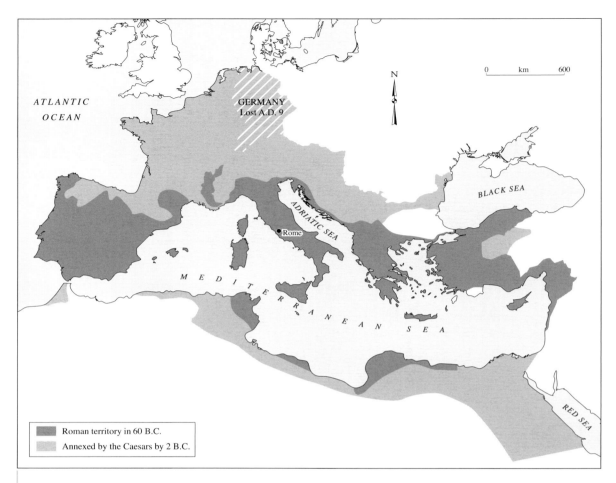

ATLANTIC
OCEAN

GERMANY
Lost A.D. 9

N

0   km   600

BLACK SEA

ADRIATIC SEA

Rome

MEDITERRANEAN SEA

RED SEA

▓ Roman territory in 60 B.C.
▓ Annexed by the Caesars by 2 B.C.

Figure 87. The Roman
Empire in 2 BC. The lighter
shading marks territories
annexed by the Caesars,
father and son.

the *optimates* in the name of the Republic. Cato's heroic suicide, the death of
Cicero and the new barbarism of the Triumvirate gave the 'tyrannicides' the
moral advantage, but the decision of power went against them at Philippi. Then
the victors fell out among themselves, until at last Caesar and Rome prevailed
over Antony and Alexandria.

Caesar Augustus tamed the senatorial elite, executing several conspirators
against his life. He gave the People protection and security, 'freedom from'
rather than 'freedom to'. In his later years, he allowed the *optimates* their due.
When he caught one of his grandsons reading Cicero, he took the book from
him, stood reading it for a long time, and gave it back with the words 'A learned
man, my boy, and a patriot too'. When he happened to be in a house Cato had
lived in, and someone criticised Cato's inflexibility, he gave a sharp answer.
'It's the mark of a good man and a good citizen not to want the constitution
changed.' What Augustus seemed to have done by 2 BC was end the enmity
without changing the constitution.

Of course it was an illusion. Already Greeks found it natural to refer to him as *basileus* ('king'), and though no Roman would have called him *rex*, they did think of him as the sole ruler. Even in the Roman Senate Messalla prayed for blessings 'on you and your house'. That in itself was change enough. And one of Augustus' steps towards retirement that year was to depute the command of his proconsular cohorts to two senior officers, the Prefects of the Praetorian Guard.

Our concern is with mythic Rome, that community of self-governing citizens protected by the god of liberty and licence. Marsyas the satyr still stood in the Roman Forum, his arm raised in salute to the Roman People, but the cult of Liber himself had been emasculated by the senatorial elite in 186 BC. Antony honoured him, but Antony was defeated, and the victor's patron god was Liber's enemy Apollo. The ancient temple of Liber was destroyed in the year of Actium, and not rebuilt.

Augustus should have remembered what his friend Horace, in prophetic mode, had written twenty years before:

> Roman, you may be innocent of guilt,
> Yet you shall pay for each ancestral crime,
> Until our mouldering temples are rebuilt
> And the gods' statues cleansed of smoke and grime.
>
> Only as servant of the gods in heaven
> Can you rule earth. . .

Horace Odes 3.6.1–5

The *pontifex maximus* should know that *all* the immortals demand their due, not just Apollo and avenging Mars.

9

CAESARS

LIBER'S REVENGE

Caesar Augustus had a daughter. At the time of her birth (39 BC) he wasn't yet Augustus, and had only been Caesar for five years. He quickly divorced her mother, Scribonia, in order to marry a younger woman, Livia Drusilla, who already had one little boy, and was pregnant with another, by her first husband Tiberius Claudius Nero. Meanwhile, Caesar's sister Octavia, who had a son and two daughters by Gaius Marcellus, a descendant of 'the sword of Rome' (p. 166 above), bore her new husband Antony two daughters before he left her for Kleopatra. And that was how it all began, with eight children born to three women in the years when young Caesar was still the junior member of the Triumvirate.

Figure 88

Figure 89

Figure 90

By the time he had sole power, two of the boys—Marcellus and Tiberius— were old enough to ride the trace-horses for his triumphal chariot. And there was another boy in the household by then—Iullus Antonius, Antony's younger son by his previous wife, named in honour of Julius Caesar and now brought up by Octavia with his half-sisters. The first of the girls to reach marriageable age, the elder Marcella, was given to Agrippa in the first year of the restored constitution, 28 BC. Three years later her brother Marcellus married Julia, the daughter of Caesar Augustus.

Marcellus was a young man full of promise. The free People elected him aedile at nineteen (an unheard-of honour), and he repaid them in the traditional way with spectacularly extravagant games. Of course his uncle paid the bills. Augustus loved shows of all kinds, and in the 20s BC Rome was in a frenzy of excitement over stars like Bathyllos and Pylades and the new mime-dancers' repertoire they had introduced from Alexandria. A star of a different kind was

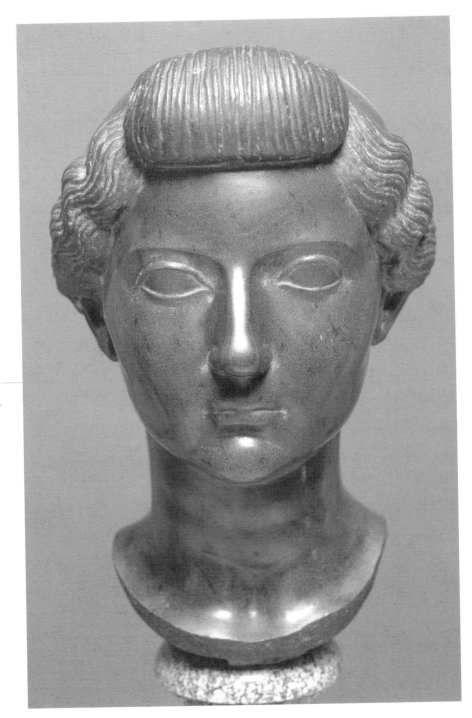

Figure 88. Livia Drusilla
(58 BC–AD 29), Augustus'
wife for fifty-one years.
When she married the
young Caesar on 17
January 38 BC she was
twelve days short of her
twentieth birthday.

Figure 89. Octavia, elder sister of Augustus (c.70–11 BC). Marble bust from Velletri (Velitrae), the home town of the Octavii.

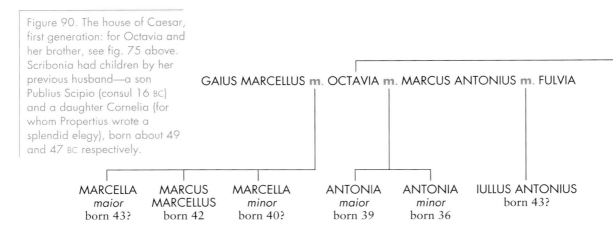

Figure 90. The house of Caesar, first generation: for Octavia and her brother, see fig. 75 above. Scribonia had children by her previous husband—a son Publius Scipio (consul 16 BC) and a daughter Cornelia (for whom Propertius wrote a splendid elegy), born about 49 and 47 BC respectively.

GAIUS MARCELLUS **m**. OCTAVIA **m**. MARCUS ANTONIUS **m**. FULVIA

MARCELLA
maior
born 43?

MARCUS
MARCELLUS
born 42

MARCELLA
minor
born 40?

ANTONIA
maior
born 39

ANTONIA
minor
born 36

IULLUS ANTONIUS
born 43?

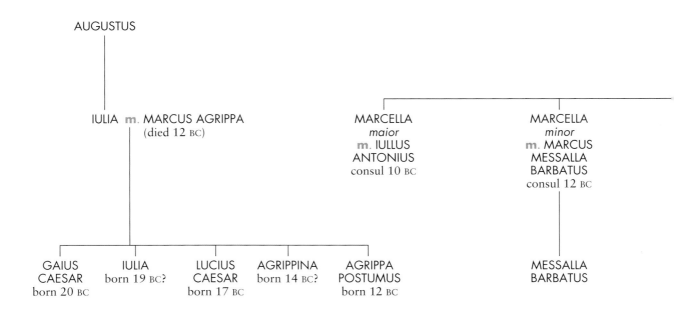

AUGUSTUS

IULIA **m**. MARCUS AGRIPPA
(died 12 BC)

MARCELLA
maior
m. IULLUS
ANTONIUS
consul 10 BC

MARCELLA
minor
m. MARCUS
MESSALLA
BARBATUS
consul 12 BC

GAIUS
CAESAR
born 20 BC

IULIA
born 19 BC?

LUCIUS
CAESAR
born 17 BC

AGRIPPINA
born 14 BC?

AGRIPPA
POSTUMUS
born 12 BC

MESSALLA
BARBATUS

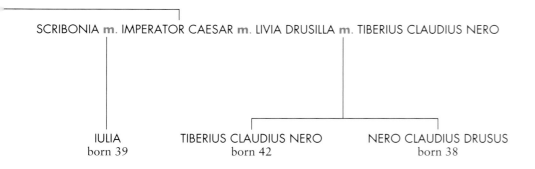

SCRIBONIA **m**. IMPERATOR CAESAR **m**. LIVIA DRUSILLA **m**. TIBERIUS CLAUDIUS NERO

IULIA
born 39

TIBERIUS CLAUDIUS NERO
born 42

NERO CLAUDIUS DRUSUS
born 38

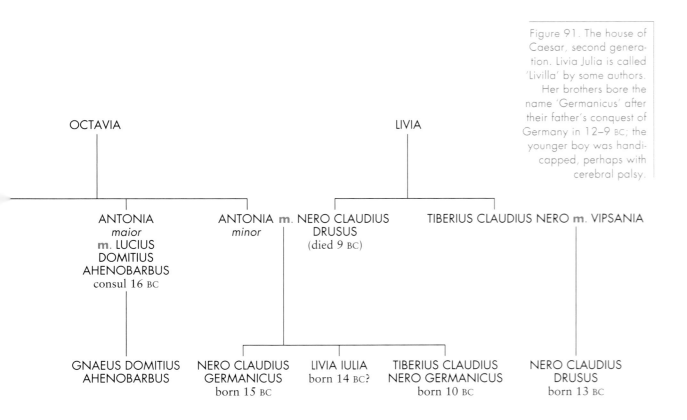

Figure 91. The house of Caesar, second generation. Livia Julia is called 'Livilla' by some authors. Her brothers bore the name 'Germanicus' after their father's conquest of Germany in 12–9 BC; the younger boy was handicapped, perhaps with cerebral palsy.

OCTAVIA

LIVIA

ANTONIA
maior
m. LUCIUS DOMITIUS AHENOBARBUS
consul 16 BC

ANTONIA
minor

m. NERO CLAUDIUS DRUSUS
(died 9 BC)

TIBERIUS CLAUDIUS NERO **m**. VIPSANIA

GNAEUS DOMITIUS AHENOBARBUS

NERO CLAUDIUS GERMANICUS
born 15 BC

LIVIA IULIA
born 14 BC?

TIBERIUS CLAUDIUS NERO GERMANICUS
born 10 BC

NERO CLAUDIUS DRUSUS
born 13 BC

the aedile's wilful, high-spirited sixteen-year-old wife, the daughter of Caesar Augustus.

Before the year was out Marcellus was dead. There was famine and plague at Rome. The Tiber flooded the city. Some god was angry. Nine years had passed since the destruction by fire of the temples of Liber and Flora, but still Augustus did not rebuild them. Instead, he tightened control of the games, putting them all under the authority of the praetors, and announced that Marcellus' memorial would be a great new theatre constructed in front of the temple of Apollo.

But who was to have the teenage widow? Who would make the princess pregnant with Augustus' grandchildren? Only Agrippa could be entrusted with that. So he divorced Marcella and married Julia. Five children were born: the two eldest boys were adopted by Augustus in 17 BC as his own sons, Gaius and Lucius Caesar. Their sisters were Julia the younger and Agrippina, and a third boy was born after his father's death and named Agrippa Postumus.

Figure 91

Meanwhile, there were other weddings and other births. Tiberius married Agrippa's daughter Vipsania; his brother Drusus married the younger Antonia; each union swiftly produced a son. Iullus Antonius married Agrippa's cast-off Marcella. Her sisters were married to favoured aristocrats outside the family—the younger Marcella to a Valerius Messalla, the elder Antonia to one of the 'bronze beards' (p. 188 above). Their children's children would be notorious.

Marriage and motherhood did not inhibit Julia's appetite for fun. Always surrounded by eager young men, she knew she could charm her father out of his disapproval. ('I have two spoilt children to put up with,' he said: 'Julia and the Republic.') She was careful with her indiscretions, and her children were so like Agrippa that she could present herself as a model wife. She was the star of the world we know through the love poetry of Ovid—cynical, sophisticated, pleasure-loving, and with none of the moral seriousness of the generation that lived through the civil wars.

One of Julia's intimates was Sempronius Gracchus, of the family of the two great martyred tribunes. Another was her cousin's husband Iullus Antonius, son of Antony and heir on his mother's side to a spectacular radical-*popularis* tradition. Her two stepbrothers, by contrast, were the sons of a man who approved of the killing of Julius Caesar; they wanted Augustus to restore the old republic and 'liberty', no doubt in the sense that Brutus had used the word

Figure 77

on the Ides of March (p. 208 above). As for Julia herself, 'I never forget,' she said, 'that I am *Caesar's* daughter.'

Augustus thought he had made such issues obsolete. He had other priorities: Agrippa was dead, and Julia was only twenty-seven. At thirty, Tiberius was now the senior man. Too bad that he loved his wife; he had to divorce her and marry Julia.

It's difficult enough to be married to someone you dislike, and who dislikes you; when two of your new stepchildren are the adopted sons of Caesar, desig-

Man About Town

We first made the acquaintance of Publius Ovidius Naso ('Ovid') in the first chapter, and throughout the book his late poem on the Roman calendar, 'The Festivals' (*Fasti*), has provided intermittent illustration of the myths of Rome.

But so far he has been wearing the eighteenth-century disguise of William Massey's translation. Now that we have reached his own time, and the mythic story in which he himself played a part, at least we can give him a contemporary voice. Here he is in Peter Green's 1982 translation, a brilliant young love poet introducing his first book—and its characteristic metre, which Massey's rhyming couplets did not try to reproduce:

> Arms, warfare, violence—I was winding up to produce a
> > Regular epic, with verse-form to match—
> Hexameters, naturally. But Cupid (they say) with a snicker
> > Lopped off one foot from each alternate line.

The poet complains, and Cupid shoots him with an arrow:

> His shafts—worse luck for me—never miss their target:
> > I'm on fire now, Love owns the freehold of my heart.
> So let my verse rise with six stresses, drop to five on the downbeat—
> > Goodbye to martial epic, and epic metre too!
> Come on then, my Muse, bind your blonde hair with a wreath of
> > Sea-myrtle, and lead me off in the six-five groove!

The girl he was in love with, the tempestuous mistress to whom he swears endless devotion (at the same time dying to bed every woman he meets), was 'Corinna', whose real identity Rome was agog to know.

If she existed, she must have been about Julia's age, and five hundred years later a learned bishop believed that she *was* Julia. That's most unlikely, but Ovid's precocious talent got him known in very high places; indeed, his patron was the same Messalla Corvinus who voiced the Senate's salute to Augustus as Father of his Country.

Certainly Ovid spoke more for Julia's generation than for that of Messalla and Augustus. No turnip-eaters' values for *him*:

> Crude simplicity's old-fashioned,
> > Rome's all gold now, possesses the vast wealth
> Of the conquered world. Consider the Capitol, past and present—
> > You'd think today's version belonged
> To a different god. Our Senate (august assembly!) now boasts
> > A worthy chamber—first built, in Tatius' reign,
> Of wattle and daub. The Palatine, where Apollo and our princes
> > Now lord it, once pastured oxen for the plough.
> Let others worship the past; I much prefer the present,
> > Am delighted to be alive today—not for
> The stubborn gold we mine, or the rare shells gathered
> > For our delight from foreign shores,
> Not for the marble quarried from crumbling mountains, the palaces
> > Pier-built over the bay, but for
> Refinement and culture, which have banished the tasteless
> > Crudities of our ancestors.

Ovid's constant subject was the game of sex: this passage comes from his famous *Art of Love*, a three-volume instruction for seduction. His readers loved it, little knowing how short a time was left for the cheerful, amoral, unworried pursuit of pleasure, and for Ovid, its prolifically brilliant spokesman. Already, Augustus had made adultery a criminal offence.

nated heirs to an unannounced monarchy of which you deeply disapprove, it becomes impossible. Tiberius stood it for five years, for most of which he and his brother were commanding Caesar's armies (Drusus died on campaign in 9 BC), extending the Roman empire to the Danube and the Elbe. In 7 BC he held his triumph and his second consulship, but the honours were hollow. Julia despised him as unworthy of her; her sons, now thirteen and ten, were old enough to know, and exploit the knowledge, that they outranked him.

The Roman People loved the glamorous princess and her growing boys. They had thought of Agrippa as one of themselves, but Tiberius was an aristocrat, haughty, taciturn, a hater of crowds. In a pointed gesture, he used the booty from his triumph to restore a monument of optimate reaction, the temple of 'Concord'; set up in the Forum after the suppression of Gaius Gracchus and his followers, it was also where Catiline's friends had been condemned to death without trial (pp. 192–3, 203 above). Julius Caesar, no doubt remembering how his own life had been threatened on the temple steps, had planned to destroy it and build a theatre on the site. But that symbolic revenge never took place, and now a patrician Claudius Nero was going to rebuild it in gleaming marble.

However, the work was soon interrupted. The proud aristocrat had had enough of his impossible marriage. In 6 BC, to Augustus' uncomprehending fury, Tiberius left Rome and went to live as a private citizen on the island of Rhodes.

Julia and her friends exploited her husband's absence in the style they knew best. One of the ways they celebrated was with nocturnal parties in the Forum, on the Rostra, under the genial gaze of Marsyas the satyr, servant of the god of liberty and licence. The Roman People were glad to see Marsyas wearing a crown of flowers the next morning, but Augustus was not amused. His health wasn't good either, and now that Julia's sons were teenagers perhaps some people were working out contingency plans. Or even planning the contingency. Augustus had rediscovered the iron law of autocracy: once your successor is known, not everyone wants to keep you alive.

We have now caught up with the end of the last chapter. Augustus has received the accolade of Father of his Country; the temple of Mars the Avenger has been dedicated; the lions have been hunted, the crocodiles killed. He has achieved consensus—that is, the end of one sort of politics and the emergence of another. The power struggle will now be within the family, and among the 'court' (aula) of relatives, friends, advisers and hangers-on that is growing up around it. There's no palace yet—the house with the laurelled doors is still conspicuously unluxurious—but 'palace politics' are dominant from now on. Republics are boys' games, but when the family is the seat of power wives and mothers have authority, and that makes them dangerous.

Colour plate 9

In 2 BC Livia Drusilla had had privileged access to Augustus for thirty-six years. Her son was in disgrace, but she still had to be listened to. In the autumn of that year Augustus destroyed his daughter. Iullus Antonius was executed for treason, Sempronius Gracchus and several others were exiled. Julia herself was banished to the prison island of Pandateria. The Roman People protested, but Augustus was adamant. 'She shall not return till fire and water mix,' he said, and was unimpressed when the citizens threw torches of burning pitch into the Tiber.

The angry gods were not finished yet. At eighteen, young Lucius Caesar was given a military command in Spain; he died on the way there, in AD 2. His brother Gaius, at twenty-one, was already in command in the East; he was wounded in a skirmish, and died in AD 4. The following year Rome was shaken by earthquakes; the Tiber flooded the city; the corn supply failed; for four years there was famine.

Augustus was devastated at the loss of his sons. He now adopted their brother, young Agrippa Postumus; but he was only fifteen, and Augustus in his middle sixties couldn't count on living that long. There had to be a mature heir. Tiberius, the stepson, was now back from Rhodes, divorced from Julia, and nursing his resentment in private life. Augustus reluctantly turned to him, and *Figure 94 (p. 242)* reshaped the house of Caesar with two more adoptions and two marriages. Julia's younger daughter (the elder was already married) was given to Tiberius' nephew Germanicus, whose sister Livia Julia married Tiberius' son. Tiberius himself adopted Germanicus, and Augustus adopted Tiberius; so the children of those two marriages would bear the name of Caesar. Meanwhile, Tiberius Caesar, as he now was, received the tribunician power as Augustus' recognised deputy and took command of the legions in Germany.

The Roman People were very unhappy. Augustus had to reassure them that his adoption of Tiberius was for the good of the Republic, however unpromising the new Caesar's temperament might seem. But popular unrest continued, not helped when Augustus disinherited young Agrippa and banished him to the island of Planasia.

Things got worse. A disastrous fire devastated much of Rome. Then a huge rebellion in the Balkans brought Tiberius in a hurry from the Rhine to the Danube, trying to prevent an invasion of Italy and keep Augustus' newly won empire together. The old man was badly shaken, and the blows kept coming. A plot was discovered to rescue Julia and young Agrippa from their confinement and use the frontier armies to install them in their rightful place. The spectre of civil war had returned.

Meanwhile, during this unhappy time the Roman People's favourite author was reinventing his repertoire. With exquisitely bad timing, the poet of seduction and hedonism had brought out his *Art of Love* just after the disgrace of Julia. Now Ovid turned to safer sex, in the great fifteen-book epic *Metamorphoses*, the western world's mythological encyclopaedia from Chaucer to Ted Hughes. He knew at least that it would outlast Augustus:

> Now stands my task accomplished. Such a work
> As not the wrath of Jove, nor fire nor sword
> Nor the devouring ages can destroy.

Ovid
Metamorphoses
15.871–873

And at the same time he was writing his poem of Roman stories, dedicated to Augustus himself:

> Since amorous themes have been my sole delight,
> Who'd think I could the serious *Fasti* write?
> But all my skill's in the poetic field;
> Verse is the only weapon I can wield,
> My arm's unfit to wave the ponderous spear
> Or guide the foaming steed to raging war;
> No helmet guards my head, nor sword my side,
> For that's an armour that I have not tried.
> But, Caesar, I'll defend thy glorious name,
> And stamp thy titles with eternal fame.

Ovid Fasti
2.7–16

And so he did; but he also gave prominence to Liber and Libera, and to sweet sexy Flora, divinities dearer to the People than to Caesar Augustus. In any case, Caesar Augustus was not going to be mollified.

Nobody knows quite what happened in AD 8. The plot to rescue Julia and Agrippa had failed; now Augustus banished his granddaughter, the younger Julia, for adultery, and her husband, Lucius Aemilius Paullus, for treason. Ovid, with his friends in high society, had seen something and not reported it. That was enough for Augustus to make an example of him. The author of *The Art of Love* spent the rest of his life in a frontier outpost near the Danube delta.

Augustus was now in his seventies. His only child and two of his three surviving grandchildren were in penal custody. He would not allow their names to be uttered, and referred to them only as his three cancers. 'Do the gods really hate the Roman People?' he wrote to Tiberius. 'If not, I pray they'll keep you safe for us, and allow you a long and healthy life.' The gods granted his prayer, though whether it was for the good of the Roman People, later generations took leave to doubt. Certainly the gods hadn't finished with Augustus. In AD 9 Germany was lost, and an army of three legions totally destroyed. Tiberius, even more indispensable now, went back to the Rhine.

At some point during these dreadful years, Augustus the *pontifex maximus* ordered the temple of Ceres, Liber and Libera and the temple of Flora to be rebuilt. But it was too late. He had made his choice fifty years before. Apollo had been generous, both to him and to Rome, but there was no avoiding the price that had to be paid—an autocracy which could be handed on only through murderous strife.

Capua, 23 August AD 14. Tiberius and Livia and their staff are making the slow journey to Rome with Augustus' coffin (he died four days ago in the Campanian town of Nola), travelling by night and resting by day to avoid the summer heat. A messenger is brought in, a centurion of the Praetorian Guard. 'Your order has been carried out, Caesar. The exile Agrippa is dead.' Tiberius is flabbergasted. 'I gave no such order. An account of this will have to be given to the Senate.'

It's a revealing moment. Tiberius Caesar was still thinking like Tiberius Claudius Nero, Roman aristocrat and old-fashioned optimate, for whom it was self-evident that the Senate had the responsibility of government. So one of the senior advisers had an urgent conversation with Livia.

Tacitus Annals
1.6.3

'Secrets of the house, friends' advice, soldiers' services—that sort of thing mustn't be made public. Bringing in the Senate weakens the *princeps*' authority. It's the condition of power that accounts are rendered to one man only.'

The message was passed on. No mention of the matter was made to the Senate.

The adviser was Sallustius Crispus, great-nephew and adopted son of Sallust the historian. Sallust had reported the *popularis* case against the arrogance of the aristocracy, and now his son was protecting the *populares*' victory in the autocratic world it had created. For the People's interests were vested in the *princeps* ('Caesar is the Republic', as Ovid put it in one of his poems from exile), and an offence against Caesar was an offence against the majesty of the Roman People, which meant treason.

The question now was, who was the true Caesar? The plan to rescue young Agrippa and take him to the Rhine army, commanded by his brother-in-law Germanicus, was reactivated as soon as Augustus' death was known, and it might have succeeded if the centurion hadn't got to the island first. Crispus had done well to give him 'Caesar's order' so promptly. Who had authorised it? Tiberius put it about that Augustus had left instructions. But Augustus never went so far as executing his own relatives, and he had made a tearful visit to Agrippa only a few months before.

Whoever was responsible (Livia is the most likely), the killing marked a watershed as fateful as that of Tiberius Gracchus 146 years before. In the new style of politics, as in the old, murder came to be recognised as an acceptable means. It wasn't always by the sword. Starvation in custody was what finished off Augustus' daughter later that year. Agrippa and Julia were the first two victims of a power game where the stakes were life or death.

How that deadly game was played out in the next fifty years is one of the most enduring of the myths of Rome, all the more powerful for being true. Its chroniclers, Cornelius Tacitus and Suetonius Tranquillus, based their accounts on good evidence, provided by people who knew what happened and in some cases helped to make it happen. Let's meet the main characters, as they were in the autumn of AD 14.

1. Divus Augustus, now among the gods; the Senate decreed his deification on 17 September. Kinship with him, above all direct descent by birth (or failing that, adoption), confers an automatic presumption of the right to rule.

2. Iulia Augusta, his widow—Livia Drusilla for the first seventy-one years of her life, but now adopted into the family of the Caesars by Augustus' will. Suspected by some of having brought about the deaths of Marcellus, Lucius, Gaius and Augustus himself in order to bring her son to power. Uniquely experienced, and now freed from the discretion required by her role as Augustus' wife.

3. Tiberius Caesar Augustus (though he rarely uses the third name), son of Divus Augustus and grandson of Divus Julius (but not by choice). Fifty-five years old, dutiful, grim, unlikeable. Disapproves of the power of the *princeps*; has accepted it only under protest and for the time being. Wants the Senate to take responsibility, but they daren't risk offending him; 'men fit to be slaves', he calls them. No sympathy with what the People likes; doesn't give shows, and will soon reverse his predecessor's tolerance of celebrity actors and their riotous fans. 'Poor Roman People,' said the dying Augustus, 'to be ground in such relentless jaws.'

4. Germanicus Caesar, Tiberius' nephew and adopted son, twenty-eight years old, in command of the Rhine army. Married to Augustus' granddaughter; Figure 94 (p. 242) they have three sons already, and will soon have three daughters too. Reacts with histrionic indignation when his legions offer to march on Rome and put him in power. Handsome, talented, everybody's darling. Tiberius views him with deep suspicion.

5. Agrippina, daughter of Agrippa and Julia, wife of Germanicus. Twenty-seven years old, brave, proud, tactless. Very conscious of her blood descent from Divus Augustus. The last of her three brothers has just been put to death; her sister languishes on a prison island. Her relations with Tiberius and his mother are tense. In Germany with her husband and her youngest boy, two-year-old Gaius. The soldiers call him 'Little Army Boot' (*Caligula*).

6. Drusus Caesar, Tiberius' son, two years younger than Germanicus and married to his sister Livia Julia. The two men get on well, and Tiberius has no need yet to decide which of his sons shall be his heir.

Germanicus' triumph in AD 17 was a time of hope. His campaigns in Germany had avenged the disaster of AD 9, and buried the remains of the three legions. Tiberius' rule was sombre and unglamorous, but he wouldn't last for ever; Germanicus and his family represented the future. Meanwhile, there were even some festivities, as the rebuilt temples of Liber and Flora were dedicated, and

Augustus the God

What did it mean to the Romans that Augustus was now a god? A poet writing at the time ended the fourth book of his epic *On the Stars* like this:

> Now man himself makes gods, and sends the stars
> Divine power: with Augustus as its *princeps*
> Heaven will grow greater.

Mere flattery? Perhaps. But here is a prose author just a few years later, dedicating to Tiberius his collection of morally exemplary stories from history:

> The other divine powers are worshipped on the basis of belief, but you appear through manifest faith like the stars your father and grandfather have become, whose glorious illumination has added such celebrated zeal to our religion: indeed, although we inherited all the other gods, we ourselves have bestowed the Caesars.

That 'zeal' (*alacritas*) is important. These new gods are as powerful as the old ones, and worshipped with no less enthusiastic devotion.

In 1979, an excavation at what had once been the village of Geyre in south-west Turkey provided startling evidence of how the new god might be visualised. This was the site of Aphrodisias, city of Aphrodite, which had a privileged status because the Caesars were descended from the goddess. Not long after Augustus' deification a group of public-spirited citizens paid for the erection of a large temple complex dedicated to 'Aphrodite the Foremother and the Augustan Gods' (or 'the divine Augusti'—*theoi Sebastoi*), and the remains of that were what was found in 1979.

In front of the temple there had been a long, narrow piazza, perhaps better thought of as a processional avenue, flanked on each side by a three-storey colonnade [fig. 92]. Between the columns in the top

Figure 92. Aphrodisias, *Sebasteion*. Reconstruction drawing, looking westwards to the temple from the monumental gate.

two storeys were sculptured panels in high relief, 180 in all, many of which were recovered by Professor Kenan Erim and his team. On the north side, the upper row evidently showed allegorical figures (Ocean, Day, etc), the lower one personified peoples and territories conquered by Augustus; the overall effect was 'a grandiose identification of the physical world with the Roman empire'. More interesting for our purposes were the panels on the south side, seamlessly combining the gods and heroes of traditional mythology in the lower row (including the she-wolf and twins), and the newly mythic characters of the story of the Caesars in the upper.

Two of the surviving panels show Divus Augustus [fig. 93]. In the first, which was immediately above the panel showing his ancestor Aeneas leaving Troy, the new god looks across at winged Victoria as she crowns a trophy above a bound barbarian captive; at Augustus' feet is the eagle normally associated with Jupiter. The second panel shows Augustus as the master of the earth and sea, the two personified elements presenting him with, respectively, a cornucopia and a steering-oar. It might be argued that since this iconography is Hellenistic, not Roman, it offers no evidence for how the Roman People imagined the new god. But it is surely self-evident that for this of all buildings the loyal burghers of Aphrodisias used a style they knew would be acceptable to the Romans.

Figure 93. Aphrodisias, panels from the *Sebasteion*, south portico. (*a*) Augustus with Nike (Victoria), trophy, captive and eagle. (*b*) Augustus with allegorical figures representing earth and sea.

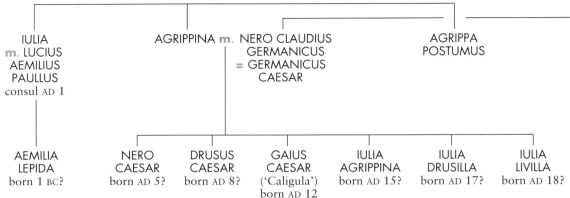

IULIA **m.** LUCIUS AEMILIUS PAULLUS consul AD 1	AGRIPPINA **m.** NERO CLAUDIUS GERMANICUS = GERMANICUS CAESAR		AGRIPPA POSTUMUS		
AEMILIA LEPIDA born 1 BC?	NERO CAESAR born AD 5?	DRUSUS CAESAR born AD 8?	GAIUS CAESAR ('Caligula') born AD 12	IULIA AGRIPPINA born AD 15?	IULIA DRUSILLA born AD 17?	IULIA LIVILLA born AD 18?

Figure 94. The house of Caesar, third generation: the surviving children of Agrippa and Julia, and the children of the younger Antonia and Tiberius' brother Nero Drusus.

Figure 95

also those of Janus and Hope (*Spes*), burnt down in a more recent fire. Symbolically, it was Germanicus who presided over the ceremony for Hope. Perhaps the bad years were over. Perhaps Germanicus would bring Liber's liberty back to the Roman People.

Two years later Germanicus was dead, in far-away Syria, and hope was dead too. In despair, the Roman People stoned the temples of the gods. They shared Germanicus' own belief that he had been poisoned. They were equally sure they knew who did it (his 'minder' Gnaeus Piso), and they had a pretty strong suspicion that Tiberius and his mother had connived at it. They greeted the returning Agrippina with desperate grief, and the returning Piso with equally desperate anger. They would have torn him to pieces if the Senate had not put him on trial—not for murder, but on a different count of treason—and he took his own life rather than face the verdict.

The popular hysteria created a difficult situation for Tiberius. He still had an adult heir, and Drusus' wife gave birth to twin boys at this very time. But that didn't help; the People saw it as a blow to Germanicus' children. The point was that Drusus, like Tiberius, was a Caesar by adoption, whereas Agrippina and her brood had the blood of Augustus in their veins, and never forgot it. Nor did the Roman People: at the funeral ceremony they prayed openly that the gods would protect the fatherless children from their enemies.

Tiberius appealed for calm and Roman self-control. In the summer (June AD 20) the People had something to cheer in the coming-of-age ceremony for Agrippina's eldest boy Nero Caesar, and his marriage to Drusus' daughter Julia.

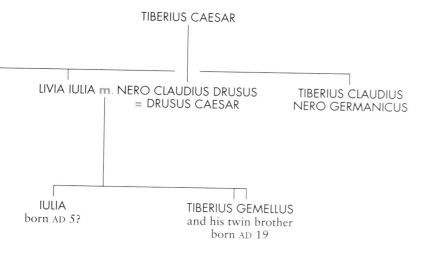

TIBERIUS CAESAR

LIVIA IULIA **m**. NERO CLAUDIUS DRUSUS
= DRUSUS CAESAR

TIBERIUS CLAUDIUS
NERO GERMANICUS

IULIA
born AD 5?

TIBERIUS GEMELLUS
and his twin brother
born AD 19

Figure 95. Guillaume Boichot, 'Agrippina with the Ashes of Germanicus'; ink drawing, c.1770. Agrippina steps ashore at Brundisium with the ashes of Germanicus and two of her six children, just as Tacitus reports. In fact, Gaius was seven and Julia Livilla only eighteen months. The grieving man must be her brother-in-law Drusus, though Tacitus says he met her not at Brundisium but at Tarracina.

The Senate Speaks

Germanicus died on 10 October AD 19. News of his death reached Rome in early December, and later that month the Senate met to decide how best to honour his memory. A year later, after the trial and suicide of Gnaeus Piso, the Senate met on 10 December AD 20 to decide how to dishonour Piso's. Archaeological exploration, legal or otherwise, in south-west Spain has recently brought to light the official records of both these meetings, inscribed on bronze and set up for the information of Rome's provincial subjects.

The honours document ('*Tabula Siarensis*', discovered in 1982) helps to explain the wholly eulogistic treatment of Germanicus in the literary sources. (Even the sceptical Tacitus, whose own narrative reveals a very mixed record of military success, compares him favourably with Alexander the Great.) The Senate proposed the erection of three honorary arches at Rome, in Syria and in Germany, each with an inscription recording Germanicus' achievements in detail, and that the obituaries read out in the Senate by Tiberius and Drusus be recorded on bronze and set up in a public place as an example to future generations. Since the 'official version' so firmly established coincided with the hero-worship of the Roman People, Germanicus remained for ever the golden boy, the one impeccable Caesar.

The Piso document (*SC de Pisone patre*, two copies discovered in the late 1980s) begins with the Senate's expression of gratitude to the immortal gods

> because they did not allow the tranquillity of the present state of the republic—
> than which nothing better can be desired and which it has fallen to our lot to enjoy
> by favour of our *princeps*—to be disturbed by the wicked plans of Gnaeus Piso.

Piso had attempted to seize the province of Syria by force after Germanicus' death. That is, he tried 'to stir up civil war, though all the evils of civil war have long since been laid to rest by the divine will of Divus Augustus and the virtues of Tiberius Caesar Augustus'.

The anxious formulation shows how far from stable the Augustan principate was still felt to be. The Senate was shocked that Roman soldiers were called 'Pisonians' (as opposed to Germanicus' 'Caesarians'); that sounded too much like the 'Pompeians and Caesarians' of sixty years before. They concluded with the hope that the soldiers would always be loyal to the house of Augustus, 'because they know that the safety of our empire has been placed in the protection of that house', and obey those of their commanders who were most devoted to the name of the Caesars, for that name 'is the source of safety for this city and the empire of the Roman People'.

They were both about fifteen; Agrippina's other sons were about twelve (Drusus Caesar) and nearly eight ('Caligula', Gaius Caesar). The People doted on them, and on their mother and their three little sisters. Tiberius was in his sixty-second year, exactly the age when it had all started to go wrong for Augustus. His security adviser now put forward a practical suggestion.

This was Aelius Seianus ('Sejanus'), the Prefect of the Praetorian Guard. When instituting the prefecture twenty years before, Augustus had been careful to share the responsibility between two men; but Tiberius trusted Sejanus totally, and gave him sole authority. Now he urged Tiberius to bring together all the nine cohorts of the Guard into a single permanent camp just outside the walls of Rome, thus concentrating the security forces where they would most be needed. Tiberius agreed, and in AD 20 the Guard moved into its new barracks beyond the Viminal Gate.

Drusus detested Sejanus, and with better reason than he knew, since his beautiful wife and the Prefect were lovers. So the next act of the drama began.

In AD 23 Drusus fell ill and died—poisoned, as it was later revealed. Tiberius had now lost both his sons. He presented Nero Caesar (eighteen) and Drusus Caesar (fifteen) to the Senate:

> 'On my behalf as well as your own, adopt and guide these youths, whose birth is so glorious—these great-grandchildren of Augustus. Nero and Drusus: these senators will take the place of your parents. For, in the station to which you are born, the good and bad in you is of national concern.'

Tacitus Annals
4.8.5

He then went on to remind the senators that he had not taken on the burden of the state indefinitely; he intended to resign it to the Senate and magistrates. Perhaps the old man still believed that was possible. But the Senate knew, Sejanus knew, and above all Agrippina and her children knew, that it could never happen while the house of Caesar was in being.

Once again, Tiberius had had enough. At sixty-seven, as he had at thirty-six, he left Rome and retired to an island. This time it was Capri, and he gave instructions by edict that his peace and quiet were not to be disturbed.

When your successor is known, not everyone wants to keep you alive. Agrippina's eldest son was already in his twenties when Tiberius withdrew. The Roman People (and the Roman armies) were now quite ready for the succession to take place, in fact the sooner the better. That could not be said openly, but even private comments were reported to Sejanus. The Prefect, as was his duty, kept Tiberius informed.

In AD 28 Agrippina's sister Julia died, after twenty years on her prison island, the final victim of the last succession crisis. The following year saw the death of Augustus' widow, Tiberius' mother, at the age of eighty-six; the funeral oration was given by her sixteen-year-old great-grandson, Gaius 'Caligula'. The eldest of his sisters, at fourteen, was now married. The new generation was growing up, but it would not grow old.

Figure 96

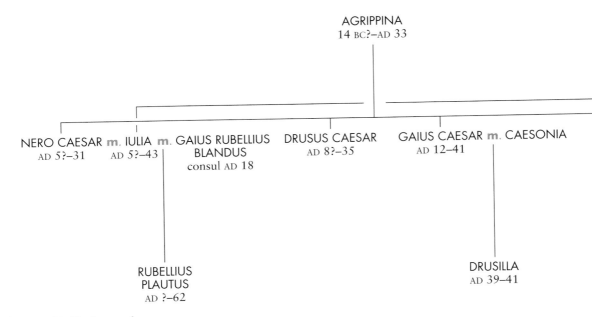

AGRIPPINA
14 BC?–AD 33

NERO CAESAR **m**. IULIA **m**. GAIUS RUBELLIUS
AD 5?–31   AD 5?–43   BLANDUS
consul AD 18

DRUSUS CAESAR
AD 8?–35

GAIUS CAESAR **m**. CAESONIA
AD 12–41

RUBELLIUS
PLAUTUS
AD ?–62

DRUSILLA
AD 39–41

Figure 96. The house of Caesar, fourth generation: doomed offspring of the two imperial widows. See fig. 91 for the younger Agrippina's husband, a grandson of Augustus' sister Octavia; and for the forgotten man, Livia Julia's handicapped brother, whose first daughter, Claudia Antonia, was born about AD 29.

Freed from his mother's demanding influence, Tiberius wrote to the Senate denouncing Agrippina and her eldest son. Despite the noisy indignation of the Roman People, they were banished to prison islands; the following year Drusus Caesar was arrested and confined to a room in one of the properties on the Palatine. Maltreatment and starvation followed, and within four years all three were dead.

Sejanus had done his work well. Now, in a carefully prepared coup, Tiberius destroyed him at the height of his power. It was a dangerous gamble, and there were warships waiting at Capri to take Tiberius to the legions if it went wrong; but Sejanus came to the temple of Apollo confident that the long letter from Tiberius that was the business of the Senate meeting would grant him the tribunician power. It didn't—and the Praetorian Guard had been given a new Prefect and a bonus of more than a year's pay each to keep them happy. Sejanus was arrested, and dragged off through the jeering crowds to the prison below the Capitol, where he was executed and his body thrown out on the steps.

The Roman People took a savage revenge. They pulled down his statues, hunted out and killed his agents and friends, and abused his corpse for three days before throwing the remains in the river. They longed for the chance to do it to Tiberius too. When the orgy of violence was over, a shrine of Libertas

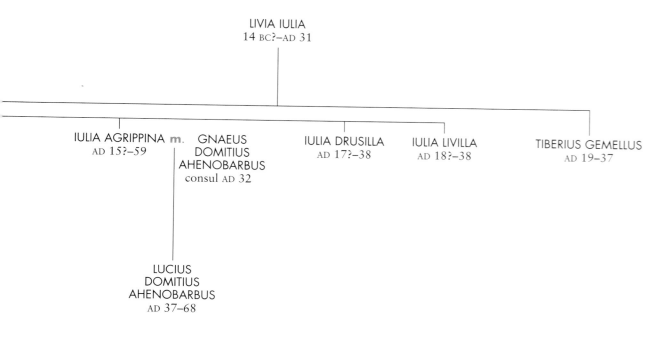

LIVIA IULIA
14 BC?–AD 31

IULIA AGRIPPINA m. GNAEUS
AD 15?–59   DOMITIUS
                   AHENOBARBUS
                   consul AD 32

IULIA DRUSILLA
AD 17?–38

IULIA LIVILLA
AD 18?–38

TIBERIUS GEMELLUS
AD 19–37

LUCIUS
DOMITIUS
AHENOBARBUS
AD 37–68

was set up in the Forum, and a festival with all the magistrates presiding. Marsyas must have smiled to see it.

The traitor princess also had to die. At twenty-seven, Drusus' widow, Sejanus' mistress, was starved to death and her memory dishonoured. Her daughter, widow of Nero Caesar, was married in due course to an undistinguished senior senator; they had a son, who lived a blameless life but in the end could not escape the doom of the Caesars.

Tiberius now had two heirs—Gaius, Germanicus' third and last son, just nineteen, and his own grandson Tiberius Gemellus, the survivor of Drusus' twins, now eleven or twelve. Both were with him on Capri, safe from the cauldron of Rome. Two things had become clear about Gaius 'Caligula': he liked dressing up, and he liked watching people suffer.

All that mattered to the Roman People was that at last the true Caesar, Augustus' great-grandson, would come into his own. Tiberius, better informed, predicted a total disaster. 'For the Roman People,' he said, 'I am bringing up a monster.' Not that he cared. He had spent his whole long life in the service of a quasi-monarchy he thought should not exist. Now, at the end of it, he was fond of quoting a line from Greek tragedy, 'When I am dead, let fire destroy the earth'. If the Romans really had to have a Caesar, he would give them one.

It has been a recurring theme in this book that one of the main media for the creation and dissemination of the myths of Rome—perhaps even the principal medium, more important than the histories and epic poems of the literary tradition—was dramatic performance, at the dedication of temples, at triumphs, at funerals, and especially at the annually recurring stage festivals (*ludi scaenici*) in honour of Jupiter, Liber, Ceres, Flora, Apollo, the Great Mother and the goddess of Victory. By the late Republic Liber had lost his games, but two new theatre festivals in honour of Divus Augustus made up for that.

The old stories were told and retold. A few of the plays that staged them—Naevius' *Romulus*, Ennius' *Sabine Women*, Accius' *Brutus* and one or two others—became classic texts, cited in our literary sources. But most play-scripts never ended up in a library. Very occasionally a reference happens to survive (as when Horace complains about the tedious triumphal procession that ended a play on the fall of Corinth), but otherwise we have to infer the existence of particular plays from the narratives of poets and historians who were influenced by them.

One thing we know for certain is that contemporary themes were always popular. Roman victories were celebrated, of course (three classic texts were Naevius on Marcus Marcellus, Ennius on Fulvius Nobilior and Pacuvius on Aemilius Paullus), but so were the great crises of internal politics; tragedies of Gaius Gracchus and Julius Caesar can be inferred from what our sources give us, and no doubt the Plebeian Games in November provided many such scenarios. Once Augustus had put an end to political strife, contemporary dramas evidently specialised in loyal praise of the *princeps* and his family; but then the new political world created crises of its own to be presented (as soon as it was safe) before the Roman People. One such play survives, and we shall come to it before long. For the moment, however, we are in AD 37.

It is the day of Tiberius' funeral, 3 April. Gaius, who was welcomed to Rome with hysterical enthusiasm a few days ago, is giving the funeral oration, with more praise of Augustus and Germanicus than of the grim old man whose corpse is to be disposed of. Tomorrow the games of the Great Mother begin, followed by those of Ceres, then those of Flora. In May there will be special games in honour of Gaius' mother and brothers, as their ashes, recovered from their prison islands, are given a final home in Augustus' mausoleum. Later in the year there will be more special games when the temple of Divus Augustus is dedicated—a duty for which Tiberius never managed to come to Rome. At all these celebrations, for the first time in fourteen years, there will be actors and dancers on the public stage. And they will have a new theme—the house of Caesar, as rich in tragic plots as the house of Atreus and the house of Tarquin.

Showbiz

During the Republic, the theatre was where the Roman People expressed its opinions most freely. There was applause or hissing as the senators came in to take their seats, and the actors could count on lively audience reaction to any lines that had a topical relevance. Cicero's letters and speeches give us the best evidence, but it was a phenomenon that went back long before his time. Wooden theatres were put up *ad hoc* for each festival, and the *optimates* successfully resisted attempts in 154 and 107 BC to build a permanent theatre, on the grounds that it would give rise to 'more sedition'.

Ambitious aediles spent huge sums decorating the theatres with prodigal extravagance (or so it seemed to moralists), and eventually the ban on a permanent structure was broken by Pompey, who dedicated his magnificent 'marble theatre' in 55 BC. Caesar's plan for a huge theatre in the Forum was never carried out, but the Theatre of Balbus, completed in 13 BC, and Augustus' splendid Theatre of Marcellus, dedicated two years later, provided Rome with 'the three theatres' recommended by Ovid as places for young women to be seen.

What went on in them was even more uninhibited than in the Republic, thanks to the riotous fans of a new theatrical genre, the danced mime. The stars were just outrageous. Augustus had one of them flogged in all three theatres when it turned out that his 'slave-boy' was a married lady with her hair cropped. 'It's in your interests, Caesar,' said another (whom Augustus had briefly banished for sedition), 'that the People should spend their leisure time on us.'

In AD 15 a centurion and several guardsmen were killed trying to keep order at the new Games of Augustus. There were constant complaints to the Senate, and not only about the riots; many gentlemen resented the fact that their wives and daughters found the star dancers sexually irresistible. In AD 23 Tiberius lost patience and banished all stage performers from Italy. The optimate censors of 115 BC had done the same, but their edict was soon reversed. Tiberius was adamant, ignoring all the pleas of the Roman People: the 'monsters of the stage' would not return while he was alive.

Of course the prohibition applied only to public shows; how people were entertained in private was up to them. On Capri, Tiberius actively encouraged young Gaius' passionate interest in acting, singing and dancing, in the hope that it might make him less sadistic in his tastes. He must have known well enough what would happen. As soon as he was dead, Gaius revoked the ban. The Roman People got their long-lost idols back, and it was the Golden Age of Saturnus all over again.

Germanicus' death-bed warning to his wife, the banquet where Sejanus tricks Drusus into drinking poison, the scene in the Senate where it dawns on Sejanus what Tiberius has done—these and many other scenes may have been created for the stage before ever they were written down in narrative histories. And once created, once presented before the eyes of the Roman People, they became the story everybody knew. Not even the most scrupulous historian could avoid being influenced by them. Our best authorities, Tacitus and Suetonius, depended on historians writing at the time of the events, and Tacitus at least was well aware that 'instant myth' was the inevitable outcome of crises within the dynasty. Not that it was necessarily untrue; the real events might be just as improbable as anything seen on the stage.

Gaius was proud of his skill as a dancer and a singer, and now that he had a captive audience he turned his public role into a continuous performance. We know from an eye-witness that like a star mime-dancer he had trained choruses to accompany him as he impersonated, in appropriate costume, one god or goddess after another. He took the idea of deified Caesars to its logical end by announcing his own divinity, and setting up a Dionysiac mystery-cult with nocturnal performance rites in worship of himself.

Figure 97

The impersonations were more than just dressing up. For the Roman People he really was Jupiter, sharing the divine bed with his sister; he really was Venus, symbol of sex and the house of Caesar; he really was Mars, escorted by armed guards to avenge and punish; and above all he really was Liber, guarantor of the Roman People's right to do what it liked, regardless of the Senate and magistrates.

The Senate and magistrates were systematically terrorised and humiliated. Again, we have eye-witness accounts: an ex-consul prostrating himself to kiss Gaius' pearl-studded slipper, grovelling in gratitude for not being executed; another, at a crowded banquet, forced to listen to his wife's sexual performance being loudly and critically discussed by Gaius; other senators and their ladies, escorting Gaius on his after-dinner stroll in the gardens, having to watch their colleagues' heads cut off before their eyes. This was what the long, contested history of Roman liberty had come to—a twenty-five-year-old living god with the power of total self-indulgence, who enjoyed dressing in silk and watching people being tortured.

The old ideology was still alive. Tiberius' first act as *princeps* had been to take the election of magistrates away from the People and allow the Senate to make the choice. Now Gaius gave the People their ancient suffrage back. But there was malice in it too: candidates would have to spend money and compromise their dignity begging the citizens to elect them. Gaius also encouraged slaves to inform on their masters, thus giving every prominent Roman the permanent fear of blackmail and denunciation. The ultimate in humiliation came when Gaius had to find ways of refilling the treasury, emptied by his irresponsible extravagance. He set aside rooms in his Palatine house as a public

Figure 97. *Sestertius* of Gaius, AD 37. Obverse: head of Gaius with laurel wreath; the legend reads C. CAESAR AVG(ustus) GERMANICVS PON(tifex) M(aximus) TR(ibunicia) POT(estate). Reverse: Gaius' three sisters, DRVSILLA, twenty or twenty-one years old, flanked by AGRIPPINA, probably twenty-two, and IVLIA (Livilla), nineteen. Drusilla was Gaius' favourite; he was said to have slept with all three, but Agrippina and Julia Livilla had to serve his friends as well. (Later, he banished them both for treason.)

The iconographic details present the sisters as goddesses, each carrying a horn of plenty (*cornucopiae*). Agrippina rests her right arm on a column, and Julia holds a rudder in her right hand; they represent the Health and Fortune of the Roman People—*Salus publica populi Romani*, whose cult was founded by Gaius Iunius 'the ploughman' (p. 130 above) in 303 BC, and *Fortuna publica populi Romani Quiritium*, whose cult dates to the last years of the war with Hannibal. Between them, Drusilla holds out an offering dish (*patera*): she may be Concordia, or Venus, or whatever friendly goddess you choose. When she died in the summer of AD 38, the Senate deified her as *Panthea*, 'all the goddesses'.

brothel, staffed it with senators' wives and boys and girls of noble family, and advertised it through the streets of Rome. Raising money was one motive, but screwing the upper class was more important: any citizens who couldn't afford the fee would be lent ready cash at the door.

Of course it couldn't go on. Gaius had to raise big taxes, and used the Praetorian Guard to enforce payment. Like Sulla and the Triumvirs, he put up proscription lists. Others besides senators were now subject to his wanton cruelty. When the crowd at the Circus Maximus protested, he shouted back 'I wish the Roman People had only one neck!' An officer of the Guard, sickened by what he had to do, went in desperation to his commander:

> 'We aren't soldiers—we're bodyguards and public executioners! We bear these arms not to defend the freedom and authority of the Romans, but to protect the man who has enslaved their bodies and their minds! Every day we kill them and torture them, polluting ourselves with blood until the time when someone at Gaius' bidding will do the same to us!'

Josephus
Antiquities 19.42

His name was Cassius Chaerea, and he cared about the enslavement of his country, 'once the freest in the world', and the authority of the laws, now abolished by Gaius.

Gaius 'Caligula' was the last of the Julius Caesars. He had soon got rid of his fellow-heir, Tiberius' grandson Gemellus, and didn't take the dangerous step of adopting an heir of his own. When Chaerea and the other officers in the plot cut him down at the Palatine Games in AD 41 (he was on his way to inspect the chorus for his own performance that evening), they assumed that the dynasty was over and the Republic would resume.

So did the Senate, who believed that night that they were in control. Meeting as free agents for the first time in three generations, they denounced the tyranny of the house of Caesar and declared all members of it public enemies, to be executed without trial. So Gaius' wife and baby daughter, grieving by the body, were killed by a Guard officer. A contemporary historian gave Caesonia a brave exit line. 'Come on,' she said, 'get the last act of the drama finished.'

9.4   THE BLOOD OF AUGUSTUS

That show was over, but elsewhere on the Palatine another was just beginning, with a most unlikely protagonist. Germanicus' handicapped brother was now forty-nine, a scholarly old buffer with a stammer and a nervous tic, who drank a bit too much. He hadn't even been a senator until Gaius made him consul, as a contemptuous joke. He wasn't a Caesar: naturally, he hadn't been adopted when his brother was, and he remained Tiberius Claudius Nero Germanicus. But he couldn't count on that keeping him safe, and he was hiding in terror when the Praetorians found him. 'Here's a Germanicus!' Ironically, it was his closeness to the Caesars that first saved his life, and then gave him the mastery *Figure 98 (p. 254)* of the world.

The People were shocked at Gaius' death. They had no interest in an optimate Republic run by the Senate, and they were glad when the Praetorians' coup put Germanicus' brother in power. The Guard's rank and file didn't share their officers' view about freedom and tyranny; they needed a Caesar to justify their existence, and when they took Claudius to the barracks and hailed him as emperor, he promised them a bonus of over five years' pay per man.

Figure 99

'Emperor' is a word we have so far avoided. Julius Caesar, the People's champion against the senatorial oligarchy, was Dictator for life; his successors in power, the heirs of the Julian house, called themselves *princeps*, 'leading citizen'. So too did Claudius—but there were two things about his sudden elevation that changed the rules of the game. He was the first to depend for his power on the Praetorian Guard; and he was the first to bear the name of Caesar not by birth or adoption but by legislative act. The family name had become the title of the Roman emperor.

Claudius also took the name 'Augustus'. His two grandmothers were Augustus' wife and Augustus' sister; but there were others in whose veins ran the blood of Augustus himself. There were also aristocrats in charge of legionary armies, who might feel that if a Claudius Nero could have supreme power, so could they. His position was precarious, but he managed to keep it for thirteen years.

Claudius had a young and beautiful wife and a baby daughter (also an older girl by a previous marriage). Valeria Messallina was herself the great-grand-daughter of Augustus' sister, and they named the baby Octavia after her. A few days after Claudius became emperor, Messallina gave birth to another child, a boy, soon to be named Britannicus after Claudius' invasion of Britain in AD 43. *Figure 100 (p. 257)* She knew how vulnerable their position was, and set about removing rivals.

Claudius had brought Gaius' sisters, Agrippina and Julia Livilla, back from

Figure 99. Aureus of Claudius, AD 41. Obverse: head of Claudius with laurel wreath; the legend reads T(iberius) CLAVD(ius) CAESAR AVG(ustus) P(ontifex) M(aximus) TR(ibunicia) P(otestate). Reverse: Praetorians' barracks, with inscription on the battlements: IMPER(ator) RECEPT(us)—the emperor is 'received' under the protection of the Praetorians.

253

Figure 98. The end-game of the Julio-Claudian dynasty. For the sake of clarity, this family tree is deliberately selective; it emphasises intermarriage with other noble families, in order to show how men with names like Silanus, Plautus and Sulla could be regarded by Nero as dangerous rivals. See fig. 90 above for the top two lines, fig. 91 for the second and third, fig. 94 for the third and fourth, fig. 96 for the fourth and fifth.

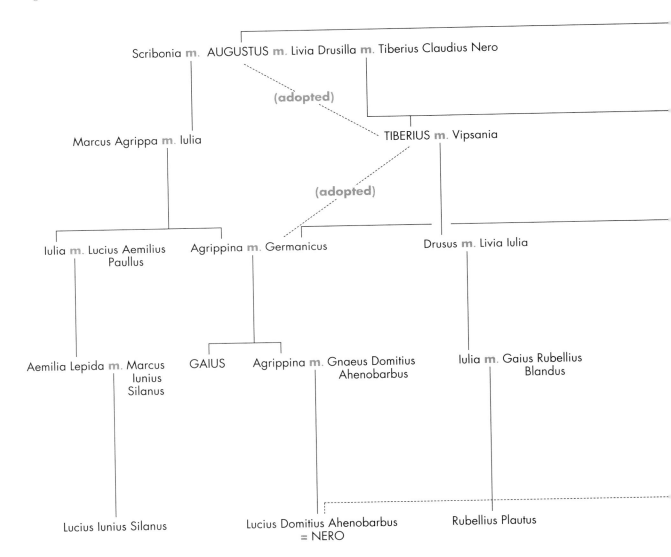

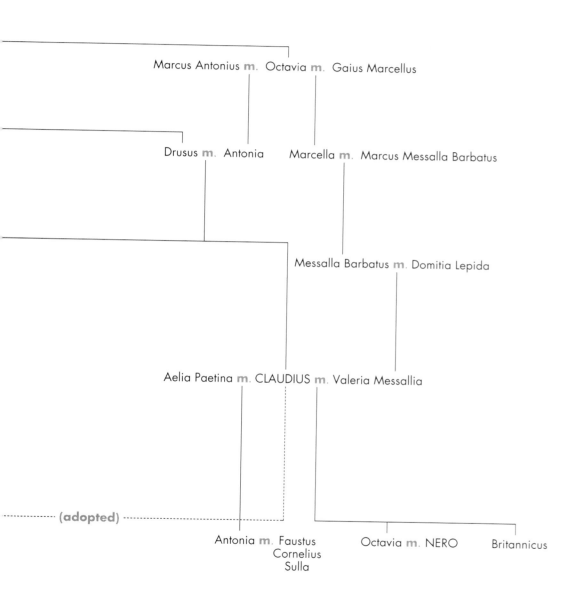

Marcus Antonius **m.** Octavia **m.** Gaius Marcellus

Drusus **m.** Antonia   Marcella **m.** Marcus Messalla Barbatus

Messalla Barbatus **m.** Domitia Lepida

Aelia Paetina **m.** CLAUDIUS **m.** Valeria Messallia

-------------- (adopted) ----------------

Antonia **m.** Faustus
Cornelius
Sulla

Octavia **m.** NERO   Britannicus

Figure 97 (p. 251) their prison islands. Still in their twenties and dangerously fertile (indeed, Agrippina already had a little boy), they were the great-granddaughters of Augustus. So too, by adoption, was Julia, daughter of Drusus the son of Tiberius. Messallina, who knew how to persuade her husband, got Julia Livilla sent back to the island and starved to death, and the other Julia executed by a guardsman's sword. She would have done the same for Agrippina, but divine anger destroyed her before she had the chance.

Venus, foremother of the Julii, used her own weapon of revenge. Messallina's intense desire for sex overcame her political judgement. Believing she could get away with anything, in AD 48 she married her latest lover, Gaius Silius, at a drunken orgy for the October wine-vintage in the imperial gardens. The revellers were dressed as satyrs and maenads, but Father Liber didn't save them when Claudius returned. (He had been in Ostia, looking after the Roman People's corn supply.) Messallina couldn't bring herself to commit suicide; the Guard officer had to kill her with his sword.

The angry goddess had avenged the divine spirit of Augustus, transfused into his blood descendants. That at least was how it seemed to those descendants themselves. Claudius knew he couldn't compete. He had already betrothed little Octavia—who was nine years old when she saw her mother's body, gashed by the tribune's sword—to Lucius Iunius Silanus, grandson of Augustus' elder granddaughter. More dangerous, though only ten years old, was Agrippina's son Lucius Domitius Ahenobarbus. Agrippina, now widowed, was about thirty-three. Whoever she married now would gain a great-great-grandson of Divus Augustus as his heir.

Claudius was her uncle; Claudius had a six-year-old son of his own; but Claudius married her, to save Rome from civil war. The Senate and People passed a law permitting the incestuous marriage 'in the public interest'. Silanus committed suicide on the wedding-day, and Octavia was betrothed to her new step-brother. The following year, AD 50, Agrippina's son was adopted as Nero Claudius Caesar. Three years after that, Octavia and Nero were married. On *that* wedding day a dreadful portent appeared: the sky seemed to be on fire.

The Roman People liked Claudius, and adored his children. But once your successor is known, not everyone wants to keep you alive. In AD 54, Nero was approaching his seventeenth birthday (in December), while Britannicus was thirteen, and would not expect to take his adult toga until the *Liberalia* the following spring. Now was the moment for an uncontested succession.

On 13 October AD 54 Jupiter called a meeting of the heavenly Senate. Claudius had turned up, asking for admission. One of the minor gods made a speech in favour. 'It's in the public interest that Romulus should have someone to eat boiled turnips with. I move that Divus Claudius be a god, and that a note to that effect be added to Ovid's *Metamorphoses*.' There was indignant opposition from Divus Augustus (it was his maiden speech):

Figure 100. The stammering scholar as super-hero: Claudius subduing Britannia. Relief panel from the south portico of the Aphrodisias *Sebasteion* (fig. 92 above).

After the disaster in AD 9, Augustus left instructions that the empire should not be extended further; but not even that trauma could halt the centuries-old tradition of Roman expansionism ('I have given them power without limit,' said Virgil's Jupiter), and Claudius needed a glorious conquest to justify his right to rule. Once the invasion was successfully achieved, he took command in person for the capture of Camulodunum (Colchester), capital of the Catuvellauni.

Seneca
Apocolocyntosis
11.4

'Was it for this that I ended the civil wars, brought peace by land and sea, founded the city on the rule of law? Who'll worship this man as a god? Who'll believe in him? Make *him* a god, and no one will believe in *you*.'

The motion was defeated. Claudius was sent down to the underworld, where Gaius Caesar claimed him as his slave.

Despite Seneca's satire, Claudius *was* deified as a god of the Roman state. But the new emperor soon ignored his cult, and got rid of his wife and children. (Seneca was Nero's tutor, but failed to convince him of the value of clemency.)

The deaths of Claudius, Britannicus and Agrippina are narrated with brilliant dramatic power by Tacitus, 'the greatest artist of antiquity', as Jean Racine called him in the preface to his play *Britannicus*. 'There is hardly one striking passage in my tragedy for which he did not give me the idea.' Was that because the story he told was already shaped for the stage? His sources will certainly have seen recent events dramatised at the theatre games—but throughout the history of the Julio-Claudians the events themselves were dramatic performances, with protagonists as histrionic as the star actors who graced their court.

One such was Paris, freed slave of Nero's aunt and now his companion in debauchery. One night he told the drunken emperor about a plot: Agrippina was going to regain her power by marrying Rubellius Plautus, who like Nero was a great-great-grandson of Augustus (pp. 254–5 above). It wasn't true, but it would soon seal the fate of both of them.

Figure 98

Another of Nero's cronies was Marcus Otho, married to the beautiful Poppaea Sabina, whose desirability he praised so often in Nero's hearing that the emperor was soon besotted by her. But Poppaea played hard to get—she wasn't going to be just a mistress—and that sealed the fate of Octavia as well. The People loved Claudius' daughter; but they liked Nero too, especially his enthusiasm for games and spectacles, and they were unaware—or chose not to see—that the glamorous young emperor and his even younger empress didn't get on.

Octavia was nineteen, and Nero twenty-two, when Poppaea's taunts goaded him into matricide. The first scheme was borrowed from the theatre, a collapsing boat in the Bay of Naples. When that failed (Agrippina swam to shore), a simpler scenario succeeded. Pretending that one of her staff had been sent to assassinate him, and not trusting the Guard to kill a daughter of Germanicus, Nero ordered the commander of the Misenum fleet to take a squad of marines to her villa and do the job there.

Did she really tell them to strike the belly that had borne Nero? Did he really come and strip the corpse, to admire his mother's figure? No one knows. But that's how the story was told (or staged), and with such people it might just be true.

As far as the Roman People knew, Claudius and Britannicus had died natural

Britannicus: a Tragedy

Claudius, resolved at last to destroy Agrippina, embraces young Britannicus. 'Grow up quickly, my boy, and I will then explain what my policy has been.' That's Robert Graves' translation of Suetonius. In Graves' novel, Claudius' policy depends on a supposed Sibylline prophecy about the Caesars and his own supposed determination to restore the Republic. Britannicus is to go secretly to the Brigantes in northern Britain, and on Nero's death 'reveal himself and return as the saviour of his country'. But Britannicus, too proud to hide, insists on staying, to succeed his father. Graves' Claudius ends his story knowing he has failed.

In fact, it is clear from Suetonius' text that for Britannicus to succeed his father is precisely what Claudius now wants. 'He that wounded you shall heal.' Britannicus shall be given his adult toga early, 'so that at last the Roman People shall have a true Caesar'. It looks like the first scene of a tragedy (though one not at all like Racine's). Next will come the banquet with the poisoned mushrooms; that and the following scenes are all from Tacitus.

Agrippina has dismissed the Praetorian Prefects who supported Britannicus, and Nero's accession is successfully stage-managed [fig. 101]. But now he's emperor, Agrippina can no longer control him. She screams at him in a fury of anger. 'Britannicus is the true heir! I'll take him to the Guards' camp! I'm Germanicus' daughter, they'll listen to me!' The next scene is a drunken party at the Saturnalia, where Nero calls on Britannicus to sing for them, and uses him as if he were a slave concubine.

At a more decorous dinner with the family, Britannicus is sitting at the boys' table, under the eye of the reclining adults. One of the servants tastes all his food and drink, but Nero's poison expert has doctored the ice-water jug. Britannicus cools his glass, drinks, and collapses in convulsions. Amid the consternation, Nero alone is unperturbed. 'An epileptic seizure. He'll soon come round.' The dinner continues, with Octavia and Agrippina concealing their horror behind carefully controlled features. Suddenly, wife and mother know what the teenage emperor is capable of.

The body is immediately cremated, and the last scene is the perfunctory funeral, as the last of the patrician Claudii goes to his fathers in a violent rainstorm that manifests the anger of the gods.

Figure 101. Emperor at sixteen: Nero crowned by Agrippina. Relief panel from the north portico of the Aphrodisias *Sebasteion* (fig. 92 above). The crown is the conqueror's laurel wreath, which is why Nero is presented not in divine nudity (compare figures 93 and 100) but as a Roman general. The reason why the figures are in such excellent condition, with no sign of weathering, is probably that the panel was taken down not long after its erection (perhaps when the news of Agrippina's 'treason' came through) and used face-down as a paving slab.

deaths, and Agrippina had been executed for treason. They welcomed Nero back to Rome, and applauded enthusiastically as a young man free of maternal disapproval was able at last to show what he could do. In modern terms, it's as if a talented rock star and racing driver was head of state. The public loved it. But they didn't like Poppaea.

Nero owed everything to the blood of Augustus transmitted by his mother. If she really had married Rubellius Plautus, Tiberius' great-grandson, any child of theirs would have had an even better title to power than his. Now she was gone, and Nero settled Plautus' business too: exile first, then assassination. He did the same for Faustus Sulla, five generations down from Sulla the dictator and dangerously married to Claudius' elder daughter Antonia. Unrivalled in descent, what Nero now needed was a son.

Octavia knew what happened to inconvenient empresses and princesses. She could have made the list:

1. Augustus' daughter Julia, banished to Pandateria at 37, starved to death at 52 (AD 14);
2. Augustus' granddaughter Julia, banished to an Adriatic island at 26, died there at 46 (AD 28);
3. Augustus' granddaughter Agrippina, banished to Pandateria at 42, starved to death at 46 (AD 33);
4. Germanicus' sister Livia Julia, starved to death in custody at 44 (AD 31);
5. Germanicus' daughter Julia Livilla, banished to Pandateria and starved to death at 23 or 24 (AD 41 or 42);
6. Tiberius' granddaughter Julia, executed at about 38 (AD 43);
7. Claudius' wife Messallina, executed at about 28 (AD 48);
8. Claudius' widow Agrippina, executed at 44 (AD 59).

She would only survive if she became pregnant by Nero before Poppaea did, and there was little chance of that.

Poppaea eventually conceived in the spring of AD 62. Octavia, now twenty-two, was immediately divorced. Nero married Poppaea in a wedding that was also a coronation—L'Incoronazione di Poppea, the triumph of raw sex over virtue and fortune, just as in Monteverdi's opera. Octavia was removed from the palace and sent away under military guard. The People of Rome, loyal to Claudius' little girl, rioted against the new empress and tore down her statues. Not since the fall of Sejanus had there been such anger on the streets. Then, on a trumped-up charge of adultery with the fleet commander, Octavia was banished to Pandateria. She was killed there on 9 June, and her head brought back as a present for Poppaea.

To win back Nero's popularity, his Praetorian Prefect Tigellinus laid on an orgy in the Campus Martius. The emperor and his party reclined on a huge raft floating in Agrippa's ornamental lake, while all around were booths and tents available for a sexual free-for-all; borrowing an idea from Gaius Caligula, the Prefect required senators' wives and daughters to offer their services. Later that year (AD 64), two-thirds of the city of Rome was destroyed by fire.

How many Roman citizens died, how many thousands were made homeless, we can only guess. Nero did his best to provide help, but the People of Rome knew his character too well. Never able to distinguish reality from imagination, he had used that marvellous backdrop of the burning city to perform 'The Fall of Troy'. People were convinced that the fire had been started on his orders. The actor emperor had lost his audience. No one now believed that the deaths of Claudius and Britannicus had been natural, or those of Agrippina and Octavia the legal punishment for treason.

Great disasters call forth prophecy. The Sibyl, who knew a thing or two about Roman autocrats, was uncharacteristically explicit: 'Aeneas' line shall end with a ruler who murders his mother.' Poppaea's child, a daughter, had died in infancy, and now, the year after the fire, Poppaea herself died (kicked by Nero in a temper) before her second pregnancy could come to term. There would be no children. The blood of Augustus had run its course.

9.5   AT LAST, A PLAY-TEXT

A plot to assassinate the last of the Caesars failed ignominiously in AD 65. Many senators were executed or forced to suicide, including two of the great names of Roman literature—Seneca, once Nero's tutor and adviser, and his nephew Marcus Lucanus ('Lucan'), once Nero's friend and fellow-poet. Lucan left unfinished a great and dreadful work, his epic poem *The Civil War*; it centred on the moment in Thessaly in 48 BC when honest Pompey failed to stop the demonic rise of Caesar, and what followed from it—the loss of Roman freedom for ever, a political system based on lies, and the worship of dead men as gods.

Meanwhile, the current tyrant could count on adulation only in the fantasy world of the court. Ever more spectacular shows, such as Nero's crowning of Tiridates as king of Parthia and the triumphal return from his tour of the Greek festivals, failed to divert the People's attention from the creation of a new palace and park from the ruins of their city, and the constant succession of conspiracies and executions. The end came when commanders of legionary armies lost their patience; in AD 68 rebellions in Gaul, Spain and Africa persuaded the Praetorian Guard that Nero wasn't worth defending.

Nero woke on 9 June, the anniversary of Octavia's execution, to find the palace almost deserted. In disguise, with just four loyal servants, he made his way out of Rome to what he hoped was a safe house. Creeping through brambles and reeds to the back of the house, they broke through the wall into a slave-bedroom in the basement. There, he resolved on suicide. 'Dead! And

To Hell with the *Populares*

Every Roman knew that the heroes of the Republic from Lucius Brutus to Scipio (our chapters 6 and 7) enjoyed eternal life among the blessed ones in the Elysian Fields. But once internal conflict became part of the Roman story (chapter 8), one might ask also who deserved punishment in hell. No doubt Cicero's epic poem on his consulship put Catiline in Tartarus. That's where we find him in Virgil, on Aeneas' prophetic shield, hanging tormented by the Furies while Cato acts as judge among the blessed. There could hardly be a clearer statement of optimate values.

The Caesars, of course, were *populares* (remember the whip in Cicero's dream, p. 204 above). But once the Augustan consensus had been achieved, writers who admired Cicero felt free to damn the People's historic champions. Writing under Tiberius, Velleius Paterculus referred to Tiberius Gracchus' 'pernicious policies' and suspected Gaius Gracchus of a plan to give himself monarchical power. His contemporary Valerius Maximus was even more explicit: Tiberius Gracchus was an enemy of the state; it was through the wisdom of the Senate that he was punished by death for daring to promote an agrarian law; Gaius Gracchus' death too was a salutary example, and both brothers deserved to be deprived of burial for having overthrown the stability of the Republic.

Such attitudes fitted Lucan's purpose perfectly. His Caesar is indeed a *popularis*, and in league with the powers of hell. In Lucan's underworld, revealed by necromancy, the blessed in Elysium include not only virtuous worthies like Decius and Curius but Sulla as well; the Gracchi and all the other *populares* are in Tartarus with Catiline, applauding Caesar's victories and demanding possession of the Elysian Fields. The *populares* won the civil war, and the autocracy of the Caesars gave the People freedom *from* by taking away the oligarchs' freedom *to*. Paradoxically, therefore, the great epic of lost liberty presupposed the ideology of right-wing politics.

Figure 102. *Denarii* issued by Galba in Spain, April–June AD 68. (*a*) Obverse: bust of the *Genius* of the Roman People (GENIO P R) with horn of plenty. Reverse: Mars the Avenger (MARTI VLTORI). (*b*) Obverse: bust of the goddess Libertas. Reverse: cap of liberty (*pilleus*) between two daggers, imitating Brutus' pre-Philippi type (fig. 77 above). The combined legends read LIBERTAS P R RESTITVTA (on this example, the R is missing beyond the right-hand dagger), either 'the liberty of the Roman People restored', or 'liberty restored to the Roman People'.

Galba at this point was using the title 'Legate of the Senate and People of Rome'; descended from an ancient patrician family, he probably saw no conflict between the liberty of the Roman People and what Brutus and the *optimates* had fought for at Philippi. Similarly Mars the Avenger, whose cult recalled the punishment of Caesar's murderers, now symbolised vengeance for Nero's victims.

Figure 102

such an artist!' The Praetorians in pursuit had orders to take him alive, for public execution, but by the time they found him he had cut his throat. His last words were 'This is honesty'.

Already, the People were dancing in the streets to celebrate their freedom. They hadn't cared when Nero attacked the Senate, but an emperor's job is to look after the citizens' welfare, and in that Nero had spectacularly failed. Now, when the Senate met in the Praetorians' barracks and recognised Galba as *princeps*, the People enthusiastically concurred. The new emperor was on his way from Spain, but already the statues of the deified Poppaea were being pulled down and those of Octavia re-erected. Galba's orders thus brought about what the People had tried to achieve six years before, though now it was only for Octavia's memory and the urn that held her restored ashes.

Galba himself entered Rome some time in October, and one of his first public engagements must have been the opening day of the People's games, the *ludi plebeii*, on 4 November. The playwrights and producers had had four months to devise their presentations of the new myth of the fallen tyrant. And now, for the first time in the whole long story, we have the text of one of their plays. It survived only because someone, at an unknown date not later than the twelfth century, thought it was by Seneca, and so it was copied and recopied along with Seneca's eight tragedies on Greek mythological subjects. On internal evidence, the date of its composition is late AD 68.

We know the date, and we can *place* it too—in just the same part of Rome as the performance we imagined for Apollo's games 278 years before (pp. 171–4 above). But what was then an open piazza, between Apollo's temple and Carmenta's Gate, is now dominated by the huge bulk of the Theatre of Marcellus, built by Augustus in memory of the beloved son of his sister Octavia. Octavia's portico stands nearby; on the other side are the tombs of the patrician Claudii; incorporated in the theatre itself is the temple of Loyalty (*Pietas*). It was in honour of Octavia that her grandson Claudius named his ill-fated daughter, and what Galba sees in the theatre on 4 November AD 68 is an act of loyalty on behalf of the People of Rome. Let's take our seats behind him.

.6 GRAND OPERA

In front of us, the elaborate stage building shows the usual three doors. The central one is the biggest and grandest, but there are torches burning and yawning guards on duty outside all three. From the window above the left-hand door comes the opening aria of the play, a woman's voice, lamenting.

> Resplendent dawn is driving from the sky
> the wandering stars, the giant Sun
> lifts up his golden hair to bring
> bright day back to the universe.
> And what must I do, overcome
> by ills so many and so great,
> but tell again the oft-told tale
> of my distresses, shed more tears
> than the sea-haunting Halcyons
> or the bird-daughters of Pandion?
> Greater than theirs my misery.
>
> Hear me, my mother, for whose fate
> my tears must ever fall, from whom
> all my afflictions spring.
> O mother, hear your daughter's cry,
> if in the house of death

any perception still remains.
Would that the age-old spinner of my fate
had cut my thread before that day
on which I wept to see
your wounded side, your face besmeared with blood.
How hateful was the light of day,
of every day thenceforth to this,
a light more dreaded than the darkest night;
while I have had to live
under a vile stepmother's rule,
to bear her spiteful enmity
and angry looks.
She was my vengeful Fury, she
lighted my marriage chamber
with Stygian torches, she destroyed
my hapless father's life;
whom once the whole world, beyond Ocean's bounds,
obeyed; whose captains put to rout
the Britons, till that day unknown and free.

And thou art dead, my father,
struck down by a wife's wickedness,
thy house and family a tyrant's slaves,
a tyrant's prisoners.

Octavia
1–33

We the audience know who the singer is. It is someone we have known and loved.

It is daybreak in the eighth year of Nero's reign. As the despairing notes of Octavia's lament die away, gradually the morning business of the city begins. It's a huge stage, 90 metres wide and deep in proportion, well able to accommodate two separate groups to act as choruses. (They don't of course use the *orchestra*; that's where Galba and the senators are sitting.) To the left, below Octavia's window, are the People of Rome, dressed more or less as we in the audience are; they are anxious, unhappy, speaking low. To the right are the courtiers in their sumptuous silks, gossiping and laughing in affected tones; they cluster around the right-hand door, from which in due course emerges Poppaea, haughty and glamorous, to receive their obsequious homage.

A woman comes forward from the group on the left. With a contemptuous look across the stage, she addresses us:

Are you impressed by the Court's splendid show?
But it's a fraud, its benefits are fragile,
and if you're really star-struck by it, see

what lurking Fortune's sudden onslaught did
to the house and family of Claudius,
whom once the world obeyed.

Octavia
34–39

She reminds us of the conquest of Britain, the murder of Claudius by Agrippina, the murder of Britannicus and Agrippina by Nero, and the grief of Octavia, Nero's adoptive sister and reluctant wife. The empress shrinks from her cruel and angry husband; they burn with hatred for each other.

Her only solace is our loyal devotion,
offered in vain; what we advise can't touch
her savage grief; her noble indignation,
strengthened by suffering, cannot be governed.
Alas, what dreadful deed our fear foresees,
and may the power of the gods prevent it!

Octavia
51–56

We know that it won't.

Octavia sings again within the palace, ending on a phrase we recognise from another of Nero's victims, Lucan: of all her family only she remains, 'the shadow of a great name'. The woman on the stage sings back; we realise that she is Octavia's nurse, and the two choruses drift offstage as the moving platform (*exostra*) brings out Octavia in her chamber for a duet followed by an iambic dialogue between the two women. The themes already introduced are elaborated in the dramatic rhetoric of Octavia's despairing rage and the nurse's vain advice that she be patient. Nero is a bloodthirsty tyrant, who hates all those of noble blood (we remember Galba's ancient family); the emperor's proud harlot now demands Octavia's head as the price of her favours; the goddess *Pietas*, whose shrine is in this very theatre, has fled from the court, her place now taken by the torch-wielding Fury of hell; the citizens of Rome are devoted to Octavia, but their power is less than the emperor's.

The nurse offers the consoling thought that Nero will get tired of Poppaea (winged *Cupido* is a fickle god), and sings an aria on Juno's tolerance of the loves of Jupiter. But that's no consolation for Octavia, and when the nurse hopes that some avenging god will manifest himself (we think of Vindex, 'the Avenger', who rebelled in Gaul), Octavia's proof of the gods' anger with the house of Claudius is the way Venus destroyed Messallina by sexual infatuation (p. 256 above). That was what brought the Furies' torches into the palace.

The *exostra* rolls back in; the choruses come on stage again. The citizens' anxious murmuring now takes musical shape, as they sing of the bad news: Nero is to take a new empress, divorced Octavia is to leave her father's palace. They feel responsible. Through fear, they have forgotten Claudius and betrayed his daughter.

Yet our forefathers knew

Octavia
291–294

true Roman virtue; they were men
in whom the seed and blood of Mars still lived.
They were the men who drove proud kings
out of this city.

They avenged Lucretia, they avenged Verginia—both victims of a tyrant's sexual desire, just as Octavia will be. We the audience are the Roman People, and these stories are the foundation legends of our liberty, told and retold on the Roman stage.

The chorus goes on to remind us of another royal palace and another tragedy of murder, as Tullia, Tarquin's queen, drives her chariot wheels over her father's body (p. 132 above). And our time too has seen such things: the chorus turns from an impious daughter to an impious son, telling the dreadful tale of Agrippina and the ship of death, her vain survival and her great last words. 'Strike this womb, that bore such a monster.' So the choral song ends, with Agrippina's grim soul escaping through the wound.

And now a man comes forward from the other chorus, the courtiers. We know from his mask that he is Seneca. Cheating Fortuna has raised him high, and he foresees his fall. The philosopher reminds us of the golden age of Saturnus, and how each subsequent epoch was more degenerate than the last.

Octavia
429–434

Vices accumulated through the ages
are drowning us, our century weighs us down.
For now crime rules, impiety exults,
and base desire for sex usurps all power.
Lust conquers all; its ever-greedy hands
plunder the whole world's wealth, to squander it.

Suddenly the guards are at attention, the central doors are opened. Enter the twenty-four-year-old emperor, with his Praetorian Prefect. 'Bring me the heads of Plautus and Sulla!' The Prefect goes.

Figure 98
(pp. 254–5)

Seneca engages his ex-pupil with a reminder of his treatise on clemency, but Nero is unimpressed. The consent of the governed? The sword will bring that about. The People must fear, and obey. Plautus and Sulla are conspiring, and must die. So must Octavia—she can follow her brother. 'What stands high, must fall.' We remember Nero's hatred of noble birth; Octavia and Britannicus were the children of a Claudius Nero and a Valeria Messallina. So Seneca's answer is aimed at the new emperor, the aristocrat Sulpicius Galba, sitting among the senators:

Octavia
472–476

This is what's good: to stand out among nobles,
protect the public interest, show mercy,
avoid fierce bloodshed, let your anger cool,
and give this world and age tranquillity.
This is true virtue, and the way to heaven.

Think of Augustus. Loyally, we applaud, and Seneca reminds Nero of the speech he wrote for him at his accession, contrasting Augustus' youth in civil war with the consensus the new emperor enjoyed. Nero's response is chilling.

> The gods have given me this, that Rome herself
> and the Senate are my slaves; unwillingly
> they beg and grovel, forced by fear of me.

Octavia
492–494

Seneca had alluded to the Augustan slogan 'saving the citizens' (which is now *Figure 82 (p. 214)* Galba's slogan too); Nero dismisses it with contempt, and gives a long and gruesome account of Augustus' own career. Killing citizens, holding power by fear—that's how Augustus found his 'way to heaven', and so will Nero, with his rivals dead and a son to deify him.

Seneca takes the opportunity: what better mother for divine offspring than Octavia, daughter of Divus Claudius, married to her brother like Juno? Yes, Poppaea is beautiful, but desire for her will pass; only virtue lasts. Besides, the People will never accept it, and a good emperor should follow the citizens' wishes. Nero's patience runs out. 'Just once, I'm going to do something Seneca disapproves of! . . . Tomorrow, I shall marry Poppaea.' He stalks back into the palace, and Seneca walks wearily off.

The guards have gone, the stage is empty, the day is over. There is silence, or only enough music to make us think of night. Suddenly, the centre of the stage opens, flame and smoke billow from the trap-door, and a ghastly figure emerges with a blazing torch in her hand.

> Through opened earth from Tartarus I come.
> My bloodstained hand has brought a torch from hell
> to light an evil wedding! Let Poppaea
> marry my son—a mother's vengeful hate
> shall turn the torches into funeral fires!

Octavia
593–597

It is Agrippina, but it is also the Fury Erinys, seeking revenge for matricide. She has a worthy death prepared for the impious tyrant—disgrace and flight, the loss of all his wealth and power. He will die 'destroyed, deserted, lacking everything', just as we know it really happened at Phaon's villa five months ago.

This horrifying spectre was once an empress and a mother. If only her baby had died innocent! He would have been welcomed by his noble ancestors, the bronze-bearded Domitii, whom now his crimes have shamed for ever. But she is guilty too, disastrous as stepmother, mother and wife. 'Why do I wait to hide my face in hell?' She plants the torch in the bracket outside Poppaea's door, and goes back down. The silence of night returns.

This time dawn comes with a bustle of activity, as slaves in imperial livery drape garlands and streamers all over the set and scatter rose petals for the royal wedding. As soon as they've gone, the courtiers in their finery appear, shrill and excited. The right-hand door is flung open and Poppaea makes her entrance. Trumpets blare, the central doors are opened, and Nero appears. The wedding formalities—the auspices, the witnessing of the contract, the joining of hands—are a sumptuous spectacle of arrogance and adulation, full of irony for us, the audience. We recognise the senators in their portrait masks as they make their obeisance: Seneca again, and Lucan and Thrasea and Petronius and Corbulo . . . The auspices are not good for *them*. We recognise too the emperor's companions and confidential staff—Locusta the poisons expert, Pythagoras, Helius, Patrobius and the rest, whom we saw only a month or two ago led in chains through the streets to execution, by order of Galba.

And now the stage is full of dancers and musicians. Tragedy becomes mime for this part of the show, as Poppaea, her orange veil seductively diaphanous, shimmies to the altar to burn incense for Venus Victrix. Soon the torches are lit for the procession, the harlot bride is brought to Nero's couch, and at last the central doors close behind them and the music dies away. A whole day has passed in celebration of power and sex.

Dawn for the third time. The chorus of citizens comes on stage, grieving amid the debris of the wedding orgy. Octavia appears from the left-hand door, banished from her father's palace. She sings:

> Weep not, my friends; this day
> of public gladness and festivity
> must not be marred by tears.
> To show your love
> and favour in my cause
> so plainly, might enrage our emperor
> and bring you sorrow for my sake.

Octavia
646–650

She tries to comfort them ('I am still Augustus' sister'), but of course it's no good. She knows, and they know, that she is doomed. She leaves the stage weeping and terrified, and the chorus—who represent us, the citizen body—reproach themselves again:

> Where is that Roman People's strength,
> the strength that broke ere now
> so many great men's power,
> that gave, in days gone by, just laws
> to our unconquered land, authority
> to men of worth,
> voted for war or peace, tamed savage tribes,
> kept captive kings in chains?
>
> Today on every side offends our eyes
> the dazzling image of Poppaea
> coupled with Nero.
> Let us not spare them!

> Tear them down to the ground!
> Down with these too true likenesses
> of her imperial highness!
> Down with her, too, from her exalted bed!
> Then on to the emperor's house
> with fire and sword!

Octavia
669–689

The torches are still burning in front of the stage building. They seize them and run out, shouting defiance.

Immediately the central doors open and Poppaea and her nurse appear. The new empress is distraught. Horrific dreams have tormented her wedding night. Ignoring the nurse's flattering reassurances, she resolves to visit the temples for prayer and sacrifice. The chorus of courtiers sings her on her way: her beauty will bring Jupiter himself out of heaven. Poppaea outshines even Helen of Troy, 'the face that launched a lamentable war and brought the throne of Phrygia to the ground'. At which ill-omened point, enter a messenger.

Call out the Guard! The People are attacking the emperor's palace, their love for Octavia has driven them to fury, they're hurling down Poppaea's statues and abusing them, they want to do the same to Poppaea herself, and if not they'll burn the palace down. As the messenger runs in to report, and the Praetorians' bugles sound behind the scene, the courtiers console themselves with a song about *Cupido*, the god of desire. His fires are more powerful than those the citizens wield. The People will be punished—but the god is dangerous, and again the courtiers remember the fall of Troy. We remember it too; we lived through it four years ago, while Nero, the last of Aeneas' descendants, watched the fires and sang.

And here he is right on cue, bursting out from the central doors with a furious monologue. He's been too soft; the People must pay for this in blood, and his sister too, who must be behind it. For this outrage, death isn't enough:

> Soon let my flames fall on the city's roofs,
> and let the guilty populace be crushed
> by fire, destruction, hunger, cruel grief . . .
> Evil must break them, burdened evermore
> beneath my yoke, or they may dare again
> to raise their eyes in sacrilege against
> my consort's face. By punishment and terror
> they'll learn to obey their emperor's merest nod.

Octavia
831–843

The Praetorian Prefect comes to report the arrest and execution of the ringleaders. Nero explodes. *That's* not enough—this rabble has attacked his palace and threatened his empress! Its punishment must be something the world will remember. We know what it will be.

Meanwhile, the emperor's wrath demands his sister's death, and his sister's head. The Prefect is horrified, but his protests are in vain. Octavia is guilty; put her on a ship, have her taken somewhere out of the way and killed. The Prefect salutes and marches off; Nero goes back into the palace.

The chorus of citizens, cowed, bruised, and fewer in number, comes slowly on to the stage. They sing of the Gracchi, their noble champions of the past, destroyed for loving the People too well. And it's still true: today's citizens will see the lady they tried to bring back to her father's court and her imperial bedroom, wretched, weeping, dragged off to her death. Better to keep your head down; it's only the great whom Fortuna destroys. We know they are wrong; they don't realise what Nero has in store for them.

Enter the soldiers, with Octavia in chains for her last aria. The tyrant and his queen will not even let her die in her native land. *Pietas* is gone, there are no gods, the Fury Erinys rules the world. The chastened chorus strengthen her with the thought that princesses and empresses before her have suffered the same fate. She accepts the verdict of Fortuna, and prays for vengeance to the gods of hell. The soldiers hustle her on to the ship, and there is one last low-key song from the citizens' chorus. May Octavia be borne by the winds to Diana's temple among the Taurians, where the barbarians are less cruel than Rome. They only kill foreigners; Rome enjoys shedding her citizens' blood.

The play is over, and we stand to applaud Galba as he leaves the theatre. Thanks to him, she got her vengeance in the end, and so did we. As we follow the champion of our freedom back through the city gate, we look to the right at the temple of Hope. It carries the name of Germanicus, another friend of the People in his time, whose early death was seen as the end of all hope for Rome. The goddess in her mercy keeps from us the knowledge of how little time Galba has got left, how soon the citizens' blood will be spilt again.

| 9.7 | **SOLDIERS ON THE RAMPAGE** |

Augustus was clever, ruthless and lucky, but even so it took him forty years to achieve the consensus that freed Rome from the fear of civil war. His great-great-grandson—not Nero, Nymphidius Sabinus—blew it in a single act.

Nymphidius was Nero's last Praetorian Prefect, and he claimed, perhaps rightly, to be an illegitimate son of Gaius Caligula. When he saw Nero was finished, he thought his moment had come and promised the Praetorians a bonus of twice what even Claudius had paid. Nothing came of it, and Nymphidius was killed. But the Praetorians wanted their money.

Galba was a hard-bitten Roman of the old school, with clear views about military discipline. 'I don't *buy* soldiers,' he said. So they killed him, openly in the middle of the Forum before the eyes of the Roman People. The murder took place at the Lacus Curtius, which marked the spot where Marcus Curtius had galloped into the chasm in heroic self-sacrifice all those centuries before (p. 149

Sporus

Sporus was a freed slave-boy in Nero's imperial household. His freedom did him little good, for he had the misfortune to be not only beautiful but also a look-alike of the empress Poppaea Sabina. When Poppaea died in AD 65, Nero had Sporus castrated and made him take her place. He simply became Poppaea: addressed by her name, attended by her maids, wearing her clothes and hairstyle, he was formally married to the emperor during the tour of Greece in 66.

'Sabina' played his role faithfully to the end. He was one of the four freedmen who went with Nero on his last desperate journey; Nero wanted to kill him, knowing how he would be treated if taken alive, but was too preoccupied with his own suicide, and Sporus fled.

They caught him, and took him straight to the bed of the Praetorian Prefect. Since Nymphidius hoped to be emperor himself, it suited him very well to inherit the imperial consort—and when Nymphidius was killed, it suited Otho too. But Otho had to go to war, and lost. When Vitellius swaggered into Rome in June AD 69, the last protection had gone.

Vitellius knew exactly what he was going to do with 'Sabina'. He had plans for a great gladiatorial show, and the arena was often used to combine entertainment for the crowd with the punishment of malefactors. As a modern expert puts it,

> the point is that the criminal is to be humiliated in his dramatic *persona* and, of course, he must suffer physically. Death is almost incidental, in that the arena's function in the context of aggravated death penalties is to provide a spectacle of suffering so severe that death must inevitably follow.

In this 'fatal charade', Sporus would play the part of the virgin Proserpina, to be ravished by the Lord of the Dead. The ravishing would be real, and the emperor could award the role of Pluto to as many gladiators as he saw fit. Rape was no doubt familiar enough to him by now, but not as a public exhibition. Sporus killed himself before the games came on.

He must have been about seventeen, a boy whose life was destroyed by men who cared only about sex and power. He too deserves to have his story told.

above). A different sort of chasm had opened now.

The question was no longer who had the right to hold power, but who had the means to seize it. The Praetorians' man was Nero's old friend Otho, husband of Poppaea. The Rhine legions wanted Aulus Vitellius, a lifelong courtier since his boyhood on Capri with Tiberius. The armies of the east supported Titus Flavius Vespasianus ('Vespasian'), a blunt, tough soldier who had just suppressed the Jewish revolt. Between them, they brought civil war back to Rome in all its horror.

Otho died honourably by suicide, hoping to be a self-sacrifice for Rome's safety like Curtius, Decius and Regulus in the old stories. Vitellius died foully by torture, inflicted in public, on the Gemonian Steps below the Capitol, by men of the Danube legions who had seized Rome for Vespasian. Already the temple of Jupiter on the Capitol was a smoking ruin, and now there was an orgy of murder and looting in Rome.

Vespasian's victory and the rule of his brief dynasty (he was succeeded first by his elder son Titus, then by his younger son Domitian) formed the subject of the first major work of Rome's greatest historian. Tacitus was about twelve years old in the 'year of the four emperors' (AD 69), and in his forties, an ex-consul, when he began the *Histories*:

Tacitus *Histories*
1.2.1, 1.3.2

> The story upon which I embark is one rich in disaster, marked by bitter fighting, rent by treason, and even in peace sinister. Four emperors perished violently. There were three civil wars . . . In short, Rome's unparalleled sufferings supplied ample proof that the gods are indifferent to our tranquillity, but eager for our punishment.

It wasn't Vespasian's fault. He was a military man from the backwoods of the Sabine country, grandson of a legionary who had fought for Pompey at Pharsalus. Bringing the virtues of his upbringing to a world that was desperately in need of them, Vespasian was the nearest imperial Rome could get to the farmer-soldiers of the middle Republic. On one occasion when he was a provincial governor, the locals pelted him with turnips; as emperor, he revoked a military officer's commission because he wore too much perfume ('you should have smelt of garlic,' he said).

Down-to-earth, unpretentious, economical, he even managed to make self-indulgent luxury unfashionable among the Roman elite. In conscious imitation of the elder Cato (pp. 180–2 above), he used the archaic powers of the censorship 'to stabilise a commonwealth tottering on the brink of ruin'. His greatest monument in Rome was what was later called the Colosseum—the Flavian Amphitheatre, a huge public arena pointedly constructed on the site of the lake in Nero's new palace grounds. 'What was the tyrant's pleasure is now the People's.'

In his seventieth year Vespasian became aware that he was becoming a god (as he sardonically put it), and he made sure that his sons would succeed him. What happened to the Julio-Claudian dynasty happened even faster to the

The Fleet Commander

On 24 August AD 79 the commander of the Misenum fleet saw a sinister cloud rising to a huge height to the east, across the Bay of Naples. There had been earth tremors for several days, so clearly something horrific was happening. He took a ship across to investigate, and to bring help to the refugees. He never returned.

The next morning his sister and her son, along with the terrified inhabitants of Misenum, tried to get away to safety. Years later the commander's nephew remembered the scene in a letter to Tacitus:

> On the landward side a fearful black cloud was rent by forked and quivering bursts of flame, and parted to reveal great tongues of fire, like flashes of lightning magnified in size . . . Soon afterwards the cloud sank down to earth and covered the sea; it had already blotted out Capri and hidden the promontory of Misenum from sight . . . Ashes were already falling, not as yet very thickly. I looked round: a dense black cloud was coming up behind us, spreading over the earth like a flood. 'Let us leave the road while we can still see,' I said, 'or we shall be knocked down and trampled underfoot by the crowd behind.' We had scarcely sat down to rest when darkness fell, not the darkness of a moonless or cloudy night, but as if the lamp had been put out in a closed room. You could hear the shrieks of women, the wailing of infants, and the shouting of men . . . Many besought the aid of the gods, but still more imagined that there were no gods left, and that the universe was plunged into eternal darkness for ever.

This was where Hercules had defeated the Giants and buried them beneath the earth (pp. 31–2 above). Now the terrified people believed they could see their huge forms in the darkness, and hear the sound of trumpets, as the Giants rose again to take their vengeance.

Did the despised Christians welcome the horror?

> 'Behold! the Lord descendeth to judgement! He maketh fire come down from heaven in the sight of men! Woe! woe! ye strong and mighty! Woe to ye of the fasces and the purple! Woe to the idolater and the worshipper of the beast!'

That's Lord Lytton, in *The Last Days of Pompeii* (1834): 'God is forth upon the wings of the elements! The new Gomorrah is doomed!'

The dead fleet commander would have had nothing but contempt for all of that. A historian and scientist as well as a soldier, and a friend of Vespasian (they were two of a kind), Gaius Plinius Secundus was a sceptical humanist. In the great *Natural History* which he dedicated to Titus, he attributes belief in the gods to mere human weakness:

> For mortal to help mortal, that is 'god'. *That* is the road to everlasting glory, the road that Roman leaders have taken, the road now trodden with heavenly step, in company with his sons, by Vespasianus Augustus, the greatest ruler of all time, as he comes to the aid of the exhausted world.

It's good to know that there were still Romans willing to live, and to die, by that noble principle.

Flavian: the generation brought up in privilege squandered the founder's achievement. Titus, the elder, was at least a successful general (it was he who destroyed Jerusalem), and so popular he was called 'the darling of the human race'; but he reigned only two years, dying before the honeymoon expired. His brief time as emperor saw great disasters—fire, plague, volcanic eruption—but if the gods were angry, it could hardly have been with him.

His brother Domitian was very different—a formidably capable ruler, but arrogant, suspicious and cruel. The soldiers strongly approved of him, for giving them action (in Germany and on the Danube), for commanding in person and for increasing their pay by a third. The senators hated him, for his ruthless elimination of men he suspected. For after a challenge to his rule by the legate of Upper Germany in AD 89, Domitian became paranoid about conspiracies. Tacitus provides a vivid eye-witness memoir of

> the Senate house under siege, the senators surrounded by a cordon of troops, and that one fell stroke that sent so many consulars to their death, so many noble ladies into banishment or exile. . . . Before long we senators led Helvidius to prison, watched in shame the sufferings of Mauricus and Rusticus, and stained ourselves with Senecio's innocent blood.
>
> Even Nero used to avert his eyes and, though he ordered abominations, forebore to witness them. The worst of our torments under Domitian was to see him with his eyes fixed upon us. Every sigh was registered against us; and when we all turned pale he did not scruple to make us marked men by a glance of his savage countenance—that blood-red countenance which saved him from ever being seen to blush for shame.

Domitian was assassinated in a palace plot organised by his chamberlain Parthenius. The conspirators had a replacement emperor ready and waiting, the elderly senator Cocceius Nerva, who took up his position that very day (18 September AD 96). The Senate was overjoyed; the Roman People were indifferent; the soldiers were furious.

The following year the Praetorian Guard mutinied, forcing Nerva to surrender the men responsible for the assassination. Their ex-Prefect was killed with a single stroke, but they took their time with Parthenius, stuffing his mouth with his severed genitals before strangling him. Nerva was compelled to announce to the Roman People his gratitude to the soldiers for their punishment of wicked criminals.

One of the consuls of that year was Cornelius Tacitus. As his greatest modern interpreter drily observed, the historian was 'adequately informed' about the realities of Roman imperial politics. Tacitus 'had heard the Praetorians baying for blood along the Roman streets', 'had seen and loathed . . . the turbulence of armed men'. He had lived through events which gave his life's work—the history of power at Rome from Augustus to Domitian—the authority and the vividness that only an insider's narrative can show. He knew how important it was. He understood very well his responsibility as the analyst of Roman tyranny. And the story he told is the last of the myths of Rome.

'If I live long enough,' he wrote, 'I have reserved for my old age the principate of Divus Nerva and the rule of Traianus ['Trajan'], a safer and more fruitful subject in a period of rare happiness, when you can think what you want and say what you think.' Tacitus' 'happy period' was picked up by his admirer Edward Gibbon at the start of *The Decline and Fall* (p. 12 above). For Nerva and his adopted successor mark a real turning point. When a man born in Spain becomes emperor, as Trajan did, the story of Rome is no longer that of a city state, with however wide dominions, but of a world empire with a cosmopolitan capital.

The first words of Tacitus' great narrative are *Urbem Romam*, 'the city of Rome'. At just the time he was writing the *Annals*, the satirist Juvenal created 'Mr Shadow' (Umbricius), a born-and-bred Roman of Rome who is leaving the city in despair. He piles his belongings on a cart and makes for the Porta Capena. There, by the fountain and grove where Numa met Egeria, he delivers his great tirade against the city, and against its current population of soldiers in hob-nailed boots, thugs, creeps and foreigners. 'I can't stand it, citizens— Rome has gone *Greek*!' And he leaves, ironically, for Greek Cumae, the home of the Sibyl. Like her, like Numa, in this new world he has become a ghost.

10

THE DREAM THAT WAS ROME

LONG PERSPECTIVES

The Romans had two different ways of thinking about 'Greeks'—by which they meant all Greek-speakers, from the Adriatic to the Red Sea. The one Umbricius took for granted saw them as opportunist hangers-on of empire, exploiting the power that ruled them and corrupting the good old honest Latin character. That was a view that went back to the elder Cato (p. 182 above) and achieved its classic statement in Horace, who could even believe that the Romans were untouched by Greek culture until the Punic Wars (p. 217 above). But the Romans also knew that Greek cultural influence went back to the very beginning. As Tacitus himself put it, the invention of writing was taught to the Greeks by Kadmos the Phoenician, and then to the Latins by Evander the Arkadian.

It's unfortunate that nineteenth- and twentieth-century classicists were prepared to believe Horace, and to dismiss the idea of Greek influence in the archaic period as a mere fable. Coupled with a romantic (and essentially racist) view of the Romans as different in kind from the imaginative and creative Greeks, that preconception caused the most influential authorities to announce that the Romans had no real mythology at all, and that what passes for it is mere literary imitation, frivolous, late and artificial. It was even suggested—and the idea is not dead yet—that while the Romans had *once* had a genuine mythology of their own, they abandoned it in a process of conscious 'demythologising'. These fantasies have been rendered untenable by archaeological excavation.

First came the discovery in 1938—though it wasn't properly published till the 1960s—of the archaic temple in the Cattlemarket, and its spectacular terra-cotta group of Hercules and Minerva (p. 28 above). Then in 1958 the bronze

Figure 9

Figure 7

Figure 2

dedication plaque for the Dioskouroi (p. 22 above) was found at Lavinium. Those two items demonstrated how familiar the Latins of the sixth century BC were with early Greek myth, and how their own cults presupposed it. But in 1989 the perspective was extended three centuries further back by the five Greek letters found scratched on a grave-marker pot in the Iron Age community which became the Latin city of Gabii (p. 13 above).

These finds make it not only possible but necessary to rethink the story-world of the Romans. Items that were previously an embarrassment, to be ignored or dismissed, now become intelligible: the Tarquins as a Corinthian dynasty; the chapels of the Argives, embedded into Roman religious ritual; the cult of Pan at the Lupercal; the very name of Rome itself, as the Greek for 'strength'. The sophisticated iconography of fourth-century BC Latin bronze-work has ceased to be an anomaly, hard to fit into the supposedly primitive pre-literary world of Rome, now that it can be read as the outcome of a long tradition. The main beneficiary of this shift of outlook is Liber, the Roman Dionysos, whose role as the symbol of the citizens' liberty now becomes apparent.

The Romans were indeed conscious that they were different; but the difference was not innate. On the contrary, it was something they *created*, by their conquest first of Italy and then of the Greek world. That too became part of their mythology, enriching their imaginative experience in a Janus-faced symbiosis of discipline and licence, authority and excess. When authority gained the upper hand, in the second century BC, the tradition of a free Republic of citizens, resisting domination by an oligarchy, was powerful enough to fight back and impose its own political solution. The consequence of *that* was an autocracy that outgrew its origins and became a monster, spawning as it did so a whole new repertoire of mythic stories.

One of them, as we saw in the previous chapter, was Nero's supposed responsibility for the great fire of Rome. Tacitus reports:

> To suppress this rumour, Nero fabricated scapegoats—and punished with every refinement the notoriously depraved Christians (as they were popularly called). Their originator, Christ, had been executed in Tiberius' reign by the governor of Judaea, Pontius Pilatus. But in spite of this temporary setback the deadly superstition had broken out afresh, not only in Judaea (where the mischief had started) but even in Rome. All degraded and shameful practices collect and flourish in the capital.
>
> First, Nero had self-acknowledged Christians arrested. Then, on their information, large numbers of others were condemned—not so much for incendiarism as for their anti-social tendencies. Their deaths were made farcical. Dressed in wild animals' skins, they were torn to pieces by dogs, or crucified, or made into torches to be ignited after dark as substitutes for daylight. Nero provided his Gardens for the spectacle, and exhibited displays in the Circus, at which he mingled with the

crowd—or stood in a chariot, dressed as a charioteer. Despite their guilt as Christians, and the ruthless punishment it deserved, the victims were pitied. For it was felt that they were being sacrificed to one man's brutality rather than to the national interest.

Tacitus Annals
15.44.2–5

We know who some of them may have been—Prisca and Aquila, Epainetos and Maria, Andronikos and the others Paul had mentioned by name in the *Epistle to the Romans*. He had urged them to obey 'the powers that be' and pay their taxes, but rendering unto Caesar the things that were Caesar's had not saved them from Nero's cruelty.

It was under Nero the Antichrist that Peter was crucified and Paul beheaded; it was under Domitian that the prophet John, in exile on the isle of Patmos, denounced Rome as 'the mother of harlots and of all the world's obscenities'. A new mythology was coming into being, irreconcilably hostile to that of Rome.

Some accommodation between the rival world-views had to be made in the fourth century, when the conversion of Constantine made the empire itself Christian, and the outsiders became the establishment. But it was only cosmetic, and no educated Christian could avoid the tension between the Scriptures and what classical art and literature took for granted. It was not that the gods didn't exist. They did: they were powerful demons, who could cut whetstones and hold water in a sieve. What was one to think of the people who honoured them throughout the long history of Rome before Constantine?

In August AD 410 Alaric and his Goths entered Rome and sacked it. It wasn't the end of the empire, but it was a shattering event. 'If Rome can perish,' wrote St Jerome, 'what can be safe?' Traditionalists blamed the disaster on the abandonment of the old gods. It was a plausible theory, which Christian apologists had to work very hard to refute. Among the polemical writings it provoked were two extensive works which became classics of the literature of Christendom.

One was the seven-book *History Against the Pagans* by the Spanish priest Orosius, which reinterpreted the whole of pre-Christian history as a catalogue of disasters from which the pagan gods conspicuously failed to protect their worshippers. A sustained negative spin is applied to the Roman tradition; Romulus, for instance, is presented as a serial killer (not only Remus but Numitor and Titus Tatius too), while the god-fearing peacemaker Numa is simply omitted from the story. Orosius' work became the standard history of antiquity for the next thousand years. The latest edition estimates that 275 medieval manuscripts still exist; by contrast, the first six books of Tacitus' *Annals* survive in one manuscript only.

Orosius dedicated his *History* to the man who had suggested it, Aurelius Augustinus ('St Augustine') of Hippo in North Africa. Augustine's own response to the sack of Rome and the subsequent polemics was the wonderful *City of God*, a much greater work in every sense. He too offered a pejorative

'Domine, quo uadis?'

The earliest account of St Peter's ministry in Rome is in the apocryphal *Acts of Peter*, written about AD 180–190. It tells the story of Peter's miracle-working contest with Simon the Magician, culminating in the scene on the Sacra Via where a large crowd had gathered to watch Simon fly. Which he did: 'everyone saw him all over Rome, passing over its temples and its hills.' Peter prayed ('Make haste, Lord') and Simon crashed to earth, breaking his leg in three places.

Among the converts Peter attracted by his victory were the four concubines of 'Agrippa the Praetorian Prefect' (their names were Agrippina, Nicaria, Euphemia and Doris), and Xanthippe, wife of 'Albinus the friend of Caesar'. Peter preached purity to them, and they gave up sex. Many other women did the same, and men too, until Rome was in an uproar. Albinus went to Agrippa and insisted that he arrest Peter as an interfering trouble-maker.

Xanthippe warned Peter that his life was in danger. He didn't want to go, but when the brethren insisted that he keep himself safe to serve the Lord, he left the city in disguise. As he was going out of the gate he saw Jesus coming in. 'Lord, where are you going?' 'I am coming to Rome to be crucified.' 'Again?' 'Yes, Peter, I am being crucified again.' Then Peter saw Jesus ascend into heaven. He turned back, rejoicing, to seek his own crucifixion.

The medieval church of *Domine quo vadis?* is on the Via Appia about half a mile outside the Porta San Sebastiano. But that was the Appian Gate of the Walls of Aurelian, which didn't exist before the 270s AD. The scene described in the Acts of Peter evidently took place at the old Porta Capena, the very place where Juvenal imagined Umbricius taking his leave of the city fifty years later. The symbolism is perfect. The satirist's creation gives way to the hagiographer's; the old Roman, born on the Aventine, departs, but Christ's disciple stays, and by his martyrdom creates the institution that will inherit the government of Rome. The secular rule of St Peter's successors lasted over a thousand years; when it ended, on 20 September 1870, Queen Victoria was fifty-one years old, and Karl Marx fifty-two.

history of Rome (in book 3), but his imaginative engagement with the great authors of the past—Cicero, Varro, Sallust, Virgil—gave him an incomparably more nuanced view of the Roman tradition.

He admires Regulus, who returned to torture and death rather than break his oath: 'our enemies are certainly right to praise a courage which rose superior to so dreadful a fate.' Of course he uses him to attack traditional religion ('this most diligent worshipper of the gods was deprived of the only country he had, because he kept his oath to them'), but the man himself is still exemplary. The Roman tradition is admirable, and deserves something better to worship:

> All this [the Christian religion] should be the object of your chief desire, you people of Rome, with all your fine natural qualities, you descendants of men like Regulus, Scaevola, the Scipios, and Fabricius. Observe how different all this is from the degraded folly and the malignant imposture of the demons. The admirable and excellent qualities which nature has bestowed on you can only come to purity and perfection through true godliness.

Augustine City of God 2.29

Augustine's target at this point is the theatre, the medium which demonstrates the immorality of the gods, but which itself is an integral part of traditional religion. The demons are depraved, but the men who worshipped them were virtuous, and that is why God gave them power throughout the world.

For Orosius, and for many other Christians, God allowed the Roman Empire to flourish merely in order to create peaceful conditions for the birth of Christ. Augustine's view is much subtler. The Romans *deserved* their empire, because of men like Marcus Curtius and Publius Decius:

> Those Roman heroes belonged to an earthly city, and the aim set before them, in all their acts of duty for her, was the safety of their country, and a kingdom set not in heaven but on earth. . . . What else was there for them to love save glory? For, through glory, they desired to have a kind of life after death on the lips of those who praised them.

Augustine City of God 5.14

God was not going to give such men eternal life. But He did give them the earthly fame they sought. As the Evangelist said, 'They have their reward'— and they had earned it:

> They took no account of their own material interests compared with the common good, that is the commonwealth and the public purse; they resisted the temptations of avarice; they acted for their country's well-being with disinterested concern; they were guilty of no offence against the law; they succumbed to no sensual indulgence. By such immaculate conduct they laboured towards honours, power and glory, by what they took to be the true way.

Augustine City of God 5.15

In a long and generous chapter, Augustine shames his Christian readers by presenting the heroes of the Roman mythic tradition one by one before their eyes. In the course of it, citing Virgil on Lucius Brutus, he pays that tradition the best compliment he can. 'These were the two motives which drove the Romans to their wonderful achievements: liberty, and the passion for the praise of men.'

ROMULUS AND REMULUS

We agreed in Chapter 1 to define myths as stories that matter enough to the community to be told and retold generation after generation. In late antiquity, what kept the myths of Rome alive were the classic texts—Virgil above all— that were read in school. A significant proportion of the raw material for this book comes from the grammarian Servius' commentary on Virgil, written about AD 400. But progressively through the fifth and sixth centuries the classical education preserved by such 'guardians of language' became as anachronistic as its main beneficiaries, the senatorial aristocracy of Italy; and by the time of the Lombard invasions and the papacy of Gregory the Great (590–604), it was effectively dead.

For centuries thereafter, the stories that were told and retold in the lands that had once been Roman were those of Scripture and the lives of saints. Of course there were still some libraries; there were still some books; there were still some people learned enough to understand them. But the stories in them would not *matter* again until the age of Dante. To get some sense of that long slumber of the myths, let's look at three works of art linked by a corrupt text.

The earliest surviving manuscript of Orosius' history, written in north Italy in the sixth century, happens to have a textual error at a crucial point. 'The city of Rome was founded in Italy on the authority of the twins Romulus and Remulus.' The other, later, manuscripts get Remus' name right; but it's clear that some early-medieval readers of the standard history of Rome may well have been misled.

At some point in the eighth century, in one of the Saxon kingdoms of eastern Britain which were now called 'English', a stranded whale provided the bone from which a master-craftsman made an intricately carved casket. On all four sides, he cut lengthy runic inscriptions round the scenes; the same may have been true of the lid, but only the central panel survives, showing a warrior called Ægili defending his wife and home against an armed band.

On the front of the casket are two symmetrical scenes, one Germanic and one biblical. To the left, Weland the smith offers a drugged cup to the daughter of his master, the Geatish king Nithad; to the right, the Magi bring gifts to the Christ-child; the inscription refers to the whale that gave the bone. On the back is a complex scene centred on the Temple at Jerusalem and the Ark of the Covenant; Titus' Romans are taking the city, and Jewish prisoners are being taken hostage, as the inscriptions make clear. As for the shorter sides, the one on the right shows the hero Sigurd and the dragon Fafnir, a horse and a woman grieving at a barrow-tomb, and the three Fates; the inscription refers to 'a group resting on a hill of grief'. What these scenes have in common is far from clear, but the one that matters to us is on the left-hand side.

Figure 103

In the centre, seen as it were from above, the she-wolf is suckling the twins. Another wolf stands guard, and the scene is witnessed by four men with spears—hunters, or shepherds? The inscription, which begins at the top left, is rendered by Michael Swanton as follows:

> Romwalus and Reumwalus, twœgen gibroþær,
> afœddæ hiæ wylif in Romæ cæstri,
> oþlæ unneg.

> Romulus and Remus, two brothers;
> a she-wolf fed them in the city of Rome,
> far from their native land.

But it's clear from the spelling of the names that the learned craftsman called them Romulus and *Remulus*. It looks as if he got the story from

Figure 103. The Franks Casket, left side panel. It came to light in the nineteenth century at Auzon, Haute-Loire, and was acquired in 1857 by Augustus Franks, later the first Keeper of British and Medieval Antiquities at the British Museum. Perhaps the theme of exile binds the scenes together: 'it is tempting to suppose,' writes Michael Swanton, 'that this casket may have been custom-made for someone—probably some young cadet of an Anglian house—leaving home, or already abroad.'

Figure 104. The Rambona diptych. The inscription at the bottom of the left-hand leaf reads ROMVLVS ET REMVLVS A LVPA NVTRITI; that on the right-hand leaf records Ageltrude's foundation of the monastery in honour of Saints Gregory, Silvester and Flavianus, and the commissioning of the ivory diptych itself by Abbot Odelricus, 'the humblest servant of the Lord'. The angel at the bottom of the right-hand leaf seems to be carrying palm-branches, like the goddess Victoria.

Orosius, who describes their ancestor Aeneas as 'a refugee from Troy'.

A northerner had to use whale-bone; in Italy, a craftsman with a seriously wealthy patron might have elephant ivory to work with. Our second item is an ivory diptych from the monastery of Rambona, in what is now the Italian region of the Marche but in the late ninth century was part of the Frankish dukedom of Spoleto. In 891 duke Wido (i.e. Guido, 'Guy') was crowned by the pope as emperor, the eighth in succession to Charlemagne; his wife Ageltrude, a Lombard princess from Benevento, was crowned empress. There was a rival emperor, Arnulf, in Germany, and when Guy died in 894 he marched south to reunify the Frankish realm. Ageltrude, acting for her son Lambert, held Rome against him; although Arnulf took the city, he suffered a stroke and had to return to Germany, leaving Ageltrude in power.

Figure 104

But Lambert died in a hunting accident in 898, and the empress retired to a life of religion and good works. One of the latter was the Rambona monastery, which is why the ivory diptych bears her name.

On the left-hand leaf is the Crucifixion according to St John's Gospel, with Mary and the disciple whom Jesus loved. Sol and Luna, the sun and moon, look on as heavenly torch-bearers, while below the hill of Golgotha, the inscription tells us, are 'Romulus and Remulus nourished by the she-wolf'. Despite the Orosian spelling, the empress's message is clear: Rome's long tradition could live on as the capital of a Christian empire.

For the third appearance of 'Remulus' we come forward a long way, to the weavers of Brussels in the later seventeenth century. A series of tapestries made at that time, illustrating the life of Romulus, hangs on the walls of Cotehele, an Elizabethan house on the Cornwall side of the Tamar estuary. It is not known how many scenes there originally were, but five survive, wholly or in part; four of them still carry their inscriptions, including 'the recognition of Romelus and Remelus' and a generalised battle scene in which 'Remelus is slain'.

Figure 105

The tapestry-makers were using traditional designs; analogous groupings can be seen in two Romulus sequences now in Vienna, which were created about 1540, and they may go back even further than that. For the recognition scene comes not from Livy or Plutarch (both of whom have only Remus present, as Romulus gets his forces together to rescue him), but evidently from Justin, a late author much read in the Middle Ages, whose version of the story allows all five characters to be present at once. Remus is brought before Amulius; the king hands the case over to Numitor, whose flocks Remus was accused of rustling; 'suddenly Faustulus arrives with Romulus and explains the boys' origin'—just as on the tapestry, where they hurry in from the country at the right-hand side.

The inscriptions too are likely to be traditional. They were evidently handed down independently of the visual designs, since the Vienna sequences have quite different texts (in good Latin and elegiac couplets); to judge by the degree of garbling, the ones used for the Cotehele tapestries had been handed down a

The Corpse Synod

One of the last acts of Pope Formosus (891–6) was to welcome the Emperor Arnulf to Rome, and administer to the citizens a loyalty oath which concluded as follows: 'I will never show to Lambert or to Ageltrude his mother any help to obtain secular power, nor will I betray this city of Rome to Lambert or to his mother Ageltrude or their men, for any consideration or argument.' A few weeks later Formosus was dead, and the stricken Arnulf on his way back to Germany.

The new occupant of the throne of St Peter was Stephen VI, Ageltrude's man. He held a synod at the Lateran to accuse his predecessor of usurpation and treason. Formosus was there in person; his body had been brought out of the tomb, dressed in pontifical robes and placed in a chair to answer the charges. (A terrified deacon was appointed to speak for him.) No doubt the empress and her son were looking on as Stephen hurled his accusations at the corpse. Formosus was found guilty. Two fingers were cut off the right hand, then the corpse was stripped and thrown into the Tiber.

The river-god was kinder to Formosus than he had been to the Gracchi. The body came ashore downstream, and was brought back and decently buried in St Peter's. By then Stephen had been overthrown, imprisoned and strangled.

long way. Their ultimate source was probably Orosius, who for his own polemical purposes identified the king deposed and killed by Romulus as Romulus' grandfather Numitor; that, presumably, is what caused the confusion in the Cotehele text. So Remus as 'Remelus' may be the last vestige of a scribal error made more than a thousand years before.

Figure 105. Tapestry at Cotehele, Cornwall. Only the top half of this scene survives, but the essential elements are all visible: the twins, as adolescents; King Amulius; his brother Numitor, the twins' grandfather; and Faustulus, who brought the boys up. The inscription, in very garbled Latin, reads: REMELVS ET ROMELVS PER FASCVLVM NVTRITIVM EORVM COGNOSVNTVR A REGE MVMTORO EORVM PATRVO. 'Through the agency of their foster-father Faustulus ["Fasculus"], Remulus and Romulus are recognised by their uncle King Numitor ["Mumtorus"];' on one of the other tapestries Numitor is called 'Munitorus'. Whoever drafted the text has confused the king with his brother, as well as mis-spelling the latter's name and describing the king as the twins' uncle instead of their great-uncle.

| 10.3 | **REPUBLICS** |

In the spring of 1300, a poet is lost in a dark forest. Wild beasts, including a she-wolf, bar his way out to the sunshine. A man meets him—or rather 'Not a man, though I was one':

Dante *Inferno*
1.70–72

> 'I was born *sub Julio*, although it was late
> And I lived in Rome under the good Augustus
> In the time of the gods who were false and told lies.'

Virgil will guide Dante through the pit of hell and the mountain of purgatory, but not beyond:

Dante *Inferno*
1.124–126

> 'Because the Emperor, who reigns up there,
> Since I was one of the rebels against his law,
> Does not wish me to enter into his city.'

At the lowest depth of the pit, in the very jaws of Dis, they will see the world's three greatest criminals, Brutus, Cassius and Judas Iscariot.

Dante's mythic Rome is still kept very firmly subordinate to the world-view of medieval Christendom. He would never have suggested, as his younger contemporary Petrarch did, that all history consists of the praise of Rome. It was Petrarch (1304–74) and the Florentine humanists Coluccio Salutati (1331–1406), Leonardo Bruni (1369–1444) and Poggio Bracciolini (1380–1459), with their eagerness to rescue whatever manuscripts of classical authors could still be found, who brought about the awakening of the myths of Rome.

Their studies were far from academic. The Italian republics, threatened by enemies on all sides, needed courage and resourcefulness, the civic virtues which enabled liberty to defy tyranny, as the Florentines defied the duke of Milan, Gian Galeazzo Visconti, in 1402. Once again the Roman stories mattered to the community. In a world inspired by antiquity, even the gods and goddesses emerged from their banishment.

Colour plates 3, 5

Colour plate 16

In 1531, when the republic of Siena was decorating its council chamber with scenes of exemplary virtue from Valerius Maximus, in neighbouring Florence a learned ex-politician's *Discourses on Livy* were posthumously published. Niccolò Machiavelli's work systematically demonstrated the relevance of the Roman republican experience to the politics of his own day. It is important, for instance, to have men

> of such reputation and exemplary behaviour that good men wish to imitate them
> and evil men are ashamed to lead a life contrary to theirs. Those men in Rome
> who produced particularly good results were Horatius Cocles, Scaevola,

Fabricius, the two Decii, Regulus Atilius, and some others, all of whom with their uncommon and worthy examples created in Rome almost the same effect that was created by the laws and institutions.

Machiavelli
Discorsi 3.1

Machiavelli was well aware of the turnip-eaters tradition. 'The most useful thing instituted in a free society,' he wrote, 'is a way to keep the citizens poor.' Look at Cincinnatus, look at Regulus:

Here, two things of great note can be seen: one, poverty, and how they were content with it; and the other, how winning honour from war was enough for these citizens, and how they left all profit to the public.

Machiavelli
Discorsi 3.25

Livy would have been delighted to know how lasting his moral message had been.

Meanwhile, Tacitus had been discovered. Filippo Beroaldo in 1515 produced the first edition of all the surviving books of the *Annals* and *Histories*, and their impact was immediate. In sixteenth-century Europe, the principate too offered paradigms for the present. From Leiden in 1581 Justus Lipsius dedicated his edition of Tacitus to the States of Holland, one of the few republics left:

Look well! He presents kings and monarchs to you, in a word the theatre of our life today. I see in one place a ruler attacking the laws and constitution, and in another subjects rebelling against the ruler. I find the ways and means of destroying liberty; I find ill-fated efforts to recover lost liberty. I read in turn of tyrants over-thrown and laid low; I read of power insecure when wielded to excess. I read too of the evils of liberty restored, disorder, rivalry between colleagues, greed, looting, wealth acquired from the people, not for the people. Tacitus, good God!, is a great and useful writer. He should be in the hands of those in whose hands are the rudder and tiller of the state.

Justus Lipsius Ad
Annales... pref.

So the versatile myths of Rome kept pace with the vicissitudes of early modern Europe.

In Elizabethan England, they even found their way back on to the stage. North's translation of Plutarch's *Lives* was published in 1579, when Shakespeare was fifteen. Twenty years later he put on the tragedy of Julius Caesar at the newly constructed Globe Theatre. Appropriately, this rendering of a Roman myth to a popular audience opens with a tribune of the *plebs* haranguing the Roman People:

> O you hard hearts, you cruel men of Rome,
> Knew you not Pompey? Many a time and oft
> Have you climbed up to walls and battlements,
> To towers and windows, yea, to chimney-tops,
> Your infants in your arms, and there have sat

The live-long day, with patient expectation,
To see great Pompey pass the streets of Rome:
And when you saw his chariot but appear,
Have you not made an universal shout,
That Tiber trembled underneath her banks
To hear the replication of your sounds
Made in her concave shores?
And do you now put on your best attire?
And do you now cull out a holiday?
And do you now strew flowers in his way
That comes in triumph over Pompey's blood?
Be gone!
Run to your houses, fall upon your knees,
Pray to the gods to intermit the plague
That needs must light on this ingratitude.

Shakespeare
Julius Caesar
Act 1, scene 1

Perhaps Shakespeare remembered from Plutarch another tribune reproaching the ungrateful People—Gaius Gracchus, on his knees in the temple of Diana, in a scene that may well have been created for an audience just like his.

After *Julius Caesar* (1599) came Jonson's *Sejanus his Fall* (1603), then *Antony and Cleopatra* (1607?), *Coriolanus* (1608?), and Jonson's *Catiline* (1611), all exploring the great themes of power, liberty and treason from the early Republic to the reign of Tiberius. Ben Jonson even had to answer to the Privy Council for his *Sejanus*. He got away with it, unlike Sir John Eliot, who ended up in the Tower of London for attacking the duke of Buckingham as a Sejanus in 1626; 'he must intend me for Tiberius,' said the king.

That was Charles I. Ominously, the following year an epic poem on civil war was published, Thomas May's translation of Lucan. Since the unfinished original ends with Caesar in desperate straits in Alexandria, May added a few lines to make it clear to his readers how the story ended:

> But he must live, until his fall may prove
> Brutus and Cassius were more just than Jove.

(In England's civil war, May was for Cromwell; he served as Secretary to Parliament and was given a state funeral in Westminster Abbey in 1650; the body was exhumed at the restoration of the monarchy.)

The ambiguity of Lucan's Caesar—demonic victor, tyrant to be killed—is conspicuous in the classic celebration of the regicide, Andrew Marvell's *Horatian Ode*:

> So restless Cromwell could not cease
> In the inglorious arts of peace,
> > But through adventurous war

> Urgèd his active star.
> And, like the three-forked lightning, first
> Breaking the clouds where it was nursed,
>   Did thorough his own side
>   His fiery way divide . . .
>
> Then burning through the air he went,
> And palaces and temples rent:
>   And Caesar's head at last
>   Did through his laurels blast.
> 'Tis madness to resist or blame
> The force of angry heaven's flame . . .

Andrew Marvell An
Horatian Ode. . .
9–16, 21–26

Caesar's head is Charles's head, but the conqueror like the lightning-fire is Caesar too, as first we meet him in Lucan's epic. Milton in 1642 had appealed to Lucius Brutus, Marcus Curtius, Gaius Fabricius, Manius Curius; naturally, the English republicans liked these old paradigms of civic virtue, but as it turned out, Caesar was not a bad parallel for the man who became Lord Protector of the Commonwealth.

In 1661, in a scene Lucan would have described with relish (and Tacitus with savage irony), Cromwell's body was dug up and decapitated. The head was stuck on a pole by Westminster Hall, and remained there throughout Charles II's reign.

> Oh happy age! Oh times like those alone
> By Fate reserved for great Augustus' throne!

So sang John Dryden in *Astraea Redux*, hailing the restored monarchy as the return of the Virgilian goddess of justice.

Stripped of his Laureateship in 1688, Dryden remained loyal to the Stuart cause even in his great translation of the *Aeneid*:

> Arms and the man I sing, who, forced by Fate
> And haughty Juno's unrelenting hate,
> Expelled and exiled, left the Trojan shore.
> Long labours, both by sea and land, he bore,
> And in the doubtful war, before he won
> The Latian realm, and built the destined town;
> His banished gods restored to rites divine,
> And settled sure succession in his line;
> From whence the race of Alban fathers come,
> And the long glories of majestic Rome.

Virgil Aeneid
1.1–7

Dryden's seventh and eighth lines expand three Latin words that mean no more than 'brought his gods to Latium'. For readers in 1695, restoration and sure succession were live issues. Then, in book 6, Anchises points out Rome's future founder in Elysium:

Virgil *Aeneid*
6.777–778

> 'See Romulus the great, born to restore
> The crown that once his injured grandsire wore.'

There's no restored crown in Virgil's text; but when those lines were published young James Edward Stuart, grandson of Charles I, was being groomed in Paris to be 'James III'.

Nothing came of that; the settlement of 1688 had ended absolute monarchy in England. An aristocratic oligarchy now held power, and continued to exploit the infinitely adaptable political paradigm of Rome. Liberty and civic virtue were constantly invoked, but without any *popularis* overtones. The *optimates* were in charge, and their hero was Cato. In 1713 Joseph Addison's tragedy *Cato* was admired by both political parties. Addison was a Whig, but his Prologue was written by the Tory Alexander Pope:

> Ev'n when proud Caesar 'midst triumphal cars,
> The spoils of nations and the pomp of wars,
> Ignobly vain and impotently great,
> Showed Rome her Cato's figure drawn in state,
> As her dead father's rev'rend image passed
> The pomp was darkened and the day o'ercast.
> The triumph ceased—tears gushed from ev'ry eye;
> The world's proud victor passed unheeded by.
> Her last good man dejected Rome adored,
> And honoured Caesar's less than Cato's sword.

Liberty, however, is a double-edged concept. For oligarchs, Roman or British, it meant freedom *to* as much as freedom *from*, and those they exploited could appeal to it too. 'Give me liberty, or give me death!' Patrick Henry's clarion-call in Richmond, Virginia, in 1775 was borrowed from Addison's *Cato*, while George Washington, who knew the play well and frequently quoted from it, even had it staged at Valley Forge to inspire the forces of the rebel colonies.

We are now in the rational, secular age of Montesquieu, Voltaire and Diderot. Except in Rome itself, and the 'Papal States' of central Italy, the thousand-year dominance of Christendom is definitively over. With the weakening of the Church's influence, the sexual frankness of the pagan gods can now come out of hiding. This is where we began, in the eruditely erotic world of Tiepolo's Flora; but it is also the heroically patriotic world of David's Sabine women and Lucius Brutus.

In 1792 Marie-Joseph de Chénier's tragedy *Gaïus Gracchus* was put on in Paris. It was nearly three years after the fall of the Bastille, but Louis XVI was still hoping to regain power. The play ends with Gracchus' suicide, and these dying words:

Figure 106. Esprit-Antoine Gibelin, 'Sacrifice to Priapus'; pen and ink drawing, c.1770. The scene combines two ancient rituals, the sacrifice of an ass to Priapus (p. 5 above) and the garlanding of the phallus for Liber Pater (p. 81 above). The beast stands at the right, with the amphora placed to catch the blood when his throat is cut, but the Bacchic *thyrsus* at the bottom left and the matron stepping up to do the honours clearly allude to the *Liberalia* ritual that so scandalised St Augustine. In reality, the lady would be wearing her best clothes for the festival, but that wouldn't do for the eighteenth century's idea of paganism. Here all the women are stark naked, matrons, musicians and slave-girls alike; the demeanour of the bearded priests, and the erotic scene on the altar, encouraged by a goat-legged Pan, give a clear enough idea of the next stage of the proceedings.

Figure 106
Colour plate 1
Colour plate 13
Figure 57 (p. 134)

'J'épargne du sang. Dieux protecteurs du Tibre,
Voici mon dernier vœu: que le peuple soit libre!'

By September the king was under arrest, his supporters had been massacred and his Prussian allies checked on the battlefield; under the stern gaze of Lucius Brutus, whose bust was set up next to the speaker's rostrum, the newly formed National Convention announced Year One of the French Republic.

Sixty years later it seemed to Karl Marx that the French Revolution had been carried out in Roman costume, by 'ghosts from the days of Rome'. At the time, however, it was much more than a charade. The heroes of the Roman Republic replaced the saints of the Roman Church as the protectors of individuals and communities. 'Our patron was St Blaise,' reported one of the deputations at the Convention; 'but a young volunteer spoke to us of Brutus; he related his actions to us, and suddenly St Blaise was dislodged and Brutus put in his place.' It was a story that still mattered, after twenty-three centuries.

What happened to the Roman Republic happened also to the French, but in a matter of years, not centuries. The *coup d'état* of 1799 gave Bonaparte power as 'first Consul'; in 1802 he became Consul for life; in 1804 he crowned himself emperor in Notre Dame. The ceremony was medieval—the insignia of Charlemagne presented by the Pope—but the realities of power were unmistakably Caesarian. It's no wonder that Napoleon detested Tacitus as a slanderer of emperors. Brutus' time had passed, but it was still Roman stories that offered a mirror to the present.

Though Napoleon conquered Europe, his empire was short-lived. After Waterloo, the French monarchy and the Pope's temporal authority were both restored. But their time too was nearly over. In 1830 popular fury in Paris caused the abdication of the reactionary Charles X. Could the same thing happen in England?

When the parliamentary reform bill came before the House of Commons in March 1831, one of those most in favour was a young Whig member called Thomas Babington Macaulay:

> Now, therefore, while everything at home and abroad forebodes ruin for those who persist in a hopeless struggle against the spirit of the age; now, while the crash of the proudest throne of the Continent is still ringing in our ears; now, while the roof of a British palace affords an ignominious shelter to the exiled heir of forty kings; now, while we see on every side ancient institutions subverted and great societies dissolved, . . . [s]ave the multitude, endangered by its own ungovernable passions. Save the aristocracy, endangered by its own unpopular power. Save the greatest and fairest and most highly civilised community that ever existed from calamities which may in a few days sweep away all the rich heritage of so many ages of wisdom and glory. The danger is terrible. The time is short.

Hansard
2 March 1831

Twelve years earlier, when the authorities in Manchester broke up a peaceful pro-reform meeting by sending in the cavalry (the 'Peterloo massacre', eleven killed, four hundred wounded), the eighteen-year-old Macaulay had explained his indignation in a letter to his father:

> My opinions, good or bad, were learnt, not from Hunt and Waithman [contemporary radicals], but from Cicero, from Tacitus, and from Milton. They are the opinions which have produced the greatest men that ever ornamented the world, and redeemed human nature from the degradation of ages of superstition and slavery.

For Macaulay as much as for Machiavelli, the Romans were a living presence.

The reform bill was eventually passed, but it wasn't enough. In May 1838 the People's Charter was published, demanding full manhood suffrage. A huge petition in its support was presented to Parliament in 1839, and rejected. Macaulay, meanwhile, was thinking about the myths of Rome.

In 1842, the year the *Lays of Ancient Rome* were published, the second petition for the Charter was presented, and again rejected.

Figure 107

The third of the *Lays* purports to be sung in the Forum in 372 BC, during the tribunes' campaign for the consulship to be opened to plebeians.

Not Just Trifles

We have already used two of Macaulay's *Lays*, 'Horatius' and 'The Battle of the Lake Regillus' (pp. 60–1 and 137 above). Shortly before the book was published, he wrote to his friend McVey Napier:

> You are acquainted, no doubt, with Perizonius' theory about the early Roman history,—a theory which Niebuhr revived, and which Arnold has adopted as fully established. I have my self not the smallest doubt of its truth. It is that the stories of the birth of Romulus and Remus, the fight of the Horatii and Curiatii, and all the other romantic tales which fill the first three or four books of Livy came from the lost ballads of the early Romans. I amused myself in India with trying to restore some of these long perished poems. Arnold saw two of them and wrote to me in such terms of eulogy that I have been induced to correct and complete them. There are four of them; and I think that, though they are but trifles, they may pass for scholar-like and not inelegant trifles.

Figure 107. Illustration from 'Virginia', in the *Lays of Ancient Rome*. Macaulay's introduction to the poem invites the reader to 'imagine himself a Plebeian who has just voted for the re-election of Sextius and Licinius... The Plebeians bear on their shoulders the two champions of liberty through the Forum. Just at this moment it is announced that a popular poet, a zealous adherent of the Tribunes, has made a new song which will cut the Claudian nobles to the heart. The crowd gathers round him, and calls on him to recite it. He takes his stand on the spot where, according to tradition, Virginia, more than seventy years ago, was seized by the pandar of Appius, and he begins his story.' The somewhat effete bard in this late edition (1884) has none of the polemical energy of the Chartist period to which the poem belongs.

In the Preface to the *Lays* Macaulay offers a 'popular exposition' of the Perizonius-Niebuhr theory. It is one of the best things ever written on the myths of Rome, a masterly presentation for the general reader of a complex scholarly hypothesis.

However, scholarship has moved on, and no one nowadays believes in the theory as Perizonius and Niebuhr stated it. The 'banquet songs' they invoked, which may indeed have been a feature of archaic Roman society, were an aristocratic phenomenon, most unlikely to result in popular traditions like those re-created by Macaulay. The minstrel in Figure 107 is not a plausible historical figure. But though the answer may be wrong, the question remains. Macaulay was right to insist that the stories of early Rome in the prose histories of Livy, Dionysios and Plutarch manifest 'that peculiar character, more easily understood than defined, which distinguishes the creations of the imagination from the realities of the world in which we live'. If ballads were not the source, what was?

As it happens, the two examples he used in his letter to Napier may offer an answer. What Plutarch says of the Romulus and Remus story, and what Dionysios says of the fight of the triplets, is that the narrative is like what you'd see on the stage; and the audience at the theatre games was the Roman People itself.

But the *Lays* don't depend on the theory that prompted their composition. They create their own world. Their narrators may be historical phantoms, but the republican ethos they convey is brilliantly imagined. That's because they are based on a profound knowledge of the ancient sources. 'To be sure,' Macaulay wrote to his sister,

> one circumstance, which will probably keep the book from ever becoming popular, will guard it from vulgar scurrility. No man who is not a good scholar can attack it without exposing himself: and there are few good scholars among the hacks of literature.

But it did become popular. It sold in hundreds of thousands, and for over a century it was where most English-speaking schoolchildren first met the Romans.

The very fact that it had a mass readership offended literary purists, and for two generations or more the *Lays* have been deeply unfashionable. I think it's time the virtues of these 'scholar-like trifles' were rediscovered.

Ye good men of the Commons, with loyal hearts and true,
Who stand by the bold Tribunes that still have stood by you,
Come, make a circle round me, and mark my tale with care,
A tale of what Rome once hath borne, and what Rome yet may bear.
This is no Grecian fable, of fountains running wine,
Of maids with snaky tresses, or sailors turned to swine.
Here, in this very Forum, under the noonday sun,
In sight of all the people, the bloody deed was done.
Old men still creep among us who saw that fearful day,
Just seventy years and seven ago, when the wicked Ten held sway.

'Virginia'
1–10

The wicked Ten were the Decemvirs of 449 BC, under whose rule the republican magistracies were suspended, including the tribunate. Appius Claudius lusted after little Virginia; in despair, her father killed her in the Forum to save her from him. The Roman People rose against Appius:

Twelve times the crowd made at him; five times they seized his gown;
Small chance was his to rise again, if once they got him down:
And sharper came the pelting; and ever more the yell
'Tribunes! we will have Tribunes!' rose with a louder swell . . .
One stone hit Appius in the mouth, and one beneath the ear;
And ere he reached Mount Palatine, he swooned with pain and fear.
His cursed head, that he was wont to hold so high with pride,
Now like a drunken man's hung down, and swayed from side to side;
And when his stout retainers had brought him to his door,
His face and neck were all one cake of filth and clotted gore.
As Appius Claudius was that day, so may his grandson be!
God send Rome one such other sight, and send me there to see!

'Virginia'
271–274,
279–286

Macaulay was careful to point out in his Preface that 'in the following poems the author speaks, not in his own person, but in the persons of ancient minstrels . . . who are in no wise above the passions and prejudices of their age and nation'. Even so, his Roman tale had a clear lesson, about the multitude and its ungovernable passions, and about the aristocracy and its unpopular power.

Expanding on Livy, Macaulay gave a fighting speech to Icilius, Virginia's fiancé:

'Now, by your children's cradles, now, by your fathers' graves,
Be men today, Quirites, or be for ever slaves! . . .
[But it's too late; we have thrown away what our ancestors gained.]
Exult, ye proud Patricians! The hard-fought fight is o'er.
We strove for honours—'twas in vain; for freedom—'tis no more.
No crier to the polling summons the eager throng;
No tribune breathes the word of might that guards the weak from wrong . . .

'Virginia' 93–94,
109–112,
143–144

[But beware of driving us too far,]
> Lest, when our latest hope is fled, ye taste of our despair,
> And learn by proof, in some wild hour, how much the wretched dare.'

In England in 1842, no one could have read that without a thought of the present.

However, the English revolution didn't happen. In Paris, a republican coup in February 1848 forced the abdication of the 'citizen king' Louis-Philippe. In London three months later, the huge crowds that accompanied the third and last petition for the Charter went home peacefully in the rain.

Elsewhere, there were thrones less secure than Victoria's. Early in 1849 Pius IX fled from Rome, and a Constituent Assembly founded the new regime with this decree:

1. The temporal power of the Papacy is suppressed *de facto* and *de iure* in the Roman States.
2. The Roman Pontiff will have all necessary guarantees for the independent exercise of spiritual power.
3. The form of Government in the Roman States will be pure Democracy, and will take the glorious name of the Roman Republic.

But if the Roman People expected fraternal aid from Paris, they were cruelly deceived. President Louis Napoleon had ambitions to do with the second French Republic what his uncle the emperor had done with the first, and he needed the Catholic vote. Within a few months General Oudinot was bombarding the Janiculum to make Rome safe again for papal rule.

A young English poet happened to be in Rome at the time. He didn't go in for politics, but even so—

A.H. Clough
Amours de
Voyage 2.20–23

> I, nevertheless, let me say it,
> Could in my soul of souls, this day, with the Gaul at the gates, shed
> One true tear for thee, thou poor little Roman Republic!
> France, it is foully done!

With his classical metre and his 'Gaul at the gates', he too had the old Romans in his head.

10.4 EMPIRES

In 1852 Louis Napoleon got his popular mandate, and became Napoleon III, emperor of France; the Second Empire lasted till the Franco-Prussian war of 1870. In 1871 the king of Prussia became Kaiser of a united Germany; the second Reich (the first had been Charlemagne's) lasted till the defeat of Germany in 1918. In 1876, by the Royal Titles Act, Queen Victoria became Empress of India; the British Empire lasted till 1947. In 1933 Adolf Hitler became Führer of the third Reich, a European empire which lasted till the defeat of Germany in 1945.

It's not surprising that in the modern world the Roman paradigm shifted from the Republic to the Empire. The old stories of republican virtue very quickly lost their exemplary power. They have no place in Theodor Mommsen's hugely influential *History of Rome*, which was published in 1854–6 and earned its author the Nobel Prize for Literature in 1902. Mommsen was an active liberal; he lost his post at Leipzig in the post-1849 reaction, and wrote most of the *History* in temporary exile in Zurich. Influenced by Macaulay, whose *History of England* had appeared in 1848, he interpreted the expulsion of the Tarquins as a 'conservative' revolution like that of 1688 in England, effected by the temporary alliance of two political parties. Lucius Brutus is not even named. 'The well-known fable,' he writes in a contemptuous footnote, 'for the most part confutes itself.' As for the Roman People,

> from the times of the Tarquins down to those of the Gracchi the cry of the party of progress in Rome was not for limitation of the power of the state but for limitation of the power of the magistrates: nor amidst that cry was the truth ever forgotten, that the people ought not to govern, but to be governed.

The Gracchi began a 'democratic-monarchical revolution' which was brought to completion by Caesar.

Figure 108

Theodor Mommsen
History of Rome
Book II, ch. 1

Figure 108. Mocking the turnip-eaters: Manius Curius 'refusing the Magnificent Gift offered by the Samnite Ambassadors' (p. 154 above), one of John Leech's illustrations in Gilbert À Beckett's *Comic History of Rome* (1852). However, the author did have a serious purpose. He ended his Preface with the hope 'that narrative in sport may be found to constitute history in earnest', and the text concludes with the following judgement on Augustus: 'He retained his position till his death—a circumstance to be attributed to the conviction that had been brought home to the popular mind, that the constant changing of the head of a State is a source of constant danger to the peace and happiness of the whole community.' Even a comic history can have lessons to teach its readers.

Mommsen's history ends with the battle of Thapsus in 46 BC, Caesar's victory over the optimate Republic. His chapter on 'the new monarchy' is an astonishing eulogy of Caesar,

Theodor Mommsen
History of Rome
Book V, ch. 11

the sole creative genius produced by Rome, and the last produced by the ancient world, which accordingly moved on in the path that he marked out for it until its sun went down.

For Mommsen, Caesar was 'the entire and perfect man'. And his legacy was still alive: 'the political life of the nations has during thousands of years again and again reverted to the lines which Caesar drew.' Good riddance to the old corrupt Republic. The modern world was the world of Empire.

The British, not surprisingly, took a similar view, though more ambivalent about the old regime. Let's listen to the Regius Professor of Modern History at Cambridge, J.R. Seeley, as he explains in 1883 how the Roman Empire has become *interesting*:

J.R. Seeley
*The Expansion of
England* 237–238

A generation ago it was the reigning opinion that there is nothing good in politics but liberty, and that accordingly in history all those periods are to be passed over and, as it were, cancelled, in which liberty is not to be found. Along with this opinion there prevailed a habit of reading history, as we read poetry, only for an exalted kind of pleasure, and this habit led us, whenever we came to a period in which there was nothing glorious or admirable, to shut the book. In those days no doubt the Roman Empire too was condemned. The Roman Republic was held in honour for its freedom; the earlier Roman Empire was studied for the traces of freedom still discernible in it.

For Seeley, all that was out of date ('obsolete' was his word). 'There are many good things in politics besides liberty; for instance, there is nationality, there is civilisation.' So now it was the Empire, not the Republic, that was 'studied with infinite curiosity and attention'.

The shift in attitude can be seen in Kipling. The children in *Puck of Pook's Hill* (1906) know Macaulay's *Lays* by heart, but the centurion Puck brings to them was defending a doomed empire nearly nine centuries after Horatius held the bridge:

Rudyard Kipling
Puck of Pook's Hill
191

Mithras, God of the Morning, our trumpets waken the Wall!
'Rome is above the Nations, but Thou art over all!'
Now, as the names are answered, and the guards are marched away,
Mithras, also a soldier, give us strength for the day!

Puck himself is a faun, though naturally much reduced from the dangerous Faunus (pp. 75–8 above). 'England,' he says, 'is a bad place for Gods.' Well, yes and no; adult readers would hear in the hymn to Mithras an echo of Kipling's most famous poem (published in *The Times* for Queen Victoria's Diamond Jubilee), which saw their own empire in a similar perspective:

God of our fathers, known of old,
      Lord of our far-flung battle-line,
Beneath whose awful hand we hold
      Dominion over palm and pine—
Lord God of Hosts, be with us yet,
Lest we forget—lest we forget!

. . .

Far-called, our navies melt away;
      On dune and headland sinks the fire:
Lo, all our pomp of yesterday
      Is one with Nineveh and Tyre!
Judge of the Nations, spare us yet,
Lest we forget—lest we forget!

Rudyard Kipling
'Recessional'
1–6, 13–18

The uneasy relationship between God and empire ('for *Thine* is the kingdom, the power and the glory') gave rise to a new dramatic genre in late-Victorian England, the 'toga play'. The best-known example, playing to huge and respectful audiences both in London and on tour, was Wilson Barrett's *The Sign of the Cross*. It opened in 1896, the year Henryk Sienkiewicz published his enormously successful novel *Quo Vadis?*, which won him the Nobel Prize for Literature in 1905. The plots of both play and novel, set in the time of Nero, turn on the redemption of an arrogant Roman officer by his love for a Christian girl. In the other great popular success of the period, Lew Wallace's *Ben-Hur: a Tale of the Christ* (novel 1880, play 1899), the arrogant Roman is defeated and crippled in the famous chariot-race, while Ben-Hur pays for a catacomb to bury Nero's victims; 'out of that vast tomb', the novel concludes, 'Christianity issued to supersede the Caesars.' Though these Roman stories were modern fictions, the empire and Nero were still myths that mattered. And the twentieth century found a new medium for them, to reach an even greater audience.

First in Italy, then in Hollywood, the novels and plays became toga films: *Quo Vadis?* in 1913, 1925 and 1951 (Peter Ustinov as Nero); *The Sign of the Cross* in 1914 and 1932 (Charles Laughton as Nero); *Ben-Hur* in 1925 and 1959. The religious theme lasted well into the new century, with Lloyd C. Douglas' best-selling novel *The Robe* becoming a Hollywood epic—as they were now called—in 1953. But despite all the innovations (*The Robe* was the first Cinemascope production), the Christian-heroine plot was now very dated. It was time to go back to the real Roman stories, and leave God out of it.

Meanwhile, what of Rome itself, which in 1870 had become the capital of the Kingdom of Italy? The end of the Pope's secular rule marked the emergence of Italy as a European Power, and like any European Power she wanted overseas colonies. Eritrea (on the Red Sea) in 1890 and Libya in 1911 provided a mini-empire, and national pride constructed an appropriately quasi-Roman

Figure 109

303

Figure 109. Air photograph of Rome about 1910, showing the monument to Victor Emmanuel II, the first king of united Italy. The building is not quite complete—the bronze four-horse chariots at each end of the great portico have still to be put in place—but already its huge size and the brightness of its Brescia marble dominate its surroundings. The architect was Giuseppe Sacconi; begun in 1885 and dedicated in 1911, its imperial pomp and grandeur symbolise the early twentieth century's myth of Rome.

architectural symbol. When the precocious Italian film industry produced the first of the great Roman screen epics (*Cabiria*, 1914), it was about Rome's conquest of African Carthage.

After 1922, the Fascist regime emphasised even more insistently the idea that modern Italy was the direct successor of the Roman Empire. Mussolini modelled himself first on Caesar and then on Augustus, taking advantage of the bimillennium of the latter's birth in 1938. Of course it was all a dream, and it died with the fall of the 'sawdust Caesar' in 1943. But it had meant something at the time. On 6 June 1944, at a cocktail party the day after Allied forces had entered Rome, Colonel George Walton of the US Fifth Army was talking to an Italian lady. 'I want to congratulate you,' she said. 'Do you realise that you are the first of the barbarians to have taken Rome from the south?'

In the post-war world, neither of the two rival superpowers could appeal to the Roman imperial paradigm, the Americans because of their national self-image as a free republic, the Russians because they had appropriated Spartacus as a founder-hero of communism (p. 201 above). The Kirk Douglas movie *Spartacus* (1960) was based on a novel which had won the Stalin Peace Prize in 1953, and its opening was picketed by right-wing protesters. But one of the fans who crossed the picket line to see it was the newly elected President John F. Kennedy, whose inauguration speech famously promised to

pay any price, bear any burden, meet any hardship, support any friend, oppose any foe to assure the survival and the success of liberty.

Spartacus was billed as showing 'the age-old fight for freedom', and anyone who wanted could see Crassus' legions as a metaphor of the Red Army. So the rebel hero could satisfy both sides; whoever the Romans symbolised, they were oppressors.

That was a message familiar to audiences from the old-fashioned 'Christian' epics, and the voice-over at the beginning of *Spartacus* was careful to place the events 'in the last century before the birth of the new faith called Christianity, which was destined to overthrow the pagan tyranny of Rome and bring about a new society'.

That of course was quite false to Howard Fast's novel, which ended with the promise that 'Rome would be torn down . . . by slaves and serfs and peasants'; but though the Marxist class struggle was unacceptable, there still had to be some prospect of freedom in the long run, or Spartacus' death would be in vain.

Rome was not wholly irredeemable. Another feature in common with the Christian epics was 'the good Roman', this time not an army officer like Vinicius in *Quo Vadis?* or Arrius in *Ben-Hur*, but a politician. The senator Gracchus, played in the film by Charles Laughton, is one of Fast's more blatant anachronisms, more recognisably a Democrat city boss than a Roman *popularis*. It is he who secures the freedom of Spartacus' wife and son, and then kills himself to escape the coming tyranny.

The last of the classic toga movies was *The Fall of the Roman Empire*; made in 1964 with a pointedly non-Christian plot, it featured Alec Guinness as the wise emperor Marcus Aurelius, whose death, supposedly in a conspiracy, marks the end of Roman virtue and idealism. So too Robert Graves' Claudius novels, made into a brilliantly successful television series in 1976, presented the unexpected emperor as a secret republican whose plans were tragically frustrated

(p. 259 above). The empire still mattered, but now it was where honesty and decency strove against ambition and irresponsible power.

Did they strive in vain? Did Rome offer any *hope*? Without the long-term consolation offered either by Christianity (at best an ambiguous champion of freedom) or by Marxism (discredited after the fall of the Soviet empire), stories of Roman heroism seemed doomed to be tragedies of liberty denied.

The Hollywood Roman-epic tradition was revived in 2000 with Ridley Scott's *Gladiator*. Truer to the history of cinema than the history of Rome, it was created out of very familiar elements. The second-century AD plot (Marcus Aurelius and Commodus) is taken from *The Fall of the Roman Empire*; like *Spartacus*, the hero is enslaved as a gladiator; his name and status—Maximus the Spanish general—come straight from Kipling; the climax in the arena where Rome is freed from tyranny is borrowed from *Quo Vadis*; and 'Senator Gracchus' reappears, two and a half centuries after his previous manifestation in *Spartacus*. What is different is the outcome.

The plot turns on the idea that Marcus Aurelius did not want his son to succeed him. The old emperor confides in Maximus:

> 'How will the world speak my name in years to come? Will I be known as the philosopher? The warrior? The tyrant? Or will I be the emperor who gave Rome back her true self? There was once a dream that was Rome. You can only whisper of it. Anything more than a whisper and the dream vanishes. . .'

He wants Maximus to be Protector of Rome, 'to give power back to the people of Rome, and end the corruption that has crippled her'. By 'the people' the film means 'the Senate'. American audiences would no doubt feel comfortable with Gracchus' explanation to the new emperor Commodus: 'The Senate *is* the people, Caesar. Chosen from the people, to speak for the people.' And so at the end, when the dying Maximus has killed Commodus, we know what his last words mean:

> 'There was a dream that was Rome. It shall be realised. These are the wishes of Marcus Aurelius.'

Senator Gracchus helps to carry the hero's body out of the arena. Unlike his predecessor, this Gracchus doesn't have to kill himself. This time, there's no need to wait for history to put things right in the long run. This tyranny has been replaced by a republic, and all is as it should be.

Of course David Franzoni, and those who later rewrote his story, could rely on the audience not knowing Gibbon. More important, after thirty-six years they would hardly remember the final scene of *The Fall of the Roman Empire*, where the Praetorians put the empire up for auction. We might complain that there's less respect now for historical authenticity, but that would be missing the point. Myth is not history (though it exploits it), and the Roman Republic of AD 193 isn't *very* much more unhistorical than the power-sharing consulship of 507 BC, or the patrician hero Camillus who rescues Rome from the Gauls. In a Roman myth for our short-term world, the good guys get to win *now*; and if that means pretending that the Praetorian Guard played no part in the imperial succession, so be it.

The dream that old Marcus can only whisper is Franzoni's contribution to a very long tradition, as I hope this chapter's headlong gallop through the centuries has shown. It matters for us in the twenty-first century—as it mattered for St Augustine, or for George Washington—that Rome was admirable for more than just her power. The passing of the modern empires has begun to bring Rome's 'true self' back into view.

0.5 BACK TO FLORA

We began by identifying a Roman story in an eighteenth-century painting. Now, looking back from a longer perspective, we can use it to pick out some characteristic features of the myths of Rome.

Colour plate 1

Flora, the goddess of spring, belongs in the uninhibited archaic world we glimpsed through the visual evidence in Chapter 5. She is a goddess of the Roman People, and the story Tiepolo knew began when the People's aediles, both aptly named Publicius, exacted large fines from wealthy landowners who had privatised public property. That was what paid for her new temple and her theatre games. This bold statement of civic values took place in the Rome which later ages most consistently admired—the city of Manius Curius, Fabricius and Regulus, who prided themselves on not being rich but were ready to give their lives for the common wealth.

If we find it hard to reconcile the cheerful sexiness of Flora's games with the firm self-discipline the Republic required, that is our problem. (The two-faced god Janus, also prominent in the mid-third century BC, is used as a metaphor in Chapter 7.) But it became the Romans' problem too, as a senatorial oligarchy in the second century exerted ever more social and political control. Flora's defiance in the Tiepolo painting—her 'triumph' was the recognition of her games in 173 BC—symbolises a rare victory for traditional values, between the emasculation of the cult of Liber, god of liberty, in 186 and the assassination of Tiberius Gracchus, tribune of the *plebs*, in 133. With empire came the power of the rich, and the subordination of the Roman People. It is good to see that at least the name of Gracchus is still remembered, after more than two millennia.

Tiepolo got the story of Flora from the last poet of free Rome. Most of Ovid's adult life was spent in the peace and prosperity achieved by Augustus, the boy with the whip who destroyed the power of the oligarchs; but you can't step in the same river twice, and Ovid soon discovered that traditional sexual frankness was unacceptable to Rome's new master. His affectionate interview with Flora is a tacit reproach to Augustus, who conspicuously declined to rebuild the temple the Publicii had paid for, after it was burned down in the year he defeated Antony.

Ovid's poem on the myths of Rome remained for ever unfinished, one of the casualties of a new loss of liberty as the true nature of the principate became apparent. It was a dynastic monarchy, and very soon a murderous tyranny. For the next great poet of Rome, the oligarchs of the late Republic had become martyred champions of freedom, the last of the Romans.

That too has been a powerful myth for posterity—perhaps too powerful, in that it privileges just one kind of liberty. The reason I have insisted in this book on Ovid and Tiepolo, Flora and Liber, Novius Plautius' engravings and Manius Curius' turnips, is to bring back into prominence what seems to me the most important thing about the myths of Rome. They were stories for the Roman People.

REFERENCES

Page numbers are given in bold.

Chapter 1

2 Tiepolo's 'Triumph of Flora': Levey 1957 (who quotes Count Algarotti's letter to Brühl); Morassi 1962.47 and fig. 354. For Flora in literature and art from the middle ages to the seventeenth century, see Held 1961; Reid 1993.1.434–42.

'Venus and Vulcan' and 'The Meeting of Antony and Cleopatra': Morassi 1962.45 (and fig. 245), 11.

3 'The sluggish ass...': Massey 1757.30–32 (I have modernised Massey's spelling and punctuation in all the quotations in the text).

The red god: for *ruber* at lines 400 ('quique ruber pauidas inguine terret aues') and 415 ('at ruber hortorum decus et tutela Priapus'), see Horace *Satires* 1.8.1–7, *Priapea* 72.2 (Parker 1988.182–3), Tibullus 1.1.17–18.

4 Bellini: Wethey 1975.143–5, cf. 29–41 (Ferrara sequence); Bull and Plesters 1990.

'Toiled...': Massey 1757.32–3.

5 'He rose...': Wilkinson 1955.283. Shakespeare picked up the simile in *Lucrece* (1594), where Tarquin gags his victim at lines 677–9: 'The wolf has seized his prey, the poor lamb cries, | Till with her own white fleece her voice controll'd | Entombs her outcry in her lips' sweet fold.'

Titian and Tarquin: Wethey 1975.180–2, 220; Donaldson 1982.13–20, plates 1–4, 13–14.

6 'The goddess...': Ovid *Fasti* 4.945–6 ('scaena ioci morem liberioris habet'); Massey 1757.245.

Cato at the games: Valerius Maximus 2.10.8 ('populus ... priscum morem iocorum in scaenam reuocauit'); cf. Seneca *Epistles* 97.8 on the 'Florales ioci nudandarum meretricum'.

'You know...': Martial 1 pref., trans. D.R. Shackleton Bailey (Loeb edition 1993).

'Fair Flora...': Ovid *Fasti* 5.183 ('mater ades florum, ludis celebranda iocosis'); Massey 1757.259. For Flora as a showgirl (*mima*) herself, cf. *Fasti* 5.347–8, with Wiseman 2002a.293–9.

8 Zephyrus story: Ovid *Fasti* 5.195–214 ('quae fuerat mihi forma graue est narrare modestae', 199).

Botticelli: Lightbown 1978.1.72–81, 2.51–3. Interpretation in terms of 'pagan mysteries', suggested by the attitude of Mercurius: Wind 1967.113–27 and figs 23–33. Chloris' name: cf. Ovid *Fasti* 5.222 ('before that the earth was monochrome').

Venus' April and Mercurius' May: Ovid *Fasti* 4.13–14, 25–8, 59–62, 85–132; 5.79–106. Names of the Graces: Hesiod *Theogony* 909; for fifteenth-century interpretations see Wind 1967.36–52 and figs 9–19.

'A flower...': Massey 1757.265–6.

9 Games of Flora: Velleius Paterculus 1.14.8 (241 BC), Pliny *Natural History* 18.285 (238 BC), Varro *De lingua Latina* 5.158, Tacitus *Annals* 2.49.1; Verrius

Flaccus, *Fasti Praenestini* on 28 April (Degrassi 1963.132–3, Scullard 1981.110).

'The task. . .': Massey 1757.268–9.

'Let none. . .': Massey 1757.270.

10 Roman peace: Pliny *Natural History* 27.3; Tacitus *Agricola* 30.6 (cf. 30.4 'nos terrarum ac libertatis extremos').

Civic virtue: Sallust *Catiline* 53.2–4; Cicero *Pro Roscio Amerino* 50, *Pro Caelio* 39; see Chapter 7.

11 Twentieth-century preconception: Wissowa 1902.23, Latte 1926.256 and 257 (my translation in each case).

CHAPTER 2

13 Gabii graffito: Peruzzi 1998.10–11, 19–22, assuming the reading *euoin*; for *eulin* (i.e. Eulinos, 'Good Spinner'), see Ridgway 1996.

euoi: e.g. Sophocles *Trachiniae* 219, Aristophanes *Lysistrata* 1294, Pausanias 4.31.4. Latin *euhoe*: e.g. Catullus 64.255, Ovid *Ars amatoria* 1.563. Euios: e.g. Euripides *Bacchae* 566, Aristophanes *Thesmophoriazusae* 993. Latin Euhius: e.g. Lucretius 5.743, Horace *Odes* 1.18.9.

Archaeological dating: Bettelli 1997.191–8.

Eighth-century context: Ridgway 1992, Burkert 1992, Osborne 1998, Malkin 1998.

14 Rumon: Servius on *Aeneid* 8.90. Albula: Ovid *Fasti* 5.646, Festus (Paulus) 4L, Servius on *Aeneid* 8.322. Tiberis: Varro *De lingua Latina* 5.30, etc. The river-god's name was Tiberinus: Cicero *De natura deorum* 3.52 (citing the augurs' *precatio*).

15 'But it was only. . .': Herodotus 2.53.1–2 (trans. A. de Sélincourt, Penguin Classics). 'Seven hundred years. . .': Ennius *Annales* fr. 154–5 Sk; Varro *De re rustica* 3.1.2. Archaeological interpretation: Cornell 1995.81. Dislike of sea: Hesiod *Works and Days* 646–94.

16 'Proto-urban' Rome: Bettelli 1997.207–19.

Rome as 'Ρώμη: Hyperochus of Cumae *FGrH* 576 F3 (Festus 328L), L. Ateius Praetextatus fr. 14 Funaioli (Servius on *Aeneid* 1.273), Plutarch *Romulus* 1.1, Solinus 1.1; allusion at Lycophron *Alexandra* 1233. Opelt 1965 assumes the association is Hellenistic; but the Romans knew Greek before the third century BC.

Nestor's cup: Ridgway 1992.55–7.

17 Hesiod on Odysseus: Eratosthenes in Strabo 1.2.14 (he found out 'by enquiry'); scholiast on Apollonius Rhodius 3.311; Hesiod *Theogony* 1011–16 (no need to assume a late addition: see Malkin 1998.86–7, 183).

For Circe as part of the more general phenomenon of far-east stories appearing also in the west, see Braund 1994.18–21; one might add Homer's *Kimmerioi* (*Odyssey* 11.14–19, Strabo 5.4.5, Pliny *Natural History* 3.61, Festus [Paulus] 37L), and the resulting 'Cimmerian Sibyl in Italy' (Lactantius *Divinae institutiones* 1.6.10 = Varro *Antiquitates divinae* fr. 56a Cardauns).

Telegony: Davies 1988.72–3, 1989.87–94. Translation of Proclus' plot-summary: Evelyn-White 1914.531.

Hero cult: suggested by Phillips 1953.55. Elpenor: Homer *Odyssey* 11.74–8, 12.10–15, Theophrastus *Historia plantarum* 5.8.3, Pliny *Natural History* 15.119. Cult of Circe at Circeii: Cicero *De natura deorum* 3.48.

Latin and Etruscan spellings: Fiesel 1928.48–56, Wüst 1936.106–9, Malkin 1998.87–8. Quintilian (1.4.16) says that 'Ulixes' comes from the Aeolian *Ulusseus*.

18 Adriatic: Malkin 1998.74–81 on Corcyra and Orikos; Plutarch *Moralia* 293a–b (*Greek Questions* 11) on Eretrians and Corinthians at Corcyra.

Odysseus in Etruria (Phillips 1953.65): Theopompus *FGrH* 115 F354, Lycophron *Alexandra* 805–6, pseudo-Aristotle p. 571 Rose (epitaph ἐπὶ 'Οδυσσέως κειμένου ἐν Τυρρηνίᾳ); cf. Plutarch *Moralia* 27e on Etruscan traditions about Odysseus.

Diomedes in Italy: e.g. Mimnermos fr. 22 West, Lykos of Rhegion *FGrH* 570 F3, Timaeus *FGrH* 566 F53, Lycophron *Alexandra* 594–632; Pearson 1988.73–5, Malkin 1998.233–57.

Rutuli as *gens Daunia*: Virgil *Aeneid* 8.146, Silius Italicus 1.291–3, 1.665–9, 8.357. Juturna as *dea Daunia*: Virgil *Aeneid* 12.785.

Herons: Lykos of Rhegion *FGrH* 570 F6, scholiast on Homer *Iliad* 5.412. Land routes: two of Diomedes' supposed foundations, Beneventum and Venafrum (Servius *auctus* on *Aeneid* 11.246), are on major routes from Apulia into Campania and Latium respectively.

Diomedes and the Palladion: Servius on *Aeneid* 2.166, 3.407 (Calabria); Cassius Hemina fr. 8 Santini = Solinus 2.14 ('in agro Laurenti'); Silius Italicus 13.30–82 (by the Tiber bank, 66); John Malalas (6.22–3, 167) puts it at Argyrippe, which he identifies as Beneventum. Aeneas and the Palladion: e.g. Dionysius of Halicarnassus 1.69.2–3 (citing Arktinos' *Ilioupersis*), 2.66.5; Ovid *Fasti* 6.434–6, *Tristia* 3.1.29.

19 Pallas and literature: Ovid *Fasti* 3.833 ('mille dea est operum, certe dea carminis illa est').

London Palladium: *Notes and Queries* 10.12 (1909) 47; *The Times* 7 Dec. 1910 p. 13, 27 Dec. 1910 p. 7; *Survey of London* 31–2 (1963) 297–300 and Plate 31b (the Palladium in 1962, with Morecambe and Wise top of the bill).

20 Aeneas and Iulii: Cato *Origines* fr. 9 Chassignet, Virgil *Aeneid* 1.267, 288 (Ascanius); Livy 1.3.2 (brother of Ascanius?); Dionysius of Halicarnassus 1.70.3–4 (son of Ascanius).

Stesichoros on Aeneas in the west: Malkin 1998.191–4. The evidence is doubted by Horsfall 1979, but needlessly, I think; in any case, the next *terminus ante quem* is about 500 BC, Hekataios *FGrH* 1 F62 on Capua founded by the Trojan Capys.

Aeneas and Odysseus as founders of Rome (Malkin 1998.194–8): Hellanikos *FGrH* 4 F84, Damastes *FGrH* 5 F3 (Dionysius of Halicarnassus 1.72.2); implied also in Lycophron *Alexandra* 1242–5.

Graikoi: Aristotle *Meteorologika* 352a; Malkin 1998.147–9.

Tusculum: Horace *Epodes* 1.29–30 ('Circaean walls') and *Odes* 3.29.8, with Porphyrio's commentary on both passages; Propertius 2.32.4, Ovid *Fasti* 3.92, 4.71; Festus 116L, Livy 1.49.9, Dionysius of Halicarnassus 4.45.1 on Tarquin's ally Octavius Mamilius; the earliest evidence is provided by the coin-types of L. Mamilius in the early second century BC and C. Mamilius Limetanus a century later (Crawford 1974.219–20, 375–7).

Rhomos, Anteias and Ardeias: Dionysius of Halicarnassus 1.72.5 (Xenagoras *FGrH* 240 F29); Strasburger 1968.11–12, Mele 1987.175. Cf. Polybius 3.22.1 (the first Carthage treaty) for Ardea, Antium and Kirkaion.

Circe's *circus*: Tertullian *De spectaculis* 8, Lydus *De mensibus* 1.12; Humphrey 1986.10–17 for the historical context (and see Chapter 3 for king Tarquinius).

Lanuvium: Appian *Civil Wars* 2.20. The eponym Lanoios, an ally of Aeneas (Fabius Pictor in *Supplementum Epigraphicum* 26.1123.3.A) looks like a later contrivance.

Covered head aetiology: Dionysius of Halicarnassus 12.16 (22), combining two versions; cf. 1.54.2 for the sacrifice to Helios. Diomedes in Calabria: Virgil *Aeneid* 3.405–7, 530–47 (allusion explained by Servius on 3.407 and 545), Plutarch *Moralia* 266a (*Roman Questions* 10). Odysseus in Latium: Festus 432L, *Origo gentis Romanae* 12.2.

21 Nautii: Varro *De familiis Troianis* fr. 1P, cited by Servius on *Aeneid* 2.166 and 5.704 (also 3.407, without the Varro reference); Dionysius of Halicarnassus 6.69.1.

Aemilii: Plutarch *Romulus* 2.3, Festus (Paulus) 22L. Cloelii: Festus (Paulus) 48L. Geganii: Servius on *Aeneid* 5.117. Sergii: Virgil *Aeneid* 5.121. Sulpicii: Suetonius *Galba* 2 (Jupiter), Crawford 1974.320 (sow of Lavinium, 106 BC). The Cloelii and Geganii, like the Iulii, came from Alba Longa (Livy 1.30.2, Dionysius of Halicarnassus 3.29.7).

22 Argonauts in Italy (Pearson 1987.62–5): Apollonius Rhodius 4.552–684 (περιώσια σήματα, 554), Diodorus Siculus 4.56.3–6 (ἐμφανῆ σημεῖα, 56.5), cf. Strabo 5.2.6. Diodorus used Timaeus (*FGrH* 566 F85), and the 'ancient authors' he refers to will have been Timaeus' own sources.

Circe on Ἀργὼ πασιμέλουσα: Homer *Odyssey* 12.70.

Formiae and Caieta: Diodorus Siculus 4.56.6, cf. Strabo 5.3.6, Festus (Paulus) 73L; Lycophron *Alexandra* 1274 and scholiasts. Laistrygonians: Cicero

Ad Atticum 2.13.2, Horace *Odes* 3.16.35 with Porphyrio's note, Pliny *Natural History* 3.59, Silius Italicus 7.410. Aeneas' nurse: Virgil *Aeneid* 7.1–4, Dionysius of Halicarnassus 1.53.3. Alternatively, Caieta was where the Trojans' ships were burned (Servius on *Aeneid* 7.1, 10.36, *Origo gentis Romanae* 10.3–4).

Amykos: the most familiar version places his realm in Bithynia, and makes Polydeukes kill him (Apollonius Rhodius 2.1–97 etc.). But he was only bound and rendered harmless in the earliest accounts, such as that of the comic poet Epicharmos about 500 BC (fr. 7 Kaibel, scholiast on Apollonius Rhodius 2.98), and that was the version preferred in fourth-century BC Latium (e.g. the Ficoroni *cista*, Chapter 5). Epicharmus' Sicilian play and the popularity of the theme in Italic art suggest that this version may have been set in the west.

Dioskourias: founded by the Dioskouroi (Pomponius Mela 1.111, Appian *Mithridatika* 101) or by their charioteers (Pliny *Natural History* 6.16, Ammianus Marcellinus 22.8.24); Braund 1994.30–33. Celtic cults as evidence: Diodorus Siculus 4.56.4.

Lavinium inscription: *ILLRP* 1271a; Weinstock 1960.112–14.

23 Rome temple: Nielsen 1993. Rome cult: Sihvola 1989. Comment by Demetrios Poliorketes: Strabo 5.3.5. Tiberius' rebuilding: Suetonius *Tiberius* 20, Dio Cassius 55.27.3–4; Sihvola 1989.88–90.

Amyklai: Servius on *Aeneid* 10.564, cf. Solinus 2.32; Spartan aetiologies for Caieta and Formiae at Strabo 5.3.6. Amunclae: Pliny *Natural History* 3.59, 8.104, Tacitus *Annals* 4.59.1; the town was proverbial for having been destroyed by silence and by snakes (Servius on *Aeneid* 10.564).

Lykourgos story: Dionysius of Halicarnassus 2.49.4–5 (citing 'local histories'). Feronia: Horace *Satires* 1.5.24 with Porphyrio's note, Virgil *Aeneid* 7.799–800, Servius *auctus* on *Aeneid* 8.564.

Sabines as Spartans: Cato *Origines* fr. 51P, Cn. Gellius fr. 10P (both cited by Servius *auctus* on *Aeneid* 8.638); Plutarch *Romulus* 16.1, *Numa* 1.3. 'Spartan' families at Rome: Silius Italicus 2.8 (Valerii), 8.412 and 15.543 (Claudii).

'Oebalian': used of the Dioskouroi by Ovid *Fasti* 5.705, Statius *Thebaid* 5.438, *Silvae* 3.2.10, Valerius Flaccus 4.294; of Helen by Ovid *Heroides* 16.128, *Remedia Amoris* 458; of Spartans in general by Virgil *Georgics* 4.125; of Tarentum (a Spartan colony) by Silius Italicus 12.451, Claudian *Carmina* 17.158; of Sabines by Ovid *Fasti* 1.260, 3.230. Oibalos: variant family trees in Pausanias 3.1.3–4, Apollodorus 3.10.4, scholiast on Euripides *Orestes* 457.

24 Servius and Servius *auctus*: Marshall 1983, Kaster 1988.169–97.

Glaukos (Gantz 1993.1.270–1): Servius *auctus* on *Aeneid* 10.564; Servius on *Aeneid* 7.796. Minos:

Herodotus 7.170.1. Galbae: Silius Italicus 8.470–1 (paternal descent), Suetonius *Galba* 2 (maternal).

25 Danae: Servius *auctus* on *Aeneid* 8.345, Pherekydes *FGrH* 3 F10–12, Servius on *Aeneid* 7.372, 410; Virgil *Aeneid* 7.372 (Turnus' descent from Inachos and Akrisios), 410 (Danae founds Ardea), 789–92 (Inachos and his daughter on Turnus' shield), 794 (Argive Rutuli).

Gorgons: Hesiod *Theogony* 274–6.

Argeus: Servius *auctus* on *Aeneid* 8.345. *Argei*: Varro *De lingua Latina* 5.45, 7.44, Dionysius of Halicarnassus 1.38.2–3 (who says there were thirty), Ovid *Fasti* 5.621–60, Festus 450–2L, Festus (Paulus) 14L; see Palmer 1970.84–97, Coarelli 1993, Carandini 1997a.395–416.

Chapels: Varro *De lingua Latina* 5.45 (*sacraria*), 5.48 (*sacellum*). Document: ibid. 5.50 ('in sacris Argeorum'), 5.52 ('ex Argeorum sacrificiis'). *Argea*: Festus (Paulus) 18L: 'Argea loca Romae appellantur, quod in his sepulti essent quidam Argiuorum inlustres uiri.'

Argive Falerii: Cato *Origines* fr. 47P (Pliny *Nat. Hist.* 3.51), Ovid *Amores* 3.13.31–5, *Fasti* 4.73–4, Solinus 2.7, Servius on *Aeneid* 7.695, 723; cf. Silius Italicus 8.474–5 (Alsium).

Argive Tibur: Horace *Odes* 2.6.5, Virgil *Aeneid* 7.670–2 (with Servius), Ovid *Fasti* 4.71, Pliny *Natural History* 16.237, Solinus 2.7.

Orestes in Aricia: Servius on *Aeneid* 2.116; see p. 124 above on the transfer of the bones of Orestes from Aricia (338 BC?) and their burial in front of the temple of Saturnus.

26 Stesichoros: Page 1973, Brize 1980; Quintilian 10.1.62. Unfortunately the surviving fragments of the *Geryoneis* cast little light on the latter part of the story.

Stesichoros' birthplace: 'Matauria in Italy' (Suda 4.433 Adler, s.v. Stesichoros), i.e. Bruttian Metaurum (Pomponius Mela 2.68, Solinus 2.11) by the river Metaurus (Strabo 6.2.9, Pliny *Natural History* 3.73); 'Matauros in Sicily' (Stephanos of Byzantium 1.437 Meineke, s.v. Matauros).

Oinotria: Pherekydes *FGrH* 3 F156 (Dionysius of Halicarnassus 1.13.1), Servius *auctus* on *Aeneid* 1.532.

Pallantion as the toe of Italy: Dionysius of Halicarnassus 19.2.1. Arkadian Pallantion: Hesiod *Ehoiai* fr. 45 MW, Pausanias 8.3.1–2 (Stesichoros fr. 182 = S85 Davies), 8.45.5; Suda 4.433 Adler, s.v. Stesichoros.

Euandros/Evander: parents Echemos and Timandra daughter of Tyndareus (Servius *auctus* on *Aeneid* 8.130, from Hesiod), or X son of Pallas and Nikostrate (Servius on *Aeneid* 8.51), or Hermes and X daughter of Ladon (Pausanias 8.43.2), or Hermes and Themis (Dionysius of Halicarnassus 1.31.1) = Mercurius and Carmentis (Virgil *Aeneid* 8.138,

335–6, *Origo gentis Romanae* 5.1), or a mortal father and Carmentis (Ovid *Fasti* 1.469–78). Nikostrate daughter of Hermes (Servius *auctus* on *Aeneid* 8.130), a prophetic nymph (Strabo 5.3.3, Servius on *Aeneid* 8.51, Servius *auctus* on *Aeneid* 8.336, *Origo gentis Romanae* 5.2) like Themis/Carmentis. Exile: Virgil *Aeneid* 8.333, Dionysius of Halicarnassus 1.31.2, Servius on *Aeneid* 8.51. Colony: Dionysius of Halicarnassus 1.31.1, Pausanias 8.43.2.

Pallantion = Palatium: Varro *De lingua Latina* 5.21, 53, Livy 1.5.1, Dionysius of Halicarnassus 1.31.4, Justin 43.1.6, Pausanias 8.43.2, Servius on *Aeneid* 8.51, *Origo gentis Romanae* 5.3.

Arkadian gods: Dionysius of Halicarnassus 1.32.3–5 (Pan Lykaios and Nike), Livy 1.5.2 (Pan Lykaios), Virgil *Aeneid* 8.343–4 with Servius (Pan Lykaios), Ovid *Fasti* 2.271–82 (Pan), 5.81–106 (Faunus, Mercurius), Justin 43.1.7 (Pan Lykaios), *Origo gentis Romanae* 5.3 (Pan). Nike as daughter of Pallas: Dionysius of Halicarnassus 1.33.1 (Arkadian story).

Lupercal = Lykaion, Lupercalia = Lykaia: Ovid *Fasti* 2.423–4, Virgil *Aeneid* 8.343–4 with Servius, Dionysius of Halicarnassus 1.32.3, 80.1, Plutarch *Romulus* 21.3, *Caesar* 61.1, *Antony* 12.1, *Moralia* 280c (*Roman Questions* 68). For Pan and the Lupercalia see Wiseman 1995b.

Temple of Victory: Wiseman 1987.187–204 and 380–1; Pensabene 1998.85–99 (previous cult site sixth to fourth century BC).

Bona Dea as Maia: Macrobius *Saturnalia* 1.12.20–1 (Cornelius Labeo).

Eratosthenes on Italian Sibyl: scholiast on Plato *Phaedrus* 244b, Clement of Alexandria *Stromateis* 1.108.3 (texts and translation in Wiseman 1995b.3, 18). Eratosthenes on Rome: *FGrH* 241 F45 (Romulus son of Ascanius). *Karmalon* from *carmen*: Wiseman 1995a.77–8.

27 'The story goes. . .': Augustine *City of God* 18.16–17 (trans. Henry Bettenson, Penguin Classics), Varro *De gente populi Romani* fr. 29 Fraccaro.

Lykaon: Hughes 1997.13–19 (based on Ovid *Metamorphoses* 1.196–243).

28 Carmenta (or Carmentis) from *carmen*: Dionysius of Halicarnassus 1.31.1, Ovid *Fasti* 1.467, Plutarch *Romulus* 21.2, *Moralia* 278c (*Roman Questions* 56), Solinus 1.10, Servius on *Aeneid* 8.51, Servius *auctus* on *Aeneid* 8.336, *Origo gentis Romanae* 5.2. Cf. Livy 1.7.8 ('a prophetess before the Sibyl came to Italy'), depending on a different Sibylline chronology from Eratosthenes'.

Shrine of Carmenta (or Carmentis) and Porta Carmentalis: Dionysius of Halicarnassus 1.32.2, Servius on *Aeneid* 8.337, Solinus 1.13.

Cattlemarket (*Forum bouarium*, Coarelli 1988): Propertius 4.9.19–20, Ovid *Fasti* 1.582, 6.477–8, Dionysius of Halicarnassus 1.40.6.

Cacus story: Virgil *Aeneid* 8.184–305, Propertius 4.9.1–20, Ovid *Fasti* 1.543–83; Livy 1.7.4–15, Dionysius of Halicarnassus 1.39–43.

Altar founded by Evander: Dionysius of Halicarnassus 1.40.2, Strabo 5.3.3, Tacitus *Annals* 15.41.1, Macrobius *Saturnalia* 3.12.4. By Hercules: Varro in Macrobius 3.6.17, Livy 1.7.11, Virgil *Aeneid* 8.271, Propertius 4.9.67–8, Ovid *Fasti* 1.581–2.

Fabius: Plutarch *Fabius* 1.1–2, Silius Italicus 6.627–36; Festus (Paulus) 77L for the *fouea*, Varro in Servius on *Aeneid* 8.51 for Pallantia. 'Herculean' Fabii: Ovid *Fasti* 2.237, *Ex Ponto* 3.3.100, Silius Italicus 2.3, 7.34, 7.44, Juvenal 8.14.

Pinarii (consuls allegedly in 489 and 472 BC, other high offices in 432, 430, 363): Servius *auctus* on *Aeneid* 8.270' (ὑμεῖς δὲ πεινάσετε), cf. Servius on *Aeneid* 8.269 (ἀπὸ τῆς πείνας), *Origo gentis Romanae* 8.1–3 (ἀπὸ τοῦ πεινᾶν); Cicero *De domo* 134, Livy 1.7.12, Dionysius of Halicarnassus 1.40.4, Virgil *Aeneid* 8.269–70, Plutarch *Moralia* 278f (*Roman Questions* 60), Festus 270L, Macrobius *Saturnalia* 1.12.28.

30 Larentia: Varro *Antiquitates divinae* fr. 220a–b (Augustine *City of God* 6.7, Tertullian *Ad nationes* 2.10.1–7); *Fasti Praenestini* on 23 December (Degrassi 1963.138–9); Plutarch *Romulus* 5.1–4, *Moralia* 272F-273B (*Quaestiones Romanae* 35); Macrobius *Saturnalia* 1.10.11–16 (putting the event in the reign of Ancus Martius).

Velabrum food market: Plautus *Curculio* 483, *Captivi* 489, Horace *Satires* 2.3.229, Martial 11.52.10, 13.32.1–2.

'Fabula': Plutarch *Moralia* 272F, Lactantius *Divinae insitituiones* 1.20.5 ('Fa‹b›ula').

Not like a mortal: Plutarch *Moralia* 273A.

Tarutius: called Tarutilius in the *Fasti Praenestini*, Carutius in Macrobius *Saturnalia* 1.10.14 and 16.

Disappeared: Varro in Augustine *City of God* 6.7 ('illa non comparente'), Plutarch *Romulus* 5.4; other sources have her die a natural death, with the sacrifice at her tomb.

Larentalia: Varro *De lingua Latina* 6.23–4, Cicero *Ad M. Brutum* 1.15.8; *Fasti Antiates maiores* (Degrassi 1963.25).

31 Hercules rationalised: Dionysius of Halicarnassus 1.34.1–2 (followers, prisoners), 1.40–42 (army), 1.43.1 (Hyperborean hostage).

Epicadus: Suetonius *De grammaticis* 12.

Argives: Varro *De lingua Latina* 5.45, Festus (Paulus) 18L, Festus 450–2L.

'Thus victor. . .': Massey 1757.288–9.

Herakles in Campania: Diodorus Siculus 4.21.5–7, Dionysius of Halicarnassus 1.44.1 (Herculaneum), Servius on *Aeneid* 8.662 (Pompeii). Giants: Pindar *Pythians* 1.15–18 (Typhon under Cumae), Strabo 5.44, 5.4.6, 5.4.9.

32 Giants' revenge (Wiseman 1992.14–21): Dio Cassius 66.22.2–23.1, cf. Pliny *Letters* 6.20.14–15 ('nusquam iam deos ullos').

Ouranos, Kronos and Zeus: Hesiod *Theogony* 154–210, 385–403, 453–506. Kronos in Taratarus: Homer *Iliad* 8.478–81, 14.203–4, 14.273–9, 15.225, Hesiod *Theogony* 850–1. Isles of the Blessed: Hesiod *Works and Days* 173a (a later interpolation), cf. 109–11 (Golden Age); Pindar *Olympians* 2.68–77.

Kronos and Saturnus: Versnel 1993.89–227.

Saturnus in Latium: Virgil *Aeneid* 8.319–27 (322 for *latere*), Ovid *Fasti* 1.235–40 (238 for *latere*), Macrobius *Saturnalia* 1.7.19–24, *Origo gentis Romanae* 1.1–3.7.

Human sacrifice (Versnel 1993.100–3, 210–27): Ovid *Fasti* 5.625–8, Dionysius of Halicarnassus 1.38.2, Macrobius *Saturnalia* 1.7.28–31.

Saturnus as civiliser: Virgil *Aeneid* 8.314–25, Plutarch *Moralia* 275a–b (*Roman Questions* 42), Festus 202L, Macrobius *Saturnalia* 1.7.25, *Origo gentis Romanae* 3.2–4. Sowing: Varro *De lingua Latina* 5.64, *Antiquitates Divinae* frr. 239–42 Cardauns, Festus 202L, Macrobius *Saturnalia* 1.10.20, Augustine *City of God* 7.13.

33 Remains of town (*castrum Saturni*): Festus 430L, Virgil *Aeneid* 8.355–8. Coinage and *aerarium*: Tertullian *Apologeticus* 10.8, Minucius Felix *Octavius* 21.5, *Origo gentis Romanae* 3.4–6. *Graeco ritu*: Dionysius of Halicarnassus 1.34.4, Festus 432L. Shackled statue: Verrius Flaccus in Macrobius *Saturnalia* 1.8.5, Minucius Felix *Octavius* 23.5.

Evander as civiliser: Dionysius of Halicarnassus 1.33.4, Festus 480L, *Origo gentis Romanae* 5.4. Alphabet: Fabius Pictor *FGrH* 809 F23, Cincius Alimentus *FGrH* 810 F6 (both in *Grammatici Latini* 6.23 Keil), Livy 1.7.8, Tacitus *Annals* 11.14.3.

Hercules commutes human sacrifice: Ovid *Fasti* 5.625–32, Dionysius of Halicarnassus 1.38.2–3. *Graecus ritus* at Ara Maxima: C. Acilius *FGrH* 813 F1 (Strabo 5.3.3), Varro in Macrobius *Saturnalia* 3.6.17, Livy 1.7.3.

Argives at Saturnia: Varro *De lingua Latina* 5.45, Dionysius of Halicarnassus 1.34.1–4.

Ovid on Ino, perhaps from a play of the second century BC (Wiseman 1998.35–51): *Fasti* 6.483–550.

Grove of Semele (or Stimula): Ovid *Fasti* 6.503, Livy 39.12.4; Cazenove 1983.56–66.

34 Servius Tullius: Ovid *Fasti* 6.475–80 (cf. 569 for Fortuna); Coarelli 1988.205–34.

35 Satyr-and-nymph antefixes: R.R. Knoop in Cristofani 1990.243–4 ('un complesso di almeno una sessantina di esemplari ricavati da più di 20 matrici'); he interprets the nymphs as maenads, but see Hedreen 1994.

Saturae palus: Virgil *Aeneid* 7.801, Silius Italicus 8.380. Satyrs: Charax of Pergamum *FGrH* 103 F1.

36 Falernus: Silius Italicus 7.162–211.

CHAPTER 3

37 Wealthy Korinthos: Strabo 8.6.20; for the Bacchiadai, or Bacchidai, see Diodorus Siculus 7.9.4, Pausanias 2.4.4; For Kypselos' coup, see Herodotus 5.92.β–ε, Nikolaus of Damascus *FGrH* 90 F57.

Aphrodite as Astarte: *SEG* 36.316; West 1997.56–7.

Eumelos: Pausanias 2.1.1; fragments in *Epicorum Graecorum fragmenta* (ed. M. Davies 1988). Helios, frr. 2–3; Poseidon, fr. 12.

38 Archias and Chersikrates, colonists of Syracuse and Corcyra: Thucydides 6.3.2, Strabo 6.2.4. Kleiklos: *SEG* 31.875; Solin 1983.

Demaratos (Blakeway 1935 for the archaeological context): Polybius 6.2.10; Cicero *De republica* 2.34, *Tusculanae disputationes* 5.109; Livy 1.34.2, Dionysius of Halicarnassus 3.46.3–5, Strabo 5.2.2, Zonaras 7.8.

Lucumo: Servius on *Aeneid* 2.278, 8.65, 8.475, 10.202; Censorinus *De die natali* 4.13.

Janiculum scene: Cicero *De legibus* 1.4, Livy 1.34.5–9, Dionysius of Halicarnassus 3.47.2–4, *De viris illustribus* 6.3–4, Zonaras 7.8.

Tarquinius gains kingdom: Polybius 6.11a.7, Cicero *De republica* 2.35, Diodorus Siculus 8.31, Livy 1.34.10–12, Dionysius of Halicarnassus 3.48, Dio Cassius 2.9, Zonaras 7.8.

Valley restructured: Ammerman 1990. Attributed to Tarquinius: Livy 1.37.6, Dionysius of Halicarnassus 3.67.5.

Neptunus Equester and Consus: Livy 1.9.6, Dionysius of Halicarnassus 1.33.2, 2.31.2–3, Plutarch *Romulus* 14.3, Tertullian *De spectaculis* 5.5, Lydus *De magistratibus* 1.30. The Consualia on 21 August was the occasion of the rape of the Sabine women, for which Romulus' signal 'Talasio' (Plutarch *Romulus* 15.2)—early Latin spelling for 'Thalassio'—may have meant 'for the sea-god!' (Aristophanes *Wasps* 1519 and *Plutus* 396 for Poseidon as *thalassios*).

Isthmian games parallel: Zevi 1995.308–9. Fortuna Virilis as the successor of a cult with temple prostitutes: Wiseman 2004.

39 Demaratos' followers: Pliny *Natural History* 35.16, 35.152; Tacitus *Annals* 11.14.3.

40 'Fair shore': Plutarch *Romulus* 20.4 (no need to assume textual corruption, as many editors do).

Floods: Le Gall 1953.9–17. The Tiber is lowest in August (dry ground for the races at the Consualia) and highest in April (flood water for the women to bathe in on Fortuna Virilis' day).

Fortuna Virilis cult: Ovid *Fasti* 4.133–62 (later combined with Venus Verticordia), *Fasti Praenestini* on 1 April (Degrassi 1963.126–7).

Myrtle grove: Servius *auctus* on *Aeneid* 8.636, Varro *De lingua Latina* 5.154. Aphrodite (Venus) and the satyrs: Ovid *Fasti* 4.141–2, Servius on *Eclogues* 7.62.

Sexual nature of 1 April ritual: Ovid *Fasti* 4.145–54. Myrtle garlands: Ovid *Fasti* 4.139–44, Plutarch *Numa* 19.2, Lydus *De mensibus* 4.65. Gifts to women on 1 April: Ovid *Ars amatoria* 1.405–6.

Tarquinius Superbus and Aristodemos 'Malakos' (on whom see Mele 1987): Cicero *Tusculanae disputationes* 3.27, Livy 2.21.5, Dionysius of Halicarnassus 6.21.3 (death); Livy 2.34.4 (heir), Dionysius of Halicarnassus 7.2.3, 7.12.1–2.

'Kymaian chronicle' on Aristodemos (Dionysius of Halicarnassus 7.3–12): Alföldi 1965.56–72.

Historicity of Tarquins: Zevi 1995, esp. 296–8.

Date of expulsion of kings: Polybius 3.22.1, probably from Eratosthenes (third century BC), who used Xerxes as a chronological marker and was interested in Roman events (*FGrH* 241 F1(a) and 45).

Vipinas brothers: Buranelli 1987.234 for the Veii dedication, 234–5 for a fifth- or fourth-century red-figure cup carrying Aule's name (evidence for a hero-cult? Cornell 1995.135).

41 Etruscan mirror: Buranelli 1987. 242–3 (also for four third-century cinerary urns with the same scene). No connection, I think, with Cacus the brigand or monster killed by Hercules in the Roman story (*pace* Small 1982). Drama: Wiseman 1994.74–5.

42 François Tomb paintings: Alföldi 1965.221–5, Thomsen 1980.68–79, Buranelli 1987.84–98, Cornell 1995.135–9, Coarelli 1996.141–51. The reconstruction of the story is Alföldi's, though like most scholars he assumes, wrongly in my opinion, that Marce Camitlnas and Cneve Tarchunies Rumach are part of it.

43 Camitlnas as Camillus: Bruun 2000.44–9.

44 Vibennae in Rome: Festus 486L, presumably from Verrius Flaccus, who was an Etruscan expert (Veronese scholiast on *Aeneid* 10.183 and 200); for the text, see Alföldi 1965.216 n.1, Cornell 1995.425–6 n.46. Tacitus *Annals* 4.65, probably from Claudius' Etruscan history.

Caelian hill: Varro *De lingua Latina* 5.46, Dionysius of Halicarnassus 2.36.2, Festus (Paulus) 38L, all attributing Caeles' visit to the time of Romulus.

Claudius (Suetonius *Claudius* 42.2 for his twenty-volume Etruscan history): Cornell 1995.133–4.

Aule (Olus Vulcentanus): Arnobius 6.7, citing among others Fabius Pictor (*FGrH* 809 F11). The corrupt text 'germani seruuli uita fuerit spoliatus et lumine' is plausibly emended to 'a germani seruulo. . .' (Coarelli 1996.153–5); cf. Cornell 1995.145, though 'his twin brother' goes beyond the evidence.

'Head of Olus' (*caput Oli*) also in Servius *auctus* on *Aeneid* 8.345; Etruscan inscription, Isidore *Origines* 15.2.31; 'king Olus', *Chronographer of AD 354* (Mommsen *MGH Chronica minora* 1) 144. Head omen without the name: Varro *De lingua Latina* 5.41, Livy 1.55.5, 5.54.7, Dionysius of Halicarnassus 4.59.2, etc.

Etruscan *haruspex* story: Dionysius of Halicarnassus 4.59.2–61.2, Pliny *Natural History* 28.15 (naming the seer Olenus Calenus), Servius *auctus* on *Aeneid* 8.345 (giving the Argiletum aetiology), Zonaras 7.11.

45 'Mastarna' as Servius Tullius: Claudius in *ILS* 212.1.22–4 (translation in Cornell 1995.133–4).

Ocrisia: chosen for Tarquinius (Zonaras 7.9), given by him to Tanaquil (Dionysius of Halicarnassus 4.1.2, Plutarch *Moralia* 323b).

Portent: Arnobius 5.18, quoting (Granius?) Flaccus; Dionysius of Halicarnassus 3.65.6 (divine *epiphaneia*), 4.2.1–3, Ovid *Fasti* 6.627–34, Pliny *Natural History* 36.24, Plutarch *Moralia* 323a–c. Identified as *Lar familiaris* by Pliny, Lar ('hero of the house') or Volcanus (Hephaistos) by Dionysius and Plutarch, Volcanus by Ovid, *di conserentes* by Arnobius.

Lares and *Genii*: Censorinus *De die natali* 3.2, quoting Granius Flaccus *De indigitamentis*; Varro *Antiquitates divinae* frr. 209 and 226 Cardauns (Arnobius 3.41, Augustine *City of God* 7.6).

Rationalising versions: Livy 1.39.5–6, Dionysius of Halicarnassus 4.1, *De viris illustribus* 7.1 (Tullius of Corniculum); Cicero *De republica* 2.37, Plutarch *Moralia* 323b (client of king); Zonaras 7.9 (before or after capture).

Flame portent: Cicero *De divinatione* 1.121, Livy 1.39.1–4, Dionysius of Halicarnassus 4.2.4, Ovid *Fasti* 6.635–6, Valerius Maximus 1.6.1, Pliny *Natural History* 2.241, Plutarch *Moralia* 323c–d, Servius on *Aeneid* 2.683, etc.

No male heirs: Dionysius of Halicarnassus 3.65.6 (inconsistent with 4.1.1 and 4.4.2, which must be from a different source). Opposition to Servius' succession: Dionysius of Halicarnassus 4.8.2, 4.10.4–6; cf. Cicero *De republica* 2.38 ('non commisit se patribus').

Palace window: Livy 1.41.4–6 (Tanaquil), Dionysius of Halicarnassus 4.5.1 (Tanaquil), Ovid *Fasti* 6.569–80 (Fortuna), Plutarch *Moralia* 273b–c (Fortuna and Tanaquil), 322e (Fortuna); for the position of the palace, see Wiseman 1998.27–30.

46 The slave-king as fortune's favourite: Plutarch *Moralia* 322c–323d.

Tenth- and ninth-century 'Rome' already outgrowing other Latin cities: Bettelli 1997.207–19, with discussion of rival archaeological models.

Ionians and Samians: *Supplementum epigraphicum Graecum* 27.671, 32.940–1017 (dedications at Gravisca); Herodotus 1.165–7 (Phokaians), Justin 43.3.4 (Phokaians ally with Rome). Samian seafaring: Herodotus 4.152.1–4 (Kolaios opens up Tartessos).

Pythagoras and Xenophanes: Guthrie 1962.146–340, 360–402.

Promathion: Mazzarino 1965.196–9, 584–6; Wiseman 1995a.57–61. Quoted by Aristotle fr. 248 Rose (a Latin translation which garbles his name as 'Promathus').

Tarchon (brother or son of Tyrrhenos): Lycophron *Alexandra* 1245–9, Cato *Origines* fr. 45P, Strabo 5.2.2, etc.

47 Tethys, 'mother of the gods' (Homer *Iliad* 14.201), borrowed from eastern cosmogony: Burkert 1992.91–3.

Citizen assembly (*comitia centuriata*): Cicero *De republica* 2.39–40, Livy 1.42.4–43.13, Dionysius of Halicarnassus 4.16–19.

'Tullius, qui libertatem ciuibus stabiliuerat': Accius *Praetextae* fr. 40R (from the *Brutus*, quoted in Cicero *Pro Sestio* 123). Abdication: Plutarch *Moralia* 323d, Livy 2.48.9; cf. Dionysius of Halicarnassus 4.9.9 (Servius promises the people an 'equal and common' constitution with justice and freedom of speech for all).

Servius as *popularis*: Dionysius of Halicarnassus 4.8.3, 4.10.1, 4.25.1; Plutarch *Moralia* 322e, Festus (Paulus) 247L, Zonaras 7.9.13. Popular grief at his death: Ovid *Fasti* 6.581–4.

48 Warlords: Cornell 1995.143–5 and fig. 17 (the late sixth-century inscription of Poplios Valesios and his *suodales* at Satricum).

'Ignobile regnum': Horace *Satires* 1.6.9. 'Regum ultimus ille bonorum': Juvenal 8.259–60, cf. Livy 1.46.3.

'My friends. . .': Empedocles *Katharmoi* fr. 102 Wright (112 Diels)—at Sicilian Akragas in the fifth century BC, but the idiom will not have varied much.

Pythagoras as quasi-god: Aristotle fr. 191 Rose. 'Tyrrhenian': Aristoxenos fr. 11 Wehrli, Aristotle fr. 190 Rose, Theopompus *FGrH* 115 F72 (Diogenes Laertius 8.1.1, Clement of Alexandria *Stromateis* 1.14). Roman citizen: Epicharmus fr. 295 Kaibel (Plutarch *Numa* 8.9)—probably not genuine, but even pseudo-Epicharmus is likely to belong to a fourth-century BC context.

49 Statues *in comitio*: Pliny *Natural History* 34.26, Plutarch *Numa* 8.10.

Pythagoras' disciples 'from the Messapians, Lucanians, Peuketians and Romans': Diogenes Laertius 8.1.14, Iamblichos *De vita Pythagorica* 34.241 (from Aristoxenos?).

'All decisions. . .': Clark 1989.60–1.

Sibyl story: Varro *Antiquitates divinae* frr. 56a (Lactantius *Institutiones* 1.6.10–11), 56c (Servius on *Aeneid* 6.72); Dionysius of Halicarnassus 4.62.1–4, Aulus Gellius 1.19, Lydus *De mensibus* 4.47, Suda s.v. *Sibylla* (p. 355 Adler), Zonaras 7.11. Dionysius, Gellius and Zonaras (also Pliny *Natural History* 13.88, Solinus 2.17, Tzetzes on Lycophron *Alexandra* 1279) attribute the story to Tarquinius Superbus, no doubt because of the arrogance of the king's reaction; all the more reason to accept Varro's version as preserving the original attribution. Varro and Gellius have the books burned before the king's eyes; Tzetzes mentions a servant. Pliny, Solinus and Lydus simplify the story by saying there were only three books, burned one at a time. The disappearance is in Dionysius, Gellius and Servius *auctus* on *Aeneid* 6.72 (not necessarily from Varro). The Sibyl's name is given by Varro and Lydus. The price in gold coins is of course an anachronism.

Attus Navius and the grape-cluster: Cicero *De divinatione* 1.31, Dionysius of Halicarnassus 3.70.2–4.

51   Tarquinius' challenge: Cicero *De divinatione* 1.32, Livy 1.36.2–5, Dionysius of Halicarnassus 3.71, Valerius Maximus 1.4.1, Festus 168–70L, etc.

Statues *in comitio*: Pliny *Natural History* 34.21–2, Livy 1.36.5, Dionysius of Halicarnassus 3.71.5. *Ficus Navia*: Festus 168–70L, with Mueller's restoration of the final sentence as '[responso haruspi]cum et diuin[is ostentis confirmabatur, quamdiu illa ficus] uiueret, libe[rtatem populi Romani incolumem man]suram'; Pliny *Natural History* 15.77. Navius mysteriously disappeared: Dionysius of Halicarnassus 3.72.3.

Numa as lawgiver: Cicero *De republica* 2.26–7, Virgil *Aeneid* 6.808–12, Livy 1.19.1, Tacitus *Annals* 3.26.4; Bruns 1909.8–11.

Numa and Egeria: Livy 1.21.3, Dionysius of Halicarnassus 2.60.5, Ovid *Metamorphoses* 15.479–84, *Fasti* 3.275–6, Plutarch *Numa* 4.1–2, 8.6, Juvenal 3.10–20, Martial 2.6.14–16 (just outside the Porta Capena).

Camenae as Muses: Livius Andronicus *Odyssey* fr. 1, Ennius *Annals* 487 Sk, etc.; Waszink 1956, Skutsch 1985.143–7, 649–50. Dinner party: Dionysius of Halicarnassus 2.60.6–7, Plutarch *Numa* 15.2.

Egeria's advice: Ovid *Fasti* 3.154 (calendar), 3.261–2 and 285–94 (Picus and Faunus, Jupiter), 4.669–70 (oracle); Plutarch *Numa* 13.1 (Picus and Faunus, Jupiter).

Jupiter Elicius story (Wiseman 1998.21–3): Valerius Antias fr. 6P (Arnobius 5.1), Ovid *Fasti* 3.295–348, Plutarch *Numa* 15.3–6; for the altar, Varro *De lingua Latina* 6.94, Livy 1.20.7.

52   Eliot's epigraph: Petronius *Satyricon* 48.7–8. Sibyl's request: Ovid *Metamorphoses* 14.101–53. Claudius: Graves 1934a ch. 1.

53   Rationalising versions: Livy 1.19.5, Dionysius of Halicarnassus 2.61.1–2, Plutarch *Numa* 4.8, 8.3–6, 15.1, 15.6 (Numa's own inventions to impress the people); Varro *Logistorici* fr. 44 Chappuis = Augustine *City of God* 7.35 (nymph Egeria an allegory for hydromancy).

Numa as Pythagorean: Ovid *Metamorphoses* 15.1–8, 60–73, 479–84. Chronological problem: Cicero *De republica* 2.28–9, Livy 1.18.2–4, Dionysius of Halicarnassus 2.59; Plutarch *Numa* 1.2–4, 8.4–10, 14.2–3, 22.3–4. Fourth century BC context: Storchi Marino 1999.

Brutus as laughing-stock: Livy 1.56.9, Dionysius of Halicarnassus 4.69.1–2, Dio Cassius 2.11.10, *De viris*

illustribus 10.2, Zonaras 7.11. *Brutus* = 'dumb': Pacuvius fr. 176R (Nonius 109L), Seneca *Letters* 121.24, etc.; *TLL* 2.2216.44–62.

Snake: Livy 1.56.4, Ovid *Fasti* 2.711–12, Zonaras 7.11; barking snake in Pliny *Natural History* 8.153. Vultures: Dionysius of Halicarnassus 4.63.2, Zonaras 7.11.

54   Brutus' offering: Livy 1.56.5–9, Dionysius of Halicarnassus 4.69.2–3, Valerius Maximus 7.3.2, Dio Cassius 2.11.10, *De viris illustribus* 10.2, Zonaras 7.11. Apollo's answer: Zonaras 7.11, cf. Pliny *Natural History* 8.153.

Siege of Ardea: Livy 1.57.1–5, Dionysius of Halicarnassus 4.64.1, Ovid *Fasti* 2.721–4. Wife's presence inferred from the vultures portent (Dionysius of Halicarnassus 4.63.2).

Greek historian: i.e. the 'chronicle of Kyme' used by Dionysius of Halicarnassus at 7.3–12 (Alföldi 1965.56–72).

Brutus' authority: Wiseman 2002b.27–32, cf. Livy 7.3.5 (from Cincius the antiquarian) on the *praetor maximus*.

Lars Porsena: Pliny *Natural History* 2.140 (Volsinii), 36.91 (tomb at Clusium). Capture of Rome: Tacitus *Histories* 3.72.1 ('dedita urbe'), Pliny *Natural History* 34.139 (treaty forbids the use of iron except for agriculture); Alföldi 1965.72–6.

Aricia campaign: Livy 2.14.5–9, Dionysius of Halicarnassus 5.36.1–2. Aristodemos and the 'Kymaian chronicle': Dionysius of Halicarnassus 7.3–12, with Alföldi 1965.56–72.

Tuscan Street (*vicus Tuscus*): Festus 486L (both versions); Livy 2.14.9, Dionysius of Halicarnassus 5.36.4 (Porsena); Varro *De lingua Latina* 5.46, Tacitus *Annals* 4.65 (Vibenna). Cf. also Propertius 4.2.49–52, Servius on *Aeneid* 5.560 (followers of Romulus' ally Lucumo).

55   What counts as truth? Cicero *De republica* 2.29, Livy 1.18.4; Plutarch *Numa* 1.4, 8.10, 22.4; Cicero *De divinatione* 1.33, 2.80.

56   Tribes: Taylor 1960.3–7; Ogilvie 1965.275, 292; Cornell 1995.173–9. But their assumption that the *tribus Claudia* was founded in 495 along with the Clustumina is unlikely: see Badian 1962.201 ('Claudia is the last of the old, Clustumina the first of the new'), Pinsent 1964.29.

Geographically named 'rural' tribes probably begin with Clustumina in 495 (cf. Livy 2.21.7); thereafter four in 387, two in 358 (though 'Poplilia' looks like a family name), two in 332, two in 318, two in 299, and two in 241 to reach the final total of thirty-one: Livy 6.5.8, 7.15.11, 8.17.11, 9.20.6, 10.9.4, *Epitome* 19.

Aimylia, daughter of Aeneas and Lavinia: Plutarch *Romulus* 2.3. Aimylos, son of Ascanius: Festus (Paulus) 22L. Sons of Pythagoras and Numa (both called Mamercus): Plutarch *Numa* 8.9–10, *Aemilius*

Paullus 2.2, Festus (Paulus) 22L.

Attus Clausus and the *tribus Claudia*: Livy 2.16.2–5, Dionysius of Halicarnassus 5.40, Plutarch *Publicola* 21.2–6 ('504 BC'); Appian *Regia* fr. 12 refers to Tarquin—perhaps Sextus, as in the Dionysius version—but not necessarily before the expulsion, as Ogilvie assumes (1965.273); Virgil *Aeneid* 7.708–9 gives the Romulus-T. Tatius context, though Servius (on 7.706) says 'post exactos reges'; Suetonius *Tiberius* 1.1 gives both versions.

57 'Gaius the Roman': Callimachus *Aitia* 4.106–7 Pfeiffer; for the missing punch-line, cf. Stobaeus 3.7.28 (Spartan warrior), Plutarch *Moralia* 331b (Philip of Macedon), Cicero *De officiis* 2.249 (Sp. Carvilius), Servius on *Aeneid* 8.646 (Horatius Cocles). According to Callimachus, the besiegers were Peuketioi, a people in the south-east of Italy, and Clement of Alexandria (*Stromateis* 4.56.3) knew a version of Lars Porsena's siege of Rome in which the king was called Peuketios; since the Peuketioi were named after the Arkadian Peuketios son of Lykaon (Dionysius of Halicarnassus 1.13.1 = Pherekydes *FGrH* 3 F156), perhaps these stories were also told in the context of Evander at Pallantion, about whom Clement certainly knew some early traditions (*Stromateis* 1.108.3).

The Sabine heifer: Plutarch *Moralia* 264c–d (*Roman Questions* 4), quoting Varro and Juba (*FGrH* 275 F91); Livy 1.45.3–7, Valerius Maximus 7.3.1; cf. *De viris illustribus* 7.10–14 (who says the farmer was a Latin and the message delivered in a dream). Juba alone gives the name of the priest (and of the Sabine, Antro Curiatius); only Plutarch and Livy (1.45.4) mention the horns on the temple.

Sergestus: Virgil *Aeneid* 5.121.

Mamurius Veturius: Varro *De lingua Latina* 6.49 (cf. Ovid *Fasti* 3.260, 382–92 for the Salian hymn); Plutarch *Numa* 13.3, Festus (Paulus) 117L.

Romulius Denter, 'Prefect of the city': Tacitus *Annals* 6.11.1.

Sex. Papirius: Pomponius in *Digest* 1.2.2.2, cf. 1.2.2.36 (Publius), Dionysius of Halicarnassus 3.36.3 (Gaius); *Digest* 50.16.144 (Granius Flaccus), Macrobius *Saturnalia* 3.11.5 for the *ius Papirianum*.

Menenius Agrippa: Dionysius of Halicarnassus 6.83.2 (in all the histories), Livy 2.32.8 (old-fashioned style); some authors gave his place in the story to Manius Valerius (Wiseman 1998.87, 89).

Battle of the triplets: Livy 1.24–5, Dionysius of Halicarnassus 3.13–20 (with different order of deaths), Manilius 1.778–9, Ampelius 20.1, *De viris illustribus* 4.5–8, Zonaras 7.6. Livy (1.24.1) knew a version where the Curiatii were the Roman triplets; cf. P. Curiatius Trigeminus, named as consul 453 BC in the Capitoline *fasti*, who appears in Dionysius (10.53.1) as P. Horatius. That version may have been an aetiology for the altar of Janus Curiatius (Dionysius

of Halicarnassus 3.22.7, Festus 380L, Bobbio scholiast 113 Stangl).

Sister: Livy 1.26, Dionysius of Halicarnassus 3.21–2, Festus 380L; Cicero *De inventione* 1.48, 2.78, *Pro Milone* 7 (with Bobbio scholiast 113 Stangl). The story of Horatius' trial by the people is clearly a later addition, and the Livian version (appointment of *duoviri*) evidently postdates 63 BC: Cloud 1977.205–9. 'Horatia's tomb' was just outside the Porta Capena (Livy 1.26.14, Dionysius of Halicarnassus 3.21.8).

58 *Tigillum Sororium*: Livy 1.26.13, Dionysius of Halicarnassus 3.22.8, Festus 380L.

Pila Horatia: Coarelli 1985.201–2. As spears: Propertius 3.3.6–7 (from Ennius), Livy 1.26.10. As pillar: Dionysius of Halicarnassus 3.22.9, Bobbio scholiast 113 Stangl.

Field of the Horatii (*campus Horatiorum*): Martial 3.47.3; cf. Dionysius of Halicarnassus 3.18.2 (3–4 stades), Livy 1.23.3 (fifth milestone), 1.25.14 (tombs).

Jupiter temple dedication: Valerius Maximus 5.10.1, Seneca *Consolatio ad Marciam* 13.1–2; Dionysius of Halicarnassus 5.35.3 for the inscription. For the 'malicious invention' story, see Cicero *De domo* 139 (calling Horatius a *pontifex*), Livy 2.8.6–8, Plutarch *Publicola* 14, Dio Cassius 3.13.3; Servius *auctus* on *Aeneid* 11.2 reports both versions.

Shrine of hero Horatius: Dionysius of Halicarnassus 5.14.1, cf. 5.16.2 (his voice rather than Faunus'?).

Cocles as 'One-eye': Pliny *Natural History* 11.150; Plautus *Curculio* 392–3, Ennius *Satires* fr. 67–8 Vahlen (Varro *De lingua latina* 7.71), Servius on *Aeneid* 8.649. The narrative sources either try to explain the significance of the name (Dionysius of Halicarnassus 5.23.2, Plutarch *Publicola* 16.5, *De viris illustribus* 11.1) or tacitly reject it (Livy 2.10.8, *oculos* plural).

Walls: Cornell 1995.198–202, 320; Coarelli 1988.35–42 for the stretch parallel to the Tiber. Dated to 378 BC by Livy (6.32.1), though he attributes the circuit wall to Servius Tullius (1.44.3); in Cocles' time, 'alia muris, alia Tiberi obiecto uidebantur tuta' (2.10.1).

'The story goes. . .': Polybius 6.55, trans. Ian Scott-Kilvert (Penguin Classics 1979), very slightly adapted.

Exemplary tale (always 'Cocles', never 'Horatius'): Cicero *De officiis* 1.61, *De legibus* 2.10, *Paradoxa Stoicorum* 1.12, Propertius 3.11.63, Virgil *Aeneid* 8.650, Manilius 1.781, Velleius Paterculus 2.6.6, Silius Italicus 10.483, Plutarch *Moralia* 317e, Juvenal 8.264, Claudian 8.406, 18.445, 28.487, Sidonius Apollinaris 5.70, 7.65.

59 Cocles survives with his arms: Livy 2.10.11 (not credible), Dionysius of Halicarnassus 5.24.3, Valerius Maximus 3.2.1 (saved by the gods), Seneca *Epistles* 120.7, Plutarch *Publicola* 16.6, Frontinus *Stratagems*

2.13.5, Florus 1.10.4, *De viris illustribus* 11.1.

Rewards: Livy 2.10.12, Dionysius of Halicarnassus 5.25.2, Plutarch *Publicola* 16.7, *De viris illustribus* 11.2. Statue: Pliny *Natural History* 34.22, Aulus Gellius 4.5.1–5; Coarelli 1983.161–9 (at the Volcanal), 174–5 (on the column at the *lapis niger* complex?).

The version that gave Cocles a gratuitous and uncomplimentary wound in the buttock (Dionysius of Halicarnassus 5.24.3, Plutarch *Publicola* 16.6)—sometimes euphemised as the thigh (Plutarch *Moralia* 317e) or the hip (Servius on *Aeneid* 8.646)—may have been trying to demote the old hero in favour of a new one (Valerius Publicola: see Wiseman 1998.83, 89); the wound could also explain why Cocles was never elected to high office or military command (Dionysius of Halicarnassus 5.25.3).

'There was. . .': Sisson 1986.225.

60 Macaulay's *Horatius*, stanzas quoted: 1, 19, 27, 29, 59. The nine gods: Dionysius of Halicarnassus 5.21.2, Pliny *Natural History* 2.138. Cocles on guard: Livy 2.10.3 ('positus forte in statione pontis'). For 'strait *path*' in stanza 29, cf. Propertius 3.11.63 (*semita*). Prayer to Tiber: Livy 2.10.11.

61 Cocles alone (*solus* or *unus*): Polybius 6.55.1, Cicero *De legibus* 2.10, *Paradoxa Stoicorum* 1.12, Valerius Maximus 3.2.1, Seneca *Epistles* 120.7, Florus 1.10.4, *De viris illustribus* 11.1, Livy *Epitome* 2 (despite Larcius and Herminius in the full text), Servius on *Aeneid* 8.646 (despite Larcius and Herminius in his note on 11.642).

Pila Horatia: Livy 1.26.10–11, Propertius 3.3.7; cf. Dionysius of Halicarnassus 3.22.9 (singular *pila* = 'column').

CHAPTER 4

63 Calendar: Michels 1967; North 1989.574–6; Cornell 1995,104–5; Beard et al. 1998.1.5–8, 2.60–77.

February from *februa*: Varro *De lingua Latina* 6.34, Ovid *Fasti* 2.19–34, Festus (Paulus) 75–6L, Plutarch *Moralia* 280b, etc.

Numa's calendar: Livy 1.19.6–7; Ovid *Fasti* 1.43–4, 3.151–4; Plutarch *Numa* 18.1–2. Modern conjectures: 'the calendar . . . can be dated to the sixth century with certainty, and perhaps even earlier' (Cornell 1995.105); 'in no case can it be proved that a festival was introduced later than the regal period' (North 1989.576); 'the period of the *decemviri* provides us with a date which is . . . more probable than most' (Michels 1967.127). In my view the fourth century is also possible.

Fragmentary calendars: Degrassi 1963 (1–28 for the *Fasti Antiates maiores*).

Phrygian cult introduced 204 BC: Livy 29.10.4–11, 29.14.5–14; Ovid *Fasti* 4.247–348. Erycina cult introduced 212 (or 215) BC: Ovid *Fasti* 4.871–6; Livy

22.9.10, 22.10.10, 23.31.9.

64 Terminus: Ovid *Fasti* 2.639–84; Dionysius of Halicarnassus 2.74.2–5; Plutarch *Numa* 16.1–2, *Moralia* 267c.

Regifugium: Ovid *Fasti* 2.685, 2.851–2 (trans. J.G. Frazer, adapted); Festus (Paulus) 347L; Ausonius 7.24.13–14; Degrassi 1963.265 (calendar of Polemius Silvius, AD 449).

Rex sacrorum: Plutarch *Moralia* 279c–d (*Roman Questions* 63), Livy 2.2.1; Beard et al. 1998.1.54–9. 'Nolle deos mutari ueterem formam': Tacitus *Histories* 4.53.1.

Equirria: Varro *De lingua Latina* 6.13; Ovid *Fasti* 2.857–60, 3.517–22; Festus (Paulus) 71L, 117L; Tertullian *De spectaculis* 5.5, Ausonius 7.24.27–8. Tiber: Le Gall 1953.11–13.

Campus Martius confiscation: Livy 2.5.2, Dionysius of Halicarnassus 5.13.2; cf. Plutarch *Publicola* 8.1, Servius on *Aeneid* 9.272. The two *Equirria* dates may represent the original dedication, supposedly by Romulus (Festus [Paulus] 71L, Tertullian *De spectaculis* 5.5), and the rededication *post reges exactos*.

Quinquatrus, fifth day (counting inclusively) after the Ides: Varro *De lingua Latina* 6.14, Festus 304–6L. Festival of Mars (*feriae Marti*): *Fasti Vaticani* (Degrassi 1963.172–3). Dance of Salii: *Fasti Praenestini* (ibid.122–3), Lydus *De mensibus* 4.55. Minerva: *Fasti Antiates maiores* [Plate 6], Ovid *Fasti* 3.809–48, Festus 134L, 306L, Ausonius 7.24.4, etc.

65 Ceres-Liber-Libera temple: Dionysius of Halicarnassus 6.17.2–4, 6.94.3 ('dedicated 493 BC', cf. Wiseman 1998.35–6); Pliny *Nat. Hist.* 35.154 (Damophilos and Gorgasos, from Varro); Vitruvius 3.3.5 (Tuscan 'araeostyle'); Cicero *In Verrem* 4.108 ('pulcherrimum et magnificentissimum').

Death of Brutus: Livy 2.6.6–9, Dionysius of Halicarnassus 5.15.1–3, Plutarch *Publicola* 9.1–2, *De viris illustribus* 10.6.

Voice in wood (Briquel 1993.79–82): Livy 2.7.2, Valerius Maximus 1.8.5 (*silua Arsia*); Dionysius of Halicarnassus 5.14.1, 5.16.1–3 (Naevian Meadow, Horatius' grove); Plutarch *Publicola* 9.4.

Castor and Pollux at Lake Regillus: Cicero *De natura deorum* 2.6, *Tusculanae disputationes* 1.28, Dionysius of Halicarnassus 6.13.1, Valerius Maximus 1.8.1a, Frontinus *Strategies* 1.11.8, Plutarch *Coriolanus* 3.4, *De viris illustribus* 16.3. Dionysius dates the battle to the fourteenth year of the Republic (494 BC on his chronological scheme); Livy has it in the eleventh, but knows of the other version (2.21.2–4).

66 Castor and Pollux in the Forum: Cicero *Tusculanae disputationes* 1.28, Dionysius of Halicarnassus 6.13.1–3, Valerius Maximus 1.8.1c, Plutarch *Coriolanus* 3.4, Lactantius *Institutiones* 2.7.9.

Thank-offering to Delphi: Diodorus Siculus 14.93.3–4; Livy 5.25.7–10, 5.28.2–4; Plutarch

Camillus 8.2–3, Appian *Italika* 8.1.

Greeks on Gallic sack: Plutarch *Camillus* 22.2–3, citing Herakleides of Pontus and Aristotle. According to the former, 'there was a story in the west that an army of Hyperboreans had captured a Greek city called Rhome, somewhere on the shores of the Great Sea'; Aristotle reported that 'Lucius' had rescued Rome—perhaps L. Furius Medullinus (Bruun 2000.57–60). Date: Polybius 1.6.1, 'in the nineteenth year after the naval battle of Aigospotamoi and the sixteenth before the battle of Leuktra' (from Timaios?).

Origins of Roman imperialism: Raaflaub 1996.

Clausus: Livy 2.16.3–5 (Attius), Dionysius of Halicarnassus 5.40.3–5 (Titus), Suetonius *Tiberius* 1.1 (Atta), Plutarch *Publicola* 21.2–6 (Appius), Servius on *Aeneid* 7.706; Wiseman 1979a.59–65. 'Condottieri': Cornell 1995.143–5. The tradition was able to incorporate the arrival of Clausus, but Valesios the warlord was only revealed in 1977.

Fabii at the Cremera: Livy 2.48–50, Dionysius of Halicarnassus 9.15, 9.18–22, Ovid *Fasti* 2.195–242, Dio Cassius 5.21, Zonaras 7.17.

Coriolanus: Livy 2.34–40, Dionysius of Halicarnassus 7.20–8.62, Plutarch *Coriolanus*, etc.

Constitution: Livy 2.1.1 (trans. A. de Selincourt, Penguin Classics 1960).

67 Local tribes and *comitia centuriata*: Livy 1.42.4–43.13, Dionysius of Halicarnassus 4.14–22; Cicero *De republica* 1.39–40, Festus (Paulus) 506L, *Oxyrhynchus Papyri* 17.2088, etc.; Cornell 1995.173–97 for detailed discussion.

Context of first secession: Sallust *Histories* 1.11M, cf. Livy 2.21.5–6.

Twelve Tables: text and translation in Crawford 1996.2.555–721 (629 on 'sale beyond the Tiber', quoted by Gellius *Noctes Atticae* 20.1.47).

68 Anna Perenna as a year goddess: Ovid *Fasti* 3.145–6 (cf. 3.657), Silius Italicus 8.200–1, Macrobius *Saturnalia* 1.12.6, Lydus *De mensibus* 4.9; Wiseman 1998.65–6. Consuls enter office: Livy 21.63.1–2, 22.1.4, 31.5.2, etc.

Adult toga (*toga uirilis*): Cicero *Ad Atticum* 6.1.12, Ovid *Fasti* 3.771–88; cf. Propertius 4.1.131–2 (*libera toga*).

Capitoline triad: Varro *Antiquitates divinae* frr. 68, 205 Cardauns; Dionysius of Halicarnassus 3.69.1, 4.61.4, etc. 'Dedicated in Year One of the Republic': Polybius 3.22.1; Livy 2.8.6–9, 7.3.8; Plutarch *Publicola* 14.

Libera as Persephone: Cicero *De natura deorum* 2.62, *In Verrem* 5.187; Dionysius of Halicarnassus 6.17.2, 6.94.3; Arnobius 5.21. Other versions: Ovid *Fasti* 3.459–516, Hyginus *Fabulae* 224.2 (Ariadne); Varro *Antiquitates divinae* fr. 93 Cardauns, *CIL* 8.15578 (Venus).

Thesmophoroi: Herodotus 6.91.2, 6.134.2, Callimachus *Aitia* 1.10, Diodorus Siculus 1.14.4, etc. (Demeter); Pindar fr. 37 Bergk (Persephone); Aristophanes *Thesmophoriazousai* 297 etc., Plutarch *Dion* 56.3, Appian *Civil Wars* 2.70 (both).

Date of Ceres-Liber-Libera temple: Dionysius of Halicarnassus 6.94.3; Wiseman 1998.35–6. Temple as archive: Livy 2.55.13 (*senatus consulta*), Pomponius in *Digest* 1.2.2.21 (*plebiscita*); for the evolution of the Senate see Cornell 2000a on the *lex Ovinia* (c. 334 BC?).

Consulship: for the view expressed here, see Wiseman 1995a.103–6 and 1996.313–15 (also p. 90 above). It depends on the assumption that the names of annual magistrates transmitted by Livy, Dionysius and the Augustan *fasti consulares* for the period 509–367 BC were the result of learned reconstruction in the second century BC, by researchers who worked on the false assumption that the consulship dated back to the beginning of the Republic, and arranged the names they found accordingly. Fabius Pictor evidently had a good chronological framework as far back as the early fourth century BC (reflected in Polybius 2.18.6–21.1); but it seems that L. Piso, writing after 120 BC, was the first historian to use annual notices with magistrates' names right from the start of the Republic (Wiseman 1979a.12–18).

Abolition of debt-enslavement (*nexum*) by *Lex Poetelia*: Livy 8.28 (326 BC), Varro *De lingua Latina* 7.105 (313 BC); cf. Cicero *De republica* 2.59, Dionysius of Halicarnassus 16.5.1–3, Valerius Maximus 6.1.9; Oakley 1998.688–91.

Marsyas: Servius on *Aeneid* 3.20 and 4.58 (*minister* of Liber, under his protection); Diodorus Siculus 3.59.2–5 (contest); Herodotus 7.26.3 (Phrygian story); Silius Italicus 8.502–5 (escape, Marsi); Pliny *Natural History* 3.108, cf. Lycophron *Alexandra* 1275 (*Phorke* = *lacus Fucinus*); Servius *auctus* on *Aeneid* 3.359, cf. Solinus 1.7 (augury).

69 Marcii: Cicero *De divinatione* 1.89, 2.113, Livy 25.12.3, Festus 162L, Festus (Paulus) 185L, Isidore *Origines* 6.8.12 (Cn. Marcius and his brother, famous prophets); Crawford 1974.377, no. 363 (Marsyas on L. Marcius Censorinus' *denarii*).

Rome statue: Horace *Satires* 1.6.115–17, with Porphyrion and ps.Acro *ad loc.*; illustrated on the 'anaglypha Traiani' reliefs; Coarelli 1985.91–119. Colonial copies: Charax of Pergamum *FGrH* 103 F31; Servius *auctus* on *Aeneid* 3.20 ('in liberis ciuitatibus') and 4.58 ('erecta manu testatur nihil urbi deesse'). Paestum: Coarelli 1985.95–100.

70 Settlement of 338 BC: Livy 8.14; Cornell 1995.347–52, Oakley 1998.538–59.

Athens: Thucydides 1.70.3–6, 6.18.3 (trans. Rex Warner, Penguin Classics 1954).

Alkibiades statue: Pliny *Natural History* 34.26,

Plutarch *Numa* 8.10.

Maenius as consul puts up a new speaker's platform, hereafter *Rostra*, decorated with the rams of captured Antiate ships, and has a column set up in his honour next to the Comitium: Pliny *Natural History* 34.20; Varro *De lingua Latina* 5.115, Livy 8.14.12, Asconius 42C; Cicero *Pro Sestio* 124, Pliny *Natural History* 7.212, Bobbio scholiast 128 Stangl. As censor in 318 sets up balconies on top of the Forum shops for spectators at shows in the piazza: Cicero *Academica* 2.70, Festus 120L, Valerius Maximus 9.12.7, Pliny *Natural History* 35.113.

Creation of circular *ekklestiasterion* (i.e. *comitium*): Humm 1999.644–75 for detailed argument and full bibliography. He demonstrates 303 BC as the *terminus ante quem* (669–75), but his argument for 338 as the *terminus post quem* (659–65) is very weak, and his own suggestion of 312 requires the improbable assumption of two major reconstructions only 26 years apart. I would prefer to identify Maenius' *Rostra* and the circular Comitium as a single phase (no. 5 in Gjerstad's sequence), and put phase 4, which Humm attributes to Maenius, somewhere in the late fifth or early fourth century (Wiseman 1986.307).

Bouleuterion: I assume that the *curia Hostilia* was originally just one of the meeting-houses of the archaic *curiae* (compare for example the *curia Acculeia*, Varro *De lingua Latina* 6.23); and that with the formation of a regular Senate in the 330s BC (Cornell 2000a), it was converted—probably rebuilt (cf. Coarelli 1983.153)—as a proper 'Senate house'.

71 'The largest trees. . .': Theophrastus *Historia plantarum* 5.8.1–3.

72 Dates for expulsion of tyrants: [Aristotle] *Athenaion politeia* 19.6 for the Pisistratids, Polybius 3.22.1 for the Tarquins (from Eratosthenes? Wiseman 2000.297). Athenian pottery at Rome: Meyer 1980.57–60.

Faunus: Dionysius of Halicarnassus 5.16.2–3 (god of *panic*). Silvanus: Livy 2.7.2, Valerius Maximus 1.8.5. Faunus as Pan: Horace *Odes* 1.17.1–4, Ovid *Fasti* 2.424, 3.84, 4.649–54.

Pan's promise: Herodotus 6.105.2–3, Pausanias 1.28.4.

Porsena: Livy 2.9–15, Dionysius of Halicarnassus 5.21–33. Cleomenes: Herodotus 5.90–93. Herodotean template: Mastrocinque 1988.32–5.

Coriolanus and Themistokles: Cicero *Brutus* 41–3, *De amicitia* 42, *Ad Atticum* 9.10.3; cf. Aulus Gellius 17.21.9–11 (Miltiades).

Kleidemos: *FGrH* 323, with Jacoby's commentary; the most extensive and revealing fragments are at Plutarch *Theseus* 19.4–7 (F17) and 27.3–4 (F18); Pausanias 10.15.5 (first Atthidographer), Tertullian *De anima* 52 (public honour). See Jacoby 1949.74–6 for the political background and Kleidemos' probable

democratic motivation.

73 Embassy to Athens to prepare law code: Livy 3.31.8, 3.32.1 and 6, 3.33.5; Dionysius of Halicarnassus 10.51.5, 10.54.3 (also Greek cities in Italy); Jerome *Chronica* 112 Helm ('452 BC'); Lydus *De magistratibus* 1.34. Cf. also Zonaras 7.18, Pomponius in *Digest* 1.2.2.4 ('Greeks', unspecified). Influence of Solon: Cicero *De legibus* 2.59, 2.64; Crawford 1996.560–1 for bibliography.

Quinquatrus and Minerva: *Fasti Antiates maiores* (Degrassi 1963.7), Ovid *Fasti* 3.809–34 (812 for her birthday), Ausonius 7.24.4, Symmachus *Epistles* 5.85.3.

Minerva temple: *Fasti Praenestini* (Degrassi 1963.122–3), Festus 134L, 306L; Richardson 1992.47 (fig. 14) for its position.

Iacchos: Aristophanes *Frogs* 316–53, etc.; scholiast on *Frogs* 479 (called son of Semele at the Athenian Lenaia); Sophocles *Antigone* 1146–54, Euripides *Bacchae* 725–6 (Dionysos). Roman parallel: Cicero *De natura deorum* 2.62 (distinguishing him from the son of Semele, cf. Wiseman 1998.41–2); Catullus 64.251–64, Virgil *Eclogues* 6.15, Ovid *Metamorphoses* 4.15 (Iacchos as Liber).

Athenian *Thesmophoria* festival: Aristophanes *Thesmophoriazusae* passim, Appian *Civil Wars* 2.70, etc.

Dionysos Eleuthereus: Pausanias 1.2.5, 1.38.8 (Eleutherai); cf. Hyginus *Fabulae* 225.1 on Eleuther, the first to set up an image and cult of Liber Pater. Eleuthereus as Liber: Alexander Polyhistor *FGrH* 273 F109 (Plutarch *Roman Questions* 104).

City Dionysia: Pickard-Cambridge 1968.101–7; West 1989. Political liberation: Seaford 1994.243–4, quoting Connor 1989; see in general Seaford 1994.238–57 on Dionysos as the god of the *polis*, destroying the royal houses of Pentheus and Lykourgos and requiring 'collective honours from all, without distinction' (Euripides *Bacchae* 208–9).

Liberalia as dramatic *ludi*: Naevius fr. 113R (Festus [Paulus] 103L), Ovid *Fasti* 3.784–6; cf. Tertullian *De spectaculis* 5.4, [Cyprian] *De spectaculis* 4.4, Ausonius 7.24.29–30.

74 Circus Maximus temple: Dionysius of Halicarnassus 6.94.3. Circus dimensions and date: Dionysius of Halicarnassus 3.68.2–4, Pliny *Natural History* 36.102; Humphrey 1986.56–131.

Aventine outside *pomerium* until AD 48: Aulus Gellius 13.14.4–7. Original *pomerium* 'per ima montis Palatini': Tacitus *Annals* 12.24.2.

Grove of Stimula: Livy 39.12.4. Semele: Ovid *Fasti* 6.503, *CIL* 6.9897. Position: Cazenove 1983.56–66. There was probably a cave there: Livy 39.13.13 ('in abditos specus'); for Bacchic *antra*, see Philodamos *Paian* 139–40 (*Collectanea Alexandrina* 169), Socrates of Rhodes *FGrH* 192 F2 (Athenaeus 4.148b),

Plutarch *Moralia* 565f-566a, Philostratus *Imagines* 1.14.3, Macrobius *Saturnalia* 1.18.3.

Dionysos son of Thyone: Philodamos *Paian* 7 (*Collectanea Alexandrina* 166), Cicero *De natura deorum* 3.58, Lydus *De mensibus* 4.51. Thyone as Dionysiac stirrer-up: scholiast on Pindar *Pythian* 3.177, Suda s.v. 'Thyone' (θύειν = ὁρμᾶν). Stimula from *stimulare*: Varro *Antiquitates divinae* fr. 130 Cardauns (Augustine *City of God* 4.11, 4.16).

Semele as Thyone: Apollodorus 3.5.3, Diodorus Siculus 4.25.4; *Anthologia Palatina* 3.1 for Hermes' participation. Thyades 'ἀπὸ τοῦ θύειν, quod est insane currere': Servius *auctus* on *Aeneid* 4.302, cf. *Etymologicum magnum* s.v. 'Thyades'. Thyades at Stimula's grove: Ovid *Fasti* 6.503, 6.514.

Summanus: Festus 254L, Pliny *Natural History* 2.138 (night lightning); Martianus Capella 2.161 ('summus Manium'), Arnobius 5.37 (Hades, rape of Persephone).

Summanus *ad cir(cum) max(imum)*: Degrassi 1963.58, 88, 186–7 (calendars for 20 June); *Notitia urbis Romae* on Regio XI (temple of Dis Pater between Mercurius and Ceres).

Mercurius cult: Ovid *Fasti* 5.99–100; cf. Dionysius of Halicarnassus 1.31.1, Virgil *Aeneid* 8.138, etc. (Evander son of Hermes). Mercurius temple: Livy 2.27.5–6, Valerius Maximus 9.3.6 (dedicated '495 BC'); Ovid *Fasti* 5.669–74 (facing Circus, near Porta Capena), Apuleius *Golden Ass* 6.8 ('retro metas Murciae').

Murcia's shrine 'sub monte Aventino': Festus (Paulus) 135L. Murcia from *murcidus*: Varro *Antiquitates divinae* fr. 131 Cardauns (Augustine *City of God* 4.16, Arnobius 4.9). Names: Varro *De lingua Latina* 5.154, Pliny *Natural History* 15.121, Plutarch *Moralia* 268e = *Roman Questions* 20 (Venus Myrtea); Servius *auctus* on *Aeneid* 8.636 (Venus Verticordia); Ovid *Fasti* 4.133–62 (Fortuna Virilis).

Chariots turn *ad Murciae*: Varro *De lingua Latina* 5.154 ('intumus circus'); Apuleius *Golden Ass* 6.8, Tertullian *De spectaculis* 8.6 ('metae Murciae'). End of maenads' run: Servius *auctus* on *Aeneid* 8.636 ('quae cum ibi Bacchanalia essent, furorem sacri ipsius murcidum faceret').

75 Satyrs and maenads: *LIMC* 8 (Supplement), 'Mainades' nos. 64, 70, 76, 80, 140a (Attic red-figure, Lucanian red-figure, Hellenistic silver, Roman mosaics).

Venus and satyrs, Fortuna Virilis on 1 April: Wiseman 2004.

Myrtle sacred to Aphrodite: Plutarch *Marcellus* 22.4, Pausanias 6.24.7; Virgil *Eclogues* 7.62, Ovid *Fasti* 4.869, Aulus Gellius 5.6.22, Pliny *Natural History* 12.3.

Bona Dea *sub saxo*: Cicero *De domo* 136, Ovid *Fasti* 5.148–58. Ban on myrtle: Plutarch *Moralia*

268d–e (*Roman Questions* 20), Arnobius 5.18 (from Butas), Macrobius *Saturnalia* 1.12.25. Poplar: Propertius 4.9.29. Ilex: Ovid *Fasti* 3.295.

Dryad: Plutarch *Caesar* 9.3 (wife of Faunus); cf. Ovid *Fasti* 4.761–2 (dangerous to see dryads, or Faunus). Queen: Lactantius *Institutiones* 1.22.9–11 (wife and sister of Faunus).

1 May ritual: Ovid *Fasti* 5.148–58, Macrobius *Saturnalia* 1.12.21 (from Cornelius Labeo). Music and dance: Propertius 4.9.23–34, Juvenal 6.314–22 (only at line 335 does he move on to the December sacrifice at the house of a magistrate). All night: implied by Juvenal 6.329 (cf. Plutarch *Caesar* 9.4).

Grotto (*antrum*): Propertius 4.9.33, Juvenal 6.328; cf. Plutarch *Caesar* 9.3 on *skenai* (tents or bowers) decked with vine-branches.

Normal abstention from wine: Cato fr. 221 Malcovati (Aulus Gellius 10.23), Dionysius of Halicarnassus 2.25.6, Valerius Maximus 6.3.9, Pliny *Natural History* 14.89–90, etc.; Bettini 1995.224–6 (228–31 on Bona Dea). Milk and honeypot: Macrobius *Saturnalia* 1.12.25, Plutarch *Moralia* 268e; cf. Lactantius *Institutiones* 1.22.11, Arnobius 5.18 (wine-jar covered over).

Satirist: Juvenal 6.316–7 ('Priapi maenades'), 317–26 (erotic stimulation), 327–34 (sex afterwards).

Identifications: Macrobius *Saturnalia* 1.12.20–23 (also Hekate); Plutarch *Caesar* 9.3 for the mother of Dionysos who may not be named (presumably Persephone, since the rites are 'Orphic in character'). *Pontificum libri*: Cornelius Labeo in Macrobius *Saturnalia* 1.12.21 (also Ops and Fatua).

Faunus son of Circe: Nonnos *Dionysiaka* 13.328–32, 37.56–60 (alluding to Hesiod's Agrios?); Wiseman 1995a.47–8. Circe and the *circus*: Tertullian *De spectaculis* 8, Lydus *De mensibus* 1.12.

Janus and Saturnus: Ovid *Fasti* 1.231–54, Macrobius *Saturnalia* 1.7.21–4, *Origo gentis Romanae* 1.3, 3.1–7; cf. Virgil *Aeneid* 8.355–8.

Saturnus' dynasty: Virgil *Aeneid* 7.45–9; Lactantius *Institutiones* 1.22.9, Arnobius 2.71. Picus and Circe: Virgil *Aeneid* 7.189–91, Plutarch *Moralia* 268f (*Roman Questions* 21), Valerius Flaccus 7.232; cf. Ovid *Metamorphoses* 14.320–434 (Circe's unwilling love-object). Faunus and Evander: Dionysius of Halicarnassus 1.31.2, Justin 43.1.6, *Origo gentis Romanae* 5.3. Faunus and Marsyas: Servius *auctus* on *Aeneid* 3.359. Latinus and Aeneas: Livy 1.1.4–10, Virgil *Aeneid* 7.45–273, etc.

Deification: Varro *Antiquitates divinae* fr. 35 Cardauns (Augustine *City of God* 4.23 etc.); cf. Macrobius *Saturnalia* 1.7.24 (Saturnus by Janus), Lactantius *Institutiones* 1.22.9 (Saturnus and Picus by Faunus), Probus on *Georgics* 1.10 (Faunus 'receptus in deorum numerum').

Prophets: Plutarch *Moralia* 268f (*Roman*

Questions 21), Pliny *Natural History* 10.40, Servius on *Aeneid* 7.190, Augustine *City of God* 18.15, etc. (Picus); Plutarch *Moralia* 268d (*Roman Questions* 20), Servius on *Aeneid* 7.47, *Origo gentis Romanae* 4.4, etc. (Faunus); Virgil *Aeneid* 7.81–103, Ovid *Fasti* 4.649–68 (oracle of Faunus), cf. Briquel 1993.85–8.

Fauna as prophetess (also called Fatua): Justin 43.1.8, Lactantius *Institutiones* 1.22.9 (from Gavius Bassus), Servius on *Aeneid* 7.47. Chaste: Varro *Antiquitates divinae* fr. 218 Cardauns (daughter), Lactantius *Institutiones* 1.22.10 (wife?), Servius *auctus* on *Aeneid* 8.314 (daughter). Beaten for drinking: Plutarch *Moralia* 268d (*Roman Questions* 20); Lactantius *Institutiones* 1.22.11, Arnobius 5.18 (both from Sextus Clodius). Deified: Lactantius *Institutiones* 1.22.9 (wife and sister), 1.22.11; Arnobius 1.36.

76 Faunus' rape of his daughter: Macrobius *Saturnalia* 1.12.24–5; cf. Plutarch *Caesar* 9.3 ('a sacred snake is enthroned with the goddess as the myth requires').

Like satyrs or Pans: Plutarch *Numa* 15.3. Faunus' horns: Ovid *Fasti* 3.312, 5.99; cf. 2.361 (*cornipes*), 5.101 (*semicaper*). Rural demigods: Ovid *Metamorphoses* 1.192–3 ('sunt mihi semidei, sunt rustica numina nymphae, faunique satyrique et monticolae Siluani'); cf. 6.392–5, *Fasti* 3.303, 3.315–16; Lucretius 4.580–9 (Sisson 1976.120).

Speakers (also called Fatui and Fatuae, Briquel 1993.81): Varro *de lingua Latina* 7.36 (quoting Ennius *Annals* fr. 207 Skutsch), Donatus on Terence *Eunuchus* 1079, Servius *auctus* on *Eclogues* 6.27, Nemesianus 2.73, Martianus Capella 2.167, etc.

Times of crisis: Cicero *De divinatione* 1.101 ('saepe etiam in proeliis fauni auditi et in rebus turbidis ueridicae uoces ex occulto missae esse dicuntur'); *De natura deorum* 2.6 ('saepe faunorum uoces exauditae'), countered at 3.15 ('faunus omnino quid sit nescio').

Literary version of Faunus (grove, grotto, prophecy): Calpurnius Siculus 1.8–135.

The Marble Faun [fig. 19]: quotation from ch. 1, penultimate paragraph. See Vance 1989.113–25 on Hawthorne's ambivalent attitude to 'pagan innocence'.

Lecherous: Horace *Odes* 3.18.1 ('nympharum fugientum amator'), cf. 3.18.6 ('Veneris sodalis'); Rutilius Namatianus *De reditu* 233–6; Augustine *City of God* 15.23, cf. Isidore *Origines* 8.11.103–4, Servius on *Aeneid* 6.775 etc. for Faunus/Fatuus as Incubo or Pan (Wiseman 1995b.6–10).

Faunus' grotto: Ovid *Fasti* 3.302, Calpurnius Siculus 1.8–9; for caves, cf. Euripides *Helen* 188–90 (Pan and nymph), Virgil *Eclogues* 6.13–26 (Silenus and Aegle the naiad). Omphale story: Ovid *Fasti* 2.303–58, esp. 307 (usually nymphs), 315–16 (grotto with spring). Illustration [fig. 20]: Zerner 1969.L.D.9.

78 Faunus, Picus and Numa: Valerius Antias fr. 6P (Arnobius 5.1), Ovid *Fasti* 3.285–354, Plutarch *Numa*

15.3–6; Wiseman 1998.21–3, Briquel 1993.82–5.

Gift of *pignus imperii*: Ovid *Fasti* 3.355–92, Plutarch *Numa* 13.1–5 (13.2 for the Muses' spring), Festus (Paulus) 117L: 'unaque edita uox omnium potentissimam fore ciuitatem quamdiu id in ea mansisset.' Camenae ('Muses') and Egeria: see p. 51 above.

79 Lupercal site: Dionysius of Halicarnassus 1.32.4; cf. 1.77.1 (grove), 1.79.9 ('a holy place arched over by a dense wood, and a hollow rock from which springs issued'). Wiseman 1994.84 for the Lupercal as 'satyr country'.

Evander: Dionysius of Halicarnassus 1.32.3–5, Ovid *Fasti* 2.271–82, etc. Lykaion and Lupercal: Ovid *Fasti* 2.423–4, Plutarch *Romulus* 21.3, etc.; implicit at Livy 1.5.1–2 and Virgil *Aeneid* 8.343–4.

Luperci drunk and naked: Cicero *Philippics* 3.12, 13.31 (Antony); Valerius Maximus 2.2.9 ('epularum hilaritate ac uino largiore prouecti'); Justin 43.1.7 (naked with goatskin capes), probably predating the goatskin loincloths (Dionysius of Halicarnassus 1.80.1, Ovid *Fasti* 5.101, Plutarch *Romulus* 21.5, etc.); Wiseman 1995b.82–3.

Striking anyone (not just women): Valerius Maximus 2.2.9 (*obuios*); Nicolaus of Damascus *FGrH* 90 F130.71; Plutarch *Romulus* 21.5, *Caesar* 61.2, *Antony* 12.1; *Origo gentis Romanae* 22.1.

Pan as Faunus: Horace *Odes* 1.17.1–4; Ovid *Fasti* 2.423–4, 3.84, 4.650–3 (cf. 2.267–8, 5.101 etc. for Faunus as the god of the Lupercalia). Contrast Livy 1.5.2 (Pan as Inuus), Justin 43.1.7 (Pan as Lupercus), etc. Silvanus as Faunus and/or Pan: *Origo gentis Romanae* 4.6, Servius *auctus* on *Georgics* 1.20, Augustine *City of God* 15.23, etc.; see Dorcey 1992.33–42, who tries (wrongly, in my view) to explain the evidence away.

She-wolf mirror: Wiseman 1995a.65–71 (and p. 325 below).

80 Guardian Lares (*Praestites*): Ovid *Fasti* 2.583–616, 5.129–36; Plutarch *Moralia* 276f (*Roman Questions* 51).

Bona Dea as Hekate: Macrobius *Saturnalia* 1.12.23. Cf. Porphyrion on Horace *Odes* 3.18.1 (Faunus as *inferus deus*); Ovid *Fasti* 2.193 (Faunus' temple founded on first day of *parentatio*).

Lares on 1 May: Ovid *Fasti* 5.129–42; Degrassi 1963.56, 87 (*Fasti Venusini* and *Esquilini*).

Underworld: Varro *Antiquitates divinae* fr. 209 Cardauns (Lares as *laruae*, their mother Mania from *manes*).

Parentatio begins on 13 February: Lydus *De mensibus* 4.29; Degrassi 1963.265 (Polemius Silvius, 'parentatio tumulorum inc[ipit]'); cf. Ovid *Fasti* 2.533–70.

Feralia: Ovid *Fasti* 2.565–84. The derivation from *ferae* is a modern conjecture; for ancient conjectures, much more far-fetched, see Varro *De lingua Latina*

6.13, Ovid *Fasti* 2.569, Paulus (Festus)75L.

Lares and Hannibal: Propertius 3.3.11 (from Ennius?); cf. Livy 26.11.2–4, Florus 1.22.44–5, Orosius 4.17.2–11 (unspecified divine aid).

Ludere, ludus etc.: Aristophanes *Frogs* 334, 375, 388, 392, 407, 411, 443, 452 (*paizein* as a recurring theme in the initiates' hymn to Iacchos). Nymphs and satyrs: e.g. Virgil *Eclogues* 6.28, Ovid *Fasti* 1.424, 6.329, [Virgil] *Culex* 19, Calpurnius Siculus 2.33, Nemesianus 3.55.

Ludere at *Liberalia*: Plautus *Casina* 980, Livy 39.15.7 ('concessus ludus et lasciuia'); cf. Plutarch *Moralia* 565f (Dionysiac *paizein*), Pliny *Natural History* 3.8. At *Lupercalia*: Livy 1.5.2 ('ludus atque lasciuia'), Varro *Antiquitates divinae* fr. 80 Cardauns, *Origo gentis Romanae* 22.1 (*ludibundi*); cf. Plutarch *Caesar* 61.2, *Antony* 12.1 (*paidia*).

Ludere and Faunus: Pliny *Natural History* 25.29 ('Faunorum ludibria'); cf. [Virgil] *Culex* 115 (Panes). And Bona Dea celebrants: Propertius 4.9.33; cf. Plutarch *Caesar* 10.2 (*paizein*).

Imitation: e.g. Varro *Antiquitates divinae* fr. 80 Cardauns (Luperci as *ludii*), Juvenal 6.324 (Bona Dea).

Ludi publici: TLL 7.1783.61–1787.77; cf. 1773.61–80 (*ludere*), 1890.17–49 (*lusus*).

81 Free speech ('libera lingua loquimur ludis Liberalibus'): Naevius fr. 113R (Festus [Paulus] 103L); cf. Ovid *Fasti* 3.784–6, Ausonius 7.24.29–30, Tertullian *De spectaculis* 5.4.

Aristotle on comedy: *Poetics* 4 (1448b.10–13), trans. T.S. Dorsch (Penguin Classics). Phallic processions: Aristophanes *Acharnians*: 241–79, Semos of Delos *FGrH* 396 F24 (Athenaeus 14.622a–d), etc.; Cole 1993, esp. 30–3 on third-century BC Delos.

Varro on *Liberalia*: *Antiquitates divinae* fr. 262 Cardauns (Augustine *City of God* 7.21), trans. H. Bettenson (Penguin Classics).

186 BC purge: Livy 39.8–19, Cicero *De legibus* 2.37, Valerius Maximus 6.3.7.

Anna Perenna: Ovid *Fasti* 3.545–656 (nymph of river Numicius at Lavinium), 358 (Themis, Io), 359–60 (Arkadian myth); cf. Dionysius of Halicarnassus 1.31.1 for Evander's mother, Wiseman 1998.66–7 for Io and the Argiletum. Grove: Martial 4.64.16–17; cf. Ovid *Fasti* 3.523–30 (meadow), Degrassi 1963.172–3 (*Fasti Vaticani*: at the first milestone on the Via Flaminia).

Old lady and cakes: Ovid *Fasti* 3.669–72 (Anna story); 3.761–70, Varro *De lingua Latina* 6.14 (*Liberalia*).

82 Forms of drama: *Tractatus Cosilinianus* 1, ultimately from Aristotle (Janko 1984.22–3, 130–1); Diomedes *Ars grammatica* 3.1.4, 3.8.1–13.2 = *Grammatici Latini* 8.482, 8.487–90 Keil, from Theophrastus.

Epicharmos: Pickard-Cambridge 1962.230–90 for evidence and discussion. Myth in Attic comedy:

Nesselrath 1990.188–241.

Tragedy: Aristotle *Poetics* 1449a.9–11; Pickard-Cambridge 1962.60–131. Satyr play: Seaford 1984.1–16. Texts and discussion on the origins of drama: Csapo and Slater 1994.89–101.

Mime: Kaibel 1899.152–81 for the fragments of Sophron; Xenophon *Symposion* 2.1, 9.2–7; Csapo and Slater 1994.369–89. Plato (*Laws* 7.816.d–e) conflates mime and comedy.

83 Chorus: Csapo and Slater 1994.349–68.

Satyrs and mime: Athenian vase paintings of about 400 BC show Dionysos being entertained by a satyr called Mimos (Simon 1982.20, fig. 2 and pl. 8) and by a *mima* dressed for a satyr play (Luce 1930.339, fig. 4); see Beazley 1963.1139–40, 1519 ('near the Talos painter' no. 5, 'the Q painter' no. 13). Plato: *Laws* 7.815c; Seaford 1984.8–9, Wiseman 2000.276–8.

Gnesippos: Kratinos fr. 256, Athenaeus 14.638d; Davidson 2000.

Rhinthon's *hilarotragoidia*: Suda s.v. 'Rhinthon'; full references and fragments in Kaibel 1899.183–9 (ibid. 191 for the *spoudogeloion* of Blaesus of Capri, whose *Satournos* was evidently a Greek play with a Latin title). Plautus: *Amphitruo* 50–63.

Sibyl's definition΄ (σπουδῇ δὲ γέλωτι μεμίχθω): Phlegon of Tralles *FGrH* 257 F 37.v.4, line 35 of the Sibylline oracle about the Secular Games.

'Origins of Roman drama': Livy 7.2 (364 BC), Horace *Epistles* 2.1.139–63, etc.; Oakley 1998.40–58.

84 Anna farce: Ovid *Fasti* 3.661–96 (695 'ioci ueteres'), with Wiseman 1998.64–74; quotation from Massey 1757.164.

85 Literary evidence for Roman popular culture: Horsfall 2003.

Singer at sacrifice: Dionysius of Halicarnassus 1.31.2 (Faunus); cf. 1.79.10 (Romulus and Remus), 8.62.3 (Coriolanus).

Vates: Lucretius 1.102–11; cf. Livy 25.1.6–12 (in the Forum); Wiseman 1994.49–67.

Praise-singer (*grassator*): Aulus Gellius 11.2.5 (from Cato's *Carmen de moribus*); cf. Festus (Paulus) 86L on *grassari* as *adulari*; Peruzzi 1998.159–60.

Funeral *praefica*: Varro *De lingua Latina* 7.70, *De vita populi Romani* fr. 110 Riposati (Nonius 93L, 212L), Plautus *Truculentus* 495–6.

Story-teller: Pliny *Letters* 2.20.1; cf. Suetonius *Divus Augustus* 74 (*aretalogi*), 78.2 (*fabulatores*), Dio Chrysostomos *Orationes* 20.10 (in the hippodrome); Wiseman 1994.33–4.

Scurra on stage: Plautus *Trinummus* 205–11, *Mostellaria* 15 ('deliciae populi'); Corbett 1986.27–43.

CHAPTER 5

87 Novius Plautius: *ILLRP* 1197 = *CIL* I² 561 (Ficoroni cista, fig. 23). Oscan *praenomen*: Livy 9.26.7 (Novius Calavius, Capua 314 BC).

Latin treaty: Cicero *Pro Balbo* 53 (visible within memory of 56 BC), Livy 2.33.9 (Sp. Cassius alone named), Dionysius of Halicarnassus 6.95.1–2; text quoted in Festus 166L.

Mountain peoples (Volsci and Aequi): Cornell 1995.304–9.

Tribunes and *concilium plebis* as regular non-military legislators: Sandberg 2001.

88 Alba *emissarium* (and Delphic oracle): Livy 5.15.2–3, 5.16.8–11; Dionysius of Halicarnassus 12.10.1–2, 12.12.2–3; Valerius Maximus 1.6.3, Plutarch *Camillus* 3–4, Zonaras 7.20. See De La Blanchère 1892.598–600 (fig. 22 from p. 599).

Gallic sack: Polybius 1.6.2–3, 2.18.2–3, 2.22.4–5; Diodorus Siculus 14.116.7, Orosius 2.19.9 (1,000 lb of gold); cf. Suetonius *Tiberius* 3.2. See also Plutarch *Camillus* 22.2–3, quoting the reactions of Herakleides of Pontos and Aristotle.

Veii and the Gauls: Cornell 1995.309–18. Veientane territory, patrician concession: Livy 5.30.8–9, 6.4.4, 6.5.8; Taylor 1960.47–9, Ziolkowski 1999.

Plautii: Münzer 1920.36–45 = 1999.39–47.

New walls: Livy 6.32.1 ('378 BC'), cf. 7.20.9 ('353 BC'); Andreussi 1996; Cornell 1995.331 and 462 n. 11, cf. 204 for relative areas enclosed.

89 'Altae moenia Romae': Virgil *Aeneid* 1.7; cf. 1.277, 2.294–5, 3.159–60, 5.737, 6.783 (prophecies of Rome); 3.85, 3.501, 5.798, 7.145 (Aeneas' destiny); 8.714–15 (Augustus and the *Romana moenia*).

Ficoroni *cista*: Dohrn 1972; Battaglia and Emiliozzi 1990.211–26, figs 297–314 (no. 68); Rouveret 1994; Simon 1996.151–61 (review of Dohrn). See Rouveret 1994.232–3 for the 'unrolling' of the frieze as in fig. 25.

E.M. Forster: 'Macolnia Shops', first published in *Independent Review* 1 (Nov. 1903) 311–18, whence Forster 1936.167–9.

90 Earliest reliable date: inferred from Polybius 2.18.6–19.7 (year-counts from Fabius Pictor?); cf. 1.5.4–6.2 and Dionysius of Halicarnassus 1.74.4.

Controversy: Plutarch *Numa* 1.1 ('Clodius'), cf. *Camillus* 22.1; Livy 6.1.2; Frier 1979.119–27.

Archaeology: Frier 1979.126, Torelli 1978.227. 'Non-existent problem': Cornell 1995.318.

Temple deposits: e.g. Livy 4.7.12, Dionysius of Halicarnassus 1.73.1. Family archives: e.g. Dionysius of Halicarnassus 1.74.5, Pliny *Natural History* 35.2–7, Festus 490L; Torelli 1996.18–22.

Reconstruction of early *fasti*: Wiseman 1979a.12–16 (on Sempronius Tuditanus, L. Cincius, Atticus, etc.). Augustan list: Degrassi 1947.1–142.

False ancestors: Cicero *Brutus* 62, Livy 8.40.4–5, Plutarch *Numa* 1.1 ('Clodius'). Consulship: Wiseman 1995a.103–7, cf. 1996.313–15 (review of Cornell 1995).

91 *Bulla*: Cicero *In Verrem* 2.1.152, Propertius

4.1.131–2, Valerius Maximus 3.1.1, Persius 5.30–1, Macrobius *Saturnalia* 1.6.8–11.

92 Hercules: Dohrn 1972.17–18, needlessly doubted by Simon 1996.158.

93 Mirror: Battaglia and Emiliozzi 1990.225–6, fig. 314; Rouveret 1994.238–40 (the egg a Pythagorean symbol?); cf. Pairault Massa 1992.135–6 (an egg labelled *Elinai*—i.e. Helen—on a fourth-century BC Etruscan vase from Orvieto).

Mopsos: Apollonius Rhodius 1.65–6, Valerius Flaccus 1.383. Winged prophet: Calchas, on a late fourth-century BC bronze mirror from Vulci (Beard et al 1998.1.21).

Oracular head: Pairault Massa 1992.156, needlessly doubted by Rouveret 1994.234. For the parallel, on an amphora of about 340 BC from the *tomba Golini* at Volsinii (Orvieto), see Pairault Massa 1992.136–7. The common but absurd idea that the head is the only visible part of Pollux's slave-boy, sitting wrapped to the chin in discarded clothing, is the result of expecting inappropriate standards of realism.

New York mirror: Peter 1890.2259–60; Bonfante 1997.32–4, no. 7 ('the winding stem of the border decoration is typical of Praenestine mirrors'). Festus (Paulus) 55L for the *nodus Herculaneus* and Iuno Cinxia.

95 Old satyr: Forster 1936.168. Satyr-play source: Simon 1996.154–7, noting Epicharmos' Sicilian comedy *Amykos*, and the stagy setting of the story on a Lucanian *hydria*.

96 Dionysos/Liber: Simon 1996.158–9, needlessly doubted by Battaglia and Emiliozzi 1990.221–2.

Lemnisci: Plautus *Pseudolus* 1265 (party), Varro in Servius on *Aeneid* 5.269 ('magni honoris'), Pliny *Natural History* 16.65. Rose crowns for drinkers: Ovid *Fasti* 5.335–46, Horace *Odes* 2.11.14–15, etc.

97 Baltimore *cista*: Battaglia and Emiliozzi 1979.41–3, figs 43–7 (no. 1).

98 Palestrina *cista*: Battaglia and Emiliozzi 1979.151–3, figs 195–200 (no. 46); Perseus with Minerva and the Gorgon-head also at Battaglia and Emiliozzi 1990.253–6, figs 354–9 (no. 76).

Pegasus on early Roman bronze: Crawford 1974.131 (no. 4.1), 136 (no. 18.2), 142 (no. 26.6), 143 (no. 27.3).

Minerva's Gorgon: Apollodorus 2.4.3 (shield, Perseus), Ovid *Metamorphoses* 4.802–3 ('pectore in aduerso').

Mirrors with *symposion* and bedroom scene: Wiseman 1995b.9–10, 2000.273 and 276–8.

Karlsruhe *cista*: Jurgeit 1999.1.528–33, 2.254–5; cf. Battaglia and Emiliozzi 1979.95–7, figs 113–17 (no. 22), where however the drawing includes the nineteenth-century additions exposed by Jurgeit 1992.

101 *Cista*-lid handles, Battaglia and Emiliozzi 1979 and 1990. (1) Arm's-length pose, man and woman: nos. 2, 6, 7, 13, 15, 19, 32 [fig. 35], 40, 43, 52, 67, 71, 79,

115. (2) Arm's-length pose, satyr and nymph: nos. 8, 18, 24, 25, 29 [fig. 36], 41, 61, 75, 76, 78, 81, 82, 95, 96, 102, 105, 108. (3) Mixed-sex wrestling: nos. 16 [fig. 37], 27, 31, 33, 66, 72, 83, 86, 92, 110, 114. (4) Female acrobat: nos. 20, 36, 45 [fig. 39], 50, 51, 54, 55, 63, 77, 85, 91, 112.

102 Bride's hair parted by *hasta caelibaris*: Ovid *Fasti* 2.560, Festus (Paulus) 55L, Plutarch *Moralia* 285c (*Roman Questions* 87), Arnobius 2.67.

Berlin *cista*: Battaglia and Emiliozzi 1979.55–6, figs 64–8 (no. 6).

Girl acrobats and comic drama: Dearden 1995, esp. plates 1a and b.

103 Performance scenes: Battaglia and Emiliozzi 1979 and 1990, nos. 45 [fig. 46], 50, 51 [fig. 40], 82 (Iphigeneia); Wiseman 2000.274–86.

104 Palestrina *cistae*: Battaglia and Emiliozzi 1979.158–62, figs 216–25 (nos. 50 and 51).

Winged girls on Rome *cista*: Battaglia and Emiliozzi 1990.312–16, figs 459–61 (no. 100).

108 Berlin *cista*: Battaglia and Emiliozzi 1979.64–5, fig. 73 (no. 9). 'Aucena' as *nomen gentilicium*: Peruzzi 1998.161–4.

109 Judgement of Paris: shown on a splendid *cista* in the Villa Giulia (Battaglia and Emiliozzi 1990.226–32, no. 69).

Rome *cista*: Battaglia and Emiliozzi 1990.277–80, figs 392–7 (no. 83). Window in stage building: Green 1995.109–10 and plate 10, cf. 111 and plate 11b for masks above the scene.

New York *cista*: Battaglia and Emiliozzi 1979.146–50, figs 185–94 (no. 45).

Sora: Livy 7.28.6. 9.23.2, 9.24.13–14, 9.43.1, 10.1.1–2.

'Aiax Ilios', i.e. Aiax Oileus: Virgil *Aeneid* 1.41, Seneca *Medea* 661, Hyginus *Fabulae* 81, etc.

111 Ajax mirror: T(h)elis as a nymph was referred to in a lost play of Ennius (fr. 368 Jocelyn), quoted by Varro (*De lingua Latina* 7.87, cf. *De re rustica* 3.9.19), who identifies her as the sea-nymph Thetis, mother of Achilles.

Vatican *cista*: Battaglia and Emiliozzi 1990.317–22, figs 462–7 (no. 101). The other named figures are SIMOS, probably Achilles' servant; (H)ERCLES, DIESPTR (Jupiter) and IVNO; and IACOR, a young man with a spear like Soresios on the New York *cista*.

112 Berlin *cista*: Battaglia and Emiliozzi 1979.56–61, figs 68–70 (no. 7); Menichetti 1994. But the scene is not a triumph.

Mezentius: Cato *Origines* fr. 12P (Macrobius 3.5.10), Varro in Pliny *Natural History* 18.284, Dionysius of Halicarnassus 1.65.2, Ovid *Fasti* 4.879–900, Plutarch *Moralia* 275e (*Roman Questions* 45).

Lyon *cista*: Battaglia and Emiliozzi 1979.108–11, figs 131–3 (no. 27); cf. 1990.200–5 (no. 66), a *cista* at

Vassar College on which CASTOR and PORLOV[CES] are named.

Pygmies by Okeanos: Homer *Iliad* 3.5–6. Usually placed in the far south (Strabo 17.2.1, Pliny *Natural History* 6.188, Pomponius Mela 3.8.1) or the far east (Aulus Gellius 9.4.10–11); cf. also Pliny *Natural History* 4.44, Juvenal 13.167–70 (Thrace), and Pliny *Natural History* 5.108–9 (Caria). It would be just as easy to place them in the far west.

Minerva: Battaglia and Emiliozzi 1979 and 1990, nos. 5, 16, 27, 29, 40, 46, 49, 59, 68, 69, 73, 74, 76, 81, 110. Victoria: nos. 5, 6, 8, 27, 31, 32, 55, 59, 66, 68, 69, 73, 75, 93, 94, 101, 117.

Evander's Victoria: Dionysius of Halicarnassus 1.32.5–33.1 (foster-sister of Minerva). Minerva on the Capitol: Dionysius of Halicarnassus 3.69.1, 4.59.1; Livy 6.29.9, 7.3.5; Pliny *Natural History* 35.108.

113 Berlin *cista*: Battaglia and Emiliozzi 1979.50–54, figs 60–3 (no. 5); Simon 1996.31–8. Ambrosia as ointment: *Homeric Hymn to Demeter* 237, Apollonius Rhodius 4.869–72, Theocritus 15.108, Ovid *Metamorphoses* 14.605–7.

114 Mars as protector of farms: Cato *De agricultura* 141. Mars Silvanus: Cato *De agicultura* 83. Faunus as son of Mars: Dionysius of Halicarnassus 1.31.2, Appian *Kings* fr. 1. Cf. Servius *auctus* on *Aeneid* 7.343: Pan Lycaeus as (a) Enyalios and (b) Liber Pater.

Late fourth-century adjustment of *Lupercalia* in warlike mode: Plutarch *Romulus* 21.6 (from Butas' *Aitia*), with Wiseman 1995b.10–13.

Mirror with she-wolf and twins: for arguments about the iconography, see Wiseman 1993 and 1995a.65–71; Carandini 1996.215 and 1997a.180–1; Wiseman 1997; Carandini 1997b; Cornell 2000b.48–9; Carandini and Cappelli 2000.98, 102–3, 233–4; Wiseman 2001.184–5; Carandini 2002.137–9; Fraschetti 2002.9–12. *Pace* Fraschetti, there is no grotto, and the left-hand bird is visibly not a woodpecker; there is no reason why Faustulus should carry a spear, or an unidentified 'demon' be represented as Mercurius; Lara is veiled because she is no longer a nymph but 'the silent *goddess*' (Ovid *Fasti* 2.583); and the supposed distinction between the Lares Praestites and the Lares of the cross-roads is refuted by Ovid's text (*Fasti* 2.615–16, 5.129–46).

Quirinus and the spear: Ovid *Fasti* 2.477–8, Festus (Paulus) 43L, Plutarch *Moralia* 285d (*Roman Questions* 87), Servius on *Aeneid* 1.292.

Lupercalia as cleansing: Varro *Antiquitates divinae* fr. 76 Cardauns, Ovid *Fasti* 2.31–2, Festus (Paulus) 75–6L, Plutarch *Romulus* 21.3, *Numa* 19.5, etc.

Quirinus from *Quirites*: Varro *De lingua Latina* 5.51, Ovid *Fasti* 2.479.

115 Settlement of 338 BC: Livy 8.14; Cornell 1995.348–52, Oakley 1998.538–59.

Quirinal as new quarter: Curti 2000.83–90.

325

Quirinus temple: vowed by L. Papirius Cursor, dictator in 325, and dedicated by his son, consul in 293 (Livy 10.46.7, Pliny *Natural History* 7.213). Myrtles: Pliny *Natural History* 15.120–1.

Mercurius: Trendall 1989.59 and fig. 85 (Lucania); Dierichs 1997.109–10 and fig. 118 (Pompeii).

116 Ovid on the Silent Goddess: *Fasti* 2.583–616 (old story, 584).

Larunda: Tacitus *Annals* 12.24.2 (with Coarelli 1983.262–4), Lactantius *Institutiones* 1.20.35. Cf. *Corpus glossatorum Latinorum* 5.30, 80, 111 ('Larunda quam quidam <Ma>niam dicunt'), with Varro *De lingua Latina* 9.61 and Macrobius *Saturnalia* 1.7.35 on Mania as the mother of the Lares; at Ovid *Fasti* 2.609, Jupiter sends her to the *Manes*. Lara from Lala: Ovid *Fasti* 2.599–602.

Performance: Wiseman 1999.199–200. Dancing girls: Ovid *Fasti* 2.590 ('medio . . . *choro*').

Almo's warning: Ovid *Fasti* 2.601–2. 'Your sister-nymph. . .': Massey 1757.97. Lara to Juno: 2.605–6 ('miserataque nuptas').

117 'Twins consequent. . .': Massey 1757.97; cf. Ovid *Fasti* 5.129–42 for Lares as guardians.

For the late fourth century as the creation period of the subject-matter of the Roman historiographical tradition, see Gabba 2000.11–23; also Dumézil 1973.114, 197, where the date is probably right regardless of Dumézil's very implausible ideas about what the creators of the tradition were actually doing.

CHAPTER **6**

119 Latin colonies: Cales 334 BC, Fregellae 328, Luceria 314, Saticula 313, Suessa Aurunca 313, Pontian islands 313, Interamna Lirenas 312, Sora 303, Alba Fucens 303, Narnia 299, Carseoli 298.

Miniature Romes: e.g. Marsyas statues at Alba Fucens and Paestum (Liberatore 1995, Coarelli 1985.95–100); district names Esquiline and Palatine at Cales, Aventine, Cermalus and Velabrum at Ariminum (*ILLRP* 1217, *CIL* 10.4641, 11.417, 419, 421); see Torelli 1999.48–9 (circular *comitium* in colonies), 71–5 ('sacred topography' at Paestum). Paestum and Ariminum were founded in 273 and 268 BC.

Roads: Via Appia 312 BC, Via Valeria 307?; the next were probably the Via Clodia in Etruria (287? 285?) and the Via Caecilia across the Apennines (283?). See Wiseman 1970.130–3 (Appia), 134–6 (Caecilia), 137 (Clodia), 139–40 (Valeria).

Aqueducts: Aqua Appia 312 BC; the next was the Anio Vetus (273 BC); Frontinus *De aquis* 1.5–6.

Economic unrest: Dio Cassius 8.37.2–4, Zonaras 8.2 (debt); Livy *Epitome* 11 (debt and secession, 289–286 BC), cf. Pomponius in *Digest* 1.2.2.8.

Temples: Quirinus vowed 325 BC, dedicated 293 (Livy 10.46.7–8, Pliny *Natural History* 7.213); Victoria begun about 307, dedicated 294 (Livy 10.33.9). Evander's Victoria temple: Dionysius of Halicarnassus 1.32.3–5.

Hercules altar and *serui publici*: Livy 9.29.9–11, Festus 290L. Epiphany and curse of Hercules: Dionysius of Halicarnassus 1.40.5, Valerius Maximus 1.1.17. Appius and Bellona: Livy 10.19.17–21.

120 Luceria colony: Livy 9.26.1–5, Diodorus Siculus 19.72.8–9. Ἄργος ἵππιον: Strabo 6.3.9, Servius on *Aeneid* 11.246.

Cavalry: Polybius 6.25.3–4; *FGrH* 839 F1.3 (lines 19–22) for the date. *Luceres*: Varro *De lingua Latina* 5.91, Cicero *De republica* 2.36, Livy 1.13.8, 1.36.2, Festus 484L. Lucerus: Festus (Paulus) 106L; cf. Virgil *Aeneid* 8.146 etc. (Rutuli as *gens Daunia*).

Iunius Bubulcus: Livy 9.20.7–9.

Trojan Minerva: Strabo 6.1.14, cf. 6.3.9. Iunius son of Daunos: Scholiast B on *Iliad* 5.412 (2.64 Erbse); Curti 1993. Diomedes as Daunos' son-in-law: Ovid *Metamorphoses* 14.458–9 and 510–11, Pliny *Natural History* 3.103.

121 Appius' books: Cicero *Brutus* 61 (speeches); Pomponius in *Digest* 1.2.2.36 (legal works, no longer extant in the second century AD); Cicero *Tusculanae disputationes* 4.4 (citing Panaetius on Appius' *carmen Pythagoreum*), [Sallust] *Epistula ad Caesarem* 1.1.2 (*carmina*); Festus 418L (*sententiae*).

Legis actiones and *fasti* published by Cn. Flavius: Cicero *Ad Atticum* 6.1.8 (Atticus was uncertain about the date); Livy 9.46.1–10, Valerius Maximus 2.5.2, Pliny *Natural History* 33.17, Pomponius in *Digest* 1.2.2.7, Macrobius *Saturnalia* 1.15.9.

Flavius as *scriba*: Piso fr. 37 Forsythe (Aulus Gellius 7.9.2), Cicero *Ad Atticum* 6.1.8 ('nec uero pauci sunt auctores. . .'), Livy 9.46.1, Valerius Maximus 2.5.2, Macrobius *Saturnalia* 1.15.9. As Appius' *scriba*: Pliny *Natural History* 33.17, Pomponius in *Digest* 1.2.2.7; cf. Livy 9.46.10.

'Faber est suae quisque fortunae': Appius in [Sallust] *Epistula ad Caesarem* 1.1.2.

Kleidemos' *Exegetika*: *FGrH* 323 F14 (Athenaeus 13.609c–d); Jacoby 1949.8–24, 75–6.

Reform of *pontifices* and augurs: Livy 10.6.3–7, 10.9.1–2 (*lex Ogulnia*, 300 BC). Livy is probably mistaken to make the pontifical college 4+4: in 210 BC, at least, it certainly had five plebeian members to four patricians (Beard 1990.35 n. 45).

Archive: the idea that the chronicle of the *pontifex maximus* predates 300 BC (e.g. Cornell 1995.14, 'we can be sure of this. . .') is based on quite inadequate evidence (Cicero *De republica* 1.25, on which see Humm 2000.106–9).

Libri pontificum: Varro *Antiquitates divinae* fr. 87 Cardauns (Servius on *Georgics* 1.21), Cicero *De domo* 136, Festus 204L, Macrobius *Saturnalia* 1.12.21, etc.; Rohde 1936. *Annales pontificum*: Cicero *De legibus* 1.2.6, *Origo gentis Romanae* pref., 17.3, 17.5, 18.3;

cf. Cicero *De oratore* 2.52, *De republica* 1.25, Aulus Gellius 4.5.6, Festus (Paulus) 113L, Macrobius *Saturnalia* 3.2.17, Servius *auctus* on *Aeneid* 1.373 (*annales maximi*); Frier 1979.

Libri augurum: Cicero *De divinatione* 1.72, *De republica* 2.54, Seneca *Epistles* 108.31, Servius *auctus* on *Aeneid* 8.95, etc.; Linderski 1986.2241–56.

Pontiffs' books: Horace *Epistles* 2.1.26 ('pontificum libros, annosa uolumina uatum').

Coalition: Livy 10.13.2–5 (298 BC); 10.16.2–8, 10.18.1–2 (296 BC).

Portents and expiation: Zonaras 8.1, where ὑπὸ τῶν μάντεων κεκρίμενα ἀπαίσια evidently refers to human sacrifice (Wiseman 1995a.117–25).

Experts on prophecy: i.e. Marcii, Publicii(?), Genucii, Minucii (Livy 10.9.2, with Wiseman 1998.103–4).

Ogulnii as aediles: Livy 10.23.11–12; see Münzer 1920.83–9 = 1999.81–6.

Mars temple: Livy 7.23.3, Ovid *Fasti* 6.191–2, *CIL* 6.10234.4. *Transuectio equitum*: Dionysius of Halicarnassus 6.13.4; cf. Livy 9.46.15, Valerius Maximus 2.2.9, *De viris illustribus* 32.3 (Q. Fabius Rullianus, censor 304 BC).

122 Statue group: Livy 10.23.12 ('ad ficum Ruminalem simulacra *infantium conditorum urbis* sub uberibus lupae'); cf. Dionysius of Halicarnassus 1.79.8 for the precinct and the bronze statue group, surviving in his day but 'of antique workmanship'.

Ficus Ruminalis: Varro *De lingua Latina* 5.54, Livy 1.4.5, Ovid *Fasti* 2.411–12, Plutarch *Romulus* 4.1, Servius on *Aeneid* 8.90, *Origo gentis Romanae* 20.4. The fig-tree in the Comitium (Ficus Navia, Festus 168L) was later identified as the *ficus Ruminalis*, miraculously transported by Attus Navius, and a replacement bronze group of the infant *conditores* was set up there (Pliny *Natural History* 15.77, Tacitus *Annals* 13.58, *CIL* 6.33856); Wiseman 1995a.72–6, cf. Coarelli 1985.33 and 89 (who I think is wrong to suppose the Comitium fig-tree the original).

Clivus Victoriae and Porta Romana: Festus 318L, with Coarelli 1983.232.

Brutus statue: Plutarch *Brutus* 1.1, Dio Cassius 43.45.4; cf. Plutarch *Brutus* 9.6, Suetonius *Divus Iulius* 80.3, Appian *Civil Wars* 2.112, Dio Cassius 44.12.3 (covered in slogans, 44 BC). Camillus statue: Asconius 29C, Pliny *Natural History* 34.23.

123 Decius' *deuotio*: Livy 10.28.6–29.7 (10.28.14 and 29.3 for the *pontifex* M. Livius); Duris *FGrH* 76 F56b, Accius *Aeneadae sive Decius* (Manuwald 2001.196–220); *Fasti Capitolini* (Degrassi 1947.38–9); Valerius Maximus 5.6.6, Juvenal 8.254–8, etc.

Deuotio formula: Livy 8.9.6–8 (Decius' father's *deuotio* in 340 BC), 10.28.15. Janus named first as doorkeeper of Olympus, and therefore controlling access of prayers to the gods (Ovid *Fasti* 1.125–6,

139–40, 171–4, Macrobius *Saturnalia* 1.9.9).

Plague and famine: Zonaras 8.1, with Wiseman 1995a.120; cf. Livy 10.47.6–7, Valerius Maximus 1.8.2, Ovid *Metamorphoses* 15.622–744, Lactantius *Institutiones* 2.7.13, *De viris illustribus* 22 (the summoning of Aesculapius in 292 BC, with Q. Ogulnius as the chief ambassador to Epidauros).

Pyrrhos: Pausanias 1.12.1 (Achilles' descendant makes war on Trojan colonists), dismissed by Erskine 2001.157–61; Justin 18.1.2 (emulating Alexander), Livy 35.14.6–9 (Hannibal's judgement), Appius *Samnite Wars* fr. 10.1 (terms).

For the Romans' use of their Trojan origin in the third century BC, see Strasburger 1968.11, Momigliano 1984.452–4, Gruen 1992.26–31; minimised by Erskine 2001.21–43, who tries systematically to argue away the evidence for Roman consciousness of Trojan origins before Caesar (2001.38, 'the sphere of historians and poets'—quite so!).

Appius' speech: Plutarch *Pyrrhus* 18.5–19.3, Appian *Samnite Wars* fr. 10.2, Zonaras 8.4; cf. Cicero *De senectute* 16 (citing Ennius), Livy *Epitome* 13, Valerius Maximus 8.13.5.

Tellus temple: Florus 1.19.2, Varro *De re rustica* 1.2.1; cf. Wiseman 1994.39–41 on Suetonius *Tiberius* 2.1 (*Italia occupata* in 268 BC?).

Kleidemos and the Atthidographers: Pearson 1942, Jacoby 1949.

124 Where the talismans were kept: Ovid *Fasti* 6.435–6 (Palladion); Aulus Gellius 4.6.1, Servius on *Aeneid* 8.3 (*ancilia*); Arnobius 6.7 (head of Aulus, 'curiosa obscuritate conclusum'); Plutarch *Moralia* 264d (*Roman Questions* 4, heifer's horns); Servius on *Aeneid* 2.116 (Orestes' ashes); Festus 324L (*quadriga*).

List of *pignora imperii*: Servius *auctus* on *Aeneid* 7.188. Great Mother's *lapis*: Livy 29.11.7. Iliona's sceptre: Virgil *Aeneid* 1.653–4.

Orestes: Euripides *Iphigeneia in Tauris* 1435–74, Servius on *Aeneid* 2.116. Diana Nemorensis: *ILLRP* 85 (cf. 83 'Diana af louco'); *ILS* 3243–5. Mirror: Servius on *Aeneid* 7.515–6. Oracle: Herodotus 1.67.2.

125 Chariot: Festus 340–2L, Plutarch *Publicola* 13, Pliny *Natural History* 8.161, 28.16, Solinus 45.15; the Porta Ratumena on the north side of the Capitol was named after the charioteer.

126 Dating 'post urbem conditam': Cicero *Brutus* 72, *Ad familiares* 9.21.2; cf. Livy 1.60.3, 3.33.1, 4.7.1, etc. 'Post reges exactos': Cicero *Brutus* 62, Varro *De re rustica* 1.2.9, Dionysius of Halicarnassus 7.1.5, Livy 7.3.8, 10.9.3, Asconius 76C, Tacitus *Annals* 11.22.4. 'Postquam Galli urbem ceperunt': Aulus Gellius 5.4.3 (from Fabius' Latin *annales*); cf. Livy 6.1.1, 7.18.1. Only the third of these eras could have been used in the third century BC, before the achievement of a continuous chronology from the beginning of the Republic.

Books of Fate (*libri fatales*): Cicero *De divinatione* 1.100, Livy 5.15.11; cf. Dionysius of Halicarnassus 12.11.2, Plutarch *Camillus* 4.3, Zonaras 7.20 ('oracles').

Date: six years (Cicero *De divinatione* 1.100) before the Gallic sack in 387 (Polybius 1.6.1–2).

Secret betrayed: Livy 5.15.4–12 (15.6 for the soldier's *religio*), Dionysius of Halicarnassus 12.11, Valerius Maximus 1.6.3, Plutarch *Camillus* 4.1–3, Zonaras 7.20; cf. Cicero *De divinatione* 1.100, a rationalised version in which the *haruspex* merely deserts to the Romans. Sceptical *patres*: Dionysius of Halicarnassus 12.12.1, cf. Plutarch *Camillus* 4.4.

Ambassador's speech: Dionysius of Halicarnassus 12.13.2–3 (Loeb translation by Earnest Cary, slightly adapted), Cicero *De divinatione* 1.100.

Vows to the gods: Livy 5.19.6, 5.23.7, Plutarch *Camillus* 5.1, 6.1; cf. Livy 5.16.11 (Apollo's request, 'bello perfecto donum amplum uictor ad mea templa portato').

127 Sappers: Diodorus Siculus 14.93.2, Livy 5.19.9–11, 5.21.4 and 10, Plutarch *Camillus* 5.3, Florus 1.12.10, Orosius 2.19.2, Zonaras 7.21.

Sacrifice story: Livy 5.21.8 (*fabula*), Plutarch *Camillus* 5.4–5 (μύθευμα).

Juno's assent: Livy 5.22.6, Dionysius of Halicarnassus 13.3, Valerius Maximus 1.8.3, Plutarch *Camillus* 6.1. Temple next to Jupiter Libertas: *Fasti fratrum Arvalium* on 1 September (Degrassi 1963.32–3), Augustus *Res gestae* 19.2.

White horses: Diodorus Siculus 14.117.6, Livy 5.23.5–6, Plutarch *Camillus* 7.1, *De viris illustribus* 23.4, Zonaras 7.21.

Forgotten vow: Plutarch *Camillus* 7.4–8.4, Appian *Italian Wars* fr. 8.1, Zonaras 7.21.

Furius' exile: Cicero *De domo* 36, Dionysius of Halicarnassus 13.5, Appian *Italian Wars* fr. 8.2, Dio Cassius 6.24.4.

Caedicius and the voice: Cicero *De divinatione* 1.101, 2.69, Livy 5.32.6–7 ('id ut fit propter auctoris humilitatem spretum'), Plutarch *Camillus* 14.1–2, Zonaras 7.23.3. *Vox diuinitus edita*: Varro *Antiquitates divinae* fr. 107 Cardauns (Aulus Gellius 16.17.2).

Fabii at Clusium: Diodorus Siculus 14.113.4, Livy 5.35.4–36.8 ('contra ius gentium arma capiunt', 36.6), Dionysius of Halicarnassus 13.12, Plutarch *Camillus* 17, *Numa* 12.6–7, Dio 7.25.1–2, Orosius 2.19.5.

Allia defeat: Diodorus Siculus 14.114, Livy 5.37.5–38.10 (5.38.1 and 6.1.12 for the commander's failure to secure the gods' approval), Plutarch *Camillus* 18.4–7, Florus 1.13.7, Orosius 2.19.6 (alleging Fabius in command).

'Dies Alliae et Fabiorum': *Fasti Antiates minores* (Degrassi 1963.208). *Dies Alliensis*: Cn. Gellius and Cassius Hemina in Macrobius 1.16.21–4, Cicero *Ad Atticum* 9.5.2, Verrius Flaccus in Aulus Gellius 5.17.2,

Livy 6.1.11–12, etc.; *Fasti Antiates maiores* and *Amiternini* (Degrassi 1963.14–15 and 188–9).

Defenceless Rome: our sources wrongly believed that the circuit wall already existed, so they had to assume a panic-stricken failure even to close the gates (Livy 5.38.10–39.2, 5.41.4, Plutarch *Camillus* 22.1, Servius on *Aeneid* 8.652, Zonaras 7.23.3–4); according to Diodorus (14.115.5) the Gauls broke down the gates.

Albinius and the Vestals: *CIL* 6.1272 (statue base from the Pantheon), Livy 5.40.7–10, Valerius Maximus 1.1.10, Plutarch *Camillus* 20.3 (fire), 21.1–2; according to Aristotle (quoted in Plutarch *Camillus* 22.3), 'Lucius' was the saviour of Rome.

Patrician commander (Q. Sulpicius): Aulus Gellius 5.17.2 (from Verrius Flaccus), Macrobius *Saturnalia* 1.16.23 (from Cn. Gellius and Cassius Hemina); Livy 5.47.9, 5.48.8, 6.1.12; Plutarch *Camillus* 28.4–5.

128 Gauls take Capitol: Ennius *Annales* 227–8 Sk (with Skutsch 1985.408); Silius Italicus 4.150–1, 6.555–6, Tertullian *Apologeticus* 40.9; cf. Varro *De vita populi Romani* fr. 61 Riposati (Nonius 800L), Lucan 5.27 and fr. 12; Skutsch 1968.138–42.

Tunnels: Cicero *Pro Caecina* 88 ('in cuniculum qua adgressi erant'), *Philippics* 3.20, Servius on *Aeneid* 8.652; cf., Lydus *De mensibus* 4.114, *De magistratibus* 1.50; Wiseman 1979b.38–40.

'Vae uictis!': Livy 5.48.8–9, Dionysius of Halicarnassus 13.9, Plutarch *Camillus* 28.4–5; Festus 510–12L makes the Roman commander Ap. Claudius.

Chronology: Aulus Gellius 5.4.3 (Fabius' *annales*, 'in the twenty-second year'); Cornell 1995.399–402.

Patrician backlash: Livy 7.17.12–18.10, 7.21.1–4, 7.22.1–3. Furii: Livy 6.42.11, 7.1.2 (praetorship created as concession to patricians, Sp. Furius elected); 7.24.11 ('dictator L. Furius Camillus ... reddidit patribus possessionem pristinam consulatus'); 7.28.1–2 (L. Furius made dictator in a year with two patrician consuls).

M. Furius: Diodorus reports a M. Furius as *tr. mil. cos. pot.* in the fourth, sixth and ninth years of the war with Veii (14.35.1, 14.44.1, 14.82.1), and again two years after the conquest (14.97.1, cf. 15.2.1). The Augustan *fasti consulares* (Degrassi 1963) name M. Furius Fusus for the first of those years ('403 BC') and M. Furius Camillus for the other three ('401, 398, 394 BC'); Livy attributes all four to Camillus, at the cost of internal incoherence (5.1.2, 5.10.1 *iterum*, 5.14.5 *iterum* again, 5.26.1). Diodorus, whose chronological scheme is now five years out, also has a M. Furius as *tr. mil. cos. pot.* in the sixth year after the Gallic sack; not in the corresponding college in Livy (6.1.8, '389 BC'), who instead has Camillus as *interrex* and dictator (6.2.5). 'Marcus' is a rare *praenomen* among the patrician Furii: the next attested example is the grandfather of P. Furius Philus, consul 223 BC.

Camillus: Livy 5.19–55, Plutarch *Camillus, De viris*

illustribus 23, etc.; for full references, and analysis of the legend in its developed literary form, see Coudry 2001 and Späth 2001. Livy 5.19.2 (*fatalis dux*), 5.23.1 ('maximum imperatorum omnium').

Camillus has the filiation 'L.f.Sp.n.' in the Augustan *fasti consulares* ('403 and 401 BC'); so too do L. Furius Medullinus, allegedly consul 413 and 409 and *tr. mil. cos. pot.* seven times between 407 and 391, and Sp. Furius Medullinus, *tr. mil. cos. pot.* '400 BC' (see the *fasti consulares* under '405 and 400 BC'). The Medullini were no doubt thought to be sons of L. Furius Medullinus, allegedly *tr. mil. cos. pot.* 432, 425 and 420 BC, and grandsons of Sp. Furius Medullinus, 'consul 464 BC'; Spurius' double *cognomen* (Medullinus in Diodorus Siculus 11.78.1, Fusus in Livy 3.4.1) makes it possible that M. Furius Fusus was thought of as a third grandson, in which case he may be the original datum on which the Camillus legend was based.

Marce Camitlnas becomes M. Furius Camillus: Bruun 2000.

Name: Festus (Paulus) 82L, Macrobius *Saturnalia* 3.8.7 on *camilli*.

Camillus dictator: Diodorus Siculus 14.93.2, Livy 5.19.2–3 ('omnia repente mutauerat imperator mutatus'), Plutarch *Camillus* 5.1, etc.

Vows: Livy 5.21.1–3, 5.22.7, 5.23.8; Dionysius of Halicarnassus 13.3.1, Plutarch *Camillus* 6.1.

Prayer and fall: Valerius Maximus 1.5.2, Plutarch *Camillus* 5.5–7; slightly different version in Livy 5.21.14–16 and Dionysius of Halicarnassus 12.14. Son's death: Livy 5.32.8, Plutarch *Camillus* 11.2.

Prosecution and exile: Cicero *De domo* 86 ('populi incitati uim iracundiamque'), *De republica* 1.4–6 (*ingrati ciues*), etc. Final prayer: Livy 5.32.9 (*ciuitas ingrata*), Dionysius of Halicarnassus 13.5, Plutarch *Camillus* 12, Appian *Italian Wars* fr. 8.2, Dio 6.24.4–6.

Juno's warning: Scholiast on Lucan 1.380 ('Moneta dicta est, quod monuisset ut Capitolium tuerentur'), cf. *Suda* s.v. Moneta; Cicero *De divinatione* 1.101, 2.69 for a rival etymology.

Gods send Gauls: Dionysius of Halicarnassus 13.6.1, Appian *Italian Wars* 8.2, Plutarch *Camillus* 13.2.

Capitol defended: Diodorus Siculus 14.115.3–4, Livy 5.39.8–12, Plutarch *Camillus* 20.2, Florus 1.7.13 ('satis constat uix mille hominum fuisse'). Manlius in command: Virgil *Aeneid* 8.652 and Servius, Florus 1.7.13, *De viris illustribus* 23.9, 24.3, Lydus *De magistratibus* 1.50; cf. Diodorus Siculus 14.116.6 (ἔνδοξος ἀνήρ), Livy 5.47.4 ('qui triennio ante consul fuerat, uir bello egregius').

Example: Livy 5.39.13, Valerius Maximus 3.2.7. *Deuotio* in Forum: Florus 1.7.9, Plutarch *Camillus* 21.2; cf. Livy 5.40.1 (*morti destinatos*), 5.41.3 ('sunt qui tradant'); Zonaras 7.23.3 (eighty). Funerals: Polybius 6.53.6–9.

129 *Atrium* scene: Livy 5.41, Valerius Maximus 3.2.7 (C. Atilius), Florus 1.7.10 and 14, Orosius 2.19.7; in Plutarch (*Camillus* 22.4–6) they are killed in the Forum; in *De viris illustribus* (23.8) the place of death is not specified.

Seven-month siege: Polybius 2.22.5, Plutarch *Camillus* 30.1; cf. Varro *De vita populi Romani* fr. 61 Riposati, Livy *Epitome* 5, Florus 1.7.15, Orosius 2.19.13 (six months); Servius on *Aeneid* 8.652 (eight months).

Fabius Dorsuo and the Vesta temple: Appian *Gallic Wars* fr. 6, from 'Causios' (Cassius Hemina?); cf. Dio 7.25.5–6 ('Kaeso Fabius', not specifying where), Florus 1.7.16 (to the Quirinal). Livy (5.46.1–3), followed by Valerius Maximus (1.1.11), makes it a family cult of the Fabii on the Quirinal, with C. Fabius Dorsuo not a priest but just a pious *iuuenis*.

Message to Camillus: Livy 5.45.4–11, Dionysius of Halicarnassus 13.6.2–4, Valerius Maximus 4.1.2, Plutarch *Camillus* 24.2–3, Appian *Gallic Wars* fr. 5, Dio 7.25.7, *De viris illustribus* 23.9 ('absens dictator dictus').

Volunteer: Livy 5.46.8–10, Dionysius of Halicarnassus 13.7.1, Plutarch *Camillus* 25; Pontius Cominius was not a patrician (Plutarch *Camillus* 25.1), and his exploit evidently pre-dates the involvement of Camillus in the story (Diodorus Siculus 14.116.3–4).

Gauls' assault: Diodorus Siculus 14.116.5–7, Livy 5.47.1–6, Dionysius of Halicarnassus 13.7.2–4, Plutarch *Camillus* 26.1–27.5, Florus 1.7.15, *De viris illustribus* 24.4.

Camillus as the gods' agent: Livy 5.49.1–5, with a ring-composition marked by *di* and *deorum opes*; Plutarch *Camillus* 29, Florus 1.7.17.

Camillus as *conditor alter*: Livy 5.49.7; Plutarch *Camillus* 31.2, cf. *Marius* 27.5.

Execution of Manlius: Diodorus Siculus 15.35.3 ('attempt at tyranny' in the equivalent to Varronian year '385 BC'); Cicero *De domo* 101, *Pro Sulla* 27, *De republica* 2.49, *Philippics* 1.32, 2.114, letter to Nepos fr. 5 (in Ammianus Marcellinus 21.16.13); Varro and Cornelius Nepos in Aulus Gellius 17.21.24; Ovid *Fasti* 6.185–90. The later annalists invented rhetorical fictions about the trial (see Wiseman 1979b), but the fact of the execution is likely to be historical.

345 BC: Livy 7.28.1–2 (consul M. Fabius Dorsuo, dictator L. Furius, *magister equitum* Cn. Manlius Capitolinus), 7.28.4–5 (Juno Moneta temple); for the temple on the site of M. Manlius Capitolinus' demolished house, see also Livy 6.20.13, Valerius Maximus 6.3.1a, Ovid *Fasti* 6.183–6 (Cicero *De domo* 101 puts the house at the *duo luci*).

130 Consul of 325 BC: Diodorus Siculus 18.2.1 (D. Iunius), Festus 458L (Iunius Scaeva); Livy 8.12.13 (Iunius Brutus), 8.29.2 (Iunius Brutus Scaeva). *Scaeva*:

Ulpian in *Digest* 21.1.12.3; cf. Aulus Gellius pref. 20, 12.13.4.

Consul of 317 BC etc.: Livy 9.20.7 and eight other passages, Valerius Maximus 8.14.6 (C. Iunius Bubulcus); *fasti consulares* on 317, 313, 312, 311, 309 and 302 BC (C. Iunius C.f.C.n. Bubulcus Brutus); Valerius Maximus 2.9.2 (C. Iunius Brutus Bubulcus). *Bubulcus*: Pliny *Natural History* 18.9–10, cf. Varro *De re rustica* 2.pref.4 (ploughman); Cicero *De divinatione* 1.57, Ovid *Tristia* 3.12.30 (ox-cart driver).

Demaratos' elder son and grandson: Livy 1.34.2–3, Dionysius of Halicarnassus 3.46.5–47.1.

Ancus' sons: Livy 1.35.1–2, Zonaras 7.8.

Collatia and Egerius: Livy 1.38.1, Dionysius of Halicarnassus 3.50.3. Has a local Latin dynasty of Egerii been incorporated into the story? Cf. Cato *Origines* fr. 58P and Festus 128L for Egerii at Aricia.

131 Servius as Tarquinius' son-in-law: Livy 1.38.4, Dionysius of Halicarnassus 3.72.7, 4.1.1, 4.3.4.

M. Iunius: Dionysius of Halicarnassus 4.68.1 (descendant of one of Aeneas' Trojans); cf. Diodorus Siculus 10.22, Livy 1.56.7, *De viris illustribus* 10.1.

Tarquinius' sons: L. Piso in the second century BC, followed by Dionysius of Halicarnassus 4.6–7 (cf. 4.1.1, 4.4.2), tried to solve the chronological impasse by making them his grandsons; Livy (1.42.2, 1.46.4) doesn't commit himself. See Forsythe 1994.227–32.

Gegania wife of Tarquinius: 'certain Roman historians' in Dionysius of Halicarnassus 4.7.4. Cf. Gegania the first Vestal (Plutarch *Numa* 10.1), Gegania the wife of Servius Tullius (Valerius Antias fr. 12P = Plutarch *Moralia* 323c), and Gegania the wife of Pinarius, in the reign of Tarquinius Superbus (Plutarch *Comparison of Lycurgus and Numa* 3.7); the Geganii were descended from Gyas the Trojan (Servius on *Aeneid* 5.117), settled in Alba, and became Roman patricians under Tullus Hostilius (Livy 1.30.2, Dionysius of Halicarnassus 3.29.7); Geganii were listed as consuls for 492, 447, 443, 440 and 437 BC, and as 'consular tribunes' for 378 and 367 BC.

Ancus' sons again: Livy 1.40–41, Dionysius of Halicarnassus 3.72–73.

Tulliae–Tarquinii marriages and murders: Livy 1.42.1–2, 1.46, Dionysius of Halicarnassus 4.28.1–30.4, Ovid *Fasti* 6.587–92, *De viris illustribus* 7.15–16.

132 Death of Servius Tullius: Livy 1.47–8, Dionysius of Halicarnassus 4.38–9, Ovid *Fasti* 6.587–610 (Massey 1757.333–4), *De viris illustribus* 7.17–19, Zonaras 7.9. *Vicus sceleratus*: Varro *De lingua Latina* 5.159, Festus 450L.

Di penates and *furiae*: Livy 1.48.7, 1.59.13; cf. Dionysius of Halicarnassus 4.40.5–6 for the curses of Servius' wife Tarquinia (and the story that they killed her too). Later suicide of Tullia: Zonaras 7.11.

Bodyguard: Livy 1.49.2, Dionysius of Halicarnassus

4.41.3, Dio Cassius 2.11.4, Zonaras 7.10. Forced labour: Cassius Hemina fr. 15P (Servius *auctus* on *Aeneid* 12.603), Livy 1.56.1–3, Dionysius of Halicarnassus 4.44. Cruel punishments: Dio Cassius 2.11.6, Isidore *Origines* 5.27.23. Killing of prominent men: Diodorus Siculus 10.22, Livy 1.49.2–5, Dionysius of Halicarnassus 4.42.1–3, Dio 2.11.2–4.

M. Iunius and his sons: Livy 1.56.7–8, Dionysius of Halicarnassus 4.68.2–69.1, Ovid *Fasti* 2.717–18, Dio Cassius 2.11.10, Zonaras 7.11.

Octavius Mamilius: Livy 1.49.9, Dionysius of Halicarnassus 4.45.1; Festus 116L for his descent.

Sextus at Gabii: Livy 1.53.4–54.7, Dionysius of Halicarnassus 4.53–8, Ovid *Fasti* 2.687–710. Sextus the eldest son: Dionysius of Halicarnassus 4.55.1, 4.64.2. The youngest: Livy 1.53.5, Ovid *Fasti* 2.691.

133 Lucius Collatinus: Fabius Pictor *FGrH* 809 F12 (Dionysius of Halicarnassus 4.64.2–3), Livy 1.57.6.

Sextus at Collatia: Diodorus Siculus 10.20.1–2, Dionysius of Halicarnassus 4.64.2–65.4 (from Gabii?). Other sources have Sextus, his brothers and Collatinus in camp at Ardea, boasting of the virtue of their respective wives, riding off to see for themselves, and finding 'the royal daughters-in-law' enjoying parties at Rome and Lucretia spinning with her maids at Collatia: Livy 1.57.5–11 ('regii iuuenes'), Ovid *Fasti* 2.723–60, Dio Cassius 2.11.13–15 (including Brutus), *De viris illustribus* 9.1–2, Servius on *Aeneid* 8.646 (calling the rapist Arruns). In that version Sextus is the youngest, and all the princes are married.

Sextus' blackmail: Diodorus Siculus 10.20.2, Livy 1.5.1–5, Dionysius of Halicarnassus 4.65.2–4, Ovid *Fasti* 2.761–812, Dio Cassius 2.11.15–17, Servius on *Aeneid* 8.646 (specifying an Ethiopian slave), Zonaras 7.11.

Lucretia's suicide, at Collatia: Diodorus Siculus 10.20.3, Livy 1.58.5–12, Ovid *Fasti* 2.813–36, Dio Cassius 2.11.18–19, Servius on *Aeneid* 8.646 (Brutus *auunculus*), Zonaras 7.11. At Rome, 'in concilio necessariorum': Dionysius of Halicarnassus 4.66–7, Valerius Maximus 6.1.1. Present: Sp. Lucretius and L. Collatinus (Lucretia's father and husband); also Brutus (Livy, Ovid, Servius, Zonaras), P. Valerius (Livy, Dionysius, Zonaras). Dionysius (4.67.3–4, 4.70.1–2) has Collatinus and Brutus present only afterwards. For Valerius, see Plate 9 and Wiseman 1998.75–89, esp. 80.

Brutus' oath: Livy 1.59.1–2, Dionysius of Halicarnassus 4.70.2–71.1, Ovid *Fasti* 2.837–46, *De viris illustribus* 10.4, Zonaras 7.11. For Brutus as *tribunus celerum*, in command of the king's cavalry (a tradition clearly inconsistent with the concealed-idiocy story), see Livy 1.59.7, Dionysius of Halicarnassus 4.71.6, Pomponius in *Digest* 1.2.2.15, Servius on *Aeneid* 8.646.

Liberty and the consulship: Sallust *Catiline* 6.7, Livy

1.60.3, Ovid *Fasti* 2.851–2, Tacitus *Annals* 1.1.1, etc.

Athenian paradigm: [Aristotle] *Athenaion politeia* 22.3–4 (Hipparchos); Cicero *De officiis* 3.40, Livy 2.2.3–10 (Collatinus); the Kollutos–Collatia parallel was pointed out by Griffiths 1998.

Brutus' sons: Polybius 6.54.5 (not named), Livy 2.3–5, Virgil *Aeneid* 6.817–23, Valerius Maximus 5.8.1, *De viris illustribus* 10.5, etc. Dionysius of Halicarnassus (5.3–12) and Plutarch (*Publicola* 3–7) follow a version in which Collatinus is still in office (cf. fig. 57) and unwilling to condemn his guilty nephews; Wiseman 1998.80–2, suggesting a date after 63 BC.

No descendants: Dionysius of Halicarnassus 5.18.1, Valerius Maximus 5.8.1 (*orbus*), Plutarch *Brutus* 1.6. Rival versions: Dionysius of Halicarnassus 6.89.1–2, 7.14–17, 7.26.3, Plutarch *Coriolanus* 7.1 (L. and T. Iunii Bruti as plebeian activists in 493–1 BC); Posidonius *FGrH* 87 F40 (the Liberator had an infant third son), Cicero *Philippics* 1.13, *Tusculanae disputationes* 4.2, etc. (M. Brutus a direct descendant).

Death of Brutus: Cicero *Tusculanae disputationes* 4.50 (*iracundia* and *odium*), Livy 2.6.5–9 (Arruns *inflammatus ira*, 6.7), Dionysius of Halicarnassus 5.15.1–2 (ὁμοίῳ δ' ἀμφότεροι θύμῳ φερόμενοι), Plutarch *Publicola* 9.1–2 (ὑπ' ἔχθους καὶ ὀργῆς), etc.

Matronae mourn: Livy 2.7.4, *De viris illustribus* 10.7.

M. Horatius: Polybius 3.22.1 (he and Brutus the first consuls); cf. Livy 2.8.5 (successor to Brutus in early authors). Sp. Lucretius: Livy 2.8.4, Dionysius of Halicarnassus 5.19.2, etc. (successor to Brutus).

134 Horatii: last attested magistrates *tr. mil. cos. pot.* in 386 and 378 BC. Lucretii: last of the patrician Lucretii Tricipitini *tr. mil. cos. pot.* in 391, 388, 383 and 381 BC.

Year Two: Livy 2.9.1, Plutarch *Publicola* 16.1–2; Dionysius of Halicarnassus (5.21.1) makes it Year Three.

Late historian (Florus 1.4.3): 'illa tria Romani nominis prodigia atque miracula, Horatius, Mucius, Cloelia, qui nisi in annalibus forent hodie fabulae uiderentur.' Cf. Livy 2.10.11 on Horatius (more *fama* than *fides*), Plutarch *Publicola* 17.1 on Mucius (variety of versions).

Horatius: Livy 2.10, Dionysius of Halicarnassus 5.22.3–25.4, Plutarch *Publicola* 16.4–7, etc.

136 For the complex reception-history of the Lucretius and Brutus stories, see Donaldson 1982 (ch. 2 on Augustine).

Lucretia guilty?: Augustine *City of God* 1.19; Donaldson 1982.21–39; for Britten's opera, see Britten et al. 1948.

137 Sextus: Livy 1.60.2 (referring back to 1.54.5–10); Dante *Inferno* 12.133–5 (cf. 28.12 on Livy); Dionysius of Halicarnassus 5.15.4, 5.22.4, 5.40.2, 5.58.4, 5.61.3, 6.5.2–5, 6.12.5. Macaulay: *Lays of Ancient Rome* (1842), 'The Battle of the Lake Regillus', stanzas

12 and 36.

138 Cloelia: Valerius Maximus 3.2.2, Florus 1.4.7, *De viris illustribus* 13.1 (horse); Livy 2.13.6, Virgil *Aeneid* 8.651, Dionysius of Halicarnassus 5.33.1, Plutarch *Publicola* 19.1, Polyaenus 8.31 (swimming); the two versions combined at Plutarch *Publicola* 19.2.

Porsena's gift: Dionysius of Halicarnassus 5.34.3, Plutarch *Publicola* 19.4, Dio Cassius 4.14. Statue: Livy 2.13.11, Dionysius of Halicarnassus 5.35.2, Seneca *Consolatio ad Marciam* 16.2, Plutarch *Publicola* 19.5; Pliny *Natural History* 34.29, citing Annius Fetialis, identifies the girl as Publicola's daughter Valeria (Wiseman 1998.84). The last patrician Cloelii to hold political office were *tr. mil. cos. pot.* and censor in 378 BC (Livy 6.31.1–2).

Rubens painting (Plate 10): McGrath 1997.1.51–2, 2.251–5 (no. 48).

'Gaius Mucius': Cicero *Pro Sestio* 48, Livy 2.12, Dionysius of Halicarnassus 5.25.4, 5.27–9, Valerius Maximus 3.3.1, Plutarch *Publicola* 17, Florus 1.4.5–6, Polyaenus 8.8, *De viris illustribus* 12, Zonaras 7.12. Patrician: Dionysius of Halicarnassus 5.25.4, 5.29.3; cf. Livy 2.12.2 (*nobilis*), 2.12.15 (*principes iuuentutis*).

The earliest known historical Mucius is Q. Mucius Scaevola, praetor in 215 BC (Livy 23.34.11, 25.3.6); for 'Scaevola' as the outcome of the Porsena story, see Livy 2.13.1, Plutarch *Publicola* 17.3, Florus 1.4.5.

Aeneas' daughters: Ennius *Annales* 34–50 Skutsch (Cicero *De divinatione* 1.40–1); cf. Servius *auctus* on *Aeneid* 1.273, Servius on *Aeneid* 6.777. The elder was the daughter of Eurydice, known to Virgil as Creusa, the wife who was left behind in Troy but preserved from captivity by Venus and the Great Mother (Pausanias 10.26.1, Virgil *Aeneid* 2.768–95).

Latin princess: Velleius Paterculus 1.8.5 (where Orelli's emendation makes Romulus the grandson of Latinus), Plutarch *Romulus* 1.3 (Romulus' mother the daughter of Lavinia).

Amulius of Alba Longa: Ennius *Annales* xxxix Skutsch (Porphyrio on Horace *Odes* 1.2.18); cf. Naevius *Lupus* in Festus 334L (Manuwald 2001.142), Naevius *Bellum Punicum* fr. 22 (Nonius 167L).

Dreams that end in tears are a good omen: Artemidorus *Oneirokritika* 2.60.

139 Rubens and Ovid: McGrath 1997.1.114–16; Ovid *Fasti* 3.1–10, 15–16 (*aperto pectore*), 21 ('Mars uidet hanc...'), 29–32 (Massey 1757.121). Palms for victory: e.g. Livy 10.47.3, Suetonius *Gaius* 32.3.

140 Ilia and Anio: Ennius *Annales* xxxix Skutsch (Porphyrio on Horace *Odes* 1.2.18), Ovid *Amores* 3.6.45–82, *Fasti* 2.598, Servius on *Aeneid* 1.273.

Twins and she-wolf: Ennius *Annales* xlii and xliv Skutsch (Virgil *Aeneid* 8.630–4 with Servius on 631, *Origo gentis Romanae* 20.3).

Acca Larentia: Licinius Macer fr. 2 Walt (Macrobius *Saturnalia* 1.10.17), Valerius Antias fr. 1P (Aulus

Gellius 7.7.5–8) and in *Origo gentis Romanae* 21.1, Livy 1.4.7, Dionysius of Halicarnassus 1.84.4, *Fasti Praenestini* on 23 December (Degrassi 1963.138–9), Ovid *Fasti* 3.55–8, 4.854, 5.453, Plutarch *Romulus* 4.3, Festus (Paulus) 106L, Lactantius *Divinae insitutiones* 1.20.1–4, Servius on *Aeneid* 1.273.

Eratosthenes on the fall of Troy as 1184 BC: *FGrH* 241 F1 (Clement of Alexandria *Stromateis* 1.138.1). Timaios on the foundation of Rome as 813 BC: *FGrH* 566 F60 (Dionysius of Halicarnassus 1.74.1, 'by what reckoning I do not know'); cf. Cato *Origines* fr. 17P (Dionysius of Halicarnassus 1.74.2), Diodorus Siculus 7.5.1, making the difference 432 or 433 years.

Alban king-list: Diodorus Siculus 7.5.6–12 (in the Armenian version of Eusebius' *Chronicle*); cf. Livy 1.3.6–10, Dionysius of Halicarnassus 1.70–1, Ovid *Metamorphoses* 14.609–21, *Fasti* 4.39–55, *Origo gentis Romanae* 17–19, etc.; Trieber 1894 for the various versions.

Numitor, Amulius and the twins: Fabius Pictor *FGrH* 809 F4, from Diokles of Peparethos (Plutarch *Romulus* 3–8, Dionysius of Halicarnassus 1.79–83); Wiseman 1995a.1–4.

Order of names: Naevius *Alimonium Remi et Romuli* (Manuwald 2001.141), Cassius Hemina fr. 14 Santini (Diomedes in *Grammatici Latini* 1.384K), Festus 332L (citing Varro), Cicero *De legibus* 1.8 ('ut aiunt, de Remo et Romulo'), Diodorus Siculus 8.3 and 8.5, *Fasti Praenestini* on 23 December (Degrassi 1963.138–9), Tacitus *Annals* 13.58, Festus (Paulus) 106L, Polyaenus 8.2, Justin 43.2.7, Servius on *Aeneid* 6.777, Lydus *De mensibus* 115 Bekker.

Pre-twin Romulus: Alkimos *FGrH* 560 F4 (Festus 326L), Kallias *FGrH* 564 F5 (Dionysius of Halicarnassus 1.72.3); perhaps implied by the *tribus Romulia* (Festus [Paulus] 331L) and the *gens Romulia* (Livy 3.33.3 MSS), though both are usually spelt 'Romilia'.

Meaning of names given in *Origo gentis Romanae* 21.5: 'Romulum autem a uirium magnitudine appellatum; nam Graeca lingua ῥώμην uirtutem dici certum est. alterum uero Remum dictum, uidelicet a tarditate, quippe talis naturae homines ab antiquis remores dici.' For Romulus, cf. Festus 326L (*uirium magnitudo*), Ovid *Fasti* 2.396 (*uigor*), Livy 1.5.3 (*uis*); for Remus, Festus (Paulus) 345L on 'remores aues in auspicio. . ., quae acturum aliquid remorari compellunt'.

Plural founders: Livy 10.23.12, Pliny *Natural History* 15.77 (Lupercal group); *CIL* 6.33856 (Comitium group); Konon *FGrH* 26 F1.48.7, Strabo 5.3.2, Justin 43.3.1, Orosius 2.4.1, Servius on *Aeneid* 6.777, Lydus *De magistratibus* 1.3, *De mensibus* 115 Bekker, Malalas 7.171.

Hero-shrine: Diodorus Siculus 37.11.1 (τοὺς κτίστας γεγενημένους τῆς Ῥώμης ἡμιθέους), Dionysius of Halicarnassus 1.79.8 and 10 (precinct, hymns).

141 Herdsmen: Cassius Hemina fr. 14 Santini (Diomedes in *Grammatici Latini* 1.384K), Diodorus Siculus 8.4.2, Valerius Maximus 2.2.9 ('diuisa pastorali turba'), *De viris illustribus* 1.4. Joint-rule plan: *Origo gentis Romanae* 23.1.

Roma or *Remora*: Ennius *Annales* fr. 77 Skutsch; for the site of 'Remuria', see Wiseman 1995a.110–17. Augury competition: Ennius *Annales* fr.72–91 Skutsch (Cicero *De divinatione* 1.107–8), with Wiseman 1995a.6–9 and 171 n. 33 (on the text).

Se deuouet: Ennius *Annales* fr. 74 Skutsch, where however Skutsch's text is inferior to that of Jocelyn (1971.62–3).

Romulus' confidence (σπουδή): Dionysius of Halicarnassus 1.86.3; cf. 1.80.3, Cicero *De republica* 2.12 (*perceleriter*), Diodorus Siculus 8.5, 8.6.1, for the same characteristic in other contexts. Remus' prophecy: *Origo gentis Romanae* 23.4, cf. Diodorus Siculus 8.5.

Light cavalry: Polybius 6.25.3–4; cf. *FGrH* 839 F1.3 (lines 19–22) for the date.

Celeres: Dionysius of Halicarnassus 2.13.2–3, Pliny *Natural History* 33.35, Festus (Paulus) 48L, Servius on *Aeneid* 11.603; as Romulus' bodyguard, cf. Livy 1.15.8, Plutarch *Romulus* 26.2, *Numa* 7.4. *Tribunus celerum* (like *magister equitum*): Pomponius in *Digest* 1.2.2.15 and 19, Lydus *De magistratibus* 1.14; cf. Dionysius of Halicarnassus 4.71.6, 4.75.1.

Celer: Valerius Antias fr. 2P (Dionysius of Halicarnassus 2.13.2), Ovid *Fasti* 4.837–44, 5.467–72, Plutarch *Romulus* 10.2, *De viris illustribus* 1.4 (centurion); Jerome (*Chronicle* on Olympiad 6.3) calls him Fabius; Wiseman 1995a.9–10.

Q. Fabius Maximus 'Rullianus' in 325 BC: Livy 8.30–6, esp. 30.4 ('seu ferox adulescens . . . seu occasione bene gerendae rei inductus'), 30.6 (charge), cf. Valerius Maximus 3.2.9 (*temere*), Dio Cassius 8.36.2 (rashness). He acted fast as aedile in 331 (Livy 8.18.5 *confestim*), and apparently rashly as consul for the second time in 310 BC (Livy 9.38.5 *temeritas*); on the latter occasion he had boldly crossed the Ciminian forest before the Senate's messengers arrived with the cautious advice that he shouldn't try it (Livy 9.36.14).

Fabius and cavalry: Valerius Maximus 2.2.9, *De viris illustribus* 32.3 (institutes *transuectio* as censor in 304 BC), cf. Livy 10.14.10–11 (fourth consulship, 297); Wiseman 1995b.10–13.

Partnership with P. Decius Mus (as consuls in 308 BC, censors in 304, consuls in 297 and 295): Livy 10.13.13, 10.22.3–4, 10.24.1–2 (*concordia*); 10.22.6 ('qui uno animo, una mente uiuerent'), 10.26.3 ('neminem omnium secum coniungi malle').

Romulus' *sulcus primigenius* (plough drawn by a bull and a cow): Dionysius of Halicarnassus 1.88.2, Ovid *Fasti* 4.825–6, Plutarch *Romulus* 11.2–3, *Moralia* 271a–b (*Roman Questions* 27). Normal

Roman custom: Cato *Origines* fr. 18P (Servius on *Aeneid* 5.755), Varro *De lingua Latina* 5.143, Dionysius of Halicarnassus 1.88.2, Festus 270–2L.

Etruscan ritual, for sacred inviolability of walls: Varro *De lingua Latina* 5.143, Plutarch *Romulus* 11.3, *Moralia* 271a-b, Festus 358L, Gaius in *Digest* 1.8.1.pref. (walls and gates *sanctae res*).

Roman military camp: Polybius 6.31.10, 6.41.10–12 (like a city); Modestinus in *Digest* 49.16.3.17–18 ('si uallum quis transcendat aut per murum castra ingrediatur, capite punitur'), Zonaras 7.3 (τὸν στρατοπέδου τάφρον τολμήσαντα διελθεῖν ... θανατοῦσθαι).

Remus' fatal jump: Diodorus Siculus 8.6.1–3, Dionysius of Halicarnassus 1.87.4, Ovid *Fasti* 4.835–44 (*nec mora* 843), 5.452 (Remus *male uelox*); cf. Ennius *Annales* fr. 92–5 Skutsch. Sanctity of the defences emphasised by Plutarch *Moralia* 271a (*Roman Questions* 27), who however makes Romulus the killer.

Decius at Sentinum: Livy 10.28.6–11 (cavalry, cf. 8.30.6–7 and Valerius Maximus 3.2.9 for Fabius in 325); 10.28.12–18 (*deuotio*). Victoria temple: Livy 10.33.9; Pensabene 1999.

142 Grave beneath altar: Vaglieri 1907.187–93; Wiseman 1995a.120–5. Interpretation: Carandini 1997a.60–1 and 66–8, Paolo Brocato in Carandini 1997a.619–21 and in Carandini and Cappelli 2000.262–3 and 285–7, Pensabene 1998.59–70, Angelelli and Falzone 1999.23–8, Wiseman 2001.188–91.

Foundation sacrifice (Sartori 1898.5–19, Wiseman 1995a.124–5): Propertius 3.9.50 ('caeso moenia firma Remo'), Florus 1.1.8 ('prima certe uictima fuit munitionemque urbis nouae sanguine suo consecrauit'); cf. Lucan 1.95 ('fraterno primi maduerunt sanguine muri') and Justin 28.2.10 ('qui denique urbem ipsam parricidio condiderint murorumque fundamenta fraterno sanguine adsperserint') for the hostile interpretation, with Romulus as the killer.

Hostile elements in foundation myth: Strasburger 1968, esp. 7–8 and 38–43; Jocelyn 1971.51–60, Wiseman 1995a.96–7.

Mother of twins: Licinius Macer fr. 2P (Malalas 7.7), Livy 1.4.2 (*culpa*), Dionysius of Halicarnassus 1.77.1, Justin 43.2.3; cf. Plutarch *Romulus* 4.2, *Origo gentis Romanae* 19.5 (rape by Amulius); Strasburger 1968.23–4.

Lupa as prostitute: Livy 1.4.7, Dionysius of Halicarnassus 1.84.4, Plutarch *Romulus* 4.3, Dio in Eustathius on *Odyssey* 24.270 (p. 1961), *Origo gentis Romanae* 21.1–2, Lactantius *Institutiones* 1.20.2, Servius on *Aeneid* 1.273, Jerome *Chronicle* on year 1221; cf. Licinius Macer fr. 2P (Malalas 7.7); Strasburger 1968.28–31.

Vultures: Livy 1.6.7, Dionysius of Halicarnassus 1.86.3–4, Valerius Maximus 1.4.pref., Plutarch

Romulus 9.5–7 (with explanation), Florus 1.1.6, *Origo gentis Romanae* 23.2–4, *De viris illustribus* 1.4, Servius on *Aeneid* 6.779; Jocelyn 1971.56–7.

Fratricide: Cicero *De officiis* 3.40–1, Horace *Epodes* 7.18–20, Livy 1.7.2 (*uolgatior fama*), Lucan 1.95, Plutarch *Romulus* 10.1, Justin 28.2.10, Minucius Felix *Octavius* 25.2, Augustine *City of God* 3.6, 15.5, Lydus *De magistratibus* 1.5, Malalas 7.1–2, Tzetzes *Chiliades* 899; rejected as *fabulosum* by Servius on *Aeneid* 6.779; Strasburger 1968.35–7.

Asylum: Virgil *Aeneid* 8.342–3, Ovid *Fasti* 3.431–4, Dionysius of Halicarnassus 2.15.3–4, Velleius Paterculus 1.8.5, Florus 1.1.9, Servius on *Aeneid* 2.7761. 'Obscura atque humilis multitudo': Livy 1.8.5, cf. 2.1.4, Strabo 5.3.2, Plutarch *Romulus* 13.2, Juvenal 8.272–5, Justin 38.7.1.

143 Slaves, outlaws, criminals: Livy 1.8.6, Plutarch *Romulus* 9.3, Minucius Felix *Octavius* 25.2, Augustine *De consensu evangelistarum* 1.19(12), *Contra Cresconium* 2.16(13); hostile tradition referred to at Dionysius of Halicarnassus 1.4.2, 1.89.1, 2.83, 7.70.1; Strasburger 1968.33–4.

Rejection of *conubium*: Livy 1.9.2–5, Ovid *Fasti* 3.189–96, Dionysius of Halicarnassus 2.30.2, Plutarch *Romulus* 9.2 (Alba), Servius *auctus* on *Aeneid* 8.635.

Mars: Cn. Gellius fr. 15P (Aulus Gellius 13.23.13), Ovid *Fasti* 3.197–8; cf. Dionysius of Halicarnassus 2.32.1, Plutarch *Romulus* 14.1 (oracles). Consus: Dionysius of Halicarnassus 2.30.3, Tertullian *De spectaculis* 5.5, Servius on *Aeneid* 8.636; cf. Festus (Paulus) 36L, Plutarch *Romulus* 14.3, etc.

Latins: Livy 1.9.8, Dionysius of Halicarnassus 2.32.2, Plutarch *Romulus* 17.1, Servius on *Aeneid* 8.638.

Signal: Livy 1.9.10, Dionysius of Halicarnassus 2.30.5, Ovid *Ars amatoria* 1.114, Plutarch *Romulus* 14.4, Servius *auctus* on *Aeneid* 8.635. 'Talasios' as Θαλάσσιος ('Neptunus!'): Wiseman 2004 on Plutarch *Romulus* 15.2.

Menfolk flee: Livy 1.19.3, Dionysius of Halicarnassus 2.30.5, Plutarch *Romulus* 14.5.

Marriage by capture: Plutarch *Romulus* 15.5, *Moralia* 271d, 285b–c (*Roman Questions* 29, 87).

Neptunus Equester: Livy 1.9.6, Dionysius of Halicarnassus 1.33.2, 2.31.2–3, Plutarch *Romulus* 14.3, Tertullian *De spectaculis* 5.5, Lydus *De magistratibus* 1.30. Consualia: Varro *De lingua Latina* 6.20, Cicero *De republica* 2.12, Livy 1.9.6, Dionysius of Halicarnassus 2.31.2, Ovid *Fasti* 3.199–200, Plutarch *Romulus* 15.5; 'in the fourth month after the founding of the city' (Fabius Pictor *FGrH* 809 F5).

Latins' war: Livy 1.10.2–11.4, Dionysius of Halicarnassus 2.32.2–36.2, Plutarch *Romulus* 16.3–17.1; Wiseman 1983.446–7.

Lowland Sabines: Velleius Paterculus 1.14.6–8 (*ciuitas sine suffragio* given in 290 BC, voting rights in

268 BC), with Taylor 1960.60–3; cf. Servius on *Aeneid* 7.709 (Romulus gives Sabines *ciuitas sine suffragio*). Mythic Sabines from Cures: Varro *De lingua Latina* 5.51, Virgil *Aeneid* 8.638, Propertius 4.4.9, Dionysius of Halicarnassus 2.36.3, 2.48.1, Ovid *Fasti* 2.135, 2.480, 3.201, *Metamorphoses* 14.778.

Common status: Velleius Paterculus 1.14.1 (historical *communio*); Plutarch *Romulus* 14.2, *Comparison of Theseus and Romulus* 6.2 (mythic κοινωνία).

Admirable motive and behaviour: Livy 1.9.14–16, Dionysius of Halicarnassus 2.30.2–5, 2.31.1, Plutarch *Romulus* 9.2, 14.2, 14.6, *Comparison of Theseus and Romulus* 6.2–3; the Greek authors insist on the absence of ὕβρις.

Rape: Sallust *Histories* 4.69.17M, Propertius 2.6.19–22, Justin 28.2.9, Augustine *City of God* 2.17, 3.13, Orosius 2.4.5; Cicero *De republica* 2.12 ('nouum quoddam et subagreste consilium'), Virgil *Aeneid* 8.635 ('raptas sine more Sabinas').

Battle in the Forum: Livy 1.12.2–3, cf. Dionysius of Halicarnassus 3.1.2, Festus 184L ('tomb of Hostilius'); Livy 1.12.3–7, Plutarch *Romulus* 18.6–7, Florus 1.1.13, cf. Dionysius of Halicarnassus 2.50.3 (Jupiter Stator temple); Piso fr. 12 Forsythe (Varro *De lingua Latina* 5.149), Livy 1.12.9–10, 1.13.5, Dionysius of Halicarnassus 2.42.4–6, Plutarch *Romulus* 18.4 (Lacus Curtius); *De viris illustribus* 2.7 ('ubi nunc forum Romanum est'). Kleidemos and the Amazons: *FGrH* 323 F18 (Plutarch *Theseus* 27.3–4).

Women's intervention: Ovid *Fasti* 3.213–28 (Massey 1757.133), Livy 1.13.1–3, Plutarch *Romulus* 19.1–6, Dio Cassius 1.5.5–7. Massey's solemn translation omits Ovid's joke about the babies: those who could cried 'Grandpa!', and those who couldn't were forced to try. Alternative version (formal embassy by the women): Cn. Gellius fr. 15P (Aulus Gellius 13.23.13), Dionysius of Halicarnassus 2.45.3–46.1; cf. Plutarch *Publicola* 1.1 (speech by Volesus Valerius).

144 Treaty and joint kingship: Cicero *De republica* 2.13, Varro *De lingua Latina* 6.68, Livy 1.13.4–8, Ovid *Fasti* 6.93–7, *Metamorphoses* 14.803–4, Dionysius of Halicarnassus 2.46.1–2, Plutarch *Romulus* 19.7.

Quirinal: Varro *De lingua Latina* 5.51, Dionysius of Halicarnassus 2.50.1, Festus 304L; Curti 2000.83–4.

Statues: Asconius 29C, Pliny *Natural History* 34.22–3.

145 *Saxum Tarpeium*: Seneca *Controversiae* 1.3.3 (description), Dionysius of Halicarnassus 7.35.4, 8.78.5 (position); Coarelli 1985.80–7. L. Tarpeius: Festus 464L (with Scaliger's supplements). Sp. Tarpeius: Plutarch *Romulus* 17.5 (Sulpicius Galba *FGrH* 92 F1), cf. Livy 1.11.6, Valerius Maximus 9.6.1.

Vestal: Varro *De lingua Latina* 5.41, Propertius 4.4; cf. Plutarch *Numa* 10.1 (on the assumption that Numa inaugurated the Vestal college). Tomb: Piso fr. 11 Forsythe (Dionysius of Halicarnassus 2.40.3),

Varro *De lingua Latina* 5.41, Propertius 4.4.1, Plutarch *Romulus* 18.1.

Family: the *lex Tarpeia*, on fines to be paid in sheep or cattle (Festus 270L), was attributed either to a consul of 454 BC (Cicero *De republica* 2.60, Dionysius of Halicarnassus 10.50.2) or to a tribune of 448 BC (Livy 3.65.1).

Offerings: Piso fr. 11 Forsythe (Dionysius of Halicarnassus 2.40.3); cf. Filocalus on 13 February (Degrassi 1963.240–1), 'uirgo Vesta(lis) parentat'.

Antigonos: *FGrH* 816 F2 (Plutarch *Romulus* 17.5); Pais 1906.97–9 and 101. Statue: Festus 496L, in the temple of Jupiter Stator dedicated in 146 BC (Velleius Paterculus 1.11.3). Creative interpretation of statues: e.g. Suetonius *Tiberius* 1.2 (Wiseman 1994.39–44); Festus (Paulus) 109L, 131L (Wiseman 1998.90–4).

Commander: Plutarch *Romulus* 17.2. Daughter: Livy 1.11.6–9, Dionysius of Halicarnassus 2.38–40 (Fabius Pictor *FGrH* 809 F6, Cincius Alimentus *FGrH* 810 F3), Valerius Maximus 9.6.1, Plutarch *Romulus* 17.2–4, Florus 1.1.12. Vestal in love: Propertius 4.4. Piso: fr. 11 Forsythe (Dionysius of Halicarnassus 2.38–40).

Basilica Paulli: Dio Cassius 49.42.2 (dedicated in 34 BC), 54.24.2–3 (rebuilt after fire in 14 BC). Frieze: Carandini and Cappelli 2000.303–19 (article by Darius A. Arya), esp. 304–5 for Tarpeia and the following scene; the latter is implausibly interpreted as a ritual offering at the tomb, but the parallel with the iconography of the 'Aldobrandini wedding' (Carettoni 1961.32–6) makes a bridal context much more likely. Aemilia: Plutarch *Romulus* 2.3.

147 Laws: Festus 260L.

'Titienses' as a cavalry regiment (*turma equitum*): Cicero *De republica* 2.36, Varro *De lingua Latina* 5.91, Festus 484L, Livy 1.13.8, *De viris illustribus* 2.11, Lydus *De magistratibus* 1.9; the Titienses, Ramnes and Luceres were also the three *tribus* of Romulus' citizen body (Ennius in Varro *De lingua Latina* 5.55, etc.).

Cults: Varro *De lingua Latina* 5.74 ('ut annales dicunt') on Ops, Flora, Vediovis, Saturnus, Sol, Luna, Volcanus, Summanus, Larunda, Terminus, Quirinus, Vortumnus, the Lares, Diana, Lucina; Dionysius of Halicarnassus 2.50.3.

Topographical definition: e.g. the Salii Collini (Dionysius of Halicarnassus 2.70.1, 3.32.4).

Tatius and the Laurentine embassy: Livy 1.14.1–3, Dionysius of Halicarnassus 2.51–2, Plutarch *Romulus* 23.1–2; cf. Festus 496L (ambassadors killed by *Titini latrones*). Tatius' tomb: Varro *De lingua Latina* 5.152, Dionysius of Halicarnassus 2.52.5, Plutarch *Romulus* 23.3, Festus 496L.

Apotheosis of Romulus: Ennius *Annales* 54–5 Sk, Horace *Odes* 3.3.15–36, Ovid *Fasti* 2.481–96, *Metamorphoses* 14.805–28; Livy 1.16.1–3, Dionysius of Halicarnassus 2.56.2, Plutarch *Romulus* 27.3 (7

July), 27.6–7; rationalised version at Cicero *De republica* 1.25 ('natura ad humanum exitum abripuit'), 2.17 (eclipse of sun), Florus 1.1.17.

Suspicions: Cicero *De republica* 2.20, Livy 1.16.4, Ovid *Fasti* 2.497–8, Plutarch *Romulus* 27.7–8, *De viris illustribus* 2.13 ('inter patres et populum seditione orta'); cf. Dionysius of Halicarnassus 2.56.3–5. Secession of 287 BC: Livy *Epitome* 11 ('post graues et longas seditiones'), Pliny *Natural History* 16.37, Augustine *City of God* 3.17.

Iulius Proculus: Ennius *Annales* 110–11 Sk (with Skutsch 1985.260–1); Cicero *De republica* 2.20, *De legibus* 1.3, Livy 1.16.5–7, Ovid *Fasti* 2.499–512, Plutarch *Romulus* 28.1–2, Florus 1.1.18, *De viris illustribus* 2.13 ('ut seditionibus abstinerent'). Ovid and Plutarch place the event on the road from Alba; Cicero and the author of *De viris illustribus* put it on the Quirinal (cf. [Plutarch] *Moralia* 313d ἐν ὄρει).

Iulii: many alleged consuls and military tribunes between 489 and 352 BC; L. Iulius Libo consul 267 BC; the Iulii start using the *cognomen* 'Caesar' with Sex. Iulius Caesar, praetor in 208 BC.

Aediles and *ludi*: Cicero *De legibus* 3.7, Livy 6.42.12–14, etc. See in general Bernstein 1998, who however wrongly follows Mommsen in dating the *ludi plebeii* and *Ceriales* to the late third century BC; see ps.Asconius 217 Stangl (*ludi plebeii*), Dionysius of Halicarnassus 6.10.1 and 6.17.2 (*ludi Ceriales*); Wiseman 1995a.133–6, 1998.35–9.

148 Acceptance of Proculus' message: 'mirum est quantum illi uiro nuntianti haec fides fuerit' (Livy 1.16.8); οὐ μὴν ἀλλὰ καὶ δαιμόνιόν τι συνεφάψασθαι πάθος ὅμοιν ἐνθουσιασμῷ (Plutarch *Romulus* 28.3).

Romulus as Quirinus: Cicero *De natura deorum* 2.62 ('quem quidem eundem esse Quirinum putant'), cf. *De officiis* 3.41.

Next time: Plutarch *Pompey* 25.4 (67 BC), Appian *Civil Wars* 2.114 (44 BC); Dionysius of Halicarnassus 2.56.3–4, Valerius Maximus 5.3.1 (Romulus killed in Senate-house); Livy 1.16.4, Plutarch *Romulus* 27.5, [Plutarch] *Moralia* 313d, Florus 1.1.17, Arnobius 1.41.5, Lactantius *Institutiones* 1.15.32–3, Augustine *City of God* 3.15 (Iulius Proculus 'subornatus a patribus').

Chapter 7

149 Curtius: Varro *De lingua Latina* 5.148 (*haruspices*, unpaid vow), Livy 7.6.1–5 ('deum monitu . . . uates canebant'), Valerius Maximus 5.6.2; cf. Dionysius of Halicarnassus 14.11 (Sibylline oracle), Pliny *Natural History* 15.78 (altar and olive), [Plutarch] *Moralia* 306f–307a, Dio Cassius 7.30.2, Zonaras 7.25.

Haydon painting (Plate 14): Pidgley 1986; Pope 1972.28–9 for Elizabeth Barrett's letter.

Cipus: Ovid *Metamorphoses* 15.565–621, Valerius Maximus 5.6.3; cf. Pliny *Natural History* 11.123 ('Actaeonem enim, et Cipum etiam in Latia historia, fabulosos reor').

150 Aelius: Varro *De vita populi Romani* fr. 94 Riposati (Nonius 835L), Valerius Maximus 5.6.4, Frontinus *Stratagems* 4.5.14, Pliny *Natural History* 10.41 (Aelius Tubero). There is a conspicuous lack of Aelii in office between C. Aelius Paetus *cos.* 286 and P. Aelius Paetus *cos.* 201; Valerius Maximus dates the event just before the battle of Cannae, but that can hardly be right (Wiseman 1995a.202 n. 38).

Decius: Livy 8.6.9–13, 8.9.1–10 (*haruspices* at 6.12 and 9.1); Accius *Aeneadae vel Decius* frr. 15–16R (Manuwald 2001.98), [Cicero] *Rhetorica ad Herennium* 4.57, Cicero *De divinatione* 1.51, *De finibus* 2.61, Valerius Maximus 1.7.3, 5.6.5, Florus 1.14.3 ('quasi monitu deorum'), *De viris illustribus* 26.4–5, etc.

295 BC portent: Zonaras 8.1 (Manius the Etruscan prophet), with Wiseman 1995a.119–20.

Aesculapius: Livy 10.31.8, 10.47.6, Valerius Maximus 1.8.2 (three years), Ovid *Metamorphoses* 15.622–744, Orosius 3.21.8, 3.22.4–5, *De viris illustribus* 22, etc.

276 BC: Orosius 4.2.2; Livy fr. 63W (Gelasius *Adversus Andromachum* 12, CSEL 35.1.457: 'Lupercalia autem propter quid instituta sunt . . . Liuius in secunda decade loquitur, nec propter morbos inhibendos instituta commemorat sed propter sterilitatem, ut ei uidetur, mulierum quae tunc acciderat exigendam'); Augustine *City of God* 3.17.

151 Romulus story: Ovid *Fasti* 2.425–52 (443–4 for the Etruscan), Massey 1757.83–6; Wiseman 1995b.14–15.

152 Flagellation for fertility: Plutarch *Caesar* 61.2, Juvenal 2.140–2, etc. For purification: Festus (Paulus) 75–6L, who associates Juno with the Lupercalia. Luperci as goats: Festus (Paulus) 49L ('crepos, id est Lupercos'); cf. 42L (*crepae* were *caprae*, so *crepi* must be *capri*).

153 Fabricius (*cos.* 282, 278) and Curius (*cos.* 290, 275, 274) as symbols of *prisca uirtus*: Cicero *Pro Caelio* 39, *Pro Plancio* 60, *De republica* 3.40, *Paradoxa Stoicorum* 48, *De amicitia* 18, 28, *De natura deorum* 2.165, *Tusculanae disputationes* 1.110, etc.; Valerius Maximus 4.3.5–6 (in the section on *abstinentia* and *continentia*).

Small farms: Dionysius of Halicarnassus 19.15.1 and 6, 19.17.4 (Fabricius, cf. Cicero *Tusculan Disputations* 3.56 on his *paupertas*); Cicero *De republica* 3.40, *De legibus* 2.3, *De senectute* 55–6, Plutarch *Cato maior* 2.1–2 (Curius).

Fabricius and the king's physician: Claudius Quadrigarius fr. 40P (Aulus Gellius 3.8.5–8); Cicero *De officiis* 1.40, 3.86, Seneca *Epistles* 120.6, Plutarch *Pyrrhus* 21.1–3, etc.; slightly different version in Valerius Antias fr. 21P (Aulus Gellius 3.8.1–4), Valerius Maximus 6.5.1. For Fabricius' reaction to Pyrrhos' offer of the post of personal adviser, see

Dionysius of Halicarnassus 19.14–18, Plutarch *Pyrrhus* 20.4.

Lokrian coins: *Lexicon Iconographicum Mythologiae Classicae* 4.2.70. Historian: Agathokles of Kyzikos *FGrH* 472 F5 (Festus 328L).

Fides Publica temple: Cicero *De natura deorum* 2.61 (A. Calatinus' triumph in 257 was probably the occasion).

Thurii story: Valerius Maximus 1.8.6 (from the section *de miraculis*); cf. Servius on *Aeneid* 3.35 ('Gradiuum quod gradum inferant qui pugnant, aut quod impigre gradiantur').

Gods love men of virtue: e.g. Cicero *De natura deorum* 2.165, Plutarch *Numa* 3.3. Virtuous men as quasi-gods: Cicero *Pro Sestio* 143 ('quos equidem in deorum immortalium coetu ac numero repono'), *Pro Caelio* 39 ('diuinis quibusdam bonis instructi').

M'. Curius: Ennius *Annales* fr. 456 Sk (Cicero *De republica* 3.6). Defeat of Pyrrhos: Plutarch *Pyrrhus* 25.2–5, etc. *Anio nouus* aqueduct: Frontinus *De aquis* 1.6.

154 Samnite embassy: Cicero *De republica* 3.40, *De senectute* 55–6, etc. Turnips: Plutarch *Cato maior* 2.2, *Moralia* 194f, Pliny *Natural History* 19.87, Athenaeus 10.419a, *De viris illustribus* 33.7 (earthenware); cf. Valerius Maximus 4.3.5. Same story attributed to Fabricius: Aulus Gellius 1.14, Frontinus *Stratagems* 4.3.2.

Romulus' turnips: Seneca *Apocolocyntosis* 9.5, Martial 13.16; Skutsch 1985.261–2 (from Lucilius?).

Serranus: Cicero *Pro Roscio Amerino* 50, *Pro Sestio* 72, Virgil *Aeneid* 6.844 (with Fabricius), Valerius Maximus 4.4.5, Pliny *Natural History* 18.20; Wiseman 1998.102, suggesting C. Atilius 'Bubulcus' (Orosius 4.12.2, Eutropius 3.3), *cos.* 245 BC.

Cincinnatus: Livy 3.26.7–9 (Penguin Classics translation by Aubrey de Sélincourt, very slightly adapted); Cicero *De senectute* 56, Valerius Maximus 4.4.7, etc.

Regulus: *De viris illustribus* 40.2 ('absente eo coniugi eius et liberis ob paupertatem sumptus publice dati'), cf. Pliny *Natural History* 18.39; Polybius 1.25–35, Diodorus Siculus 23.11–15 (15.1–2 on folly, arrogance and nemesis), perhaps deriving from the pro-Carthaginian historian Philinos of Akragas (*FGrH* 174 F4). Torture of Bodostar and Hamilcar: Diodorus Siculus 24.12.

155 George Washington as Cincinnatus: Wills 1984, esp. 13 (Benjamin West and George III), 197 (Joseph Banks), 225–32 (Houdon's statue [fig. 65]). Byron: McGann 1981.265–6 and 456–7 (stanzas written in 1814 but only published in the 1831 edition of Byron's works).

158 Regulus' mission, return and torture: Sempronius Tuditanus fr. 5P, Aelius Tubero fr. 9P (both in Aulus Gellius 7.4); Cicero *De senectute* 75, *De officiis* 1.39, 3.104, *De finibus* 1.65, Seneca *Dialogues* 1.3.9

(paradigm of *fides*); Livy *Epitome* 18, Florus 1.18.23–6, Eutropius 2.24.2–25.3, Orosius 4.10.1 (mission also *de pace*); Valerius Maximus 1.1.14 (approval of gods), 9.2.ext.1 (Carthaginian cruelty); Augustine *City of God* 1.15, 3.18.

Winged Fides: Ennius *Tragedies* fr. 350 Jocelyn (Cicero *De officiis* 3.104, 'o Fides alma apta pinnis. . .').

Cicero's use of Regulus: *De officiis* 3.99–111 ('illis quidem temporibus aliter facere non potuit', 111).

Temple dates: Festus 228L (Consus, Vortumnus), Tacitus *Annals* 2.49.1–2 (Janus, Flora, Spes), Florus 1.14.2 (Tellus), 1.15.1 (Pales), Ovid *Fasti* 6.193–4 (Tempestates), Servius *auctus* on *Aeneid* 12.139 (Juturna), Cicero *De natura deorum* 3.52 (Fons), Livy 24.10.9, (Volcanus, 214 BC *terminus ante quem*). For Feronia and the Nymphae see respectively Coarelli 1995 and Manacorda 1996.

Roman devotion to gods: e.g. Sherk 1969.214–15, a praetor's letter to Teos in 193 BC ('we are convinced for many reasons that our honouring of the gods is manifest to all'); Sherk 1969.226, a consul's letter to Delphi in 189–188 BC ('because it is our ancestral custom to revere the gods and honour them as the source of all good').

Volcanus (Hephaistos): Homer *Iliad* 1.597–600 (laughter), *Odyssey* 8.266–366 (cuckold); Ovid *Fasti* 4.153–4 (sleeping draught).

159 Metellus and the Vesta temple: Valereius Maximus 1.4.5; Livy *Epitome* 19, Dionysius of Halicarnassus 2.66.3–4, Ovid *Fasti* 6.437–54, Orosius 4.11.9; Pliny (*Natural History* 7.141) says he was blinded, but that was an invention of the rhetorical schools (Seneca *Controversiae* 4.2, with Wiseman 1979a.32–3).

Pales: Florus 1.15.1 (Regulus); Ovid *Fasti* 4.723–82, esp. 744 (*rustica*), 746 (*siluicola*), 752 (nymphs and Pan), 761–2 (Dryads and Faunus); [Virgil] *Culex* 19–20 (Naiads), Statius *Thebaid* 6.110–13 (nymphs and Silvanus), Nemesianus *Eclogues* 1.66–9 (Faunus, nymphs, Flora), 2.55–6 (Silvanus); Servius on *Georgics* 3.1 and 3.294 (goddess of pasture).

'In days of old. . .': Ovid *Fasti* 3.779–82 (Massey 1757.171); cf. 1.205–8 (Janus on the *priscum tempus*).

Feronia: Servius on *Aeneid* 7.799 and 8.564 (*nympha Campaniae*), Strabo 5.2.9 (*lucus Feroniae*); Varro *Antiquitates divinae* fr. 222 Cardauns (Servius *auctus* on *Aeneid* 8.564), identifying her as *Libertas*; Livy 22.1.18 (portents, 217 BC).

Juturna: Varro *De lingua Latina* 5.71, Virgil *Aeneid* 12.138–46, with Servius on 12.139 ('iuxta Numicum fluuium'); Ovid *Fasti* 1.708, Valerius Maximus 1.8.1, etc. (*lacus Iuturnae*).

160 Elysium nymphs: Ovid *Fasti* 5.197–8 ('ubi audis rem fortunatis ante fuisse uiris'), 273–4 (human sexuality part of Flora's power), 347–54 (showgirls); see Wiseman 2002a.293–9.

Flora and Liber: Ovid *Fasti* 5.331–46 (*liberior iocus* 332, cf. 4.946); Ampelius 9.11 ('secundus Liber ex merone at Flora'), with Wiseman 1998.41–2.

Flora, Juno and Mars: Ovid *Fasti* 5.229–60.

Pomona: Ovid *Metamorphoses* 14.623–771. Vortumnus: Propertius 4.2; Festus 228L and *Fasti triumphales* for 264 BC (M. Fulvius Flaccus' triumph over Volsinii).

Flamen Pomonalis: Varro *De lingua Latina* 7.45, Festus 144L; cf. Festus 296L for her cult centre *in agro Solonio*.

'This was her love. . .': Melville 1986.344.

Flora and Priapus: Martial 10.92.11–12.

161 Janus and Cranae: Ovid *Fasti* 6.101–30 (Massey 1757.302), an old story ('obscurior aeuo fama', 103–4). Her technique is reminiscent of Myrrhine's teasing of Kinesias in Pan's cave (Aristophanes *Lysistrata* 904–53).

Carna: Ovid *Fasti* 6.131–68 (her rescue of the infant Proca); Macrobius *Saturnalia* 1.12.31–3 (temple allegedly founded by L. Brutus).

Janus as ruler: Ovid *Fasti* 1.233–54; *Origo gentis Romanae* preface ('a Iano et Saturno conditoribus') and 3.1–7, Macrobius *Saturnalia* 1.7.19–24, both exploiting Virgil *Aeneid* 8.355–8; Plutarch *Numa* 19.6, *Moralia* 268a, 269a, 274f (*Roman Questions* 19, 22, 41) on Janus as the bringer of agriculture and civilised life.

Janus allegorised: Lydus *De mensibus* 4.1–2 (quoting Labeo, Longinus, Messalla, Varro, Fonteius, Gavius Bassus, Lutatius etc.); Macrobius *Saturnalia* 1.9.2–16 (quoting Xenon, Nigidius, Cornificius, Gavius Bassus, Messalla, Varro); cf. also Ovid *Fasti* 1.103–14 (Chaos), 115–20 and Martial 10.28.1 (controller of universe).

Doorkeeper: Ovid *Fasti* 1.125–40 (for the Horae, see Homer *Iliad* 5.749–51 = 8.393–5), Macrobius *Saturnalia* 1.9.9; cf. Gavius Bassus in Lydus *De mensibus* 4.2 (go-between for prayers).

Named first in prayers: Ovid *Fasti* 1.171–4, Martial 8.8.3, Macrobius *Saturnalia* 1.9.3, 1.16.25, *Origo gentis Romanae* 3.7; e.g. Livy 8.9.6 (Decius' *deuotio* prayer in 340 BC).

Janus in the Forum: e.g. Varro *De lingua Latina* 5.165 (Piso fr. 15 Forsythe), Livy 1.19.2–3, Ovid *Fasti* 1.257–8 and 277–85, Velleius Paterculus 2.38.3, Plutarch *Numa* 20.1–2, Procopius *Bellum Gothicum* 1.25 (describing the shrine); Coarelli 1983.89–97.

Porta Ianualis: Varro *De lingua Latina* 5.164–5 (unnecessarily dissociated from the Palatine by Forsythe 1994.185–7), Ovid *Fasti* 1.265, *Metamorphoses* 14.780–1; cf. Macrobius *Saturnalia* 1.9.17 (putting the gate 'sub radicibus collis Viminalis'). The idea of a Romulean defensive wall across the Forum at this point is also implied by Plutarch *Romulus* 11.1–2 on Romulus' *mundus* (cf.

Ovid *Fasti* 4.821–5); Wiseman 2001.190.

162 Boiling water story: Ovid *Fasti* 1.259–76, *Metamorphoses* 14.775–804 (nymphs, 785–92); Macrobius *Saturnalia* 1.19.17–18, Servius on *Aeneid* 1.291, Servius *auctus* on *Aeneid* 8.361. In the *Metamorphoses* version it is Venus who notices Juno's trick; for the nymphs below the *arx*, cf. Propertius 4.4.25 (and 4.4.3–6 for Silvanus' grove); Janus' two faces symbolised the union of the two peoples and their two kings (Servius on *Aeneid* 1.291, 12.198).

Cranae/Carna as *dea cardinis*: Ovid *Fasti* 6.101–2, 127–8; cf. Augustine *City of God* 4.8, 6.7 (Cardea).

Janus and Camasene: Servius *auctus* on *Aeneid* 8.330. Janus and Venilia: Ovid *Metamorphoses* 14.333–4 (320–32 for Picus and the nymphs of Latium, 332–41 for Canens). Janus and Juturna: Arnobius 3.29. In a different narrative mode, Venilia is the mother of Turnus (Virgil *Aeneid* 10.76), and so presumably also of Juturna (*Aeneid* 12.138); according to Servius (on *Aeneid* 6.90 and 12.29) she is the sister of Latinus' wife Amata.

163 Beardless Janus coins: Crawford 1974.133 no. 14.1 (*as*, 280–76 BC); 141 no. 25.4 (*as*, 241–35 BC); 144–7 nos. 28–34 (*quadrigati*). Crawford describes the image as 'Janiform head of Dioscuri', but I think that is mistaken: see Wiseman 1995a.158 and 219 n. 35 (unnecessarily tentative).

Bearded Janus coins: Crawford 1974.147–258 and 304–71, listing 107 issues of *asses* between '225–17' and 146 BC (nos. 35.1–219.2), and 21 more between 114 and 84 BC (nos. 290.2–355.1). Long-term circulation: Crawford 1985.72, 260–1.

'Heads or ships': Ovid *Fasti* 1.229–40, Plutarch *Moralia* 274f (*Roman Questions* 41); Macrobius *Saturnalia* 1.7.22, *Origo gentis Romanae* 3.4–5 (Janus first to strike coins).

Janus' antiquity: Ovid *Fasti* 1.103, 'nam sum res prisca'.

164 Vesta and Jupiter (Hestia and Zeus): Hesiod *Theogony* 454.

Tuccia: Livy *Epitome* 20 (date and condemnation); Dionysius of Halicarnassus 2.69.1–3, cf. 68.1–2 for the context (Vesta's epiphanies); Valerius Maximus 8.1.abs.5 (prayer); Pliny *Natural History* 28.12 (date corrupted in MSS), cf. 28.10 for the context (the power of words and prayer); Tertullian *Apologeticus* 22.12, Augustine *City of God* 10.16, 22.11 (miracles of pagan *daemones*). See Mueller 2002.50–2.

Conception of Scipio: Silius Italicus 13.615–49 (cf. 498–502, prophesied in the Sibylline oracles rejected by Tarquin); historical version in Livy 26.19.7 ('famam in Alexandro magno prius uolgatam, et uanitate et fabula parem'), Valerius Maximus 1.2.1 ('Ioue genitus credebatur'), Dio 16.57.39 (φήμην ἔλαβεν), *De viris illustribus* 49.1 ('Iouis filius creditus').

Jupiter temple: Livy 26.19.5, *De viris illustribus* 49.2–3 (dogs). Reputation: Polybius 10.2.5–13, cf. 10.5.5–6; Livy 26.19.3–9. For the Scipio legend in general see Walbank 1967 (= 1985.120–37), who convincingly argues that the main elements were in place before the mid-second century BC.

Hannibal's oath: Polybius 3.11.4–7, Livy 21.1.4, 35.19.3–4. Hannibal's dream: Silenos *FGrH* 175 F2 (Cicero *De divinatione* 1.49), Valerius Maximus 1.7.ext.1.

Trasimene casualties: Fabius Pictor *FGrH* 809 F22 (Livy 22.7.2–4), Polybius 3.84.7.

Twin temples: Livy 22.9.9–10 (instruction in *fatales libri*), 22.10.10 (vow), 23.31.9 (dedication, 215 BC).

165 Eryx cult: Diodorus 4.83.4–7 (83.6, Roman magistrates μεταβάλλουσιν εἰς παιδιὰς καὶ γυναικῶν ὁμιλίας), Strabo 6.2.6.

Founded by Aeneas: Virgil *Aeneid* 5.759–60; cf. Dionysius of Halicarnassus 1.53.1 where 'Elymos' must refer to Eryx), Tacitus *Annals* 4.43.4 (Tiberius *consanguineus*).

Cannae casualties: Livy 22.49.15; cf. 25.6.13 ('50,000'), Polybius 3.117.4 ('70,000', perhaps a Carthaginian estimate).

Scipio and the conspiracy: Livy 22.53 ('fatalis dux huiusce belli' 53.6, cf. 5.19.2 on Camillus); Valerius Maximus 5.6.7, Silius Italicus 10.415–48, *De viris illustribus* 49.5, Orosius 4.16.6.

Polybian project: Polybius 1.1.5 (Penguin Classics translation by Ian Scott-Kilvert), 6.2.3, 39.8.7. Position of book 6: Polybius 3.2.2–6, 3.118.9; cf. 6.2.1–7 (character best seen in the aftermath of disaster). See in general Walbank 1972.130–56.

Mixed constitution: Polybius 6.11–14; cf. Cicero *De republica* 1.41–55, 1.69. Tacitus (*Annals* 4.33.1) regarded it as merely an intellectual construct, hard to realise and impossible to sustain.

John Adams: quoted in Chinard 1933.209. See in general Richard 1994.123–68.

Bipolar model: the evidence is infinite, but see for instance Cicero *Pro Roscio Amerino* 136, *Pro Sestio* 96; Caesar *Civil War* 1.22.5; Sallust *Catiline* 38.1–3, *Jugurthine War* 41.6–42.1, *Histories* 1.11M; Tacitus *Dialogus* 36.3, *Histories* 2.38.1–2.

166 Sword and shield: Posidonius *FGrH* 87 F42 (Plutarch *Marcellus* 9.4, *Fabius Maximus* 19.3).

Homeric Marcellus: Plutarch *Fabius Maximus* 19.2 (trans. J. and W. Langhorne, 1770).

Single combat: *Fasti triumphales* for 222 BC (Degrassi 1947.550), Livy *Epitome* 20, Propertius 4.10.39–44 (Virdomarus claims descent from Brennus), Virgil *Aeneid* 6.855–9, Plutarch *Marcellus* 6.3–7.3 and *Romulus* 16.7 (calling the king 'Britomartus'), Festus 204L, etc.

Naevius' *Clastidium*: Varro *De lingua Latina* 7.107, 9.78; Manuwald 2001.134–41.

Archimedes at Syracuse: Plutarch *Marcellus* 14.3–17.7 and 19.4–6 (trans. of 19.6 by J. and W. Langhorne, 1770).

Εὕρηκα: Vitruvius *De architectura* 9.pref.10. Δός μοι ποῦ στῶ: Pappus of Alexandria *Mathematika* 1060.3–4.

Fabius' age and ancestry: Sumner 1973.30–2. His strategy: Polybius 3.89.1–90.6. Unpopular: Livy 22.15.1, 22.23.3, 44.22.10.

'Unus homo nobis cunctando restituit rem': Ennius *Annales* 363 Sk, Virgil *Aeneid* 6.846; quoted by Cicero (*Ad Atticum* 2.19.2, *De officiis* 1.84), Livy (30.26.9), Augustus (Suetonius *Tiberius* 21.5, letter to Tiberius), and many others.

167 Polybius on Rome: 3.118.9 (ἰδιότης), 6.3.3 (ποικιλία), 6.11a (lost 'archaeologia'), 6.47.1 (ἔθη καὶ νόμοι).

Citizen army: Polybius 6.52.5–7. Funeral: Polybius 6.53–4 (translation of 53.10 and 54.3–6 by Ian Scott-Kilvert, Penguin Classics).

Procession: Diodorus Siculus 31.25.2, Dionysius of Halicarnassus 7.72.12 (satyr-dancers), Suetonius *Vespasian* 19.2; Flower 1996.97–106.

168 Belief in gods (δεισιδαιμονία): Polybius 6.56.6–12 (56.8 ἐκτετραγώδηται, 56.11 τῇ τοιαύτῃ τραγῳδίᾳ); Mazzarino 1966.61–2.

Myths of Hades: Polybius 6.56.12, cf. Diodorus Siculus 1.2.2. Furies: Cicero *Pro Roscio Amerino* 66–7, *In Pisonem* 46, *De haruspicum responso* 39, *De legibus* 1.40.

Gods on stage: Plautus *Amphitruo* 41–4.

Effect of funeral orations: Polybius 6.54.2 (trans. Ian Scott-Kilvert, Penguin Classics); cf. Sallust *Jugurthine War* 4.5–6.

169 Delphi mission: Livy 22.57.5, 23.11.1–3 (translations from Fontenrose 1978.259); 'lasciuiam a uobis prohibetote' at 23.11.3. Pictor: Appian *Hannibalic War* 27.

Prophets and holy men (*uates et sacrificuli*): Livy 25.1.8 (Rome 213 BC); cf. Theopompus *FGrH* 115 F248 (Metapontum *c*.355 BC), *Epistles of Diogenes* 38.2 (Olympia fourth century BC), Apuleius *Metamorphoses* 2.13–4 (Corinth second century AD).

Complaint of *boni* and Senate's crackdown: Livy 25.1.9–12, 25.12.3.

The *carmina Marciana*: Livy 25.12.2–15 (translations adapted from W.F. Roberts, Everyman Library 1912); cf. Cicero *De divinatione* 1.89 ('Marcios quosdam fratres nobili loco natos'), 1.115 (Marcius *uates*), 2.113 (Marcii *uates*, plural); Festus 162L ('in carmine Cn. Marci uatis').

170 Hannibal's camp at the Anio: Polybius 9.5.9 (40 stades, i.e. five miles), Livy 26.10.3 (three miles), Appian *Hannibalic War* 38 (32 stades, i.e. four miles), Eutropius 3.14.1 (four miles).

Panic: Polybius 9.6.1–4, Livy 26.9.6–8, Silius Italicus 12.545–50.

Consuls' defence: Polybius 9.6.5–9. Gods' defence: Livy 26.11.4 ('in religionem ea res apud Poenos uersa est'), Florus 1.22.44–5, Silius Italicus 12.574–730, Zonaras 9.6 (ὦ Κάνναι Κάνναι).

171 'Salua res est, saltat senex': Festus 436–8L, quoting Verrius Flaccus; for the *parasiti Apollinis*, cf. Martial 9.28.9 and *ILS* 5186, 5189, 5193–4, 5196, 5200, 5201, 5209a, 5275 (mainly second century AD).

Nonae Caprotinae play: Varro *De lingua Latina* 6.18 (reading *togata praetexta* with the MSS); discussion in Coarelli 1997.38–46, Wiseman 1998.8–11, Manuwald 2001.66–71.

Ludi Apollinares dates: Degrassi 1963.477–8.

Tutula play scenario: based on Plutarch *Romulus* 29.3–5, *Camillus* 33.2–5, Polyaenus 8.30, Macrobius 1.11.35–40, Polemius Silvius on 7 July (*CIL* I² p. 269); cf. Ovid *Ars amatoria* 2.258, [Plutarch] *Moralia* 313a (*FGrH* 286 F1), who have Gauls rather than Latins as the enemy.

172 Slave-girls in mistresses' clothes: Ausonius 14.16.9–10. *Caprificus* in Campus Martius: Historia Augusta *Marcus Aurelius* 13.6; Coarelli 1997.56–7, 180–1. Sacrifice: Varro *De lingua Latina* 6.18 (*mulieres*), Macrobius *Saturnalia* 1.11.36 ('liberae pariter ancillaeque'). Use of branches and sap: Varro *De lingua Latina* 6.18, Macrobius *Saturnalia* 1.11.40; explained by Coarelli 1997.39–40. Sheets hung on boughs: Plutarch *Romulus* 29.6, *Camillus* 33.6 (and implied in the aetiological story). Feast, play, joking: Plutarch *Romulus* 29.6, *Camillus* 33.6.

Letter of Philip V: *Sylloge inscriptionum Graecarum*³ 543, translated in Austin 1981.118.

173 Togas worn by women in early Rome: Nonius 867L (citing Afranius fr. 182R), Varro *De vita populi Romani* fr. 44 Riposati; Servius on *Aeneid* 1.282.

174 *Liberior iocus*: Ovid *Fasti* 4.496, 5.332.

Scipio's election: Livy 26.18.6–19.2 ('quattuor et uiginti ferme annos natus', 18.7).

Carthago Nova and Neptunus: Polybius 10.11.7 (Scipio's dream), 10.14.11–12 (effect on troops); Livy 26.45.9.

'Continence of Scipio': Livy 26.50 (cf. 26.49.14 on 'mea populique Romani disciplina'), Valerius Maximus 4.3.1, Frontinus *Stratagems* 2.11.5, Silius Italicus 15.268–82, etc. The story must pre-date Valerius Antias (fr. 25P, A. Gellius 7.8.6), who claims that it was false and Scipio kept her as his concubine. Paintings: Pigler 1974.2.424–9 (181 examples).

Sibylline books, 205 BC: Livy 29.10.4–8, Ovid *Fasti* 4.255–62, Silius Italicus 17.1–4.

Embassy: Livy 29.11.1–8 (11.5–6 and 8 for Delphi and the *uir optimus*), Ovid *Fasti* 4.263–72; cf. Diodorus Siculus 34.33.2 (text unfortunately corrupt), who attributes the 'best man' requirement to the Sibyl.

175 Sacred stone: Livy 29.11.7, Appian *Hannibalic War* 56.

Nasica 'qui uir optimus a senatu iudicatus est': Cicero *De haruspicum responso* 27, Livy 29.14.6–9 (doesn't know on what criterion), Velleius Paterculus 2.3.1, Valerius Maximus 8.15.3 (*sanctissimus*), Pliny *Natural History* 7.120, Silius Italicus 17.6–7, Appian *Hannibalic War* 56, Dio Cassius 17.61 (εὐσεβὴς καὶ δίκαιος), etc.

Q. Claudia 'quae matronarum castissima putabatur': Cicero *De haruspicum responso* 27 (with Wiseman 1979a.95–9); cf. Diodorus Siculus 34.33.2, where the name Valeria suggests a revisionist version by Valerius Antias (cf. Wiseman 1998.75–89), and Ovid *Fasti* 4.260 (*casta manu*), who like Diodorus attributes the requirement to the Sibyl.

Q. Claudia miracle story: Ovid *Fasti* 4.291–328 (Massey 1757.200–1); Propertius 4.11.51–2, Pliny *Natural History* 7.120, Silius Italicus 17.23–45, Suetonius *Tiberius* 2.3, Appian *Hannibalic War* 56, etc. A later development made her a Vestal Virgin accused of unchastity, like Tuccia: Statius *Silvae* 1.2.245–6 (*uirgo*), Herodian 1.11.4, *De viris illustribus* 46.1–2.

177 Q. Claudia play: Ovid *Fasti* 4.326 ('mira sed et scaena testificata loquar') and 4.310 ('ad rigidos promptaque lingua senes'); Massey omits 326 and mistranslates 310.

Ludi Megalenses and Cybele cult: Cicero *De haruspicum responso* 24 ('more institutisque maxime casti, sollemnes, religiosi'), Lucretius 2.618–23, Dionysius of Halicarnassus 2.19.3–5, Aulus Gellius 2.24.2 (dinners of *principes ciuitatis*), etc. See Beard et al 1998.1.97–8 and 164–6, 2.43–9.

Trojan ancestress: Ovid *Fasti* 4.247–76, with an allusion at 274 to Aeneas' ships (Virgil *Aeneid* 3.5–6, 9.80–9). Ida: Hesiod *Theogony* 1010 (Aeneas' birthplace), Hellanikos *FGrH* 4 F31 (Dionysius of Halicarnassus 1.47.3–6, Trojan survivors).

Generals' prayers: Virgil *Aeneid* 10.252–5; Cicero *De haruspicum responso* 28 ('ut. . . nostri imperatores maximis et periculosissimis bellis huic deae uota facerent'), Plutarch *Marius* 31.1.

Son of Jupiter: Silius Italicus 17.653–4 ('nec uero, cum te memorat de stirpe deorum | prolem Tarpei mentitur Roma tonantis').

Chapter 8

179 'When all the world': Lucretius 3.834–7 (trans. Cyril Bailey, 1947).

Flamininus: Polybius 18.46 (Isthmian Games scene), Plutarch *Titus Flamininus* 12.6–7 (Delphi dedications).

180 Post-Magnesia diplomacy: Livy 37.45.8–12.

Booty: Livy 34.52.2–11 (triumph of T. Flamininus, 194 BC), 37.46.3–4 (of Manius Acilius, 190), 37.59.3–6 (of L. Scipio, 189), 39.6.6–7.3 (of Cn. Manlius, 187); see especially 39.6.7, 'luxuriae enim peregrinae origo ab exercitu Asiatico inuecta in urbem est'.

M. Cato: Livy 39.40.4 and 9–11 (trans. Henry Bettenson, Penguin Classics); Plutarch *Cato maior* 2.1–2 (Curius' cottage); 3.5–7, 11.1–2, 15.1–2, 18.1 (Scipio); 17.1–5, 19.2 (Flamininus). See Astin 1978.59–77 on the political disputes of 190–184 BC.

Censorship: Astin 1978.78–103, esp. 91–8 for his attack on luxury; Plutarch *Cato maior* 19.4 for the Salus temple statue (doubted by Astin 1978.103 n.89).

181 Cato on fish: Plutarch *Cato maior* 8.1 (cf. Polybius 31.25.5a, where the reference is to a jar of pickled fish from the Black Sea).

Fish at Macellum: Plautus *Aulularia* 373, *Pseudolus* 169, *Rudens* 979–81; cf. Terence *Eunuchus* 255–7 ('macellum. . . cuppedinarii. . . piscatores'). Forum Cuppedinis: Varro *De lingua Latina* 5.146. 179 BC censors: Livy 40.51.5.

Equitius and Romanius: Varro fr. 121 Funaioli (Donatus on Terence *Eunuchus* 255–7, Festus [Paulus] 42L), and *De lingua Latina* 5.147; Festus (Paulus) 112L for the censors.

182 Cato on Greeks: Pliny *Natural History* 29.13–14, cf. Plutarch *Cato maior* 23.2; Astin 1978.170–8, esp. 171 (translation), 173–4 (luxury).

Pergraecari: Plautus *Bacchides* 813, *Mostellaria* 22–4 (Segal 1968.33) and 960, *Poenulus* 603, *Truculentus* 88; see Segal 1968 passim, esp. 32–41.

Bacchanalia: Livy 39.8–19, esp. 8.3 ('Graecus ignobilis. . . sacrificulus et uates'), 12.4 (*lucus Stimulae*), 15.3 (consul's speech, trans. P.G. Walsh, 1994), 16.4 ('ad rem publicam opprimendam'), 16.6–9 (Roman v. alien *religio*), 17.4 ('magnus terror urbe tota fuit'), 17.6 (7,000 men and women), 18.5 (majority executed). 'Conspiracy' (*coniuratio*): Livy 39.8.3, 14.4, 14.8, 16.5, 18.3; *ILLRP* 511.34 ('De Bacanalibus quei foideratei esent').

Wine and sex: Livy 39.8.5–6, 10.7, 13.10–11, 15.9. Play-acting: Livy 39.13.12–13; cf. Plautus *Casina* 980 ('nunc Bacchae nullae ludunt').

Senate: Livy 39.14.3–8, 17.1–4, 18.8–9; for the ideological context see Wiseman 1994.35–43. Popular: Livy 39.13.14 (*multitudo ingens*).

Numa's books: Pliny *Natural History* 13.84–7, citing the various versions in Cassius Hemina, Piso, Tuditanus, Varro and Valerius Antias; Livy 40.29.2–14, Plutarch *Numa* 22.2–5, etc.; Gruen 1990.163–70, Goldberg 1995.124–30.

Villa Lante painting (fig. 70): Gnann 1996.

183 Hercules and the Muses: Cicero *Pro Archia* 27, Ovid *Fasti* 6.799–800 and 811–12, Pliny *Natural History* 35.66, Eumenius *Panegyrici Latini* 9(4).7–8.

Pomponius Musa coins (fig. 71): Crawford 1974.437–9, no. 410.

Homer and Ennius: Lucretius 1.120–6, Cicero *Academica* 2.51, Porphyrio on Horace *Epistles* 2.1.51,

scholiast on Persius 6.11; Goldberg 1995.89–92. Three hearts: Aulus Gellius 17.17.1.

Naevius (died 201 BC): Cicero *De senectute* 50 (*Bellum Punicum* written in his old age); Macrobius *Saturnalia* 6.2.31, Servius *auctus* on *Aeneid* 4.9 (Dido and Anna); Nonius 760L (Dido[?] asks Aeneas how he left Troy); see Goldberg 1995.51–6.

Muses: Varro *De re rustica* 1.1.4 ('ut Homerus et Ennius'); *De lingua Latina* 7.20 (Ennius *Annales* fr. 1 Sk), cf. 7.25 (fr. 487 Sk, identifying them with the Latin Camenae).

Ennius' citizenship: Cicero *Brutus* 79.

'Yearly records': cf. Ennius *Annales* frr. 154–5 Sk (years from foundation), 304–6 Sk (consular date).

185 Prose historians: Q. Fabius Pictor, L. Cincius Alimentus, P. Cornelius Scipio, A. Postumius Albinus (*FGrH* 809–12); Badian 1966.2–7.

Recitations: for Ennius recitals, see Suetonius *De grammaticis* 2.1 (Q. Vargunteius), Aulus Gellius 18.5.2–4 (in the theatre at Puteoli). That early Roman epic was primarily an oral mode is shown by the fact that Naevius' *Bellum Punicum* was only edited as a seven-book text fifty years or so after the poet's death (by C. Octavius Lampadio, Suetonius *De grammaticis* 2.2); for the parallel with Homeric ῥαψῳδίαι, see Pfeiffer 1968.115–16 and Kaster 1995.65.

'Moribus antiquis res stat Romana uirisque': Ennius *Annales* fr. 156 Sk (Cicero *De republica* 5.1); cf. fr. 363 and 456 Sk, on Manius Curius and Fabius Cunctator.

'New cleverness' (*noua sapientia*): Livy 42.47.1–9 (*moris antiqui memores* 47.4, cf. 47.6 for *fides* and the Pyrrhos story).

Aemilius Paullus monument (fig. 72): Kähler 1965, Holliday 2002.91–6.

Castor and Pollux epiphany: Cicero *De natura deorum* 2.6, 3.11, Valerius Maximus 1.8.1 (P. Vatienus of Reate); Suetonius *Nero* 1.1 (L. Domitius). The alternative version (Florus 1.28.14–15, Minucius Felix *Octavius* 7.3) has them announce the victory itself at the Lacus Iuturnae in Rome—an exact doublet of the story of the battle of Lake Regillus three centuries earlier.

Royal galley: Livy 45.35.3, Plutarch *Aemilius Paullus* 30.2. Triumph: Plutarch *Aemilius Paullus* 32.4–34.7, Livy 45.40.1–8. Pydna and Rome's world power: Polybius 3.3.8–9.

186 Scipio stemma (fig. 73): Münzer 1920.102 = 1999.98.

187 Scipio Aemilianus: Polybius 31.25.2–8 (trans. Ian Scott-Kilvert, Penguin Classics).

Policy debate: Diodorus Siculus 34/35.33.3–6; Livy *Epitome* 49, Florus 1.31.4–5, Plutarch *Cato maior* 27.1–3, Appian *Libyka* 69, Augustine *City of God* 1.30; Astin 1967.276–80.

Scipio and Polybios: Polybius 38.21.1–3, cf. Diodorus 32.24, Appian *Libyka* 132; Astin 1967.282–7.

188 Bronze beards: Plutarch *Aemilius Paullus* 25.2–4 (Lake Regillus story); Suetonius *Nero* 1.1, Tertullian *Apologeticus* 22.12 (context not given).

Nero's ancestors: Velleius Paterculus 2.10.2 (cf. 2.72.3), Suetonius *Nero* 1.5; Syme 1970.33–4, 1986.155–7.

189 C. Laelius in 140 BC: Plutarch *Tiberius Gracchus* 8.4; Astin 1967.307–10.

Agrarian law and deposition of M. Octavius: Plutarch *Tiberius Gracchus* 8–12, Appian *Civil Wars* 1.7–12; Astin 1967.190–210. Tiberius on the tribunate: Plutarch *Tiberius Gracchus* 15, cf. Appian *Civil Wars* 1.12.51.

'The catastrophe' (Astin 1967.211–26): Valerius Maximus 3.2.17 (an *exemplum* of bravery in civilian life); [Cicero] *Ad Herennium* 4.55.68 (to illustrate vivid narrative—*demonstratio* or ἐνάργεια); cf. Velleius Paterculus 2.3.1–3, Plutarch *Tiberius Gracchus* 16–19, Appian *Civil Wars* 1.14–16.

191 Cornelia: Seneca *Consolatio ad Marciam* 16.3 (twelve children), Plutarch *Tiberius Gracchus* 1.4 (Ptolemy's offer), Valerius Maximus 4.4.pref.1 (jewels story).

Sempronia's marriage: Plutarch *Tiberius Gracchus* 4.4 (before 146 BC), Valerius Maximus 6.2.3. Sons' education: Cicero *Brutus* 104, 211, Tacitus *Dialogus* 28.5, Plutarch *Tiberius Gracchus* 1.5, 8.5 ('How long. . .?').

Aemilianus' reply: Plutarch *Tiberius Gracchus* 21.4 (Homer *Odyssey* 1.47), Velleius Paterculus 2.4.4 (*iure caesum*). His death (Astin 1967.240–1): Appian *Civil Wars* 1.20.83 (Cornelia and Sempronia); cf. Livy *Epitome* 59, Orosius 5.10.9–10 (Sempronia only), Cicero *De republica* 6.12 ('impias propinquorum manus').

Rival claims about Cornelia's politics: Plutarch *Gaius Gracchus* 13.2. Letters: Nepos fr. 1–2 OCT ('miscenda atque perturbanda re publica'); see Horsfall 1989.41–3 and 125–6.

Statue (fig. 74): Plutarch *Gaius Gracchus* 4.3, Pliny *Natural History* 34.31, *CIL* 6.31610; Coarelli 1996.280–99.

192 Never before: Velleius Paterculus 2.3.3, Plutarch *Tiberius Gracchus* 20.1, Appian *Civil Wars* 1.2.4, 1.17.71.

Gracchus' supporters: Livy *Epitome* 58, Plutarch *Tiberius Gracchus* 19.6 ('more than three hundred'), 20.2 (Tiber), Appian *Civil Wars* 1.16.70, Orosius 5.9.3 ('two hundred'), etc.

Subsequent executions: Sallust *Jugurthine War* 32.7 ('in plebem Romanam quaestiones habitae sunt'), Velleius Paterculus 2.7.3, Valerius Maximus 4.7.1, Plutarch *Tiberius Gracchus* 20.3, etc.

Sacrosanctity of tribunes: Dionysius of Halicarnassus 6.89.3–4, Livy 3.55.6–10, Festus 422L, etc. Deputation to Enna: Cicero *In Verrem* 4.108.

Liber, the Senate and the urban praetor: Livy 39.18.8–9; *ILLRP* 511.4–9 and 16–21.

Senate's resolution: Cicero *In Catilinam* 1.4, *Philippics* 8.14, Plutarch *Gaius Gracchus* 14.3; Lintott 1999.89–93.

Consul's military action and the death of Gaius Gracchus: Plutarch *Gaius Gracchus* 13–17, Appian *Civil Wars* 1.25–6, Orosius 5.12.5–9, etc.

Concordia temple: Plutarch *Gaius Gracchus* 17.6, Appian *Civil Wars* 1.26.120, Augustine *City of God* 3.25.

Early version of the 'demagogue' Sp. Cassius: Cicero *De republica* 2.60, where *ut audistis* implies a source earlier than the dramatic date of 129 BC (Ogilvie 1965.338 suggests Fabius Pictor); Cassius enjoyed *summa apud populum gratia*, but was put to death *cedente populo* after a trial before a quaestor (another anachronism: Ogilvie 1965.344–5).

Early version of the 'demagogue' Sp. Maelius: Cincius Alimentus *FGrH* 810 F4 (Dionysius of Halicarnassus 12.4.2–6); Maelius was killed by a private citizen, Servilius Ahala, who was pursued by the furious populace until he explained he was acting on the Senate's orders.

Historians writing in Latin: Badian 1966.7–15 on Cato, Cn. Gellius, L. Piso and C. Fannius, though I think he is wrong to classify Piso separately from 'the Gracchan historians' (Forsythe 1994.32–6 on the date of Piso's *Annales*).

193 Sp. Cassius and land distribution: Livy 2.41, Dionysius of Halicarnassus 8.69–79, Valerius Maximus 5.8.2 ('qui tribunus plebis agrariam legem primus tulerat'), etc.

Sp. Maelius and grain distribution: Cicero *Pro Milone* 72, Livy 4.13–16, Dionysius of Halicarnassus 12.1–4; cf. Wiseman 1998.99–101 on the historiographical development of the episode.

Teaching by example: e.g. Sempronius Asellio fr. 2P (Aulus Gellius 5.18.9), Livy pref. 10, Valerius Maximus 1 pref.

Cassius, Maelius, Gracchus: Cicero *De amicitia* 36–7, *De republica* 2.49 (both with a dramatic date of 129 BC); cf. *In Catilinam* 1.3, *Pro Milone* 72 (Maelius and Ti. Gracchus).

Memory of the Gracchi: Plutarch *Gaius Gracchus* 17.6 (Concordia as *discordia*), 18.2 (shrines), 19.1–2 (Cornelia). Cornelia's pride in her dead sons: Seneca *Consolatio ad Marciam* 16.3, *Consolatio ad Helviam* 16.6.

Tribune's speech (C. Memmius, 111 BC): Sallust *Jugurthine War* 31; for the clique, cf. 31.1 (*opes factionis*), 31.2 (*superbia paucorum*), 31.9 (*pauci nobiles*), 31.19 (*pauci potentes*).

194 'Nine Tribunes' Pyre': Dio 5.22 = Zonaras 7.17 (murderous patricians about 470 BC); Festus 180L (white stone, near the Circus, military tribunes in 487); Valerius Maximus 6.3.2 (P. Mucius and his colleagues in 486).

Penalty for non-election of successors: Diodorus Siculus 12.25.3 (at the restitution of the tribunate after the Decemvirs).

Beccafumi painting (Plate 16): Sanminiatelli 1967 no. 47i.

195 Sallust as tribune (52 BC): Asconius 37C, 49C. Burning of Senate house: Cicero *Pro Milone* 90, Asconius 33C, Dio Cassius 40.49.3.

Cicero's republic: Cicero *De legibus* 3.9 (tribunes), 3.10 (Senate: 'eius decreta rata sunto. . . is ordo uitio uacato, ceteris specimen esto'); discussion at 3.19–32, esp. 26 (Quintus and Atticus on the tribunate), 28 (Senate as *dominus publici consilii*).

δημοκρατία and ἀριστοκρατία: Diodorus Siculus 34/35.25.1 (Posidonius *FGrH* 87 F111b), Plutarch *Gaius Gracchus* 5.3, Appian *Civil Wars* 1.103.478, etc.: see Ste. Croix 1981.322–3, Pelling 2002.211–17.

Roman equivalents: Cicero *De republica* 1.42–3, *Pro Sestio* 96, etc.: Hellegouarc'h 1963.484–565.

Cicero's admission: Cicero *De legibus* 3.29 ('non de hoc senatu nec his de hominibus qui nunc sunt, sed de futuris, si forte his legibus parere uoluerint, haec habetur oratio').

Sallust's diagnosis: Sallust *Catiline* 10.3–4, *Jugurthine War* 41.7 (trans. S.A. Handford, Penguin Classics).

196 People v. Senate: Sallust *Catiline* 4.2, 38, 54; *Jugurthine War* 4.7–8, 40.5, 41.5, etc. *Popularis* spokesmen: Sallust *Catiline* 20, 33; *Jugurthine War* 31, 85; *Histories* 1.55M, 3.48M.

Party strife to civil war: Sallust *Jugurthine War* 5.2, *Histories* 1.12M; cf. Velleius Paterculus 2.3.3 (on the murder of Ti. Gracchus, 'hoc initium in urbe Roma ciuilis sanguinis gladiorumque impunitatis fuit'), Appian *Civil Wars* 1.55.240, 1.60.269 (on Sulla's march on Rome).

Trumpet: Plutarch *Sulla* 7.3.

Sulla's march on Rome: Appian *Civil Wars* 1.55–60 (translation by Horace White, Loeb ed.), Plutarch *Sulla* 8–9, etc.

Tribunes' powers abolished: Appian *Civil Wars* 1.59.267 (88 BC), 1.100.467 (81 BC). Sulla's dictatorship: Appian *Civil Wars* 1.98–9.459–63.

Villa Publica: Livy 4.22.7, Varro *De re rustica* 3.2.4; Coarelli 1997.164–75 (esp. 174–5 on *frumentationes*).

Seven thousand citizens: Seneca *De clementia* 1.12.2, Augustine *City of God* 3.28; cf. [Sallust] *Epistula ad Caesarem* 4.1 (*plebs Romana*), Livy *Epitome* 88 (8,000 *dediticii*), Valerius Maximus 9.2.1 ('four legions of the opposite party'), Strabo 5.4.11 (3–4,000 Samnites), Plutarch *Sulla* 30.1–2 (6,000), *De uiris illustribus* 75.10 (9,000 *dediticii*), Orosius 5.21.1 (3,000).

Sulla's comment: Seneca *De clementia* 1.12.2, Plutarch *Sulla* 30.3.

197 Cimbri and Teutoni: Strabo 7.2.1–3, Tacitus *Germania* 37.1–2; Pliny *Natural History* 2.167

(Jutland). Wagons: Strabo 7.2.3, Plutarch *Marius* 11.2, 27.2–3, Florus 1.38.16–17.

Challenge to *superbia nobilitatis*: Sallust *Jugurthine War* 5.2 (exemplified against Marius at 64.1). Marius and the *nobiles*: Sallust *Jugurthine War* 84–5.

Soothsayer: Sallust *Jugurthine War* 63.1, Plutarch *Marius* 8.4.

Cimbri in control of Transpadana: Plutarch *Marius* 24.2. Marius' victories: Florus 1.38, Plutarch *Marius* 15–27. Third founder: Plutarch *Marius* 27.5 (Livy 5.49.7 for Camillus as the second).

Sixth and seventh consulships: Appian *Civil Wars* 1.29–32 and 71–5. Biographer's verdict: Plutarch *Marius* 2.3 (trans. Bernadotte Perrin, Loeb ed.).

198 Sulla's innovation: Velleius Paterculus 2.28.3 ('primus ille, et utinam ultimus. . .'), Florus 2.9.25 ('noui generis edictum'), Appian *Civil Wars* 1.95.442.

Proscription lists: Valerius Maximus 9.2.1 (final total), Plutarch *Sulla* 31.3, Orosius 5.21.3; cf. Appian *Civil Wars* 1.95.442 (40 senators, 1,600 *equites*).

Torture: Plutarch *Cato minor* 3.2, Appian *Civil Wars* 1.2.8; most notoriously M. Marius Gratidianus at the tomb of the Lutatii (Sallust *Histories* 1.44M, Livy *Epitome* 88, Valerius Maximus 9.2.1, Seneca *De ira* 3.18.1–2, etc.).

In the street: Cicero *Pro Roscio Amerino* 89 (at the Lacus Servilius), Appian *Civil Wars* 1.95.443.

Severed heads: Asconius 84C, Lucan 2.160–73. Forum: Seneca *De providentia* 3.7–8 (Lacus Servilius), Plutarch *Sulla* 32.2. Rostra: Dio Cassius 30–35.109.21. Sulla's house: Valerius Maximus 3.1.2, Plutarch *Cato minor* 3.3.

Marius' ashes: Cicero *De legibus* 2.56, Valerius Maximus 9.2.1. Marius' monuments: Suetonius *Divus Iulius* 11 ('a Sulla disiecta').

Sulla's constitution: Cicero *De legibus* 3.22, Velleius Paterculus 2.30.4, Appian *Civil Wars* 1.100.467, etc. (tribunes); Cicero *In Verrem actio prima* 37, Velleius Paterculus 2.32.3, etc. (juries).

Restored republic: Cicero *Pro Roscio Amerino* 139 ('dum necesse erat resque ipsa cogebat, unus omnia poterat, qui postea quam magistratus creauit legesque constituit, qua cuique procuratio auctoritasque est restituta').

Roscius case: Cicero *Brutus* 312 ('prima causa publica'), Plutarch *Cicero* 3.2–4.

Cicero on the *causa nobilitatis*: *Pro Roscio Amerino* 135–42, esp. 136–7 ('quis enim erat qui non uideret humilitatem cum dignitate de amplitudine contendere. . .?'). Translation of 139 ('nostri isti nobiles nisi uigilantes et boni et fortes et misericordes erunt. . .') by Rawson 1975.24.

Cicero and ἀριστοκρατία: Plutarch *Cicero* 22.1, probably from Cicero's Greek monograph on his consulship (Pelling 2002.47).

Cicero as *popularis*: Q. Cicero *Commentariolum*

petitionis 53; e.g. Cicero *In Verrem* 5.175 (70 BC), *Pro lege Manilia* 1–2 and 63–4 (66 BC), Asconius 74–8C (65 BC).

Crowd (*corona*) around court: Cicero *Brutus* 290, Catullus 53, Seneca *Epistles* 114.12, Tacitus *Dialogus* 20.3, etc.

Peroration on *crudelitas*: Cicero *Pro Roscio Amerino* 154 ('populum Romanum . . . domestica crudelitate laborare').

199 Licinius Macer: Sallust *Histories* 3.48M (his speech in 73 BC). Text and commentary in Walt 1997; political analysis in Ogilvie 1965.7–12, Wiseman 2002b.295–302.

Rape by Amulius: *Origo gentis Romanae* 19.5. Lykaina: John Malalas 7.7.178–80 (from 'Licinius, the Roman chronicler').

Quarrel and riot: *Origi gentis Romanae* 23.5 (from Licinius Macer's Book I); cf. Livy 1.6.4 ('auitum malum, regni cupido'), 1.7.2, Dionysius of Halicarnassus 1.85.4–5 (στάσις, πλεονέκτημα), 1.87.1–2 (ἔρις, φιλονεικία).

Death of Romulus: Livy 1.16.4 (cf. 1.15.8 'multitudini gratior fuit quam patribus'), 2.56.4, Valerius Maximus 5.3.1, Plutarch *Romulus* 27.5, [Plutarch] *Moralia* 313d, Florus 1.1.17, Arnobius 1.41.5; Dionysius and Valerius Maximus put the murder in the Senate house, no doubt influenced by the Ides of March 44 BC (cf. Appian *Civil Wars* 2.114.476 for the parallel).

200 Iulius Proculus lying: implied by Livy 1.16.5 ('consilio. . . unius hominis'), explicit in Lactantius *Institutiones* 1.15.32–3, Augustine *City of God* 3.15 ('subornatus a patribus').

'Tyrannical' Romulus: Dionysius of Halicarnassus 2.56.3, Plutarch *Romulus* 26.1–2, 27.1–2, Appian *Civil Wars* 2.114.476.

67 BC: Plutarch *Pompey* 25.4; C. Piso's rash remark is the earliest evidence for this version of Romulus' death, and the reason for attributing it to Licinius Macer's recently published history.

Origin of the 'struggle of the orders': Livy 2.23.1–9, Dionysius of Halicarnassus 6.26.1–2; I have borrowed a paragraph from Wiseman 2002b.296–7.

Licinius as first tribune: Livy 2.33.2, Dionysius of Halicarnassus 6.89.1; contrast Asconius 77C (citing Sempronius Tuditanus, Cicero and Atticus); Forsythe 1994.292–3. Macer on Licinii: Livy 7.9.5 ('quaesita ea propriae familiae laus').

Licinius as first plebeian consul: *De viris illustribus* 20.2 (surely from Macer); contrast Livy 6.42.9, 7.1.1–2, and the *fasti consulares* for 366 BC (Degrassi 1947.32–3).

Brutal creditors: Sallust *Catiline* 33.1 (63 BC); cf. *Histories* 1.11M (early Republic), 3.48.26–7M (Macer's speech), with Wiseman 2002b.297–300.

Pompey and the backlash: Sallust *Catiline* 38.1–39.2.

201 Spartacus (Bradley 1989.83–101): Plutarch *Crassus* 8–11, Appian *Civil Wars* 1.116–20 (116.542 for the figure 70,000). Proverbial enemy: Cicero *De haruspicum responso* 26, *Philippics* 4.15; Horace *Epodes* 16.5, *Odes* 3.14.19; cf. Eutropius 6.7.2 for Spartacus and Hannibal.

Modern views: Montesquieu *Pensées* 174 and 2194 (Masson 1950.59, 659), Marx-Engels 1985.265; Rubinsohn 1987 (p. 6 for Stalin), Koestler 1939 (quotation from ch. 12), Fast 1952 (dedication quoted); Shaw 2001.14–24. Spartacus on stage and screen: Wyke 1997.34–72, Futrell 2001.

Reality: Appian *Civil Wars* 1.116.540 (free men), 120.559 (crucifixions).

202 Marius' trophies (65 BC, Caesar aedile): Velleius Paterculus 2.43.4, Suetonius *Divus Iulius* 11, Plutarch *Caesar* 6.1–4 (all emphasising optimate hostility). Murder court (64 BC): Suetonius *Divus Iulius* 11, Dio Cassius 37.10.2–3.

Revenues: Plutarch *Pompey* 45.3 (from 50 million to 135 million *denarii*). Tribunes' programme: Cicero *De lege agraria* 2.7–10 (*populares*), 2.11 (planning sessions), 2.31 (Gracchan precedent); Dio Cassius 37.25.4 (debt and land); Gelzer 1968.43 n. 1 for Caesar's involvement.

Italy: Cicero *In Catilinam* 2.6 (Apulia, Etruria, Picenum, *ager Gallicus*), *Pro Sulla* 53 (Etruria, Umbria, Picenum, *ager Gallicus*), *Pro Sestio* 9 (Capua, Pisaurum, *ager Gallicus*); Sallust *Catiline* 27.1 (Etruria, Picenum, Apulia), 30.2–5 (Capua, Apulia, Etruria, Picenum), 42.1 (Cisalpine Gaul, Picenum, Bruttium, Apulia); Suetonius *Divus Augustus* 3.1 (Thurii in Lucania); Dio Cassius 37.41.1 (many rebellions, places not specified).

Not against the Republic: Sallust *Catiline* 33.1 ('deos hominesque testamur, imperator, nos arma neque contra patriam cepisse. . .'), 33.3 (secession precedent); cf. *Jugurthine War* 31.6, 31.17, *Histories* 1.11M, 1.55.23M, 3.48.1M for the *plebs armata*.

203 Etruria rising: Sallust *Catiline* 28.4, 30.1. Catiline: Sallust *Catiline* 5.1–7 (character), Cicero *Pro Murena* 50–1 ('dux et signifer calamitosorum'). *Fasces*: Sallust *Catiline* 36.1. Eagle: Cicero *In Catilinam* 1.24, 2.13, Sallust *Catiline* 59.3.

Catiline's army: Sallust *Catiline* 56.1–3 (two legions); cf. Plutarch *Cicero* 16.4, Appian *Civil Wars* 2.7 (20,000 men).

Casualties: Dio Cassius 37.40.1, cf. Sallust *Catiline* 61.5–7 (no prisoners). Catiline's head: Dio Cassius 37.40.2; cf. Cicero *Pro Flacco* 95 (his tomb decorated in 59 BC).

Failed coup: Cicero *In Catilinam* 3, Sallust *Catiline* 39.6–55.6, etc.

Caesar: Cicero *In Catilinam* 4.9 ('is in re publica uiam quae popularis habetur secutus est'), Plutarch *Caesar* 7.4–8.4; Sallust *Catiline* 49.4 (threatened), 51

(Senate speech).

'The little army. . .': Beesly 1865.183, para-phrasing Sallust *Catiline* 61.3–6; Wiseman 1998.121–34 on Beesly. The programme of the new journal was announced in the *Saturday Review*, 25 March 1865, p. 362.

204 *Pontifex maximus*: Plutarch *Caesar* 7.1–3, etc.; cf. Ovid *Fasti* 3.699, 5.573 ('priest of Vesta').

Caesar in 59 BC: Suetonius *Divus Iulius* 22.2 (taunt), Cicero *Pro Flacco* 95 (Catiline's tomb); Gelzer 1968.71–101.

Cicero's dream: Suetonius *Divus Augustus* 94.9, Dio Cassius 45.2.2; the different dream reported in Plutarch *Cicero* 44.2–4 is usually attributed to Q. Catulus (Suetonius *Divus Augustus* 94.8, Dio Cassius 45.2.3–4); cf. also Nigidius Figulus' prophecy at the boy's birth (Dio Cassius 45.1.3–5).

Clodius' death and funeral: Asconius 31–36C.

Threat to tribunes: Caesar *Civil War* 1.1–5. Caesar's declaration: Caesar *Civil War* 1.22.5.

205 Rubicon scene: Plutarch *Caesar* 32.4–6 (from Asinius Pollio), cf. Suetonius *Divus Iulius* 31.2 (bridge), Appian *Civil Wars* 2.35; for the apparition, see Suetonius *Divus Iulius* 32, with Wiseman 1998.60–3 (a satyr-play scenario with Pan?).

Caesar's daughter, Pompey's wife: married 59 BC (Cicero *Ad Atticum* 2.17.1, Velleius Paterculus 2.44.3), died in childbirth 54 BC (Dio Cassius 39.64).

'Strike at the face' (*faciem feri*): Florus 2.13.50; Plutarch *Pompey* 69.2–3, 71.3–5, *Caesar* 42.2, 45.1–3; Appian *Civil Wars* 2.76.318, 2.78.328; cf. Horace *Odes* 2.1.20 (so the scene comes from Asinius Pollio).

Six thousand dead: Plutarch *Caesar* 46.2, *Pompey* 72.3, Appian *Civil Wars* 2.82.346 (Asinius Pollio fr. 2b P). 'Hoc uoluerunt': Suetonius *Divus Iulius* 30.4, Plutarch *Caesar* 46.1 (Asinius Pollio fr. 2a P).

Caesar and Pompey's head: Livy *Epitome* 112, Valerius Maximus 5.1.10, Plutarch *Pompey* 80.5, Dio Cassius 42.8.1, etc.

'The vast trunk': Virgil *Aeneid* 2.557–8 (trans. Robert Fitzgerald); Servius' commentary gives the Pompey connection, which must be from Pollio (Morgan 2000.52–5).

Pollio as tribune (47 BC): Plutarch *Antony* 9.1–2. His life and work: Morgan 2000, Woodman 2003.196–213. His style: Suetonius *De grammaticis* 10.6 ('ut noto *ciuilique* et proprio sermone utatur').

Pollio witness of Africa campaign: Plutarch *Caesar* 52.6.

206 Cato's character: Cicero *Pro Murena* 3 ('grauissimus atque integerrimus uir'), *Ad Atticum* 2.1.8 ('as if he were living in Plato's republic'); Plutarch *Cato minor* 4.1, 6.3, 13.1–2 etc.

Caesar's clemency: Cicero *Ad Atticum* 9.7c.1, 9.16.1–2, Caesar *Civil War* 3.98.2, etc. Pollio on *atrox*

animus: Horace *Odes* 2.1.24.

Cato and Caesar: Sallust *Catiline* 53.2–54.6 (rival paradigms of *uirtus*), Valerius Maximus 5.1.10 (each envying the other's glory).

Caesar and Brutus: Plutarch *Brutus* 4–6, *Caesar* 54.2, Suetonius *Divus Iulius* 50.2, 82.2, Appian *Civil Wars* 2.112.467–8, Dio Cassius 41.63.6.

L. Brutus and Ahala (fig. 76): Cicero *Ad Atticum* 2.24.3, 13.40.1, *Brutus* 331, *Philippics* 2.26; Plutarch *Brutus* 1.1–5; Crawford 1974.455–6, no. 433.

Bodyguard: Suetonius *Divus Iulius* 86.1 (quotation from 86.2), Appian *Civil Wars* 2.109.454–5, Dio Cassius 44.7.4.

207 Twenty-three wounds: Appian *Civil Wars* 4.8.34 (Triumvirs' decree), Suetonius *Divus Iulius* 82.2–3 (one mortal).

'Fear not. . .': Massey 1757.165. Ovid and Vesta: Ovid *Fasti* 3.697–710; cf. *Metamorphoses* 15.843–51, where it is Venus who rescues Caesar's soul and puts it among the stars.

Funeral and will: Appian *Civil Wars* 2.143–7; Suetonius *Divus Iulius* 84, Plutarch *Brutus* 20.1–7, *Antony* 14.3–4, Dio Cassius 45.35.2–4, 45.50.

Hero shrine: Cicero *Ad Atticum* 14.15.1, *Philippics* 1.5, 2.107; Suetonius *Divus Iulius* 85, Appian *Civil Wars* 3.2–3, Dio Cassius 45.51.1–2; Weinstock 1971.364–7.

July: Cicero *Ad Atticum* 16.1.1, Dio Cassius 45.7.2; Weinstock 1971.152–8. Star: Virgil *Eclogues* 9.47, Horace *Odes* 1.12.46–7, Ovid *Metamorphoses* 15.845–50; Pliny *Natural History* 2.93–4, Servius *auctus* on *Eclogues* 9.46 (from Augustus' memoirs); Suetonius *Divus Iulius* 88, Dio Cassius 46.7.1, etc.; Weinstock 1971.370–84.

To free the Republic: Augustus *Res gestae* 1.1 ('rem publicam a dominatione factionis oppressam in libertatem uindicaui').

Vultures: Dio Cassius 46.46.2–3; cf. Suetonius *Divus Augustus* 95, Obsequens 69. *Haruspex*: Appian *Civil Wars* 4.4.15.

People's vote: Augustus *Res gestae* 1.4 ('populus . . . creuit').

Triumvirs' proscription decree: Appian *Civil Wars* 4.8.33 (trans. Horace White, Loeb ed.).

Livy on Cicero's remains: Seneca *Suasoriae* 6.17.

Victor's myth: Ovid *Fasti* 3.705–10 (*iusta arma*, 710), 5.569–78 (*pia arma*, 569).

208 Divus Iulius at Philippi: Valerius Maximus 1.8.8; cf. Plutarch *Brutus* 36.6–7 and 48.1, *Caesar* 69.5–7 ('thou shalt see me at Philippi').

Parricide: Valerius Maximus 1.5.7, 6.4.5; cf. 1.8.8, 3.1.3, 6.8.4 (Cassius). Calendar: *Fasti Praenestini* 23 October (Degrassi 1963.134–5), 'Bruto occiso'.

Brutus and liberty (fig. 77): Crawford 1974.518, no. 508.3; Dio Cassius 47.43.1 (watchword at Philippi); Syme 1939.205 on Philippi as 'the last struggle of the Free State'; Wirszubski 1950.87–91.

Rioting: Dio Cassius 48.9.4–5, 48.31.5–6, Appian *Civil Wars* 5.18.73, 5.67–8, etc.

Freedom and the Republic: Appian *Civil Wars* 5.19.74, 30.118, 39.159–61, 43.179, 54.227–8 (L. Antonius, 41–40 BC).

Perugia massacre: Seneca *De clementia* 1.11.1 ('arae Perusinae'), Suetonius *Divus Augustus* 15 ('scribunt quidam. . .'), Dio Cassius 48.14.4 (λόγος γε ἔχει).

Impious Caesar and Apollo: Suetonius *Divus Augustus* 70.1 (70.2 for the famine, Appian *Civil Wars* 5.67 etc.). Caesar could also be thought of as the son of Apollo: Domitius Marsus 8 Courtney, Suetonius *Divus Augustus* 94.4, Dio Cassius 45.1.2.

Apollo the Torturer: Suetonius *Divus Augustus* 70.2; Wiseman 2000.291–3. Antony in Asia Minor: Plutarch *Antony* 24.3–4 (Ephesus), 26.3 (Cilicia).

Fratricide: Livy 1.7.2 (*uolgatior fama*); cf. Cicero *De officiis* 3.40–1, Lucan 1.95, Plutarch *Romulus* 10.1, Augustine *City of God* 3.6, etc.; Wiseman 1995a.10–16.

Poet: Horace *Epodes* 7: cf. *Odes* 2.7.9–12 for Philippi.

209 Agrippa as boyhood friend: Nikolaos of Damascus *FGrH* 90 F127.7.16, Velleius Paterculus 2.59.5.

Kleopatra: Walker and Higgs 2001.

Alexandria: Diodorus Siculus 17.52.5; Nikolaos of Damascus *FGrH* 90 F130.20.68, Suetonius *Divus Iulius* 79.3 (Caesar's alleged plan).

Provinces transferred (34 BC): Plutarch *Antony* 54.3–6, Dio Cassius 49.1–3.

Expiry of Triumvirate: Augustus *Res gestae* 7.1 ('per continuos annos decem'), Livy *Epitome* 132.

Antony's plans: Livy *Epitome* 132, Velleius Paterculus 2.82.4. Cleopatra's hopes: Dio Cassius 50.5.4, Horace *Odes* 1.37.6–12, Propertius 3.11.31–2, Florus 2.21.2.

Oath of allegiance to Caesar: Augustus *Res gestae* 25.2 ('tota Italia sponte sua'), Suetonius *Divus Augustus* 17.2 ('coniurandi cum tota Italia').

Declaration of war: Dio Cassius 50.4.4–5, 50.6.1 (not against Antony); but cf. Suetonius *Divus Augustus* 17.2 (Antony declared a public enemy).

Republic: Virgil *Aeneid* 8.678–9 ('agens Italos in proelia Caesar | cum patribus populoque'). Apollo: Virgil *Aeneid* 8.704–5, Propertius 4.6.15–68; Thucydides 1.29.3, Suetonius *Divus Augustus* 18.2, Dio Cassius 51.1.2.

Flight of Kleopatra: Horace *Odes* 1.37.12–21, Virgil *Aeneid* 8.707–13, Velleius Paterculus 2.85.3, Florus 2.21.8.

'Aegyptus in potestatem populi Romani redacta': *Fasti Praenestini* 1 August (Degrassi 1963.134–5), Macrobius *Saturnalia* 1.12.35 (27 BC *senatus consultum*), *ILS* 91 (10–9 BC obelisks); cf. Augustus *Res gestae* 27.1 ('Aegyptum imperio populi Romani adieci').

Thanksgiving: *Fasti fratrum Arvalium, Praenestini*

and *Amiternini* for 1 August (Degrassi 1963.30–1, 134–5, 190–1): 'quod eo die Imp. Caesar Divi f. rem publicam tristissimo periculo liberauit'.

'Re publica conseruata': *ILS* 81 (29 BC, inscription from triumphal arch). Treasury: Velleius Paterculus 2.39.2 (almost equal to the revenue from Gaul).

Law: Ulpian in *Digest* 1.17.1; cf. Tacitus *Annals* 12.60.2, Strabo 17.1.12. Ban on senators: Tacitus *Annals* 1.59.3, cf. *Histories* 1.11.1.

Tribunes' powers: Augustus *Res gestae* 10.1 ('sacrosanctus in perpetuum ut essem et quoad uiuerem tribunicia potestas mihi esset per legem sanctum est'); Appian *Civil Wars* 5.132.548, Dio Cassius 49.15.5–6, Orosius 6.18.34 (36 BC); Dio Cassius 51.19.6 (30 BC), 53.32.5 (23 BC).

Restoring law and justice (fig. 78): Rich and Williams 1999; cf. Millar 2000.6–7, who suggests the reading '[quod leges et iura] p. R. rest[it]u[it]' in the *Fasti Praenestini* item on the oak-leaf crown (13 January, Degrassi 1963.112–3).

210 Ptolemy and the body of Alexander: Diodorus Siculus 18.28.3–6, Strabo 17.1.8. Alexandria: Fraser 1972. Successor kingdoms: Davis and Kraay 1973.

Essayist: Lucian *De saltatione* 37.

Mime and Alexandria: Cicero *Pro Rabirio Postumo* 35 ('ab eis mimorum argumenta nata sunt'), Athenaeus 1.20d (Bathyllus from Alexandria), Philo *In Flaccum* 34, 38, 72, 85; cf. Ovid *Tristia* 1.2.79–80, Statius *Silvae* 5.5.66–9.

Theatre-mad: Philo *Quod omnis probus liber sit* 141 (Loeb ed. vol. 9 p. 91)—audience enthusiasm for Euripides on liberty.

Pantomimus: Beacham 1999.141–6; Lucian *De saltatione* 29–30 (singers), 63 (chorus), 68 (actor and singers).

A Roman by a Roman: Plutarch *Antony* 77.4 (Spencer 1964.281 for the 1579 translation). Alexandrian sources: Plutarch *Antony* 77.2 (eye-witnesses), 82.2 (Olympos, the queen's physician).

Kleopatra narrative: Plutarch *Antony* 77–87 (Spencer 1964.279–94). Charmion speech (North spells the name correctly): Plutarch *Antony* 85.4 (Spencer 1964.292).

Art of the ὀρχηστής: Lucian *De saltatione* 67 (trans. H.W. and F.G. Fowler, 1905).

'Squeaking Cleopatra': *Antony and Cleopatra* 5.2.219.

211 Triumph: Dio Cassius 51.21.5–9 (triple triumph, therefore triple arch?); Degrassi 1947.344–5, 1963.208 (date, in *Fasti triumphales Barberiniani* and *Antiates*).

Divus Iulius dedication: Dio Cassius 47.18.4, 51.22.2 (vowed 42 BC, dedicated 29 BC); Degrassi 1963.180–1, 190–1, 208 (date, in *Fasti Allifani, Amiternini* and *Antiates*).

28 BC consulship: Dio Cassius 53.1.1–3 (κατὰ τὰ

πάτρια... ὥσπερ ἐν τῇ ἀκριβεῖ δημοκρατίᾳ). Turning point marked by *lustrum*: Augustus *Res gestae* 8.2, Degrassi 1947.254–5 (*Fasti Venusini*).

Popularity of Agrippa: Dio Cassius 53.23.1–4, 53.27.4, 53.31.4, 54.29.3–4; cf. 54.15.1, 54.29.6 (resentment of *optimates*); Seneca *Controversiae* 2.4.13, Tacitus *Annals* 1.3.1 (*ignobilitas*).

Arch (fig. 79): *ILS* 81 ('Senatus populusque Romanus | imp. Caesari diui Iuli f. cos. quinct.| cos. design. Sext. Imp. Sept. | re publica conseruata'); Dio Cassius 51.19.1, with Rich 1998.97–115. *Fasti triumphales* and *consulares* (figs 79 and 80): Degrassi 1947.1–87 and plates I-LIV.

Engineer: Vitruvius 1.pref.1 ('cum... triumpho uictoriaque tua ciues gloriarentur... populusque Romanus et senatus liberatus timore amplissimis tuis cogitationibus consiliisque gubernaretur...'); cf. 1.pref.2 (artillery), 8.6.2 (aqueducts).

212 28–27 BC: Augustus *Res gestae* 34 (trans. Brunt and Moore 1967.35–7, adapted); cf. Rich and Williams 1999.190–1. For the shield (fig. 81), see Galinsky 1996.80–90.

Old Republic: Velleius 2.89.3 ('prisca illa et antiqua rei publicae forma reuocata'); cf. Birley 2000.724–40. Elections: e.g. Horace *Odes* 3.1.10–14, Velleius Paterculus 2.91.3. Legislation: e.g. Frontinus *De aquis* 2.129.

Peace and concord: Livy 9.19.17 ('modo sit perpetuus huius qua uiuimus pacis amor at ciuilis cura concordiae'); Ovid *Fasti* 6.91–2 (Concordia as 'placidi numen opusque ducis').

214 Freedom from fear: Horace *Odes* 3.14.14–16, cf. 4.15.17–20.

Corona ciuica (fig. 82): Pliny *Natural History* 16.7–14, Aulus Gellius 5.6.11–15.

'All these...': Massey 1757.46, slightly adapted; strangely, Massey translated 'sancta uocant augusta patres' as 'all sacrifices are *divine* decreed', and deliberately ignored all Ovid's word-play on *augusta... auget... augeat*.

'Augustus': Suetonius *Divus Augustus* 7.2 ('non tantum nouo sed etiam ampliore cognomine, quod loca quoque religiosa, et in quibus augurato quid consecratur, augusta dicantur'); Florus 2.34.66 ('sanctius et reuerentius uisum est nomen Augusti, ut scilicet iam tum, dum colit terras, ipso nomine et titulo consecraretur'); Dio Cassius 53.16.8 (ὡς καὶ πλεῖόν τι ἢ κατὰ ἀνθρώπους ὤν).

Divus Iulius altar: Appian *Civil Wars* 1.4.17. Divine Caesar: Cicero *Philippics* 5.43; Virgil *Eclogues* 1.6–8, *Georgics* 1.24–42, 1.503–4, 3.16, 4.562; Vitruvius 1.pref.1 ('diuina...mens et numen'); Horace *Odes* 1.2.41–52 (cf. 25–6 for the prayers of the Roman People), 3.25.3–6, 4.5.33–6; Dio Cassius 53.27.3 (on the dedication of the Pantheon in 25 BC); Galinsky 1996.312–31, Gradel 2002.109–16.

Romulus proposal: Suetonius *Divus Augustus* 7.2 ('quibusdam censentibus...'), Florus 2.34.66 ('tractatum in senatu'); cf. Dio Cassius 53.16.6, who says it was what Caesar wanted, but was too suggestive of kingship.

Proposer (L. Munatius Plancus, consul 42 BC): Suetonius *Divus Augustus* 7.2; Velleius Paterculus 2.67.3–4.

215 Ennius allusion: Suetonius *Divus Augustus* 7.2 (Ennius *Annales* 155 Sk).

Golden Age: Virgil *Eclogues* 4.4–10 ('iam regnat Apollo'), *Aeneid* 6.791–5; Galinsky 1996.90–121.

Apollo temple: Velleius Paterculus 2.81.3, Dio Cassius 49.15.5, 53.1.3 (vowed 36 BC, dedicated 28 BC); *Fasti Antiates* 9 October (Degrassi 1963.209). Magnificence: Asconius 90C (*nobilissima*); Virgil *Aeneid* 8.720, Propertius 2.31.9–11 (marble, *quadriga*); Ovid *Tristia* 3.1.59–60 (*sublimia*). Temple and house: Zanker 1983.21–7.

Liber and Flora: Dio Cassius 50.10.3–4 (fire), Tacitus *Annals* 2.49.1 (reconstruction only in AD 17); Wiseman 2000.293–4.

Restoration of temples in 28 BC: Augustus *Res gestae* 20.4; cf. Livy 4.20.7 ('templorum omnium conditor aut restitutor'), Suetonius *Divus Augustus* 30.2, Dio Cassius 53.2.3–4.

Puritanical: Augustus *Res gestae* 8.5 (exemplary legislation); Propertius 2.7.1–6, Horace *Carmen saeculare* 17–20, Suetonius *Divus Augustus* 34.1, Tacitus *Annals* 3.25.1, 3.28.2–3, etc.; Galinsky 1996.121–40.

Horace and Liber: *Odes* 1.1.29–32, 1.19.1–4, 2.19.1–8, 3.25. Horace and Faunus: *Odes* 1.17.1–12, 2.17.27–30, 3.18.

'Roman Odes': Horace *Odes* 3.1–6, a single sequence and perhaps a single poem (Griffiths 2002.73–9); 3.1.1–4 (*sacerdos*), 3.2.13 (*dulce et decorum*), 3.5.10–12 (shield and Vesta), 3.5.13–56 (Regulus), 3.6.32–44 (farmer-soldiers), 3.6.45–8 (trans. Michie 1964.165).

Aeneas and Evander: Virgil *Aeneid* 8.18–369. Aeneas' shield: *Aeneid* 8.608–731, trans. Sisson 1986.228.

216 Immortality: Virgil *Aeneid* 9.448–9, Horace *Odes* 3.30.7–9. *Vates*: Virgil *Aeneid* 7.41, cf. *Eclogues* 9.32–6; Horace *Epodes* 16.66, *Odes* 1.1.35, 4.6.44, etc.

Prophecies: Virgil *Aeneid* 1.279; 6.847–54 (trans. Sisson 1986.170–1); cf. *Aeneid* 1.283–5, 6.836–40 and Horace *Odes* 3.3.57–68 for the conquest of Greece as defining Rome's empire.

217 Horace on Roman peasants: *Epistles* 2.1.139 (*agricolae prisci*), 156–7, 161–3.

'Monumentum aere perennius': Horace *Odes* 3.30.1. Virgil and Horace as school texts: Juvenal 7.227, Ausonius 8.56–7, 11.21.8. Stamped on the memory: Orosius 1.18.1 (plot of the *Aeneid* 'ludi litterarii disciplina nostrae quoque memoriae inustum'), cf.

Augustine *City of God* 1.3; Comparetti 1895.28–33.

218 Forum Augustum (fig. 83): Augustus *Res gestae* 21.1 (*ex manibiis*), Ovid *Fasti* 5.545–98; Galinsky 1996.197–213. Date: Suetonius *Divus Augustus* 29.1 (Forum opened before Mars Ultor temple), Macrobius *Saturnalia* 2.4.9 (slow progress), Velleius Paterculus 2.100.2 (Mars Ultor temple dedicated 2 BC); Rich 1998.86–9.

219 Statues: Ovid *Fasti* 5.563–6 ('claraque dispositis acta subesse uiris'), Suetonius *Divus Augustus* 31.5 ('qui imperium populi Romani ex minimo maximum reddidissent'), Historia Augusta *Alexander Severus* 28.6 ('summorum uirorum statuas. . . additis gestis'). Augustus' edict: Suetonius *Divus Augustus* 35.1.

Pantheon: *CIL* 6.896 (27 BC), Dio 53.27.2–3 (25 BC, statues). Statues and *elogia*: Dio Cassius 54.1.1; *CIL* 6.1272, with Cozza 1983 (the only other known example is of the elder Caesar's daughter Iulia).

Augustus as *pontifex maximus*: Augustus *Res gestae* 10.2, Ovid *Fasti* 3.415–28; *Fasti Maffeiani* and *Praenestini* and *Feriale Cumanum* for 6 March (Degrassi 1963.74, 120–1, 279); Bowersock 1990.

Augustalia (fig. 84): *Fasti Amiternini* 12 October (Degrassi 1963.194–5), Augustus *Res gestae* 11, Dio Cassius 54.10.3.

221 Pontifical archive: Servius *auctus* on *Aeneid* 1.373, with Frier 1979.27–37, 193–200 (properly cautious in suggesting the Augustan context, which seems to me inescapable). Four certain fragments of the 80–book edition are known, three of them (*Origo gentis Romanae* 17.3, 17.5, 18.3) from Book 4 on Ascanius and the Alban kings.

Sibylline and other prophecies: Suetonius *Divus Augustus* 31.1, cf. Dio Cassius 54.17.2.

Agrippa as Remus: Virgil *Aeneid* 1.292–3 with Servius' commentary ('uera tamen hoc habet ratio, Quirinum Augustum esse, Remum pro Agrippa positum').

Constant partner: as consul in 28 and 27 BC (see the coin-legend in fig. 78[a] above for Virgil's '*iura dabunt*'); *censoria potestas* in 28 BC (Augustus *Res gestae* 8.2, *Fasti Venusini* in Degrassi 1947.254–5); *tribunicia potestas* from 18 BC onwards (Dio Cassius 54.12.4 and 28.1); presidency of the Secular Games in 17 BC (Augustus *Res gestae* 22.2).

222 Empire of the Roman People: Augustus *Res gestae* preface ('orbem terrarum imperio populi Romani subiecit'). Agrippa's world map probably made a similar boast: 'Aethicus' in *Geographi Latini minores* 71 Riese, ('senatum populumque Romanum totius mundi dominos. . .'), with Wiseman 1992.41–2.

Virgil on the *iuuenis*: *Eclogues* 1.42, *Georgics* 1.500; cf. Horace *Odes* 1.2.41.

Census: Augustus *Res gestae* 8.2–3 ('lustrum solus feci'), Ovid *Fasti* 6.647 (7 BC). *Lustrum*: Livy 1.44.1–2, Dionysius of Halicarnassus 4.22.1–2.

Prayer: Valerius Maximus 4.1.10.

Regiones and *uici*: Pliny *Natural History* 3.66; Dio Cassius 55.8.6–7, Suetonius *Divus Augustus* 30.1; Fraschetti 1990.255–68.

Lares cult: Dionysius of Halicarnassus 4.14.3–4, Ovid *Fasti* 5.129–46; *ILS* 3612–21, 9250; Hano 1986.2338 and 2353–4 (on *ILS* 3613, fig. 85), Galinsky 1996.300–10, Lacey 1996.180–6 (but Lacey's association of the *Genius Augusti* with Liber Pater is without foundation), Gradel 2002.116–39.

Domestic cult (fig. 86): e.g. *ILS* 3604–5; Orr 1978.1563–75 (*Lares* and *Genius*), Gradel 2002.36–44; Plautus *Aulularia* 2–5, Cicero *De republica* 5.7 (*Lares familiares*), Servius on *Aeneid* 5.85 (snake as *genius loci*), etc.

Genius: Censorinus *De die natali* 3.1 ('Genius est deus cuius in tutela ut quisque natus est uiuit').

Tribunicia potestas: Augustus *Res gestae* 10.1, Tacitus *Annals* 1.2.1 ('ad tuendam plebem'), 3.56.2, ('summi fastigii uocabulum'), Dio Cassius 53.17.10 (yearly grant), 53.32.5–6; Lacey 1996.100–16 and 154–68.

Corn supply: Augustus *Res gestae* 5.2, 15.1, Dio Cassius 54.1.3–4; Rickman 1980.60–4 and 179–85.

Augustus as proconsul: Dio Cassius 53.17.4; Alföldy 2000.179–81 (edict of Augustus 'trib. pot. VIII et procos.' discovered in 1999). Praetorian cohorts: Dio Cassius 53.11.5, Suetonius *Divus Augustus* 49.1; Keppie 1983.33–5 for the prehistory of the Praetorian Guard.

Popular anxieties: Manilius *Astronomica* 2.600, 5.119–24, 5.220–2.

Dialogue: Suetonius *Divus Augustus* 42.1–2, 65.3; Dio Cassius 55.9.2–3, 55.9.10, 55.13.1. Edicts: Suetonius *Divus Augustus* 28.2, 31.5 (explanation), 42.2, 53.1, 56.2 (rebukes). Public speeches: e.g. Suetonius *Divus Augustus* 40.5.

Retirement: Seneca *De brevitate vitae* 4.2–4 (letter to the Senate).

Coming of age (L. Caesar's *toga uirilis*): Suetonius *Divus Augustus* 26.2. Mars temple: Augustus *Res gestae* 21.1, Dio Cassius 55.10.1–5. Shows: Augustus *Res gestae* 22.2 and 23, Dio Cassius 55.10.6–8 (cf. 55.10.11 for *ludi scaenici*).

223 Embassy: Suetonius *Divus Augustus* 58.1.

Concordia on 5 February: *Fasti Antiates maiores* (Plate 6) 'Concord(iae) in Capit(olio)', *Fasti Praenestini* 'Concordiae in arce' (Degrassi 1963.4, 118–19); Livy 23.21.7 (dedicated 216 BC); *pace* Lacey 1996.194, the Concordia temple Tiberius had vowed to restore was not this one but Opimius' 'work of Discord' (p. 193 above).

Show, laurel wreaths, Senate scene: Suetonius *Divus Augustus* 58.1–2 ('uniuersi repentino maximoque consensu'); cf. Augustus *Res gestae* 35.1 ('senatus et equester ordo populusque Romanus uniuersus'), Ovid *Fasti* 2.127–32; Ando 2000.145–8 on consensus.

Presiding consul (M. Plautius Silvanus): cf. Dio Cassius 53.1.1 for the monthly alternation of the *fasces*. Augustus must have held them in January, March and May—for the opening ceremonial (Ovid *Fasti* 1.71–88, etc.), for Lucius' *toga uirilis*, and for the dedication of Mars Ultor.

Messalla at Philippi: Velleius Paterculus 2.71.1, Plutarch *Brutus* 40.1–4, Tacitus *Annals* 4.34.4.

'Quod bonum faustumque sit' formula: cf. Livy 42.30.10 (171 BC), *ILS* 112.6–10 (AD 11), Dio Cassius 58.3.4 (AD 97).

224 Conspirators: Velleius Paterculus 2.88, 2.91.2–4, Suetonius *Divus Augustus* 19.1, Tacitus *Annals* 1.10.4 (M. Lepidus in 30 or 29 BC, L. Murena and Fannius Caepio in 22, M. Egnatius in 19). Protection: Tacitus *Annals* 1.2.1 ('ad tuendam plebem').

Augustus on Cicero and Cato: Plutarch *Cicero* 49.3 (λόγιος ἀνήρ, ὦ παῖ, λόγιος καὶ φιλόπατρις); Macrobius *Saturnalia* 2.4.18 ('quisquis praesentem statum ciuitatis commutari non uolet et ciuis et uir bonus est').

225 *Princeps* as βασιλεύς: Antipater of Thessalonica 40.5 Gow-Page (*Anthologia Palatina* 10.25.5), about 8 BC; cf. Macrobius *Saturnalia* 2.7.19 (attributed to Pylades); Mason 1974.120–1. Sole ruler: e.g. Horace *Epistles* 2.1.1 ('cum tot sustineas et tanta negotia *solus*').

Praetorian Prefects: Dio Cassius 55.10.10.

Self-governing: Manilius *Astronomica* 5.315–16 (magistrates as servants of the *populus*).

'Roman, . . .': Michie 1964.161–3.

CHAPTER **9**

227 Birth of Julia: Dio Cassius 48.34.3; the allegation that he divorced Scribonia on the very day of the birth may be from an Antonian source. Compare Tacitus *Annals* 1.10.5, 5.1.2, 12.6.2, Suetonius *Divus Augustus* 62.2 on the supposed removal of Livia from her husband by force (contradicted by Velleius Paterculus 2.79.2, 2.94.1, Dio Cassius 48.44.3, Suetonius *Tiberius* 4.3); Flory 1988.

Octavia's daughters: Plutarch *Antony* 87.2; Syme 1986.141–4, though 40 is more likely than 39 for the birth of the younger Marcella (Dio Cassius 48.31.3 for her pregnancy in the autumn), if the elder Antonia was born in 39.

Marcellus and Tiberius at the triumph (29 BC): Suetonius *Tiberius* 6.4.

Iullus Antonius: Plutarch *Antony* 87.1; for 'Iullus' as a name of the patrician Iulii, cf. Dionysius of Halicarnassus 8.1.1, 8.90.5 etc. (Syme 1986.398, 'Marcus Antonius advertised posthumous loyalty to Caesar the Dictator').

Marriages: Dio Cassius 53.1.2 (Marcella and Agrippa). 53.27.5 (Julia and Marcellus).

Marcellus: Velleius Paterculus 2.93.1, Seneca

Consolatio ad Marciam 2.3 (his virtues); Dio Cassius 53.28.3–4 (election); Tacitus *Annals* 1.3.1, cf. Dio Cassius 53.30.2 and 31.2–4 (Augustus' favour).

Games: Propertius 3.18.13–20, Velleius Paterculus 2.93.1 ('munificentissimo munere'), Pliny *Natural History* 19.24, Dio Cassius 53.31.2–3 (Augustus' subsidy).

Augustus and the theatre: Tacitus *Annals* 1.54.2, Suetonius *Divus Augustus* 43–5, esp. 45.1 ('studio spectandi ac uoluptate'), cf. Ovid *Tristia* 2.511–14. Pylades, Bathyllos etc.: Dio Cassius 54.17.4–5, Seneca *Controversiae* 3.pref.10, Macrobius *Saturnalia* 2.7.12–19, Athenaeus 1.20d–e, Jerome *Chronicle* Olympiad 189.3 (22–21 BC), etc.; Beacham 1999.142–6.

232 Marcellus' death: Virgil *Aeneid* 6.860–86, Propertius 3.18. Plague, famine, flood: Dio Cassius 53.33.4–5, 54.1.1–2. Angry god: Propertius 3.18.8 ('deus hostis').

Tightened control: Dio Cassius 54.2.3–5. New theatre: Dio Cassius 53.30.5–6, Augustus *Res gestae* 21.1 ('ad aedem Apollinis'). The foundations had supposedly been laid by Caesar the dictator (Dio Cassius 43.49.2–3), but Augustus says he bought the site from private owners, so it must have been a new project; Caesar's plan for a huge theatre 'Tarpeio monti accubans' (Suetonius *Divus Iulius* 44.1) has nothing to do with it.

Agrippa and Julia: Dio Cassius 54.6.5 (21 BC), Plutarch *Antony* 87.2–3 (Marcella remarried to Iullus Antonius). Children: Suetonius *Divus Augustus* 64.1; Dio Cassius 54.18.1 (adoption of Gaius and Lucius, 17 BC). Marriages and children of the Marcellae: Syme 1986.143–52.

Julia and Augustus: Macrobius *Saturnalia* 2.5.1–9.

Sempronius Gracchus: Velleius Paterculus 2.100.5, Tacitus *Annals* 1.53.3. Iullus Antonius: Velleius Paterculus 2.100.4, Tacitus *Annals* 3.18.1, 4.44.3, Dio Cassius 55.10.15; his mother Fulvia was married to P. Clodius, C. Curio and Antony (Cicero *Philippics* 2.11), and from the same noble family as C. Gracchus' ally M. Fulvius Flaccus, killed in 121 BC.

Father of Tiberius and Drusus: Suetonius *Tiberius* 4.1 (proposed in the Senate that the 'tyrannicides' be rewarded). Drusus on the 'pristinus rei publicae status': Suetonius *Divus Claudius* 1.4. Drusus to Tiberius on Augustus and *libertas*: Suetonius *Tiberius* 50.1, cf. Tacitus *Annals* 1.33.2. Brutus and *libertas*: Appian *Civil Wars* 2.119, etc.

Caesar's daughter: Macrobius *Saturnalia* 2.5.8. Tiberius' divorce: Suetonius *Tiberius* 7.2–3.

233 'Arms, warfare . . .': Ovid *Amores* 1.1.1–4 and 25–30; Green 1982.86–7. 'Corinna': Ovid *Amores* 2.17.29, *Ars amatoria* 3.538, *Tristia* 4.10.59–60. Devotion: *Amores* 1.3. Every woman he meets: *Amores* 2.4.

Chronology: Ovid *Tristia* 4.10.5–6 (born 43 BC), 4.10.57–60 (first *Amores* poems about 26 BC?).

234 Learned bishop: Sidonius Apollinaris *Carmina* 23.158–61. High places: Ovid *Tristia* 3.4.4 ('nomina magna'); *Ex Ponto* 1.7.28–9, 2.3.75–8 (Messalla Corvinus).

'Crude simplicity's ...': Ovid *Ars amatoria* 3.118–28; Green 1982.217.

Adultery (*lex Iulia de adulteriis coercendis*, 18 BC): Horace *Odes* 4.5.21–2, Suetonius *Divus Augustus* 34.1; Crawford 1996.781–6.

235 Julia and Tiberius: Tacitus *Annals* 1.53.1 ('fuerat in matrimonio Tiberii florentibus Gaio et Lucio Caesaribus spreueratque ut imparem'). Her sons: Velleius Paterculus 2.99.2, Dio Cassius 55.9.1–2.

Tiberius and Julia: Suetonius *Tiberius* 7.2 ('Iuliae mores improbaret'), 10.1 ('uxoris taedio'); Tacitus *Annals* 6.51.2 ('impudicitiam uxoris tolerans aut declinans').

Tiberius' arrogance: Suetonius *Tiberius* 68.3 (Augustus' view), Tacitus *Annals* 1.4.3, 1.10.7. His taciturnity: Suetonius *Tiberius* 68.3; Tacitus *Annals* 1.24.1, 4.1.2, 4.52.3. His dislike of crowds: Tacitus *Annals* 1.76.4 ('taedium coetus'), 4.57.2 ('uitare coetus').

Opimius' Concordia temple: Dio Cassius 55.8.2; Cicero *In Catilinam* 3.21, *Philippics* 2.19, Sallust *Catiline* 46.5, 49.4 (63 BC); cf. Cicero *Pro Sestio* 26 (recall of Cicero).

Caesar's plan: Suetonius *Divus Iulius* 44.1; the 'theatrum summae magnitudinis Tarpeio monti accubans' must have required the destruction of the temple.

Tiberius' withdrawal: Suetonius *Tiberius* 10 (10.2 for Augustus' complaint of desertion, 68.3 for Augustus on Tiberius' ingratitude and arrogance).

Marsyas and *licentia*: Seneca *De beneficiis* 6.32.1, Pliny *Natural History* 21.9; cf. Velleius Paterculus 2.100.3 on Julia's *luxuria* and *licentia*, 'quidquid liberet pro licito uindicans'. Augustus' health: Suetonius *Tiberius* 11.1.

Aula, literally the atrium or reception-hall: Horace *Odes* 2.10.8, 2.18.31, *Epistles* 1.1.87. Imperial court: Seneca *De ira* 2.33.2, [Seneca] *Octavia* 285, etc.; Suetonius *Gaius* 19.3 (*interiores aulici*); Wallace-Hadrill 1996.

Augustus' unluxurious house: Suetonius *Divus Augustus* 72.1.

236 Treason: Pliny *Natural History* 7.149 (Julia's *consilia parricidii*), Seneca *De brevitate vitae* 4.6, Tacitus *Annals* 1.10.4 (cf. 3.18.1, 4.44.3), Dio Cassius 55.10.15; Velleius Paterculus (2.100.4) says Iullus committed suicide. Gracchus and the others: Velleius Paterculus 2.100.5, Tacitus *Annals* 1.53.

Roman People: Suetonius *Divus Augustus* 65.3 ('deprecanti saepe p. R. et pertinacius instanti'), Dio Cassius 55.13.1.

Lucius and Gaius: Velleius Paterculus 2.102.3, Tacitus *Annals* 1.3.3, Suetonius *Divus Augustus* 65.1,

Dio Cassius 55.10a.8–9.

AD 5 calamities: Dio Cassius 55.22.3. Famine AD 5–8: Dio Cassius 55.26.1–2, 55.27.1, 55.31.3–4, 55.33.4.

Adoptions: Velleius Paterculus 2.103.3 and 104.1; Suetonius *Divus Augustus* 65.1, *Tiberius* 15.2, *Gaius* 1.1 and 4; Dio Cassius 55.13.2. Marriages: Suetonius *Gaius* 7 (Germanicus and Agrippina), Tacitus *Annals* 4.3.3 (Drusus and Livia Julia), etc.

Roman People: Velleius Paterculus 2.104.1, Suetonius *Tiberius* 21.3 ('rei publicae causa'); Suetonius *Tiberius* 68.3 ('saepe apud senatum ac populum professus'), cf. Tacitus *Annals* 1.10.7 (to Senate).

Popular unrest: Dio Cassius 55.27.1, 55.31.3 (AD 6–7). Agrippa Postumus: Velleius Paterculus 2.112.7, Suetonius *Tiberius* 65.1 and 4, Tacitus *Annals* 1.3.4, Dio Cassius 55.32.1–2.

Fire: Dio Cassius 55.26.4 (AD 6). Pannonian rebellion: Velleius Paterculus 2.110.2–112.6 (110.6 for Augustus' fear), Pliny *Natural History* 7.149, Dio Cassius 55.29–30.

Plot: Suetonius *Divus Augustus* 19.2 ('Iuliam filiam et Agrippam nepotem ex insulis quibus continebantur rapere ad exercitus'); in fact, Julia had by now been moved to Rhegium on the mainland (Tacitus *Annals* 1.53.1, Suetonius *Divus Augustus* 65.3).

237 'Now stands ...': Ovid *Metamorphoses* 15.871–3, trans. Melville 1986.379. 'Since amorous themes. . .': Massey 1757.57–8; cf. *Tristia* 2.549–52 for the dedication.

'Thy titles': e.g. *Fasti* 1.590–616 (*Augustus*), 2.119–32 (*pater patriae*), 3.415–28 (*pontifex maximus*), 4.673–6 (*imperator*).

Liber: e.g. *Fasti* 3.459–516 (*Libera*), 3.713–90, 6.481–8. Flora: *Fasti* 4.943–8, 5.183–378. Liber and Flora together: *Fasti* 5.331–54 (on the *liberior iocus* of Flora's games).

Julia's adultery: Pliny *Natural History* 7.149, Suetonius *Divus Augustus* 65.1 and 4, Tacitus *Annals* 3.24.2–3, 4.71.4 (AD 8). Paullus' treason: Suetonius *Divus Augustus* 19.1, with Syme 1986.117–25.

Ovid's banishment: *Tristia* 2.103–4, 207 ('duo crimina, carmen et error'), 3.5.49–52, 3.6.11–15, etc.; Green 1982.44–59.

Three cancers: Suetonius *Divus Augustus* 65.4. Letter to Tiberius: Suetonius *Tiberius* 21.7 ('si non p. R. perosi sunt'). Gods' hostility: Tacitus *Annals* 4.1.2 ('deum ira in rem Romanam'), cf. 16.16.2, *Histories* 1.3.2.

Varus disaster: Velleius Paterculus 2.117–19, Pliny *Natural History* 7.149, Suetonius *Divus Augustus* 23, Dio Cassius 56.18–24 (24.2 for divine anger).

Temples rebuilt: Tacitus *Annals* 2.49.1 (dedicated AD 17); cf. Ovid *Tristia* 5.3, addressed to Liber about AD 11.

238 Killing of Agrippa: Tacitus *Annals* 1.6, with

Woodman 1998.23–39; cf. Suetonius *Tiberius* 22, Dio Cassius 57.3.5–6. The placing of the scene at Capua on 23 August is a guess: see Levick 1976.69–70 for the chronology. Barrett (2002.69) puts it at Nola, Woodman (1998.37–9) at Rome; the former makes the centurion's mission impossibly fast, the latter improbably slow.

Sallust's great-nephew: Tacitus *Annals* 1.6.3 ('particeps secretorum'), 3.30.2–3.

Caesar as the Republic: Ovid *Tristia* 4.4.15 ('quia res est publica Caesar'). Treason (*maiestas*): Cicero *De inventione* 2.53, Ulpian in *Digest* 48.4.1.1, etc.; Tacitus *Annals* 1.72.2–3.

Plot reactivated: Tacitus *Annals* 2.39.1–2. Augustus and Agrippa: Tacitus *Annals* 1.5.1, Dio Cassius 56.30.1; cf. Tacitus *Annals* 1.6.2 ('in nullius umquam suorum necem durauit'); Levick 1976.64–5.

Death of Julia: Tacitus *Annals* 1.53.2, cf. 3.19.3, Suetonius *Tiberius* 50.1.

239 17 September: *Fasti Amiternini* and *Fasti Viae dei Serpenti* (Degrassi 1963.192–3, 214–5), 'diuo Augusto honores caelestes a senatu decreti'.

Iulia Augusta: Velleius Paterculus 2.71.3, Tacitus *Annals* 1.8.1, Dio Cassius 56.46.1; Barrett 2002.148–51. Suspicions of murder: Dio Cassius 53.33.4 (Marcellus), 55.10a.10 (Lucius and Gaius, cf. Tacitus *Annals* 1.3.3), 56.30.1–2 (Augustus, cf. Tacitus *Annals* 1.5.1).

Tiberius 'Augustus': Suetonius *Divus Augustus* 101.2, *Tiberius* 26.2, Dio Cassius 57.2.1 and 8.1; Levick 1976.247 n. 11.

Tiberius on power of *princeps*: Tacitus *Annals* 1.72.1–2, 3.69.4–5 ('satis potentiae'), Suetonius *Tiberius* 29. Under protest: Tacitus *Annals* 1.11–13, with Woodman 1998.40–69; cf. Suetonius *Tiberius* 24–5, Dio Cassius 57.2–3. For the time being: Suetonius *Tiberius* 24.2, Tacitus *Annals* 4.9.1.

Senate: Tacitus *Annals* 3.65, 4.6.2, etc.; Suetonius *Tiberius* 26–31.

People's tastes: Tacitus *Annals* 1.54.2, 1.76.4, 4.62.2; Suetonius *Tiberius* 47; Beacham 1999.157–68. Actors: Velleius Paterculus 2.126.2 ('compressa theatralis seditio'), Valerius Maximus 2.4.1 (theatres as *urbana castra*); Tacitus *Annals* 1.54.2, 1.77, 4.14.3; Suetonius *Tiberius* 37.2, Dio Cassius 56.47.2, 57.21.3.

Relentless jaws: Suetonius *Tiberius* 21.2 (trans. Levick 1976.68).

Germanicus: Suetonius *Gaius* 3–4, Tacitus *Annals* 1.33. Legions' offer: Velleius Paterculus 2.125.1–3, Tacitus *Annals* 1.31.1, 1.35.3–5, Suetonius *Gaius* 1.1. Tiberius' suspicion: Tacitus *Annals* 1.7.6, 1.52.1, 1.69.3–5, 2.5.1, etc.

Agrippina: Suetonius *Gaius* 7; Tacitus *Annals* 1.33, 1.69.1 ('femina ingens animi'). Blood of Augustus: Tacitus *Annals* 1.40.3, 2.71.4, 3.4.2, 4.51.2.

Caligula: Tacitus *Annals* 1.41.2, 1.69.4; Seneca *De*

constantia animi 18.4–5, Suetonius *Gaius* 9, Dio Cassius 57.5–6.

Drusus and Germanicus: Tacitus *Annals* 2.43.6, cf. 3.56.3 (Tiberius' impartiality between them), Ovid *Ex Ponto* 4.13.31–2, Strabo 6.4.2 (joint assistants of Tiberius). Drusus' exact age is uncertain: born in 14 or 13 BC? I follow Levick (1976.30, 236 n. 62) in assuming the latter.

Temple dedications: Tacitus *Annals* 2.49. It is usually supposed, on the strength of Dio Cassius 50.10.3, that Janus and Hope were also burned down in 31 BC; but they were a long way from the Circus Maximus, and the calendars imply that the temple of Hope was in being on 1 August 30 BC (Degrassi 1963.489). It is easier to suppose that they were destroyed in the AD 6 fire, and that Dio was misled by a reference in his source to the rededication of Hope in the same year as those of Liber and Flora.

240 New gods: Manilius *Astronomica* 4.934–5; Valerius Maximus pref., with Mueller 2002.11–20 (translation from p. 13). Enthusiasm: e.g. *CIL* 10.3757 (*ILS* 137), Tacitus *Annals* 1.73.2, Fronto *Epistles* 4.12.6; Gradel 2002 (esp. 110–12, 198–209, 216–24, 266–9), rightly emphasising private worship of the living emperor.

Aphrodisias *Sebasteion*: Smith 1987. 'Foremother' ('Ἀφροδίτην Προμήτορα θεῶν Σεβαστῶν, on a statue-base in front of the entrance): Reynolds 1986.111–13.

241 Arrangement of panels: Smith 1987.95–8 (quotation from p. 96). Augustus reliefs (fig. 94): Smith 1987.101–6, Plates IV-VII.

242 Hope and liberty: Tacitus *Annals* 1.33.2 ('in Germanicum fauor et spes'), 2.82.2 ('populum Romanum aequo iure complecti'), both in the context of 'reddere libertatem'. End of hope: Tacitus *Annals* 3.4.1 ('populus . . . nihil spei reliquum clamitabant').

Reaction to Germanicus' death: Suetonius *Gaius* 5–6, Tacitus *Annals* 2.82. Germanicus' belief: *SC de Pisone patre* 27–9 (Damon and Takács 1999.18–19), Tacitus *Annals* 2.70–2.

Return of Agrippina (fig. 95): Tacitus *Annals* 3.1–2.

Drusus' twins: Tacitus *Annals* 2.84, cf. 4.15.1 (death of one in AD 23).

Prayer for Agrippina's children: Tacitus *Annals* 3.4.2, cf. 3.17.2 for Tiberius and Livia as the enemies. Appeal for calm: Tacitus *Annals* 3.6.2–3 (*firmitudo* and *constantia*).

Nero Caesar: Tacitus *Annals* 3.29.3, Suetonius *Tiberius* 54.1; *Fasti Ostienses* on AD 20 (Degrassi 1947.186–7), ten days after Drusus' triumph *ex Illyrico*.

244 Senate records: Crawford 1996.507–43 (*Tabula Siarensis*, text at 515–18, translation at 527–9), Damon and Takács 1999.13–41 (text and translation); for the chronology, see Woodman and Martin 1996.67–78.

Germanicus and Alexander: Tacitus *Annals* 2.73.1–3.

Senate's proposals: *Tabula Siarensis* a.9–34 (arches), b.2.11–20 (*libelli* of Tiberius and Drusus); Crawford 1996.515–16, 517–18.

Piso's treason: *SC de Pisone patre* 12–15, 45–7 (Damon and Takács 1999.14–17, 20–21, translation very slightly adapted).

'Pisonians': *SC de Pisone patre* 55–7 (Damon and Takács 1999.38–9). 'Pompeians': e.g. Velleius Paterculus 2.52.3–4 (48 BC), 2.62.1 and 5, 2.63.3, 2.65.1 (43 BC), 2.73.2 (41 BC); Seneca *De ira* 3.30.5 (44 BC); Seneca *Controversiae* 10.pref.5 (late Augustus); Tacitus *Annals* 4.34.3 (Augustus on Livy).

Soldiers' loyalty: *SC de Pisone patre* 160–5 (Damon and Takács 1999.38–9, translation slightly adapted), 'cum scirent *salutem* imperii nostri in eius domus custodia positam esse . . . *salutare* huic urbi imperioque p. R. nomen Caesarum'.

245 Sejanus: Dio Cassius 57.19.6 (sole command, single camp AD 20); Tacitus *Annals* 1.24.2 (*magna auctoritas* with Tiberius already in AD 14), 4.1–2.

Drusus and Sejanus: Tacitus *Annals* 4.3.2–3, 4.7. Death of Drusus: Tacitus *Annals* 4.8.1, 4.11.2, Dio Cassius 57.22.1–4.

Tiberius' speech: Tacitus *Annals* 4.8.2–5 (trans. Michael Grant, Penguin Classics); cf. Dio Cassius 57.22.4a. Reminder: Tacitus *Annals* 4.9.1, cf. Suetonius *Tiberius* 24.2.

Tiberius' retirement: Tacitus *Annals* 4.57–8, 4.67.1–3 (67.1 for the edict); Suetonius *Tiberius* 39–41.

Agrippina and Nero Caesar: Tacitus *Annals* 4.59.3–60.3 ('uelle id populum Romanum, cupere exercitus'), 4.67.3–4 ('perfugere ad Germaniae exercitus . . . populumque ac senatum auxilio uocare'), 4.70.4.

AD 28–9: Tacitus *Annals* 4.71.4 (Julia), 4.75 (younger Agrippina married), 5.1 (Livia).

246 Fate of Agrippina, Nero and Drusus: Tacitus *Annals* 5.3–5, Suetonius *Tiberius* 58.22.4–5. Roman People: Tacitus *Annals* 5.4.2–4, 5.5.

Sejanus: Dio Cassius 58.5–10 (58.13.1 for the ships), Suetonius *Tiberius* 65, Josephus *Jewish Antiquities* 18.181–2. Guard: Dio Cassius 58.9.2–5; Suetonius *Tiberius* 48.2 (1,000 *denarii* each), cf. Tacitus *Annals* 1.17.6 (two *denarii* per day).

People's revenge: Dio Cassius 58.11–12 (esp. 11.5, 12.1, 12.4), Valerius Maximus 9.11.ext.4 ('populi Romani uiribus obtritus'), Juvenal 10.56–81.

'Tiberius in Tiberim!': Suetonius *Tiberius* 75.1, cf. 66 ('iustissimo ciuium odio'), 72.2 ('ut uim multitudinis caueret'). *Libertas*: Dio Cassius 58.12.4–5.

247 Livia Julia: Dio Cassius 58.11.7, Tacitus *Annals* 6.2.1. Marriage of Drusus' daughter to Rubellius Blandus (AD 34): Tacitus *Annals* 6.27.1; cf. 14.22.1 for their son.

Heirs on Capri: Tacitus *Annals* 6.46.5, Suetonius *Gaius* 10.1, Dio Cassius 58.23.2–3. Gaius' tastes:

Suetonius *Gaius* 11.

Tiberius' fatalism: Suetonius *Gaius* 11 ('se natricem p. R. . . . educare'), Dio Cassius 58.23.3–4.

248 Liber's games: Ovid *Fasti* 3.784–6.

Ludi Augustales: *Fasti Amiternini* on 5 and 12 October (Degrassi 1963.194–5), fig. 84 above; *Tabula Hebana* 50–4 (Crawford 1996.521 and 531–2 for text and translation); Tacitus *Annals* 1.15.2–3, 1.54.2, Dio Cassius 56.46.4.

Ludi Palatini: *Fasti* of Filocalus and Silvius on 17–22 January (Degrassi 1963.238–9, 264); Josephus *Jewish Antiquities* 19.75–102, Tacitus *Annals* 1.73.3, Suetonius *Gaius* 56.2, Dio Cassius 56.46.5.

Historical plays (*fabulae praetextae*): Manuwald 2001, Kragelund et al. 2002. Classic texts: fragments and allusions in Manuwald 2001.131–248. Corinth play: Horace *Epistles* 2.1.187–93 and scholiasts (Manuwald 2001.71–5).

Inference: Wiseman 1998.1–63 for discussion and possible examples. Poets: e.g. Ovid *Fasti* 4.326. Historians: e.g. Livy 1.46.3, 5.21.9; Dionysius of Halicarnassus 3.18.1, 9.22.3; Plutarch *Romulus* 8.7.

Roman themes: Manilius *Astronomica* 5.477–85 ('scaenisque *togatos* aut magnos heroas aget'). Contemporary politics: e.g. Cornelius Gallus in Cicero *Ad familiares* 10.32.3, with Kragelund et al. 2002.29–34 and 94–5.

Gaius Gracchus: Plutarch *Gaius Gracchus* 14.4–16.5, with Wiseman 1998.52–9, Beness and Hillard 2001. Julius Caesar: Appian *Civil Wars* 2.146–7.606–12, with Weinstock 1971.353–7.

Praise of *princeps*: Phaedrus 5.7.57, Suetonius *Divus Augustus* 89.3, Pliny *Panegyricus* 54.1–2.

Funeral speech: Dio Cassius 59.3.8. Date: *Fasti Ostienses* on AD 37 (Degrassi 1947.190–1).

Ashes of Agrippina, Nero Caesar and Drusus Caesar: Suetonius *Gaius* 15.1, Dio Cassius 59.3.15. Date inferred from Germanicus' birthday on 24 May (*CIL* 6.2028.c.31).

Divus Augustus temple: Dio Cassius 59.7.1–2 (30–31 August, coinciding with Gaius' birthday), Suetonius *Tiberius* 47.1, *Gaius* 21.

249 Theatre demonstrations: Cicero *Pro Sestio* 106 ('de re publica populi Romani iudicium et uoluntas'), 119 ('uniuersi populi iudicium'), *Ad Quintum fratrem* 2.15.2 ('theatri significationes'), *Ad Atticum* 14.3.2 ('populi ἐπισημασίαν'), *Philippics* 1.36–7 ('consentientem populi Romani uniuersi uoluntatem'). Examples: Cicero *Pro Sestio* 105 (Gracchi), Plutarch *Cicero* 13.3 (63 BC), Cicero *Ad Atticum* 1.16.11 (61 BC), 2.19.3 (59 BC), *Pro Sestio* 115–16 (58 BC), 117–23 (57 BC), *In Pisonem* 65 (55 BC), *Ad familiares* 8.2.1 (51 BC), Velleius Paterculus 2.79.6 (31 BC).

Optimates: Appian *Civil Wars* 1.28.125 on 107–106 BC (ὡς τόδε στάσεων ἄρξον ἑτέρων), with North 1992; cf. Livy *Epitome* 48, Velleius Paterculus

1.15.3, Valerius Maximus 2.4.2, Augustine *City of God* 1.31 and Orosius 4.21.4 on 154 BC.

Moralists: Livy 7.2.13 (*insania*), Valerius Maximus 2.4.6 (*lautitia*), Pliny *Natural History* 36.5, 36.113–20.

Pompey's theatre: Asconius 1C (date), *Fasti Amiternini* on 12 August (Degrassi 1963.190–1, 'in theatro marmoreo'), Vitruvius *De architectura* 3.3.2 ('ad theatrum lapideum'), etc.

Caesar's plan: Suetonius *Divus Iulius* 44.1; not to be confused with the alleged Caesarian foundations of the theatre of Marcellus (Dio Cassius 48.49.2–3).

Augustan dates: Dio Cassius 54.25.2 (Balbus), Pliny *Natural History* 8.65 (Marcellus); cf. Ovid *Ars amatoria* 3.394 ('terna theatra'), Suetonius *Divus Augustus* 45.4 ('trina theatra').

Mime-dancers: Macrobius *Saturnalia* 2.7.12–19, Dio Cassius 54.17.4–5 (Pylades' comment), Suetonius *Divus Augustus* 45.4. Their groupies: Seneca *Epistles* 47.17 ('nobilissimos iuuenes mancipia pantomimorum'), Tacitus *Annals* 1.77.4 (senators and *equites*).

Riots: Tacitus *Annals* 1.54.2, Dio Cassius 56.47.2 (AD 14); Tacitus *Annals* 1.77.1 (AD 15); Velleius Paterculus 2.126.2 ('theatralis seditio'), Valerius Maximus 2.4.1 ('ciuili sanguine'). Senate: Tacitus *Annals* 1.77.2–3, 4.14.3 ('multa ab iis in publicum seditiose, foeda per domos temptari'); cf. Dio Cassius 57.21.3 (women).

Banished: Suetonius *Tiberius* 37.2, Tacitus *Annals* 4.14.3 (cf. 1.74.2, 'populum . . . ad duriora uertere'), Dio Cassius 57.21.3; Cassiodorus *Chronicle* on 115 BC. Pleas: Suetonius *Tiberius* 37.2. Monsters: Valerius Maximus 2.4.1 ('scaenica portenta').

Gaius on Capri: Suetonius *Gaius* 11 ('scaenicas saltandi canendique artes'), Philo *De legatione* 42; *pace* Barrett 1989.31, this is not contradicted by Philo *De legatione* 14 on Gaius' unluxurious upbringing.

Ban revoked: Dio Cassius 59.2.5. Golden Age: Philo *De legatione* 13, cf. Suetonius *Gaius* 13.

250 Drama scenes: Tacitus *Annals* 2.72.1 ('alia secreto per quae ostendere credebatur metum ex Tiberio'), 4.10.2–3 ('haec uulgo iactata'), Dio Cassius 58.10.

Instant myth: Tacitus *Annals* 4.11.2 ('quamuis fabulosa et immania credebantur, atrociore semper fama erga dominantium exitus'); cf. 3.19.2, 11.27.

Gaius as singer and dancer: Philo *De legatione* 42, Suetonius *Gaius* 11, 54, Dio Cassius 59.5.5, 59.29.6. Actor companions (Apelles and Mnester): Philo *De legatione* 203–6, Suetonius *Gaius* 33, 36.1, 55.1, Dio Cassius 59.5.2–4. See in general Beacham 1999.168–86.

Audience, performance: Philo *De legatione* 79, 111, 351, 359, 368; Seneca *De beneficiis* 2.12.1 ('in conspectu principum'), *De constantia animi* 18.2 ('in conuiuio, id est in contione').

Eye-witness: Philo *De legatione* 96 (χοροί συγκεκροτημένοι), 77–113 (gods); also Suetonius *Gaius* 52, Dio Cassius 59.26.5–8 (gods and goddesses). For the *choroi*, cf. Manilius *Astronomica* 5.484, Phaedrus 5.7.25, Lucian *De saltatione* 63.

Divinity: Philo *De legatione* 75–7, 162 etc.; Josephus *Jewish Antiquities* 19.4–6, Suetonius *Gaius* 22.2–4, Dio Cassius 59.26.5–28.8; Gradel 2002.146–59.

Mystery-cult: Josephus *Jewish Antiquities* 19.30, 71–2, 104; Suda 1.503 Adler (s.v. 'Gaios'). Dionysiac: Philo *De legatione* 79, 96, Dio Cassius 59.26.7 (playing a maenad), Aurelius Victor *De Caesaribus* 3.10 (Liber with *chorus Bacchanalis*); Gaius called himself ὁ νέος Διόνυσος (Athenaeus 4.148d).

Nocturnal performance: Suetonius *Gaius* 54.2, 57.4, Dio Cassius 59.5.5; cf. Suetonius *Gaius* 22.4, Dio Cassius 59.26.5 and 27.6 (Luna as Gaius' divine bedfellow).

Jupiter: Dio Cassius 59.26.5 and 9, Aurelius Victor *De Caesaribus* 3.10 (*ob incestum*); cf. Suetonius *Gaius* 52 (golden beard). Jupiter Latiaris: Suetonius *Gaius* 22.2, Dio Cassius 59.28.5.

Sisters: Josephus *Jewish Antiquities* 19.204 (Drusilla only); Suetonius *Gaius* 24, Dio Cassius 59.3.6, Aurelius Victor *De Caesaribus* 3.10, Orosius 7.5.9. Exile of Agrippina and Julia Livilla: Suetonius *Gaius* 29.2, Dio Cassius 59.22.6–8. Coin image (fig. 97): Sutherland 1987.72–4 (though the traditional identification of Agrippina as 'Securitas' seems to me arbitrary).

Full cult title of Salus: e.g. *CIL* 6.5034.16. Of Fortuna: e.g. *Fasti Caeretani* on 25 May (Degrassi 1963.67). Foundation dates: Livy 10.1.9, 34.53.5–6. Drusilla as Panthea: Dio Cassius 59.11; cf. Suetonius *Gaius* 24.2, Seneca *Consolatio ad Polybium* 17.5.

Venus: Suetonius *Gaius* 52, Dio Cassius 59.26.6, Aurelius Victor *De Caesaribus* 3.12. Mars (and escort): Philo *De legatione* 97. Liber: Athenaeus 4.148d; cf. Philo *De legatione* 79, 88, 96, Dio Cassius 59.26.6, Aurelius Victor *De Caesaribus* 3.10.

Senate: Seneca *De ira* 3.19.1–2, Josephus *Jewish Antiquities* 19.2, 19.50, Philo *De legatione* 108; Suetonius *Gaius* 26.2, 28, 30.2, 35.1, 48.2, 49.1; Dio Cassius 59.16.1–7, 59.18.1–5, 59.25.5, 59.26.2–3, 59.27.1; Aurelius Victor *De Caesaribus* 3.9. Magistrates: Suetonius *Gaius* 26.3, 32.3; Dio Cassius 59.20.1–3.

Eye-witness: Seneca *De beneficiis* 2.12, *De constantia animi* 18.2, *De ira* 3.18.4; cf. Suetonius *Gaius* 32.1 (executions), 36.2 (sexual taunts).

Self-indulgence: Philo *De legatione* 190 ('youth with absolute power is an evil that can't be fought'), Seneca *Consolatio ad Helviam* 10.4 ('summa uitia in summa fortuna'), Josephus *Jewish Antiquities* 19.201 ('once he had his fill of power, he used it for one purpose only, the pursuit of outrageous violence'), Suetonius *Gaius*

29.1 ('memento mihi omnia et in omnes licere').

Silk: Suetonius *Gaius* 52, Dio Cassius 59.26.10; cf. Seneca *De constantia animi* 18.3 (*perlucidus*).

Torture: Seneca *De ira* 18.3 ('non quaestionis sed animi causa'), 19.1–2, *De beneficiis* 4.31.2 ('sanguinis humani auidissimus'), Josephus *Jewish Antiquities* 19.43 ('not justice but his own pleasure'), Suetonius *Gaius* 11, 30.1, 32.1, 33.

Tiberius and the elections: Velleius Paterculus 2.124.3 ('primum principalium operum'), 2.126.2 ('summoto e foro seditio, ambitio campo'); Tacitus *Annals* 1.15.1 ('senatus largitionibus ac precibus sordidis exsolutus'). Gaius and the elections: Suetonius *Gaius* 16.2, Dio Cassius 59.9.6, 59.20.3–4 (later reversed).

Slaves: Josephus *Jewish Antiquities* 19.12–14, Suda 1.503 Adler (s.v. 'Gaios').

252 Brothel: Suetonius *Gaius* 41.1, Dio Cassius 59.28.9–10 ('the crowd enjoyed his licentiousness').

Taxes: Josephus *Jewish Antiquities* 19.25–9, Suetonius *Gaius* 40, Dio Cassius 59.28.8–11. Proscription: Dio Cassius 59.18.2–3.

One neck: Seneca *De ira* 3.19.2, Suetonius *Gaius* 30.2, Dio Cassius 59.13.6–7 (anger at informers).

'We aren't soldiers . . .': Wiseman 1991.8. Rule of law: Josephus *Jewish Antiquities* 19.57, cf. 19.190, etc.; Wiseman 1992.1–3 for the ideology.

Tiberius Gemellus: Philo *De legatione* 23–30, Suetonius *Gaius* 23.3, Dio Cassius 59.8.1.

Ludi Palatini: Josephus *Jewish Antiquities* 19.75, Suetonius *Gaius* 56.2; cf. Dio Cassius 56.46.5. Gaius' performance: Suetonius *Gaius* 54.2, 57.4. Chorus: Josephus *Jewish Antiquities* 19.104, Suetonius *Gaius* 58.1–2, Dio Cassius 59.29.6, 60.7.2.

Republic to resume: Josephus *Jewish Antiquities* 19.54, 79, 100, 183 (Chaerea on freedom); Wiseman 1992.1–13.

Senate meeting: Josephus *Jewish Antiquities* 19.167–84 (consul's speech); Orosius 7.6.3 ('de abrogando imperio ac re publica in antiquum ordinem restituenda euertendaque penitus Caesarum uniuersa familia'), Aurelius Victor *De Caesaribus* 3.16.

Caesonia and daughter: Josephus *Jewish Antiquities* 19.190–200 (199, ἐπὶ τελειώσει τοῦ δράματος), Suetonius *Gaius* 59.

Early life and character of Claudius: Suetonius *Divus Claudius* 2–9, Dio Cassius 60.2; Levick 1990.11–28 (who however consistently tries to make him more significant than the sources say).

Scholarly: Josephus *Jewish Antiquities* 19.164 and 213, Suetonius *Divus Claudius* 3.1, 40.3–42.2, Tacitus *Annals* 6.46.1, Dio Cassius 60.2.1. Drink: Suetonius *Divus Claudius* 5, 33.1, 40.1, Tacitus *Annals* 11.37.1, 12.67.1.

Found by Praetorians: Josephus *Jewish Antiquities* 19.162–4 and 212–26 ('Γερμανικὸς μὲν οὗτος', 217); Suetonius *Divus Claudius* 10.1–2, Dio Cassius

60.1.2–3. Mastery of the world: [Seneca] *Octavia* 26.

253 People's view: Josephus *Jewish Antiquities* 19.115, 158–9, 228 (cf. 189, 191, 272 for a more pro-senatorial version, and Wiseman 1991.xii-xiv on Josephus' sources); Suetonius *Divus Claudius* 10.4.

Praetorians' view: Josephus *Jewish Antiquities* 19.162–5, 214–15, 223–5; cf. Tacitus *Histories* 1.5.1 ('miles urbanus longo Caesarum sacramento imbutus'), *Annals* 14.7.4 ('praetorianos toti Caesarum domui obstrictos').

Bonus: Josephus *Jewish Antiquities* 19.247 (5,000 *denarii*), Suetonius *Divus Claudius* 10.4 (15,000 *sestertii* = 3,750 *denarii*); cf. Tacitus *Annals* 1.17.6 (two *denarii* per day).

Coin-type (fig. 99): Sutherland 1987.74–7.

Claudius as the first Roman emperor: C.E. Stevens in Levick 1990.41.

Legislative act, not directly attested but necessarily inferred: Levick 1990.42, who however alleges that 'blood relationship with Gaius justified his assuming it instantly', which I think is seriously misleading (Wiseman 1987.377). No doubt there was a senatorial resolution followed by a vote of the People (cf. Dio Cassius 60.1.4 and 3.2).

Legionary armies: Wiseman 1987.88–92. Civil war of AD 42: Suetonius *Divus Claudius* 13.2, 35.2, Dio Cassius 60.15.3–4.

Claudius' wives and children: Suetonius *Divus Claudius* 26–7, esp. 26.2 (with Syme 1986.147) on Messallina's descent, 27.2 on the birth of Britannicus.

Claudius in Britain: Suetonius *Divus Claudius* 17.1–2, Dio Cassius 60. 19–21; for Augustus' instruction, see Tacitus *Annals* 1.11.4, Dio Cassius 56.33.5–6.

256 Aphrodisias relief (fig. 100): Smith 1987.115–17, Plates XIV–XV.

The two Julias: Seneca *Apocolocyntosis* 10.4 ('proneptes . . . alteram ferro alteram fame'), Suetonius *Divus Claudius* 29.1, Dio Cassius 60.4.1 (recall), 60.8.5, 60.18.4.

Agrippina: Tacitus *Annals* 11.21.1 (Messallina distracted by 'nouo et furori proximo amore'). Anger of Venus: [Seneca] *Octavia* 253–68.

Messallina's promiscuity: Pliny *Natural History* 10.172, Juvenal 6.115–32, Dio Cassius 60.18.1–3, 60.31.1, Aurelius Victor *De Caesaribus* 4.5–7 (all referring to public prostitution). Particular adulterers: Pliny *Natural History* 29.8, Tacitus *Annals* 11.28.1, 11.30.2, Dio Cassius 60.22.3–5, 60.28.2–4.

Silius: Tacitus *Annals* 11.12.2–3, 11.26.1–31.1; Dio Cassius 60.31.3.

Messallina's wedding party: Tacitus *Annals* 11.31.2 ('strepente circum procaci choro') –38.2. Claudius' business in Ostia: Dio Cassius 60.31.4.

'Divine spirit transfused': Tacitus *Annals* 4.52.2 (citing Agrippina on her mother, 53.2).

L. Silanus: Suetonius *Divus Claudius* 27.2, Dio

Cassius 60.5.7; Seneca *Apocolocyntosis* 10.4 (Augustus' *abnepos*); for the Silani (his brothers died under Nero) see Syme 1986.191–2.

Agrippina as necessary empress: Tacitus *Annals* 12.2.3.

Senate and People: Tacitus *Annals* 12.5.2–7.1, Suetonius *Divus Claudius* 26.3, Dio Cassius 60.31.8 (cf. 60.32.2 for popular approval of Agrippina).

Silanus' suicide, betrothal of Octavia: Tacitus *Annals* 12.3.2–4.3, 12.8.1–9.2, Suetonius *Divus Claudius* 29.1–2, Dio Cassius 60.31.8.

Adoption: Tacitus *Annals* 12.25.1, Suetonius *Nero* 7.1. Marriage: Tacitus *Annals* 12.58.1 (AD 53). Portent: Dio Cassius 60.33.2 (Xiphilinus), Zonaras 11.10.

Popularity: Suetonius *Divus Claudius* 12.3, 21.5 (Claudius), 27.2 (Britannicus); Tacitus *Annals* 13.15.1 (Britannicus), 14.59.4, 14.60.5–61.2 (Octavia).

Scene in heaven: Seneca *Apocolocyntosis* 9.5 (Diespiter speech), 10–11 (Divus Augustus), 15.2 (Gaius). Deification of Claudius: Tacitus *Annals* 12.69.3, Suetonius *Divus Claudius* 45 ('honorem a Nerone destitutum abolitumque').

258 Seneca as tutor: Tacitus *Annals* 13.2.1, Suetonius *Nero* 7, etc. Clemency: Seneca *De clementia* 1.1, 1.11, 2.1–2.

Racine (second preface, 1676): 'J'avais copié mes personnages d'après le plus grand peintre de l'antiquité, je veux dire Tacite. Et j'étais alors si rempli de la lecture de cet excellent historien qu'il n'y a presque pas un trait éclatant dans ma tragédie dont il ne m'ait donné l'idée.'

Paris: Tacitus *Annals* 13.19.3–20.1 (cf. 22.2, Paris 'ualidior apud libidines principis'); for aunt Domitia see Syme 1986.159–62.

Poppaea: Tacitus *Annals* 13.45–6 ('acri iam principis amore ad superbiam uertens', 46.2), 14.1; Dio Cassius 61.11.1–2.

Enthusiasm for games (*ludi*): Tacitus *Annals* 13.24.1 and 25.4, Suetonius *Nero* 26.2, Dio Cassius 61.8.2–3 (AD 55–6); details in Champlin 2003.68–77. Popularity of Nero as a second Gaius: Dio Cassius 61.5.1–2.

Boat attempt: [Seneca] *Octavia* 309–55, Tacitus *Annals* 14.3–6, Suetonius *Nero* 34.2–3; Dio Cassius 61.12.2 (theatre) –14.3.

Murder, last words: [Seneca] *Octavia* 356–76, Tacitus *Annals* 14.7–8, Suetonius *Nero* 34.3, Dio Cassius 61.13.4–5. Stripped corpse: Tacitus *Annals* 14.9.1 ('some say'), Suetonius *Nero* 34.4, Dio Cassius 61.14.2.

259 'Grow up quickly . . .': Suetonius *Divus Claudius* 43 (trans. Robert Graves, Penguin Classics 1957), Dio Cassius 60.34.1; Graves 1934b ch. 32.

Agrippina and Nero: Tacitus *Annals* 12.42.1 (Prefects), 12.69.1 (accession), 13.14.2–3. 'Crowning'

relief (fig. 101): Smith 1987.127–30, Plates XXIV–XXVI.

Saturnalia: Tacitus *Annals* 13.15.2 (song), cf. 13.17.2 (*stuprum*).

Poison: Tacitus *Annals* 13.15.3–5 (a scene with Nero, Locusta the poisoner, and the Guard cohort commander), 13.16–17 (dinner and funeral); Suetonius *Nero* 33.2–3.

261 Welcome back: Tacitus *Annals* 14.13.2.

Nero's talents: Tacitus *Annals* 14.14–16, Suetonius *Nero* 11–12, 20–2, Dio Cassius 61.19–21, etc.; Beacham 1999.206–29.

Rubellius Plautus: Tacitus *Annals* 14.22 (exile, AD 60), 14.57.1–59.3 (death, AD 62) Faustus Sulla: Tacitus *Annals* 13.23.1 (Antonia), 13.47 (exile, AD 58), 14.57 (death, AD 62).

Poppaea supplants Octavia: Tacitus *Annals* 14.59.3–64.2 (61.1 for riots); Suetonius *Nero* 35.1–3 ('improbante diuortium populo'), cf. 46.1 for Nero's dream of dead Octavia and the *multitudo* of ants.

Tigellinus' orgy (Champlin 2003.153–60): Tacitus *Annals* 15.37.1–3, Dio Cassius 62.15; on Tacitus' narrative see Woodman 1998.168–79.

262 Fire: Tacitus *Annals* 15.38–41 (39.1–2 for relief efforts), Suetonius *Nero* 38 (under the heading of *crudelitas* [26.1] against the *populus*), Dio Cassius 62.16.1–18.2.

While Rome burned: Tacitus *Annals* 15.39.3 (*Excidium Troiae*), Suetonius *Nero* 38.2 (*Halosis Ilii*), Dio Cassius 62.18.1 (Ἅλωσις Ἰλίου). Actor emperor: Champlin 2003.53–83.

Sibyl: Dio Cassius 62.18.4.

Poppaea: Tacitus *Annals* 15.23.1–3 (baby dies, AD 63), 16.6.1 (death, AD 65), Suetonius *Nero* 35.3, Dio Cassius 62.28.1–2.

Failed plot: Tacitus *Annals* 15.48–74 (with Woodman 1998.190–217), Suetonius *Nero* 36 ('nobilissimo cuique exitium destinauit'), Dio Cassius 62.24.27.

Seneca: Tacitus *Annals* 15.60.2–63.3, Suetonius *Nero* 35.5, Dio Cassius 62.25. Lucan: Tacitus *Annals* 15.70, Martial 7.21, Statius *Silvae* 2.7.100–1.

Epic: Lucan *Civil War* 5.385–6 (lies), 7.432–6 (liberty), 7.457–9 (dead men deified), 7.638–45 (future tyranny).

Crowning of Tiridates: Suetonius *Nero* 13 (a *spectaculum*), Dio Cassius 63.1–6; Champlin 2003.221–9. Return from Greek tour: Suetonius *Nero* 25.1–2, Dio Cassius 63.19.2–21.1; Champlin 2003.229–34.

Conspiracies and executions: Tacitus *Annals* 16.7–35 ('ciuium exitus', 16.16.1), Suetonius *Nero* 36.1–2, Dio Cassius 62.26, 63.17; Pliny *Letters* 3.5.5, 5.5.3; Griffin 1984.171–82. Nero's war on the Senate: Suetonius *Nero* 43.1, Dio Cassius 63.15.1, 63.27.2.

Rebellions: Suetonius *Nero* 40–4, 47.1, *Galba* 9.2–10.3, Dio Cassius 63.22–5 and 27.1; Sutherland 1987.103–9.

Praetorian Guard: Plutarch *Galba* 2.2, 14.2, Tacitus *Histories* 1.5.1.

Nero's last hours: Suetonius *Nero* 47.3–49.4, Dio Cassius 63.27.3–29.2—probably from Cluvius Rufus (on whom see Wiseman 1991.111–17), but the ultimate source must be one of Nero's four companions.

263 Romans in Elysium: [Virgil] *Culex* 358–71; cf. Virgil *Aeneid* 6.756–853 (waiting for metempsychosis), Manilius *Astronomica* 1.777–99 (Milky Way), Silius Italicus 13.703–31 ('loca amoena piorum'), etc.

Cicero's epic (Goldberg 1995.148–54): Cicero *Ad Atticum* 2.3.4, *De divinatione* 1.17–22. Catiline and Cato: Virgil *Aeneid* 8.666–70; cf. 1.148–53, 6.815–16, 11.336–41 for optimate attitudes in the *Aeneid*.

Admiration of Cicero: Velleius Paterculus 2.66.2–5, Valerius Maximus 5.3.4 ('caput Romanae eloquentiae').

Tiberius Gracchus: Velleius Paterculus 2.3.2 ('perniciosa consilia'), Valerius Maximus 4.7.1 ('inimicus patriae'), 7.2.6b ('sapientia senatus'). Gaius Gracchus: Velleius Paterculus 2.6.2 ('regalis potentia'), Valerius Maximus 9.4.3 ('bono exemplo').

Gracchi attack *status ciuitatis*: Valerius Maximus 6.3.1d; cf. Velleius Paterculus 2.6.3 (Gaius Gracchus leaves nothing *in eodem statu*).

Lucan and the *populares*: Lucan *Civil War* 1.268–71, 4.799–802 (Curio); 3.52–8 (Caesar and the fickle mob); 7.574–85, 7.760–1 (Pharsalus as the victory of the *plebs* over the *nobilitas*). Caesar and the infernal gods: Lucan *Civil War* 7.168–71, 7.768–86, etc.

Underworld: Lucan *Civil War* 6.778–99.

264 'Qualis artifex pereo' (trans. Robert Graves, Penguin Classics) and 'Haec est fides': Suetonius *Nero* 49.1 (cf. Dio Cassius 63.29.2), 49.4. Champlin (2003.50–1) believes that Nero said 'What an artisan I am in my dying', a rueful comment on the *ad hoc* grave he and his companions were trying to construct; but on that translation *pereo* seems redundant (contrast Graves' emphasis on the word). In any case, what matters for our purpose is not what Nero may have meant at the time, but how the famous last words (τὸ θρυλούμενον ἐκεῖνο, says Dio) contributed to his myth.

Galba (fig. 102): Suetonius *Galba* 10.1, Plutarch *Galba* 5.2 ('legatus senatus populique Romani'); Sutherland 1984.204–5 nos. 17 and 20, Plate 23.

Celebration of freedom: Dio Cassius 63.29.1, Zonaras 11.13. Emperor's job: Tacitus *Annals* 15.36.3–4, Suetonius *Divus Vespasianus* 18, etc.

Recognition of Galba: Suetonius *Galba* 11, Dio Cassius 63.29.6. Statues and remains restored: Dio Cassius 64.3.4c (Zonaras 11.14).

265 Playwrights: Tacitus *Dialogus* 11.2 (with Kragelund et al. 2002.38–40 and 95–8) on Curiatius Maternus' *Nero*. [Seneca] *Octavia*: Kragelund et al. 2002.41–51;

date established independently by Barnes 1982 and Kragelund 1982.38–52.

Octavia's portico: Festus 188L. Claudian tombs: Suetonius *Tiberius* 1.1, *CIL* 6.1282; La Rocca 1987.365–8. Pietas temple: Pliny *Natural History* 7.121, *Fasti Amiternini* on 1 December (Degrassi 1963.198–9).

'Resplendent Dawn . . .': [Seneca] *Octavia* 1–33, trans. E.F. Watling, Penguin Classics.

267 'Her only solace . . .': *Octavia* 51–6; I think *nostra* (51, 53) and *noster* (55) are genuinely 'our', not 'my'.

Shadow of a great name: *Octavia* 71, Lucan *Civil War* 1.135.

Exostra: Cicero *De provinciis consularibus* 14, where the casual allusion implies familiarity; unfortunately not included among the Roman stage devices discussed in Beacham 1991.169–83.

Noble blood: *Octavia* 88, cf. 148–9 (Silanus), 168–9 (Britannicus), 471–2, 495–6 (Sulla and Plautus), 505–6, 641, 884; cf. Plutarch *Galba* 5.2, Tacitus *Histories* 1.15.1 for Galba and the *nobiles*.

Proud harlot: *Octavia* 125–33. Pietas and Erinys: *Octavia* 160–3, cf. 911–13 (*pietas* of the Roman People, 52, 286, 674).

Citizens v. emperor: *Octavia* 183–5, cf. 572–9, 646–50, 792–805, 820–56, 877–98 (*fauor ciuium*, 183, 648, 792); see Kragelund et al. 2002.45–50.

Nurse: *Octavia* 196–221 (219–20 for Octavia as Juno, 'soror Augusti coniunxque'). Avenger: *Octavia* 254–69 (*vindex deus*, 255).

'Yet our forefathers . . .': *Octavia* 273–303 (291–4 trans. E.F. Watling, Penguin Classics).

268 Tullia: 304–8, cf. Livy 1.46.3 ('tulit et Romana regia sceleris tragici exemplum'). Agrippina: 309–76, fifty years or so before Tacitus *Annals* 14.4–8.

Seneca: 377–436. Plautus and Sulla: 437–9.

Dialogue with Nero: 440–592 (Watling's translation of 471).

269 Saving the citizens (*ob ciues seruatos*): Sutherland 1984.43–4, 47 (Augustus), 211–12 (Augustus re-used in AD 68), 235, 241 (Galba); *Octavia* 444, 495 ('seruare ciues'). Nero on Augustus: 504–29.

Agrippina: 593–645. 'Through opened earth . . .': 593–7 (Watling's translation of 593). 'Why do I wait . . .?': 644.

270 Wedding: described in retrospect at 699–702; Treggiari 1991.161–70. Portrait masks: Dio Cassius 63.9.5. Nero's staff: Plutarch *Galba* 17.2, Dio Cassius 64.3.4.

Poppaea as *uictrix*: *Octavia* 131, 672–3 (cf. 300, 'uictrix dira libido').

Octavia and citizens: 646–89; translation of 646–50 and 669–89 by E.F. Watling, Penguin Classics. For the chronological problem (which day is dawning?), see Kragelund et al. 2002.87, 99–100; I still resist Kragelund's solution, because it would involve an implausible 24–hour gap between the citizens' attack on the palace and the messenger's report of it.

271 Poppaea and nurse: 690–777 (Watling's translation of 776–7). Messenger and courtiers: 778–819 ('regna euertit Priami, claras diruit urbes', 816–17).

Nero and Prefect: 820–76.

272 Sister's head: 861 'dirum caput', cf. 133 and Tacitus *Annals* 14.64.2; just before his suicide (Suetonius *Nero* 49.4), Nero desperately begged his companions not to let the Praetorians take his head.

Citizens' chorus: 877–98. Octavia in chains: 899–981.

Temple of Hope (*Spes in foro Holitorio*): Livy 25.7.6 (just outside the Porta Carmentalis), Tacitus *Annals* 2.49.2 (rededicated by Germanicus). Germanicus and *libertas*: Tacitus *Annals* 1.33.2 ('fauor et spes'), 2.82.2, 3.4.2 ('nihil spei reliquum').

Nymphidius: Plutarch *Galba* 2.1–2 (7,500 *denarii* per man), 8–9 (imperial ambitions), 13–14 (death). Descent from Caligula: Tacitus *Annals* 15.72.2, Plutarch *Galba* 9.1–2.

Galba on Praetorians' demands: Tacitus *Histories* 1.5, Suetonius *Galba* 16.1, Plutarch *Galba* 18.2, Dio Cassius 64.3.3.

Death of Galba: Tacitus *Histories* 1.40–42, Suetonius *Galba* 19–20, Plutarch *Galba* 26.1–27.3, Dio Cassius 64.6.1–4.

273 Sporus (Champlin 2003.145–50): Dio Chrysostomos *Orations* 21.6–7, Suetonius *Nero* 28, 46.2, Dio Cassius 62.28.2–3, 63.12.3–4.

Last scene with Nero: Suetonius *Nero* 48.1, 49.3, Dio Cassius 63.27.3, [Aurelius Victor] *Epitome de Caesaribus* 5.7, John of Antioch 92M, Zonaras 11.13.

Nymphidius and Otho: Plutarch *Galba* 9.3, Dio Cassius 64.8.3. Vitellius' plan: Dio Cassius 65.10.1; Coleman 1990 (quotation from p. 69); Champlin 2003.147–8 for Proserpina (though ὕβριν in Dio's text shows that it was no mere stage performance).

274 Vitellius on Capri: Suetonius *Vitellius* 3.2 ('inter Tiberiana scorta').

Otho and the heroes of *deuotio*: Dio Cassius 64.13.2.

Death of Vitellius: Tacitus *Histories* 3.84.4–85, Suetonius *Vitellius* 17 ('minutissimis ictibus excarnificatus'). Danube legions: Tacitus *Histories* 3.71–2 (burning of Capitol temple), 4.1 (loot and murder).

'The story upon which . . .': Tacitus *Histories* 1.2.1, 1.3.2 (trans. Kenneth Wellesley, Penguin Classics, very slightly adapted).

Vespasian: Tacitus *Histories* 2.5.1 ('antiquis ducibus par'); Suetonius *Divus Vespasianus* 4.3 (turnips), 8.3 (garlic), 12–16, 22; Dio Cassius 66.11.

Luxury unfashionable: Tacitus *Annals* 3.55.4. Censorship (AD 73–4): Suetonius *Divus Vespasianus* 8.1 ('prope afflictam nutantemque rem p. stabilire').

Colosseum: Martial *De spectaculis* 1–2 ('deliciae populi quae fuerant domini', 2.12). Other public

works: Suetonius *Divus Vespasianus* 9.1, Dio Cassius 66.10.1–3.

Becoming a god: Suetonius *Divus Vespasianus* 23.4, Dio Cassius 66.17.3. Succession: Suetonius *Divus Vespasianus* 25, Dio Cassius 66.12.1.

275 Vesuvius: Pliny *Letters* 6.16, 6.20 (translation of 6.20.9, 11, 13–15 by Betty Radice, Penguin Classics); Dio Cassius 66.23.1 (Giants); Lytton 1834 Book V chapters 5 and 7.

Pliny and Vespasian: Pliny *Letters* 3.5.9. Pliny on 'god' (*quaestio de deo*): *Natural History* 2.14–27; quotation from 2.18 (cf. Marcus Aper in Tacitus *Dialogus* 17.3, 'Vespasianus rem publicam fouet').

276 Titus: Suetonius *Divus Titus* 1 ('amor ac deliciae generis humani'), 5.2 (Jerusalem), 8.3 (disasters).

Domitian: Suetonius *Domitian* 6 (wars), 7.3 (soldiers' pay), 10–13 (character); discussion of his campaigns in Jones 1992.126–59.

Antonius Saturninus rebellion and aftermath: Suetonius *Domitian* 6.2, 10.5, Dio Cassius 67.11.1–3.

Senators: Tacitus *Agricola* 45.1–2 (trans. Harold Mattingly, Penguin Classics rev. ed. 1970); Pliny *Panegyricus* 48.3–5, 76.3–4, etc.

Palace plot: Suetonius *Domitian* 16–17, Dio Cassius 67.15–17, [Aurelius Victor] *Epitome de Caesaribus* 11.11–12. Varied reactions: Suetonius *Domitian* 23 (probably a first-hand observation).

Mutiny: Pliny *Panegyricus* 5.7–6.2, [Aurelius Victor] *Epitome de Caesaribus* 12.6–8.

Tacitus: Pliny *Letters* 2.1.6 (consulship), with Syme 1958.70, 640–2; quotations from Syme 1958.130, 194.

277 Historian's responsibility: Tacitus *Histories* 3.51.2 ('exempla recti aut solacia mali'), *Annals* 4.33.1–2. 'If I live . . .': Tacitus *Histories* 1.1.4.

Umbricius: Juvenal 3.1–20, 60–1 ('non possum ferre, Quirites, Graecam urbem'), 248 ('in digito clauus mihi militis haeret'), etc.

CHAPTER **10**

279 Alphabet: Fabius Pictor *FGrH* 809 F23, Tacitus *Annals* 11.14.3; cf. Livy 1.7.8, Hyginus *Fabulae* 277.2; Gabba 2000.159–64.

Influential authorities: e.g. Wissowa 1902, Latte 1926, Rose 1928. ch. 11 ('Italian Pseudo-Mythology'). Refuted by Feeney 1998.47–75—but even he, by concentrating on *literature*, may give the unwary reader the impression that it all began in the late third century BC.

'Demythologising': see Gabba 2000.187–9 for a convenient summary, and Carandini 2002.133, 137, 162 etc. for a modern version of the idea.

280 Christians in AD 64: Tacitus *Annals* 15.44.2–5, trans. Michael Grant (Penguin Classics); Champlin 2003.121–6. Victims: *Romans* 13.1–6 ('powers that be'), 16.13–15 (names).

281 Peter and Paul: Eusebius *History of the Church* 2.25; *Acta apostolorum apocrypha* 1–234 Lipsius. Antichrist: Champlin 2003.17–21.

John's prophecy: *Revelation* 1.9 (Patmos), 17–18 (denunciation of Rome, quotation from 17.5). Date: Irenaeus *Against Heresies* 5.30.3.

Demons: e.g. Tertullian *Apologeticus* 22–3 (22.12 for miracles), Augustine *City of God* 10.16, 22.10–11.

Sack of Rome: Jerome *Epistles* 123.16 (trans. Brown 1967.289).

Negative spin: Orosius 1.pref.10 ('quaecumque aut bellis grauia aut corrupta morbis aut fame tristia aut terrarum motibus terribilia aut inundationibus aquarum insolita aut eruptionibus ignium metuenda aut ictibus fulminum plagisque grandinum saeua uel etiam parricidiis flagitiisque misera per transacta retro saecula'); 2.4.2–8 on Romulus and no Numa.

Manuscripts: Arnaud-Lindet 1990.lxvii–lxviii ('le "manuel" d'histoire universelle le plus prisé par les clercs du Moyen-Âge'). Dedication: Orosius 1.pref.1 and 8–10.

282 'Domine, quo uadis?': *Acts of Peter* 31–6 = *Acta apostolorum apocrypha* 80–91 Lipsius; translation in Hennecke 1965.314–18 (275 for the date). Umbricius and the Aventine: Juvenal 3.84–5.

283 Augustine and pagan authors: O'Daly 1999.234–55.

Augustine on the Roman tradition: *City of God* 1.15, 2.29 (translations by Henry Bettenson, Penguin Classics).

Attack on theatre: Augustine *City of God* 1.32–3, 2.8–10, 6.6–7; Orosius 3.4.4–5, 4.21.5–6.

God-given empire: Augustine *City of God* 5.12–19. Roman empire and the birth of Christ: Orosius 6.22.5–11; cf. Origen *Contra Celsum* 2.30, Eusebius *History of the Church* 4.26.7–8 (quoting Melito of Sardis).

Empire deserved: Augustine *City of God* 5.14–15, 5.18 (translations by Henry Bettenson, Penguin Classics); *Matthew* 6.2, Virgil *Aeneid* 6.819–23.

284 'Guardians of language': Kaster 1988.70–95.

Gregory the Great: Llewellyn 1971.78–108, Brown 2003.190–215.

Remulus: Orosius 2.4.1, with the *apparatus criticus* at *Corpus scriptorum ecclesiasticorum Latinorum* 5.88 ('urbs Roma in Italia a Romulo et Remulo geminis auctoribus condita est'): for the *Laurentianus* pl 65.1, see Arnaud-Lindet 1990.lxx–lxxi.

'English': Brown 2003.351–2 on the name used by Bede.

285 The Franks casket (fig. 103): Swanton 1999.7 (date), 9–14 (front scene), 14–16 (left-hand side), 16–19 (back), 19–22 (right-hand side), 23–5 (lid). The back scene is shown in reverse in Carandini and Cappelli 2000.240.

286 Rambona diptych (fig. 104): Goldschmidt 1914.86–7 (no. 181, plate 84); Presicce 2000.108. The inscrip-

tions on the cross are from John 19.19–21 and 26–7.

287 Aeneas as refugee: Orosius 1.18.1 ('Aeneae Troia profugi').

Ageltrude: Leporace 1960, Llewellyn 1971.286–96.

Cotehele tapestries: Lemmey 1999; cf. Mahl 1965.12–13 and figs 4–5 for the recognition scene on the Vienna tapestries.

Recognition scene: Justin 43.2.10 ('repente Faustulus cum Romulo superuenit; a quo origine cognita puerorum ...'); contrast Livy 1.5.3–7, Plutarch *Romulus* 7.1–8.6. Justin in the Middle Ages: Reynolds 1983.197–9.

288 The corpse synod: Liudprand of Cremona *Antapodosis* 1.28–31; Auxilius *In defensionem sacrae ordinationis Papae Formosi* 1.10 (Dümmler 1866.71); Llewellyn 1971.291–3.

289 Numitor as deposed king: Orosius 2.4.3.

290 Virgil the guide: Dante *Inferno* 1.70–2 and 124–6 (trans. Sisson 1981.49–50), 34.61–9.

Petrarch: 'Totius humanae magnificentiae supremum domicilium Roma est... Quis enim magnificum, quaeso, legit umquam aliquid, aut audiuit, sine nomine et gloria urbis Romae?' (Bufano 1975.1196).

Gods and goddesses: Seznec 1953.

Machiavelli: *Discourses on Livy* 3.1, 3.25 (trans. Julia Conaway Bondanella and Peter Bondanella, World's Classics).

291 Tacitus: R.J. Tarrant in Reynolds 1983.406–9. Lipsius: text and translation in Morford 1993.138. For the 'Tacitism' of the late sixteenth and seventeenth centuries, see Burke 1969.

Early modern Europe: 'The enthusiasm for Tacitus coincides approximately with the age of religious wars in Europe, 1559–1648, and with the longer-term rise of courts and of absolute monarchy. Tacitus described a period of civil war, and emperors with unlimited power' (Burke 1969.168).

292 Shakespeare: *Julius Caesar* 1.1.36–55; cf. Plutarch *Gaius Gracchus* 16.5 (Wiseman 1998.55); ingratitude also at the death of Cassius Chaerea (Josephus *Jewish Antiquities* 19.272).

Jonson and the Privy Council: Ayres 1983 (the trial of Silius in Act 3 of *Sejanus*, based on Tacitus *Annals* 4.18–20, also alluded to the notorious trial of Ralegh in 1603). Sir John Eliot: Burke 1969.161–2.

May's Lucan and its context: Norbrook 1999.23–50.

293 Marvell: *An Horatian Ode upon Cromwell's Return from Ireland* (1650) lines 9–16, 21–6; cf. Lucan *Civil War* 1.143–57.

Milton: Wolfe 1953.640 (Brutus), 792 (Curtius), 855 (Fabricius and Curius).

Dryden: Hammond 1999.84–92 (*Astraea Redux*), 231–3 (*Aeneid* 1.1–7), 249–60 ('restoration'), 277–8 (*Aeneid* 6.777–8).

294 Liberty and civic virtue: Ayres 1997.1–29 (cf. Cato in

Act 4 of Addison's play: 'Oh, liberty! Oh, virtue! Oh, my country!').

Patrick Henry: Litto 1966.444–5 (*Cato* Act 2: 'It is not now a time to talk of aught | But chains, or conquest; liberty, or death'). Washington: Litto 1966.441–2, 447 (Valley Forge); Richard 1994.57–60.

Chénier's *Gaius Gracchus*: Thom 1995.38–9 for its reception.

295 Brutus and the National Convention: Parker 1937.139–42, citing *Le moniteur* 42 (2 November 1793) 314 for the obsolescence of St Blaise at Ris.

Individuals: Keaveney 1990 on the revolutionary Babeuf, who took the names first of Camillus and then of Gracchus.

Marx's comment (in 'Der 18te Brumaire des Louis Napoleon', 1852): Marx-Engels 1979.104.

296 Napoleon on Tacitus: Mellor 1993.157–8.

'Now, therefore. . .': *Hansard* (third series) 2.1204–5, 2 March 1831.

'My opinions. . .': Pinney 1974–81.1.133 (September 1819). For 'Macaulay's Rome', see Edwards 1999 (who however ignores the political background).

297 'You are acquainted. . .': Pinney 1974–81.4.44 (14 July 1842). For the Perizonius-Niebuhr theory see Momigliano 1957; Horsfall 2003.96–8 for judicious scepticism.

298 'Peculiar character': Macaulay 1842.6–7. Alternative theory: Wiseman 1994.12–16, 1995a.129–33; Plutarch *Romulus* 8.7, Dionysius of Halicarnassus 3.18.1. Theatre audience as *populus Romanus*: e.g. Cicero *Pro Sestio* 106, 116, *In Pisonem* 65, *Ad Atticum* 2.19.3, 14.3.2.

'To be sure. . .': Pinney 1974–81.4.67–8 (29 October 1842). Popular success (293,000 copies sold by 1912): Gray 1984.80–91.

299 'Now, by your children's cradles. . .': 'Virginia', lines 93–4, 109–12, 143–4; cf. Livy 3.45.6–11.

300 English non-revolution: Prochaska 2000.69–85.

Roman Republic foundation decree: *House of Commons Parliamentary Papers* 1851.lvii.156–7.

English poet: Arthur Hugh Clough, 'Amours de Voyage' canto 2, lines 20–23 (Mulhauser 1974.104). Cf. William Cowper, 'Boadicea: an Ode' (1782), line 20: 'Hark! The Gaul is at her gates!'

301 Comic history (fig. 108): À Beckett 1852.v (Preface), 146 (Curius), 308 (Augustus).

Mommsen's *History* and its background: Wiedemann 1996. Quotations from Mommsen 1854–6.book II ch. 1 (on the end of the monarchy) and

Book V ch. 11 (on Caesar) are by W.P. Dickson, whose translation was published in 1862–75.

302 'A generation ago. . .': Seeley 1883.237–8; for the background see Hingley 2000.19–27.

The 'centurion of the Thirtieth': Kipling 1906.137–225; cf. Rivet 1978 for the historical background.

'Mithras, God of the Morning. . .': Kipling 1906.191 = 1940.523 ('Hymn of the XXX Legion, circa AD 350').

Puck as Faun: Kipling 1906.143, cf. 15 ('bad country for Gods'). For Fauns in England from the 1890s to the 1920s, see Jenkyns 1980.188–91 (also Hutton 1999.43–51 for Pan).

303 'God of our fathers. . .': Kipling 1940.328–9 ('Recessional', first and third stanzas); cf. Carrington 1955.263–8 for its reception.

Toga plays: Mayer 1994.2–11 (Victorian imperial background), 104–88 (*The Sign of the Cross*), 189–290 (play of *Ben-Hur*); Wyke 1997.110–18 (*Quo Vadis?*).

Toga films: Mayer 1994.312–21; Wyke 1997.14–33 (history of the genre), 110–46 (*Quo Vadis?* and *The Sign of the Cross*).

304 Italy and imperial Rome: Wyke 1997.18–22, 1999a (before 1922), 1999b ('sawdust Caesar'); Stone 1999 (Fascism and *romanità*). For Mussolini and Roman archaeology, see Manacorda and Tamassia 1985.

305 Colonel Walton at the party: Adleman and Walton 1968.284.

The message of *Spartacus*: Wyke 1997.63–72 (71 for Kennedy), Futrell 2001.77 (publicity), 97–9. Novel: Fast 1952, penultimate paragraph.

Post-war American movies: Winkler 2001; also Winkler 1995 on *The Fall of the Roman Empire*, 'the most intelligent of all Roman epics'.

306 Maximus the general: Kipling 1906.155–6, 158–60, 183–9, 197–202, 206–17.

Senator Gracchus: at Gram 2000.37 (dialogue omitted in the film) Marcus refers to him as 'that fat man in Rome'—not right for Derek Jacobi, but a clear allusion to the fat Gracchus of *Spartacus* (novel and film).

'How will the world. . .': Gram 2000.49–50 (I quote the film version, not quite the same as in the book).

'To give power. . .': Gram 2000.51. 'The Senate *is* the people. . .': Gram 2000.111.

Maximus' last words: I quote the film version, added to Gram 2000.225.

BIBLIOGRAPHY

À Beckett 1852: Gilbert Abbott À Beckett, *The Comic History of Rome, from the Founding of the City to the End of the Commonwealth*. London: Bradbury and Evans.

Adleman and Walton 1968: Robert H. Adleman and Colonel George Walton, *Rome Fell Today*. Boston: Little, Brown.

Alföldi 1965: Andrew Alföldi, *Early Rome and the Latins* (Jerome Lectures series 7). Ann Arbor: University of Michigan Press.

Alföldy 2000: Géza Alföldy, 'Das neue Edikt des Augustus aus El Bierzo', *Zeitschrift für Papyrologie und Epigraphik* 131: 177–205.

Ammerman 1990: A. Ammerman, 'On the Origins of the Roman Forum', *American Journal of Archaeology* 94: 627–46.

Ando 2000: Clifford Ando, *Imperial Ideology and Provincial Loyalty in the Roman Empire*. Berkeley: University of California Press.

Andreussi 1996: M. Andreussi, '"Murus Servii Tullii"; mura repubblicane', in Eva Margareta Steinby (ed.), *Lexicon Topographicum Urbis Romae* 3, H–O (Rome: Quasar): 319–24.

Angelelli and Falzone 1999: Claudia Angelelli and Stella Fanzone, 'Considerazioni sull'occupazione protostorica nell'area sud-occidentale del Palatino', *Journal of Roman Archaeology* 12: 5–32.

Arnaud-Lindet 1990: Marie-Pierre Arnaud-Lindet (ed.), *Orose, Histoires (Contre les Païens)*, vol. 1. Paris: Les Belles Lettres.

Astin 1967: A.E. Astin, *Scipio Aemilianus*. Oxford: Clarendon Press.

Astin 1978: Alan E. Astin, *Cato the Censor*. Oxford: Clarendon Press.

Austin 1981: M.M. Austin (ed.), *The Hellenistic World from Alexander to the Roman Conquest: A Selection of Ancient Sources in Translation*. Cambridge University Press.

Ayres 1983: Philip J. Ayres, 'Jonson, Northampton, and the "Treason" in *Sejanus*', *Modern Philology* 80: 356–63.

Ayres 1997: Philip Ayres, *Classical Culture and the Idea of Rome in Eighteenth-Century England*. Cambridge University Press.

Badian 1962: E. Badian, review of Taylor 1960, *Journal of Roman Studies* 52: 200–210.

Badian 1966: E. Badian, 'The Early Historians', in T.A. Dorey (ed.), *Latin Historians* (London: Routledge and Kegan Paul): 1–38.

Barnes 1982: Timothy D. Barnes, 'The Date of the *Octavia*', *Museum Helveticum* 39: 215–17.

Barrett 1989: Anthony A. Barrett, *Caligula: The Corruption of Power*. London: Batsford.

Barrett 2002: Anthony A. Barrett, *Livia: First Lady of Imperial Rome*. New Haven: Yale University Press.

Battaglia and Emiliozzi 1979: Gabriella Bordenache Battaglia and Adriana Emiliozzi, *Le ciste prenestine*, I Corpus: 1.1. Rome: Consiglio nazionale delle ricerche.

Battaglia and Emiliozzi 1990: Gabriella Bordenache Battaglia and Adriana Emiliozzi, *Le ciste prenestine*, I Corpus: 1.2. Rome: Consiglio nazionale delle ricerche.

Beacham 1991: Richard C. Beacham, *The Roman Theatre and its Audience*. London: Routledge.

Beacham 1999: Richard C. Beacham, *Spectacle Entertainments of Early Imperial Rome*. New Haven: Yale University Press.

Beard 1990: Mary Beard, 'Priesthood in the Roman Republic', in Mary Beard and John North (eds), *Pagan Priests: Religion and Power in the Ancient World* (London: Duckworth): 19–48.

Beard, North and Price 1998: Mary Beard, John North and Simon Price, *Religions of Rome*, two volumes: 1 *A History*, 2 *A Sourcebook*. Cambridge University Press.

Beazley 1963: J.D. Beazley, *Attic Red-Figure Vase-Painters*, ed. 2. Oxford: Clarendon Press.

Beesly 1865: E.S. Beesly, 'Catiline as a Party Leader', *Fortnightly Review* 1.2 (1 June 1865): 167–84.

Beness and Hillard 2001: J.L. Beness and T.W. Hillard, 'The Theatricality of the Deaths of C. Gracchus and Friends', *Classical Quarterly* 51: 135–40.

Bernstein 1998: Frank Bernstein, *Ludi publici: Untersuchungen zur Entstehung und Entwicklung der öffentlichen Spiele im republikanischen Rom* (Historia Einzelschriften 119). Stuttgart: Franz Steiner.

Bettelli 1997: Marco Bettelli, *Roma, la città prima della città: i tempi di una nascita* (Studia archeologica 86). Rome: L'Erma di Bretschneider.

Bettini 1995: M. Bettini, 'In vino stuprum', in Oswyn Murray and Mabuela Tecusan (eds), *In Vino Veritas* (London: British School at Rome): 224–35.

Birley 2000: A.R. Birley, 'Q. Lucretius Vespillo (cos. ord. 19)', *Chiron* 30: 711–48.

Blakeway 1935: Alan Blakeway, 'Demaratus', *Journal of Roman Studies* 25: 129–45.

Bonaria 1965: Mario Bonaria (ed.), *Romani mimi*. Rome: Ateneo.

Bonfante 1997: Larissa Bonfante (ed.), *Corpus speculorum Etruscorum, USA 3: New York, Metropolitan Museum of Art*. Rome: L'Erma di Bretschneider.

Bowersock 1990: G.W. Bowersock, 'The Pontificate of Augustus', in Kurt A. Raaflaub and Mark Toher (eds), *Between Republic and Empire: Interpretations of Augustus and his Principate* (Berkeley: University of Claifornia Press): 380–94.

Bradley 1989: Keith R. Bradley, *Slavery and Rebellion in the Roman World 140 BC–70 BC*. Bloomington: Indiana University Press.

Braund 1994: David Braund, *Georgia in Antiquity: a History of Colchis and Transcausian Iberia 550 BC–AD 562*. Oxford: Clarendon Press.

Briquel 1993: Dominique Briquel, 'Les voix oraculaires', in O. de Cazenove and J. Scheid (eds), *Les bois sacrés: actes du colloque international* (Naples: Centre Jean Bérard): 77–90.

Britten et al. 1948: Benjamin Britten, Ronald Duncan, John Piper, Henry Boys, Eric Crozier and Angus McBean, *The Rape of Lucretia: A Symposium*. London: The Bodley Head.

Brize 1980: Philip Brize, *Die Geryoneis des Stesichorus und die frühe griechische Kunst* (Beiträge zur Archäologie 12). Würzburg: Konrad Triltsch.

Brown 1967: Peter Brown, *Augustine of Hippo: A Biography*. London: Faber and Faber.

Brown 2003: Peter Brown, *The Rise of Western Christendom: Triumph and Diversity, AD 200–1000*, second edition. Oxford: Blackwell.

Bruns 1909: Carolus Georgius Bruns, *Fontes iuris Romani antiqui: leges et negotia*, ed. 7. Tübingen: Mohr.

Brunt and Moore 1967: P.A. Brunt and J.M. Moore (eds), *Res gestae divi Augusti: The Achievements of the Divine Augustus*. Oxford University Press.

Bruun 2000: Christer Bruun, '"What every man in the street used to know": M. Furius Camillus, Italic Legends and Roman Historiography', in Christer Bruun (ed.), *The Roman Middle Republic: Politics, Religion and Historiography c.400–133 BC* (Acta Instituti Romani Finlandiae 23, Rome): 41–68.

Bufano 1975: Antonietta Bufano (ed.), *Opere latine di Francesco Petrarca*. Turin: Unione tipografico-editrice torinese.

Bull and Plesters 1990: David Bull and Joyce Plesters, *The Feast of the Gods: Conservation, Examination, and Interpretation* (Studies in the History of Art 40). Washington DC: National Gallery of Art.

Buranelli 1987: Francesco Buranelli (ed.), *La tomba François di Vulci*. Rome: Quasar.

Burke 1969: P. Burke, 'Tacitism', in D.A. Dorey (ed.), *Tacitus* (London: Routledge and Kegan Paul): 149–71.

Burkert 1992: Walter Burkert, *The Orientalizing Revolution: Near Eastern Influence on Greek Culture in the Early Archaic Age*. Cambridge, Mass.: Harvard University Press.

Carandini 1996: Andrea Carandini, 'Rango, ritualità e il mito dei Latini', *Ostraka* 5.2: 215–22.

Carandini 1997a: Andrea Carandini, *La nascita di Roma: Dèi, Lari, eroi e uomini all'alba di una civiltà*. Turin: Einaudi.

Carandini 1997b: Andrea Carandini, 'Sullo specchio con lupa, Romolo e Remo (di nuovo a proposito di T.P. Wiseman)', *Ostraka* 6.2: 445–6.

Carandini 2002: Andrea Carandini, *Archeologia del mito: Emozione e ragione fra primitivi e moderni* (Saggi 849). Turin: Einaudi.

Carandini and Cappelli 2000: Andrea Carandini and Rosanna Capelli (eds), *Roma: Romolo, Remo e la fondazione della città*. Milan: Electa.

Carettoni 1961: G. Carettoni, 'Il fregio figurato della

Basilica Emilia', *Rivista dell'Instituto nazionale d'archeologia e storia dell'arte* 19 (n.s. 10): 5–78.

Carrington 1955: Charles Carrington, *Rudyard Kipling: His Life and Work*. London: Macmillan.

Cazenove 1983: Olivier de Cazenove, 'Lucus Stimulae: les aiguillons des Bacchanales', *Mélanges de l'École française de Rome (Antiquité)* 95: 55–113.

Champlin 2003: Edward Champlin, *Nero*. Cambridge, Mass.: Harvard University Press.

Chinard 1933: Gilbert Chinard, *Honest John Adams*. Boston: Little, Brown.

Clark 1989: Gillian Clark (trans.), *Iamblichus: On the Pythagorean Life* (Translated Texts for Historians 8). Liverpool University Press.

Cloud 1977: J.D. Cloud, 'Livy's Source for the Trial of Horatius', *Liverpool Classical Monthly* 2: 205–13.

Coarelli 1983: Filippo Coarelli, *Il foro romano: periodo archaico*. Rome: Quasar.

Coarelli 1985: Filippo Coarelli, *Il foro romano: periodo repubblicano e augusteo*. Rome: Quasar.

Coarelli 1988: Filippo Coarelli, *Il foro boario dalle origini alle fine della repubblica*. Rome: Quasar.

Coarelli 1993: F. Coarelli, 'Argei, sacraria', in Eva Margareta Steinby (ed.), *Lexicon Topographicum Urbis Romae* 1, A–C (Rome: Quasar): 120–5.

Coarelli 1995: F. Coarelli, 'Feronia, aedes', in Eva Margareta Steinby (ed.), *Lexicon Topographicum Urbis Romae* 2, D–G (Rome: Quasar): 247–8.

Coarelli 1996: Filippo Coarelli, *Revixit ars: arte e ideologia a Roma dai modelli ellenistici alla tradizione repubblicana*. Rome: Quasar.

Coarelli 1997: Filippo Coarelli, *Il Campo Marzio dalle origini alla fine della repubblica*. Rome: Quasar.

Cole 1993: Susan Guettel Cole, 'Procession and Celebration at the Dionysia', in R. Scodel (ed.), *Theatre and Society in the Classical World* (Ann Arbor: University of Michigan Press): 25–38.

Coleman 1990: K.M. Coleman, 'Fatal Charades: Roman Executions Staged as Mythological Enactments', *Journal of Roman Studies* 80: 44–73.

Comparetti 1895: Domenico Comparetti, *Vergil in the Middle Ages* (trans. E.F.M. Benecke, Italian original 1872). London: Sonnenschein.

Connor 1989: W.R. Connor, 'City Dionysia and Athenian Democracy', *Classica et Mediaevalia* 40: 7–32.

Corbett 1986: P.B. Corbett, *The Scurra* (Scottish Classical Studies 2). Edinburgh: Scottish Academic Press.

Cornell 1995: T.J. Cornell, *The Beginnings of Rome: Italy and Rome from the Bronze Age to the Punic Wars (c.1000–264 BC)*. London: Routledge.

Cornell 2000a: T.J. Cornell, 'The *Lex Ovinia* and the Emancipation of the Senate', in Christer Bruun (ed.), *The Roman Middle Republic: Politics, Religion and Historiography c.400–133 BC* (Acta Instituti Romani Finlandiae 23, Rome): 69–89.

Cornell 2000b: Timothy J. Cornell, 'La leggenda della nascita di Roma', in Andrea Carandini and Rosanna Cappelli (eds), *Roma: Romolo, Remo e la fondazione della città* (Milan: Electa): 45–51.

Coudry 2001: Marianne Coudry, 'Camille: construction et fluctuations de la figure d'un grand'homme', in Marianne Coudry and Thomas Späth (eds), *L'invention des grands hommes de la Rome antique: Die Konstruktion der grossen Männer Altroms* (Paris: De Boccard): 47–81.

Cozza 1983: Lucos Cozza, 'Le tegole di marmo del Pantheon', in *Città e architettura nella Roma imperiale* (Analecta Romana Instituti Danici, supplement 10, Odense University Press): 109–18.

Crawford 1903: Francis Marion Crawford, *Ave Roma Immortalis: Studies from the Chronicles of Rome*, ed. 2. London: Macmillan.

Crawford 1974: Michael H. Crawford, *Roman Republican Coinage*. Cambridge University Press.

Crawford 1985: Michael H. Crawford, *Coinage and Money under the Roman Republic: Italy and the Mediterranean Economy*. London: Methuen.

Crawford 1996: M.H. Crawford (ed.), *Roman Statutes* (BICS Supplement 64), two volumes. London: Institute of Classical Studies.

Cristofani 1990: Mauro Cristofani (ed.), *La grande Roma dei Tarquinii: catalogo della mostra*. Rome: L'Erma di Bretschneider.

Csapo and Slater 1994: Eric Csapo and William J. Slater, *The Context of Ancient Drama*. Ann Arbor: University of Michigan Press.

Curti 1993: Emmanuele Curti, 'The Use of Myth in Roman Propaganda', unpublished paper given at a conference in London, 23 November 1993.

Curti 2000: Emmanuele Curti, 'From Concordia to the Quirinal: Notes on Religion and Politics in Mid-republican/Hellenistic Rome', in Edward Bispham and Christopher Smith (eds), *Religion in Archaic and Republican Rome and Italy* (Edinburgh University Press): 77–91.

Damon and Takács 1999: Cynthia Damon and Sarolta Takács (eds), *The senatus consultum de Cn. Pisone patre: Text, Translation, Discussion* (American Journal of Philology 120.1). Baltimore: Johns Hopkins University Press.

Davidson 2000: James Davidson, '*Gnesippos paigniagraphos*: the Comic Poets and the Erotic Mime', in David Harvey and John Wilkins (eds), *The Rivals of Aristophanes: Studies in Athenian Old Comedy* (London: Duckworth and Classical Press of Wales): 41–64.

Davies 1988: Malcolm Davies (ed.), *Epicorum Graecorum fragmenta*. Göttingen: Vandenhoeck and Ruprecht.

Davies 1989: Malcolm Davies, *The Epic Cycle*. Bristol Classical Press.

Davis and Kraay 1973: Norman Davis and Colin M. Kraay, *The Hellenistic Kingdoms: Portrait Coins and History*.

London: Thames and Hudson.

Dearden 1995: C.W. Dearden, 'Pots, Tumblers and Phlyax Vases', in Alan Griffiths (ed.), *Stage Directions: Essays in Ancient Drama in Honour of E.W. Handley* (BICS Supplement 66, London: Institute of Classical Studies): 81–6.

Degrassi 1937: Atilius Degrassi (ed.), *Inscriptiones Italiae*, XIII *Fasti et elogia*, fasc. 3 *Elogia*. Rome: Libreria dello stato.

Degrassi 1947: Atilius Degrassi (ed.), *Inscriptiones Italiae*, XIII *Fasti et elogia*, fasc. 1 *Fasti consulares et triumphales*. Rome: Libreria dello stato.

Degrassi 1963: Atilius Degrassi (ed.), *Inscriptiones Italiae*, XIII *Fasti et elogia*, fasc. 2 *Fasti anni Numani et Iuliani*. Rome: Istituto poligrafico dello stato.

De La Blanchère 1892: M.-R. de La Blanchère, 'Emissarium', in Ch. Daremberg and Edm. Saglio (eds), *Dictionnaire des antiquités grecques et romaines* 2.1 (Paris: Hachette): 597–603.

Dierichs 1997: Angelika Dierichs, *Erotik in der römischen Kunst*. Mainz: von Zabern.

Dohrn 1972: Tobias Dohrn, *Die Ficoronische Ciste in der Villa Giulia in Rom* (Monumenta artis Romanae 11). Berlin: Gebr. Mann.

Donaldson 1982: Ian Donaldson, *The Rapes of Lucretia: A Myth and its Transformations*. Oxford: Clarendon Press.

Dorcey 1992: Peter F. Dorcey, *The Cult of Silvanus: A Study in Roman Folk Religion* (Columbia Studies in the Classical Tradition 20). Leiden: Brill.

Dumézil 1973: Georges Dumézil, *Mythe et épopée* III, *Histoires romaines*. Paris: Gallimard.

Dümmler 1866: Ernst Dümmler, *Auxilius und Vulgarius: Quellen und Forschungen zur Geschichte des Papstthums im Anfange des zehnten Jahrhunderts*. Leipzig: S. Hirzel.

Edwards 1999: Catharine Edwards, 'Translating Empire? Macaulay's Rome', in Catharine Edwards (ed.), *Roman Presences: Receptions of Rome in European Culture, 1789–1945* (Cambridge University Press): 70–89.

Erskine 2001: Andrew Erskine, *Troy Between Greece and Rome: Local Tradition and Imperial Power*. Oxford University Press.

Evelyn-White 1914: Hugh G. Evelyn-White (trans.), *Hesiod, the Homeric Hymns and Homerica* (Loeb Classical Library). London: Heinemann.

Fast 1952: Howard Fast, *Spartacus*. London: Bodley Head.

Feeney 1998: Denis Feeney, *Literature and Religion at Rome: Cultures, Contexts, and Beliefs*. Cambridge University Press.

Fiesel 1928: Eva Fiesel, *Namen des griechischen Mythos im Etruskischen*. Göttingen: Vandenhoeck and Ruprecht.

Flory 1988: Marleen Flory, '*Abducta Neroni uxor*: The Historiographical Tradition of the Marriage of Octavian and Livia', *Transactions of the American Philological Association* 118: 343–59.

Flower 1996: Harriet I. Flower, *Ancestor Masks and Aristocratic Power in Roman Culture*. Oxford: Clarendon Press.

Fontenrose 1978: Joseph Fontenrose, *The Delphic Oracle: Its Responses and Operations, with a Catalogue of Responses*. Berkeley: University of California Press.

Forster 1936: E.M. Forster, *Abinger Harvest*. London: Edward Arnold.

Forsythe 1994: Gary Forsythe, *The Historian L. Calpurnius Piso Frugi and the Roman Annalistic Tradition*. Lanham MD: University Press of America.

Fraschetti 1990: Augusto Fraschetti, *Roma e il principe*. Rome: Laterza.

Fraschetti 2002: Augusto Fraschetti, *Romolo il fondatore* (Quadrante Laterza 112). Rome: Laterza.

Fraser 1972: P.M. Fraser, *Ptolemaic Alexandria*. Oxford: Clarendon Press.

Frier 1979 (= 1999): Bruce W. Frier, *Libri annales pontificum maximorum: The Origins of the Annalistic Tradition* (Papers and Monographs of the American Academy in Rome 27). Rome: American Academy (ed. 2 1999, Ann Arbor: University of Michigan Press).

Futrell 2001: Alison Futrell, 'Seeing Red: Spartacus as Domestic Economist', in Sandra R. Joshel, Margaret Malamud and Donald T. McGuire, jr. (eds), *Imperial Projections: Ancient Rome in Modern Popular Culture* (Baltimore: Johns Hopkins University Press): 77–118.

Gabba 2000: Emilio Gabba, *Roma arcaica: storia e storiografia* (Storia e letteratura 205). Rome: Edizioni di storia e letteratura.

Galinsky 1996: Karl Galinsky, *Augustan Culture: An Interpretive Introduction*. Princeton University Press.

Gantz 1993: Timothy Gantz, *Early Greek Myth: A Guide to Literary and Artistic Sources*, two volumes. Baltimore: Johns Hopkins University Press.

Gelzer 1968: Matthias Gelzer, *Caesar: Politician and Statesman* (trans. Peter Needham). Oxford: Blackwell.

Gnann 1996: Achim Gnann, 'Zur Beteiligung des Polidoro da Caravaggio an der Ausmalung des Salone der Villa Lante', in Eva Margareta Steinby (ed.), *Ianiculum—Gianicolo: Storia, topografia, monumenti, leggende dall'antichità al rinascimento* (Acta Instituti Romani Finlandiae 16, Rome): 237–59.

Goldberg 1995: Sander M. Goldberg, *Epic in Republican Rome*. New York: Oxford University Press.

Goldschmidt 1914: Adolph Goldschmidt, *Die Elfenbeinskulpturen aus der Zeit der karolingischen und sächsischen Kaiser*, vol. 1. Berlin: B. Cassirer.

Gradel 2002: Ittai Gradel, *Emperor Worship and Roman Religion*. Oxford: Clarendon Press.

Gram 2000: Dewey Gram, *Gladiator* (based on a screenplay by David Franzoni, John Logan and William Nicholson, story by David Franzoni). London: Penguin.

Graves 1934a: Robert Graves, *I, Claudius*. London: Arthur Barker.

Graves 1934b: Robert Graves, *Claudius the God*. London:

Arthur Barker.

Gray 1984: Donald J. Gray, 'Macaulay's *Lays of Ancient Rome* and the Publication of Nineteenth-Century British Poetry', in James R. Kincaid and Albert J. Kuhn (eds), *Victorian Literature and Society: Essays Presented to Richard D. Altick* (Ohio State University Press): 71–93.

Green 1982: Peter Green, *Ovid: The Erotic Poems*. Harmondsworth: Penguin.

Green 1995: J.R. Green, 'Theatrical Motifs in Non-Theatrical Contexts on Vases of the Later Fifth and Fourth Centuries', in Alan Griffiths (ed.), *Stage Directions: Essays in Ancient Drama in Honour of E.W. Handley* (BICS Supplement 66, London: Institute of Classical Studies): 93–121.

Griffin 1984: Miriam T. Griffin, *Nero: The End of a Dynasty*. London: Batsford.

Griffiths 1998: Alan Griffiths, 'Where Did Early Roman History Come From?', unpublished paper given at a conference in Bristol, 15 July 1998.

Griffiths 2002: Alan Griffiths, 'The *Odes*: just where do you draw the line?', in Tony Woodman and Denis Feeney (eds), *Tradition and Contexts in the Poetry of Horace* (Cambridge University Press): 65–79.

Gruen 1990: Erich S. Gruen, *Studies in Greek Culture and Roman Policy* (Cincinnati Classical Studies n.s. 7). Leiden: E.J. Brill.

Gruen 1992: Erich S. Gruen, *Culture and National Identity in Republican Rome* (Cornell Studies in Classical Philology 52). Ithaca, NY: Cornell University Press.

Guthrie 1962: W.K.C. Guthrie, *A History of Greek Philosophy*, I *The Earlier Presocratics and the Pythagoreans*. Cambridge University Press.

Hammond 1999: Paul Hammond, *Dryden and the Traces of Classical Rome*. Oxford University Press.

Hano 1986: Michel Hano, 'A l'origine du culte impérial: les autels des Lares Augusti', in H. Temporini and W. Haase (eds), *Aufstieg und Niedergang der römischen Welt* 2.16.3 (Berlin: De Gruyter): 2333–81.

Hedreen 1994: Guy Hedreen, 'Silens, Nymphs and Maenads', *Journal of Hellenic Studies* 114: 47–69.

Held 1961: Julius S. Held, 'Flora, Goddess and Courtesan', in M. Meiss (ed.), *De artibus opuscula: Essays in Honour of E. Panofsky* (New York University Press): 201–18.

Hellegouarc'h 1963: J. Hellegouarc'h, *Le vocabulaire latin des relations et des partis politiques sous la république* (Publications de la Faculté des Lettres et Sciences Humaines de l'Université de Lille, 11). Paris: Les Belles Lettres.

Hennecke 1965: E. Hennecke, *New Testament Apocrypha*, vol. 2 (edited by W. Schreemelcher, English translation by R. McL. Wilson). London: Lutterworth Press.

Hingley 2000: Richard Hingley, *Roman Officers and English Gentlemen: The Imperial Origins of Roman Archaeology*. London: Routledge.

Holliday 2002: Peter J. Holliday, *The Origins of Roman Historical Commemoration in the Visual Arts*. Cambridge University Press.

Horsfall 1979: Nicholas Horsfall, 'Stesichorus at Bovillae?', *Journal of Hellenic Studies* 99: 26–48.

Horsfall 1989: Nicholas Horsfall, *Cornelius Nepos: A Selection, including the Lives of Cato and Atticus*. Oxford: Clarendon Press.

Horsfall 2003: Nicholas Horsfall, *The Culture of the Roman Plebs*. London: Duckworth.

Hughes 1997: Ted Hughes, *Tales from Ovid*. London: Faber and Faber.

Humm 1999: Michel Humm, 'Le comitium du forum romain et la réforme des tribus d'Appius Claudius Caecus', *Mélanges de l'École française de Rome (Antiquité)* 111: 625–94.

Humm 2000: Michel Humm, 'Spazio e tempo civici: riforma delle tribù e riforma del calendario alla fine del quarto secolo a.C.', in Christer Bruun (ed.), *The Roman Middle Republic: Politics, Religion and Historiography c.400–133 BC* (Acta Instituti Romani Finlandiae 23, Rome): 91–119.

Humphrey 1986: John H. Humphrey, *Roman Circuses: Arenas for Chariot Racing*. London: B.T. Batsford.

Hutton 1999: *The Triumph of the Moon: A History of Modern Pagan Witchcraft*. Oxford University Press.

Jacoby 1949: Felix Jacoby, *Atthis: The Local Chronicles of Ancient Athens*. Oxford: Clarendon Press.

Janko 1984: Richard Janko, *Aristotle on Comedy: Towards a Reconstruction of Poetics III*. London: Duckworth.

Jenkyns 1980: Richard Jenkyns, *The Victorians and Ancient Greece*. Oxford: Blackwell.

Jocelyn 1971: H.D. Jocelyn, 'VRBS AVGVRIO AVGVSTO CONDITA: Ennius ap. Cic. *Div.* 1.107 (= *Ann.* 77–96 V²)', *Proceedings of the Cambridge Philological Society* n.s. 17: 44–74.

Jones 1992: Brian W. Jones, *The Emperor Domitian*. London: Routledge.

Jurgeit 1992: Fritzi Jurgeit, 'Interventi ottocenteschi sulla cista di Karlsruhe', *Bollettino d'arte* 74–5: 85–94.

Jurgeit 1999: Fritzi Jurgeit, *Die etruskischen und italischen Bronzen im Badischen Landesmuseum Karlsruhe* (Terra Italia 5), two volumes. Rome: Gruppo editoriale internazionale.

Kähler 1965: Heinz Kähler, *Der Fries vom Reiterdenkmal des Aemilius Paullus in Delphi* (Monumenta artis Romanae 5). Berlin: Mann.

Kaibel 1899: Georgius Kaibel (ed.), *Comicorum Graecorum fragmenta*, I fasc. 1. Berlin: Weidmann.

Kaster 1988: Robert A. Kaster, *Guardians of Language: The Grammarian and Society in Late Antiquity*. Berkeley: University of California Press.

Kaster 1995: Robert A. Kaster, *C. Suetonius Tranquillus De Grammaticis et Rhetoribus*. Oxford: Clarendon Press.

Keaveney 1990: Arthur Keaveney, 'The Three Gracchi: Tiberius, Gaius and Babeuf', in *La storia della storiografia europea sulla rivoluzione francese* (Istituto storico per l'età moderna e contemporanea, Rome): 417–32.

Keppie 1983: Lawrence Keppie, *Colonisation and Veteran Settlement in Italy 47–14 BC*. London: British School at Rome.

Kipling 1906: Rudyard Kipling, *Puck of Pook's Hill*. London: Macmillan.

Kipling 1940: *Rudyard Kipling's Verse: Definitive Edition*. London: Hodder and Stoughton.

Koestler 1939: Arthur Koestler, *The Gladiators*. London: Jonathan Cape.

Kragelund 1982: Patrick Kragelund, *Prophecy, Populism, and Propaganda in the 'Octavia'* (Opuscula Graecolatina 25). Copenhagen: Museum Tusculanum.

Kragelund et al. 2002: Patrick Kragelund *et alii*, 'Historical Drama in Ancient Rome: Republican Flourishing and Imperial Decline?', *Symbolae Osloenses* 77: 5–105.

Lacey 1996: W.K. Lacey, *Augustus and the Principate: The Evolution of the System* (Arca 35). Leeds: Francis Cairns.

La Rocca 1987: Eugenio La Rocca, 'L'adesione senatoriale al "consensus": i modi della propaganda augustea e tiberiana nei monumenti "in circo Flaminio"', in *L'Urbs: espace urbain et histoire* (Collection de l'École française de Rome 98, Rome): 347–72.

Latte 1926: Kurt Latte, 'Über eine Eigentumlichkeit der italischen Gottesvorstellung', *Archiv für Religionswissenschaft* 24: 244–58.

Le Gall 1953: Joël Le Gall, *Le Tibre fleuve de Rome dans l'antiquité*. Paris: Presses universitaires de France.

Lemmey 1999: Pamela Lemmey, 'Romulus in Cornwall: the Cotehele Tapestries'. University of Exeter MA dissertation.

Leporace 1960: T. Gasparrini Leporace, 'Ageltrude', *Dizionario biografico degli italiani* 1: 384–6.

Levey 1957: Michael Levey, 'Tiepolo's "Empire of Flora"', *The Burlington Magazine* 99: 89–91.

Levick 1976: Barbara Levick, *Tiberius the Politician*. London: Thames and Hudson.

Levick 1990: Barbara Levick, *Claudius*. London: Batsford.

Liberatore 1995: Daniela Liberatore, 'Un Marsia nel Foro di Alba Fucens? Una proposta di identificazione', *Ostraka* 4: 249–55.

Lightbown 1978: Ronald Lightbown, *Sandro Botticelli*, two volumes. London: Paul Elek.

Linderski 1986: J. Linderski, 'The Augural Law', in *Aufstieg und Niedergang der römischen Welt* 2.16.3 (Berlin: De Gruyter): 2146–312.

Lintott 1999: Andrew Lintott, *The Constitution of the Roman Republic*. Oxford: Clarendon Press.

Litto 1966: Fredric M. Litto, 'Addison's *Cato* in the Colonies', *William and Mary Quarterly* 23: 431–49.

Llewellyn 1971: Peter Llewellyn, *Rome in the Dark Ages*. London: Faber and Faber.

Luce 1930: Stephen Bleecker Luce, 'Attic Red-Figured Vases and Fragments at Corinth', *American Journal of Archaeology* 34: 334–43.

Lulof 1996: Patricia S. Lulof, *The Ridge-Pole Statues from the Late Archaic Temple at Satricum* (Scrinium 9, Satricum 5). Amsterdam: Thesis publishers.

Lytton 1834: The Right Hon. Lord Lytton, *The Last Days of Pompeii*. London: R. Bentley.

Macaulay 1842: Thomas Babington Macaulay, *Lays of Ancient Rome*. London: Longmans, Green and Co.

Mahl 1965: Elisabeth Mahl, 'Die Romulus und Remus-Folgen der Tapisseriensammlung des Kunsthistorischen Museums', *Jahrbuch der Kunsthistorischen Sammlungen in Wien* 61: 7–40.

Malkin 1998: Irad Malkin, *The Returns of Odysseus: Colonization and Ethnicity*. Berkeley: University of California Press.

Manacorda 1996: D. Manacorda, 'Nymphae, aedes', in Eva Margareta Steiny (ed.), *Lexicon Topographicum Urbis Romae* 3, H–O (Rome: Quasar): 350–1.

Manacorda and Tamassia 1985: Daniele Manacorda and Renato Tamassia, *Il piccone del regime*. Rome: Curcio.

Manuwald 2001: Gesine Manuwald, *Fabulae praetextae: Spuren einer literarischen Gattung der Römer* (Zetemata 108). Munich: C.H. Beck.

Marshall 1983: P.K. M[arshall], 'Servius', in L.D. Reynolds (ed.), *Texts and Transmission: a Survey of the Latin Classics* (Oxford: Clarendon Press): 385–8.

Marx-Engels 1979: Karl Marx, Frederick Engels, *Collected Works* (English translation), vol. 11. London: Lawrence and Wishart.

Marx-Engels 1985: Karl Marx, Frederick Engels, *Collected Works* (English translation), vol. 41. London: Lawrence and Wishart.

Mason 1974: Hugh J. Mason, *Greek Terms for Roman Institutions: A Lexicon and Analysis* (American Studies in Papyrology 13). Toronto: Hakkert.

Massey 1757: William Massey (trans.), *Ovid's Fasti, or the Romans Sacred Calendar, translated into English Verse*. London: George Keith, at the Bible and Crown in Gracechurch St.

Masson 1950: André Masson (ed.), *Oeuvres complètes de Montesquieu*, vol. 2. Paris: Nagel.

Mastrocinque 1988: Attilio Mastrocinque, *Lucio Giunio Bruto: Ricerche di storia, religione e diritto sulle origini della repubblica romana*. Trento: edizioni La Reclame.

Mayer 1994: David Mayer, *Playing Out the Empire: Ben-Hur and Other Toga Plays and Films, 1883–1908*. Oxford: Clarendon Press.

Mazzarino 1965: Santo Mazzarino, *Il pensiero storico classico*, I. Bari: Laterza.

Mazzarino 1966: Santo Mazzarino, *Il pensiero storico classico*, II.1. Bari: Laterza.

McGann 1981: Jerome J. McGann (ed.), *Lord Byron: The Complete Poetical Works*, vol. 3. Oxford: Clarendon

Press.

McGrath 1997: Elizabeth McGrath, *Rubens: Subjects from History* (Corpus Rubenianum Ludwig Burchard 13), two vols. London: Harvey Miller.

Mele 1987: Alfonso Mele, 'Aristodemo, Cuma e il Lazio', *Quaderni del Centro di studio per l'archaeologia etrusco-italica* 15: 155–77.

Mellor 1993: Ronald Mellor, *Tacitus*. New York: Routledge.

Melville 1986: A.D. Melville (trans.), *Ovid Metamorphoses*. Oxford University Press.

Menichetti 1994: Mauro Menichetti, '*Praenestinus Aeneas*: il culto di Iuppiter Imperator e il trionfo su Mezenzio quali motivi di propaganda antiromana su una cista prenestina', *Ostraka* 3.1: 7–30.

Meyer 1980: Jørgen Chr. Meyer, 'Roman History in Light of the Import of Attic Vases to Rome and Etruria in the Sixth and Fifth Centuries BC', *Analecta Romana Instituti Danici* 9: 47–68.

Michels 1967: Agnes Kirsopp Michels, *The Calendar of the Roman Republic*. Princeton University Press.

Michie 1964: James Michie (trans.), *The Odes of Horace*. London: Rupert Hart-Davies.

Millar 2000: Fergus Millar, 'The First Revolution: Imperator Caesar, 36–28 BC', in *La révolution romaine après Ronald Syme: Bilans et perspectives* (Entretiens sur l'antiquité classique 46, Geneva: Fondation Hardt): 1–30.

Momigliano 1957: Arnaldo Momigliano, 'Perizonius, Niebuhr and the Character of Early Roman Tradition', *Journal of Roman Studies* 47: 104–14.

Momigliano 1984: Arnaldo Momigliano, *Settimo contributo alla storia degli studi classici e del mondo antico* (Raccolta di studi e testi 161). Rome: Edizioni di storia e letteratura.

Mommsen 1854–6: Theodor Mommsen, *Römische Geschichte*. Berlin: Weidmann.

Morassi 1962: Antonio Morassi, *A Complete Catalogue of the Paintings of G.B. Tiepolo*. London: Phaidon Press.

Morford 1993: Mark Morford, 'Tacitean *prudentia* and the Doctrines of Justus Lipsius', in T.J. Luce and A.J. Woodman (eds), *Tacitus and the Tacitean Tradition* (Princeton University Press): 129–51.

Morgan 2000: Llewellyn Morgan, 'The Autopsy of C. Asinius Pollio', *Journal of Roman Studies* 90: 51–69.

Mueller 2002: Hans-Friedrich Mueller, *Roman Religion in Valerius Maximus*. London: Routledge.

Mulhauser 1974: F.L. Mulhauser (ed.), *The Poems of Arthur Hugh Clough*, second edition. Oxford: Clarendon Press.

Münzer 1920: Friedrich Münzer, *Römische Adelsparteien und Adelsfamilien*. Stuttgart: Metzler.

Münzer 1999: Friedrich Münzer, *Roman Aristocratic Parties and Families* (trans. Thérèse Ridley). Baltimore: Johns Hopkins University Press.

Nesselrath 1990: Heinz-Günther Nesselrath, *Die attische mittlere Komödie: ihre Stellung in der antiken Literaturkritik und Literaturgeschichte*. Berlin: De Gruyter.

Nielsen 1993: I. Nielsen, 'Castor, aedes, templum', in Eva Margareta Steinby (ed.), *Lexicon Topographicum Urbis Romae* I, A–C (Rome: Quasar): 242–5.

Norbrook 1999: David Norbrook, *Writing the English Republic: Poetry, Rhetoric and Politics, 1627–1660*. Cambridge University Press.

North 1989: J.A. North, 'Religion in Republican Rome', in F.W. Walbank et al. (eds), *The Cambridge Ancient History*, VII part 2 (ed. 2) *The Rise of Rome to 220 BC* (Cambridge University Press): 573–624.

North 1992: J.A. North, 'Deconstructing Stone Theatres', in *Apodosis: Essays Presented to Dr. W.W. Cruickshank to Mark his Eightieth Birthday* (London, St Paul's School): 75–83.

Oakley 1998: S.P. Oakley, *A Commentary on Livy Books VI–X*, vol. II *Books VII and VIII*. Oxford: Clarendon Press.

O'Daly 1999: Gerard O'Daly, *Augustine's City of God: A Reader's Guide*. Oxford: Clarendon Press.

Ogilvie 1965: R.M. Ogilvie, *A Commentary on Livy Books 1–5*. Oxford: Clarendon Press.

Opelt 1965: Ilona Opelt, 'Roma = 'Ρώμη und Rom als Idee', *Philologus* 109: 47–56.

Orr 1978: David G. Orr, 'Roman Domestic Religion: the Evidence of the Household Shrines', in H. Temporini and W. Haase, *Aufstieg und Niedergang der römischen Welt* 2.16.2 (Berlin: De Gruyter): 1557–91.

Osborne 1998: Robin Osborne, 'Early Greek Colonisation? The Nature of Greek Settlement in the West', in Nick Fisher and Hans van Wees (eds), *Archaic Greece: New Approaches and New Evidence* (London: Duckworth): 251–69.

Page 1973: Denys Page, 'Stesichorus: the *Geryoneïs*', *Journal of Hellenic Studies* 93: 138–54.

Pairault Massa 1992: Françoise-Hélène Pairault Massa, *Iconologia e politica nell'Italia antica: Roma, Lazio, Etruria dal VII al I secolo a.C.* (Biblioteca di archeologia 18). Milan: Longanesi.

Pais 1906: Ettore Pais, *Ancient Legends of Roman History*. London: Swan Sonnenschein.

Palmer 1970: Robert E.A. Palmer, *The Archaic Community of the Romans*. Cambridge University Press.

Parker 1937: Harold T. Parker, *The Cult of Antiquity and the French Revolutionaries: A Study in the Development of the Revolutionary Spirit*. University of Chicago Press.

Parker 1988: W.H. Parker, *Priapeia: Poems for a Phallic God*. London: Croom Helm.

Pearson 1942: Lionel Pearson, *The Local Historians of Attica* (Philological Monographs 11). Philadelphia: American Philological Association.

Pearson 1987: Lionel Pearson, *The Greek Historians of the West: Timaeus and his Predecessors* (Philological Monographs of the APA 35). Atlanta GA: Scholars

Press.

Pelling 2002: Christopher Pelling, *Plutarch and History: Eighteen Studies*. London: Classical Press of Wales and Duckworth.

Pensabene 1998: Patrizio Pensabene, 'Vent'anni di studi e scavi dell'Università di Roma "La Sapienza" nell'area sud-ovest del palatino (1977–1997)', in Carlo Giavarini (ed.), *Il Palatino: area sacra sud-ovest e Domus Tiberiana* (Studia archaeologica 95, Rome: L'Erma di Bretschneider): 1–154.

Pensabene 1999: P. Pensabene, 'Victoria, aedes', in E.M. Steinby (ed.), *Lexicon Topographicum urbis Romae 5*, T–Z (Rome: Quasar): 149–50.

Peruzzi 1998: Emilio Peruzzi, *Civiltà greca nel Lazio preromano* (Studi dell'Accademia Toscana 'La Columbaria' 165). Florence: Leo S. Olschki.

Peter 1890: R. Peter, 'Hercules', in W.H. Roscher (ed.), *Ausführliches Lexikon der griechischen und römischen Mythologie*, I (Leipzig: Teubner): 2253–98.

Pfeiffer 1968: Rudolf Pfeiffer, *History of Classical Scholarship from the Beginnings to the End of the Hellenistic Age*. Oxford: Clarendon Press.

Phillips 1953: E.D. Phillips, 'Odysseus in Italy', *Journal of Hellenic Studies* 73: 53–67.

Pickard-Cambridge 1962: Sir Arthur Pickard-Cambridge, *Dithyramb, Tragedy and Comedy*, revised ed. by T.B.L. Webster. Oxford: Clarendon Press.

Pickard-Cambridge 1968: A.W. Pickard-Cambridge, *The Dramatic Festivals of Athens*, revised ed. Oxford: Clarendon Press.

Pidgley 1986: Michael Pidgley, *The Tragi-Comical History of B.R. Haydon's 'Marcus Curtius Leaping into the Gulf'*. Exeter College of Art and Design.

Pigler 1974: A. Pigler, *Barockthemen: eine Auswahl von Verzeichnissen zur Iconographie des 17. und 18. Jahrhunderts*. Budapest: Akadémiai Kiadó.

Pinney 1974–81: Thomas Pinney (ed.), *The Letters of Thomas Babington Macaulay*, six volumes. Cambridge University Press.

Pinsent 1964: John Pinsent, 'Cincius, Fabius, and the Otacilii', *Phoenix* 18: 18–29.

Pope 1972: Willard Bissell Pope (ed.), *Invisible Friends: The Correspondence of Elizabeth Barrett Browning and Benjamin Robert Haydon 1842–1845*. Cambridge, Mass.: Harvard University Press.

Presicce 2000: Claudio Parisi Presicce, *La lupa capitolina* (catalogue of exhibition at the Palazzo Caffarelli, Musei Capitolini, June–October 2000). Milan : Electa.

Prochaska 2000: Frank Prochaska, *The Republic of Britain 1760–2000*. Harmondsworth: Penguin.

Raaflaub 1996: Kurt A. Raaflaub, 'Born to be Wolves? Origins of Roman Imperialism', in R.W. Wallace and E.M. Harris (eds), *Transitions to Empire: Essays in Greco-Roman History, 360–146 BC, in Honor of E. Badian* (Norman: University of Oklahoma Press): 273–314.

Rawson 1975: Elizabeth Rawson, *Cicero: A Portrait*. London: Allen Lane.

Reid 1993: Jane Davidson Reid (with the assistance of Chris Rohmann), *The Oxford Guide to Classical Mythology in the Arts, 1300–1990s*, two volumes. New York: Oxford University Press.

Reynolds 1983: L.D. Reynolds (ed.), *Texts and Transmission: A Survey of the Latin Classics*. Oxford: Clarendon Press.

Reynolds 1986: Joyce Reynolds, 'Further Information on Imperial Cult at Aphrodisias', *Studii Clasice* 24: 109–17.

Rich 1998: J.W. Rich, 'Augustus' Parthian Honours, the Temple of Mars Ultor and the Arch in the Forum Romanum', *Papers of the British School at Rome* 66: 71–128.

Rich and Williams 1999: J.W. Rich and J.H.C. Williams, '*Leges et Iura P.R. Restituit*: A New Aureus of Octavian and the Settlement of 28–27 BC', *Numismatic Chronicle* 159: 169–213.

Richard 1994: Carl J. Richard, *The Founders and the Classics: Greece, Rome, and the American Enlightenment*. Cambridge, Mass.: Harvard University Press.

Richardson 1992: L. Richardson, jr., *A New Topographical Dictionary of Ancient Rome*. Baltimore: Johns Hopkins University Press.

Rickman 1980: Geoffrey Rickman, *The Corn Supply of Ancient Rome*. Oxford: Clarendon Press.

Ridgway 1992: David Ridgway, *The First Western Greeks*. Cambridge University Press.

Ridgway 1996: David Ridgway, 'Greek Letters at Osteria dell'Osa', *Opuscula Romana* 20: 87–97.

Rivet 1978: A.L.F. Rivet, 'Rudyard Kipling's Roman Britain', *The Kipling Journal* 45 (206): 5–15.

Rohde 1936: G. Rohde, *Die Kultsatzungen der römischen Pontifices* (Religionsgeschichtliche Versuche und Vorarbeiten 25). Berlin: Töpelmann.

Rose 1928: H.J. Rose, *A Handbook of Greek Mythology, Including its Extension to Rome*. London: Methuen.

Rouveret 1994: Agnès Rouveret, 'La ciste Ficoroni et la culture romaine du IVe s. av. J.-C.', *Bulletin de la Societé Nationale des Antiquaires de France* 1994: 225–42.

Rubinsohn 1987: Wolfgang Zeev Rubinsohn, *Spartacus' Uprising and Soviet Historical Writing* (trans. John G. Griffith). Oxford: Oxbow.

Sandberg 2001: Kaj Sandberg, *Magistrates and Assemblies: A Study of Legislative Practice in Republican Rome* (Acta Instituti Romani Finlandiae 24). Rome: Institutum Romanum Finlandiae.

Sanminiatelli 1967: Donato Sanminiatelli, *Domenico Beccafumi*. Milan: Bramante.

Sartori 1898: P. Sartori, 'Ueber das Bauopfer', *Zeitschrift für Ethnologie* 13: 1–54.

Scullard 1981: H.H. Scullard, *Festivals and Ceremonies of the Roman Republic*. London: Thames and Hudson.

Seaford 1984: Richard Seaford, *Euripides Cyclops, with Introduction and Commentary*. Oxford: Clarendon Press.

Seaford 1994: Richard Seaford, *Reciprocity and Ritual: Homer and Tragedy in the Developing City-State*. Oxford: Clarendon Press.

Seeley 1883: J.R. Seeley, *The Expansion of England: Two Courses of Lectures*. London: Macmillan.

Segal 1968: Erich Segal, *Roman Laughter: The Comedy of Plautus*. Cambridge, Mass.: Harvard University Press.

Seznec 1953: Jean Seznec, *The Survival of the Pagan Gods: The Mythological Tradition and its Place in Renaissance Humanism and Art* (Bollingen Series 38). New York: Pantheon.

Shaw 2001: Brent D. Shaw, *Spartacus and the Slave Wars: A Brief History with Documents*. Boston: Bedford/St Martin's.

Sherk 1969: Robert K. Sherk (ed.), *Roman Documents from the Greek East: Senatus consulta and epistulae to the Age of Augustus*. Baltimore: Johns Hopkins University Press.

Sihvola 1989: Juha Sihvola, 'Il culto dei Dioscuri nei suoi aspetti politici', in Eva Margareta Steinby (ed.), *Lacus Iuturnae*, I (Rome: De Luca): 76–91.

Simon 1982: Erika Simon, *The Ancient Theatre* (trans. C.E. Vafopoulou-Richardson). London: Methuen.

Simon 1996: Erika Simon, *Schriften zur etruskischen und italischen Kunst und Religion*. Stuttgart: Franz Steiner.

Sisson 1976: C.H. Sisson (trans.), *Lucretius De Rerum Natura: The Poem on Nature*. Manchester: Carcanet.

Sisson 1981: C.H. Sisson (trans.), *Dante: The Divine Comedy*. London: Pan.

Sisson 1986: C.H. Sisson (trans.), *Virgil: The Aeneid*. Manchester: Carcanet.

Skutsch 1968: Otto Skutsch, *Studia Enniana*. London: Athlone Press.

Skutsch 1985: Otto Skutsch, *The Annals of Quintus Ennius*. Oxford: Clarendon Press.

Small 1982: Jocelyn Penny Small, *Cacus and Marsyas in Etrusco-Roman Legend* (Princeton Monographs in Art and Archaeology 44). Princeton University Press.

Smith 1987: R.R.R. Smith, 'The Imperial Reliefs from the Sebasteion at Aphrodisias', *Journal of Roman Studies* 77: 88–138.

Solin 1983: Heikki Solin, 'Varia onomastica: V. Κλεῖκλος', *Zeitschrift für Papyrologie und Epigraphik* 51: 180–2.

Späth 2001: Thomas Späth, 'Erzählt, erfunden: Camillus. Literarische Konstruktion und soziale Normen', in Marianne Coudry and Thomas Späth (eds), *L'invention des grands hommes de la Rome antique: Die Konstruktion der grossen Männer Altroms* (Paris: De Boccard): 341–412.

Spencer 1964: T.J.B. Spencer, *Shakespeare's Plutarch: The Lives of Julius Caesar, Brutus, Marcus Antonius and Coriolanus in the Translation of Sir Thomas North*. Harmondsworth: Penguin.

Ste. Croix 1981: G.E.M. de Ste. Croix, *The Class Struggle in the Ancient Greek World*. London: Duckworth.

Stibbe et al. 1980: C.M. Stibbe, G. Colonna, C De Simone, H. Versnel, *Lapis Satricanus: Archaeological, epigraphical, linguistic and historical aspects of the new inscription from Satricum* (Archeologische Studiën van het Nederlands Instituut te Rome, Scripta Minora 5). The Hague: Ministerie van Cultur, Recreatie en Maarschappelijk Werk.

Stone 1999: Marla Stone, 'A Flexible Rome: Fascism and the Cult of *romanità*', in Catherine Edwards (ed.), *Roman Presences: Receptions of Rome in European Culture, 1789–1945* (Cambridge University Press): 205–20.

Storchi Marino 1999: Alfredina Storchi Marino, *Numa e Pitagora: sapientia constituendae civitatis*. Naples: Liguori Editore.

Strasburger 1968: Hermann Strasburger, *Zur Sage von der Gründung Roms* (Sitzungsberichte der Heidelberger Akademie 1968.5). Heidelberg: Carl Winter Universitätsverlag.

Sumner 1973: G.V. Sumner, *The Orators in Cicero's Brutus: Prosopography and Chronology* (Phoenix Supplementary volume 11). University of Toronto Press.

Sutherland 1984: C.H.V. Sutherland, *The Roman Imperial Coinage*, revised ed., vol. 1. London: Spink.

Sutherland 1987: C.H.V. Sutherland, *Roman History and Coinage 44 BC–AD 69*. Oxford: Clarendon Press.

Swanton 1999: Michael Swanton, *Opening the Franks Casket* (Fourteenth Brixworth Lecture). University of Leicester Department of Adult Education.

Syme 1939: Ronald Syme, *The Roman Revolution*. Oxford: Clarendon Press.

Syme 1958: Ronald Syme, *Tacitus*. Oxford: Clarendon Press.

Syme 1970: Ronald Syme, 'Domitius Corbulo', *Journal of Roman Studies* 60: 27–39.

Syme 1986: Ronald Syme, *The Augustan Aristocracy*. Oxford: Clarendon Press.

Taylor 1960: Lily Ross Taylor, *The Voting Districts of the Roman Republic* (Papers and Monographs of the American Academy in Rome 20). Rome: American Academy.

Thom 1995: Martin Thom, *Republics, Nations and Tribes*. London: Verso.

Thomsen 1980: Rudi Thomsen, *King Servius Tullius: A Historical Synthesis* (Humanitas 5). Copenhagen: Gyldendal.

Torelli 1978: Mario Torelli, 'Il sacco gallico di Roma', in *I Galli e l'Italia* (Rome: De Luca), 226–8.

Torelli 1996: Mario Torelli, 'Riflessioni sulle registrazioni storiche in Etruria', *Eutopia* 5.1–2: 13–22.

Torelli 1999: Mario Torelli, *Tota Italia: Essays in the Cultural Foundation of Roman Italy*. Oxford: Clarendon Press.

Treggiari 1991: Susan Treggiari, *Roman Marriage: Iusti Coniuges from the Time of Cicero to the Time of Ulpian*.

Oxford: Clarendon Press.

Trendall 1989: A.D. Trendall, *Red-Figure Vases of South Italy and Sicily: A Handbook*. London: Thames and Hudson.

Trieber 1894: Conrad Trieber, 'Zur Kritik des Eusebios: 1. Die Königstafel von Alba Longa', *Hermes* 29: 124–42.

Vaglieri 1907: D. Vaglieri, 'Regione X: scoperte al Palatino', *Notizie degli scavi* 1907: 185–205.

Vance 1989: William L. Vance, *America's Rome*, vol. I *Classical Rome*. New Haven: Yale University Press.

Versnel 1993: H.S. Versnel, *Transition and Reversal in Myth and Ritual* (Studies in Greek and Roman Religion 6.2). Leiden: Brill.

Walbank 1967: F.W. Walbank, 'The Scipionic Legend', *Proceedings of the Cambridge Philological Society* n.s. 13: 54–69.

Walbank 1972: F.W. Walbank, *Polybius* (Sather Classical Lectures 42). Berkeley: University of California Press.

Walbank 1985: Frank W. Walbank, *Selected Papers: Studies in Greek and Roman History and Historiography*. Cambridge University Press.

Walker and Higgs 2001: Susan Walker and Peter Higgs (eds), *Cleopatra of Egypt: from History to Myth*. London: British Museum Press.

Wallace-Hadrill 1996: Andrew Wallace-Hadrill, 'The Imperial Court', in Alan K. Bowman, Edward Champlin, Andrew Lintott (eds), *The Cambridge Ancient History* ed. 2, vol. 10 (Cambridge University Press): 283–308.

Walt 1997: Siri Walt, *Der Historiker C. Licinius Macer: Einleitung, Fragmente, Kommentar* (Beiträge zur Altertumskunde 103). Stuttgart and Leipzig: Teubner.

Waszink 1956: J.H. Waszink, 'Camena', *Classica et Mediaevalia* 17: 139–48.

Waszink 1979: J.H. Waszink, *Opuscula Selecta*. Leiden: Brill.

Weinstock 1960: Stefan Weinstock, 'Two Archaic Inscriptions from Latium', *Journal of Roman Studies* 50: 112–18.

Weinstock 1971: Stefan Weinstock, *Divus Julius*. Oxford: Clarendon Press.

West 1989: M.L. West, 'The Early Chronology of Attic Tragedy', *Classical Quarterly* 39: 251–4.

West 1997: M.L. West, *The East Face of Helicon: West Asiatic Elements in Greek Poetry and Myth*. Oxford: Clarendon Press.

Wethey 1975: Harold E. Wethey, *The Paintings of Titian*, vol. III *The Mythological and Historical Paintings*. London: Phaidon Press.

Wiedemann 1996: Thomas Wiedemann, 'Mommsen, Rome and the German *Kaiserreich*', in Theodor Mommsen, *A History of Rome under the Emperors* (London: Routledge): 36–47.

Wilkinson 1955: L.P. Wilkinson, *Ovid Recalled*. Cambridge University Press.

Wills 1984: Garry Wills, *Cincinnatus: George Washington and the Enlightenment*. Garden City, NY: Doubleday.

Wind 1967: Edgar Wind, *Pagan Mysteries in the Renaissance*, enlarged and revised ed. Harmondsworth: Penguin.

Winkler 1995: Martin M. Winkler, 'Cinema and the Fall of Rome', *Transactions of the American Philological Association* 125: 135–54.

Winkler 2001: Martin M. Winkler, 'The Roman Empire in American Cinema after 1945', in Sandra R. Joshel, Margaret Malamud and Donald T. McGuire, jr (eds), *Imperial Projections: Ancient Rome and Modern Popular Culture* (Baltimore: Johns Hopkins University Press): 50–76.

Wirszubski 1950: Ch. Wirszubski, *Libertas as a Political Idea at Rome During the Late Republic and Early Empire*. Cambridge University Press.

Wiseman 1970: T.P. Wiseman, 'Roman Republican Road-Building', *Papers of the British School at Rome* 38: 122–52.

Wiseman 1979a: T.P. Wiseman, *Clio's Cosmetics: Three Studies in Greco-Roman Literature*. Leicester University Press.

Wiseman 1979b: T.P. Wiseman, 'Topography and Rhetoric: the Trial of Manlius', *Historia* 28: 32–50.

Wiseman 1983: T.P. Wiseman, 'The Wife and Children of Romulus', *Classical Quarterly* 33: 445–52.

Wiseman 1986: T.P. Wiseman, review of Coarelli 1985, *Journal of Roman Studies* 86: 307–8.

Wiseman 1987: T.P. Wiseman, *Roman Studies Literary and Historical*. Liverpool: Francis Cairns.

Wiseman 1991: T.P. Wiseman, *Flavius Josephus: Death of an Emperor* (Exeter Studies in History 30). University of Exeter Press.

Wiseman 1992: T.P. Wiseman, *Talking to Virgil: A Miscellany*. University of Exeter Press.

Wiseman 1993: T.P. Wiseman, 'The She-Wolf Mirror: an Interpretation', *Papers of the British School at Rome* 61: 1–6.

Wiseman 1994: T.P. Wiseman, *Historiography and Imagination: Eight Essays on Roman Culture*. University of Exeter Press.

Wiseman 1995a: T.P. Wiseman, *Remus: A Roman Myth*. Cambridge University Press.

Wiseman 1995b: T.P. Wiseman, 'The God of the Lupercal', *Journal of Roman Studies* 85: 1–22.

Wiseman 1996: T.P. Wiseman, 'What Do We Know About Early Rome?', *Journal of Roman Archaeology* 9: 310–15.

Wiseman 1997: T.P. Wiseman, 'The She-Wolf Mirror (Again)', *Ostraka* 6.2: 441–3.

Wiseman 1998: T.P. Wiseman, *Roman Drama and Roman History*. University of Exeter Press.

Wiseman 1999: T.P. Wiseman, 'The Games of Flora', in Bettina Bergmann and Christine Kondoleon (eds), *The Art of Ancient Spectacle* (Studies in the History of Art 56, New Haven: Yale University Press): 195–203.

Wiseman 2000: T.P. Wiseman, 'Liber: Myth, Drama and Ideology in Republican Rome', in Christer Bruun (ed.), *The Roman Middle Republic: Politics, Religion and Historiography c.400–133 BC* (Acta Instituti Romani Finlandiae 23, Rome): 265–99.

Wiseman 2001: T.P. Wiseman, 'Reading Carandini', *Journal of Roman Studies* 91: 182–93.

Wiseman 2002a: T.P. Wiseman, 'Ovid and the Stage', in Geraldine Herbert-Brown (ed.), *Ovid's Fasti: Historical Readings at its Bimillennium* (Oxford University Press): 275–99.

Wiseman 2002b: T.P. Wiseman, 'Roman History and the Ideological Vacuum', in T.P. Wiseman (ed.), *Classics in Progress: Essays on Ancient Greece and Rome* (Oxford University Press for the British Academy): 285–310.

Wiseman 2003: T.P. Wiseman, 'The Legend of Lucius Brutus', in Mario Citroni (ed.), *Memoria e identità: la cultura romana costruisce la sua immagine* (Studi e testi 21, Università degli studi di Firenze): 21–38.

Wiseman 2004: T.P. Wiseman, 'The Kalends of April', in W.V. Harris and E. Lo Cascio (eds), *Noctes Campanae* (Naples: Edipuglia):

Wissowa 1902: Georg Wissowa, *Religion und Kultus der Römer* (Handbuch der klassischen Altertumswissenschaft 5.4). Munich: C.H. Beck.

Wolfe 1953: Don M. Wolfe (ed.), *The Complete Prose Works of John Milton*, vol. 1. New Haven: Yale University Press.

Woodman 1998: A.J. Woodman, *Tacitus Reviewed*. Oxford: Clarendon Press.

Woodman 2003: A.J. Woodman, 'Poems to Historians: Catullus 1 and Horace, *Odes* 2.1', in David Braund and Christopher Gill (eds), *Myth, History and Culture in Republican Rome* (University of Exeter Press): 191–216.

Woodman and Martin 1996: A.J. Woodman and R.H. Martin, *The Annals of Tacitus Book 3* (Cambridge Classical Texts and Commentaries 32). Cambridge University Press.

Wüst 1936: Ernst Wüst, 'Odysseus', in Wilhelm Kroll (ed.), *Real-Encyclopädie der Classischen Altertumswissenschaft* 17 (Stuttgart: J.B. Metzler): 1905–96.

Wyke 1997: Maria Wyke, *Projecting the Past: Ancient Rome, Cinema, and History*. New York: Routledge.

Wyke 1999a: Maria Wyke, 'Screening Ancient Rome in the New Italy', in Catherine Edwards (ed.), *Roman Presences: Receptions of Rome in European Culture, 1789–1945* (Cambridge University Press): 188–204.

Wyke 1999b: Maria Wyke, 'Sawdust Caesar: Mussolini, Julius Caesar, and the Drama of Dictatorship', in Maria Wyke and Michael Biddiss (eds), *The Uses and Abuses of Antiquity* (Bern: Peter Lang): 167–88.

Zanker 1983: Paul Zanker, 'Der Apollontempel auf dem Palatin: Ausstattung und politische Sinnbezüge nach der Schlacht von Actium', in *Città e architettura nella Roma imperiale* (Analecta Romana Instituti Danici, supplement 10, Odense University Press): 21–40.

Zerner 1969: Henri Zerner, *The School of Fontainebleau: Etchings and Engravings*. London: Thames and Hudson.

Zevi 1995: Fausto Zevi, 'Demarato e i re "corinzi" di Roma', in A. Storchi Marino (ed.), *L'incidenza dell'antico: studi in memoria di Ettore Lepore*, I (Naples: Luciano editore): 291–314.

Zimmer 1987: Gerhard Zimmer, *Spiegel im Antikenmuseum* (Bilderheit der Staatlichen Museen Preussischer Kulturbesitz 52). Berlin: SMPK.

Ziolkowski 1999: Adam Ziolkowski, 'La scomparsa della clientela arcaica: un'ipotesi', *Athenaeum* 87: 369–82.

ILLUSTRATION CREDITS

Colour Plates

Plate 1. Giovanni Battista Tiepolo, 'The Empire of Flora', c. 1743, oil on canvas, 28¼ × 35 in.; Fine Arts Museums of San Francisco, Gift of the Samuel H. Kress Foundation.

Plate 2 (a). Giovanni Battista Tiepolo, 'Sketch for Venus and Vulcan', 1765–6; John G. Johnson Collection (J# 287), Philadelphia Museum of Art.

Plate 2 (b). Giovanni Battista Tiepolo, 'The Meeting of Antony and Cleopatra'; © National Gallery of Scotland (NG 91).

Plate 3. Giovanni Bellini and Titian, 'The Feast of the Gods'; Widener Collection (1942.9.1), © Board of Trustees, National Gallery of Art, Washington.

Plate 4. Titian, 'Tarquin and Lucretia' (Fitzwilliam Museum, Cambridge); The Bridgeman Art Library.

Plate 5. Sandro Botticelli, 'Primavera' (Galleria degli Uffizi, Florence); The Bridgeman Art Library (BEN 558).

Plate 6. Drawn by Delphine Jones (after Degrassi 1963).

Plate 7. Tomasso Laureti, 'La battaglia del Lago Regillo'; Roma, Musei Capitolini; Archivio Fotografico dei Musei Capitolini.

Plate 8 (a). Vatican, Museo Gregoriano Etrusco (inv. 14962-18212); photo P. Zigrossi. © Monumenti musei e gallerie pontifiche.

Plate 8 (b). © Musée d'art et d'histoire, Ville de Genève (inv. 23471); photo Ives Siza.

Plate 9. Jacques-Antoine Beaufort, 'The Oath of Brutus' (Musée municipal Frederic Blandin, Nevers); Roger-Viollet, Paris; The Bridgeman Art Library (RVI 103898).

Plate 10. Peter Paul Rubens (Schüler und Nachahmer), 'Die Flucht der Cloelia'; Staatliche Kunstsammlungen Dresden, Gemäldegalerie (inv. 1016A).

Plate 11. Peter Paul Rubens, 'Mars and Rhea Silvia'; Sammlungen des Fürsten von und zu Liechtenstein, Vaduz (inv. 122).

Plate 12. Pietro da Cortona, 'The Rape of the Sabine Women'; Pinacoteca Capitolina, Rome; studio fotografico Antonio Idini.

Plate 13. Jacques-Louis David, 'Les Sabines' (Louvre, Paris); The Bridgeman Art Library (GIR 18914).

Plate 14. Benjamin Robert Haydon (1786–1846), 'Curtius Leaping into the Gulf' (Exeter City Museums and Art Gallery); The Bridgeman Art Library (EX 17106).

Plate 15. Benjamin West (1728–1820), 'The Departure of Regulus', 1769; The Royal Collection (RCIN 405416, OM 1152, GIII 158); © Her Majesty Queen Elizabeth II.

Plate 16. (a) Sala del Concistoro, Palazzo Pubblico, Siena; (b) Domenico Beccafumi, 'Il tribuno Publio Muzio manda i colleghi al rogo'. © Comune di Siena; Foto LENSINI Siena, nos. 1306 (*a*), 304 (*b*).

Figures in text

p. xiv   © *The New Yorker*.

p. 7   *The Works of Henry Purcell Vol 20* (ed. Ian Spink, 1998) p. 49, by permission of Novello and Company Ltd, London.

Figs. 1–4. Maps by András Bereznay: www.historyonmaps.com

Fig. 5. Peruzzi 1998.20 (fig. 2b), by permission of Casa Editrice Leo S. Olschki, Florence.

Fig. 6. *Pithekoussai* I (Monumenti Antichi, serie monografica vol. IV, Rome 1993), tavv.72–3, by permission of the Accademia Nazionale dei Lincei.

Fig. 7. Stibbe et al. 1980.47 (fig. 3), by permission of Prof. Giovanni Colonna.

Fig. 8. Crawford 1903.63 (drawing signed 'Wadham 1902').

Fig. 9. Roma, Musei Capitolini; Archivio fotografico dei Musei Capitolini.

Fig. 10. Lulof 1996.169, by permission of Dr P.S. Lulof and the Netherlands Institute in Rome.

Fig. 11. Anderson Photos, Rome.

Fig. 12. *Etruskische Spiegel* 5, no. 127.

Fig. 13. Holliday 2002.67, by permission of Peter J. Holliday and Kevin W. Davis.

Fig. 14. Museo Archeologico, Florence; The Bridgeman Art Library (scene 3 ALI 214590-1, scene 4 ALI 212367). © Fratelli Alinari, 2003.

Fig. 15. Duomo, Siena; The Bridgeman Art Library (ALI 212365). © Fratelli Alinari, 2003.

Fig. 16. Stibbe et al. 1980, Plate 1, by permission of the Netherlands Institute in Rome.

Fig. 17. Soprintendenza archeologica per le provincie di Salerno, Avellino e Benevento.

Fig. 18. © British Museum (neg. 243939).

Fig. 19. Museo Capitolino, Rome; The Bridgeman Art Library (ALI 212366). © Fratelli Alinari, 2003.

Fig. 20. The Devonshire Collection, Chatsworth; reproduced by permission of the Duke of Devonshire and the Chatsworth Settlement Trustees. Photograph: Photographic Survey, Courtauld Institute of Art.

Fig. 21. *Monumenti dell'Instituto* 11, 3.1.

Fig. 22. De La Blanchère 1892.599.

Fig. 23. German Archaeological Institute, Rome (neg. DAI 69.2799).

Fig. 24. F. Ritschl, *Priscae Latinitatis monumenta epigraphica* (1862), I(a).

Fig. 25. Drawn by Sean Goddard.

Fig. 26. *Etruskische Spiegel* 2, no. 171.

Fig. 27. *Etruskische Spiegel* 5, no. 147.

Fig. 28. The Walters Art Museum, Baltimore (54.136).

Fig. 29. Istituto per l'archeologia etrusco-italica.

Fig. 30. © British Museum (neg. 113583).

Fig. 31. *Etruskische Spiegel* 5, no. 43.

Fig. 32. Soprintendenza archeologica per l'Etruria meridionale.

Fig. 33. Drawing by Dr F. Jurgeit Blanck.

Fig. 34. Zimmer 1987.32, by permission of the Staatliche Museen zu Berlin (Antikensammlung, Misc. 6240).

Fig. 35. © British Museum (neg. PS261598).

Fig. 36. © British Museum (neg. C-2445).

Fig. 37. Nationalmuseet, Copenhagen.

Fig. 38. *Archäologische Zeitung* 20 (1862), Taf. 164–5.

Fig. 39. The Pierpont Morgan Library, New York (AZ046a–AZ046b).

Fig. 40. Istituto per l'archeologia etrusco-italica.

Fig. 41. Soprintendenza archeologica per l'Etruria meridionale; Museo nazionale di Villa Giulia (inv. 13133, neg. 224535).

Fig. 42. *Etruskische Spiegel* 5, no. 45.

Fig. 43. *Monumenti dell'Instituto* 6–7, 55.

Fig. 44. Drawn by Sean Goddard.

Fig. 45. *Monumenti dell'Instituto* Supplement, 15–16.

Fig. 46. *Monumenti dell'Instituto* 9, 22–3; by permission of the British Library (748.h.3).

Fig. 47. *Etruskische Spiegel* 5, no. 120.

Fig. 48. *Monumenti dell'Instituto* 10, 29.

Fig. 49. *Monumenti dell'Instituto* 9, 24–5.

Fig. 50. *Monumenti dell'Instituto* 9.58–9.

Fig. 51. © British Museum (neg. 062709).

Fig. 52. Museum für Kunst und Gewerbe, Hamburg (neg. F1283/13).

Fig. 53. Museo Nazionale, Naples (neg. 200839).

Fig. 54. © British Museum (neg. 104105).

Fig. 55. © British Museum (neg. 230591).

Fig. 57. Thaw Collection, The Pierpont Morgan Library, New York.

Fig. 58 (a). Thaw Collection, The Pierpont Morgan Library, New York.

Fig. 58 (b). Roma, Musei Capitolini (inv. MC.1183/S); Archivio Fotografico dei Musei Capitolini.

Fig. 59. Drawing by George Scharf jun. (p. 107 of the 1847 edition of Macaulay's *Lays of Ancient Rome*).

Fig. 60. © British Museum (neg. 343627).

Fig. 61. American Academy in Rome (Fototeca Unione no.1182).

Fig. 62 (a and b). © British Museum (neg. 096582).

Fig. 62 (c). © British Museum (neg. 247439).

Fig. 63. Soprintendenza archeologica di Roma.

Fig. 64. *Etruskische Spiegel* 3, no. 123.

Fig. 65. The State Capitol of Virginia, Richmond; The Bridgeman Art Library (SSI 82996).

Fig. 66. © British Museum (neg. 280779).

Fig. 67. © British Museum (neg. 310902).

Fig. 68. © British Museum (neg. 189883).

Fig. 69. German Archaeological Institute, Rome (neg. DAI 38.1602).

Fig. 70. Bibliotheca Hertziana, Rome (neg. U.Pl. C8462).

Fig. 71. © British Museum (neg.s 137729 [centre], 164137, 164138, 164139, 164140, 164141, 164142, 164143, 115701, 176623 [clockwise]).

Fig. 72. Holliday 2002.93, by permission of Peter J. Holliday and Kevin W. Davis.

Fig. 74. German Archaeological Institute, Rome (neg. DAI 76.328).

Fig. 76 (a). © British Museum (neg. 117444).

Fig. 76 (b). © British Museum (neg. 362606).

Fig. 77. © British Museum (neg. 096599).

Fig. 78 (a). © British Museum (neg. 288569).

Fig. 78 (b). © British Museum (neg. 232268).

Fig. 79. Degrassi 1947, Plate IX; © Istituto poligrafico dello stato, Rome.

Fig. 80. Roma, Musei Capitolini (inv. MC.3342/S); Archivio Fotografico dei Musei Capitolini.

Fig. 81. Musée de l'Arles antique.

Fig. 82. © British Museum (neg. 362607).

Fig. 83. Degrassi 1937.xxv; © Istituto poligrafico dello stato, Rome.

Fig. 84. Soprintendenza Antichità, Chieti.

Fig. 85. German Archaeological Institute, Rome (neg. DAI 34.73).

Fig. 86. Photo Michael Larvey.

Fig. 87. Map by András Bereznay: www.historyonmaps.com

Fig. 88. Musée du Louvre, Paris (Peter Willi); The Bridgeman Art Library (PWI 98001).

Fig. 89. German Archaeological Institute, Rome (neg. DAI 40.1187).

Fig. 92. Prof. R.R.R. Smith.

Fig. 93. Smith 1987 Plates IV and VI, by permission of Prof. R.R.R. Smith and the Roman Society.

Fig. 95. Musée des Beaux-Arts de Lille (inv. W.3533).

Fig. 97. © British Museum (neg. 82034).

Fig. 99. © British Museum (neg. 115079).

Fig. 100. Smith 1987 Plate XIV, by permission of Prof. R.R.R. Smith and the Roman Society.

Fig. 101. Smith 1987 Plate XXIV, by permission of Prof. R.R.R. Smith and the Roman Society.

Fig. 102 (a). © British Museum (neg. 362608).

Fig. 102 (b). © British Museum (neg. 362609).

Fig. 103. © British Museum (neg. 104669).

Fig. 104. Musei Vaticani: Museo Sacro, raccolta già della Biblioteca Apostolica Vaticana (inv. 62442); neg. xxxvi.26.73/1.

Fig. 105. © The National Trust.

Fig. 106. Musée des Beaux-Arts de Lille (inv. W.3566).

Fig. 107. Drawing by J.R. Weguelin in the 1884 edition of Macaulay's *Lays of Ancient Rome*.

Fig. 108. À Beckett 1852.146.

INDEX

References in **bold** are to the main discussion (or narrative) of the relevant items.